E vely
c/o Ira

D1145276

Ewing Galloway

La fameuse Tour Eiffel et la magnifique porte du Trocadéro.

THE
NEW CHARDENAL

BY

W. H. GROSJEAN

FORMER HEAD OF THE FRENCH DEPARTMENT OF THE LANGUAGE
INSTITUTE OF NEW YORK

1951

ALLYN AND BACON

BOSTON   NEW YORK   CHICAGO
ATLANTA   SAN FRANCISCO   DALLAS

PRINTED IN THE UNITED STATES OF AMERICA

PREFACE

The New Chardenal retains the qualities that have made the original book for so many years the most popular and successful textbook for elementary instruction in French — simplicity, thoroughness, and careful gradation. In rewriting the book the author has taken advantage of his long use of the original *Chardenal* in the classroom to make the work still simpler and to add numerous devices which experience has proved to be a help both to pupil and to teacher.

Conversational French is emphasized throughout, and the readings are connected, sensible, idiomatic, and interesting. To introduce conversational work as early as possible the regular conjugations and the different tenses of the verbs have been brought forward so that when the student reaches Lesson 27, the present, past indefinite, imperfect, future, and future anterior have already been covered.

The New Chardenal gives special attention to vocabulary building, especially in useful, modern words. Cognates are emphasized and a classified vocabulary of some 400 useful words is included in the appendix.

The pronunciation of French sounds is treated in a practical way at the beginning of the book with cuts showing the position of lips and teeth for the more difficult sounds. This treatment enables the student, with the help of a pocket mirror, to reproduce correctly the sounds given by the instructor in the classroom.

The grammar rules have been explained at length and in a simple and attractive way which experience has shown will appeal to the student. The inductive method has been used wherever it has proved more effective than the deductive. Drawings and graphs illustrate the more important rules, thus helping to fix them in the pupil's mind.

Each lesson has connected reading which illustrates the grammatical points. These readings are either bright anecdotes or "conversations suivies" in which everyday French idioms are introduced. These conversations may be acted as little plays, the instructor calling before the class as many pupils as are needed and having them act either with or without the book. This work is supplemented by lists of conversational idioms in a number of lessons. As these sentences are short, they can be used for unison oral work, half the class taking one part, the other half the other part.

The exercises form the backbone of the book. Direct questions accustom the pupil to use naturally and correctly everyday conversational idioms. Some 200 new, short, modern exercises have been added. But perhaps the Exercices-Revue constitute the main feature of *The New Chardenal*. Beginning with Lesson 9, each lesson contains an exercicerevue of positive, negative, and interrogative sentences referring to the ten or fifteen preceding lessons, thus keeping constantly in the pupil's mind the important points of the ground already covered. In this way the student reviews each lesson about ten times.

The irregular verbs are dealt with more than twenty lessons earlier than in the former *Chardenal*. They are introduced little by little in three tenses, present, imperfect, and future. As the past participle is also given, the compound tenses may be easily formed. Only those verbs in common use are treated in the lessons, but a complete table where all are fully conjugated will be found in the appendix.

The appendix contains a complete résumé of grammar, the above-mentioned table of irregular verbs, 200 verbal idioms constantly used in French conversation, a unique section on translation helps, a classified vocabulary of

400 useful words, and the official French rules of syntax and orthography.

Some forty drawings by an eminent Parisian artist illustrate the lessons. There are also thirty-five full-page photographs of the most interesting places and monuments in France.

JULY 4, 1929   W. H. G.

TABLE DES MATIÈRES

vjj

TABLE DES ILLUSTRATIONS

THE NEW CHARDENAL

INTRODUCTION

The Alphabet

a	b	c	d	e	f	g	h	i
a	*bé*	*cé*	*dé*	*e* [1]	*effe*	*gé*	*ache*	*i*

j	k	l	m	n	o	p	q	r
ji	*ka*	*elle*	*emme*	*enne*	*o*	*pé*	*ku*	*erre*

s	t	u	v	w		x	y	z
esse	*té*	*u*	*vé*	*double vé*		*iks*	*i grec*	*zèd*

Orthographic Signs

Accents. — Three orthographic marks are called accents, — the acute (´), the grave (`), and the circumflex (^).

The acute accent, **accent aigu,** is used only over the vowel *e* (**é**), which then has the sound of *a* in *late*. As **été, vérité.**

The grave accent, **accent grave,** is used chiefly over the vowel *e* (**è**), which then has nearly the sound of *e* in *met*. As **près, père.** It is used over *a* and *u* merely to distinguish certain words which are otherwise spelled alike, and does not alter the pronunciation. As **à** (*to*) from **a** (*has*); **là** (*there*) from **la** (*the* or *her*); **où** (*where*) from **ou** (*or*).

The circumflex accent, **accent circonflexe,** is used on any vowel, which is then long. As **âge, tête, île, dôme, bûche.** It frequently indicates that a letter, often *s*, has been dropped, as in **île,** *isle;* **hâte,** *haste.*

It distinguishes **dû** (*owed*) from **du** (*of the*), **sûr** (*sure*) from **sur** (*upon*), **mûr** (*ripe*) from **mur** (*wall*).

---

[1] In repeating the alphabet, **e** is also pronounced like **é**; in spelling a word, an unaccented **e** is given the sound of **e** in **le.** See page xvi.

These accents do not imply any stress of voice on the syllable where they occur.

L'apostrophe, the apostrophe, ('), indicates that one of the vowels, **a, e,** or **i,** has been dropped before a word beginning with a vowel or *h mute.*

a is elided only in the article or pronoun **la** ; as **l'âme** for **la âme.**

e is elided in **le, je, me, te, se, de, ce, ne, que** (but when **je, ce, le,** and **la** come directly after the verb, either as subjects or objects, no elision takes place) ; in **jusque** and **lorsque** ; in **puisque** and **quoique** before **il, ils, elle, elles, on, un, une** ; in **quelque** before **un, une** ; and in **entre** in compound words.

i is elided only in **si** before **il** or **ils.**

No elision occurs before **onze, onzième, oui, huit, huitième.**

Le trait d'union, the hyphen, (-), marks the connection between two or more words or parts of a word.

The hyphen is used between the verb and the pronouns **je, moi, nous, tu, toi, vous, il, ils, elle, elles, le, la, les, lui, leur, y, en, ce, on,** when they are placed after a verb of which they are subjects or objects.   The other cases of its use will be noticed as they occur.

La cédille, the cedilla, (ç), is put under **c** when it has the sound of *s* before **a, o,** or **u.   As français, garçon, reçu.**

Le tréma, the diæresis, (¨), is placed over the second of two vowels to show that it begins a new syllable.   As **naïf** (na-if), **Noël** (no-el).

Pronunciation

Most French sounds have no English equivalents.   In the following pages on pronunciation, intended only to supplement the work of the teacher by furnishing examples for the use of both teacher and pupil, the word *like* means *somewhat like,* when French and English sounds are compared.

A glance at the cuts on the following pages will enable the pupil, with the help of a mirror, to shape his mouth in the right way to pronounce correctly the sounds given by the instructor in the class.

Important note. — In pronouncing French words, *always* stress lightly the last syllable, except when the word ends with an unaccented **e**, in which case the accent or stress is on the syllable before the last.

par-*ler'*   a-ni-*mal'*   ma-*da'*-me

Simple Vowels

a is an agreeable sound in all languages, especially in French. Except when the circumflex accent is placed over it, **a** is always short and clear.

The sound is nearly the same as *a* in the English words *hat, rat, fat.*

To make the sound correctly, open the mouth halfway, pushing the tip of the tongue against the lower teeth.

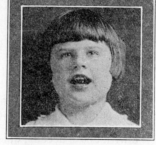

a

fat . . . . at . . . . **a**
rat . . . . at . . . . **a**
hat . . . . at . . . . **a**

Practice drill: baba, pacha, table, sable, banal, madame, malade, parade, cassable, La Marne, palissade, caravane, cavalcade, Alaska, Panama.

a with the circumflex accent has a longer, broader sound, as in the English word *parlor.*

The circumflex accent usually indicates the suppression of the letter s formerly used in the old French : **haste — hâte, paste — pâte.**

Practice drill: bâtir, âme, âge, blâme, pâtre, âne, lâche, tâche, Pâques.

e, unaccented, has a sound nearly like *u* in *hut, nut,* or *but,* or like *e* in *the* in the colloquial expression *the* days of *the* week.

To make the sound **e** correctly, the mouth must be open just enough to show the central upper teeth.

but	. . . . .	ut	. . . . .	e
cut	. . . . .	ut	. . . . .	e
hut	. . . . .	ut	. . . . .	e

e

Practice drill: le, je (zjuh), de, ne, petit, tenir, relire, demi, repas, venir, relatif, devenir.

When **e** unaccented ends a word of more than *one* syllable, it is silent, the preceding consonant only being sounded, although in singing it makes a separate syllable: **bri-*se*** (bree-zuh).

Examples of mute **e** in English are found in: lik¢, tim¢, som¢.

Practice drill: cachemir¢, camarad¢, corsag¢, rag¢, ramag¢, salad¢, parad¢, tapag¢, partag¢.

e with acute accent, **é,** is pronounced nearly like the English *a* in *baby, late,* or like *ay* in *day, bay, hay,* or like *ey* in *they.* But it is a single sound, not a diphthong as in English, which gives the sound of *ee* at the end: *they = thā-ee.*

é is of common occurrence in French, as the past participle of ninety per cent of French verbs ends with **é.**

é

To enunciate a sound corresponding to the French **é,** smile, partly opening the lips so as to show the teeth, and say quickly: *hay, hay, hay,* **é, é, é.**

Practice drill: dé, été, pré, bébé, marché, décédé, délassé, ménagé, crénelé, hérédité, liberté, préparé, égalité, élevé, généralité, répété, dégénéré.

If we notice that **-er, -ez,** and **-ai** (all endings of French verbs) are sounded exactly like **é,** we shall realize the importance of the correct pronunciation of that sound.

Practice drill: parl**er**, pass**er**, march**er**, lav**er**, parl**ez**, pass**ez**, march**ez**, lav**ez**, parl**ai**, pass**ai**, march**ai**, lav**ai**.

e with a grave accent, **è,** has almost the same sound as in the English word *ebb.*

To make the sound **è** correctly, open the mouth so as to show half of the upper and half of the lower teeth.

è

```
let   . . . .  et  . . . .  è
met   . . . .  et  . . . .  è
set   . . . .  et  . . . .  è
```

Practice drill: après, très, règle, élève, liège, père, mère, frère, sévère, bipède, lèvre, genèse, homogène, cafetière, blasphème.

Correct enunciation of **è** is very important, because the endings **-ais, -ait, -est,** and **-et,** as well as **es** and **ai** (not as verb endings) are sounded like **è**. **e** unaccented has also the sound of **è** when it comes before **c, f, l, r, s, t.**

Practice drill: français, anglais, jamais, Calais, distrait, parfait, lait, poulet, chaise, fraise, des, les, c'est, mes, ses, chef, sec, fer, sel, belle.

e with a circumflex accent, **ê,** is a little more open than the **è,** and is nearly the sound made when one imitates the bleating of a sheep. The circumflex accent often indicates the suppression of the letter **s** formerly used in the old French: **teste** — **tête, feste** — **fête.**

Practice drill: même, grêle, frêle, rêve, fête, tête, bête, crête, chêne, bêler, forêt, carême.

i is sounded like *ee* in the English word *bee*. The French **i** is *much softer* than the English *i* in *machine*. To make the sound **i** correctly, smile broadly, widening the mouth until the teeth show plainly.

Practice drill: dire, rire, lire, cire, mire, difficile, risible, acide, salive, cilice, midi, ici, fini, merci, visibilité.

i

i with a circumflex accent, **î,** is sounded a little longer than **i** unaccented, almost like *ee* in *feel*. Here too, the circumflex accent has taken the place of the **s** formerly used in the old French : **isle — île.**

Practice drill: île, dîme, dîner, gîte, abîme, épître.

o, at the beginning or in the middle of words, must be pronounced like *u* in the English words *rub, fun.*

Practice drill: globe, mode, robe, joli, monotone, téléphone, personne, monopole, octobre, ordonné, octogone, obole.

o before **s,** and in words ending in **o** or **ot** is pronounced like an English *o*.

Practice drill: rose, pose, chose, pot, mot, cachot, piano, Roméo, Figaro.

o with the circumflex accent, **ô,** is sounded like a long *o* (*home*).

Practice drill: dôme, cône, rôti, drôle, môle, rôle, ôter, trône.

Note. — **o** is silent in **paon, taon, faon,** and **Laon.**

u is the most difficult of the vowels to pronounce, for that sound is not found in English.

With the lips a little more closed than for whistling, say *ee* as in *feet* and prolong the sound. (By all means avoid saying *oo* or *eeoo*.)

Practice drill: du, dur, sur, pur, une, brune, bitume, fortune, numéro, tubulure, opuscule, minuscule, culture, murmure, sulfure.

u with the circumflex accent, **û,** is sounded like **u,** but is a bit longer.

Practice drill: dû, fût, sûr, mûr, chûte, piqûre, brûlure, bûche, mûrir.

y, Greek *ι,* when initial, when between two consonants, or when forming a syllable by itself, is sounded like the ordinary French **i.**

Practice drill: type, style, gypse, physique, mystique, Ypres, rythmique, pyrite, gymnastique.

u

y between two vowels is sounded like a double **i: ii.**

Practice drill: payer, payable, croyable, essayer.

Diphthongs and Combined Vowels

The union of two vowels creating a new sound is called a diphthong.

ai is sounded like **é** when at the end of words : **mai, quai, j'ai, gai;** and like **è** when followed by **s, d** or **t: mais, laid, fait.**

Note. — Some corruptions have occurred in this rule, but, fortunately, in very few instances; for example, **vrai** is pronounced **vrè** (instead of **vré**) and **je sais** is generally pronounced **je sé** (instead of **je sè**).

ei is sounded like **è : reine, neige, seigle.**

au and **eau** are sounded like **ô,** or nearly like **o** in the English word *home:* **cause, sauce, beau, chapeau, cadeau.**

eu and **œu** have no equivalent in English ; shape your mouth as indicated in the cut for the pronunciation of **e** (showing the two central upper teeth) then push the lips forward and drawl slightly : **peu, jeu, nœud.**

When this diphthong is followed by **f, l, r,** or **v,** it has a sound somewhat similar to *u* in *fur* or to *i* in *sir:* **bœuf, œuf, seul, sœur, peur, veuve, neuve.**

oi is sounded somewhat like *wa* in *was,* but the sound should be plain and clear.   Imitate the barking of a little dog, opening the mouth plainly as in accompanying cut.

Practice drill: moi, toi, soi, quoi, foi, loi, roi, voir, poire, boire, oiseau, toiture, coiffer, moineau, boîte.

oi

ou is sounded like *oo* in *tool* or *fool.*   To pronounce correctly, push the lips forwards as in pouting; this way you will *avoid* saying *aou* as in the English word *out.*

Practice drill: fou, mou, route, coupe, double, course, souple, loupe, couple, bourse, moule, coucou.

ia is sounded like *ia* in the English word *cordial:* **liane, miasme, trivial, piastre, Diane.**

ie is sounded like *ee* in the English word *fee:* **vie, mie, lie, partie, pharmacie, anomalie.**

ua, ui, and **uo** have no equivalent in English.   The *u* is pronounced first, *lightly* with a slight whistling sound, the second letter, *a, i,* or *o,* being sounded more strongly: **nu*a*ge, mu*a*ble, lu*i*, cu*i*re, du*o*.**

ou

The Nasal Sounds

m and **n,** when final or before a consonant, lose their value as consonants and form with the preceding vowel a nasal

sound which is a true vowel. These sounds have no exact
equivalents in English; and in pronouncing them, care must
be taken that *no consonant m, n, or ng be heard.*

They are divided into four
groups:

An, am, en, em, ean. — These
five sounds have the same pronunciation. (**m** is found before **b** or **p**.)

To pronounce correctly **an, am,
en, em, ean,** relax the lower jaw,
keep the mouth open, throw the
sound up into the back of the nasal
passage, but do *not* prolong the
sound into *ng:*

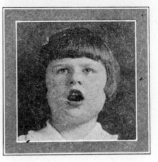

en

want	ant	**an**
chance . . .	ance . . .	**an**
France . . .	ance . . .	**an**

Practice drill: France, danse, lance, manche, fantaisie, fanfare,
pensif, pendant, enfant, avance, empire, semblable, aventure,
moment, attentif, Angleterre, Jean, rendre, entendre, ensemble,
campagne, prétendre, amplitude,
lentement, tempérament.

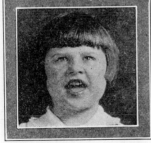

In, ain, ein, im, aim, and **eim**
are pronounced alike and have
somewhat the sound of *an* in *fan*
or *can* without, however, sounding
the *n.* When that sound is
uttered, the face or at least the
mouth should show a slight expression of disgust.

in

Practice drill: vin, pin, fin, pain,
bain, teinte, simple, timbre, demain, faim, Américain, syntaxe,
plein, instinct, rein, serin, festin, symbole.

Note. — **en** coming after **i** has the sound of **in,** the **i** being pronounced separately: **bien, rien, mien, lien, sien, chien.**

On, om. — The sound **on** (**om**) is pronounced somewhat like *on* in *song, wrong,* without sounding *ng.*

To produce that sound correctly, round out the lips and push the sound half through the mouth, half through the nose.

Practice drill: mon, ton, son, non, don, bonbon, pardon, chanson, raison, combinaison, compensation, fronton, pondération, contrepoison.

on

Un, um. — The French sound **un** (**um**) may be attained by saying over and over the word *lunch,* dropping the *nch* every other time : *lunch, lu, lunch, lu,* etc. To have an exact idea of the correct pronunciation of the sound **un,** press the nostrils lightly (see cut) and say *hun* without sounding the *n.* The trial should then be repeated without the help of the fingers.

Practice drill: un, brun, chacun, lundi, humble, alun, parfum, emprunter, tribun, embrun, importun, humblement.

Consonants

French consonants are pronounced as in English except the following :

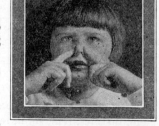

c before **e, i, y,** or **ç** (**c** cedilla) is sounded like *s.* In any other case, it is sounded like *k:* **ce, ici, ciment, cygne, ça, garçon; caverne, colosse, curé.**

g before **e, i, y** is sounded like *s* in *pleasure;* in other cases, like *g* in *go:* **geste, gilet, gymnastique; gant, gothique, guide.**

un

h is always silent : **homme, honneur, habit.**

j   is sounded like *s* in *pleasure:* **je, j'ai, Jeanne.**

s   between two vowels is sounded like *z:* **raser, pose, musique, bise.**

r   is always guttural in French : **rire, rare, recrue, reproduire.**

ch, qu, th, compound consonants, are respectively sounded *sh, k, t:* **chic, quelque, thé.**

Note. — Final consonants are generally silent in French, except **c, f, l, r: sec, chef, sel, fer.**

Liquid Sounds

ill is sounded like *ey* in *beyond:* **fille, famille, habiller.** However, in words beginning with **ill, mill,** and **vill,** and in **tranquille** the **ill** is not liquid, and **ll** has its regular sound : **illustre, village, mille.**

il at the end of a word, and when preceded by a vowel, has the same sound as liquid **ill: corail, soleil, fauteuil.**

gn is sounded like *ni* in *onion,* or *gn* in *mignonette:* **signal, magnifique, montagne, ligne.**

Note. — There are very few exceptions to these rules.

Division of Syllables

In the body of a word each syllable must if possible begin with a consonant ; as **mo-ra-li-té, a-ma-bi-li-té.**

If there are two consonants, the division usually takes place between the two ; as **hom-me, vil-le, par-tir, en-ten-du.** But if the second is **l** or **r** (and the first is neither **l** nor **r**), or if the two are **ch, ph, th,** or **gn,** the division takes place before the two ; as **é-gli-se, ta-bleau, é-cri-re, a-che-ter, am-phi-thé-â-tre, no-tre, vi-gne.**

As **h** is never heard in pronunciation, the consonant which precedes it is always carried, in speaking, to the following vowel ; as **i-nhu-main, i-nha-bi-té.**

The compound consonant **x** (= **ks** or **gz**) always goes with the preceding vowel ; as **ex-il.**

quatre, papa, Canada, table, blâmer, ananas, passer, vérité,
venir, garçon, dame, arbre, samedi, pied, objet, secret, ici,
midi, école, hôte, ôter, rue, général, mangea, rossignol, science,
pays, puis, appuyer, fléau, haïr, je hais, haïssant, paille, tailleur,
œil, leur, demeure, patience, question, nation, enfant, jambe,
bien, rien, le sien, moyen, juin, grognon, lundi, humble, soleil.

Exceptions, Similarities, etc.

à, a, as

la, là

ou, août

soi, soie, sois

est (*is*), est (*east*)

mer, mère

votre, le vôtre

non, nom

bon, bonne

rien, reine

plein, pleine

faim, femme

sais, ses, ces

mes, mais, maïs

au, eau

des, dès

pré, prés, près

lui, Louis

cou, coup

moi, mois

moins, moine

sel, selle, celle

cn, an, âne, un

mil, mille

fils, fil, fille

ville, village

gentil, gentille

le haut, l'eau

la hauteur, l'auteur

les hauteurs, les auteurs

la haine, laine

le héros, l'héroïne

les héros, les zéros

le huit, lui

tache, tâche

ennemi, ennui

lac, tabac, estomac

net, nette

clef, clé

œuf, œufs

bœuf, bœufs

cœur, chœur, sœur

je donnai, je donnais

tous (*adj.*), tous (*pron.*)

Jésus, Christ

Jésus-Christ

The Linking of Words (La Liaison)

The last consonant of a word, standing before a word beginning with a vowel or **h** mute and closely connected with it in
sense, is often carried over to it in pronunciation.

In such cases **s** and **x** have the sound of **z, d** that of **t, c** and **g** that of **k,** and **f** that of **v.** As **mes‿amis, ils‿ont, aux‿ armes, grand‿homme, avec‿elle, rang‿élevé, neuf‿ans.** In carrying over the **n** of a nasal, the sound of the nasal must be retained, and the **n** sounds as if it were the first letter of the following word : **mon enfant = mon nenfant; un homme = un nhomme.**

This linking of words, called **liaison,** is necessary in public speaking or reading; in conversation it generally takes place only when the words thus joined cannot do without each other. It cannot occur before **oui, onze,** or **onzième.** The t of **et** is _never_ linked to the following word.

Final **m, n, p,** or **r** of a noun is not usually carried over. Beyond certain general principles, it is impossible to lay down rules. In reading, the number of **liaisons** will vary, according to the style of the composition, the shades of thought, pauses, euphony, and the taste of the reader.

EXAMPLES OF LIAISON : Ce petit‿enfant est très‿aimable. _This little child is very lovable._

Leurs‿amis ne sont pas‿encore arrivés. _Their friends have not arrived yet._

Quels jours‿heureux ! _What happy days !_

Que dit‿on ? _What do they say?_

Quand‿avez-vous‿été chez‿eux ? _When were you at their house ?_

Je les‿ai vus de temps‿en temps. _I saw them from time to time._

Ça m'est‿égal. _That makes no difference to me._

Elle répond‿à ses questions‿amusantes. _She answers his amusing questions._

Ils‿aiment‿à lire et à écrire. _They like to read and write._

Il a beaucoup‿étudié. _He has studied a great deal._

Il est bien‿heureux, tout‿heureux. _He is very happy, quite happy._

Capital Letters

Except at the beginning of a sentence, capital letters, **lettres majuscules,** are not used for the names of the months and of the days of the week : as **avril, lundi ;** for any word used as an adjective: as **un officier français** ; for any word used to signify rank or position: as **empereur, roi, duc, général, cardinal, docteur, abbé, maire,** etc.

Punctuation Marks

The marks of punctuation most frequently used are:

le point	.	le point d'exclamation	!
le virgule	,	le trait d'union	-
le point (et) virgule	;	la parenthèse	( )
les deux points	:	les guillemets	" "
le point d'interrogation	?	les points de suspension	...

Expressions for Classroom Use

1. **Monsieur (M.),** *Sir, Mr.*
2. **Madame (Mme),** *Madam, Mrs.*
3. **Mademoiselle (Mlle),** *Miss.*
4. **Bonjour,** *Good morning, good day.*
5. **Bonsoir,** *Good evening.*   6. **Au revoir,** *Good-by.*
7. **Bon amusement,** *Enjoy yourself.*
8. **Bonne chance,** *Good luck to you.*
9. **Au plaisir,** *Until I have the pleasure of seeing you again.*
10. **A demain,** *Good-by, until to-morrow.*
11. **Un peu de silence, s'il vous plaît,** *Quiet, please.*[1]
12. **Tenez-vous droit,** *Stand erect.*[1]
13. **Prenez vos livres,** *Take your books.*
14. **Ouvrez vos livres,** *Open your books.*
15. **Quelle leçon?** *What lesson?*
16. **Quelle page?** *What page?*
17. **Lisez,** *Read.*   18. **Lisez à haute voix,** *Read aloud.*
19. **Pas si vite,** *Not so fast.*

---

[1] These expressions and a number of other "Expressions de conversation" were suggested by Miss Tatiana Boldyreff, of Battle Creek College, Michigan.

20. **Parlez plus haut,** *Speak louder.*
21. **C'est cela, c'est très bien,** *That's it, very good.*
22. **C'est mal, c'est très mal,** *That's bad, very bad.*
23. **Comment dites-vous?** *How do you say?*
24. **Vous prononcez mal,** *You pronounce badly.*
25. **Écoutez,** *Listen.*
26. **Prononcez⌣après moi,** *Pronounce after me.*
27. **A la bonne heure,** *Good! Fine!*
28. **Continuez,** *Continue, proceed.*
29. **S'il vous plaît,** *If you please.*
30. **Plaît-il?** *What do (did) you say?*
31. **Pardon,** *I beg your pardon.*
32. **Merci,** *Thank you.*
33. **Il n'y a pas de quoi,** ⎫
34. **De rien,**   ⎬ *Don't mention it, you are welcome.*
                ⎭
35. **Allez⌣au tableau,** *Go to the blackboard.*
36. **Écrivez,** *Write.*
37. **En⌣anglais,** *In English.*
38. **En français,** *In French.*
39. **Allez⌣à votre place,** *Go to your seat.*
40. **Traduisez,** *Translate.*
41. **Faites⌣attention,** *Pay attention, look out!*
42. **Répétez,** *Repeat.*
43. **Répétez⌣ensemble,** *Repeat together.*
44. **Commencez la lecture,** *Begin the reading.*
45. **Suivant,** *Next.*
46. **Comprenez-vous?** *Do you understand?*
47. **Vous comprenez, n'est-ce pas?** *You understand, do you not?*
48. **Oui, monsieur, je comprends,** *Yes, Sir, I understand.*
49. **Non, madame, je ne comprends pas,** *No, Madam, I don't understand.*
50. **Savez-vous?** *Do you know?*
51. **Non, mademoiselle, je ne sais pas,** *No, Miss, I don't know.*

52. **Levez la main,** *Raise your hand.*
53. **Répondez à ma question,** *Answer my question.*
54. **Répondez en français,** *Answer in French.*
55. **Défense de parler anglais,** *Speaking English prohibited.*
56. **Qu'est-ce que c'est?** *What is it?*
57. **Où sommes-nous?** *Where are we?*
58. **Au haut de la page,** *At the top of the page.*
59. **Au bas de la page,** *At the bottom of the page.*
60. **Au milieu de la page,** *In the middle of the page.*
61. **Quel mot, quelle phrase?** *What word, what sentence?*
62. **Vous êtes en retard,** *You are late.*
63. **Vous vous trompez,** *You are mistaken.*
64. **A qui le tour?** *Whose turn is it?*
65. **C'est à moi,** *It is my turn.*
66. **Regardez,** *Look.*
67. **Voyez-vous les fautes?** *Do you see the mistakes?*
68. **Est-ce clair?** *Is that clear?*
69. **Est-ce correct?** *Is that correct?*
70. **Apprenez par cœur,** *Memorize, study by heart.*
71. **Permettez!** *Allow me!*
72. **Pas du tout,** *Not at all.*
73. **Récitez la leçon,** *Recite the lesson.*
74. **Levez-vous,** *Get up, stand up.*
75. **Asseyez-vous,** *Be seated.*
76. **Dites-moi,** *Tell me.*
77. **Corrigez les fautes,** *Correct the mistakes.*
78. **Voilà, c'est bien simple!** *There you are, that's very simple.*
79. **Ce n'est pas difficile,** *That is not difficult.*
80. **Que faites-vous?** *What are you doing?*
81. **Cela ne fait rien,** *That does not matter.*
82. **C'est assez,** *That's enough.*
83. **C'est fini,** *That's finished (the lesson is over).*
84. **C'est tout,** *That's all.*
85. **Cela suffit,** *That will do.*

An Easy Way to Increase One's Vocabulary

A great many words are identical in both English and French. Most of these words have the following endings:

-ace, -ice.*	populace, police.
-ant, -ent.	arrogant, content, prudent.
-acle.	spectacle, miracle, obstacle.
-ade.*	cavalcade, parade.
-al.	festival, loyal, royal.
-ance,* -ence.*	balance, innocence.
-able, -ible.	durable, capable, visible.
-ge, -gue.	cortège, privilège, monologue, intrigue.
-ile.*	docile, pile, mobile.
-ine.*	marine, sardine.
-ion.*	position, commission, direction.
-ude.*	multitude, solicitude.

A great many other words have just a slight change in the ending:

-acy	⎫	-atie,*	democratie (see), autocratie.
-ary, -ory		-aire, -oire,	militaire, gloire.
-ancy, -ency,		-ance, -ence,*	constance, décence.
-ia,		-ie,*	pneumonie, Californie.
-ic, -cal,		-ique,*	identique, musique, biblique.
-ine,	change	-in,	félin, ravin.
-ist,	into	-iste,	anarchiste, liste.
-ive,		-if,	intensif, attentif, pensif.
-or,		-eur,	ardeur, professeur, acteur.
-ous,		-eux,	désireux, harmonieux.
-ty, after a vowel,		-té,*	beauté, hospitalité.
y, after a conson.	⎭	-ie,*	orgie, monarchie.

* The nouns ending with the termination marked with a (*) are usually feminine.

THE NEW CHARDENAL

1ère Leçon: L'article défini

Tel père, tel fils. — *Like father, like son.*[1]

Observe the different forms of the definite article:

le livre, *the book.*   l'élève, *the pupil.*
la table, *the table.*   l'homme, *the man.*

There is no neuter gender in French.   All nouns are either masculine or feminine.   The gender of a noun is shown by the article.

Always learn the article with each noun.

The singular definite article *the* is translated in French by:

le before a masculine noun beginning with a consonant,
la before a feminine noun beginning with a consonant,
l' before a noun (m. or f.) beginning with a vowel or **h** mute.

Note. — The apostrophe is not a sign of separation of sound, but of union.   **L'élève** is pronounced **lélève.**

Attention! The definite article is repeated before each noun it modifies.

Vocabulaire

le professeur, *the teacher.*   la femme, *the woman, the wife.*
l'élève, *the pupil.*   la table, *the table.*
l'homme, *the man.*   la plume, *the pen.*
le livre, *the book.*   la règle, *the ruler.*
le crayon, *the pencil.*   la craie, *the chalk.*

montrez-moi, *show me.*   voici, *here is, here are.*
donnez-moi, *give me.*   voilà, *there is, there are.*
aussi, *also, too.*   et, *and.*

---

[1] Literally, *Such a father, such a son.*

Lecture

1. Le professeur; voici le professeur.   2. L'élève; voilà
l'élève.   3. Montrez-moi le crayon.   4. Voici le crayon.
5. Donnez-moi le livre.   6. Voici le livre.   7. Voici la
règle.   8. Voici la table, la règle et la plume.   9. Montrez-moi aussi le livre et le crayon.   10. Voici le livre et
voilà le crayon.

Exercices

A. *Remplacez les tirets par l'article qui convient.* (*Replace
the dashes by the suitable article.*)

1. —— règle. 2. —— plume. 3. —— homme.
4. —— crayon. 5. —— femme. 6. Voici —— table.
7. Voilà —— livre. 8. Donnez-moi —— craie. 9. Montrez-moi —— professeur.   10. Voici —— crayon,
—— plume et —— règle.

B. *Traduisez en français.* (*Translate into French.*)
1. The man, the pen, the book.   2. The woman, the table, the chalk.   3. The teacher and the pupil.   4. Show me the book.   5. There is the book.   6. Give me the pencil.   7. Here is the pencil.   8. Show me also the table.   9. There is the table.   10. Give me the book.
11. Here are the book, pencil, and pen.   12. Show me the man and woman.   13. There are the man and woman.

Exercice de prononciation.   Le son " a " (as in *cat*)

ba, da, ma, la, ta, sa, va, lala, dada, mama, tata, tralala, Panama, caravane, malade, carnaval, Canada, salade, partage, madame, banal, amalgame, Trafalgar, Madagascar.

*   *   *   *   *   *   *

2ᵉ Leçon: L'article indéfini

Petit à petit, l'oiseau fait son nid. — *Little by little the bird builds its nest.*

Observe the different forms of the indefinite article :

un livre, *a book.*	**un élève,** *a pupil.*
une table, *a table.*	**une boîte,** *a box.*

The singular indefinite article *a* or *an* is translated by :

> **un** before a masculine noun,
> **une** before a feminine noun.

When the masculine noun begins with a vowel or **h** mute, the **n** of **un** is carried over and pronounced with the next word, just as if that word itself began with **n**.

> **Un élève** is pronounced **un nélève.**
> **Un homme** is pronounced **un nomme.**

Attention ! The indefinite article is repeated before each noun it modifies.

Vocabulaire

un tableau, *a blackboard.*	une boîte, *a box.*
un plumier, *a pencil box.*	une chaise, *a chair.*
un pupitre, *a desk.*	une porte, *a door.*
un papier, *a paper.*	une fenêtre, *a window.*
un canif, *a penknife.*	une gomme, *an eraser.*

Lecture

1. Une table et une chaise. 2. Une porte et une fenêtre.
3. Un crayon, une plume et un papier. 4. Donnez-moi
une gomme. 5. Voici un crayon et une gomme. 6. Montrez-moi un tableau. 7. Voilà un livre. 8. Montrez-moi aussi un canif. 9. Voici un canif. 10. Voici un
homme et voilà une femme.

Exercices

A. *Remplacez les tirets par l'article indéfini qui convient:*
1. —— professeur et —— élève. 2. —— livre, ——
crayon et —— gomme. 3. —— porte, —— fenêtre et
—— tableau. 4. —— pupitre, —— table et —— chaise.
5. Donnez-moi —— papier et —— crayon. 6. Montrez-moi
—— plumier, —— boîte, —— plume et —— canif. 7. Donnez-moi —— livre, —— règle, —— crayon et —— chaise.

B. *Traduisez en français:*
1. A woman, a pupil. 2. A professor, a man. 3. A
table and a chair. 4. A window and a door. 5. Show
me a pencil box. 6. Give me a penknife. 7. Here is a
book. 8. Here is a box and a pencil. 9. There is a blackboard. 10. There are a pen, ruler, and eraser.

Exercice de prononciation. **Le son " i "** (as in *machine*)

midi, ici, fini, risible, difficile, Paris, merci, civil, défini,
cilice, pacifique, discipline, rigide, activisme, ministre.

* * * * * * *

3ᵉ Leçon: Présent de l'indicatif du verbe AVOIR,
to have

C'est le premier pas qui coûte. — *It is the first step that costs.*

---

j'ai, *I have.*	**nous‿avons,** *we have.*
tu as, *thou hast.*	**vous‿avez,** *you have.*
il a, *he has.*	**ils‿ont,** *they* (m.) *have.*
elle a, *she has.*	**elles‿ont,** *they* (f.) *have.*

The French word for *I* is **je**. Before a vowel or silent **h**, **je** becomes **j'**. Instead of **je ai**, we say **j'ai**.

Note. — **Vous,** like the English *you,* may be either singular or plural. **Tu** is a familiar form used in addressing members of one's family, intimate friends, children, or animals. **Vous** should always be used in the exercises of this book unless otherwise directed.

Vocabulaire

le père, *the father.*	**un frère,** *a brother.*
la mère, *the mother.*	**une sœur,** *a sister.*
un fils (feess), *a son.*	**l'ami,** *the friend* (m.).
une fille, *a daughter, girl.*	**l'amie,** *the friend* (f.).
l'enfant, *the child.*	**le garçon,** *the boy.*

Lecture

1. J'ai un ami.   2. Tu as une sœur.   3. Nous avons une fille.   4. Elle a un fils.   5. Vous avez un frère. 6. Le père et la mère ont un fils.   7. Ils ont aussi une fille. 8. L'enfant a un père et une mère.   9. Le garçon a un ami et une amie.   10. Il a aussi une sœur.

Exercices

A. *Remplacez les tirets par la forme convenable du verbe* **avoir:**

1. Nous —— un fils et une fille.   2. Elle —— aussi un enfant.   3. Vous —— un ami et une amie.   4. Ils —— un frère et une sœur.   5. Elles —— un père et une mère. 6. Le garçon —— le livre.   7. Tu —— la boîte.   8. Vous —— un crayon et nous —— le papier.

B. *Traduisez en français:*

1. The teacher has a son.   2. He has a son.   3. The pupil has a pencil.   4. You have also a book.   5. They have the paper and a pencil.   6. They (*f.*) have a father and mother.   7. We have the book, ruler, paper, and pen. 8. She has a father, mother, and brother.

Exercice de prononciation.   **Le son "u"** (see *Introduction*)

mu, mur, murmure, su, sur, pu, pur, du, dur, prune, rhume, lune ; j'ai vu une plume sur le pupitre.

Prononcez rapidement: mu, mi, mi, mu, su, si, si, su, ru, ri, bu, bi, bibi, bubu, lilili, lululu, turlututu.

Conversation

— Bonjour,[1] monsieur, madame, mademoiselle!	Good day, sir, madam, miss!

---

[1] **Bonjour,** *good day,* is used in French all day long until sunset. Therefore both *good morning* and *good afternoon* are translated **Bonjour.**

LA TOMBE DU SOLDAT INCONNU À PARIS.

— Comment allez-vous?	How do you do?
— Très bien, merci; et vous?	Very well, thank you; and you?
— Pas trop mal, merci; mais mon frère est malade.	Pretty well, thank you; but my brother is ill.
— Oh! C'est dommage! Je regrette beaucoup.	Oh! That's too bad! I am very sorry.

*   *   *   *   *   *   *

4e Leçon: Présent de l'indicatif du verbe AVOIR, forme interrogative

A bon chat, bon rat. — *Tit for tat.*[1]

ai-je?	*have I?*	**avons-nous?**	*have we?*
as-tu?	*hast thou?*	**avez-vous?**	*have you?*
a-t-il?	*has he?*	**ont-ils?**	*have they* (m.)?
a-t-elle?	*has she?*	**ont-elles?**	*have they* (f.)?

Note that in the above questions, where the subject is a personal pronoun, the verb comes first and the pronoun follows, just as in English. In French, the verb and the pronoun are connected by a hyphen.

Note also the euphonic -t-. This -t- is added in the third person singular whenever the verb ends in a vowel (**e** or **a**).

Vocabulaire

l'oncle, *the uncle.*	**le neveu,** *the nephew.*
la tante, *the aunt.*	**la nièce,** *the niece.*
le cousin, *the cousin.*	**la grammaire,** *the grammar.*
la cousine, *the cousin* (f.).	**l'encre** (f.), *the ink.*
vu, *seen.*	**Jean,** *John.*
perdu, *lost.*	**Jeanne,** *Jane.*
trouvé, *found.*	**Louis,** *Louis.*
pris, *taken.*	**Louise,** *Louise.*
	oui, *yes.*

---

[1] Literally, *For a good cat a good rat.*

Lecture

1. Ai-je une grammaire? 2. Oui, monsieur, vous‿avez‿ une grammaire. 3. Jeanne, avez-vous‿un‿oncle et une tante? 4. Oui, madame, j'ai un‿oncle et une tante. 5. As-tu l'encre, Louis? 6. Oui, mademoiselle, j'ai pris l'encre et la plume. 7. Ont-ils un cousin et une cousine? 8. Avons-nous‿un neveu et une nièce? 9. Avez-vous vu le canif? 10. A-t-il trouvé la règle et le crayon? 11. Ont-ils perdu le plumier? 12. A-t-elle pris la grammaire?

Exercices

A. *Mettez les phrases suivantes à la forme interrogative. (Turn the following sentences into questions.)*

1. J'ai un fils. 2. Nous avons la plume. 3. Elle a un oncle et une tante. 4. Tu as un cousin. 5. Il a la grammaire. 6. Vous avez une nièce. 7. Ils ont perdu la règle. 8. Nous avons trouvé le papier. 9. Elle a pris l'encre.

B. *Traduisez en français :*

1. Have you a father and mother? 2. Have they a son and a daughter? 3. Has he an uncle and aunt? 4. Has she a nephew and a niece? 5. Have you taken the grammar? 6. Has he found the ink? 7. Have you (*2d pers. sing.*) seen a box, John? 8. Have we lost the ruler and the chalk? 9. Louise, have you taken the pencil? 10. Have they (*f.*) seen the cousin (*m.*) and the cousin (*f.*)?

Exercice de prononciation. Le son " e " (as in *her*)

le, me, ne, de, se, re, ne, que, le petit, le menu, le me ne, je se re, (*quickly*) le me ne je, se re ne que. (*Repeat 5 times.*)

Conversation

— Bonsoir, monsieur, madame, mademoiselle !	Good evening, sir, madam, miss !
— Comment vous portez-vous ce soir ?	How are you this evening ?
— Je me porte très bien, merci, et vous ?	I am very well, thank you, and you ?
— Comment va votre sœur ?	How is your sister ?
— Elle a mal à la tête.	She has a headache.
— C'est très désagréable.	It is very disagreeable.

* * * * * * *

5ᵉ Leçon : Présent de l'indicatif du verbe AVOIR, forme négative

---

Il n'a pas inventé la poudre. — *He will never set the river on fire.*[1]

---

je n'ai pas, *I have not.*
tu n'as pas, *thou hast not.*
il n'a pas, *he has not.*
elle n'a pas, *she has not.*

nous n'avons pas, *we have not.*
vous n'avez pas, *you have not.*
ils n'ont pas, *they* (m.) *have not.*
elles n'ont pas, *they* (f.) *have not.*

Ne   Verb   *Pas*

Not is expressed by *two* words in French, **ne** and **pas**. They are placed one on either side of the verb, **ne** before, **pas** after.

---

[1] Literally, *He didn't invent gunpowder.*

Ne becomes **n'** before a verb beginning with a vowel or **h** mute.

Observe the following constructions :

> Je *n'*ai *pas* **vu**.   *I have not seen.*
> Il *n'*a *pas* **pris**.   *He has not taken.*

In compound tenses, **ne** and **pas** come one on either side of the *auxiliary verb;* in other words, **pas** comes before the past participle (**vu,** *seen,* and **pris,** *taken,* in the present case).

Le féminin des adjectifs. — Feminine of adjectives. —
Note the change in the adjective :

> **un petit garçon,** *a little boy.*
> **une petite fille,** *a little girl.*

An adjective agrees in gender with its noun.

Adjectives, like the indefinite article, **un,** form their feminine by adding **e** mute to the masculine singular. However, to show that the adjective is feminine, the consonant preceding the mute **e** is strongly sounded. *Example :* **peti-tt** for **petite, gran-dd** for **grande.**

Adjectives ending in **e** mute do not change in the feminine.

> **un jeune homme,** *a young man.*
> **une jeune femme,** *a young woman.*

Vocabulaire

petit (m.), **petite** (f.), *little, small, short.*	**jeune,** *young.*
grand (m.), **grande** (f.), *large, tall, great, big.*	**la leçon,** *the lesson.*
joli (m.), **jolie** (f.), *pretty.*	**que?** *what?*
méchant (m.), **méchante** (f.), *naughty, wicked.*	**de,** *of, from.*
gentil (m.), **gentille** (f.), *nice.*	**non,** *no.*
qu'avez-vous? *what have you?*	**très,** *very.*

Lecture

1. Je n'ai pas la petite chaise.   2. Il n'a pas la grande règle.   3. L'homme a une gentille petite fille.   4. Jean, avez-vous perdu la grande gomme?   5. Non, monsieur, je n'ai pas perdu la gomme.   6. Le professeur a une méchante petite nièce.   7. La jeune cousine a une très jolie tante.

8. Vous n'avez pas la grande chaise.   9. Ils n'ont pas perdu la petite boîte.   10. Elles n'ont pas vu la jeune sœur de Louis.

Exercices

A. *Mettez les phrases suivantes à la forme négative:*

1. Il a le joli papier.   2. J'ai la petite grammaire.
3. Vous avez le joli canif.   4. Elle a perdu la grande boîte.
5. Nous avons pris la petite plume.   6. Elles ont trouvé le grand crayon.   7. Ils ont vu la gentille jeune fille.

B. *Traduisez en français:*

1. Have you the small ruler?   2. No sir, I have not the small ruler.   3. What have you?   4. We have the large ruler.   5. She has not the small grammar.   6. They have not a pretty niece.   7. Show me a young girl.   8. There is the naughty girl!   9. We have not seen the young woman.   10. He has lost the large pen.

Exercice de prononciation

Séparez en syllabes. (*Separate into syllables.*) (Syllables, in French, begin whenever possible with a consonant.)

professeur, élève, fenêtre, pupître, perdu, enfant, une, ami, cousine.

Liaison: Le petit‿enfant; nous‿avons‿un petit‿ami.

Expressions de conversation

Pardon, monsieur, madame, mademoiselle.	Pardon me, sir, madam, miss.
Que dites-vous?	What do you say?
Je vous demande pardon.	I beg your pardon.
Cela ne fait rien.	It does not matter.
Merci bien, merci beaucoup.	Thank you, thank you very much.
Merci mille fois.	Thank you a thousand times.
C'est‿assez.	That's enough.
Cela suffit.	That will do.

6e Leçon: Présent de l'indicatif du verbe AVOIR, forme négative-interrogative

Nécessité n'a pas de loi. — *Necessity knows no law.*

n'ai-je pas? *have I not?*

n'as-tu pas? *hast thou not?*

n'a-t-il pas? *has he not?*

n'a-t-elle pas? *has she not?*

n'avons-nous pas? *have we not?*

n'avez-vous pas? *have you not?*

n'ont-ils pas? *have they* (m.) *not?*

n'ont-elles pas? *have they* (f.) *not?*

In the negative-interrogative form, **ne** always precedes the verb, and **pas** comes after the *pronoun subject.* In other words, it is simply the interrogative form (**ai-je**) conjugated with **ne** preceding, and **pas** following.

Yes — *Si*. — In answering affirmatively to a negative question, **si** should be used instead of **oui**.

N'avez-vous pas la grammaire? *Have you not the grammar?*

Si, j'ai la grammaire. *Yes, I have the grammar.*

Questions avec un nom comme sujet. — Questions with a noun subject. — When the subject of an interrogative sentence is a noun (or any other pronoun except a personal pronoun) that noun is placed before the verb and the verb is followed by **il, elle, ils,** or **elles,** according to the gender and number of the noun subject.

Le professeur a-t-*il* la grammaire? *Has the professor the grammar?*

La tante a-t-*elle* une fille? *Has the aunt a daughter?*

Place des adjectifs. — Position of adjectives. — French adjectives usually follow the noun they modify. Only a limited number of adjectives are placed before the noun; some of those (nearly one half) were given in the preceding lesson. (For complete list, see Lesson 20.)

un homme riche, *a rich man.* **une leçon facile,** *an easy lesson.*

Le Palais du Luxembourg à Paris.

Vocabulaire

riche, *rich.*   facile, *easy.*
pauvre, *poor.*   difficile, *difficult.*
charmant (m.), charmante (f.), *charming.*

Lecture

1. N'avez-vous pas une gentille petite fille?   2. Le professeur n'a-t-il pas une tante très riche?   3. N'a-t-elle pas une sœur charmante?   4. Si madame, elle a une sœur charmante et très jolie.   5. N'avez-vous pas vu la jeune cousine de Louise?   6. N'ont-ils pas une mère très pauvre? 7. N'avons-nous pas une leçon difficile?   8. Si mademoiselle, nous avons une leçon très difficile.   9. N'ont-elles pas trouvé la grande règle?   10. N'a-t-elle pas pris la petite gomme?

Exercices

A. *Mettez les phrases suivantes à la forme interrogative :*

1. Vous n'avez pas la craie.   2. Je n'ai pas le grand papier.   3. Elles n'ont pas l'encre.   4. Nous n'avons pas vu le professeur.   5. Il n'a pas pris la petite grammaire. 6. Vous n'avez pas perdu la grande plume.   7. Elle n'a pas trouvé la jolie règle.   8. L'homme a un fils.   9. La fille a une mère.   10. Louise a une jeune cousine.

B. *Traduisez en français :*

1. The professor has not the pen, he has the pencil. 2. Has he not the large book?   3. Yes, he has the large book.   4. Have you not seen the naughty little girl? 5. Has he not a charming little niece?   6. Yes, he has a charming niece.   7. Hasn't Jane the grammar?   8. We have not the grammar.   9. Hasn't the man a pretty daughter?   10. Yes.   11. I have not seen the child. 12. Have they (*f.*) not taken the small ruler?   13. Have you not a difficult lesson?   14. Have they not found the pencil, paper, and pen?

Exercice de prononciation. Le son " o " (between *not* and *nut*)

robe, mode, sobre, octobre, porte, poche, homme, parole, commode, l'or, bonne, donne, école, protocole, monotone.

Conversation

Paul.	Bonjour, Jean !	Good day, John !
Jean.	Bonjour, Paul !	Good day, Paul !
Paul.	Comment ça va-t-il ?	How are you (*familiar*)?
Jean.	Pas trop mal, merci ; et vous ?	So-so, thank you ; and you?
Paul.	Pourquoi " pas trop mal "?	Why do you say " so-so "?
Jean.	J'ai un rhume, et je vais chez (shay) le médecin.	I have a cold, and I am going to the doctor.
Paul.	Au revoir, Jean.	Good-by, John.
Jean.	Au revoir, Paul.	Good-by, Paul.

Note. — In this conversation and those which will follow, a pupil should take the part of Paul and another the part of Jean. These useful and practical drills should be repeated several times, then in unison, the left side of the class taking the part of Paul and the right side the part of Jean.

* * * * * * *

7ᵉ Leçon : Présent de l'indicatif du verbe ÊTRE, *to be*

La parole est d'argent, le silence est d'or. — *Speech is silver, silence is gold.*

Forme affirmative	Forme interrogative
je suis, *I am.*	**suis-je?** *am I?*
tu es, *thou art.*	**es-tu?** *art thou?*
il est, *he is.*	**est-il?** *is he?*
elle est, *she is.*	**est-elle?** *is she?*
nous sommes, *we are.*	**sommes-nous?** *are we?*
vous êtes, *you are.*	**êtes-vous?** *are you?*
ils sont, *they* (m.) *are.*	**sont-ils?** *are they* (m.)?
elles sont, *they* (f.) *are.*	**sont-elles?** *are they* (f.)?

How to translate

It *is*

il est	elle est
when the noun for which **il** stands is masculine singular.	when the noun for which **elle** stands is feminine singular.

Où est *le* livre?
Il est sur la table.

Où est *la* plume?
Elle est sur la table.

Vocabulaire

l'école (f.), *the school.*
à l'école, *at school.*
la salle de classe, *the classroom.*
la cour, *the court, yard.*
sur, *on.*

la maîtresse, *the teacher* (f.).
dans, *in.*
où? *where?*
qui? *who?*

Lecture

1. L'école est grande, la cour est petite.   2. Nous sommes à l'école.   3. Le professeur est-il dans la salle de

classe? 4. Oui, madame, il est dans la salle de classe.
5. Qui est la maîtresse? 6. Vous_êtes la maîtresse. 7. Où
est le livre? 8. Il est sur le pupitre. 9. Le père de Louis
est-il riche? 10. La mère de Jeanne est-elle pauvre?
11. La salle de classe est-elle grande? 12. Non, elle est
petite.

Exercices

A. *Remplacez les tirets par les pronoms qui conviennent:*

1. Où est la plume? —— est sur le pupitre. 2. Où est
le crayon? —— est aussi sur le pupitre. 3. Où est la
salle de classe? —— est dans l'école. 4. Où est le tableau? —— est dans la salle de classe.

B. *Traduisez en français:*

1. The grammar is difficult. 2. Is it difficult? 3. Is
the pupil young? 4. Louise, are you short? 5. No, I
am tall, I am a big girl. 6. Where is the class? 7. The
class is in the classroom. 8. Where is the classroom?
9. The classroom is in the school. 10. Is the blackboard
in the classroom? 11. Yes, it is in the classroom. 12. Is
the grammar small? 13. No, madam, it is large.

Exercice de prononciation. " e " before c, f, l, r, s, t
(*e* as in *set*)

bec, sec, nef, pelle, sel, belle, fer, cher, Albert, des, mes,
reste, nette, mettre, secret.
Séparez en syllabes: école, exercice, salle, classe, vocabu-
laire, traduisez, remplacez, lecture.

Expressions de conversation

Parlez-vous français, ma-dame?	Do you speak French, madam?
Très peu, monsieur, et très mal.	Very little, sir, and very badly.

A qui le tour?	Whose turn is it?
C'est à moi.	It is my turn.
Non, c'est à vous.	No, it is your turn.
Je vous demande pardon, c'est à moi.	I beg your pardon, it is my turn.
C'est bien.	That's all right. (Very well.)

* * * * * * *

8ᵉ Leçon: Présent de l'indicatif du verbe ÊTRE

Pauvreté n'est pas vice. — *Poverty is no crime.*

FORME NÉGATIVE	FORME NÉGATIVE-INTERROGATIVE
je ne suis pas, *I am not.*	**ne suis-je pas?** *am I not?*
tu n'es pas, *thou art not.*	**n'es-tu pas?** *art thou not?*
il n'est pas, *he is not.*	**n'est-il pas?** *is he not?*
elle n'est pas, *she is not.*	**n'est-elle pas?** *is she not?*
nous ne sommes pas, *we are not.*	**ne sommes-nous pas?** *are we not?*
vous n'êtes pas, *you are not.*	**n'êtes-vous pas?** *are you not?*
ils ne sont pas, *they* (m.) *are not.*	**ne sont-ils pas?** *are they* (m.) *not?*
elles ne sont pas, *they* (f.) *are not.*	**ne sont-elles pas?** *are they* (f.) *not?*

Pluriel des noms et des adjectifs. — Plural of nouns and adjectives. — As a general rule, the plural of *nouns* and *adjectives* is formed by adding a *silent* **s** to the singular.   The **s** being silent, a special article is necessary to prevent confusion in the spoken language.   That article is **les** which is substituted for **le, la,** and **l'**.

> Le grand frère, *the big brother.*
> *Les* grand**s** frère**s**, *the big brothers.*
> La petite sœur, *the little sister.*
> *Les* petite**s** sœur**s**, *the little sisters.*

Accord des adjectifs. — Agreement of adjectives. —
(1) An adjective modifying two or more masculine nouns must be masculine plural.

(2) An adjective modifying two or more feminine nouns must be feminine plural.

(3) An adjective modifying two or more nouns of *different* genders must be *masculine* plural.

(1) **Le père et le fils sont grands.**   *The father and son are tall.*
(2) **La mère et la fille sont grandes.**   *The mother and daughter are tall.*
(3) *Le* **père et** *la* **mère sont grands.**   *The father and mother are tall.*

How to translate

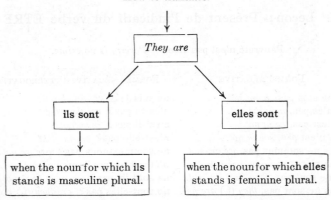

Où sont les livres?   **Où sont les plumes?**
Ils **sont sur la table.**   *Elles* **sont sur la table.**

Attention! When *they are* stands for two nouns of *different* genders (masculine and feminine), it is translated by ***ils sont***.

Les crayons (m.) **et les plumes** (f.) **sont-*ils* bons?**   **Oui,** *ils* **sont bons.**
Are the pencils and pens good?   *Yes, they are good.*

Vocabulaire

le banc, *the bench.*	**assis, assise** (f.), *seated.*
l'exercice (m.), *the exercise.*	**debout,** adv., *standing.*
malade, *ill, sick.*	**ou,** *or.*
ici, *here.*	**là,** *there.*

Le Grand Lac, au Bois de Boulogne à Paris.
Vue de Paris, prise de St. Gervais.

Lecture

1. Êtes-vous à l'école, Louis? 2. Oui, monsieur, je suis à l'école. 3. Où est Jean? 4. Il n'est pas ici, mademoiselle, il est dans la cour. 5. Les élèves ne sont-ils pas debout dans la cour? 6. Non, madame, ils sont assis sur les bancs dans la salle de classe. 7. Le professeur et la petite fille sont-ils ici? 8. Qui est là, dans la cour? 9. Jeanne est dans la cour, mademoiselle, elle est malade. 10. Les exercices et les leçons ne sont-ils pas difficiles? 11. Si, ils sont très difficiles. 12. Avez-vous un crayon ou une plume?

Exercices

A. *Remplacez les tirets par les pronoms qui conviennent:*

1. Où sont les bancs? —— sont dans la salle de classe.
2. Où sont les grandes règles? —— sont sur la table.
3. Où sont les plumes et les crayons? —— sont dans le plumier. 4. Où sont les exercices et les leçons? —— sont dans la grammaire.

B. *Mettez les phrases suivantes au pluriel:*

1. Je suis sur la chaise. 2. Le petit garçon n'est pas assis. 3. Le grand crayon est-il dans la petite boîte? 4. L'élève n'est-il pas dans la salle de classe? 5. Tu es ici et il est là.

C. *Traduisez en français:*

1. Where am I? 2. Where are we? 3. Where are you? 4. Are you not in the classroom? 5. I am not in the classroom. 6. Is the book on the table? 7. Are the pupils seated on the benches or on the chairs? 8. Who is there? 9. Is Jane seated or standing? 10. Am I not the professor and are you not the pupils? 11. The professor and Jane are tall. 12. Louise and John are short.

Exercice de prononciation. Le son " é " (*may*)

é, é, et, bé, cé, dé, été, décidé, préféré, liberté, égalité, fraternité, j'ai répété, j'ai préféré, j'ai décidé.

Liaison : les_élèves, les_enfants, les_exercices, les_enfants sont_assis.

Expressions de conversation

M'en voulez-vous?	Are you angry with me?
Pas le moins du monde !	Not in the least !
Je ne vous_en veux pas.	I am not angry with you.
Est-ce bien vrai?	Is it really true?
C'est la pure vérité.	It is absolutely true.
J'en doute.	I doubt it.
N'en doutez pas je vous prie.	Take my word for it. (*Literally*, Do not doubt it, I beg of you.)

*   *   *   *   *   *   *

9e Leçon : Possession

Loin des yeux, loin du cœur. — *Out of sight, out of mind.*[1]

> **le livre de Jeanne,** *Jane's book.*
> **les enfants de la femme,** *the woman's children.*

The apostrophe followed by *s* ('*s*), used to denote possession in English, is not employed in French. There is no possessive case for nouns ; the preposition **de** is used instead. Therefore, such expressions as : *the man's house, the pupil's book*, should be translated by : *the house* OF *the man, the book* OF *the pupil*.

Note that the word signifying the possessor *always follows* the thing possessed.

---

[1] Literally, *Far from the eyes, far from the heart.*

Contraction de l'article défini avec la préposition *de*. — Study the following sentences :

le livre *du* professeur, *the professor's book.*
les livres *des* professeurs, *the professors' books.*
les enfants *de l'*homme et *de la* femme, *the children of the man and woman.*

The preposition **de,** *of, from,* can *never* be followed by the articles **le** or **les.**

> De le is contracted into du.
> De les is contracted into des.

No contraction occurs when **de** is followed by **la** or **l'**.

Attention! The preposition **de,** alone or contracted with the article, *must be repeated* before each noun it governs.

Vocabulaire

la maison, *the house.*	**acheté,** *bought.*
la chambre, *the room.*	**parlé,** *spoken.*
le salon, *the parlor.*	**fermé,** *closed.*
la salle à manger, *the dining room.*	**ouvert,** *open.*
le médecin, *the doctor.*	**mis,** *put.*
l'avocat, *the lawyer.*	**reçu,** *received.*
la famille, *the family.*	**un, une,** *one.*
la poche, *the pocket.*	**deux,** *two.*
la lettre, *the letter.*	**trois,** *three.*
le mouchoir, *the handkerchief.*	**quatre,** *four.*
la montre, *the watch.*	**bien,** *well.*

c'est bien, *that's all right.*

Lecture

1. La maison du père du médecin est très grande.
2. Nous sommes dans la maison du cousin de Louise.
3. Avez-vous fermé la porte du salon?   4. Oui, madame,
et j'ai ouvert les fenêtres de la salle à manger.   5. C'est bien,
Marie, merci.   6. Nous avons reçu deux lettres de l'oncle
et de la tante du fils du professeur.   7. Elles sont sur la
table de la chambre de Jeanne.   8. Henri, vous êtes un
méchant garçon, vous avez mis le mouchoir de Paul dans la
poche de Charles.   9. J'ai vu la montre de la jeune fille,
elle est très jolie.   10. Il a parlé du médecin, de l'avocat et
du professeur.   11. Qui a mis les livres des enfants sur les
chaises du salon?   12. A-t-il acheté les plumes des élèves?

Exercices

A. *Remplacez les tirets par* **de** *et un article défini.*

1. Qui a fermé les fenêtres —— chambre, —— salon et
—— salle à manger?   2. Nous avons parlé —— famille
—— élèves —— professeur.   3. Jeanne, avez-vous le mouchoir —— garçon?   4. Montrez-moi la maison —— nièces
—— médecin.   5. La famille —— avocat n'est-elle pas
grande?   6. Elle a reçu une lettre —— cousines ——
professeur.

B. *Traduisez en français:*

1. The parlor, of the parlor, the parlors, of the parlors.
2. The pocket, of the pocket, the pockets, of the pockets.
3. Of the lawyer, of the lawyers.   4. The child, of the
child, of the children.   5. The family, of the family, of the
families.   6. John's father is ill.   7. The professor's book
is lost.   8. Are not the young girls Paul's sisters?

Exercice-revue

1. The blackboard, a desk, the eraser.   2. Show me the
box, pens, and ink.   3. I have a little cousin; she is very

nice.   4. The grammar is difficult.   5. Have you not taken a book into the classroom?   6. Good day, sir, how do you do?   7. There are the naughty little boys.   8. Are they not in the class?   9. Here is an exercise ; it is (a) difficult (one).   10. Charles, where are you?   11. I am here, madam, in the yard.   12. Who is seated in the room?

Exercice de prononciation.   Le son " è " (*met*)

è, ê, les, des, mes, mère, père, très, mais, jamais, il est Français, fête, bête, rêve.

Prononcez rapidement : et est, et est, et est, est et, est et, est et, et et, est est, mé mè, té tè, ré rè, mémé, mèmè, me mé mè, se sé sè.

Attention ! Ils‿ont, ils sont : il a, il est.

Conversation

EN ROUTE	EN ROUTE
M. P. Pardon, monsieur ; n'êtes-vous pas monsieur Morris?	Pardon me, sir ; are you not Mr. Morris?
M. K. Non ; je suis monsieur Kelly.	No ; I am Mr. Kelly.
M. P. Oh ! monsieur Kelly de la maison Jones and Kelly de Boston?	Oh ! Mr. Kelly of Jones and Kelly of Boston?
M. K. Parfaitement, monsieur.	Yes, sir.
M. P. Je suis‿enchanté de faire votre connaissance.	I am delighted to make your acquaintance.
M. K. A qui ai-je l'honneur de parler?	To whom have I the honor of speaking?
M. P. Je suis monsieur Picard, professeur de français à New-York.	I am Mr. Picard, teacher of French in New York.

M. K. Enchanté, monsieur ; vous_allez_à Paris?

Delighted, sir ; are you going to Paris?

M. P. Oui, monsieur ; et vous_aussi?

Yes, sir ; and you too?

M. K. Certainement ; je désire visiter la jolie capitale de la France.

Certainly. I want to visit the attractive capital of France.

M. P. Je suis Parisien et je connais Paris comme ma poche ; si je puis vous_être utile, je suis_entièrement_à votre disposition.

I am a Parisian and I know Paris as I know my own pocket. If I can be of any use to you, I am entirely at your service.

M. K. Merci, monsieur ; vous_êtes bien_aimable.

Thank you, sir ; you are very kind.

*   *   *   *   *   *   *

10e Leçon : Contraction de l'article défini avec la préposition *à*

Petite pluie abat grand vent. — *A soft answer turneth away wrath.*[1]

Study the following sentences :

J'ai donné le livre *au* professeur.   *I gave the book to the professor.*

J'ai donné les livres *aux* professeurs.   *I gave the books to the professors.*

J'ai donné les livres *à* l'homme et *à la* femme.   *I gave the books to the man and woman.*

The preposition **à,** *to, at,* can *never* be followed by the articles **le** or **les.**

> The combination **à le** is contracted into **au.**
> The combination **à les** is contracted into **aux.**

---

[1] Literally, *Little rain stills great wind.*

No contraction occurs when **à** is followed by **la** or **l'**.

Attention! The preposition **à**, alone or contracted with the article, *must be repeated* before each noun it governs.

Vocabulaire

le jardin, *the garden.*
le voisin, *the neighbor.*
la voisine, *the neighbor* (f.).
la balle, *the ball.*
vendu, *sold.*
donné, *given.*
écrit, *written.*

hier, *yesterday.*
déjà, *already.*
cinq, *five.*
six (sees), *six.*
sept (set), *seven.*
huit, *eight.*
neuf, *nine.*

dix (dees), *ten.*

Lecture

1. N'avez-vous pas parlé au professeur hier?   2. Non, mais j'ai parlé au fils et à la fille du voisin du professeur. 3. Louis, avez-vous montré la jolie balle aux neveux du médecin?   4. Non, mère, j'ai perdu la balle dans le jardin de la voisine.   5. Vous êtes un méchant garçon, vous avez déjà perdu sept ou huit balles!   6. Jean a-t-il écrit une petite lettre au cousin de Louise?   7. Le professeur a-t-il vendu la maison au fils du médecin ou à l'oncle de l'avocat?

8. Il a vendu la maison à la tante de Charles. 9. Avez-vous donné les balles aux enfants? 10. Nous avons donné cinq balles aux petits garçons et six livres aux grandes filles.

Exercices

A. *Remplacez les tirets par la préposition* à *ou* de *et l'article:*

1. (to the) J'ai parlé —— professeur. 2. (of the) J'ai parlé —— professeur. 3. (to the) Ont-ils parlé —— voisins? 4. (to the) A-t-elle parlé —— enfant? 5. (of the) N'avez-vous pas parlé —— enfants? 6. (to the) Nous avons parlé —— amis (of the) —— voisine. 7. (to the) Vous avez parlé —— père et —— mère (of the) —— neveu —— avocat. 8. (of the) A-t-elle reçu une lettre —— oncle —— fils —— professeur? 9. (to the) Ils ont donné dix livres —— fils —— fille et —— nièces (of the) —— oncle —— médecin.

B. *Traduisez en français:*

1. We have written a letter to the lawyer. 2. Have you not given the big ball to the little boy? 3. Where is it? 4. I have given the ball to the neighbor's son. 5. Who has spoken to the doctor's wife? 6. Has she not written to the brother or son of the lawyer? 7. Has he sold the house to the doctor or to the doctor's neighbor? 8. Has John spoken to the woman's nephew or son?

C. *Traduisez rapidement:*

1. To the boy, to the friend (*f.*), to the friend (*f.*), to the family, to the neighbors. 2. The man, to the man, the men, to the men. 3. To the woman, the women, to the women. 4. To the brother, to the brothers. 5. To the father, to the child. 6. Of the nephew, of the man, of the aunt, of the boys. 7. Of the friend (*m.*), of the friend (*f.*), of the friends (*f.*). 8. Of the boy, to the boy, of the boys, to the boys. 9. From the father, to the father.

LE PANTHÉON À PARIS.

Le Panthéon à Rome.

10. From the child, to the child.   11. The children, from the children, to the children.

Exercice-revue

1. A father, mother, son, and daughter.   2. There is the paper, pen, and pencil.   3. The eraser is in the large box on the small table.   4. It is (a) large (one).   5. Good evening, miss, are you not the professor's cousin?   6. Has not Louise taken the pen and ink?   7. She has spoken to Charles, Henry, Jane, the professor, and the doctor.   8. Are not the pupils seated on the benches in the classroom.   9. Is not the pencil very small?

Exercice de prononciation.   Les sons " oi " (*wah*) et " ou "
(*oo*)

moi, toi, loi, soi, roi, quoi, trois, bois, fois, joie, pois, soif, voir, revoir, noir, boîte, (*quickly*) ma moi, ta toi, la loi, sa soi.
mou, fou, cou, nous, vous, coucou, toujours, route, cour.
Liaison : Ils‿ont‿étudié leurs‿histoires.

Conversation

Au téléphone	At the telephone
M. K. Louvre trente-quatre-cinquante, s'il vous plaît, mademoiselle.	Louvre 34-50, if you please, miss.
Mlle. Voilà, monsieur.	Here it is, sir.
M. K. Allo, allo !	Hello, hello !
M. P. Allo, j'écoute. A qui ai-je l'honneur. . . .	Hello, I am listening. To whom have I the honor of speaking?
M. K. C'est monsieur Kelly.	This is Mr. Kelly.
M. P. Oh ! Bonjour, monsieur ; vous‿êtes‿à Paris ?	Oh ! Good morning, sir. You are in Paris?

M.K. Oui ; comment_allez-vous, monsieur Picard?

M. P. Très bien merci ! A quel hôtel êtes-vous descendu?

M. K. Je suis_au Ritz. Voulez-vous dîner_avec moi ce soir?

M. P. Avec grand plaisir ; à quelle heure?

M. K. A sept heures, si cela vous convient.

M. P. Entendu ; à ce soir, à sept heures dans la salle à manger de l'Hôtel Ritz.

M. K. C'est cela ; au plaisir de vous voir !

Yes ; how do you do, Mr. Picard?

Very well, thank you. At which hotel are you staying?

I am at the Ritz. Will you dine with me this evening?

With much pleasure ; at what time?

At seven o'clock, if that suits you.

Agreed ; till this evening at seven o'clock in the dining room of the Hotel Ritz.

That's it. I am looking forward to the pleasure of seeing you.

*   *   *   *   *   *   *

11ᵉ Leçon : Première conjugaison

Qui aime bien, châtie bien. — *Spare the rod and spoil the child.*[1]

French verbs are divided into *three* conjugations according to the ending of their infinitive.

Those ending in **er** belong to the *first* conjugation. The past participle is formed by changing the ending **er** into **é**.

Donner, *to give;* **donné,** *given*

[1] Literally, *Who loves well, chastises well.*

Présent de l'indicatif

je donne, *I give, I am giving, I do give.*
tu donnes, *thou givest.*
il donne, *he gives.*
elle donne, *she gives.*

nous donnons, *we give.*
vous donnez, *you give.*
ils donnent, *they* (m.) *give.*
elles donnent, *they* (f.) *give.*

Observe the terminations of the present indicative of the verbs of the first conjugation.

SINGULIER			PLURIEL		
e	es	e	ons	ez	ent (silent)

Note. — Emphatic and progessive forms like *I do speak, I am speaking* do not exist in French.

Impératif

SINGULIER	PLURIEL	
donne, *give* (thou).	donnons, *let us give.*	donnez, *give.*

The imperative of any regular verb is formed from the present indicative. In the first conjugation, **s** of the second person singular is dropped.

FORME INTERROGATIVE DU PRÉSENT

Do I give? Am I giving? etc. (Note 1)

donné-je? (See Note 2.)	or	est-ce que je donne?
donnes-tu?	or	est-ce que tu donnes?
donne-t-il? (See Note 3.)	or	est-ce qu'il donne?
donne-t-elle?	or	est-ce qu'elle donne?
etc.		etc.

FORME NÉGATIVE DU PRÉSENT

I do not give, I am not giving, etc.

je ne donne pas.	nous ne donnons pas.
tu ne donnes pas.	vous ne donnez pas.
il (elle) ne donne pas.	ils (elles) ne donnent pas.

Notes. — (1) The auxiliary verbs *to do, to be* (*am, is, are*), used in English to ask questions, do not exist in French. Instead, the position of the verb and the pronoun is reversed.

(2) The form of the first person, **donné-je,** *do I give,* is seldom used in general, and never in conversation. Instead, we say : **Est-ce que je donne.**

(3) In the third person singular of questions, the letter -t- is always added between the verb and the pronouns **il** and **elle** for euphony's sake (Lesson 4).

Le gallicisme *Est-ce que* (*Is it that*). — Any statement can be turned into a question by placing **Est-ce que** before it.

Est-ce que is the form corresponding to the English auxiliary verb *do :*

Est-ce que { vous parlez français?
Do { *you speak French?*

Vocabulaire

chanter, *to sing.*	**la chanson,** *the song.*
danser, *to dance.*	**l'histoire** (f.), *the story.*
raconter, *to tell, to relate.*	**la danse,** *the dance.*
écouter, *to listen.*	**ie téléphone,** *the telephone.*
parler, *to speak.*	**mais,** *but.*
sonner, *to ring.*	**la musique,** *the music.*
montrer, *to show.*	**pourquoi,** *why.*
téléphoner, *to telephone.*	**parce que,** *because.*

trouver, *to find.*
laisser, *to leave.*
aimer, *to like, to love.*
le sac, *the bag.*
le cadeau, *the gift.*

intéressant, *interesting.*
français, -e, *French.*
maintenant, *now.*
beaucoup, *much, very much.*
laissé, *left.*

à bientôt, *see you soon.*

Note the idiom :
    Comment trouvez-vous la musique ?
    How do you like (what do you think of) the music?

Lecture

1. Est-ce que madame Duval chante?   2. Non, mais la sœur du professeur chante très bien.   3. Jeanne et Louise dansent-elles?   4. Certainement, elles aiment beaucoup la danse.   5. Et vous, est-ce que vous ne dansez pas? 6. Écoutez ! Le téléphone sonne.   7. Qui téléphone maintenant?   8. Allo, j'écoute.   9. Bonjour, mademoiselle, comment allez-vous?   10. Vous avez laissé un petit sac sur une des chaises du salon?   11. Mais oui, j'ai trouvé le sac, il est ici.   12. Mais certainement, vous parlez très bien français.   13. Au revoir, mademoiselle, à bientôt.

Exercices

A. *Traduisez en français :*

1. Do you speak French?   2. Yes, sir, I speak French. 3. Are you speaking French now?   4. No, sir, I am not speaking French now.   5. John is singing and Alice is dancing.   6. Do you find the lessons difficult?   7. No, I like the lessons very much (very much the lessons). 8. Louis, you are not listening.   9. I beg your pardon, sir, I am (listening).   10. The professor is telling a story ; he speaks very well.   11. The pupils are listening; they like the story.   12. Leave the watch on the table now, and telephone to the doctor.

B. *Traduisez rapidement:*

1. He speaks, he is speaking. 2. Do I speak, am I speaking? 3. I do speak, I am speaking. 4. She does not speak. 5. She is not speaking. 6. Are we speaking? 7. Are we not speaking? 8. Why do you not speak? 9. Why do they speak? 10. They are not speaking. 11. Speak. 12. Do not speak. 13. Let us speak. 14. Why are they (*f.*) not speaking?

Exercice-revue

1. Where are we now? 2. Are you not in the parlor? 3. Jane, where have you put John's ball? 4. It is here, mother, in the garden. 5. Who has spoken to the neighbor's cousin? 6. Have Louise and Mary lost John's penknife? 7. Is the woman's bag on the parlor('s) table? 8. Here are the little girls, they are charming. 9. Have they (*f.*) telephoned to the lawyer's daughters?

Exercice de prononciation. Le son " en — an "

ban, dan, fan, lan, man, nan, ren, dans, banc, tante, encre, lent, lentement, parent, dansant, pendant, pensant, enfant, plan, dent, camp, France, certainement, parfaitement, franchement.

Liaison: les‿enfants, les‿élèves, les‿avocats, les‿oncles.

Conversation

DANS LA SALLE À MANGER DE L'HÔTEL RITZ

M. K. Ah! Vous voilà! Bonjour, cher monsieur!

M. P. Bonjour, monsieur, je suis charmé de vous revoir !

M. K. Voici une petite table près de la fenêtre.

M. P. Oui, nous sommes très bien placés pour regarder le jardin.

M. K. Garçon! La carte, s'il vous plaît.

Le G. Voici le menu, monsieur ; il est très bon, nous‿ avons‿un dîner‿excellent‿aujourd'hui.

M. K. Monsieur Picard, voulez-vous le dîner régulier, ou préférez-vous manger‿à la carte?

M. P. Pour parler franchement, je préfère manger‿à la carte ; et vous?

M. K. Moi aussi. Garçon, donnez-nous la carte du jour.

*   *   *   *   *   *   *

12ᵉ Leçon : Les adjectifs possessifs

Qui m'aime, aime mon chien, *Love me, love my dog.*

Observe the following forms of the possessive adjectives :

my { **mon** masculine **ma** feminine **mes** plural for both	*thy* { **ton** masculine **ta** feminine **tes** plural for both

his, her, its { **son** + masculine noun
sa + feminine noun
ses + plural noun (*m.* and *f.*)

our { **notre** masculine **notre** feminine **nos** plural	*your* { **votre** masculine **votre** feminine **vos** plural

their { **leur** masculine
leur feminine
leurs plural

1. The function of an adjective is to modify a noun. French adjectives agree in gender and number with the

nouns they modify (Lesson 6). The same rule applies to possessive adjectives. They *must* take the gender and number of the *following noun* (the object possessed), taking under *no consideration the gender of the possessor.*

A boy, speaking of his pen, should say **ma plume,** because **plume** is a feminine noun. Therefore,

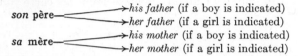

son père———→*his father* (if a boy is indicated)
   ———→*her father* (if a girl is indicated)
sa mère———→*his mother* (if a boy is indicated)
   ———→*her mother* (if a girl is indicated)

2. For the sake of euphony, **mon, ton, son** are used, instead of **ma, ta, sa,** before a feminine noun beginning with a vowel or **h** mute.

son‿école.   **mon‿histoire.**

Attention! The possessive adjectives are repeated before each noun they modify.

Ma **plume,** *mon* **crayon et** *mes* **livres.** *My pen, pencil, and books.*

Conversation

Avant la classe

Paul. Dites donc (*Say*), Charles, n'avez-vous pas vu mon crayon?

Charles. Non, Paul, je n'ai pas vu votre crayon. Voulez-vous ma plume?

Paul. Non, merci, vous êtes bien aimable (*very kind*).

Charles. Où avez-vous laissé votre crayon?

Paul. J'ai laissé mon crayon à la maison (*at home*), je suppose.

Charles. Vos livres sont-ils dans votre pupître?

Paul. Oui, et voici la plume de Jean. Il a mis sa plume, sa règle, sa gomme et ses livres dans mon pupître.

Charles. Qui a pris mon encre?

Paul. Louis a pris votre encre. Qu'en dites-vous?
(*What do you say to that?*)

Charles. Cela ne fait rien. (*It does not matter.*) Où
sont nos exercices?

Paul. Voici nos exercices, ils sont faciles.

Charles. Votre sœur a-t-elle raconté son histoire à son
oncle?

Paul. Bien sûr! (*Surely!*) Il a été (*been*) très content.

Charles. Voici notre professeur; écoutons la leçon maintenant.

Exercices

A. *Questions sur la conversation:*

1. Avez-vous perdu vos livres?   2. Où Paul a-t-il laissé
son crayon?   3. A-t-il pris la plume de Charles?   4. Où
sont vos livres?   5. Où Jean a-t-il mis sa plume et sa règle?
6. Charles a-t-il donné son encre à Jean?   7. Qui a pris
son encre?   8. Où sont leurs exercices?   9. Écoutez-
vous votre professeur quand (*when*) il parle?   10. Qui a
raconté son histoire?

B. *Remplacez les tirets par un adjectif possessif:*

1. J'écoute —— professeur.   2. Tu écoutes —— père.
3. Il écoute —— mère.   4. Elle écoute —— frère.
5. Nous écoutons —— amis.   6. Vous écoutez —— professeurs.   7. Ils écoutent —— enfants.   8. Elles écoutent
—— élèves.   9. Écoutez —— professeur.   10. N'écoutons
pas —— amis.

C. *Traduisez rapidement:*

1. his pencil, her pencil, his pencils, her pencils.
2. his pen, her pen, his pens, her pens.
3. her story, his story, her ink, her uncle.
4. his friend (*f.*), her friend (*m.*), her father, his aunt.
5. her exercise, his exercise, his exercises, her child.

D. *Traduisez en français:*

1. We are in our classroom. 2. I like my school. 3. She likes her book. 4. Don't you like her story? 5. Certainly, her story is very interesting. 6. We have lost our books. 7. Have you left your books in your desk? 8. My desk is in my classroom. 9. Where has she put her pencil, pen, and bag? 10. Here is her bag, but I have not her paper and ink. 11. Our exercises are in our book. 12. Sing your song now. 13. My children have lost their ball. 14. It does not matter.

Exercice-revue

1. My little brother is sick. 2. I am very sorry; is he very sick? 3. Have you telephoned to the doctor? 4. Yes, but he is not home. 5. Where is he? 6. The lawyer's daughter is also ill. 7. Have you given the exercises to the professor? 8. Speak to the children. 9. They are not here. 10. Are they not here? 11. No, they are in the neighbor's garden. 12. They like the neighbor's son.

Exercice de prononciation. Le son " on "

mon, ton, son, bon, don, non, long, font, rond, vont, bonbon, ronron, ponton, bonjour, bonsoir, pardon, garçon, melon, ballon.

ba, be, bi, bo, bu, ban, bon.

sa, se, si, so, su, san, son.

Expressions de conversation

Dites donc.	I say ; By the way ; Tell me.
Ici on parle français.	French spoken here.
Qu'en dites-vous?	What do you say to that?
Je n'en crois rien.	I don't believe it.
C'est comme ça.	It is a fact.
Je pense que oui.	I think so.
Je pense que non.	I don't think so. I think not.

La Place de l'Opéra à Paris.

13e Leçon : Pronoms possessifs

Les bons comptes font les bons amis. — *Short accounts make long friends.*

Observe the difference between the possessive adjectives and pronouns.

ADJECTIFS		PRONOMS	
Masculin Singulier			
my	mon	*le* mien	*mine*
thy, your	ton	*le* tien	*thine, yours*
his, her, its	son	*le* sien	*his, hers, its*
our	notre	*le* nôtre	*ours*
your	votre	*le* vôtre	*yours*
their	leur	*le* leur	*theirs*
Feminin Singulier			
my	ma	*la* mienne	*mine*
thy, your	ta	*la* tienne	*thine, yours*
his, her, its	sa	*la* sienne	*his, hers, its*
our	notre	*la* nôtre	*ours*
your	votre	*la* vôtre	*yours*
their	leur	*la* leur	*theirs*
Masculin Pluriel			
my	mes	*les* miens	*mine*
thy, your	tes	*les* tiens	*thine, yours*
his, her, its	ses	*les* siens	*his, hers, its*
our	nos	*les* nôtres	*ours*
your	vos	*les* vôtres	*yours*
their	leurs	*les* leurs	*theirs*
Feminin Pluriel			
my	mes	*les* miennes	*mine*
thy, your	tes	*les* tiennes	*thine, yours*
his, her, its	ses	*les* siennes	*his, hers, its*
our	nos	*les* nôtres	*ours*
your	vos	*les* vôtres	*yours*
their	leurs	*les* leurs	*theirs*

Distinguish carefully between possessive adjectives and possessive pronouns. The chart on the preceding page shows the differences *in form*. Note that the pronoun is *always* preceded by the definite article ; the adjective, *never*.

In use, the adjective is *always* followed by a noun ; the pronoun, *never*. As the pronoun replaces a noun, it must take the gender and number of that noun.

J'ai perdu mes *livres* et *elle* a perdu *les siens*. *I have lost my books and she has lost hers.*

   Masc. plur.   3d per.   3d per. Masc. plur.

Vous avez vos plumes et j'ai les miennes. *You have your pens and I have mine.*

Voici mon crayon, où est le vôtre ? *Here is my pencil, where is yours?*

Elle a vendu son sac et Jeanne a donné le sien à sa cousine. *She has sold her bag and Jane has given hers to her cousin.*

Louise a raconté son histoire ; Jean, racontez-moi la vôtre maintenant. *Louise has told her story; John, tell me yours now.*

J'ai chanté ma chanson, pourquoi Paul ne chante-t-il pas la sienne ? *I sang my song, why doesn't Paul sing his?*

Vos crayons et les nôtres sont dans mon pupître. *Your pencils and ours are in my desk.*

Attention! " *A friend of mine.*" Expressions like :

a friend of mine } should be changed to { *one of my friends,* **un de mes amis.**
a book of hers } { *one of her books,* **un de ses livres.**

Lecture

1. Avez-vous vu ma plume ? 2. Votre frère a-t-il trouvé la sienne ? 3. Oui, il a trouvé la sienne. 4. Jeanne a son joli sac, montrez-moi le vôtre, Alice. 5. Voici le mien, regardez le sien. 6. Le sac de notre voisine est très grand, le mien est très petit. 7. J'ai perdu mes livres, avez-vous les vôtres ? 8. Non, j'ai laissé les miens à l'école. 9. Louise

et Marie, ont-elles aussi laissé les leurs à l'école?   10. Oui,
elles ont mis les leurs dans leurs pupîtres.   11. Une de
mes amies a donné un cadeau à la fille de notre docteur.
12. Pourquoi Louis donne-t-il nos plumes à sa tante?
13. Il ne donne pas les nôtres, il donne les siennes.

Exercices

A. *Complétez les phrases suivantes avec le pronom entre
parenthèses :*

1. (yours) Les enfants sont ——.   2. (mine) Avez-vous
vu ——.   3. (his) La grande maison est ——.   4. (hers)
Le petit sac est ——.   5. (theirs) Voici votre balle, où est
——?   6. (ours) La grande école est ——.   7. (his) J'ai
écrit ma lettre, a-t-il écrit ——.   8. (hers) L'exercice est
——.   9. (mine) Avez-vous pris ——?   10. (yours) Vous
avez laissé —— à l'école.

B. *Mettez les phrases suivantes au singulier :*

1. Nous avons fermé nos portes et les siennes.   2. Ils ont
reçu leurs lettres et nous avons reçu les nôtres.   3. Elles
ont mis leurs livres sur les tables et nous avons mis les nôtres
sur les pupîtres.   4. Nous avons ouvert nos fenêtres et les
vôtres.   5. Fermez les miennes et les siennes.

C. *Traduisez en français :*

1. Has she taken your bag?   2. No, she has not taken
mine.   3. She has taken yours.   4. I beg your pardon,
she has taken yours also.   5. My pens are here, where are
yours?   6. Mine are in my pencil box.   7. Mary hasn't
hers.   8. A friend of mine is here.   9. Here are two books
of yours, Mary.   10. Where is your chair?   11. Mine is
here; where is his?   12. My ink is poor (*mauvaise*) ;
is poor too.   13. They have lost two pencils of hers.

Exercice-revue

1. Is he rich? 2. Is she not nice? 3. Do you not like your little cousin? 4. Has your sister not lost the lawyer's papers? 5. Give your ball to the child. 6. Do not give the penknife to the little girl. 7. Here is the children's book. 8. Show me the doctor's house. 9. It is not very large. 10. Speak to the doctor. 11. Where is he? Is he not in the parlor? 12. No, he is speaking to the professor in the dining room.

Exercice de prononciation. Le son " in," " ein," " ain," " aim "

fin, lin, pin, bain, daim, faim, main, nain, pain, peint, rein, saint, teint, vain, saint Augustin, Rintintin.

banban, bonbon, binbin.
dandan, dondon, dindin.

Expressions de conversation

Comment vous appelez-vous?	What is your name?
Je m'appelle Jean Valjean.	My name is Jean Valjean.
Ayez la bonté de parler plus haut.	Kindly speak louder.
Pas si vite, s'il vous plaît.	Not so fast, please.
Parlez plus lentement.	Speak more slowly.
Oui, c'est ça.	Yes, that's it.
Je vous remercie.	I thank you.
Il n'y a pas de quoi.	Don't mention it, you are welcome.

* * * * * * *

14ᵉ Leçon : Passé indéfini ou passé composé

Les petits ruisseaux font les grandes rivières — *Great oaks from little acorns grow.*[1]

Compare the French with the English in the following sentences :

J'ai perdu ma montre. *(je perdis)*	I LOST *my watch.*
Elle a vu son oncle.	*She* SAW *her uncle.*
Avez-vous trouvé la maison ?	DID YOU FIND *the house?*

The past indefinite (perfect), called in French **passé indéfini** or **passé composé,** is the conversational past tense of the French language.

It is very simply formed with the present indicative of the auxiliary verb **avoir** (sometimes **être**) and a past participle.

Important Note. — The auxiliary verb *do* does not exist in French. The French say : *Speak you French?* instead of : *Do you speak French?* (Lesson 9). The past form *did* has therefore no equivalent, and the auxiliary verb *have* is used instead.

Did you lose your pencil? ⎫ become ⎧ *Have you lost your pencil?*
Did she give her book? ⎭   ⎩ *Has she given her book?*

Attention! Many English verbs have identical forms for past tense and past participle : *I lost, I have lost; I bought, I have bought; I closed, I have closed.* Both these tenses, the past and the perfect, are translated in French by the past indefinite : **j'ai perdu, j'ai acheté, j'ai fermé.** *Never say:* **je perdu, j'acheté, je fermé.**

Vocabulaire

eu (pronounced **u**), *had.*	**la connaissance,** *the acquaintance.*
été, *been.*	**faire la connaissance,** *to make the acquaintance of.*
accepter, *to accept.*	
jouer, *to play.*	**le matin,** *the morning.*
préférer, *to prefer.*	**mais certainement,** *yes indeed.*

[1] Literally, *Little brooks make great rivers.*

rester, *to stay, to remain.*
le plaisir, *the pleasure.*
avec plaisir, *with pleasure.*
quand, *when.*
la soirée, *the evening, evening party.*

penser, *to think.*
vendu, *sold.*
à ravir, *admirably.*
à propos, *by the way.*
cela va sans dire, *that goes without saying.*

à la maison, *at home.*

Conversation

La soirée de Madame Legrand

Robert. Avez-vous été à la soirée de madame Legrand hier?

Jacques. Oui, j'ai été à sa soirée et j'ai eu le plaisir de faire la connaissance de votre gentille cousine.

Robert. Quand avez-vous reçu l'invitation de madame Legrand?

Jacques. Elle a téléphoné à ma mère hier matin, et nous avons accepté son invitation avec plaisir.

Robert. Avez-vous trouvé la soirée intéressante?

ELLE A CHANTÉ.   NOUS AVONS DANSÉ.   ILS ONT JOUÉ.

Jacques. Oui, la soirée a été charmante. Madame Legrand et sa nièce ont chanté, sa fille a joué du piano; elles ont eu un grand succès.

Robert. Avez-vous aussi dansé?

Jacques. Mais certainement. J'ai dansé avec votre cousine, elle danse à ravir.

Robert. Monsieur votre père a-t-il aussi dansé?

Jacques. Non ; monsieur Legrand, mon père, ma tante, et mon oncle ont joué au bridge. A propos, et vous? Pourquoi n'avez-vous pas été à la soirée? Madame Legrand a invité votre famille, je pense.

Robert. Cela va sans dire ! Ma mère et madame Legrand sont deux amies inséparables ; mais ma petite sœur est malade, et nous avons préféré rester à la maison.

Exercices

A. *Questions sur la conversation :*

1. Qui a donné une soirée? 2. Qui a été à la soirée de Mme Legrand? 3. Avez-vous été à sa soirée? 4. Jacques a-t-il eu le plaisir de faire la connaissance de la mère de Robert? 5. Comment (*how*) Mme Legrand a-t-elle invité la mère de Jacques? 6. Comment Jacques a-t-il trouvé la soirée? 7. Pourquoi a-t-il trouvé la soirée charmante? 8. Pourquoi M. Legrand et ses amis n'ont-ils pas dansé? 9. Mme Legrand a-t-elle invité la mère de Robert et pourquoi? 10. Pourquoi Robert n'a-t-il pas été à la soirée?

B. *Traduisez en français :*

1. He lost his handkerchief yesterday. 2. We bought a present. 3. When did you buy your present? 4. I bought mine yesterday. 5. Did you speak to the professor? 6. No, I spoke to his brother. 7. Haven't you found your books? 8. No, but I found hers. 9. When your brother told his story, why did you not listen? 10. I did listen. 11. Haven't they sold their house to their neighbors? 12. The little girl left her ball in my garden. 13. Mother, I found your bag ! 14. How did you like Mrs. Legrand's evening party? 15. Did you play bridge? 16. That goes without saying.

Exercice-revue

1. I lost my exercise. 2. Did you lose yours? 3. Mary has put hers in her book. 4. She has written to her neighbor. 5. Does she speak French? 6. Why does she not speak French to the doctor's son? 7. The doctor's little boy does not speak French. 8. Here is my present, show me yours. 9. I have lost mine and she has lost hers. 10. We found ours. 11. Have they already written their letters? 12. He has written his, but I have not written mine. 13. Speak to the girl's uncle now. 14. Let us not sing, let us dance. 15. With pleasure.

Exercice de prononciation. Le son " un "

un, chacun, aucun, lundi, brun, parfum, quelqu'un, alun, tribun, embrum.

un an, an un, un an, an un, un an, an un, man mun, lan lun.

ban bon bin bun.   dan don din dun.   ran ron rin run.
san son sin sun.   van von vin vun.   tan ton tin tun.

* * * * * * *

15e Leçon : Adjectifs démonstratifs

L'habit ne fait pas le moine. — *Clothes do not make the man.*[1]

Observe the different forms of the demonstrative adjectives :

ce **crayon,** *this* (or *that*) *pencil.*
cet **homme et** *cet* **enfant,** *this* (or *that*) *man and child.*
cette **maison,** *this* (or *that*) *house.*
ces **hommes,** *ces* **femmes et** *ces* **enfants,** *these* (or *those*) *men, women, and children.*

---

[1] Literally, *The garment doesn't make the man.*

The forms of the demonstrative adjective in the singular are :

this — that
- **ce,** before a masculine noun beginning with a consonant.
- **cet,** before a masculine noun beginning with a *vowel* or **h** *mute*.
- **cette,** before a feminine noun.

The only form of the demonstrative adjective in the plural is :

ces, *these — those,* before any plural noun, masculine or feminine.

Note. — When the demonstrative adjectives **ce, cet, cette** refer to *one* thing they are translated either *this* or *that;* **ce livre** may be translated *this book* or *that book.*

Similarly, **ces** is used for *these* or *those* when referring to *one* set of persons or things ; **ces hommes** is translated in English *these men* or *those men.*

The forms -*ci* (contraction of *ici,* here) and -*là,* there. — Study this example :

Ce livre-*ci* est grand, *ce* livre-*là* est petit.   *This book is large, that book is small.*

When *two* things or two sets of things are contrasted, as *this* and *that, these* and *those,* the distinction is made by adding **-ci** (*this, these*) and **-là** (*that, those*) to the nouns which follow the demonstratives.   Compare the English, *this book here, that book there.*

Attention!   The demonstrative adjective is repeated before each noun it modifies (like the article, the preposition, and possessive adjectives).

Vocabulaire

apporter, *to bring.*
regarder, *to look, to look at.*
préparer, *to prepare.*
gronder, *to scold.*
quelquefois, *sometimes.*

Lecture

1. Avez-vous préparé cet exercice?   2. Non, il est très difficile, regardez!   3. Oui, cet exercice-ci est difficile, mais cet exercice-là est facile.   4. Donnez-moi ce crayon. 5. Non, mon ami, ce crayon est le mien.   6. Où avez-vous trouvé cette grande règle?   7. Regardez ces enfants, ils jouent dans la cour de cette école.   8. Ce professeur gronde ses élèves quand ils n'ont pas préparé leurs leçons.   9. Jean a-t-il préparé cette leçon hier?   10. Non, et il a été grondé. 11. Ces grandes balles sont-elles les vôtres?   12. Non, cette balle-ci est la mienne.   13. Louis, apportez-moi ces grands livres.   14. Ces livres-ci ou ces livres-là?   15. Ces livres-là.

Exercices

A. *Remplacez les grands tirets par l'adjectif démonstratif qui convient et les petits tirets par* -ci *ou* -là.

1. —— exercice est facile.   2. —— plume est petite. 3. —— enfants sont méchants.   4. Où avez-vous trouvé —— balle?   5. —— crayon — est grand, —— crayon — est petit.   6. Comment trouvez-vous -—— livres?   7. —— maison — est la maison de —— femme —, —— maison — est la maison de —— femme —.   8. —— élève prépare ses leçons.   9. Quand avez-vous acheté —— chaise —? 10. —— homme — est le père de —— petit garçon — et —— homme — est l'oncle de —— petite fille —.

B. *Traduisez en français:*

1. Is that little girl a cousin of yours?   2. No, madam, that little girl is this boy's sister.   3. Are those three boys your friends?   4. Yes, sir, those boys are my friends. 5. Do you play sometimes with that big ball?   6. Who found that pretty handkerchief?   7. My father bought those houses yesterday.   8. These houses or those houses? 9. Who put these books on that desk?   10. This table is

Paris et la Seine. Vue prise de la Tour Eiffel.

mine, that table is his.   11. Listen! Did that telephone ring?   12. Why did you not speak French when you telephoned to the professor?   13. Tell me that story please. 14. I told that story yesterday, why did you not listen?

Exercice-revue

1. Are your exercises difficult?   2. Yes, mine are difficult, but yours are easy.   3. How do you like your lesson? 4. It is difficult, but very interesting.   5. Let us speak French when we are in the classroom.   6. Does the professor speak French to his pupils?   7. Yes, when he gives the lesson, he speaks French to the pupils.   8. Jane has her book and John has his.   9. Here is my bag, where are theirs?   10. There are theirs on the small table.   11. Do you play with your neighbor's son?   12. Why yes, Louis is a friend of mine.   13. Is he not a friend of your sister too? 14. Yes, Louis is also my sister's friend.

Exercice de prononciation. Le son " eu " fermé

feu, jeu, peu, deux, ceux, veut, peut, queue, bleu, adieu, lieu, heureux, malheureux, peureux, monsieur, Europe, il pleut, deux yeux bleus.   Adieu, monsieur, à jeudi.

Conversation
Paris

M. A.   Montrez-moi le plan de Paris.

M. B.   Voici le plan de la jolie ville de Paris.

M. A.   J'aime beaucoup votre plan, il est clair et très complet.

M. B.   Paris est divisé en vingt districts ou arrondissements.

M. A.   Voici une rivière.

M. B.   Oui, la Seine est une grande rivière ; elle divise la capitale en deux parties.

M. A. Les rues de Paris sont-elles intéressantes?

M. B. Oh! Mais oui, très intéressantes ; la beauté des avenues, des grands boulevards et des maisons est remarquable.

(à suivre, *to be continued*)

* * * * * * *

16ᵉ Leçon : Nombres cardinaux

Un homme averti en vaut deux. — *Forewarned is forearmed.*[1]

un, une	1	six (seess)	6	onze	11	seize (sehz)	16
deux	2	sept (set)	7	douze	12	dix-sept (deess)	17
trois	3	huit (weet)	8	treize	13	dix-huit (deez)	18
quatre	4	neuf	9	quatorze	14	dix-neuf (deez)	19
cinq	5	dix (deess)	10	quinze	15	vingt (vin)	20

Prononciation. — The pronunciation of French numerals is irregular and requires attention.

Un, une is the only cardinal number having a feminine, probably because it means also *a, an*, when used as an article. The **n** of **un** is slightly sounded when the following word begins with a vowel or **h** mute :

    un‿enfant.   un‿homme.

Deux The final letter, **x**, is silent when the number stands alone or when it is followed by a noun beginning with a consonant :

    deux livres.   deux plumes.

When the following word begins with a vowel or **h** mute, the **x** is carried over with the sound of **z** :

    deux‿enfants.   deux‿hommes.

Trois The same rules apply to the final **s** in **trois** as to the final **x** in **deux**.

---

[1] Literally, *A man warned is worth two.*

Quatre The **e** of **quatre** is always silent. When the noun following begins with a vowel or silent **h,** the **r** of **quatre** is linked with the following word as if it were *one word.*

> **Quatre enfants** is pronounced **quatrenfan.**
> **Quatre hommes** is pronounced **quatromm.**

Cinq When **cinq** stands alone, the **q** is sounded (like *k*). The **q** is also sounded when the next word begins with a vowel or **h** mute:

> **cinq‿enfants.** **cinq‿hommes.**

Before a noun beginning with a consonant, the **q** is silent:

> **cinq** (sin) **livres.** **cinq** (sin) **plumes.**

Six When the number stands alone, the **x** is sounded like double **s.** When followed by a noun beginning with a vowel or **h** mute, the **x** is carried over like a **z**:

> **six‿enfants.** **six‿hommes.**

Before a noun beginning with a consonant, the **x** is silent:

> **six** (si) **livres.** **six** (si) **plumes.**

Sept In colloquial and everyday French, the **t** is generally sounded. Some people do not sound the **t** when the following noun begins with a consonant and say: **sè livres,** for **sept** (set) **livres.**

It is best to sound the **t** to avoid any possible confusion with **ces** or **ses.**

Huit The same rules apply to **huit** as to **cinq.**

Neuf Same as **sept.** Although the **f** of **neuf** is generally dropped before a word beginning with a consonant, many people sound it.

It is best not to sound the **f.**

> **Neuf livres** should be pronounced **neu livres.**

Before a vowel or **h** mute, the **f** is given the sound **v** for euphony:

> **Neuf enfants** $\big\}$ should be pronounced $\Big\{$ **neuvenfan.**
> **Neuf hommes** **neuvomm.**

When **neuf** stands alone, the **f** is sounded.

Dix Apply the same rules as to **six.**

Note. — The numbers are numeral adjectives.

Vocabulaire

compter, *to count.*
jusqu'à, *as far as.*
penser, *to think.*
prononcer, *to pronounce.*
expliquer, *to explain.*
combien de, *how many.*
beaucoup de, *many, much.*
pas du tout, *not at all.*
mal, *badly.*
l'arbre (m.), *the tree.*
la feuille, *the leaf.*
la fleur, *the flower.*
la rose, *the rose.*
toujours, *always.*

la tulipe, *the tulip.*
la violette, *the violet.*
le muguet, *the lily-of-the-valley.*
la couleur, *the color.*
blanc (blanche), *white.*
noir, *black.* noire (f)
rouge, *red.*
bleu, *blue.* bleue (f)
jaune, *yellow.*
vert, *green.* verte (f)
violet, *purple.* violet (f)
brun, *brown.* brune (f)
gris, *gray.* grise (f)
rose, *pink.*

Il y a, *there is, there are.*   Y a-t-il? *Is there, are there?*
De quelle couleur est . . . ?   *What color is . . . ?*

Adjectives of color always follow their nouns.

Le chat noir, *the black cat.*   le livre bleu, *the blue book.*

Attention! **Combien** and **beaucoup,** when followed by *a noun,* always take **de** or **d'** (never **des**).

combien *de* livres.   beaucoup *de* livres.

DIFFERENCE BETWEEN

Il y a   and   **Voilà**
There is, there are.   *There is, there are.*

Il y a, *there is,* or *there are,*
simply makes a statement:
Il y a un livre sur ma table,
there is a book on my table.

Voilà points out an object and
answers the questions, where
is? where are? *There is my
book,* voilà mon livre.

Lecture

1. Regardez! Il y a beaucoup de fleurs dans le jardin du
médecin.   2. Voilà ses roses et ses tulipes; elles sont
superbes!   3. Combien d'arbres y a-t-il dans son jardin?
4. Il y a douze petits arbres.   5. De quelle couleur sont

les tulipes? 6. Elles sont blanches, rouges, jaunes et violettes. 7. Les tulipes sont-elles quelquefois vertes, bleues et grises? 8. Je ne pense pas, mais il y a une tulipe brune dans le jardin de ma tante. 9. Les feuilles des arbres sont vertes maintenant. 10. Le muguet et la violette sont deux petites fleurs charmantes.

11. A propos, hier notre professeur a expliqué les nombres dans la classe de français. 12. Nous avons compté jusqu'à 20. 13. Comptons de 1 à 20. 14. Vous ne prononcez pas bien les nombres : trois, cinq, six, huit et neuf. 15. Et vous, vous prononcez mal : douze, seize, dix-sept et dix-neuf.

Exercices

A. *Nommez les nombres pairs* (even numbers) *de 2 à 20.*
B. *Nommez les nombres impairs* (odd numbers) *de 1 à 20.*
C. *Traduisez en français :*

1. There are many flowers in my uncle's garden. 2. Look! There are five roses. 3. What colors are those flowers? 4. They are pink, red, and yellow. 5. What color is the lily-of-the-valley? 6. Are there many flowers and trees in that garden? 7. There are many trees, but there are not many flowers. 8. Look at that small tree, its leaves are yellow and brown. 9. By the way, you spoke of numbers, give me five numbers from 2 to 20. 10. With pleasure, here are five numbers : seven, thirteen, fifteen, eighteen, and nineteen. 11. Very well.

Exercice-revue

1. I like your flowers; they are very pretty. 2. Where are yours? Are they not on the table in the dining room? 3. Did you not speak to the professor's wife yesterday? 4. No, but I telephoned to the professor: his wife is ill. 5. That's too bad; I am very sorry. 6. How did you like the lawyer's wife's evening party? 7. I do not like her parties, but yours are always very interesting. 8. Don't

you like hers? 9. No, not at all. 10 Mary, are you listening to my story? 11. No, I am not listening, I am speaking to John. 12. Is John here? 13. Yes, he is playing in the court with his ball and mine. 14. Why does he play with your ball when he has his?

Exercice de prononciation. Le son "eu" ouvert (as in *fur, sir*)

leur, fleur, neuf, bœuf, œuf, beurre, malheur, cœur, feuille, meuble, seul, menteur, chanteur.

leu leur, peu peur, eux œuf, ceux seul, nœud neuf.

Conversation

PARIS (*suite*)

M. A. Regardez le plan à gauche.

M. B. Ah! Voici le fameux Bois de Boulogne! Est-il intéressant à visiter?

M. A. Certainement. Le Bois de Boulogne est le grand parc extérieur de Paris, et le petit parc intérieur est le jardin du Luxembourg. Il y a beaucoup de statues dans ce parc.

M. B. Voici aussi une grande maison.

M. A. Oui, le Palais du Sénat est dans le jardin du Luxembourg, et voilà l'Observatoire. Il est exactement situé à l'endroit où passe la ligne méridienne de Paris.

M. B. Vous connaissez certainement Paris comme votre poche. Vos explications sont très intéressantes.

* * * * * * *

17e Leçon : Deuxième conjugaison

Il n'y a pas de rose sans épines. — *There is no rose without a thorn.*

French verbs whose infinitive ends in **-ir** belong to the second conjugation. The past participle of those verbs ends in **-i.**

Fin*ir*, *to finish;* **fin*i*,** *finished*

Présent de l'indicatif de **fin*ir*** : *I finish, I am finishing, I do finish*

je fin*is*	nous fin*iss*ons
tu fin*is*	vous fin*iss*ez
il fin*it*	ils fin*iss*ent

The present indicative of all regular verbs of the second conjugation is formed by changing the ending **-ir** of the infinitive into :

SINGULIER	PLURIEL
-is, -is, -it	**-*iss*ons, -*iss*ez, -*iss*ent**

Note. — In order to avoid any confusion between the verbs of the second conjugation and those of the first, note that **iss** is inserted (in the plural) between the root and the endings: **-ons, -ez, -ent.**

Impératif

SINGULIER	PLURIEL
fin*is*, *finish*	**fin*iss*ons,** *let us finish* **fin*iss*ez,** *finish*

Vocabulaire

punir, *to punish.*	**l'encrier** (m.), *the inkwell.*
agir, *to act, to behave.*	**les vêtements** (m.), *clothing.*
rougir, *to blush.*	**la robe,** *the dress.*
remplir, *to fill.*	**la rue,** *the street.*
salir, *to soil.*	**la ville,** *the city, town.*
bâtir, *to build.*	**principal,** *principal, main.*
choisir, *to choose.*	**content,** *pleased, glad, content.*
autre, *other.*	**naturellement,** *naturally, of course.*
travailler, *to work.*	**faites attention,** *look out, pay attention.*

Lecture

1. Le professeur punit le petit Paul parce qu'il ne travaille pas bien. 2. Punit-il aussi les autres élèves? 3. Naturellement, il punit les autres élèves quand ils agissent mal. 4. Jean, pourquoi rougissez-vous? 5. Je rougis parce que

je n'ai pas fini mon exercice.   6. Vous n'agissez pas bien,
mon ami, je ne suis pas content.   7. Louise, remplissez
votre encrier.   8. Faites attention ! Vous salissez votre
robe.   9. Jeanne et Louise salissent toujours leurs robes.
10. Quand vous salissez vos vêtements, agissez-vous bien?
11. Non, quand nous salissons nos vêtements, nous agissons
mal et notre mère n'est pas contente.   12. Jean, où votre
père bâtit-il une maison?   13. Il bâtit une maison dans la
rue principale de la ville.

Exercices

A. *Remplacez les tirets par les terminaisons qui conviennent :*

1. Je fin— mon exercice.   2. Nous fin— les nôtres.
3. Il chois— un livre.   4. Vous chois— les vôtres.   5. Elle
sal— sa robe.   6. Vous roug— toujours.   7. Ils sal—
leurs vêtements.   8. Nous bât— cette grande maison.
9. Ne rempl— pas ces encriers.   10. Fin— nos leçons.

B. *Traduisez en français :*

1. When we act badly, our professor is not pleased.
2. Why does this mother punish her two little girls?   3. Because they always play (play always) with the ink and soil
their dresses.   4. Alice always blushes when she speaks
French.   5. I blush when you punish my little brother.
6. Finish your lesson now ; your sister has finished hers.

C. *Traduisez rapidement :*

1. They choose ; they are choosing.   2. They do not
choose ; they are not choosing.   3. Are you choosing?
4. Are you not choosing?   5. We choose ; we have not
chosen.   6. Does she not choose?   7. I do not choose.

Exercice-revue

1. Look at that child.   2. Did you speak to this boy's
father and mother?   3. The professor gives a lesson to the
boys and girls.   4. Doesn't he give his lesson in the class-

La Cathédrale de Notre-Dame à Paris.

room?   5. There are nineteen desks and seventeen pupils in this classroom.   6. There are the pupils, and there is the professor.   7. 7, 9, 11, 12, 13, 15, 16, 17, 20.   8. This book is hers.   9. Where is mine?   10. Here is yours. 11. Where did you put his?

Exercice de prononciation.   Le son " o " fermé, " o," " au," " eau " (as in *home*)

au, lot, mot, pot, l'eau, tôt, beau, chapeau, bureau, rideau, manteau, bateau, aura, Laura, audace, marteau, cadeau.

Liaison : Les‿amis de nos‿amis sont nos‿amis.   Vos‿enfants‿ont‿écouté mon‿histoire.   Ils‿ont.   Ils sont.

Expressions de conversation

Eh bien ! Paul, vous êtes en retard !	Well, Paul, you are late !
Dépêchez-vous !	Hurry up !
Nous n'avons pas de temps à perdre.	We have no time to lose.
Allons ! En route !	Now then, let's be on our way !
Bon voyage et bonne chance !	A pleasant journey and good luck !

*   *   *   *   *   *   *

18e Leçon : Nombres cardinaux

Une fois n'est pas coutume. — *Once does not make a habit.*[1]

20 vingt (vin)	25 vingt-cinq (sound t)	30 trente
21 vingt *et* un (vinté un)	26 vingt-six (sound t)	31 trente *et* un
22 vingt-deux (sound t)	27 vingt-sept (sound t)	32 trente-deux
23 vingt-trois (sound t)	28 vingt-huit (sound t)	40 quarante
24 vingt-quatre (sound t)	29 vingt-neuf (sound t)	41 quarante *et* un

---

[1] Literally, *One time is not custom.*

42 quarante-deux	61 soixante *et* un	80 quatre-vingts
50 cinquante	62 soixante-deux	81 quatre-vingt-un
51 cinquante *et* un	70 soixante-dix	90 quatre-vingt-dix
52 cinquante-deux	71 soixante (*et*) onze	91 quatre-vingt-onze
60 soixante	72 soixante-douze	92 quatre-vingt-douze

100 cent   101 cent un

1000 mille   1001 mille un

1,000,000 un million   1,000,000,000 un milliard

(1) **Un** always becomes une before a feminine noun: **vingt et une maisons.**

(2) **Et** must be used in 21, 31, 41, 51, 61, and may be used in 71, but is never used in 81 or 91.

(3) Except where **et** is used, hyphens connect the different parts of any French number under 100, either when that number is alone (**trente-sept**) or when it is part of a large number (**deux cent trente-sept**).

(4) Neither *a* nor *one* is expressed before **cent** or **mille.**

(5) The t of **vingt** is pronounced only in the numbers 21 to 29 inclusive. The t of **cent** is silent in 101, 102, etc.

(6) **Quatre-vingt** and the multiples of **cent** add s, except when followed by another numeral or used in a date or as an ordinal : **trois cent quatre-vingts; quatre cents; sept cent quatre-vingt-dix-sept; page quatre-vingt.**

(7) **Mille** never adds s; **quatre mille,** *four thousand.* It becomes **mil** in dates ; **l'an mil huit cent douze** (or **dix-huit cent douze**), *the year 1812.*

(8) **Un million** and **un milliard** are followed by **de** before a noun.

Vocabulaire

le jour, *the day.*	**la seconde,** *the second.*
la semaine, *the week.*	**l'hôtel de ville** (m.), ⎫
le mois, *the month.*	**la mairie,** ⎬ *the city-hall.*
le trimestre, *the trimester.*	**l'habitant,** *the inhabitant.*
le semestre, *the semester.*	**la bibliothèque,** *the library.*
l'an (m.), **l'année** (f.), *the year.*	**la gare,** *the station.*
le siècle, *the century.*	**l'église,** (f.), *the church.*
l'heure (f.), *the hour.*	**font,** *make.*
la minute, *the minute.*	**fois,** *times.*
environ, *about.*	**plus de,** *more than* (before numbers)

Lecture

Paris

Paris est une grande ville, très importante et très intéressante. Elle est divisée en 20 arrondissements (*wards*) ou districts ; chaque (*each*) arrondissement a son hôtel de ville ou mairie. A Paris il y a 57 portes, 33 ponts, 2000 rues et boulevards, 9 ambassades, 41 légations, 51 consulats, 12 gares, 88 églises, 8 synagogues, 5 temples et une mosquée, 19 cimetières, et 23 hôpitaux. Paris a 17 banques, 15 musées, 7 parcs, 41 théâtres et 50 music-halls, salles de concert, cabarets artistiques, dancings et cinémas. Il y a aussi 78 bureaux de police, 124 bureaux de poste et plus de 200 stations de métro (*subway*). Paris a 5 universités et 1300 écoles. La bibliothèque nationale possède 2,500,000 volumes et plus de 3,000,000 de manuscrits et documents historiques. La population de cette grande ville est de 3,125,612 habitants. Le nombre d'Américains demeurant (*living*) en permanence à Paris est d'environ 35,000.

Exercices

A. *Remplacez les tirets par les nombres qui conviennent :*

1. —— secondes font une minute.   2. —— minutes font deux heures.   3. —— heures font un jour.   4. —— jours font une semaine.   5. —— jours font un mois.   6. —— semaines font une année.   7. —— mois font aussi une année.   8. —— mois font un trimestre et —— mois font un semestre.   9. —— jours font une année.   10. —— ans font un siècle.

B. *Lisez* (read) *les nombres et traduisez les phrases en français :*

1. 5, 7, 9.   2. 12, 14, 17.   3. 13, 16, 21.   4. 28, 31, 36.   5. 41, 51, 61.   6. 70, 71, 77.   7. 79, 81, 88. 8. 91, 96, 99.   9. 100, 101, 105.   10. 121, 139, 172. 11. 666, 871, 973, 999.   12. 1000, 1001, 42,795, 69,978. 13. There are 397 pages (page) in my book.   14. Are there 3,000,000 inhabitants in (*à*) Paris?

Exercice-revue

1. Isn't that little girl very charming?   2. Are you not one of the professor's pupils?   3. Hasn't she lost a book of yours?   4. Here is a book of hers.   5. No, that book is mine.   6. I do not speak of that book; I speak of this book near the window.   7. Yes, this book is mine and that book is hers.   8. Did you not speak to John?   9. His mother is not here, but there are his uncle and aunt.   10. What colors are those tulips?   11. They are red, yellow, pink, white, and purple.   12. A friend of mine has a black tulip in his garden.

Exercice de prononciation.   Le son " ou " + une voyelle

Always sound a *w* before the vowel following **ou** : **Lou-is** = *Lou-wi.*

oui, bouée, jouer, mouette, louer, fouet, Louise, troué, prouesse, doué, alouette, silhouette, noué.

ba, be, bi, bo, bu, beu, bou, boi.

Liaison : Les‿élèves‿ont parlé à leurs‿amis.   Les‿amis sont‿ici.

Expressions de conversation

Ah ! Comme je suis content de vous voir !	How glad I am to see you !
Vous avez une mine superbe !	You look fine !
Faites attention !	Look out !
Que voulez-vous dire ?	What do you mean ?
Attention au chien !	Beware of the dog !
Oh ! Chien qui aboie ne mord pas.	Barking dogs do not bite. (A dog that barks does not bite.)
C'est vrai, vous avez raison.	That's true, you are right.

*   *   *   *   *   *   *

19e Leçon : Nombres ordinaux

Echanger n'est pas voler. — A fair exchange is no robbery.

1st	premier, première.	19th	dix-neuvième.
2d	deuxième, second, e (f.).	20th	vingtième.
3d	troisième.	21st	vingt et unième
4th	quatrième.	30th	trentième.
5th	cinquième.	31st	trente et unième.
6th	sixième.	40th	quarantième.
7th	septième.	41st	quarante et unième.
8th	huitième.	50th	cinquantième
9th	neuvième.	51st	cinquante et unième.
10th	dixième.	60th	soixantième.
11th	onzième.	61st	soixante et unième.
12th	douzième.	70th	soixante-dixième.
13th	treizième	71st	soixante et onzième.
14th	quatorzième.	72d	soixante douzième.
15th	quinzième.	80th	quatre-vingtième.
16th	seizième.	81st	quatre-vingt-unième.
17th	dix-septième.	90th	quatre-vingt-dixième.
18th	dix-huitième.	91st	quatre-vingt-onzième.

1000th millième	100th centième.	1,000,000th millionième.

dernier, dernière (f.), *last.*

Abbreviations : premier, 1er; première, 1ère; deuxième, 2e; troisième, 3e; *etc.*

With the exception of **premier** (*first*) and **second** (*second*), an ordinal number is formed by adding -ième to the cardinal number. In adding -ième to form the ordinal, drop final -e of the cardinal, insert u after q, or change f to v: quatre, quatrième; cinq, cinquième; neuf, neuvième.

Attention! Before **huit** or **huitième, onze** or **onzième,** l' is never used for le or la, and final consonants are never linked: le huitième mot; la onzième leçon; les onze livres; du huit, not de l'huit.

Vocabulaire

dimanche, *Sunday.*		vendredi, *Friday.*
lundi, *Monday.*		samedi, *Saturday.*
mardi, *Tuesday.*		le matin, *the morning.*
mercredi, *Wednesday.*		le temps, *the time.*
jeudi, *Thursday.*		commencer, *to begin.*

janvier, *January.*	août, *August.*
février, *February.*	septembre, *September.*
mars, *March.*	octobre, *October.*
avril, *April.*	novembre, *November.*
mai, *May.*	décembre, *December.*
juin, *June.*	la saison, *the season.*
juillet, *July.*	nommez, *name.*

aujourd'hui, *to-day.*

Les saisons

le printemps, *the spring.*	l'automne, *the autumn.*
au printemps, *in spring.*	en automne, *in autumn.*
l'été, the *summer.*	l'hiver, *the winter.*
en été, *in summer.*	en hiver, *in winter.*

The names of the days, months, and seasons are all masculine. The names of days and months are not capitalized.

In expressions like *last week, last month, last Tuesday,* **dernier** follows the noun: **la semaine dernière, le mois dernier, mardi dernier.**

Lecture

LES DIVISIONS DU TEMPS

Il y a douze mois dans une année. Les douze mois sont : janvier, février, mars, avril, mai, juin, juillet, août, septembre, octobre, novembre et décembre. Janvier est le premier mois de l'année ; décembre est le dernier. Dimanche est le premier jour de la semaine, mercredi est le quatrième, samedi est le septième. Les mois de janvier, mars, mai, juillet, août et décembre ont trente et un jours. Avril, juin, septembre et novembre ont trente jours. Février a vingt-huit ou vingt-neuf jours.

Les quatre saisons sont : le printemps, l'été, l'automne, et l'hiver. Le printemps est la saison des fleurs. Le premier [1] janvier est le 1er jour de l'année et le 31 [1] décembre est le 365e jour de l'année.

---

[1] The French use cardinal numbers in dates and titles of sovereigns except **premier,** *first.*

Exercices

A. *Remplacez les tirets par le nombre ordinal qui convient:*

1. Jeudi est le —— jour de la semaine. 2. Dimanche est le —— et samedi le ——. 3. Novembre est le —— mois de l'année. 4. Février est le —— et août est le ——. 5. Six est la —— partie de trente. 6. Sept est la —— partie de soixante trois. 7. Un est la —— partie de cent. 8. Une seconde est la —— partie d'une minute. 9. Une semaine est la —— partie d'un an. 10. Le 31 décembre est le —— jour de l'année.

B. *Traduisez en français:*

1. First, fifth, tenth. 2. Second, third, seventh. 3. The sixth, the eighth, the eleventh. 4. The sixteenth, the nineteenth, the twenty-first. 5. The 31st sentence of the 41st lesson is difficult. 6. The spring begins the 21st (of)[1] March and ends the 20th (of) June. 7. Have we the seventeenth lesson to-day? 8. I lost my watch last Saturday. 9. The pupils are at school the first five (five first) days of the week. 10. The sixth and (the) seventh days of the week, Saturday and Sunday, they are not at school; they are at home.

Exercice-revue

1. Finish your exercises, my children. 2. We like this exercise; it is not difficult, it is easy. 3. I do not like mine, because it is difficult. 4. He has finished his lesson. 5. They are choosing a present for their father and mother. 6. Look out, Jane! You are soiling your white dress. 7. Yes, I soiled mine too, last week, with that ink. 8. Give your small ball to that poor man's son. 9. Why don't you listen when I speak? 10. I beg your pardon, I always listen (listen always) when you speak. 11. Where has

---

[1] *Of* and *on* in dates are not translated in French.

your father built a house? 12. There is his house.
13. There are many beautiful houses in this town.
14. There are my uncle's houses.

Exercice de prononciation. **Le son " gn "** (*onion, mignonette*)

digne, dignité, campagne, magnifique, Espagne, Espagnol,
montagne, vigne, signe, agneau, borgne, lorgnette.

Divisez en syllabes: avocat, fini, écoutez, téléphoner,
regardez, jardin, certainement.

Une anecdote

TOUT DE SUITE [1] (TOOT-SWEET)

Une Anglaise entre un jour dans un restaurant à Paris. Le
garçon demande :

— Madame désire?

— Donnez-moi, euh . . . euh. . . .

La dame qui ne parle pas français saisit (*grabs*) la carte et
montre un plat (*dish*) au hasard (*at random*).

— Aussi une tasse de café, garçon, café, café.

Le garçon apporte le plat et la tasse de café, et retourne
à la cuisine.

— Garçon, garçon, crie la dame.

Le garçon arrive.

La dame montre son café et dit : " Euh . . . euh . . .
sugar, sugar."

Le garçon remarque qu'il a oublié le sucre et dit vivement
(*says quickly*) : Tout de suite, madame, tout de suite.

— " Too sweet," murmure la dame, " too sweet ! Why,
there is not a bit of sugar in it ! "

* * * * * * *

[1] *Right away, immediately.*

Ewing Galloway

L'Université de Paris.

20ᵉ Leçon : Comparaison des adjectifs

Il n'est pire sourd que celui qui ne veut pas entendre. — *There is none so deaf as he who will not hear.*

Je suis grand.   *I am tall.*

Je suis	*plus*			*que* Paul.	*I am taller than Paul.*
Je suis	*moins*	grand		*que* Paul.	*I am less tall than Paul.*
Je suis	*aussi*			*que* Paul.	*I am as tall as Paul.*
Je ne suis pas *si*				*que* Paul.	*I am not so tall as Paul.*

The comparison of French adjectives is made by means of :

plus, for the comparative of superiority
moins, for the comparative of inferiority   } + adjective + **que**
aussi, for the comparative of equality

Note. — When the sentence is negative, **si** (instead of **aussi**) is used.

Superlatif des adjectifs. — The superlative is formed by placing the definite article or the possessive adjective before **plus** or **moins** of the comparative, and dropping **que.**

Jean est *le plus grand* de la classe.   *John is the tallest in the class.*
Voici *le moins intéressant* de mes livres.   *Here is the least interesting of my books.*
Marie a *sa plus belle* robe.   *Mary has her most beautiful dress.*

Attention !   After a superlative, *in* is translated by **de.**

Comparatifs irréguliers. — Three adjectives have irregular comparative and superlative forms :

bon, *good;* **meilleur,** *better,* **meilleure** (f. s.), **meilleurs** (m. p.), etc.; **le meilleur,** *the best.* **Bon** is irregular only in its comparative of superiority; the others are regular : **moins bon que, aussi bon que.**

petit, *small* { **plus petit,** *smaller;* **le plus petit,** *the smallest.*
{ **moindre,** *less;* **le moindre,** *the least.*

mauvais, *bad* { **plus mauvais,** *worse, poorer;* **le plus mauvais,** *the worst, the poorest.*
{ **pire,** *worse, more evil, more wicked;* **le pire,** *the worst, the most evil, the most wicked.*

Note. — Generally **moindre** is used to denote *less in importance,* while **plus petit** refers to size.

Position du superlatif. — In English, the superlative always comes before the noun. In French, it follows the same rule as the positive if it is an adjective which precedes its noun. If, however, the adjective is one of those which generally follows the noun, the superlative also follows and the definite article is repeated.

Positive	Superlative
la belle saison.	la plus belle saison.
la saison froide.	la saison *la* plus froide.

The following adjectives usually precede their nouns :

beau, *beautiful.*	**gentil,** *nice.*	**joli,** *pretty.*	**petit,** *small.*
bon, *good.*	**grand,** *large.*	**long,** *long.*	**vieux** (*m.*),
cher, *dear.*	**gros,** *big.*	**mauvais,** *bad.*	**vieille** (f.), } *old.*
court, *short.*	**jeune,** *young.*	**méchant,** *wicked.*	**vilain,** *ugly.*

Vocabulaire

bon, bonne (f.), *good, kind.*	**chaud,** *warm, hot.*
mauvais, *bad, poor* (quality).	**froid,** *cold.*
beau, belle (f.), *beautiful.*	**long, longue** (f.), *long.*
vieux, vieille (f.), *old.*	**court,** *short.*
haut, *high.*	**autre,** *other.*

Lecture

1. Ma tante est plus jeune que mon oncle. 2. Cet homme-ci est moins riche que cet homme-là. 3. L'été est plus chaud que le printemps. 4. L'été est la plus chaude des saisons. 5. Louise est aussi grande que Jeanne, mais elle n'est pas si jolie. 6. Charles est le meilleur élève de la classe. 7. Le 21 juin est le plus long jour de l'année, et le 21 décembre est le plus court. 8. Votre maison est plus haute que la mienne. 9. Oui, ma maison est la plus haute et aussi la plus vieille de la rue. 10. Paul est mon meilleur ami. 11. Louise a sali sa plus belle robe. 12. Voilà l'homme le plus riche de la ville.

Exercices

A. *Donnez les trois formes du comparatif des adjectifs suivants :*

grand	bon	petit	beau	chaud
haut	vert	froid	court	vieille
vieux	jeune	belle	joli	aimable

B. *Remplacez les tirets par un adjectif au superlatif :*

1. Louise est —— de mes amies.   2. La rose est —— des fleurs.   3. Cette maison est —— de la rue.   4. Ces hommes sont —— de la ville.   5. L'hiver est —— des saisons.   6. Juillet est le mois —— de l'année.   7. Cet exercice est —— de la leçon.

C. *Traduisez en français :*

1. My book is better than yours.   2. My books are better than yours.   3. My pen is better than yours.   4. My pens are better than yours.   5. This little boy is younger than that little girl.   6. We are not as rich as our neighbor. 7. Louise is less beautiful than her sister Marie.   8. Are you not taller than your cousin?   9. Yes, I am taller. 10. Who built the largest house in that street?   11. You chose my prettiest flowers.   12. You have the easiest exercise in the book.   13. The leaves of the trees are greener in spring than in autumn.   14. This exercise is not as easy as that exercise.

Exercice-revue

1. I am playing.   2. She is acting badly.   3. Are there 375 pupils in your school?   4. No, there are 347 pupils, 216 boys and 131 girls.   5. They have, they are.   6. Six children, six books, six.   7. Four, four friends, four roses. 8. Seven bags, seven men, seven.   9. Eight, eight tulips, eight children.   10. My garden's eleven trees are green now.   11. These pens, pencils, and papers are mine.   12. I

spoke to her father yesterday. 13. We are building a house in that long street. 14. I lost a book of mine.

C'EST LÀ, JUSTE EN FACE.

Conversation

PERDU!

A. Pardon, monsieur, j'ai perdu mon chemin.

B. En quoi puis-je vous être utile?

A. Où est le bureau de poste?

B. C'est là juste en face, de l'autre côté de la rue.

A. Est-ce possible? Merci mille fois, monsieur, vous êtes bien aimable.

B. Il n'y a pas de quoi. Bonjour, monsieur.

A. Au revoir, monsieur, et merci encore une fois.

* * * * * * *

21ᵉ Leçon : Comparaison des adverbes

Mieux vaut tard que jamais. — *Better late than never.*

		Je parle vite.		*I speak fast.*	
Je parle	*plus*		*que* Jean.	*I speak faster than John.*	
Je parle	*moins*	vite	*que* Jean.	*I speak less fast than John.*	
Je parle	*aussi*		*que* Jean.	*I speak as fast as John.*	
Je ne parle pas *si*			*que* Jean.	*I do not speak so fast as John.*	

Adverbs are compared like adjectives, by placing **plus, moins,** and **aussi** before the adverb.

Note. — When the sentence is negative, **si** (instead of **aussi**) is used.

Superlatif des adverbes. — The superlative of adverbs is formed by placing **le** before the comparative and dropping **que.** An adverb being invariable, the article is *always* **le.**

le plus souvent, le moins souvent.

Comparatifs irréguliers. — The adverbs **bien, mal, peu,** corresponding to the adjectives **bon, mauvais, petit,** are irregularly compared :

bien, *well.*	mieux, *better.*	le mieux, *the best.*
mal, *badly, ill.*	pis, *worse.*	le pis, *the worst.*
peu, *little.*	moins, *less.*	le moins, *the least.*

Note. — The other comparatives of **bien** and **mal** are made regularly.

Position des adverbes. — Adverbs in French always follow the verb in simple tenses, and usually in compound tenses.

A few adverbs, **bien, mal, toujours, souvent, beaucoup,** especially the first three, stand between the auxiliary verb and the past participle.

Il parle lentement.	*He speaks slowly.*
Il a parlé lentement.	*He has spoken slowly.*
Il a bien parlé.	*He has spoken well.*

Vocabulaire

mériter, *to deserve.*	poliment, *politely.*
la récompense, *the reward.*	lentement, *slowly.*
aimable, *amiable, kind, lovable.*	vite, *quick, fast.*
poli, *polite.*	souvent, *often.*

bien, *very.*

Lecture

1. Bravo, Louise, vous avez très bien chanté ! 2. Ai-je mieux chanté que la semaine dernière? 3. Bien sûr ! (*surely*), vous avez beaucoup mieux chanté. 4. Vous méritez une récompense ; choisissez la plus belle de ces fleurs. 5. Merci, vous êtes bien aimable, je choisis cette rose rouge, elle est plus jolie que ces tulipes. 6. Louis, parlez poliment quand vous parlez à votre vieille tante. 7. Je parle poli-

ment, je suis toujours poli. 8. Quand nous parlons français, nous parlons toujours lentement. 9. Jean parle mieux que Paul, mais Charles parle le mieux des trois. 10. Marie ne travaille pas si bien que Jeanne. 11. Jeanne travaille toujours bien. 12. Elle a toujours fini ses leçons plus vite que sa sœur. 13. Agit-elle souvent mal? 14. Non, elle agit toujours très bien.

Exercices

A. *Mettez les adverbes suivants aux 3 formes du comparatif et au superlatif:*

souvent	bien	mal
poliment	lentement	vite

B. *Remplacez les tirets par le comparatif de l'adverbe indiqué:*

1. (well) Louise travaille —— que son frère. 2. (slowly) Elle parle —— que Jeanne. 3. (often) Nous dansons —— que vous. 4. (politely) Ils agissent —— que vos frères. 5. (fast) Parlez ——. 6. (well) Je parle —— que Charles.

C. *Traduisez en français:*

1. Young, younger, youngest. 2. Good, better, best. 3. Well, better, best. 4. Cold, colder, coldest. 5. As warm as. 6. I am as tall as my friend John. 7. Is he not taller than you? 8. This man is more polite than that man. 9. Do you speak more slowly than his sister? 10. No, sir, I speak faster and I speak better. 11. Is the 20th lesson more or less difficult than the 21st? 12. Surely, it is more difficult; the 20th lesson is the most difficult of the last lessons. 13. The 13th lesson is better than the 30th. 14. It is also shorter.

Exercice-revue

1. Are you finishing your last lessons now? 2. How many pages are there in your book? 3. There are 479

pages.   4. Paris has a population of 3,000,000 inhabitants.
5. Are there many schools in that big city?   6. There are
one thousand schools.   7. We saw Paris last year.   8. I
bought a house.   9. We danced yesterday.   10. They
spoke to the professor.   11. In summer and in spring.
12. In winter and in autumn.   13. How glad I am to see
you!

UNE PREMIÈRE PARIS, S'IL VOUS PLAÎT.

Conversation

A LA GARE

Le voyageur.   Où est le guichet (*ticket office*)?

Le facteur.   C'est là-bas à gauche.

Le voyageur.   Une première Paris, s'il vous plaît.

L'employé.   Simple ou aller et retour?

Le voyageur.   Aller seulement.   A quelle heure le train
direct?

L'employé.   A dix heures juste.

Le voyageur.   Sur quelle voie (*track*)?

L'employé.   La voie quatre.

Le facteur.   Par ici, monsieur.

*   *   *   *   *   *   *

22ᵉ Leçon : Les pronoms relatifs

Dis-moi qui tu hantes et je te dirai qui tu es. — *A man is known by the company he keeps.*[1]

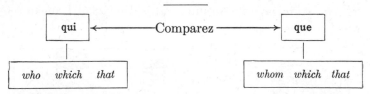

qui	**que**
who which that	*whom which that*

Le monsieur *qui* chante.	**Le monsieur *que* vous regardez.**
Le livre *qui* est sur la table.	**Le livre *que* vous avez perdu.**

When the pronoun is used as a *subject*, use **qui**.

When the pronoun is used as an *object*, use **que**.

Attention! (1) The relative pronoun, often omitted in English, *is never omitted in French.* To translate literally *the man I saw, the book he has* would be incorrect. The French say :

The man WHOM *I saw.*	**L'homme *que* j'ai vu.**
The book WHICH *he has.*	**Le livre *qu'il* a.**

(2) **Que** becomes **qu'** before a vowel or **h** mute. **Qui** never changes.

(3) *Which* or *that* should be translated by **qui** when it comes immediately before the verb, and by **que** when a noun or a pronoun comes between *which* or *that* and the verb. See examples above.

Vocabulaire

la bague, *the ring.*	**remarquer,** *to notice.*
le bracelet, *the bracelet.*	**demeurer,** *to live, to dwell.*
le collier, *the necklace.*	**le plancher,** *the floor.*

---

[1] Literally, *Tell me with whom you associate and I will tell you who you are.*

Lecture

1. Avez-vous remarqué le joli bracelet que Madame Duval a reçu? 2. Qui est Madame Duval? 3. Regardez la dame qui est près de la porte. 4. Le professeur a une bague qui est très jolie. 5. J'ai vu le collier qu'elle a donné à Jeanne. 6. J'ai vu un collier qui est très joli. 7. Il a perdu le livre que j'ai montré à Louise. 8. Non, monsieur, voilà le livre que vous avez montré. 9. Le livre qui est sur la table est le mien. 10. L'histoire qu'il raconte est très intéressante. 11. Les enfants qui sont dans la salle de classe sont mes élèves. 12. Où est le bracelet que vous avez trouvé sur le plancher? 13. Voici le bracelet que j'ai trouvé.

Exercices

A. *Remplacez les tirets par le pronom relatif* qui *ou* que :

1. Avez-vous apporté le livre —— est dans le salon? 2. J'ai trouvé le mouchoir —— vous avez perdu. 3. Le monsieur —— parle est le médecin. 4. Le monsieur —— vous avez vu est le père de Jean. 5. L'avocat —— demeure dans cette maison est l'ami de mon père. 6. Où a-t-elle mis le cadeau —— j'ai acheté? 7. La bague —— il a est plus belle que la vôtre. 8. Elle a laissé dans la salle à manger le collier —— vous avez apporté. 9. Les élèves —— écoutent le professeur sont polis. 10. Aimez-vous l'histoire —— votre ami raconte?

B. *Traduisez en français:*

1. Here is the book I received from John's father. 2. It is very beautiful; it is better than mine which is on the table. 3. Louis, did you find the bag I left on the chair? 4. No, mother, but there is the bag which Jane found on the floor. 5. Show me that bag she found, my little (one). 6. Look at the boy who plays with your sister in the garden. 7. The big ball which is in our garden is mine. 8. The stories the

professor tells are more interesting than the stories which are in our book.　9. The gentleman whom you saw at Mrs. Duval's evening party and who is here to-day is our doctor. 10. The children whom you like and who speak French well are the lawyer's daughters.

Exercice-revue

1. The young man who lives in my house speaks French better than you.　2. Does he speak English too? 3. Does he speak English as well as French?　4. No, he does not speak English as well as French.　5. How many trees are there in your garden?　6. Our trees are better than yours; they are higher too.　7. Yes, but my flowers are more beautiful than yours.　8. Why isn't the professor at home to-day?　9. Because he is at school; he has many classes to-day.　10. There is his mother; she is very old. 11. She is as old as my father.　12. No, she is older. 13. Who is speaking to your sister's friend?　14. 75, 321, 892.　15. 1st, 31st, 79th.

Expressions de conversation

Ne m'interrompez pas, s'il vous plaît.	Don't interrupt me, please.
Permettez. . . .	Allow me. . . .
Vous me coupez toujours la parole.	You don't let me say a word.
Parlez à voix basse.	Speak in a low voice.
M'entendez-vous?	Do you hear me?
Me comprenez-vous?	Do you understand me?
En voilà assez !	Enough of it !
Jamais !　Au grand jamais !	Never in your life !

*　　*　　*　　*　　*　　*　　*

La Cathédrale de Notre-Dame à Paris.

Une des portes de la Cathédrale de Notre-Dame à Paris.

23ᵉ Leçon : Troisième conjugaison

Ne vendez pas la peau de l'ours avant de l'avoir tué. — *Do not count your chickens before they are hatched.*[1]

All verbs ending in **re** belong to the third conjugation.
The past participle is formed by changing the ending **re** into **u**.

Rend**re**, *to give back;* rend**u**, *given back.*

Présent de l'indicatif

FORME AFFIRMATIVE

je rends, *I give back, I am*
tu rends. *giving back, I do*
il rend. *give back,* etc.
elle rend.
nous rendons.
vous rendez.
ils rendent.
elles rendent.

FORME INTERROGATIVE

est-ce que je rends? *do I give back?*
rends-tu? etc.

FORME NÉGATIVE

je ne rends pas, *I do not give back.*
tu ne rends pas, etc.

The endings of the Present Indicative are :

SINGULIER	PLURIEL
-s, -s, -(t)	-ons, -ez, -ent

Impératif

SINGULIER	PLURIEL	
rends, *give back.*	rendons, *let us give back.*	rendez, *give back.*

Vocabulaire

rendre, *to give back.*
vendre, *to sell.*
attendre, *to wait, to wait for.*
entendre, *to hear.*
perdre, *to lose.*
répondre à, *to answer.*

comprenez-vous? *do you understand?*
je comprends, *I understand.*
le jouet, *the toy, plaything.*
je ne sais pas, *I do not know.*
l'occasion (f.), *the opportunity.*
probablement, *probably.*

encore, *again, yet, still.*

[1] Literally, *Don't sell the bear's skin before killing the bear.*

Lecture

1. Louis, je ne comprends pas pourquoi vous restez à la maison. 2. N'entendez-vous pas? 3. Pourquoi ne répondez-vous pas à votre tante? 4. J'attends mon ami Charles. 5. Vous perdez votre temps ; Charles est encore malade. 6. Rendez les jouets à votre petite sœur et jouez avec le fils du voisin. 7. Je n'aime pas jouer avec le fils du voisin, il perd toujours mes jouets. 8. Quand vendent-ils leur maison? 9. Je ne sais pas, ils attendent une bonne occasion. 10. Ils ont déjà perdu deux occasions. 11. Nous répondons toujours aux questions de nos maîtres.

Exercices

A. *Conjuguez :*

1. J'attends mon frère, tu attends ton frère, etc.
2. Je n'attends pas ma mère, tu . . ., etc.
3. Je réponds à mon professeur, tu . . ., etc.
4. Est-ce que je vends ma maison, vends-tu . . ., etc.
5. J'attends mon père et j'entends ma mère, tu . . ., etc.

B. *Traduisez en français :*

1. Are you waiting for your cousin? 2. No, I am waiting for my brother. 3. John is waiting for his, too. 4. By the way, did you answer your brother's letter? 5. Certainly, I always answer my brother's letters. 6. Look, there is Paul's ball in our garden. 7. Yes, he always loses his toys. 8. His father is selling his house. 9. Why does he sell that beautiful house? 10. I did not hear your question. 11. He lost one thousand dollars, and that is too bad.

C. *Traduisez rapidement :*

1. You are losing ; are you not losing? 2. She loses ; is she not losing? 3. She lost ; she has not lost. 4. I am waiting ; are you waiting? 5. Wait ; do not wait. 6. Is he waiting? 7. Are they waiting? 8. Let us wait ; let us not wait. 9. Do I hear? 10. Do I not hear? 11. Have they heard? 12. They hear ; they wait.

Exercice-revue

1. Show me the beautiful bracelet you received from your
aunt.   2. Why do you blush?   3. I lost the bracelet I
received.   4. Oh! That's too bad, I am very sorry.
5. Jane, bring me the book which is on the table in the
dining room.   6. That book is more interesting than mine.
7. Yes, it is better than yours.   8. Do you like the summer
better than the spring?   9. No, I like the spring better,
because it is not so hot as the summer.   10. Is not John a
good pupil?   11. Yes.   12. Louis is a better pupil than
John, but Charles is the best pupil in the class.   13. 28,979.
14. 1000 is the thousandth part of one million.   15. November is the 11th month of the year.   16. Let us not
punish that child; he is ill.

Expressions de conversation

Entrez sans sonner.	Walk in.
Attention à la peinture !	Wet paint !
Ça y est; j'ai sali mes vête-ments.	There it is; I soiled my clothes.
Ma foi, c'est bien fait !	My word, it serves you right !
Dieu merci ! Ce n'est pas grave.	Thank goodness ! that's not serious.
Mon Dieu, non !	Gracious, no !
Qu'est-ce que ça fait?	What does it matter?

*   *   *   *   *   *   *

24ᵉ Leçon : L'article partitif

Paris n'a pas été fait en un jour. — *Rome was not built in a day.*

Observe the following meanings of **du, de la, de l', des.**

Je désire *du* **pain,** *de la* **viande,** *de l'***eau et** *des* **fruits.** *I want
(some) bread, (some) meat, (some) water and (some) fruit.*

Le sens partitif. — *Some* or *any*, whether expressed or understood before a noun in English, is regularly expressed in French by the preposition **de** + the definite article, namely :

du, de la, de l', des.

Note. — Like the definite article, the partitive article is repeated before each noun it limits. (See example above.)

Observe the following changes :

J'ai *de* bons crayons, mais je n'ai pas *de* plumes.   *I have (some) good pencils, but I have no(t any) pens.*

When the noun is preceded by an adjective (see Lesson 20 and also new rules, page 358), or *when the verb is negative*, **du, de la, de l',** and **des,** *some, any, no,* become **de** (or **d'**), the article being omitted.

Le sens général du nom. — Observe the difference between the following two sentences :

J'aime *les* livres.   *I like books.*
J'achète souvent *des* livres.   *I often buy books.*

In the first example, we say **J'aime les livres** because it means : *I like books, generally speaking.*   But we say **J'achète des livres** because I do not buy books, generally speaking, but only some particular books.

A noun used in a general sense takes the definite article in French.

Notice the difference between the general and the partitive sense in the following sentence :

***Les* chiens et *les* chats sont *des* animaux utiles à *l'*homme.**   *Dogs and cats are animals useful to man.*

Four articles are used in French and none in English. Dogs in general and cats in general are some of the particular animals useful to man in general.

Vocabulaire

dîner, *to dine.*
la carte du jour, *the bill of fare.*
le potage, *the soup.*
le poisson, *the fish.*
la viande, *the meat.*
le rosbif, *the roastbeef.*
le poulet, *the chicken.*
le légume, *the vegetable.*
la salade, *the salad.*
le fruit, *the fruit.*
le dessert, *the dessert.*
le pain, *the bread.*
le lait, *the milk.*

la boisson, *the drink.*
l'eau minérale, *mineral water.*
le café, *the coffee.*
le thé, *the tea.*
la crème, *the cream.*
le fromage, *the cheese.*
le poivre, *the pepper.*
le sel, *the salt.*
la moutarde, *the mustard.*
le sucre, *the sugar.*
les hors-d'œuvre, *the relish.*
le pot, *the pot, jar.*
près de, *near.*

DONNEZ-MOI DU POTAGE, DU POISSON . . .

Conversation

AU RESTAURANT

M. Loriot.   Garçon, avez-vous une petite table près de la fenêtre ?

Le garçon.   Voici une petite table pour deux.   Ces messieurs désirent dîner ?

M. Loriot.   Donnez-nous la carte du jour.   Bien, merci.

M. Allard.   Donnez-moi aussi une carte.

M. Loriot.   Du potage, du poisson, du rosbif, des légumes et des fruits.

Le garçon.   Très bien ; et monsieur ?

M. Allard.   Des hors-d'œuvre, du poulet, de la salade, du dessert et du fromage.

Le garçon. Bien, monsieur.

M. Allard. Ne désirez-vous pas de salade, monsieur Loriot?

M. Loriot. Non, je n'aime pas la salade. Et vous, n'aimez-vous pas les fruits?

M. Allard. J'aime beaucoup les fruits, mais quand je mange de la salade, je ne mange pas de fruits.

Le garçon. Et comme boisson, messieurs?

M. Loriot. De l'eau minérale.

M. Allard. De la limonade.

Le garçon. Ces messieurs désirent du café? Une demitasse?

M. Loriot. Du café au lait.

M. Allard. J'aime mieux du thé et de la crème.

M. Loriot. Garçon, mettez (*put*) aussi du sel, du poivre et de la moutarde sur la table. Il n'y a pas de pain ; et où est le sucre?

Le garçon. Voici, monsieur ; le poivre, le sel et le sucre. La moutarde est dans ce petit pot bleu ; j'apporte le pain dans une minute.

M. Allard. Ah! Voici le potage et les hors-d'œuvre, commençons.

Exercices

A. *Conversation sur la lecture.*

1. Où monsieur Loriot et monsieur Allard sont-ils?
2. Demandent-ils une grande table? 3. Où désirent-ils une table? 4. Que demandent-ils aussi au garçon?
5. Que choisit M. Loriot? 6. Et M. Allard? 7. Pourquoi M. Loriot ne désire-t-il pas de salade? 8. Et pourquoi M. Allard ne mange-t-il pas de fruits? 9. Qu'est-ce que ces messieurs ont demandé comme boisson? 10. Aimez-vous mieux la limonade que l'eau minérale? 11. M. Loriot a-t-il demandé du thé au garçon? 12. Qu'est-ce que M. Allard a commandé?

B. *Remplacez les tirets par l'article partitif ou par* **de.**

1. Donnez-moi —— papier et —— encre.   2. Il n'y a pas —— encre dans cet encrier.   3. Notre voisine vend —— poisson et notre voisin vend —— viande.   4. Le frère de notre voisin ne vend pas —— poisson, il vend —— légumes.   5. Ma jeune amie Louise a toujours —— belles robes blanches.   6. Y a-t-il —— muguets dans ce jardin? 7. Non, il n'y a pas —— muguets, mais il y a —— violettes, —— tulipes rouges et —— belles roses.

C. *Traduisez en français :*

1. Coffee is better than tea.   2. Do you like cream? 3. Do you want cream in your tea?   4. Have you any sugar in your coffee?   5. No, thank you, I do not like sugar.   6. Have you bought any flowers for your mother? 7. Waiter, bring us some chicken and salad.   8. Sorry, sir, we have no chicken to-day.   9. We have fish.   10. We do not like fish.   11. Give me some roast beef and vegetables.   12. Any soup, sir?   13. Yes, bring me some soup.   14. There are no flowers on this table.   15. We did not buy any flowers.   16. Did Mrs. Dulac put any sugar in her coffee?   17. Yes, she took sugar and cream : she likes sugar and cream.   18. Have you any friends in this large city?   19. No, I have no friends here.   20. Good books are always good friends.

Exercice-revue

1. Do you hear your mother?   2. No, but I hear my father ; he is speaking to the doctor's son.   3. Give me back my pen and ink, please.   4. What do you think of that fish? 5. It is very good, I think.   6. Why does that little boy always act badly?   7. He does not act worse than the other boys.   8. Where did you put the present you received from the neighbor's daughter?   9. The flowers which are on that table are mine.   10. Where is the little red handker-

chief that your mother bought for you? 11. Did you not see the large houses my father and my uncle are building in the main street? 12. This house is higher than that house. 13. It cost (*coûter*) 57,900 dollars. 14. This house is the highest and the most beautiful in the city. 15. Is this man richer than that man? 16. Yes, he is richer, he has $1,000,000.

* * * * * * *

25e Leçon : L'imparfait de l'indicatif

C'est bonnet blanc et blanc bonnet. — *It is six of one and half a dozen of the other.*[1]

Study the imperfect of the regular and auxiliary verbs.

1
Donner

je donn*ais,* I *gave,* I *was giving,*
tu donn*ais.* I *used to give.*
il (elle) donn*ait.*
nous donn*ions.*
vous donn*iez.*
ils (elles) donn*aient.*

2
Finir

je finiss*ais,* I *finished,* I *was*
tu finiss*ais.* *finishing,* I *used*
il (elle) finiss*ait. to finish.*
nous finiss*ions.*
vous finiss*iez.*
ils (elles) finiss*aient.*

3
Rendre

je rend*ais,* I *gave back,* I *was giving*
tu rend*ais.* *back,* I *used to give back.*
il (elle) rend*ait.*
nous rend*ions.*
vous rend*iez.*
ils (elle) rend*aient.*

---

[1] Literally, *It is white cap and cap white.*

Avoir	Être
j'av*ais*, *I had, I used to have*	j'ét*ais*, *I was, I used to be.*
tu av*ais*.	tu ét*ais*.
il (elle) av*ait*.	il (elle) ét*ait*.
nous av*ions*.	nous ét*ions*.
vous av*iez*.	vous ét*iez*.
ils (elles) av*aient*.	ils (elles) ét*aient*.

The endings of the imperfect are :

-ais, -ais, -ait, -*i*ons, -*i*ez, -aient.

Formation de l'imparfait. — The easiest way to form the imperfect of *all* verbs with the exception of **être** (*to be*) is to drop the ending **ons** of the first person plural of the present indicative and add the endings of the imperfect.

FIRST PERSON PLURAL PRESENT INDICATIVE

nous donn*ons*   nous finiss*ons*   nous rend*ons*

Emploi de l'imparfait. — The imperfect tense is second to the past indefinite in importance among the French past tenses.   It is used :

1. To express a continuous past action :
    When we lived in Paris . . .

2. The repetition of the same past action :
    I used to go to church every . . .

3. To denote a past action going on when another action took place :
    I was writing when I received your letter.

4. To express a state of being in the past :
    When *I was young, I was* poor.

When to translate an English past by the imperfect. — An almost infallible way to decide how to translate correctly a past tense such as *I spoke* from English into French is to see if that past tense can be replaced by *I was speaking* or *I used to speak* without the meaning of the sentence being changed.

| When *I spoke* has the meaning of | $\left\{\begin{array}{c} I\ was\ speaking \\ or \\ I\ used\ to\ speak \end{array}\right\}$ | use the imperfect: **Je parlais.** |
| When *I spoke* has the meaning of | $\left\{\begin{array}{c} I\ did\ speak \\ or \\ I\ have\ spoken \end{array}\right\}$ | use the past indefinite: **J'ai parlé.** |

In other words, the imperfect answers the questions : *What was happening, what used to happen?* while the past indefinite answers the question : *What has happened, what did happen?*

Vocabulaire

passer, *to pass, to spend.*
passer le temps, *to spend the time.*
visiter, *to visit.*
déjeuner, *to breakfast.*
luncher (lunshay), *to lunch.*
quitter, *to quit, leave.*
rester, *to remain.*
si, *if; so.*
à l'américaine, *the American way.*

à la française, *the French way.*
souper, *to sup.*
en ville, *in town (down town).*
le soir, *the evening.*
la soirée, *the evening hours.*
régulièrement, *regularly.*
malheureusement, *unfortunately.*
je prenais, *I used to take.*
l'arrivée (f.), *the arrival.*

il y avait, *there was, there were.*

Idiomatic expressions

Used in the following conversation.

tiens! *well!*
quelles nouvelles? *what news?*
ces derniers temps, *lately.*
en voilà une surprise! *that's a surprise!*
vous plaisantez! *you are joking!*
nullement, c'est comme ça, *no, sir, that's a fact.*
à l'heure, *by the hour.*

bien entendu! *of course!*
en voilà une idée! *the idea!*
mais non! *surely not!*
c'est cela, *that's it.*
à un de ces jours, *see you one of these days.*
à bientôt, *see you soon.*
ah! non, par exemple! *I should say not!*

Conversation

UNE RENCONTRE

A. Tiens! Voilà Bob! Quelles nouvelles? Où étiez-vous ces derniers temps?

B. Bonjour, Al ; mais j'étais à Paris !

A. Non ! vous plaisantez !

B. Nullement, c'est comme ça.

EN VOILÀ UNE SURPRISE !

A. En voilà une surprise ! Racontez-moi votre voyage. Comment passiez-vous le temps à Paris ?

B. Un jour je visitais les musées, un autre jour, je prenais un taxi à l'heure et je visitais les monuments et les curiosités de cette belle ville ; le temps passait vite.

A. Et le soir, restiez-vous à l'hôtel ?

B. Ah ! Non, par exemple ! Je passais mes soirées au théâtre, à l'opéra ou quelquefois dans les cinémas.

A. Dîniez-vous régulièrement à l'hôtel ?

B. Non, je déjeunais à l'hôtel, mais je dînais en ville.

A. Lunchiez-vous à l'américaine ?

B. Bien entendu, mais après le théâtre, je soupais à la française.

A. Où soupiez-vous, à l'hôtel ?

B. Mais non, en voilà une idée ! A Paris on (*they*) soupe dans les restaurants de nuit.

A. Avez-vous vu Madame X—— quand vous étiez à Paris ?

B. Malheureusement non. Elle a quitté la ville le jour de mon arrivée.

A. Voici mon omnibus. Au revoir, cher ami, à un de ces jours.

B. C'est cela ; à bientôt !

Exercices

A. *Remplacez les tirets par l'imparfait du verbe entre parenthèses :*

1. (rencontrer, saluer) Quand nous —— ce monsieur, il —— toujours ma mère.   2. (être, perdre) Quand vous —— à Paris, vous ne —— pas votre temps.   3. (rougir, parler) Pourquoi cette jeune fille —— -elle hier quand votre mère ——?   4. (complimenter, porter) Parce que ma mère —— Jeanne sur la jolie robe qu'elle ——.   5. (avoir, chanter, danser) Il y —— beaucoup de jeunes filles qui —— et —— très bien à la soirée de Mme Duval.   6. (avoir, jouer) Y —— -il des messieurs qui —— au bridge?   7. (être, perdre) Quand j'—— petit, je —— toujours mes jouets.   8. (être, danser) Quand elles —— jeunes, Marie —— mieux que sa sœur.   9. (avoir) Il y —— moins d'élèves à l'école l'année dernière que cette année-ci.

B. *Traduisez en français :*

1. When I was in (à) Paris last year, I used to visit the museums.   2. Were you answering your friend's letter when the telephone rang?   3. Where were you yesterday when I telephoned?   4. I was here.   5. No, you were not here.   6. If you were here, why did you not answer? 7. When my sister was young, she used to sing very well. 8. Did she sing better than your mother?   9. Oh! yes, she sang much better.   10. We were waiting for an omnibus when we saw your father.   11. Where were you waiting for an omnibus?   12. Were you not waiting for an omnibus near our house?   13. Was your sister choosing a present when she lost her bag?   14. They used to punish their little girl when she soiled her dress.

C. *Traduisez rapidement :*

1. They had; they have.   2. They were; they are. 3. They used to wait; they do wait.   4. They sold; they

have sold; they sell. 5. I sell; I used to sell. 6. We always used to sing when we were young. 7. Do you have? Did you have? 8. She is choosing; she was choosing. 9. She was not choosing; she was acting better.

Exercice-revue

1. Give me some bread. 2. We have no bread. 3. You have no bread, that's too bad. 4. Where is the book which was on this table this morning? 5. I did not see that book, but here is a book which is very interesting. 6. You always choose good books. 7. Your house is certainly the most beautiful in this street. 8. We are building another house, larger than this house in the main street. 9. Do you like large houses? 10. Name the days of the week. 11. Name the months of the year. 12. Name the seasons. 13. The flowers; flowers. 14. Salt; the salt. 15. Soup, fish, and dessert. 16. Tea is not as good as coffee. 17. Did you put sugar and milk in her coffee? 18. She does not like sugar, but she likes cream. 19. 183, 973. 20. 999.999.

* * * * * * *

26e Leçon : L'adjectif TOUT

Ne mettez pas tous vos œufs dans le même panier. — *Don't put all your eggs in one basket.*

The adjective **tout** (*m. s.*), **toute** (*f. s.*), **tous** (*m. pl.*). **toutes** (*f. pl.*), *every, all, whole*, precedes the article when the latter is present.

tout homme, *every man.*	toute femme, *every woman.*
tout enfant, *every child.*	toute la journée, *all day (long).*
tout le monde, *everybody.*	toute la matinée, *all morning.*
tous les deux, ⎫ *both.*	toute la soirée, *all evening.*
tous deux, ⎭	toute l'année, *all year (long).*

tous les hommes, *all men.*
tous les jours, *every day.*
tous les mois, *every month.*
tous les ans, *every year.*
tous les jeudis, *every Thursday.*

toutes les semaines, *every week.*
toutes les femmes, *all women.*
toutes les deux, *both* (f.).
toutes les fois (que), *every time.*
tout le temps, *all the time.*

Tout enfant est capricieux.
Tous les chiens sont fidèles.
Toute la classe est punie.

Every child is capricious.
All dogs are faithful.
The whole class is punished.

Tout is used in the singular without the article when the noun modified is used to personify or represent a whole class of people, animals, or things ; otherwise the article is always present. See the examples above.

Attention! Of, often used after *all* in English, is always omitted in French.

All of her friends are here to-day. **Tous ses amis sont ici aujourd'hui.**

Use of **an, année; jour, journée.**

An is used in a general sense to mention a definite number of years.

Année is used, most of the time in the singular, when speaking of a particular year: **cette *année*-ci, l'*année* dernière**, etc., or when speaking of the duration of the time rather than of a definite length of time: **J'ai passé une *année* à Paris.**

Jour, matin, soir are used when speaking of the division of time: **Il y a sept *jours* dans une semaine. Le *matin*, nous déjeunons, le *soir*, nous dînons.**

Journée, matinée, soirée are used when the speaker refers to the duration of the day, morning, and evening. **Nous avons passé la *journée* à la campagne. J'ai travaillé toute la *matinée*, et j'ai passé la *soirée* au théâtre.**

Matinée also means a day performance at the theater.

Soirée also means an evening party.

Vocabulaire

la campagne, *the country.*
à la campagne, *in(to) the country.*
la mer, *the sea.*
au bord de la mer, *at the seashore.*
quelque chose, *something.*
fidèle, *faithful.*

l'après-midi (m. and f.), *the afternoon.*
le monde, *the world.*
l'occasion, *the occasion, opportunity.*
le chien, *the dog.*

Lecture

1. Toutes les écoles sont fermées tous les samedis et tous les dimanches. 2. Les écoles françaises sont-elles aussi fermées tous les samedis? 3. Non, le (*on*) samedi, les écoles françaises sont ouvertes toute la journée, mais elles sont fermées tous les jeudis après-midi. 4. Hier, nous n'avons pas bien travaillé à l'école et toute la classe a été punie. 5. Pas possible! Tout le monde a été puni? 6. Oui, tous les élèves. 7. Louis ne travaille pas bien, il est puni tous les jours. 8. Mon frère aussi était puni tout le temps quand il était à l'école. 9. Jean était ici hier soir, et nous avons travaillé, tous les deux, toute la soirée. 10. Où passez-vous l'été cette année? 11. Tous les ans, nous passons l'été à la campagne. 12. Passez-vous tout l'été à la campagne? 13. Non, pas tout l'été. 14. Nous passons tout le mois d'août au bord de la mer.

Exercices

A. *Conversation sur la lecture:*

1. Les écoles françaises sont-elles ouvertes tous les jours de la semaine? 2. Qui a été puni hier? 3. Quand Jean et son ami ont-ils travaillé? 4. Jean passe-t-il souvent l'été à la campagne? 5. Quand Louis était-il puni? 6. Qui est dans la salle de classe? 7. Qui aime la mer?

B. *Traduisez en français:*

1. I have been in all the rooms of that large white house. 2. Did you visit the whole house? 3. Yes, the whole house. 4. All of my friends are here to-day, let us play. 5. They always are here every Saturday. 6. Every good pupil prepares all of his lessons and all of his exercises every day. 7. Everybody is here now, let us begin the lesson. 8. When you were in Paris, did you speak French all the time? 9. Of course, I spoke French every time (that) I

had the opportunity. 10. Yesterday, I spent the whole day in my garden. 11. I like your garden, all of your flowers are so pretty ! 12. Here are Paul and Charles, both of them are good pupils. 13. All the children are at the seashore every summer. 14. Every dog is faithful.

Exercice-revue

1. Is John more polite than Louis? 2. Who is the best pupil in your class? 3. Last year, Paul was the best pupil in the class. 4. This year he is the second and I am the first. 5. You deserve a reward ; here is a pretty little penknife that I bought for you. 6. Where is the necklace that was in that box this morning? 7. The necklace you had yesterday? 8. No, the necklace I received from my uncle. 9. You always lose something. 10. No, but I think I lost my necklace and my ring this time. 11. Wait a minute, I hear Jane. 12. Yes, here is Jane. Where were you? 13. You were losing your time again. 14. No, I was waiting for Mary in the street. 15. Do not wait in the street, wait here. 16. Were you answering your brother's letter when I rang [the bell]?

Une anecdote

RÉPONSE INATTENDUE

Dans une ville du midi (*south*) de la France que beaucoup de touristes visitaient en hiver, la porte d'un hôtel portait l'inscription suivante :

Ici on parle anglais, allemand, russe, italien, espagnol.

Un Anglais entre et demande l'interprète. — Nous n'avons pas d'interprète, répond le garçon. — Comment, dit l'Anglais, mais alors, qui parle toutes les langues mentionnées sur la porte? — Mais . . . les voyageurs, monsieur, répond le garçon.

* * * * * * *

27ᵉ Leçon : Futur et futur antérieur

Un tiens vaut mieux que deux tu l'auras. — *A bird in the hand is worth two in the bush.*

PREMIÈRE CONJUGAISON

Donner: je donnerai, -ras, -ra, -rons, -rez, -ront.   *I shall* or *will give*, etc.

DEUXIÈME CONJUGAISON

Finir: je finirai, -ras, -ra, -rons, -rez, -ront.   *I shall* or *will finish*, etc.

TROISIÈME CONJUGAISON

Rendre: je rendrai, -ras, -ra, -rons, -rez, -ront. *I shall* or *will give back*, etc.

The future tense is formed by adding to *the whole infinitive* the endings :

-ai, -as, -a, -ons, -ez, -ont,

except that the **e** of the infinitive of the verbs of the 3d conjugation is dropped before the endings of the future.

Attention!   There is always a " grrrowl " in *all* persons of the *future* in *all* verbs.

Historical Note. — The endings of the future are made of the old present indicative of the verb **avoir**. Even now, in some parts of France the country people say : **nous ons, vous ez,** for : **nous avons** and **vous avez.**

Avoir

j'aurai, *I shall* or *will have.*
tu auras.
il aura.
nous aurons.
vous aurez.
ils auront.

Être

je serai, *I shall* or *will be.*
tu seras.
il sera.
nous serons.
vous serez.
ils seront.

Le futur antérieur. — The future perfect is formed with the future of the auxiliary verb **avoir** (sometimes **être**) and the past participle of the verb.

j'aurai donné, *I shall have given.*
j'aurai fini, *I shall have finished.*
j'aurai rendu, *I shall have given back.*

j'aurai eu, *I shall have had.*
j'aurai été, *I shall have been.*

Emploi du futur. — The future and future perfect are used as in English. They must also be used after **quand** and **lorsque** (*when*), **aussitôt que** and **dès que** (*as soon as*) when futurity is implied, even though the present or perfect be used in English.

The future perfect is always used when it is necessary to show that a future action must take place immediately before another future action. (Example 2.)

1. **Je finirai quand il arrivera.** *I shall finish when he arrives.*
2. **Je jouerai quand j'aurai fini ma leçon.** *I will play when I have finished my lesson.* (Literally: *When I shall have finished my lesson.*)

Aller (irregular), *to go;* participe passé, **allé,** *gone*

Présent	Imparfait	Futur
je vais, *I go, I am going,*	j'allais, *I went, I was going,*	j'irai, *I shall go.*
tu vas.　*I do go.*	tu allais.　*I used to go.*	tu iras.
il va.	il allait.	il ira.
nous allons.	nous allions.	nous irons.
vous allez.	vous alliez.	vous irez.
ils vont.	ils allaient.	ils iront.

Impératif

Singulier	Pluriel	
va, *go.*	allons, *let us go.*	allez, *go.*

Vocabulaire

sous peu, *in a little while.*
demain, *to-morrow.*
précisément, *precisely.*
ensemble, *together.*
volontiers, *willingly.*
prochain, *next* (in time).
quelques, *a few.*

l'invité, *the guest.*
arriver, *to arrive.*
le départ, *the departure.*
il y aura, *there will be.*
y aura-t-il? *will there be?*
ce soir, *this evening, to-night.*
après, *later, then.*

aller bien, *to be well.*

Expressions idiomatiques

de tout cœur, *very willingly.*
cela va sans dire, *that goes without saying.*

jamais de la vie! *I should say not!*
entendu! *agreed!*

en famille, *with one's family.*
beaucoup de monde, *many people.*
sans faute, *without fail.*

à demain soir! *see you to-morrow night!*
bien des choses, *kind regards.*

Conversation

Une invitation par téléphone

Jean.   Allo, Paul !   Nous allons à la campagne sous peu.

Paul.   Voilà une bonne idée !   Quand irez-vous à la campagne? . . .   Oh ! la semaine prochaine. . . .   Serez-vous à la maison ce soir ou demain soir?

Jean.   Oui, j'allais précisément vous proposer (*to propose to you*) de passer la soirée ensemble demain.

ALLO, PAUL !

Paul.   Mais volontiers, j'accepte de tout cœur votre bonne invitation, cela va sans dire.

Jean.   Vous raconterez votre dernier voyage à Paris, et nous parlerons de notre prochain départ.

Paul.   Y aura-t-il beaucoup de monde?

Jean.   Non, nous dînerons en famille, mais après le dîner nous aurons la visite de quelques invités.   Quand tout le monde sera ici, nous déciderons comment nous passerons la soirée.   Madame Mireille chantera, mon frère jouera du piano et après je suppose que nous danserons.

Paul.   Je serai sans faute à votre soirée; j'arriverai à neuf heures quand vous aurez fini de dîner.

Jean. Jamais de la vie, vous dînerez avec nous à sept heures.

Paul. Entendu, cher ami, à demain soir et merci. Bien des choses à madame votre mère.

Exercices

A. *Mettez les verbes suivants au futur, à la personne indiquée :*

je marcher	nous entendre	elle vendre	tu attendre
il bâtir	ils agir	nous finir	nous écouter

B. *Traduisez en français :*

1. My kind regards to your father. 2. Will they go to the opera together? 3. No, his mother will stay home, she is not well. 4. I thought she was better. 5. She will be better next week, and then she will go to the country. 6. Will you be at home to-night? 7. No, I shall not be home. 8. When we have danced, she will play bridge. 9. When John is here, we always play bridge. 10. When John is here, we shall tell anecdotes. 11. When will you sell your house? 12. I will not sell my house; will he sell his? 13. No, he will wait until next year. 14. As soon as he has spoken, we shall go into the dining room and we shall eat a little. 15. Will there be many people at Mrs. Dupont's evening party next week? 16. No, there will not be many people.

Exercice-revue

1. Do you eat salad every day? 2. Yes, I like salad. 3. And you, don't you like salad? 4. Yes, very much. 5. When I was in (*en*) France I used to take fruit every day. 6. Is (are) fruit(s) good in France? 7. Mine were very good. 8. I spoke French yesterday with the professor's little boy; he speaks very well. 9. Did you hear the professor last week? 10. Yes, he spoke very well. 11. Where did you spend the evening yesterday? 12. I

spent the whole day at home and the evening at the theater.
13. Do you understand French?   14. No, and if (*si*) you
speak French, you are losing your time, because I do not
understand.   15. The gentleman who passes there, on the
other side of the street, is our doctor.   16. Where does he
live?   17. He lives in that small house, near the park.

*   *   *   *   *   *   *

28e Leçon : Participe passé avec ÊTRE

Réfléchissez avant d'agir.   *Look before you leap.*[1]

Study the following sentences :

> **Il est allé à la campagne.**
> **Elle est allée à la campagne.**
> **Ils sont allés à la campagne.**
> **Elles sont allées à la campagne.**

Most French verbs form their compound tenses with **avoir**
(Lesson 14). However, some verbs, denoting motion or
change of condition, use the verb **être** to form their compound
tenses.

Attention!   Note that the verb **être** in this particular case
is translated by *to have* in English.

Accord du participe passé conjugué avec *être*. — The past
participle conjugated with **être** agrees in gender and number
with the *subject*.

The following are the most common past participles which
are conjugated with **être**.

allé, *gone.*   **entré (dans),** *entered, gone into.*
venu, *come.*   **sorti,** *gone out, come out.*
revenu, *come back, returned.* **resté,** *remained, stayed.*

---

[1] Literally, *Reflect before acting.*

devenu, *become.*
arrivé, *arrived, happened.*
parti, *gone away, set out, left.*
rentré, *come back* (in the house, home)

retourné, *gone back, returned.*
tombé, *fallen.*
né, *born.*
mort, *died* (adj., *dead*).

Vocabulaire

pas encore, *not yet.*
entendre dire que, *to hear that.*
faire une visite, *to visit* (a person).
ordonner, *to order, to prescribe.*
il y a huit jours, *a week ago.*

le repos, *the rest.*
absolu, *absolute, complete.*
en deuil, *in mourning.*
le (la) même, *the same.*
car (conj.), *for.*

il y a (before a period of time), *ago.*

Conversation

A.   Quand êtes-vous allés à la campagne cette année?

B.   Je suis parti le 1er juin et je suis revenu le 11 septembre ; nous sommes donc restés trois mois et onze jours.

A.   Êtes-vous revenus avec les Delagrange?

B.   Non, ils sont arrivés il y a huit jours.

A.   Avez-vous entendu dire que leur petite fille est retournée à la campagne?

B.   Mais non, sa mère est venue ici il y a quatre ou cinq
jours et n'a pas parlé de cela (*that*).

A.   L'accident n'était pas encore arrivé. Sa fille est
tombée sur la (*her*) tête jeudi dernier, et le médecin a
ordonné un repos absolu.

B.   Savez-vous que la famille de notre voisin est en deuil?

A.   Non, qu'est-il arrivé (*what happened*)?

B.   La tante de Jean est venue ici hier faire une visite ;
elle est entrée dans le salon, mais elle est sortie tout de suite,
car elle est devenue malade ; elle a pris un taxi et est rentrée ;
sa sœur a téléphoné qu'elle est morte dans la soirée.

A.   Oh ! C'est dommage ! Était-elle très vieille?

B.   Non, elle est née il y aura exactement cinquante ans
demain.

Exercices

A. *Traduisez en français :*

1. Did you go to school this morning?   2. No, I did not go out to-day.   3. Why did you stay home?   4. Because yesterday I fell, and I am still a little ill.   5. Has your mother gone away?   6. Yes, she went to Boston, but she has already come back.   7. Do you hear?   Who entered the dining room?   8. My aunt and my sister have entered, I think.   9. Is your aunt in town?   10. Yes, she arrived yesterday with my mother.   11. My mother went to the station, but they stayed home.   12. My aunt has become very old.   13. The last time (that) she came, she was much younger.   14. When she returned two years ago, she fell very sick, and then my uncle died.   15. Was he old? When was (is) he born?   16. He was born in 1885.

Exercice-revue

1. Will you be here to-morrow?   2. I shall be home all day.   3. I shall be here too ; we shall prepare our lessons together.   4. With pleasure, and when we have finished our lessons, we shall go to the movies.   5. Will your father go to the country next Sunday?   6. Yes, we go to the country every Sunday.   7. When we went to the country last year, we always stayed two days, Saturday and Sunday.   8. I shall wait for my brother and then we shall go home together. 9. Who brought these beautiful flowers which are on the table?   10. When we go to the country, we always bring flowers.   11. Will your uncle sell his house?   12. Yes, he will sell his house as soon as he has found a house in town. 13. Mine will build a house in this street, when he has the money.   14. I saw your father in a taxi yesterday, where was he going?   15. He was going to the theater ; he was late.

*   *   *   *   *   *   *

29ᵉ Leçon : Noms et adverbes de quantité

C'est beaucoup de bruit pour rien. — *Much ado about nothing.*

Observe the use of the preposition **de** in the following sentences :

Voulez-vous une tasse *de* café?   *Will you have a cup of coffee?*
J'ai trop *de* café.   *I have too much coffee.*
Nous avons beaucoup *de* (not **des**) livres.   *We have many books.*

After nouns of quantity, French uses the preposition **de** (*of*) without the article, exactly as in English.

After adverbs of quantity, where English omits *of*, French requires **de**. *Do not* use **des**, even if the following noun is plural.

De becomes **d'** before a noun beginning with a vowel or **h** mute.

Attention! **De** is always repeated before each noun.

Vouloir, *to want, to wish;* participe passé, **voulu**

PRÉSENT	IMPARFAIT	FUTUR
je veux, *I wish.*	je voulais, *I was wishing.*	je voudrai, *I shall wish.*
tu veux.	tu voulais.	tu voudras.
il veut.	il voulait.	il voudra.
nous voulons.	nous voulions.	nous voudrons.
vous voulez.	vous vouliez.	vous voudrez.
ils veulent.	ils voulaient.	ils voudront.

Vocabulaire

la douzaine, *the dozen.*
la livre, *the pound.*
la demi-livre, *the half-pound.*
la tasse, *the cup.*
le verre, *the glass.*
la bouteille, *the bottle.*
la carafe, *the carafe.*
le panier, *the basket.*

combien de, *how much, how many.*
beaucoup de, *much, many, a great deal.*
trop de, *too, too much, too many.*
tant de, *so much, so many.*
autant de, *as much, as many.*
assez de, *enough.*
plus de. *more.*
moins de, *less.*

le morceau, *the piece, morsel.*

un peu, *a little, few.*

la sauce, *the gravy.*

la fraise, *the strawberry.*

vide, *empty.*

peu de, *little.*

bu, *drunk.*

au lieu de + infin., *instead of.*

taquiner, *to tease.*

plein, *full.*

l'avis (m.), *the opinion.*

Beaucoup is never preceded by a modifier like très or trop, but it is possible to say beaucoup plus (*much more* or *far more*), beaucoup moins (*much less* or *far less*), and beaucoup trop (*far too, far too much, far too many*).

Assez always precedes the noun; assez de fleurs, *flowers enough.*

Autant, and not tant, is used both affirmatively and negatively in a comparison:

Il n'a pas autant de plumes que de crayons. *He has not so many pens as pencils.*

Vous avez tant de beaux tableaux! *You have so many beautiful pictures!*

Peu, *little,* denotes quantity, while petit denotes size; as a noun, peu is always masculine: un peu d'eau, *a little water.*

Expressions idiomatiques

mes petits, *my little ones.*

v'lan! *bang!*

attrape! *take that!*

bien élevé, *well behaved.*

mon chéri, *my darling* (m.).

ma chérie, *my darling* (f.).

Conversation

A TABLE

Le papa. Mangez, mes petits; voici un peu de soupe.

La maman. J'ai acheté une douzaine de petits pains (*rolls*), une demi-livre de fromage et un panier de fraises.

Jeanne. Bravo! J'adore les fraises!

Le papa. Jeanne, nous ne demandons pas votre avis.

Louis (à sa sœur). V'lan, attrape!

La maman. Louis, finissez votre soupe au lieu de taquiner votre sœur.

Jeanne (à son frère). V'lan, attrape aussi!

Le papa. Silence, les enfants. Oh! Voici un magnifique rosbif.

Louis. Je veux un grand morceau de rosbif et beaucoup de sauce !

Le papa. Vous mangerez le morceau que vous aurez.

Jeanne. Maman, Louis a plus de rosbif que moi (*I*).

La maman. Naturellement vous avez moins de rosbif que Louis, vous n'êtes pas si grande que votre frère.

Le papa. Ma chérie, donne-moi un peu de légumes s'il te plaît. Comment ! Cette carafe d'eau est déjà vide ?

VOUS MANGEREZ LE MORCEAU QUE VOUS AUREZ.

La maman. Louis a déjà bu trois verres d'eau, et cette après-midi il a bu deux tasses de thé et une bouteille de limonade.

Le papa. C'est trop de liquide ; vous avez pris assez d'eau maintenant, Louis.

Louis. Maman, je n'ai pas autant de fraises que Jeanne.

La maman. Mais si, comptez : une, deux, trois, quatre, cinq, six.

Louis. Oui, mais les miennes sont plus petites que les siennes !

Le papa. Pas tant de remarques, s'il vous plaît. Finissez votre dessert et allez jouer tous les deux dans le jardin.

Exercices

A. *Conversation sur la lecture :*

1. Qu'est-ce que la maman a acheté ? 2. Que dit Louis à sa sœur ? 3. Ne veut-il pas de rosbif ? 4. Pourquoi

Alphonse Daudet (1840–1897) : Romancier et auteur dramatique.   Ses recueils de nouvelles, notamment les Lettres de
mon Moulin et les Contes du Lundi, sont considérés, à juste
titre, comme des chefs-d'œuvre.

Victor Hugo (1802–1885) : Le plus illustre des poètes français
du XIXe siècle.   Le nombre et l'importance de ses œuvres,
leur influence sur son époque font de lui une des plus grandes
personnalités de son siècle.

Guy de Maupassant (1850–1893) : Ecrivain réaliste, sobre et
robuste, d'un style châtié et précis.

Jules Verne (1828–1905) : Romancier scientifique.   Auteur
de romans scientifiques et géographiques dénotant un esprit
créateur et inventif d'une vision rare.   Cinquante ans d'avance,
il avait conçu le sous-marin et le dirigeable.

Anatole France (1844–1924) de son vrai nom Anatole François
Thibault : Poète et littérateur.   Ecrivain de premier ordre, au
style impeccable, à l'esprit souple et complexe.

Alexandre Dumas (1803–1870) : Le plus célèbre de tous les
romanciers français.

Jeanne a-t-elle reçu moins de rosbif que son frère? 5. Louis a-t-il beaucoup bu? 6. A-t-il plus de fraises que sa sœur?

B. *Traduisez en français :*

1. Have you meat enough? 2. I have too much cheese and too little bread. 3. Will you have a cup of tea and a little cream? 4. With pleasure, thank you. 5. I have cream enough, thanks. 6. One or two pieces of sugar? 7. One piece of sugar, please. 8. How many dozen baskets of strawberries does your neighbor sell? 9. Charles, you have made (*fait*) many mistakes (*faute*, f.) in the exercise, too many mistakes. 10. Bring me a bottle of mineral water and a glass of lemonade. 11. We want more lemonade, sir. 12. How many pounds of vegetables do you buy every day? 13. I bought as many pounds of vegetables to-day as yesterday. 14. I wanted to buy fruit also, but I had not money enough. 15. Give me a little more of that tea please.

Exercice-revue

1. Everybody likes good friends. 2. Shall we go to the theater to-morrow evening? 3. I went yesterday. 4. The singers (*chanteurs*) who sang were not good. 5. The opera they were singing was very interesting. 6. Were there many people? 7. Do you go to the opera every week? 8. Yes, we go every Friday. 9. Last year, every time (that) we were going to the opera, my sister used to fall ill. 10. Is your father out (gone out)? 11. Yes, he left for Boston this morning. 12. My brother will not be here to-day. 13. When do you want to have your French lesson? 14. I want to have a lesson every day. 15. All right, you will have a lesson every day; I shall be here all day to-morrow.

* * * * * * *

30e Leçon : Pronoms personnels. Régime direct

Vouloir, c'est pouvoir. — *Where there's a will there's a way.*

When personal pronouns are direct objects of a verb, they take the following forms :

	SINGULIER	PLURIEL
1st person	**me**, *me.*	**nous**, *us.*
2d person	**te**, *thee (you).*	**vous**, *you.*
3d person (m.)	**le**, *him, it.*	**les**, *them.*
3d person (f.)	**la**, *her, it.*	

Me, te, le, la become **m', t', l'** before a verb beginning with a vowel or **h** mute.

Place des pronoms régimes directs. — Observe the position of the direct object pronouns in the following *affirmative* sentences :

Je *le* vois.	*I see* IT.
Je *l'*ai vu.	*I did see* IT.
Me voici.	*Here* I *am.*
La voilà.	*There* SHE *is.*

All personal pronouns, direct objects of a verb, are placed *immediately before* that verb in simple tenses, and *immediately before* the auxiliary verb in compound tenses.

These pronouns are also placed before **voici** and **voilà**.

Study the following *negative* sentences :

Je ne *le* vois pas.
I do not see IT.
Je ne *l'*ai pas vu.
I did not see IT.

Note that in the negative form, **ne,** the first part of the negation, precedes the object pronoun, which follows the general rule and comes *immediately before the verb.*

Observe the position of the pronoun in the following *interrogative* sentences :

> **Vous** aime-t-elle ?   *Does she love* YOU?
> **Vous** a-t-elle aimé ?   *Did she love* YOU?

In the interrogative form, the object pronoun begins the sentence, because it must be placed *immediately before the verb.*

Study the following *negative-interrogative* sentences :

> **Ne** *vous* aime-t-elle pas ?   *Doesn't she love* YOU?
> **Ne** *vous* a-t-elle pas aimé ?   *Didn't she love* YOU?

In the negative-interrogative form, **ne** begins the sentence in order to leave the object pronoun *immediately before the verb.*

Pouvoir, *to be able, can, may;* participe passé, **pu**

Présent	Imparfait	Futur
je peux or je puis, *I can,*	je pouvais, *I was able,*	je pourrai, *I shall*
tu peux. *I am able.*	tu pouvais. *I could.*	tu pourras. *be*
il peut.	il pouvait.	il pourra. *able.*
nous pouvons.	nous pouvions.	nous pourrons.
vous pouvez.	vous pouviez.	vous pourrez.
ils peuvent.	ils pouvaient.	ils pourront.

Pouvoir is conjugated like **vouloir.**

Note. — *Can I* is expressed in French by **Puis-je.**

Vocabulaire

> **blâmer,** *to blame.*   **gronder,** *to scold.*
> **louer,** *to praise.*   **chercher,** *to look for.*

Lecture

1. Préparez-vous votre leçon de français?   2. Oui, je la prépare.   3. Préparez-vous aussi vos exercices?   4. Oui, je les prépare, les voici.   5. Qui vous gronde?   6. Nos parents nous grondent quand nous ne les écoutons pas. 7. J'ai pris votre livre et je l'ai mis dans la bibliothèque :

l'avez-vous cherché? 8. Je vous remercie ; je comprends maintenant pourquoi je ne pouvais pas le trouver ce matin. 9. Mon cousin est arrivé, l'avez-vous vu? 10. Non, je ne l'ai pas vu, mais je l'attends. 11. Votre professeur vous punit-il quelquefois? 12. Oui, il nous punit assez souvent. 13. Me voici, que voulez-vous? 14. Pourquoi la blâmez-vous? 15. Je ne la blâme pas, je la loue.

Exercices

A. *Employez tous les pronoms régimes directs dans les phrases suivantes :*

1. Il laisse.
2. Il remarque.
3. Ils blâment.
4. Elle gronde.
5. Il accepte.
6. Ils ne regardent pas.
7. Elles n'acceptent pas.
8. Ne blâme-t-il pas?
9. Cherche-t-elle?
10. Voici. 11. Voilà.

B. *Conjuguez :*

1. Je le regarde. 2. Je ne le regarde pas. 3. Je ne la vends pas. 4. Je le veux. 5. Je l'ai fini. 6. Je ne l'ai pas vendu. 7. La vendrai-je? 8. L'ai-je trouvé? 9. Je ne le voulais pas. 10. Ne les attendrai-je pas?

C. *Remplacez les noms en italique par les pronoms qui conviennent :*

1. Je veux *mon livre*. 2. Je veux *ma plume*. 3. Je veux *mes crayons*. 4. Je ne veux pas *mes plumes*. 5. Pourquoi ne voulez-vous pas *vos plumes?* 6. Elle n'a pas pris *les livres*. 7. Il n'a pas vu *Paul*. 8. Entendez-vous la *musique?* 9. Attendons-nous *Jeanne?* 10. Je ne comprends pas *la question*. 11. Aimez-vous *les fruits?* 12. Je n'aime pas *les légumes*.

D. *Traduisez en français :*

1. I like him, her, it, you, them. 2. You like me, him, us, them. 3. Do you like us? 4. Does she not like you?

5. Why don't you like her, me, them, him, us?   6. He is looking for you.   7. He is looking at you.   8. You are not looking at me, him, her, us, them.   9. They do not look for me, him, her, it (*m.*), it (*f.*), us, them, you. 10. Will you not look at us, them, him, her, me, it.

Exercice-revue

1. Her father is my uncle's best friend.   2. I lost, I bought, I noticed, I found.   3. I do hear, I am hearing. 4. Do we finish? Are we finishing?   5. This pencil and that pencil are my sister's pencils.   6. Five, five strawberries, five children.   7. What colors are those flowers? 8. 51, 106, 591.   9. I am the tallest boy in my class. 10. Here is the most difficult exercise in the grammar. 11. Do not speak so fast.   12. She found the bag you lost. 13. They went to the seashore.   14. I do not want any coffee, thank you.   15. I always lose my pen.   16. Dogs and cats are useful animals.   17. Both went to school this morning.   18. We shall go to pay a visit to our aunt to-morrow.

Conversation

En visite

M. Legrand.   Monsieur Dumoulin est-il à la maison?

La bonne.   Oui, monsieur ; qui dois-je annoncer?

M. Legrand.   Voici nos cartes.

La bonne.   Merci, monsieur, voulez-vous entrer dans le salon?

Mr. Smith.   Quelle jolie maison !   Quel chic !

M. Dumoulin.   Bonjour, mon vieux camarade !   Quelle agréable surprise !

M. Legrand.   Bonjour, cher Gaston.   Je te présente un de mes amis, Stanley Smith, un jeune Américain.

M. Dumoulin. Enchanté de faire votre connaissance, monsieur.

Mr. Smith. Tout le plaisir est pour moi, monsieur.

(*à suivre*)

* * * * * * *

31e Leçon : Pronoms personnels. Régimes indirects

Je ferai d'une pierre deux coups. — *I shall kill two birds with one stone.*[1]

When the personal pronouns are used as indirect objects of a verb, that is, *when they are the object of the preposition à, to,* understood, they have the following forms :

SINGULIER	PLURIEL
1st person **me,** *to me.*	**nous,** *to us.*
2d person **te,** *to thee (you).*	**vous,** *to you.*
3d person **lui,** *to him, to her, to it.*	**leur,** *to them* (m. and f.).

Note. — 1. Notice that the indirect object pronouns differ from the direct object pronouns only in the 3d person (sing. and plur.).

2. The preposition **à,** *to,* is *not* expressed in French since it is included in the pronoun itself.

Position des pronoms régimes indirects. — Observe in the following sentences the position of the personal pronouns used as indirect objects :

Je *vous* parle.	*I speak to* YOU.
Elle *me* parle.	*She speaks to* ME.
Nous ne *lui* avons pas parlé.	*We didn't speak to* HIM (or *to* HER).
Lui parlerez-vous ?	*Will you speak to* HIM (or *to* HER) ?
Ne *leur* parlez-vous pas ?	*Don't you speak to* THEM ?

Like the direct object pronouns, the indirect object pronouns are placed *immediately before the verb* in single tenses and *immediately before the auxiliary* verb in compound tenses,

[1] Literally, *I shall make two blows with* [*of*] *one stone.*

whether the sentences are affirmative, negative, or interrogative.

Faire (irregular), *to do, to make;* participe passé, **fait**

Présent	Imparfait	Futur
je fais, *I do, I am doing, I*	je faisais.	je ferai, *I shall do or*
tu fais. *make or am making.*	tu faisais.	tu feras. *make.*
il fait.	il faisait.	il fera.
nous faisons.	nous faisions.	nous ferons.
vous *faites.*	vous faisiez.	vous ferez.
ils font.	ils faisaient.	ils feront.

IMPÉRATIF

SINGULIER	PLURIEL	
fais, *make, do.*	faisons, *let us make or do.*	faites, *make, do.*

Vocabulaire

envoyer, *to send.*
espérer, *to hope.*
obéir (à),[1] *to obey.*
désobéir (à),[1] *to disobey.*
prêter, *to lend.*
refuser, *to refuse.*
le costume, *the suit.*
télégraphier, *to telegraph.*

emprunter, *to borrow.*
le télégramme, *the telegram.*
la somme, *the sum.*
pressé, *in a hurry.*
promis, *promised.*
comme vous voilà fait, *how odd you look!*
comme ça, *like that, this way.*
hier soir, *last night, last evening.*

Lecture

1. Quand avez-vous écrit à votre frère?   2. Je lui ai
écrit une lettre hier.   3. Je pensais que vous lui aviez
envoyé un télégramme.   4. Je lui télégraphierai s'il ne me
répond pas immédiatement.   5. Pourquoi êtes-vous si
pressé?   6. Je lui ai demandé mille dollars et il m'a promis
de les envoyer avant la fin du mois.   7. J'espère qu'il ne
vous refusera pas cette petite somme.   8. Lui avez-vous

---

[1] Contrary to the English usage, *obey* and *disobey* require the preposition **à**, *to,* when followed by a noun.   Therefore, when a pronoun is
used instead of a noun, that pronoun should be in the dative case, *i.e.,*
it should be an indirect object pronoun.

expliqué pourquoi vous voulez lui emprunter cet argent? 9. Oui, je lui ai écrit que Louis m'a emprunté de l'argent et qu'il ne peut pas me rendre toute la somme que je lui ai donnée. 10. Où est votre petit garçon? Ah! le voici. 11. Comme vous voilà fait! Vous m'avez encore désobéi, vous avez sali votre nouveau costume. 12. Non, père, je ne vous ai pas désobéi, je vous obéis toujours. 13. Qui vous a sali comme ça alors? 14. Je suis tombé dans le jardin. 15. Une autre fois, faites attention quand vous jouez.

Exercices

A. *Remplacez les tirets par les six pronoms régimes indirects :*

1. Il —— parle. 2. Elle —— donne un livre. 3. Ils —— ont répondu. 4. —— donne-t-il un livre? 5. Elle ne —— a pas écrit. 6. Ne —— ont-ils pas obéi?

B. *Conjuguez :*

1. Je lui parlais. 2. Je ne leur obéirai pas. 3. Lui ai-je écrit? 4. Ne leur répondrai-je pas? 5. Je ne lui vendrai pas ma maison.

C. *Remplacez les mots en italique par les pronoms régimes indirects qui conviennent :*

1. Je montre cette lettre *à mon ami*. 2. Vous obéissez *à vos parents*. 3. Elle rend les exercices *aux élèves*. 4. Nous vendrons notre maison *au voisin*. 5. Je ne parle pas *au professeur*. 6. Pourquoi n'avez-vous pas donné les fleurs *à votre tante?* 7. Je parlais *au médecin* quand vous êtes entré. 8. Nous obéissons toujours *à nos parents*. 9. N'avez-vous pas désobéi *à votre mère?* 10. Si, j'ai désobéi *à ma mère*.

D. *Traduisez en français :*

1. I speak to her, to you, to him, to them. 2. We spoke to you, to them, to him, to her. 3. Has she not spoken to us, to me, to her, to them, to you? 4. They obey us, them,

you, him.   5. Does he bring us coffee and sugar?   6. He
did not bring me any coffee.   7. Did I show you my new
suit?   8. Why don't you answer me?   9. Why didn't you
answer them?   10. Did she read (*lu*) that letter to you?
11. I sold him my house.   12. Didn't you show us your
beautiful necklace?   13. Did you telegraph him or did you
telephone him?   14. I wrote them.   15. He brought us
beautiful roses.

Exercice-revue

1. I want it.   2. I do not want it.   3. Why don't you
want it?   4. Do they want it?   5. We used to go to the
country every summer.   6. Can you do it?   7. Can you
not do it?   8. Did you see him last Sunday at church?
9. No, I saw him yesterday at the opera.   10. Will you stay
here all day to-morrow?   11. No, but I shall be home all
morning.   12. When did she come to school?   13. When
did she arrive?   14. My father and mother left for Paris
last week.   15. Here are a dozen rolls and a big piece of
cheese, will you eat?   16. No thanks, I do not like cheese.
17. That young girl has become very pretty, but she is in
mourning.

Conversation

EN VISITE (*suite*)

M. Dumoulin. Mais asseyez-vous, je vous prie. Voici
des cigares, des cigarettes, faites comme chez vous. Vous
arrivez de New-York?

M. Legrand. Oui, directement. Nous avons débarqué il
y a trois jours.

M. Dumoulin. A quel hôtel êtes-vous descendus?

M. Legrand. Nous sommes dans un petit hôtel à Montmartre.

M. Dumoulin. Ce vieux Legrand! Toujours le bohême
des temps passés! Êtes-vous pour longtemps à Paris?

M. Legrand. Pas moi ; je quitte Paris dans deux jours ; mais mon ami reste ici.

M. Dumoulin. Ah ! Vous restez à Paris, monsieur Smith?

Mr. Smith. Oui, monsieur ; je désire étudier à la Sorbonne.

M. Dumoulin. Oh ! Mais c'est très bien ! Vous êtes le bienvenu dans notre beau Paris ; et comme vous êtes un ami de Legrand, vous savez, en France, les amis de nos amis sont nos amis.

Mr. Smith. Vous êtes bien aimable, monsieur, je ne sais comment vous remercier.

(à suivre)

* * * * * * *

32e Leçon : Pronoms régimes avec l'impératif

Aide-toi, le ciel t'aidera. — *Heaven helps those who help themselves.*

Observe the following sentences :

Montrez-*moi* le livre.	*Show* ME *the book.*
Montrez-*le* à votre frère.	*Show* IT *to your brother.*
Montrez-*lui* le livre.	*Show* HIM *the book.*

We have seen in the two preceding lessons that the personal pronouns used as direct or indirect objects are placed immediately before the verb. The **only exception** to that rule occurs when the mood of the verb is the *imperative affirmative.* Then the pronouns are placed *immediately after* the verb as in English.

Note. — A pronoun, whether subject or object, when placed after the verb, is connected with it by a hyphen.

When placed after the verb, **me** and **te** become **moi** and **toi.** The other pronouns do not change their form.

Observe the following negative sentences :

Ne *me* montrez pas le livre.   *Don't show* ME *the book.*
Ne *le* montrez pas à votre frère. *Don't show* IT *to your brother.*
Ne *lui* montrez pas le livre.   *Don't show* HIM *the book.*

With the *negative imperative*, the pronoun objects are placed before the verb, following the general rule.

Vocabulaire

féliciter, *to congratulate.*
envoyer, *to send.*
l'anniversaire (m.), *the birthday.*

consulter, *to consult.*
l'ordonnance (f.), *the prescription.*
sage, *good* (speaking of a child).

Lecture

1. Je suis le premier de ma classe ; félicitez-moi.   2. Je vous félicite, mon ami.   3. Il est le premier de sa classe ; félicitez-le.   4. Elle est la première de sa classe ; félicitez-la.   5. Nous sommes les meilleurs élèves de notre classe ; félicitez-nous.   6. Ils sont méchants ; grondez-les.   7. Voici le médecin, consultez-le et demandez-lui une ordonnance.   8. Parlez-lui tout de suite, il est pressé.   9. Donnez-moi votre plume, j'ai perdu la mienne.   10. Répondez-nous quand nous vous parlons.   11. Regardez-la ; pourquoi ne la regardez-vous pas?   12. Envoyez-lui un petit cadeau pour son anniversaire.   13. Prêtez-moi dix dollars, s'il vous plaît.   14. Avec plaisir, les voici.   15. Expliquez-leur pourquoi vous ne leur avez pas écrit.   16. Ne me télégraphiez pas, téléphonez-moi.   17. Si vous n'aimez pas cette robe, refusez-la.   18. Non, ne la refusez pas ; acceptez-la et donnez-la à votre sœur.   19. Blâmez-nous, ne les blâmez pas.   20. Louons-les.

Exercices

A. *Mettez à la forme affirmative :*

1. Ne nous parlez pas.   2. Ne me regardez pas.   3. Ne les écoutons pas.   4. Ne nous obéissez pas.   5. Ne les con-

sultez pas.   6. Ne la félicitez pas.   7. Ne me répondez
pas.   8. Ne le blâmez pas.   9. Ne leur refusez pas.
10. Ne lui parlez pas.

B. *Mettez à la forme négative :*

1. Grondez-la.   2. Désobéissez-moi.   3. Parlez-leur.
4. Faites-le.   5. Donnez-lui.   6. Montrez-les.   7. Con-
sultez-nous.   8. Vendez-lui.   9. Perdez-le.   10. Ré-
pondez-leur.   11. Prêtez-moi.

C. *Traduisez en français :*

1. Here is a basket of fruit, carry it.   2. Give it to your
mother.   3. Don't give it to the children.   4. There are
the best pupils in the class, look at them and congratulate
them.   5. Tell them that we shall give them a good reward.
6. Here is a little souvenir (*m.*) from Paris, accept it please.
7. I accept it with pleasure, thousand thanks.   8. Don't
give him your ball, leave it here.   9. Scold her if she is not
good.   10. Don't blame them, blame me.   11. Give us
back our exercises, we will finish them.   12. Finish them
quickly, but finish them well.   13. Here is the doctor's
prescription, do not lose it.   14. Answer me politely.
15. If you cannot go to Mrs. Dulac's evening party, telephone her.

Exercice-revue

1. Let us both go to the park.   2. Go if you want, but I
can't.   3. Why can't you?   4. Here is your little son ;
does he disobey you sometimes?   5. Sometimes ! He dis-
obeys me all the time !   6. As soon as I finish my lesson, I
shall go home.   7. Will your sister give a party Sunday
evening?   8. Did I put too much cream in your tea?
9. Not at all ! I love cream !   10. How many dozen
boxes of pens can she buy?   11. When were (are) you
born?   12. I was born on May the 1st (the 1st May),
1915.   13. You have become very tall, you are taller than

your sister. 14. She went away a week ago with a friend
(*f.*) of hers. 15. She has too many friends and not money
enough.

Conversation

EN VISITE (*suite*)

M. Dumoulin. Et toi, Edmond, pourquoi retournes-tu si
vite?

M. Legrand. Je représente l'université de Pennsylvanie à
la Convention Internationale des Professeurs à Genève. Je
suis en voyage d'affaires.

M. Dumoulin. Je comprends ; c'est dommage.

M. Legrand (se levant). Et maintenant, en route ! Nous
avons beaucoup de choses à faire. Je cherche une bonne
pension bourgeoise pour Mr. Smith.

M. Dumoulin. Monsieur Smith, vous serez toujours le
bienvenu dans cette maison, et je suis entièrement à votre
disposition si je puis vous être utile.

Mr. Smith. Merci mille fois, monsieur, vous êtes trop
aimable. Au revoir, monsieur.

M. Legrand. Au revoir, Gaston.

M. Dumoulin. Au revoir, messieurs, au plaisir ! Bon
voyage, Edmond !

(*Fin*)

*   *   *   *   *   *   *

33ᵉ Leçon : Noms de matière.   Place des adjectifs

Qui ne dit mot, consent. — *Silence gives consent.*

Observe the following constructions :

une robe de soie, *a silk dress.*
une montre d'or, *a gold watch.*

Instead of adjectives denoting material, the French use
adjective phrases made up of the preposition **de** + a noun.

Therefore, the noun of the material always follows the name of the object.

Notice the position of the adjectives in the following sentences :

> un chapeau noir, *a black hat.*
> un costume espagnol, *a Spanish costume.*
> une table ronde, *a round table.*

As already mentioned (Lessons 6 and 16), adjectives usually follow their nouns in French, especially those denoting color, shape, size, nationality, religion.

Dire (irregular), *to say, to tell;* participe passé, **dit,** *said.*

PRÉSENT	IMPARFAIT	FUTUR
je dis, *I say, I am say-*	je disais, *I was saying, I said,*	je dirai, *I shall*
tu dis. *ing, I do say.*	tu disais. *I used to say.*	tu diras. *say.*
il dit.	il disait.	il dira.
nous disons.	nous disions.	nous dirons.
vous *dites.*	vous disiez.	vous direz.
ils disent.	ils disaient.	ils diront.

IMPÉRATIF

SINGULIER	PLURIEL	
dis, *say.*	disons, *let us say.*	dites, *say.*

Vocabulaire

anglais, *English.*
allemand, *German.*
italien, *Italian.*
espagnol, *Spanish.*
rond, *round.*
carré, *square.*
le magasin, *the store.*
oublier, *to forget.*
le gant, *the glove.*
offrir, *to offer.*
le chapeau, *the hat.*
la cravate, *the tie.*
l'or, *the gold.*
l'argent, *the silver.*
l'acier, *the steel.*
le marbre, *the marble.*
la soie, *the silk.*
là-bas, *over there.*
la dentelle, *the lace.*
le velours, *velvet.*
la paille, *the straw.*
le cuir, *the leather.*
la peau, *the skin, kid.*
le rayon, *the shelf, counter.*
la cuiller, *the spoon.*
la fourchette, *the fork.*
la langue, *the language.*
faire des emplettes, *to shop.*

un magasin de nouveautés, *a department store.*
y aller, *to go there;* allons-y, *let us go there;* allez-y, *go there.*

Lecture

DANS UN MAGASIN DE NOUVEAUTÉS

A. Où puis-je acheter des cravates de soie et des gants de peau?

B. Là-bas, dans cette grande maison blanche.

A. Allons-y ensemble, si vous voulez.

B. Mais certainement, je désire aussi faire des emplettes.

VOUS TROUVEREZ ICI TOUS LES LIVRES QUE VOUS VOULEZ.

A. Nous voici dans le plus grand magasin de nouveautés de la ville.

B. Voici le rayon des livres. Vous trouvez ici tous les livres que vous voulez, des livres français, anglais, italiens, espagnols et allemands.

A. Je désire un chapeau de paille. Je veux aussi acheter un sac de cuir brun et un joli mouchoir de dentelle pour ma mère.

B. Il y a de très jolis sacs de cuir dans ce magasin.

A. La semaine dernière, pour son anniversaire, ma sœur a reçu une petite montre d'or, une robe de crêpe de Chine rose et un joli chapeau de velours noir.

B. Regardez cette petite table de marbre carrée.

A. Aimez-vous mieux les tables carrées que les tables rondes?

B. Non, mais cette table carrée est très originale.

A. Ne m'avez-vous pas dit que vous vouliez acheter une cuiller et une fourchette d'argent pour votre charmant bébé?

B. Si, j'allais l'oublier !

A. Permettez-moi de vous offrir ce petit cadeau comme souvenir.

B. Vous êtes mille fois trop aimable ; j'accepte avec le plus grand plaisir.

Exercices

A. *Remplacez les mots anglais par les mots français en observant l'accord et la position :*

1. Elle a perdu son (lace) mouchoir. 2. Montrez-moi votre (pretty, silver) montre. 3. Ce (Spanish) costume est très original. 4. Les (gold) plumes sont-elles meilleures que les (steel) plumes ? 5. Voilà une (beautiful, green) robe. 6. Où sont vos (kid) gants ? 7. Ils sont sur mon (old, straw) chapeau. 8. Je ne peux pas trouver ma (black, silk) cravate ; elle était ce matin sur cette (small, round) table. 9. Avez-vous pris vos (French) livres ? 10. La (German) langue est-elle plus difficile que la (English) langue ?

B. *Traduisez en français :*

1. When we want kid gloves, silk ties, and a straw hat, we go in a department store. 2. Here is beautiful white lace. 3. Yes, it is very beautiful, I like it. 4. You told me that you wanted a leather bag for your niece. 5. Have you any leather bags, not too large ? 6. Certainly, madam ; what color do you want the bag ? 7. Show me blue, brown, and green bags. 8. Here is a beautiful French bag that we received from Paris last week. 9. Did you put your brown velvet dress in that large gray box ? 10. My friend wants some Spanish and German books ; where can he buy them ? 11. Have you good steel pens ? 12. How do you like this little square marble table ? 13. Gracious ! (*Mon Dieu!*) I lost my large yellow bag ! 14. What had you in that yellow bag ? 15. There were a gold ring, a lace handkerchief, two silver spoons, and all my money, $75.

Exercice-revue

1. Do not wait for me all the time.   2. I do wait for you every Sunday.   3. I lost all of my gloves.   4. We shall go to the store together.   5. My mother went to the store an hour ago.   6. As soon as she has returned, we shall leave.   7. Let us wait for her.   8. Certainly, we shall wait for her, I want to speak to her.   9. Yesterday we went out at 10 o'clock and we came back at 6 (o'clock) ; we spent the whole day in the park.   10. When was your little niece born?   11. She was born the 21st of July, 1927. 12. She is younger than mine.   13. Will you have a glass of cold water or a cup of tea?   14. How many watches and rings have you?   15. Show them.   16. Do not show them here.   17. There is Charles ; I do not like him, he teases me all the time.   18. Does he tease you?   19. Do not speak to him.   20. Does he not speak to you?

*   *   *   *   *   *   *

34e Leçon : Participe passé avec AVOIR

La nuit porte conseil. — *The night brings counsel.*

Study the following sentences :

(1) **Nous avons** $\boxed{\text{écrit}}$ ───────→les lettres.

(2) **Les lettres**←───── que nous avons $\boxed{\text{écrites}}$.

When conjugated with **avoir** the past participle remains unchanged when the object follows the verb (Example 1) or when there is no object, as in **Nous avons écrit.**

But when the object precedes the verb, the past participle agrees in *gender and number* with that object (Example 2).

Study the following sentence :

Il a $\boxed{\text{vu}}$ ─────→les lettres←───── que j'ai $\boxed{\text{écrites}}$.

In the above example, **lettres** is the object of two different verbs : *to see* and *to write.* The past participle **vu** remains unchanged because the object **lettres** follows the verb ; but the past participle **écrites** takes the feminine plural because its object **que,** standing for **lettres,** is feminine plural and *precedes the verb.*

Attention! Before writing a past participle of a verb conjugated with **avoir,** *always locate the direct object.*

Vocabulaire

le fleuriste, *the florist.*	**la photographie,** *the photograph.*
la pivoine, *the peony.*	**l'absence** (f.), *the absence.*
la jonquille, *the jonquil.*	**le vestibule,** *the vestibule, foyer.*
le franc, *the franc.*	**payer,** *to pay, to pay for.*
pendant, *during.*	**corriger,** *to correct.*

un petit mot, *a short note.*

Lecture

1. Où avez-vous mis les fleurs que le fleuriste a apportées? 2. Je les ai mises dans le grand vase bleu. 3. Aimez-vous les fleurs que j'ai commandées? 4. Mais oui, les fleurs que vous avez choisies sont très jolies. 5. Combien avez-vous payé les pivoines et les jonquilles? 6. Je les ai payées dix francs. 7. Les roses et les tulipes que vous avez demandées à votre oncle qui demeure à la campagne, sont-elles arrivées? 8. Non, pas encore, il les aura probablement oubliées. 9. J'ai reçu sa photographie, l'avez-vous vue? 10. Non, je ne l'ai pas vue, où est-elle? 11. La voilà ; je l'ai reçue ce matin et je l'ai mise sur le piano. 12. Julie, madame Dupont est-elle venue pendant mon absence? 13. Oui, madame, elle est venue, mais elle est partie tout de suite. 14. N'a-t-elle pas laissé un petit mot? 15. Si, madame, voilà la lettre qu'elle a écrite. 16. Avez-vous ouvert les fenêtres du salon? 17. Non, je ne les ai pas encore ouvertes. 18. Ouvrez-les maintenant et dans une heure, vous les fermerez.

Exercices

A. *Remplacez les tirets par les lettres qui manquent :*

1. Avez-vous achet— des cravates?   2. Oui, regardez les jolies cravates que j'ai achet—.   3. Avez-vous vu— les fleurs que ma sœur a reç— ce matin?   4. Qui les a envoy—? 5. Montrez-moi la bague d'or que vous avez trouv—. 6. Ne l'avez-vous pas encore montr— à votre mère?

B. *Mettez au pluriel :*

1. J'ai perdu le livre qu'il m'a donné.   2. Il a trouvé le crayon que j'ai perdu.   3. Où est le jeune garçon que j'ai vu?   4. Voici la cuiller d'argent qu'il a reçue.   5. Il est allé à l'école.   6. Je suis parti.   7. As-tu corrigé l'exercice que j'ai fini?   8. Non, je ne l'ai pas encore corrigé.

C. *Répondez négativement aux questions suivantes en remplaçant chaque nom par un pronom personnel :*

1. Avez-vous reçu ma lettre?   2. Avez-vous écrit les lettres?   3. Avez-vous mis les fleurs sur la table?   4. Avez-vous acheté vos robes de dentelle?   5. A-t-il pris vos roses? 6. Avons-nous vendu notre maison?   7. Ont-ils mangé les fraises?   8. Ont-elles oublié les violettes?

D. *Traduisez en français :*

1. Did you receive the letters I sent you from Paris? 2. Yes, I received them, thank you.   3. Did you receive mine?   4. No, I did not receive them.   5. Show me the dresses and hats you bought in Paris.   6. Here they are ; how do you like them?   7. Here is the dress I have chosen for my sister.   8. Did she like it?   9. She has not seen it yet.   10. Where did I put the flowers I brought? 11. Did you not leave them in the vestibule?   12. Yes, they are there, are they not pretty !

Exercice-revue

1. When you finish your lesson, show it to your father. 2. He will not look at it.   3. Here is the page of the book I

was looking for.   4. Where is the bottle of ink which was on this little marble table?   5. Here are paper, pens, and ink; work if you wish.   6. Have you any blue pencils? 7. Jane, give her a good blue pencil.   8. Jane is (gone) out, sir.   9. When did she leave?   10. She left an hour ago and has not come back yet.   11. You have already too many pencils.   12. All of my pencils are poor.   13. Were you speaking to the doctor when I saw you?   14. No, I was saying to the professor that my son was working well. 15. Did you tell him that we shall not go to his evening party to-morrow night?   16. I shall tell him to-morrow morning that we cannot go.

Une anecdote

Le mot "impossible" n'est pas français

Louis.   Je trouve mes leçons de français très difficiles.

Jean.   Mais non, elles ne sont pas difficiles, pas du tout !

Louis.   Je vous assure qu'elles sont très, très difficiles ; les pronoms par exemple sont impossibles !

Jean.   Le mot "impossible" n'est pas français a dit Napoléon.

Louis.   Par exemple ! (*the idea!*)   Mais le mot est dans le dictionnaire !

Jean.   Mais oui, bien entendu (*surely*), mais il y a une anecdote sur Napoléon et le mot "impossible."

Louis.   Racontez-moi l'anecdote, s'il vous plaît.

Impossible ! Ce mot n'est pas français.

LE TOMBEAU DE NAPOLÉON À L'HÔTEL DES INVALIDES À PARIS.

Le Palais du Louvre à Paris.

Jean. Avec plaisir. Voici l'anecdote ; écoutez.

Un jour, Napoléon donne à un jeune lieutenant un ordre difficile à exécuter.

L'officier hésite et murmure : " Sire, l'exécution de cet ordre est impossible !

— Impossible ! crie Napoléon furieux. Impossible ! ce mot n'est pas français ! "

*   *   *   *   *   *   *

35ᵉ Leçon: Pluriels irréguliers des noms et des adjectifs

Après la pluie, le beau temps. — *After a storm comes a calm.*[1]

We learned in Lesson 8 that the great majority of nouns and adjectives form their plural, as in English, by adding an **s** (silent) to the singular :

le joli collier,   **les jolis colliers.**

However, there are certain groups of nouns and adjectives which form their plural irregularly.

1. Observe the following nouns and adjectives :

SINGULAR	PLURAL
le fils, *the son.*	**les fils,** *the sons.*
la voix, *the voice.*	**les voix,** *the voices.*
le nez, *the nose.*	**les nez,** *the noses.*
gris, *gray.*	**gris,** *gray.*
heureux, *happy.*	**heureux,** *happy.*

Nouns ending in **s, x, z,** and adjectives ending in **s** and **x** in the singular remain unchanged in the plural.

2. Observe the following nouns and adjectives :

SINGULAR	PLURAL
le rideau, *the curtain.*	**les rideaux,** *the curtains.*
un cheveu, *a hair.*	**les cheveux,** *the hair.*
beau, *beautiful.*	**beaux,** *beautiful.*

---

[1] Literally, *After the rain, fair weather.*

Nouns ending in **au, eau,** and **eu,** and adjectives ending in **eau** form their plural by adding **x** instead of **s.** Exception : the adjective **bleu** takes **s : bleus.**

3. Observe the following nouns and adjectives :

Singular	Plural
le cheval, *the horse.*	les chevaux, *the horses.*
égal, *equal.*	égaux, *equal.*

Nouns and adjectives in **al** change **al** into **aux.**

4. There are also several irregular plurals of nouns which follow no fixed rules. Here are the most common of those nouns :

(*a*)

Singular	Plural
le travail, *the work.*	les travaux.
le corail, *the coral.*	les coraux.
le vitrail, *stained glass (window).*	les vitraux.

(*b*)

Singular	Plural
le ciel, *the sky, heaven.*	les cieux (see-yeu).
l'œil (m.) (le-y[es]), *the eye.*	les yeux (lè zee-yeu).

(*c*) Seven nouns in **ou** take **x** instead of **s.** The most common are :

le bijou, *the jewel.*	le joujou, *the toy.*
le chou, *the cabbage.*	le caillou, *the pebble.*

Their plurals are :

les bijoux, les choux, les joujoux, les cailloux.

(For complete list, see page 368.)

Savoir (irregular), *to know (a fact), to know how;* participe passé, **su,** *known*

Présent	Imparfait	Futur
je sais, *I know.*	je savais, *I knew.*	je saurai, *I shall know.*
tu sais.	tu savais.	tu sauras.
il sait.	il savait.	il saura.
nous savons.	nous savions.	nous saurons.
vous savez.	vous saviez.	vous saurez.
ils savent.	ils savaient.	ils sauront.

IMPÉRATIF

SINGULIER	PLURIEL	
sache, *know.*	sachons, *let us know.*	sachez, *know.*

Vocabulaire

l'animal (m.), *the animal.*
le cheval, *the horse.*
le chameau, *the camel.*
le lionceau, *the cub.*
l'éléphant, *the elephant.*
la trompe, *the trunk.*
le singe, *the monkey.*
l'oiseau (m.), *the bird.*
le sable, *the sand.*
le général, *the general.*
le vaisseau, *the ship.*
le pays, *the country.*
le métal, *the metal.*
loin de là, *far from it.*

la noix, *the nut.*
loyal, *loyal.*
frugal, *frugal.*
oriental, *oriental.*
égal, *equal.*
la nourriture, *the food.*
gros, *stout, big.*
doux, *sweet, gentle.*
brillant, *bright, shiny.*
nommer, *to name.*
gratter, *to scratch.*
l'ange (m.), *the angel.*
le désert, *the desert.*
tard, *late.*

Lecture

AU JARDIN DES PLANTES

Paul.   Est-ce que le Jardin des Plantes est le plus important de tous les jardins zoologiques?

Jean.   Non, loin de là, mais il est très joli, bien arrangé, et très intéressant.   Voici un des plus gros éléphants du monde. Regardez, il a mis sa trompe dans la poche de ce vieux général!

Paul.   Savez-vous que les éléphants sont des animaux très doux et très loyaux?

Jean.   Oui, dans les pays orientaux, ils font tous les travaux de transportation.

Paul.   Regardez les vaisseaux du désert.

Jean.   Que voulez-vous dire?

Paul.   Mais les chameaux!   Ne savez-vous pas que les chameaux sont des animaux très frugaux, qu'ils peuvent

VOICI LA CAGE DES SINGES.

rester des journées sans eau et aussi sans nourriture, qu'ils marchent vite et facilement dans le sable?

Jean. Oui, j'avais oublié la métaphore. Ah ! Voici la cage des singes. Regardez-les. Comme ils cassent facilement les noix que les enfants leur donnent. Regardez ce petit singe qui gratte le nez de sa mère !

Paul. Voici un lion magnifique et trois lionceaux. Ils jouent comme des chats ; leurs yeux sont brillants.

Jean. Allons voir les oiseaux, ils sont si jolis !

Paul. Il est déjà tard, nous n'aurons pas le temps aujourd'hui, nous continuerons notre visite la semaine prochaine.

Jean. A vos ordres, mon ami. Nous avons un omnibus de l'autre côté du Pont d'Austerlitz ; nous serons à la maison dans une demi-heure.

Exercices

A. *Conversation sur la lecture :*

1. Nommez les animaux mentionnés dans le texte. 2. Les éléphants sont-ils de petits animaux? 3. Les éléphants sont-ils méchants? 4. Que font les éléphants dans les pays orientaux? 5. Comment Paul nomme-t-il les chameaux? 6. Que font les singes dans leur cage? 7. Comment nommez-vous les jeunes lions? 8. Comment sont leurs yeux? 9. Pourquoi nos deux amis ne vont-ils pas voir les oiseaux? 10. Quand seront-ils à la maison?

B. *Mettez au pluriel :*

1. Le vitrail de cette église est très beau.   2. Je n'ai pas vu le cheval du général.   3. J'aime ce bijou et le corail. 4. Je finis mon travail.   5. Il a laissé son chapeau gris dans le vestibule.   6. Son fils est très heureux.   7. La voix de cet oiseau est très pure.   8. Le soldat est loyal au général et à son pays.   9. Le pays oriental est très beau.   10. Son fils est plus grand que son neveu.

C. *Traduisez en français :*

1. Gold and silver are metals.   2. This young lady (*dame*) has beautiful jewels.   3. Do you like horses? 4. I like all animals.   5. There are many beautiful birds in tropical (*tropical*) countries.   6. These two generals always have gray horses.   7. Let us finish our works.   8. The little children think that there are angels in the heavens. 9. Everybody likes loyal friends.   10. What color are your eyes ; are they blue?   11. My friend lost all of her hair (*plur.*).   12. Did you read the newspapers this morning?   13. Yesterday, I bought beautiful lace curtains (rideau, *m.*).   14. Do you know that the American boats are very big?   15. Yes, I know it.

Exercice-revue

1. Tell her the story.   2. I didn't tell them the story. 3. Why did you not tell them the story?   4. Because I have forgotten it.   5. Where are the steel pens you brought home.   6. I lost them.   7. Did you lose them or did you give them to the professor's nephew?   8. I go ; I am going ; I was going.   9. I used to go ; I was willing ; I can't. 10. I was not able to do it.   11. I shall not be able to do it. 12. I shall not do it.   13. She went ; she has gone ; she used to go.   14. We shall go ; you will be able to do it. 15. Say it ; tell him ; don't tell him.   16. 4, 75 ; 19, 50 ; 79, 95.   17. The 31st of December is the 365th day of the year.

Expressions de conversation

Bonne chance !	Good luck !
Bon amusement !	Have a good time !
Bon gré, mal gré.	Willing or not willing.
A quoi bon !	What is the use !
A vrai dire.	To tell the truth.
A tour de rôle.	By turn.

Une charade

Mon premier est un métal précieux,
Mon dernier est un habitant des cieux.
Mon tout est un fruit délicieux.

* * * * * * *

36ᵉ Leçon : Les pronoms personnels disjoints (disjunctive)

Au royaume des aveugles les borgnes sont rois. — *In the realm of the blind the one-eyed are kings.*

		SINGULIER	PLURIEL
1st	person	**moi,** *I, me.*	**nous,** *we, us.*
2d	person	**toi,** *thou, thee.*	**vous,** *you.*
3d	person (m.)	**lui,** *he, him.*	**eux,** *they, them.*
3d	person (f.)	**elle,** *she, her.*	**elles,** *they, them.*

The personal pronouns mentioned in Lessons 30, 31, and 32 are called *conjunctive* because they are closely joined to a verb as subject or object. The above pronouns are called *disjunctive* because they are not closely connected with the verb either as subject or as object.

Study the following sentences :

(1) **Irez-vous avec moi ?**	*Will you go with me?*
J'irai sans vous.	*I will go without you.*
Elle n'est pas chez elle.	*She is not at home.*

(2) Qui le dit? **Moi.**	*Who says it? I (do).*
(3) **Moi, je le ferai.**	*I will do it.*
(4) **Qui est là? C'est lui.**	*Who is there? It is he.*
(5) **Il est plus grand que moi.**	*He is taller than I.*

The disjunctive pronouns are used : (1) mainly after a preposition, (2) when the verb is not expressed or is understood, (3) for emphasis or in apposition with the subject, (4) after **ce** + **être** as logical subject (*i.e.* when **être** is immediately followed by a pronoun), (5) after **que** in comparisons.

Pronoms emphatiques. — The disjunctive pronouns, although rather emphatic when used alone, are made more intensive by the addition of the adjective **même,** *self*.

moi-même.	nous-mêmes.
toi-même.	vous-même(s) *s. and pl.*
lui-même.	eux-mêmes.
elle-même.	elles-mêmes.

Emploi de *n'est-ce pas.* — When *yes* is expected as an answer to a question, or when the speaker believes that the person to whom he speaks will agree with him, the question may be asked by adding **n'est-ce pas?** to the statement.

Vous partirez avec moi, n'est-ce pas? *You will leave with me. will you not?*

Vous ne partirez pas sans moi, n'est-ce pas? *You will not leave without me, will you?*

N'est-ce pas? means *is it not?* But according to the tense used in English, it may mean : *do you not, does he not, will they not, are you not, have we not, would you not, shall he not,* etc.

Vocabulaire

avant, *before* (time).
devant, *before* (place).
après, *after* (time).
derrière, *behind.*
entre, *between.*
sans, *without.*

pour, *for.*
à cause de, *on account of.*
fixer, *to fix.*
le tour, *the turn.*
le dentiste, *the dentist.*
marcher, *to walk.*

avec, *with.*

le mari, *the husband.*

malgré, *in spite of, against the will of.*

chez, *at, to the house of.*

quant à, *as for.*

ni moi non plus, *nor I, neither do I.*

allons! en route! *let's be on our way.*

à tantôt, *see you soon.*

passer, *to pass.*

courageux, *courageous.*

ce n'est pas gentil, *that is not nice.*

étudier, *to study.*

la gravure, *the picture.*

Chez means *at, to,* and *in the house of, office of,* or *place of business of,* and is followed by a disjunctive pronoun, a proper noun, a profession, a trade or cognate :

chez moi, chez Smith, chez le dentiste, chez la modiste, chez ma tante.

Attention! **De** is never used after **chez** and **malgré,** but is used after **près.**

Lecture

A. Ah vous voilà ! J'allais partir sans vous.

B. Entre nous, ce n'était pas gentil de partir avant moi.

A. Mais, mon ami, je ne voulais pas être en retard à cause de vous ! Vous savez qu'avec ce dentiste, quand vous n'êtes pas chez lui à l'heure fixée, vous perdez votre tour.

B. Allons, en route !

A. Regardez la dame qui est devant nous.

B. Madame Duval, n'est-ce pas?

A. Oui, c'est elle ; elle est avec son mari ; nous allons passer la soirée chez eux ce soir. Marchons derrière eux.

B. Je n'aime pas aller chez le dentiste, et vous?

A. Ni moi non plus! Je vais chez lui malgré moi. Il demeure près de chez nous, mais il y a un an que je n'ai pas été chez lui.

B. Quant à moi, je pense qu'il y a deux ans !

A. Nous voici arrivés, voulez-vous passer avant ou après moi?

B. Non, passez le premier ; vous êtes plus courageux que moi.

A. Voici un magazine pour vous ; regardez les gravures, le temps passera plus vite. A tantôt.

Exercices

A. *Remplacez les tirets par un pronom disjoint :*

1. Voici monsieur Lorand, nous sommes invités chez —— demain. 2. Voulez-vous aller avec ——? 3. Nos parents travaillent pour ——. 4. Les enfants ne savent pas que leurs parents travaillent pour ——. 5. ——, je parlerai, ——, vous écouterez. 6. Louise est plus grande que ——. 7. —— parle, ——, nous écoutons.

B. *Traduisez en français :*

1. For them (*m.*) ; for them (*f.*) ; for themselves (*m.*) ; for themselves (*f.*). 2. Of me ; of him ; of her. 3. Of you ; of them (*m.*) ; of us. 4. At my house ; at our house. 5. At his house ; at her house. 6. At your house ; at their (*m.*) house. 7. At the professor's ; at the lawyer's. 8. She came to our house without them (*m.*) and in spite of them (*m.*). 9. We went away after him and came back before him. 10. After you, my friend. 11. Who is the best pupil in your class, you or he? 12. I shall do that work for you, if you want. 13. No, thank you, I will do it myself. 14. I am studying French with her. 15. The man who is near you is very old. 16. I fell on account of him. 17. My brothers are ill, we will go to the country without them. 18. You said that I lost your pencil, but I know that you lost it yourself. 19. Nor we either (she, you).

Exercice-revue

1. Name the seasons. 2. Name the days of the week. 3. Name the months of the year. 4. How do you form the three comparative forms in French? 5. Give the difference between better (*adj.*) and better (*adv.*). 6. When is **si** used instead of **aussi** in a comparative form? 7. How do you translate *in* after a superlative? 8. When is **moindre** used in preference to **plus petit?** 9. When is **si** used instead of **oui?** 10. What is the position of adverbs

in French? 11. Name the partitive articles. 12. Is there any change in their form when the verb is negative? 13. Are these articles used when the noun is taken in a general sense? 14. How do you know when *I danced* should be translated by the perfect or the imperfect? 15. How do you translate **tout?** Give an example for each translation. 16. How is the future formed? 17. What is always found in the future? 18. How is the future perfect formed and when is it used?

* * * * * * *

37ᵉ Leçon: Verbes en –OIR

Quand on parle du loup, on en voit la queue. — *Speak of angels and you will hear the flutter of their wings.*[1]

French verbs were formerly divided into four conjugations according to their endings : **-er, -ir, -oir, -re.** But some twenty years ago, modern grammarians began to discard, from the regular conjugations, the verbs ending in **-oir,** as there are less than 20 verbs in that conjugation and only 7 of these are conjugated alike ; namely, those ending in **-evoir.** Therefore, the former third conjugation has disappeared from modern grammars.

The seven verbs ending in **-evoir** are : **recevoir,** *to receive;* **devoir,** *to owe, to be obliged, must;* **apercevoir,** *to see, to perceive;* **décevoir,** *to deceive;* **percevoir,** *to perceive, to collect;* **concevoir,** *to conceive;* and **redevoir,** *to owe again.* They are here mentioned in their order of importance.

The past participle ends in **-u.**

reçu, dû, aperçu, déçu, perçu, conçu, redû.

[1] Literally, *When one speaks of a wolf, one sees his tail.*

Recevoir, *to receive;* participe passé, **reçu**

PRÉSENT	IMPARFAIT	FUTUR
je reçois, *I receive,*	je recevais, *I was receiving,*	je recevrai, *I shall* or
tu reçois. *I am re-*	tu recevais. *I used to*	tu recevras. *will*
il reçoit. *ceiving.*	il recevait. *receive.*	il recevra. *receive.*
nous recevons.	nous recevions.	nous recevrons.
vous recevez.	vous receviez.	vous recevrez.
ils reçoivent.	ils recevaient.	ils recevront.

IMPÉRATIF

SINGULIER	PLURIEL	
reçois, *receive.*	recevons, *let us receive,*	recevez, *receive.*

Devoir, *to owe;* participe passé, **dû**

PRÉSENT	IMPARFAIT	FUTUR
je dois, *I must, I owe,*	je devais, *I was obliged,*	je devrai, *I shall owe,*
tu dois. *I am obliged.*	tu devais. *I owed.*	tu devras. *I shall be*
il doit.	il devait.	il devra. *obliged.*
nous devons.	nous devions.	nous devrons.
vous devez.	vous deviez.	vous devrez.
ils doivent.	ils devaient.	ils devront.

IMPÉRATIF

SINGULIER	PLURIEL	
dois, *owe.*	devons, *let us owe.*	devez, *owe.*

Note. — Notice the ç before o and u to keep the sound s all through the conjugation of **recevoir**. Notice also the û in the past participle **dû** of **devoir** to distinguish it from **du**, *of the.*

Emploi du pronom indéfini *on.* — Observe the following :

On **vend des pommes dans ce magasin.** *They sell apples in this store.*
Ici *on* **parle français.** *French is spoken here.*

The indefinite pronoun **on,** *one, we, you, they, somebody, people,* etc., even when plural in meaning, is used *only* as subject of a verb in the *third person singular.*

The disjunctive form of **on** is **soi.**

The form **l'on** may be used instead of **on** whenever it sounds better. It is often used after **et, ou, où, que, lorsque, pourquoi, si,** etc., but not when the following word begins with **l.**

Vocabulaire

la pomme, *the apple.*

la poire, *the pear.*

la pêche, *the peach.*

la prune, *the plum.*

l'abricot (m.), *the apricot.*

la cerise, *the cherry.*

l'orange, *the orange.*

le journal, *the newspaper.*

de temps en temps, *from time to time.*

le marché, *the market.*

au marché, *at* or *in the market.*

surtout, *especially.*

drôle, *funny, odd, queer.*

un peu plus longtemps, *a little longer.*

sur votre chemin, *on your way.*

plusieurs, *several.*

Lecture

1. Oh! les beaux fruits! Regardez ces pommes, ces poires, ces pêches et ces cerises! 2. Recevez-vous souvent des fruits? 3. Oui, tous les ans nous recevons des fruits plusieurs fois. 4. Dans un mois, nous recevrons des prunes et des abricots. 5. Quand ma tante demeurait à la campagne, je recevais aussi des fruits de temps en temps. 6. Maintenant, je dois acheter tous les fruits que je veux manger. 7. Trouve-t-on beaucoup de fruits au marché? 8. Oui, on trouve surtout des pêches et des abricots. 9. Peut-on déjà acheter des oranges? 10. Jeanne! On a apporté les fleurs que j'ai commandées ce matin, n'est-ce pas? 11. Non, madame, on ne les a pas encore apportées. 12. C'est drôle, on devait les apporter tout de suite. 13. Je pense que je devrai téléphoner au fleuriste. 14. Oui, téléphonez-lui, il les a certainement oubliées.

Exercices

A. *Conversation sur la lecture :*

1. Nommez les fruits que vous aimez. 2. Où trouve-t-on tous les fruits que l'on désire? 3. Que doit-on faire quand on ne reçoit pas de fruits de ses parents ou de ses amis? 4. Vous aimez les fruits, n'est-ce pas? 5. Que devait-on apporter tout de suite? 6. Pourquoi ne les a-t-on pas apportées?

B. *Traduisez en français :*

1. He owes ten francs to his brother.   2. You owe twenty francs to your cousin, I think.   3. We shall receive a letter from my father to-morrow.   4. When we were in Paris last year, we used to receive an American newspaper every week.   5. One is happy when one receives a good book.   6. When must you go home?   7. I must go now. 8. Can't you stay a little longer?   9. The florist is on your way, will you enter his store?   10. Why, yes ; with pleasure, and I will tell him that you have not yet received the flowers you have ordered.   11. Good-by, until to-morrow. . 12. Jane, do they sell fruit in the store near our house? 13. Yes, madam, they sell fruit and vegetables in that store. 14. I think that store is French ; I have seen on the window the words : "French spoken here."

C. *Traduisez rapidement :*

1. I receive ; I am not receiving.   2. We receive ; let us not receive.   3. One receives ; one does not receive. 4. She receives ; she owes ; she must ; she has to.   5. We are not receiving ; we must not.   6. They used to receive ; they had to.   7. I will be obliged ; I will not receive. 8. She was not receiving ; was she not obliged?   9. Will he have to ; will he receive?   10. One must not receive.

Exercice-revue

1. Name all the past participles conjugated with **être.** 2. What is the agreement of those past participles? 3. Draw a parallel between the agreement of the past participles conjugated with **avoir** and those conjugated with **être.** 4. What always follows a noun or an adverb of quantity? Give five examples of each.   5. What is the definition of a pronoun and what is the agreement?   6. What is a personal pronoun?   7. For what does a personal pronoun stand? 8. Name the personal pronoun subjects.   9. Name the

personal pronouns used as direct objects.   10. Name the
personal pronouns used as indirect objects.   11. Name
the disjunctive personal pronouns.   12. What is the difference between a conjunctive and a disjunctive pronoun?
13. Where are the conjunctive pronouns placed?   14. Is
there any exception?   15. How are adjectives of material
formed in French?

Une anecdote

DU TAC AU TAC (*TIT FOR TAT*)

Note. — **Réfléchir,** means *to reflect,* but also *to think.*
   Poli, means *polite,* but also *polished, smooth in surface.*

Napoléon III était marié avec une princesse espagnole, la
princesse Eugénie, très jolie, très intelligente, mais très

SAVEZ-VOUS **LA** DIFFÉRENCE QU'IL Y A ENTRE CE MIROIR ET VOUS?

souvent distraite (*absent-minded*).   Napoléon, qui adorait
sa femme, aimait la taquiner à ce sujet (*on that ground*).

 Un jour il entre dans le boudoir de l'impératrice, qu'il
trouve assise devant son miroir.

 — Savez-vous,[1] Eugénie, la différence qu'il y a entre ce
miroir et vous?

 — La différence entre mon miroir et moi?   Non, je ne sais
pas.

---

[1] In the French aristocracy it was not customary to use **tu** with
friends and relatives.

— Eh bien, c'est très simple ; votre miroir réfléchit et vous ne réfléchissez pas.

— Voilà certainement un compliment très aimable.   Mais vous, savez-vous la différence qu'il y a entre mon miroir et vous?

— Non, répond Napoléon surpris.

— Eh bien, c'est très simple, mon miroir est poli et vous ne l'êtes pas !

*   *   *   *   *   *   *

38e Leçon: Le pronom partitif EN

Qui ne risque rien n'a rien. — *Nothing venture, nothing have.*[1]

En, *some, any,* is used chiefly as a partitive pronoun.   It takes the place of a noun used in a partitive sense, that is, of a noun preceded by the partitive articles **du, de la, de l', des.**

Avez-vous du pain?   Oui, j'*en* ai.   *Yes I have* (SOME).
Avez-vous des légumes?   Non, je n'*en* ai pas.   *No, I haven't* (ANY).

Note. — The pronouns *some* or *any* are often omitted in English, but their French equivalent **en** is always expressed.

Let us not confuse *some* and *any* preceding a noun with *some* and *any* used as pronouns.

$$some \text{ and } any \text{ with a noun} = \begin{cases} \textbf{du} \\ \textbf{de la} \\ \textbf{des} \end{cases}$$

$$some \text{ and } any \text{ without a noun} = \quad \textbf{en}$$

When **en** means *some* or *any,* expressed or understood in English, it is strictly a partitive pronoun, because it refers to a part of the whole and never to the whole itself.

When referring to the whole, **le, la, les** should be used.

---

[1] Literally, *Who risks nothing has nothing.*

Study the following chart so as to see the difference between the use of the pronouns **le, la, les,** and the pronoun **en.**

Pronoms *le, la, les*	Pronom *en*
Mangez-vous *le* pain? Oui, je *le* mange.	Mangez-vous *du* pain? Oui, j'*en* mange.
Mangez-vous *la* viande? Oui, je *la* mange.	Mangez-vous *de la* viande? Oui, j'*en* mange.
Mangez-vous *les* légumes? Oui, je *les* mange.	Mangez-vous *des* légumes? Oui, j'*en* mange.

Notice that **en** never changes.

Place du pronom *en.* — As **en** is a conjunctive pronoun, it is placed *immediately* before the verb like any other conjunctive pronoun. However, when the verb is in the *imperative affirmative,* it is placed after the verb as are all conjunctive pronouns (Lesson 32).

Vous avez des cerises, donnez-*en* à votre frère. *You have cherries, give some to your brother.*

Vocabulaire

prendre, *to take.*
l'appartement (m.), *the apartment.*
le tiroir, *the drawer.*
ne . . . plus, *no more, no longer.*

admirer, *to admire.*
la course, *the errand.*
la confiture, *the jam, preserve.*
l'accueil (m.), *the welcome.*

infiniment, *exceedingly, very much.*

Lecture

LE FIVE O'CLOCK TEA

Mme Allard. Encore un peu de thé, chère amie?
Mme Miran. Non, merci, je n'en désire plus.
Mme Allard. Et toi, Suzanne, en veux-tu?
Mme Simon. Oui, Mariette, j'en prendrai encore, merci.

Mme Allard.   De la crème, madame Drolet?

Mme Drolet.   Non, merci, je n'en prends pas, je préfère du citron.

Mme Allard.   En voici, servez-vous (*help yourself*).   Et vous, madame Smith, un peu de confiture?

Mme Smith.   Merci bien, madame, j'en ai encore.

Mme Allard.   Avez-vous des amis américains à Paris?

Mme Smith.   J'en avais, mais je n'en ai plus ; ils sont déjà retournés à New-York.   J'admire vos fleurs, madame, elles sont superbes ; en recevez-vous tous les jours?

Mme Allard.   J'en reçois tous les deux jours ; j'en ai ainsi tout le temps dans mon salon et dans ma salle à manger.

AVEZ-VOUS DES AMIS AMÉRICAINS À PARIS?

Mme Smith.   Avez-vous des enfants, madame?

Mme Allard.   Non, je n'en ai pas, c'est pourquoi nous avons un si petit appartement.

Mme Smith.   Il est petit, mais il est adorable !

Mme Allard.   Comment, vous partez déjà !   Et toi aussi, Suzanne?

Mme Simon.   Oui, chère amie, nous avons encore quelques courses à faire avant le dîner.

Mme Smith.   Madame, je vous remercie infiniment de votre charmant accueil.   J'espère que vous me ferez le grand plaisir de dîner chez moi demain soir, avec madame Simon.

Mme Allard.   Mais certainement, madame, tout le plaisir sera pour nous.

Exercices

A. *Conjuguez à haute voix:*

1. J'en‿ai, tu en‿as, il en‿a, elle en‿a, nous‿en‿avons, vous‿en‿avez, ils‿en‿ont, elles‿en‿ont. 2. Je n'en‿ai pas, tu n'en‿as pas, etc. 3. En‿ai-je, en‿as-tu, en‿a-t-il? etc. 4. N'en‿ai-je pas, n'en‿as-tu pas, etc.

B. *Remplacez les mots en italique par* **en :**

1. Voulez-vous *de la limonade?* 2. Je veux *de l'eau.* 3. Je ne veux pas *de fromage.* 4. Elle donne *des bonbons* à la petite fille. 5. Pourquoi donne-t-elle *des bonbons?* 6. Donnez *des bonbons* à cet enfant. 7. Elle n'a pas *de bonbons.* 8. Elle ne peut pas donner *des bonbons* quand elle n'a pas *de bonbons.* 9. Avez-vous *de l'argent?* 10. Non, nous n'avons pas *d'argent.*

C. *Traduisez en français:*

1. Have you any books? 2. No, I haven't any. 3. Has she any? 4. Yes, she has some. 5. We have some too. 6. He has not any. 7. Why has he not any? 8. He is too poor to buy any. 9. That's too bad; why don't you give some to that poor boy? 10. Don't you want any? 11. I want some. 12. What are you doing? 13. I have no paper and I am looking for some. 14. You will find some in that drawer. 15. No, there isn't any. 16. That is strange, I thought there was some. 17. No, look yourself, the drawer is empty. 18. I have some in my room, I will bring some. 19. Here is some. 20. I found some. 21. Give some to John. 22. Don't give any to your sister.

Exercice-revue

1. Where are the white horses you bought last month? 2. How much did you pay [for] them? 3. It is not to me that you must ask (*faire*) that question. 4. Why not to you? 5. Because it is not I who paid [for] them. 6. Here

is my father, it is he who bought them.   7. Ask him how much he paid [for] them.   8. I paid more than 30,000 francs.   9. That is a great deal of money for two horses. 10. Yes, but they are very beautiful.   11. You must be very pleased, are you not?   12. Here is a very pretty gold ring that I received from my mother yesterday for my birthday.   13. You like jewels, don't you?   14. Yes, to speak frankly, I must say that I do (like them).   15. My mother knows it, and every year, I receive something from her.

*   *   *   *   *   *   *

39e Leçon : Le pronom partitif EN (*suite*)

Un point fait à temps en épargne cent. — *A stitch in time saves nine.*

We learned in the preceding lesson that the partitive pronoun **en** means *some* or *any* (expressed or understood in English) and stands for a noun preceded by a partitive article : **du, de la,** or **des.**

Besides this, **en** has several other uses.

Study the following sentences :

Combien *de* chapeaux avez-vous?
    How many hats have you?

(1) **J'*en* ai quatre.**
    I have four (of them).

Avez-vous acheté assez *de* crayons?
    Did you buy enough pencils?

(2) **J'*en* ai acheté [1] beaucoup.**
    I bought many.

Avez-vous reçu beaucoup *de* fruits?
    Have you received many fruits?

(3) **J'*en* ai reçu un panier.**
    I received a basket.

Avez-vous besoin *de* ce livre?
    Do you need this book?

(4) **Oui, j'*en* ai besoin.**
    Yes, I need it.

When
  (1) after a number (**un, deux** etc. . . . .)
  (2) after an adverb of quantity,
  (3) after a noun of quantity,
  (4) after a verb requiring **de,**
the noun limited is not mentioned, that noun must be represented by **en,** placed before the verb.

In those cases, **en** means *of it, of them.*

Attention! **En** always represents an expression with **de.**

---

[1] Notice that the past participle does not agree with **en.**

Voir (irregular), *to see;* participe passé, vu

PRÉSENT	IMPARFAIT	FUTUR
je vois, *I see, I do see,*	je voyais, *I saw, I used to see,*	je verrai, *I shall*
tu vois. *I am seeing.*	tu voyais. *I was seeing.*	tu verras. *see.*
il voit.	il voyait.	il verra.
nous voyons.	nous voyions.	nous verrons.
vous voyez.	vous voviez.	vous verrez.
ils voient.	ils voyaient.	ils verront.

IMPÉRATIF

SINGULIER	PLURIEL	
vois, *see.*	voyons, *let us see.*	voyez, *see.*

Vocabulaire

le besoin, *the need.*
avoir besoin de, *to need.*
la honte, *the shame.*
avoir honte de, *to be ashamed of.*
la peur, *the fear.*
avoir peur de, *to be afraid of.*

bien aise, *very glad.*
le porte-monnaie, *the purse.*
la banane, *the banana.*
la caisse, *the case.*
un ananas, *a pineapple.*
sûr, *sure.*

Lecture

1. Combien d'ananas y a-t-il dans ces deux caisses? 2. Il y en a cinquante dans cette caisse-ci, mais dans cette caisse-là il y a des bananes. 3. Avez-vous besoin de ces fruits? 4. Non, je n'en ai pas besoin, et vous? 5. Moi, j'en ai besoin. 6. En avez-vous besoin ce soir? 7. Jeanne a-t-elle mangé beaucoup de prunes? 8. Elle en a mangé dix. 9. N'en a-t-elle pas honte? 10. Non, elle dit qu'elles étaient très petites et que Louise en a mangé plus qu'elle. 11. Et vous, combien en avez-vous mangé? 12. J'en ai pris trois. 13. C'est bon, j'en suis bien aise. 14. Avez-vous beaucoup d'argent? 15. Mon porte-monnaie en est plein. 16. Jean n'est pas encore arrivé, je pense qu'il est malade. 17. J'en ai peur. Voilà son frère. 18. Jean est malade, n'est-ce pas? 19. C'est cela! J'en étais sûr!

Exercices

A. *Conjuguez à haute voix :*

1. J'en ai, tu . . ., etc.   2. Je n'en ai pas, tu . . . etc.   3. En ai-je, etc.   4. N'en ai-je pas, etc.

B. *Répondez aux questions suivantes en employant le pronom* **en** *:*

1. Combien de minutes y a-t-il dans une heure?   2. Combien de jours y a-t-il dans une semaine?   3. Combien de mois y a-t-il dans une année?   4. Combien de livres de cerises avez-vous achetées?   5. Avez-vous assez d'eau dans votre verre?   6. En voulez-vous encore?   7. N'en veut-elle pas?   8. Avez-vous besoin de cette encre?

C. *Mettez à la forme négative :*

1. Vous en avez beaucoup.   2. Nous en voulons. 3. Elle en a peur.   4. Ils en ont besoin.   5. En avez-vous assez?   6. En as-tu honte?   7. Donnez-en à Charles. 8. Cherchez-en.   9. Nous en avons besoin.   10. J'en vois deux.

D. *Traduisez en français :*

1. How many books have you in your library?   2. I have seventy-five.   3. Do you need these blue pencils? 4. I do.   5. Do you?   6. Has he money enough? 7. His pockets are full.   8. I think he has too much. 9. I am afraid so (of it).   10. He has lost all of his money. 11. Is he not ashamed of it?   12. No, he says that he is glad of it.   13. How many roses did the florist bring? 14. He brought twenty.   15. You said that you wanted a pound of cheese?   16. No, I want two pounds.   17. I haven't any.   18. Here are good apples, will you have one? 19. Give some to that little boy.   20. We have no bananas to-day, but we will have some to-morrow.

Exercice-revue

1. I shall receive many letters next week. 2. When I have received them, I shall show you the most interesting. 3. Here is Jane, go with her to the florist. 4. We do not know where he lives. 5. You will find him, his store is opposite the lawyer's house. 6. Must we go now? 7. Yes, go at once, and tell him that I want flowers to-morrow too, red roses and white tulips. 8. Very well, we shall tell him. 9. Be careful, do not soil your pretty silk dress. 10. No, mother, I will be careful. 11. I do it. 12. We do not do it. 13. They will tell him. 14. Don't tell him. 15. Don't say it. 16. Is that book for me? 17. Have you any money? 18. No, I haven't any. 19. Nor I.

* * * * * * *

40ᵉ Leçon : Le temps

On prend plus de mouches avec du miel qu'avec du vinaigre. — *There are more flies to be caught with honey than with vinegar*

Quel temps fait-il? *What kind of weather is it?*	**Il fait lourd.** *The weather is sultry.*
Il fait beau (temps). *It is fine (weather).*	**Il fait des éclairs.** *It is lightening.*
	Il fait de l'orage. *It is thundering.*
Il fait mauvais. *It is bad weather.*	**Il fait frais.** *It is cool.*
Il fait chaud. *It is warm.*	**Il pleut.** *It is raining.*
Il fait froid. *It is cold.*	**Il pleuvait.** *It was raining.*
Il fait du vent. *It is windy.*	**Il a plu.** *It has rained.*
	Il pleuvra. *It will rain.*
Il fait du soleil. *It is sunny.*	**Il neige.** *It is snowing.*

Vocabulaire

l'imperméable, *the raincoat.*
la pluie, *the rain.*
le parapluie, *the umbrella.*
la canne, *the cane.*

changer, *to change.*
subitement, *suddenly.*
neiger, *to snow.*
pleuvoir, *to rain.*

la **casquette**, *the cap.*
le **tonnerre**, *the thunder.*
l'**orage**, *the thunderstorm.*
la **neige**, *the snow.*
la **chance**, *the luck.*

incertain, *uncertain.*
mettre (past participle, **mis**), *to put, to put on.*
faire une promenade, *to take a walk*

Prendre (irregular), *to take;* participe passé, **pris**, *taken*

Présent	Imparfait	Futur
je prends.	je prenais, *I was taking.*	je prendrai, *I shall take.*
tu prends.	tu prenais.	tu prendras.
il prend.	il prenait.	il prendra.
nous prenons.	nous prenions.	nous prendrons.
vous prenez.	vous preniez.	vous prendrez.
ils prennent.	ils prenaient.	ils prendront.

Impératif

Singulier	Pluriel	
prends, *take.*	prenons, *let us take.*	prenez, *take.*

Lecture

Une promenade remise

La maman. Allons, mes enfants, en route ! Il fait beau, il fait du soleil, nous allons faire une grande promenade dans le parc.

Charles. Où ai-je mis mon chapeau de paille et ma canne ?

Nous allons faire une grande promenade.

La maman. Non, Charles, mets ta casquette et prends ton imperméable ou un parapluie ; il fait lourd, et on ne sait pas, il peut faire de l'orage.

Charles. Il fait chaud pour mettre une casquette.

La maman. Oui, mais s'il fait de l'orage, il fera du vent, il fera frais et il pleuvra.

Jeanne. Il a plu hier toute la journée et il pleuvait encore ce matin, il ne pleuvra pas cette après-midi.

La maman. Ce n'est pas sûr. Il fait beau, mais le temps est incertain ; après la pluie d'hier, il fait trop chaud aujourd'hui. Le temps change si subitement en cette saison.

Jeanne. Écoutez ! Le tonnerre ! Il fait des éclairs !

La maman. Voyez-vous ? J'avais peur de cela (*that*). Nous resterons à la maison. Fermez toutes les fenêtres, voilà l'orage qui arrive.

Charles. Quel dommage !

Jeanne. C'est toujours comme ça (*that*), nous n'avons pas de chance !

La maman. Il va faire très mauvais ; nous ne pourrons pas faire cette promenade aujourd'hui. Jouez dans votre chambre, et si vous êtes sages, nous irons au cinéma ce soir.

Exercices

A. *Questions sur la lecture :*

1. Pourquoi la maman décide-t-elle de faire une promenade avec ses enfants? 2. Pourquoi conseille-t-elle (*advise*) à Charles de prendre son imperméable? 3. Que répond Charles? 4. Qu'arrivera-t-il s'il fait de l'orage? 5. Pourquoi Jeanne dit-elle qu'il ne pleuvra pas? 6. Pourquoi la mère des enfants ne pense-t-elle pas comme Jeanne? 7. Qu'est-ce qu'il fait subitement? 8. Les enfants ont-ils fait leur promenade?

B. *Remplacez les tirets par le temps convenable du verbe entre parenthèses :*

1. (pleuvoir) Il ——. 2. ——-il hier soir? 3. Non, mais il —— demain. 4. (faire) Il —— froid ici. 5. Il ne —— pas froid aujourd'hui, mais il —— froid demain.

6. ——-il —— du soleil ce matin? 7. Oui, il —— très
beau ce matin, et maintenant il —— de l'orage. 8. ——-il
du vent au bord de la mer? 9. Quel temps ——-il?
10. Il —— lourd.

C. *Traduisez en français et répondez aux questions:*
1. When is it warm? 2. What kind of weather is it?
3. Is the weather sultry? 4. Is it not cold in January?
5. Is it colder in April than in December? 6. When does
it snow? 7. Was it raining this morning? 8. Will it
snow to-morrow? 9. Did it snow yesterday? 10. Do
you take your umbrella when it rains? 11. Does it often
thunder in winter? 12. Why does it not thunder in winter? 13. Was it windy this morning, when you went out?
14. What kind of weather was it? 15. What kind of
weather will it be to-morrow?

Exercice-revue

1. Conjugate orally: j'en ai, tu . . ., etc. 2. Je n'en ai
pas, tu . . ., etc. 3. We receive three newspapers
every day. 4. Did you see all of my mother's jewels?
5. Are they not beautiful? 6. They are very beautiful, I
like them. 7. Has your sister any? 8. No, she hasn't
any yet, she is too young. 9. Will you give her a ring for
her birthday? 10. No, if she wants one, she can buy it
herself, she has money. 11. And you, haven't you any?
12. I have a little, but I have not too much. 13. One
never has too much, does one? 14. I am losing all my
hair, what am I going to do? 15. I don't know; why
don't you go to the doctor? 16. I went to his office
yesterday, but I forgot to speak of it. 17. Speak of it
when you see him. 18. I will (speak of it).

Expressions idiomatiques

Faites ce que vous voudrez.   Do as you please.
Faites comme chez vous.   Make yourself at home.

Faites venir un médecin.	Send for a doctor.
Faites entrer ce monsieur.	Show the gentleman in.
Faites votre malle.	Pack your trunk.
Faites de votre mieux.	Do your best.

*   *   *   *   *   *   *

41ᵉ Leçon : Emplois de la négation

Ce n'est pas la mer à boire. — *It is not so very difficult.*[1]

(1) We learned in Lesson 24 that the partitive articles **du, de la, des** (*some, any*, expressed or understood in English) are expressed by the single word **de** when the verb is negative.

Je n'ai pas *d'***argent.**	*I haven't any money.*
Ne voulez-vous pas *de* **fleurs?**	*Don't you want any flowers?*

(2) Study the following sentences :

Il n'a *ni* **parents** *ni* **amis.**	*He has neither relatives nor friends.*
Il est *sans* **amis.**	*He is without friends.*

After **ni . . . ni,** *neither . . . nor*, and after **sans,** *without*, **de, du, de la, des** are omitted, as in English.

Attention! When **ni . . . ni** is used with a verb, **ne** is always found before that verb.

(3) Study the following sentences :

Avez-vous *jamais* **vu** *des* **lions?**	*Have you ever seen lions?*
N'avez-vous *jamais* **vu** *de* **lions?**	*Have you never seen lions?*
Jamais.	*Never.*

Jamais, used alone or without a verb, means *never*. With a verb preceded by **ne** it means also *never*. With a verb, but *without* **ne,** it means *ever* and has not a negative meaning.

As to position, **ne . . . jamais** follows the same rule as **ne . . . pas.**

---

[1] Literally, *It is not like drinking the sea.*

(4) Observe the following constructions :

Il *n'a que* des amis.   *He has only (nothing but) friends.*
Nous *n'*avons vu *que* des amis.   *We have seen only (nothing but)*
friends.

After **ne . . . que,** *only, nothing but,* both **de** and the
article, that is to say, **du, de la, des,** are used.

Notice that, when the tense is compound, **que** comes after
the past participle.

Attention! **Pas** is omitted with **ne . . . que** and **ne . . .**
jamais.

Vocabulaire

le **tailleur,** *the tailor.*
le **complet,** *the suit* (3 pieces).
le **veston,** *the coat.*
le **gilet,** *the vest.*
le **pantalon,** *the trousers.*
la **jaquette,** *the cutaway.*
le **smoking,** *the tuxedo.*
l'**habit,** *the full dress.*
la **manche,** *the sleeve.*
le **pardessus,** *the overcoat.*
essayer, *to try on.*
la **chaussure,** *footwear.*
la **bottine,** *the high shoe.*
le **soulier,** *the low shoe.*
la **pantoufle,** *the slipper.*
la **chaussette,** *the sock.*
le **linge,** *the linen.*

la **chemise,** *the shirt.*
le **sous-vêtement,** *the underwear.*
le **cache-nez,** *the muffler.*
sur mesures, *on measure.*
tout fait, *ready made.*
aller bien, *to fit.*
léger, *light* (in weight).
lourd, *heavy* (in weight).
étroit, *narrow, tight.*
large, *wide, loose.*
clair, *light* (in color).
foncé, *dark* (in color).
prêt, *ready.*
presque, *almost.*
chic (invariable), *smart.*
parfait, *perfect.*
l'**étalage,** *display, show-window.*

Lecture

LES VÊTEMENTS D'HOMME

Paul. Votre tailleur vous a-t-il envoyé votre complet
hier?

Jean. Non, je ne l'ai reçu que ce matin ; voulez-vous le
voir?

Paul. Mais oui, montrez-moi votre acquisition.

Jean.   Voici le veston, le gilet et le pantalon.

Paul.   Vous va-t-il bien?   Mettez le veston.

Jean.   Il me va à la perfection ; je n'ai jamais eu de complet si bien fait.   Il n'est ni trop étroit ni trop large, ni trop léger ni trop lourd, ni trop foncé ni trop clair.   Les manches ne sont ni trop longues ni trop courtes, il est parfait.

Paul.   Il est certainement très chic ; je l'aime beaucoup. A propos, avez-vous jamais commandé des chaussures sur mesures?

Jean.   Jamais.   Je ne commande ni bottines, ni souliers, ni pantoufles sur mesures ; j'achète toujours mes chaussures toutes faites.

Paul.   Et votre linge : chemises, cols, sous-vêtements, etc.

Jean.   Non, je ne commande ni chemises ni cols sur mesures.   Vous ai-je dit que j'ai aussi acheté un pardessus?

Paul.   Non.   L'avez-vous aussi acheté chez votre tailleur?

Jean.   Non, je l'ai acheté chez Dormeuil.   Je passais devant chez lui ; le pardessus était à l'étalage ; je suis entré, je l'ai essayé, et comme il m'allait bien, je l'ai pris.

Paul.   Vous voilà prêt pour votre voyage à Paris.

Jean.   Oui, presque.   Je n'attends plus que mon smoking ; ma jaquette est prête, mon habit aussi, et le tailleur m'apportera demain mon costume de voyage.   Je ne dois acheter qu'une demi-douzaine de paires de chaussettes, une casquette et un cache-nez.   Voulez-vous sortir avec moi? Nous les achèterons ensemble.

Paul.   Avec plaisir.   Voici ma canne, voilà votre chapeau, en route !

Exercices

A. *Questions sur la lecture :*

1. Jean a-t-il reçu son complet hier?   2. Pourquoi est-il content de son nouveau complet?   3. Comment Paul

LE SACRÉ-CŒUR DE MONTMARTRE À PARIS, FROM LA RUE LAFITTE.

trouve-t-il le complet de son ami? 4. Est-ce que Jean
commande jamais ses bottines sur mesures? 5. Et ses
chemises et ses cols? 6. Comment a-t-il acheté son pardessus? 7. Doit-il encore acheter beaucoup de choses?

B. *Traduisez en français:*

1. These men are very poor, they have neither high shoes
nor low shoes. 2. They have only slippers. 3. She has
no crêpe de Chine, she has only lace. 4. Has she enough?
5. We have no gloves. 6. Have you collars only? 7. We
have neither gloves nor collars. 8. I have no umbrella.
9. Will you not have mine? 10. No, thank you, I have
already lost one. 11. Do you ever return (give back) the
umbrellas you borrow? 12. Almost never, I always lose
them. 13. Not always, but sometimes. 14. Do you
ever order your shirts on measure? 15. Never. 16. How
many canes have you? 17. I have only one. 18. He
has neither muffler nor cap. 19. I never wear any muffler.
20. Never? 21. Never.

Exercice-revue

1. He has money, but I haven't. 2. Have you? 3. I
have. 4. Has he? 5. He hasn't. 6. How much have
you? 7. I have a good deal. 8. One never has enough.
9. For him. 10. With her. 11. Without us. 12. Behind me. 13. At their (*m.*) house. 14. At my house.
15. After her. 16. With him. 17. I see you, him, her,
them. 18. There is the professor who punishes me every
day. 19. She lost the blue silk handkerchief that Jane
gave her. 20. One must go to the doctor when one is ill.
21. We shall go for a walk to-morrow if the weather is fine.
22. If it rains, we shall stay home. 23. When you go to
the doctor, tell him that I want to see him. 24. All right,
I will tell him that you want to see him.

Expressions idiomatiques

Si j'ai bonne mémoire.	If I recollect rightly.
S'il en est ainsi.	If such is the case.
Si bon vous semble.	If you think best.
Tant mieux !	So much the better !
Tant pis !	So much the worse !

*   *   *   *   *   *   *

42ᵉ Leçon : Adjectifs interrogatifs

Pierre qui roule n'amasse pas mousse. — *A rolling stone gathers no moss.*

Study the following questions :

(1) *Quel* livre avez-vous ?	*What book have you?*
(2) *Quelles* fleurs aime-t-elle ?	*What flowers does she like?*
(3) *Quel* est le nom de votre ami ?	*What is your friend's name?*

The interrogative adjective **quel,** *which, what,* has the following forms :

SINGULIER $\begin{cases} \text{quel (m.)} \\ \text{quelle (f.)} \end{cases}$ PLURIEL $\begin{cases} \text{quels (m.)} \\ \text{quelles (f.)} \end{cases}$

Quel, as a rule, immediately precedes the noun it modifies. With **être,** however, the noun may stand after the verb (Example 3).

Observe the use of **quel** in the following sentences :

Quel malheur!	*What a misfortune!*
Quelle différence!	*What a difference!*

The interrogative adjective **quel** is sometimes used in exclamatory form, and in that case is translated in English by *what a,* but the *a* is never expressed in French.

Connaître (irregular), *to know;* participe passé, connu

Présent	Imparfait	Futur
je connais, *I know.*	je connaissais, *I was*	je connaîtrai, *I shall*
tu connais.	tu connaissais. *knowing.*	tu connaîtras. *know.*
il connaît.	il connaissait.	il connaîtra.
nous connaissons.	nous connaissions.	nous connaîtrons.
vous connaissez.	vous connaissiez.	vous connaîtrez.
ils connaissent.	ils connaissaient.	ils connaîtront.

Impératif

Singulier	Pluriel	
connais, *know.*	connaissons, *let us know.*	connaissez, *know.*

Distinction between *savoir* and *connaître*. — Savoir means *to know through the mind, to have learned, to know that something is so, to know how to.* It never has a person for its object and it may be followed by a conjunction or a verb.

Savez-vous votre leçon ?	*Do you know your lesson?*
Je sais qu'elle est ici.	*I know that she is here.*
Il sait lire et écrire.	*He knows how to read and write.*

Connaître means *to be acquainted with, to know by sight* or by the other senses, *to recognize.* It may have a person or thing for its object, but can never be followed by a conjunction or a verb.

Nous connaissons ce monsieur.	*We know that gentleman.*
Je connais le dictionnaire de Littré.	*I know Littré's dictionary.*

Je *connais* cette dame, mais je ne *sais* pas son nom. *I know that lady, but I don't know her name.*

Vocabulaire

un Parisien, *a Parisian.*	perfectionner, *to perfect.*
un Américain, *an American.*	reconnaître, *to recognize.*
le conseil, *the advice.*	permettre, *to permit, to allow.*
conseiller, *to advise.*	exactement, *exactly.*
l'accent, *the accent.*	raisonnable, *reasonable.*
le genre, *the kind.*	gauche, *left.*
le prix, *the price, cost.*	la partie, *the part.*
l'idée (f.), *the idea.*	la rive, *the bank.*

le **numéro,** *the number.*
la **pension bourgeoise,** *the board-*
   ing house.
l'**adresse** (f.), *the address.*
l'**annuaire téléphonique** (m.), *the*
   telephone directory.
      descendre à l'hôtel, *to stop at a hotel.*

Lecture

Dans le train Cherbourg-Paris

M. X.   Pardon, monsieur, puis-je fermer cette fenêtre ;
il fait beaucoup de vent.

M. Z.   Mais certainement, monsieur.

M. X.   Vous êtes Parisien, n'est-ce pas ?   Vous avez
exactement le même accent qu'un Parisien que je connais.

A quel hôtel descendrez-vous ?

M. Z.   Oui, monsieur, je suis né à Paris ; et vous, de quel
pays êtes-vous ?

M. X.   Je suis Américain, je vais à Paris pour la première
fois.

M. Z.   A quel hôtel descendrez-vous ?

M. X.   Je ne sais pas encore ; pouvez-vous me donner un
conseil ?

M. Z.   Quel genre d'hôtel voulez-vous ?   Quel prix désirez-
vous payer ?

M. X.   Je n'ai pas la moindre idée des hôtels et des prix.
On m'a conseillé d'aller dans une pension bourgeoise où je
pourrai perfectionner le peu de français que je sais.   Quelles
sont les meilleures pensions de la capitale et quels en sont les
prix ?

M. Z.   Il y en a beaucoup.   La pension Mailly est très connue.

M. X.   Quels sont les prix de cette pension?

M. Z.   Je ne sais pas exactement, mais dans les pensions bourgeoises, les prix sont toujours raisonnables.

M. X.   Dans quelle partie de la ville est cette pension, dans quelle rue?

M. Z.   Je sais que c'est sur la rive gauche, mais je ne sais ni quelle rue, ni quel numéro.

M. X.   Quel dommage !

M. Z.   Quand nous arriverons à Paris, nous trouverons l'adresse dans l'annuaire téléphonique.

M. X.   Merci mille fois, monsieur.   Permettez-moi de me présenter ; voici ma carte.

M. Z.   Merci, monsieur, voici la mienne.

Exercices

A. *Questions sur la lecture :*

1. Où sont les deux messieurs qui parlent?   2. A quel hôtel M. X va-t-il descendre?   3. Quel conseil lui a-t-on donné?   4. Que demande-t-il à M. Z?   5. M. Z sait-il dans quelle rue est la pension Mailly?   6. Que dit M. X quand M. Z ne peut pas lui donner l'adresse de la pension?

B. *Traduisez en français :*

1. On what table did I leave my gloves?   2. Which gloves?   3. Which gloves?   The brown gloves I bought yesterday.   4. In what store did you buy them?   5. I bought them in the (*au*) Bon Marché where I bought shoes also.   6. What a large store !   7. What shoes did you buy?   8. In what store do they sell the best shoes in Paris? 9. What a question !   There are so many stores in Paris ! 10. In which boarding house did you stop?   11. To what theater are we going to-night?   12. I do not know yet ; what kind of theater do you like?   13. When shall we go to

the museum? 14. What a good idea! Let us go this afternoon. 15. Do you know it? Do you know in what street is the museum? 16. No, but I will find it. 17. Are you sure of it? 18. I am.

Exercice-revue

Conjugate in unison: j'en‿ai, etc.; je n'en‿ai pas, etc.; en‿ai-je? etc.; n'en‿ai-je pas? etc. 1. What are you doing? 2. Why don't you obey me? 3. Look at me and don't speak to him. 4. Where did he put his straw hat? 5. Do you know that I received half a dozen silver spoons yesterday? 6. I received them for Mary's birthday. 7. Did you see the doctor's beautiful gray horses? 8. No, I have not seen them. 9. There they are, in front of his door. 10. Gold and silver are metals. 11. Do that exercise for me, please. 12. No, do it yourself. 13. I must go to his house now. 14. If you must go, I will go with you, if it is not raining. 15. It is not raining, but it is windy, the weather is bad. 16. Here are apples, will you have some. 17. No thanks, I don't want any. 18. Why don't you want any? 19. Because I have already eaten some. 20. I eat some every day.

Une anecdote

LE JEU DE MOTS

Calino,[1] notre imbécile national, était un jour dans une maison avec quelques autres invités. C'était l'heure du thé, et un des messieurs qui désirait faire un compliment à la maîtresse de maison qui lui donnait une tasse de thé, dit :

— Madame, vous êtes comme cette tasse, vous êtes pleine de bon thé (bonté).

---

[1] In France, Calino is a fictitious person who is supposed to make blunders all the time.

Ce jeu de mots spirituel obtint (*received*) beaucoup de succès.

Quelques jours plus tard, Calino dînait dans une autre maison, et saisissant la première occasion de faire une de ses gaffes (*blunders*) habituelles, dit à sa voisine, à la fin du dîner :

— Madame, vous êtes comme cette tasse, vous êtes pleine de bon café !

La dame, naturellement n'a pas compris le compliment, et Calino cherche encore maintenant pourquoi son jeu de mots n'a pas eu de succès.

* * * * * * *

43ᵉ Leçon : Pronoms démonstratifs

Tout nouveau, tout beau. — *A new broom sweeps clean.*

In Lesson 15, we learned the demonstrative adjectives, **ce, cette, ces,** and noticed that they are always followed *immediately* by a noun, for the function of an adjective is to modify a noun.

A pronoun, as we know, takes the place of a noun. Therefore, a demonstrative pronoun *cannot be followed immediately* by a noun, because, like any other pronoun, it replaces a noun, and takes the gender and number of the noun for which it stands.

Study now the following examples :

(1) **Voici mon livre et *celui de* ma sœur.** *Here is my book and my sister's.*

(2) **Voici *celui qui* était sur la table.** *Here is the one which was on the table.*

(3) **Voici *celui que* j'ai acheté.** *Here is the one I bought.*

(4) ***Celui-ci* est meilleur que *celui-là*.** *This one is better than that one.*

The demonstrative pronouns are never used alone, but are always found in one of the following forms :

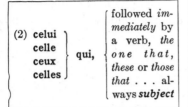

> (1) celui
> celle
> ceux
> celles } de + a noun, *that of, the one of, those of*

> (2) celui
> celle
> ceux
> celles } qui, { followed *im-mediately* by a verb, *the one that, these* or *those that . . .* always **subject**

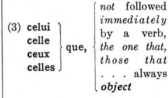

> (3) celui
> celle
> ceux
> celles } que, { *not* followed *immediately* by a verb, *the one that, those that . . .* always **object**

> (4) celui
> celle
> ceux
> celles } -ci, *this, this one, these*

> (4) celui
> celle
> ceux
> celles } -là, *that, that one, those*

The latter form (4) is used when a sharp distinction is to be emphasized between persons or objects referred to.

Omission du pronom anglais. — The demonstrative pronoun is sometimes omitted in English, but is always expressed in French. The only way to translate *John's* or *my sister's* in French is : *That* or *those of John ;* **celui, celle, ceux** or **celles de Jean,** and **celui, celle,** etc., **de ma sœur,** according to the gender and number of the thing possessed by John or by my sister.

Vocabulaire

le mercier, *the haberdasher.*
la qualité, *the quality.*
la toile, *the linen.*
le coton, *the cotton.*
l'usage, *the wear.*
la main, *the hand.*

en main(s), *in hand.*
magnifique, *magnificent, beautiful.*
solide, *strong.*
l'assortiment, *the set, collection.*
cher (adv.), *expensive, dear.*
souple, *pliant, soft.*

Lecture

CHEZ LE MERCIER

Le mercier. Bonjour, monsieur. Monsieur désire . . .?

Le client. Je désire des chemises et des gants.

Le mercier. Voici deux qualités de chemises ; celles-ci sont en toile, celles-là sont en coton. Celles qui sont en toile sont plus solides que celles qui sont en coton ; cela va sans dire.

Le client. Naturellement. Combien coûte celle que j'ai ici ?

Le mercier. Celle-là ne coûte que 35 francs, trois pour 100 francs.

Le client. Ça me va. Maintenant montrez-moi des gants.

Le mercier. En voici un magnifique assortiment.

Le client. Combien coûtent ceux-ci ?

Le mercier. Ceux-là coûtent 50 francs. Ils sont bons, mais ils ne sont pas de la meilleure qualité. Ceux-ci sont excellents, ils coûtent un peu plus cher, mais vous en aurez meilleur usage.

Le client. Ils sont de la même couleur que ceux de mon frère ; en avez-vous de couleur grise ?

Le mercier. Mais certainement ; en voici des gris clair,[1] des gris foncé [1] et des gris acier. Essayez cette paire ; non, pas celle-là, celle-ci ; celle que vous avez en main est trop petite. Voyez comme ils sont beaux et souples.

Le client. C'est bien, je prends ceux-ci. Envoyez-moi les chemises cette après-midi ou demain ; voici mon adresse.

Le mercier. C'est entendu. Au revoir, monsieur, merci bien.

Exercices

A. *Remplacez les tirets par un pronom démonstratif suivi de* **de, qui, que, ci** *or* **là** :

1. Voici ma canne et —— mon frère.   2. Voici ma canne et —— était dans le vestibule.   3. Voici ma canne et ——

---

[1] When two adjectives are put together to express a color, both are invariable (see grammar summary p. 371).

mon frère a reçue hier. 4. Quelle est votre canne ——
ou ——? 5. Vos bijoux sont plus beaux que —— ma
sœur. 6. Son pardessus est plus foncé que —— j'ai acheté.
7. Les robes de ma sœur sont plus chic que —— Marie.
8. —— arrive en retard perd sa place (*proverb*).

B. *Mettez au pluriel :*

1. Quel livre prenez-vous, celui-ci ou celui-là? 2. Je
prendrai celui que vous me donnerez. 3. Ce cheval-ci est
celui du médecin, ce cheval-là est celui de l'avocat. 4. Ouvrez cette porte-ci et fermez celle-là. 5. Celui qui travaille
sera récompensé. 6. Voici mon chapeau et celui de mon
frère.

C. *Traduisez en français :*

1. What gloves do you want, these or those? 2. I want
those that you have in [your] hand. 3. Your muffler is
prettier than Paul's. 4. His hair is not as dark as my
cousin's. 5. Where is your bag and Jane's? 6. This is
mine, that one is Jane's. 7. Here is your book, did you
read the one I gave you last week? 8. I bought two boxes
of candy, this one is for your mother, that one is for
your aunt. 9. These overcoats are larger than those.
10. Is that one your father's? 11. Yes, and this one is
my brother's. 12. I like this one better than the one
which is in the tailor's window.

Exercice-revue

1. I cannot write, I have neither paper nor pen. 2. Here
is a pen ; as for the paper, you will find some in that drawer.
3. No, there isn't any. 4. Here is some. 5. Have you
ever been in Paris? 6. Never, but I will go next summer.
7. You will never regret your trip. 8. What kind of weather
is it in Paris, is it warm? 9. It is not very warm, but it
often rains. 10. What is the name of that gentleman?
11. I don't know ; I don't know him. 12. Do you need

La Grande Corniche à la Côte d'Azur.

this umbrella?   13. No, I don't need it; give it to your brother.   14. Thank you, he will need it, I think it will rain.   15. I am sure of it.   16. Has your father many flowers in his garden?   17. He has more than 200.   18. There are no more in mine.   19. There were so many last year.   20. Why are there not any this year?   21. I cannot tell you why.

Locutions idiomatiques

A la bonne heure !	Good for you !
Laissez-moi tranquille !	Let me alone !
Ne faites pas attention à cela.	Don't mind that.
Vous n'y êtes pas.	You are wide of the mark.
Vous y êtes !	You have hit it !

*   *   *   *   *   *   *

44e Leçon: Les pronoms démonstratifs CE, CECI, CELA

Vous mettez la charrue devant les bœufs. — *You put the cart before the horse.*

1. Observe the use of **ce, ceci, cela** in the following sentences :

*C'*est facile.	*That's easy.*
Ceci est facile, mais *cela* est difficile.	*This is easy, but that is difficult.*
Voulez-vous *ceci* ou *cela?*	*Will you have this or that?*
Aimez-vous *ça?*	*Do you like that?*

Ce is used as subject of **être** and refers to something vague, indefinite.

Ceci and **cela** are used instead of **ce** in contrasts.   **Ceci** and **cela** are invariable, have neither gender nor number, and refer to something pointed out in fact or in thought, but not named, while **celui-ci, celui-là,** etc. (preceding lesson) take the place of a noun or pronoun plainly mentioned before.

Ça is the familiar or colloquial form of **cela.**

2. Note the use of **c'est** and **ce sont** (not : il est, elle est, ils sont, elles sont) in the following sentences :

C'est mon cousin.	*He is my cousin.*
Ce sont mes cousins.	*They are my cousins.*
C'est ma sœur.	*She is my sister.*
C'est mon panier.	*It is my basket.*
C'est le mien.	*It is mine.*
C'est le plus grand.	*It (he) is the largest.*

He is, she is, it is, they are are generally expressed by **c'est** and **ce sont** before a *noun,* a *pronoun,* or a *superlative.*

C'EST LUI.   C'EST ELLE.   CE SONT EUX.   CE SONT ELLES.

3. Notice the use of the disjunctive pronouns after **c'est** and **ce sont** :

C'est moi, *it is I.*   **C'est nous,** *it is we.*
C'est toi, *it is thou (you).*   **C'est vous,** *it is you.*
C'est lui, *it is he, he is the one.*   **Ce sont eux,** *it is they* (m.).
C'est elle, *it is she, she is the one.*   **Ce sont elles,** *it is they* (f.).

INTERROGATIVE

Est-ce moi? *is it I?*   **Est-ce nous?** *is it we?*
Est-ce toi? *is it thou (you)?*   **Est-ce vous?** *is it you?*
Est-ce lui? *is it he?*   **Est-ce eux?** *is it they* (m.)?
Est-ce elle? *is it she?*   **Est-ce elles?** *is it they* (f.)?

Observe that **c'est** is used before all these forms, except the third person plural affirmative : **ce sont eux (elles)**. Note that **est-ce** is used with *all* forms.

Attention! **C'est nous qui demeurons ici.** *It is we who live here.* Notice the agreement of the verb with the antecedent of **qui** in sentences with the construction **c'est** + a disjunctive pronoun.

4. Notice also the following expressions :

C'est bien.　　　*That's all right.*　　　*C'est* à vous.　　　*It's your turn.*

C'est is also used before an adverb or a preposition.

C'est and *il est,* **before an adjective.** — **C'est** is used when the adjective finishes the sentence. **Je ne fais pas cela parce que** *c'est* **difficile.**

Il est is used when the sentence does not finish with the adjective. *Il est* **difficile de faire cela.**

Mettre (irregular), *to put;* participe passé, **mis,** *put*

Présent	Imparfait	Futur
je mets, *I put.*	je mettais, *I was putting.*	je mettrai, *I shall put.*
tu mets.	tu mettais.	tu mettras.
il met.	il mettait.	il mettra.
nous mettons.	nous mettions.	nous mettrons.
vous mettez.	vous mettiez.	vous mettrez.
ils mettent.	ils mettaient.	ils mettront.

Impératif

Singulier	Pluriel	
mets, *put.*	mettons, *let us put.*	mettez, *put.*

Vocabulaire

cependant. *however.*　　　　　　　　remarquable, *remarkable.*
au contraire, *to the contrary.*　　　généreux, *generous.*
　　　　　　venir, *to come.*

Lecture

1. Est-ce vous, Paul?　　2. Oui, c'est moi.　　3. Qui sont ces messieurs?　　4. Ce sont nos voisins.　　5. Connaissez-

vous M. Gaillard? C'est le plus célèbre de tous nos avocats.
6. Voyez-vous ces dames? Ce sont mes sœurs. 7. Qui sont
ces enfants? 8. Ce sont les miens. 9. New-York est
une grande ville, c'est la plus grande de ce pays. 10. C'est
à vous que je parle, répondez-moi. 11. Est-ce à moi que
vous parlez? 12. Comment trouvez-vous ceci? 13. Je
n'aime pas cela. 14. C'est joli cependant. 15. Vous
voulez faire cela? 16. Mais, mon ami, c'est impossible!
17. Non, c'est difficile, mais ce n'est pas impossible.
18. Il est très possible de le faire. 19. C'est bien, c'est
bien, faites-le si vous pensez que c'est si facile. 20. Est-ce
Henri qui doit venir? 21. Non, ce n'est pas lui, c'est son
frère. 22. C'est le meilleur de mes amis. 23. C'est aussi
le mien. 24. Il est plus jeune que vous, n'est-ce pas?
25. Oui, il est plus jeune que moi et que vous; c'est le plus
jeune de tous mes amis.

Exercices

A. *Remplacez les tirets par un pronom démonstratif:*

1. —— est très bien. 2. Ceci est bon, —— est mauvais.
3. —— est facile, cela est difficile. 4. Est- —— votre ami?
5. Oui, —— est mon meilleur ami. 6. —— sont mes
cousines qui sont arrivées. 7. —— ne sont pas mes cousins.

B. *Remplacez les tirets par* **ce** *ou* **il, elle, ils, elles** *selon le
cas.*

1. Qui est- ——? —— est mon oncle, —— est bon et
aimable. 2. —— est vrai, —— est plus généreux que le
mien, —— est le plus généreux des hommes. 3. Quel beau
chien, est- —— le vôtre? 4. Non, —— n'est pas le mien,
mais je le connais, —— est très intelligent, —— est un chien
remarquable. 5. Est- —— aussi intelligent que celui de
votre cousin? 6. —— est plus intelligent que le sien, ——
est le plus intelligent de tous les chiens.

C. *Traduisez en français:*

1. Do not take those books, they are not yours.   2. I beg your pardon, they are mine.   3. Why do you do that? 4. When will you finish this?   5. Who is there? Is it you, John?   6. No, it is I, Paul.   7. Is it your turn?   8. No, it is her turn.   9. Now, it is mine.   10. Is it possible? 11. Here is an interesting book, is it yours?   12. It is a French book, isn't it?   13. No, that is a Spanish book. 14. It is the best of my books.   15. What a beautiful woman ! Who is she?   16. She is my aunt.   17. She is here for five or six days.   18. Is she richer than your mother?   19. Yes, she is much richer ; she is the richest woman in our family.

Exercice-revue

1. Here are flowers, give some to your mother.   2. I do not want to give any.   3. You must give some.   4. You have neither roses nor tulips, you have only jonquils. 5. Where are those you received this morning?   6. I gave them to my cousin (*f.*).   7. Do you know the gentleman who is in front of you?   8. No, I don't know him.   9. Do they sell shirts, collars, kid gloves, and silk ties at this haberdasher?   10. I cannot buy all that, I have only ten dollars. 11. Don't you think this suit is better than that one? 12. Yes, it is better than the one you have.   13. Buy it if you like it.   14. I lost my handkerchief, let us look for it. 15. Look for it yourself, I must go home now, I think it will rain.   16. Here is my muffler and my brother's.   17. Go without me, I will arrive later.   18. Good-by, see you soon.

Locutions idiomatiques

Cela se peut.	That may be.
Ça ne se peut pas.	That cannot be.
C'est bien vrai.	That's very true.

Ça ne vaut pas la peine.   It is not worth while.
C'est trop fort !   That is going too far !
C'est bonnet blanc et blanc   It is six of one and half a
    bonnet.   dozen of the other.

*   *   *   *   *   *   *

45e Leçon : L'heure. — Fractions

Une hirondelle ne fait pas le printemps. — *One swallow does not make a summer.*

Quelle heure est-il ?   *What time is it?*
Il est midi.   *It is twelve o'clock, noon.*
Il est minuit.   *It is midnight.*
Il est une heure.   *It is one o'clock.*
Il est trois heures cinq.   *It is five after three.*
Il est quatre heures et quart.   *It is a quarter after four.*
Il est cinq heures et demie.   *It is half past five.*
Il est six heures moins vingt-cinq.   *It is five thirty-five.*
Il est sept heures moins un quart.   *It is a quarter of seven.*
Il est huit heures moins cinq.   *It is five minutes of eight.*
Il est neuf heures juste.   *It is exactly nine o'clock.*
A quelle heure ?   *At what time?*
Vers sept heures.   *About seven o'clock.*
A dix heures précises (**sonnant**).   *At ten o'clock sharp (striking).*
Ma montre avance.   *My watch is fast.*
Ma montre retarde.   *My watch is slow.*

Attention ! **Il est** is *always* used to translate *it is*, in reference to the time of the day.

Notes. — (1) As in English, any number of minutes may go with the preceding hour; although, after half past, especially after 35 past, the next hour is usually named, *less* (**moins**) the number of minutes to complete the hour.

(2) *O'clock* is very often omitted in English, but **heure** or **heures** is always mentioned in French. **Minutes,** however, is generally omitted.

(3) **Midi** and **minuit** are used for twelve o'clock; we never say **douze heures.**

Quelle heure est-il ?

IL EST UNE HEURE.

IL EST TROIS HEURES
CINQ.

IL EST QUATRE HEURES
ET QUART.

IL EST CINQ HEURES
ET DEMIE.

IL EST CINQ HEURES
TRENTE-CINQ.

IL EST SEPT HEURES
MOINS UN QUART.

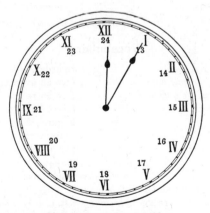

UNE HORLOGE FRANÇAISE.

(4) In France, railroad time tables are figured on the 24-hour basis, from 1 to 24. This avoids the A.M. and P.M. of the American time tables. A train leaving at 1.22 P.M. will be scheduled as leaving at 13.22. The time between midnight and 1 A.M. is mentioned as zero hour. A train may leave at 0.05. Many new French watches and clocks have a double dial, as illustrated in the picture on page 163.

Fractions. — Fractions are expressed, as in English, with a cardinal number for the numerator and an ordinal for the denominator except for $\frac{1}{2}$, $\frac{1}{3}$, and $\frac{1}{4}$.

$\frac{1}{2}$ **un demi,** *one half.*
$\frac{1}{3}$ **un tiers,** *one third.*
$\frac{1}{4}$ **un quart** (kahr), *one quarter.*

$\frac{1}{5}$ **un cinquième,** *one fifth.*
$\frac{3}{7}$ **trois septièmes,** *three sevenths.*
$\frac{5}{8}$ **cinq huitièmes,** *five eighths.*

Partir (irregular), *to set out, to leave;* participe passé, **parti**

Présent	Imparfait	Futur
je pars, *I set out,*	je partais, *I was setting*	je partirai, *I shall set out,*
tu pars. *I leave.*	tu partais. *out, I was*	tu partiras. *I shall leave.*
il part.	il partait. *leaving.*	il partira.
nous partons.	nous partions.	nous partirons.
vous partez.	vous partiez.	vous partirez.
ils partent.	ils partaient.	ils partiront.

Impératif

Singulier	Pluriel
pars, *leave.*	partons, *let us leave.* partez, *leave.*

Vocabulaire

l'heure, *the hour.*
la demi-heure, *the half hour.*
le quart d'heure, *the quarter.*
l'horloge, *the clock.*
tôt, *early.*
tard, *late.*
il est tard, *it is late.*
depuis, *since.*
avancer, *to be fast.*

retarder, *to be late.*
être en avance, *to be early.*
être en retard, *to be late.*
être à l'heure, *to be on time.*
la gare, *the station.*
le train, *the train.*
par le train de, *by the train of.*
manquer, *to miss.*
longtemps, *long, long time.*

comment se fait-il? *how is it?*
casser la croûte, *to break a crust, to have a bite.*
un coup de téléphone, *a telephone call, a ring.*

Lecture

A LA GARE

Louis. Tiens Jean !   Que faites-vous ici, à la gare, à cette heure ?

Jean. J'attends mon père qui arrive à 5 h. 30.   Et vous ? Comment se fait-il que vous voilà avec deux valises ?   Vous partez ?

Louis. Vous l'avez dit !   Je pars pour Stockholm.

Jean. Par quel train partez-vous ?

Louis. Par le train de 6 h. 10.   Je sais que je suis en avance, mais je n'ai rien mangé depuis ce matin et je veux casser la croûte au buffet.

Jean. Je comprends maintenant pourquoi vous êtes ici si tôt.   A quelle heure arriverez-vous à Stockholm ?

Louis. Demain à 8 h. 15.

Jean. Pourquoi n'avez-vous pas pris le train de nuit ? Celui de minuit est le meilleur.

Louis. C'est exact, mais il n'y avait plus de places. Quelle heure est-il ?

Jean. J'ai 5 h. 20 à ma montre, mais je pense que ma montre retarde.

Louis. Il n'est pas si tard ; votre montre avance.   Où est l'horloge ?   Ah, la voilà.   Regardez, il n'est que 5 h. 12. Vous avancez de huit minutes.   Allons au buffet.

Jean. Non, j'ai demandé si le train de Calais était en retard, et l'on m'a répondu qu'il était à l'heure.

Louis. Vous avez encore plus d'un quart d'heure si le train n'arrive qu'à 5 h. 30.

Jean. Non, Louis, merci ; allez-y sans moi, et ne restez pas trop longtemps au buffet ; ne manquez pas votre train.

Louis. Au revoir, alors ; je vous donnerai un coup de téléphone dès que je serai revenu.

Jean. C'est cela. Au revoir, Louis ; bon voyage !

Exercices

A. *Questions sur la lecture :*

1. A quelle heure le père de Jean arrive-t-il?   2. Par quel train Louis part-il?   3. A quelle heure arrivera-t-il? 4. Quelle heure est-il à la montre de Jean?   5. Est-ce que la montre de Jean retarde?   6. De combien de minutes sa montre avance-t-elle?   7. Quelle heure est-il à l'horloge de la gare?   8. Que fera Louis quand il sera revenu de Stockholm?   9. Que va-t-il faire au buffet?

B. *Give the correct time, assuming the clocks on page 163 are:*

1. 7 minutes slow.   2. 13 minutes slow.   3. 20 minutes slow.   4. 25 minutes slow.   5. 3 minutes fast. 6. 10 minutes fast.   7. 20 minutes fast.

C. *Traduisez en français :*

1. At what time do you go to school?   2. Are you always on time?   3. I am always early, but Paul is often late. 4. We have our French lesson at 9.45.   5. The lesson finishes $\frac{3}{4}$ of an hour later.   6. What time will it be $\frac{3}{4}$ of an hour later?   7. It will be 10.30.   8. We have also a class from 10.30 till 11.15.   9. At what time do the lessons finish?   10. They finish at noon and the pupils go home. 11. What time is it now by your watch?   12. Is it not 10 o'clock sharp?   13. No, sir, your watch is slow. 14. What time is it by the school clock?   15. It is 10.10. 16. It is late, is it not?   17. The lesson will be finished in

half an hour.   18. By what train will you go to the country next Saturday?   19. We always leave by the 8.24 train. 20. Tell me why you leave so early?   21. Because if we miss that train, there is no train before 11.50.   22. I understand ; you do not want to arrive too late.

Exercice-revue

1. I was going.   2. We do go.   3. She was not going. 4. What do you want?   5. I do, I am doing.   6. I was doing, I used to do.   7. What was she doing?   8. Do it. 9. Don't do it.   10. Let us do it.   11. We used to say. 12. We shall not say.   13. We shall not do it.   14. We shall not put.   15. Does he know?   16. Will he know? 17. I see you.   18. No, you don't see me.   19. Take that.   20. I will take it.   21. She used to take it. 22. They take it.   23. Let us see.   24. Put that here.

*   *   *   *   *   *   *

46ᵉ Leçon : Dates. — Age. — Plus-que-parfait

C'est chercher une aiguille dans une botte de foin. – *It is like hunting for a needle in a haystack.*

Study the following expressions :

Quel jour du mois est-ce aujourd'hui ?	*What day of the*
Quel jour du mois sommes-nous aujourd'hui ?	*month is it to-day?*
Quel jour du mois avons-nous aujourd'hui ?	
C'est aujourd'hui le 11 mars.	*It is March 11th.*
C'était hier le dix.	*Yesterday was the 10th.*
Ce sera demain le douze.	*To-morrow will be the twelfth.*
Il y a huit jours.	*A week ago.*
Il y a quinze jours.	*A fortnight ago.*
D'aujourd'hui en huit.	*A week from to-day.*
D'aujourd'hui en quinze.	*A fortnight from to-day.*
De samedi en huit.	*A week from Saturday.*
De dimanche en quinze.	*A fortnight from Sunday.*

En (dans) quel mois?	*In what month?*
Au mois de septembre.	*In the month of September.*
En septembre.	*In September.*
Napoléon Premier (1er).	*Napoleon the First.*
Henri IV. Louis XIV.	*Henry the Fourth. Louis the Fourteenth.*

In dates and titles of sovereigns, cardinal numbers are used, except for the *first*.

Attention!   **C'est,** not **il est,** is used in dates.

Study the following sentence and compare the two languages :

Napoléon 1er est mort le 5 mars 1821.   *Napoleon the First died on the 5th of March, 1821.*

The English words *on* and *of* used with dates and *the* in titles are not translated in French.

Age. — In expressions denoting age, **avoir** is used in French instead of **être** in English.

Quel âge avez-vous?	*How old are you?*
J'ai vingt ans.	*I am twenty (years old).*
A l'âge de trente ans.	*At the age of 30.*
Elle est plus âgée que moi de [1] cinq ans.	*She is older than I by 5 years.*

Plus-que-parfait. — The pluperfect is formed with the imperfect of **avoir** (sometimes **être,** Lesson 28) and the past participle of the verb conjugated.

j'avais donné, *I had given.*	j'étais allé, *I had gone.*
j'avais fini, *I had finished.*	j'étais parti, *I had left.*
j'avais rendu, *I had given back.*	j'étais tombé, *I had fallen.*

j'avais eu, *I had had.*
j'avais été, *I had been.*

Emploi du plus-que-parfait. — The pluperfect is used to denote that a past action was entirely finished when another past action took place. It is used, like the English past perfect, to express what *had* happened.

J'avais fini ma lettre quand vous avez téléphoné.   *I had finished my letter when you telephoned.*

[1] In comparison, **de** is used instead of **que** before a number.   In this case **de** = *by* in English.

Ewing Galloway

L'Hôtel de Ville de Paris.

Vocabulaire

Pâques (f. pl.), *Easter*.
la fête de Pâques, *Easter holiday*.
la Noël, *Christmas*.
Je n'y manquerai pas. *I will not fail*.

même, *same*.
le calendrier, *the calendar*.
la fête, *the birthday, holiday*.
un jour de fête, *a holiday*.

Lecture

Conversation

Louise.   Quel jour du mois est-ce Pâques, cette année?

Jeanne.   Je ne sais pas, la fête de Pâques ne tombe pas le même jour tous les ans comme la Noël ; mais c'est toujours un dimanche.

Louise.   Je pense que c'est d'aujourd'hui en huit, c'est-à-dire dimanche prochain.

Jeanne.   Regardons le calendrier.   Non, c'est d'aujourd'hui en quinze.   Ce sera le 17 avril, cette année.

Louise.   C'était hier la fête de mon père, il est né le 3 avril.

Jeanne.   Quel âge a-t-il?

Louise.   Il a 43 ans.   Votre père est-il plus jeune que lui? En quel mois est-il né?

Jeanne.   Mon père a 41 ans, il est donc plus jeune que le vôtre de 2 ans.   Il est aussi né en avril.

Louise.   Savez-vous que ma tante est arrivée de Paris il y a huit jours?

Jeanne.   Non, je ne le savais pas.

Louise.   Si ; elle est arrivée le 29 mars, et dimanche en quinze nous partons avec elle à la campagne où elle a une jolie maison.

Jeanne.   Je ne savais pas qu'elle avait acheté une maison à la campagne.

Louise.   Si ; elle l'avait déjà achetée quand nous avons acheté la nôtre.

Jeanne.   N'est-ce pas un peu tôt pour aller à la campagne? il fait encore froid en avril.

Louise. Non, nous sommes aujourd'hui le 4 ; dimanche ce sera le 9 ; nous partirons donc dimanche le 24 ; il fera déjà chaud. Nous allons toujours à la campagne au mois d'avril. J'espère que vous passerez une semaine ou deux chez nous cet été.

Jeanne. Mais certainement, je n'y manquerai pas ; vous êtes trop aimable.

Exercices

A. *Questions sur la lecture :*

1. Quel jour tombe la Noël? 2. Quel jour était-ce hier? 3. Quel jour le père de Louise est-il né? 4. Quel âge a le père de Jeanne? 5. De combien est-il plus jeune que celui de Louise? 6. Quand la tante de Louise est-elle arrivée de Paris? 7. Quand part-elle à la campagne? 8. Quand avait-elle acheté une maison?

B. *Translate into French :*

1. What day of the month is it to-day? 2. What day of the month was it yesterday? 3. What day of the month will it be to-morrow? 4. What day of the month will it be a week from to-morrow? 5. What day of the month was it a week ago? 6. Yesterday (it) was my birthday. 7. Mine was a fortnight ago. 8. Next Wednesday is a holiday. 9. Where were you a week ago? 10. Where will you be a week from to-day? 11. In what month were you born? 12. Do you know in what month Louis XVI was born? 13. No, but I know when Napoleon the First died. 14. Was it in March? 15. Yes, it was on March the 5th, 1821. 16. Had you finished your exercises when Mary went to your house? 17. Yes, I had finished them. 18. In what month do you go to the country? 19. We will go in a fortnight from to-day. 20. My cousins (*f.*) went to the seashore a week ago. 21. How old are you? 22. I will be 16 to-morrow. 23. I was (*use past indef.*) 15 yesterday and

my little brother was 10 a fortnight ago. 24. I am 4 years older than he.

Exercice-revue

1. Is it at twelve o'clock that your train leaves? 2. Take your overcoat and muffler with you because it is cold. 3. I shall take neither overcoat nor muffler. 4. Which suitcase will you take, this one or that one? 5. Must I take one? 6. Some one rings [the bell]. 7. See who it is. 8. Who is it? 9. It is the tailor; he brought your blue suit. 10. Which suit? 11. The one I gave him last week. 12. That's all right, put it in that suitcase. 13. Who are these children whom I hear? 14. They are your nieces and nephews. 15. They came to say good-by to you. 16. Don't put my gloves there; I need them. 17. You never wear (porter) any. 18. Close that window, it is too windy here. 19. Do you need this? 20. Yes, put that in my suitcase too.

* * * * * * *

47ᵉ Leçon: CE QUI — CE QUE

Tout vient à point à qui sait attendre. — *Everything comes to him who waits.*

The demonstrative pronoun **ce** combined with the relative pronouns **qui** or **que** translates the English pronoun *what* when the latter means *that which*. In this locution **qui** and **que** follow the rules given in Lesson 22.

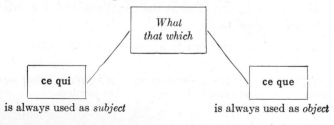

Study the following sentences :

Je vois *ce qui* est sur la table.	*I see what is on the table.*
Je vois *ce que* vous mettez sur la table.	*I see what you put on the table.*

In both cases, a whole clause is the object of the verb **je vois.** In the first sentence, *what* is the subject of the clause ; therefore, it must be translated by **ce qui.** In the second sentence, *you* is the subject of the clause, and *what* is the object ; therefore, it must be translated by **ce que.**

Other examples :

Ce qui est beau est agréable à regarder. *What is beautiful is agreeable to look at.*

Ce que vous dites est intéressant. *What you say is interesting.*

Dites-moi *ce qui* vous amuse. *Tell me what amuses you.*

Donnez-moi *ce que* vous avez. *Give me what you have.*

Donnez-moi *tout ce qui* est là. *Give me everything that is there.*

Donnez-moi *tout ce que* vous avez. *Give me all you have.*

Everything that or *all that* (*singular*) is expressed by **tout ce qui,** when *that* is subject, and by **tout ce que,** when *that* is object.

Study the following sentences :

Ce qui m'amuse, *c'est* ce joli tableau. *What amuses me is that beautiful picture.*

Ce qui m'intéresse, *c'est* ce qu'il dit. *What interests me is what he says.*

Notice that in these two examples, **ce** (**c'**) is used to repeat the preceding subject. This is the usual construction, when the subject is a clause.

Venir, *to come ;* participe passé, **venu,** *come*

Présent	Imparfait	Futur
je viens, *I come.*	**je venais,** *I was coming.*	**je viendrai,** *I shall come.*
tu viens.	**tu venais.**	**tu viendras.**
il vient.	**il venait.**	**il viendra.**

Présent	Imparfait	Futur
nous venons.	nous venions.	nous viendrons.
vous venez.	vous veniez.	vous viendrez.
ils viennent.	ils venaient.	ils viendront.

Impératif

SINGULIER   PLURIEL

viens, *come.*   venons, *let us come.*   venez, *come.*

Vocabulaire

le canotage, *boating.*
le canot, *row boat.*
protéger, *to protect.*
pour, *in order to* (+ infin.).
vouloir dire, *to mean.*
impatient, *impatient.*
ennuyer, *to annoy, to bother.*

le rendez-vous, *appointment.*
contre, *against.*
maintenir, *to maintain, to keep.*
l'équilibre, *the balance.*
facilement, *easily.*
peut-être, *perhaps, may be.*
la laine, *the wool.*

Lecture

PROJET DE PARTIE DE CANOTAGE

Jean.   Dites-moi ce que vous ferez demain.

Paul.   Je ferai tout ce que vous voudrez.

Jean.   Ce que je veux faire, c'est une partie de canotage.

Paul.   C'est entendu.   Je n'ai jamais fait de canotage et cela m'intéresse beaucoup.   Dites-moi ce que je dois prendre avec moi.

Jean.   Prenez simplement ce qui est nécessaire pour vous protéger contre le froid : votre sweater et votre casquette.

Paul.   Oh non ! pas mon sweater ; c'est un sweater de laine.

Jean. Mon ami, ce qui est en laine est chaud, et c'est ce que nous devons avoir quand nous reviendrons ; il sera déjà tard et il fera probablement froid.

Paul. Oh ! je comprends ce que vous voulez dire. Nous prendrons nos sweaters avec nous, mais nous ne les mettrons que quand nous aurons fini la partie de canotage.

Jean. A quelle heure partirons-nous ? Vers midi et demi, une heure ?

Paul. Voilà ce que je ne puis pas vous dire maintenant, car je ne sais pas exactement à quelle heure nous déjeunerons, et c'est ce qui m'ennuie.

Jean. Prenons rendez-vous pour deux heures alors.

Paul. Je pense que c'est ce qui sera le mieux. Je suis impatient de voir ce que je pourrai faire dans un canot.

Jean. Ce qui est le plus difficile, c'est de maintenir son équilibre, ce que vous ferez facilement si vous faites attention à tout ce que je vous dirai et à tout ce que je vous montrerai.

Paul. Alors, à demain à deux heures, peut-être avant.

Jean. C'est cela, je vous attendrai. A demain, au revoir !

Exercices

A. *Remplacez les tirets par le pronom* **ce qui** *ou* **ce que :**

1. Je sais ―― vous désirez. 2. Il ne comprend pas ―― vous dites. 3. Avez-vous vu ―― est sur la table? 4. Voici ―― m'intéresse. 5. Je veux savoir ―― vous avez fait hier. 6. Montrez-moi ―― est dans votre poche. 7. Montrez-moi ―― vous avez dans votre poche. 8. Répétez ―― vous avez dit. 9. ―― l'intéresse, ce n'est pas ―― vous dites, mais ―― vous faites. 10. Nous savons ―― vous amuse. 11. Avez-vous ―― je vous ai demandé? 12. ―― est fait est fait. 13. ―― vous racontez est très drôle, mais je ne comprends pas ―― vous voulez dire. 14. Savez-vous ―― c'est que cet objet? 15. Je ne comprends pas ―― vous ennuie.

B. *Traduisez en français:*

1. I know what you say. 2. All that I say is true.
3. What happens now was foreseen (*prévu*) twenty years
ago. 4. Tell me what you have heard. 5. He knows
what amuses you. 6. We know what you want. 7. They
lost everything that was in their pockets. 8. We lost all
that we had in our pockets. 9. We gave what we had.
10. What is in the book and what you say are two different
things. 11. Guess (*deviner*) what I received this morning.
12. I cannot guess what you have received. 13. I lost
what I had in my purse, and that annoys me. 14. What is
lost is lost, forget it. 15. Look at that box, do you know
what it is? 16. I do not know what you mean. 17. What
I mean is this : I cannot do what is impossible. 18. They
say she never says what she thinks. 19. All that interests
me in this house are these beautiful books. 20. Everything
that you say is interesting.

Exercice-revue

1. Had you already spoken to him when she came?
2. No, I had not seen him yet. 3. I am glad of it.
4. How old is that gentleman? 5. I do not know exactly
how old he is, but I think he must be 60. 6. At what time
will you go to Mr. Lenoir's house? 7. At a quarter of
eight, when we will be sure that they have finished their
dinner. 8. I think they will have finished their dinner at
that time. 9. That is not sure, let us go a little later.
10. Do you like this room better than that one? 11. No,
I like this one better. 12. I lost my purse and the theater
tickets, what do you think of that? 13. That is very sad.
14. Have you ever lost your money? 15. I never lose any
money because I never have any. 16. Conjugate : **j'en ai,
tu . . .,** etc. 17. Conjugate : **je n'en ai pas, tu . . .,** etc.
18. Conjugate : **en ai-je, . . .,** etc. 19. Conjugate : **n'en
ai-je pas, . . .,** etc. 20. Very well, I congratulate you.

48ᵉ Leçon : Conditionnel présent et passé

Si jeunesse savait, si vieillesse pouvait. — *If youth but knew, and age but could.*

Première conjugaison

Donner: je donner*ais*, *-rais*, *-rait*, *-rions*, *-riez*, *-raient*. *I should or would give,* etc. . . .

Deuxième conjugaison

Finir: je finir*ais*, *-rais*, *-rait*, *-rions*, *-riez*, *-raient*. *I should or would finish,* etc. . . .

Troisième conjugaison

Rendre: je rendr*ais*, *-rais*, *-rait*, *-rions*, *-riez*, *-raient*. *I would or should give back,* etc.

Formation. — The conditional is formed by adding to *the whole infinitive* the endings of the imperfect :

-ais, -ais, -ait, -ions, -iez, -aient,

which are the abbreviated forms of the imperfect of the auxiliary verb **avoir** (**j'avais, tu avais,** etc. See Lessons 25 and 27).

The **e** of the infinitive of the verbs of the 3d conjugation is dropped before the endings : **rendre, je rendrais.**

Attention! As in the future, there is always a " grrrowl " in the conditional.

Avoir	Être
j'aur*ais*, *I would or should have.*	je ser*ais*, *I should or would be.*
tu aur*ais*.	tu ser*ais*.
il aur*ait*.	il ser*ait*.
nous aur*ions*.	nous ser*ions*.
vous aur*iez*.	vous ser*iez*.
ils (elles) aur*aient*.	ils (elles) ser*aient*.

Conditionnel passé. —

j'aurais donné, *I should have given.*
j'aurais fini, *I should have finished.*
j'aurais rendu, *I should have given back.*

> *je serais* allé, *I should have gone.*
> *je serais* parti, *I should have left.*
> *je serais* entré, *I should have entered.*
>
> *j'aurais* eu, *I should have had.*
> *j'aurais* été, *I should have been.*

Formation et emploi. —

The past conditional is formed with the conditional of the auxiliary verb **avoir** (sometimes **être,** Lesson 28) and the past participle of the verb.

The conditional is used to translate the English *should* and *would,* and the conditional past to translate *should have* and *would have.*

Sequence of tenses in conditional sentences. — Study carefully the following examples :

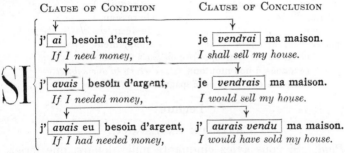

CLAUSE OF CONDITION	CLAUSE OF CONCLUSION
j' ai besoin d'argent,	je vendrai ma maison.
If I need money,	*I shall sell my house.*
j' avais besoin d'argent,	je vendrais ma maison.
If I needed money,	*I would sell my house.*
j' avais eu besoin d'argent,	j' aurais vendu ma maison.
If I had needed money,	*I would have sold my house.*

Conditional sentences have two clauses : a condition introduced by **si,** *if,* and a conclusion. Neither the future nor the conditional is used in clauses of condition or " *if* clauses." They are used *only* in the conclusion.

Therefore, our sequence of tenses will be the following :

Condition (*If*) { Present ⟶ Future / Imperfect ⟶ Conditional / Pluperfect ⟶ Conditional past } Conclusion

Attention! French conditions and conclusions are just like English except that *only three tenses* can be used after **si :**

the PRESENT, IMPERFECT, and PLUPERFECT, *no matter what tenses are used in English.*

In translations from English into French, when in doubt about the tense to use after **si,** as only three tenses can be used in French, proceed by elimination.

For instance : *If he would speak.* The verb *would speak* is not a present ; neither is it a pluperfect ; therefore, it can *only* be an imperfect, which is the sole tense left.

NOTE. *Si* becomes *s'* before the vowel **i.**

Vocabulaire

le château, *the castle.*	**placer,** *to place, to invest.*
tout d'abord, *at the very first.*	**la valeur,** *the security, value.*
un beau jour, *one fine day.*	**l'intérêt** (m.), *the interest.*
les affaires (f. pl.), *business.*	**pour cent,** *per cent.*
réussir, *to succeed.*	**vivre,** *to live.*
la mission, *the mission.*	**la rente,** ⎫ *the income.*
la poule, *the hen.*	**le revenu,** ⎭
dépenser, *to spend.*	**le désir,** *the desire, the wish.*
reparler, *to speak again.*	**simplement,** *simply.*

vivre de ses rentes, *to live on one's income.*
revenons à nos moutons, *let us return to our subject.*
faire des châteaux en Espagne, *to build castles in the air.*

Lecture

CHÂTEAUX EN ESPAGNE

Paul. Si vous aviez cinquante mille dollars, que feriez-vous?

Louis. Si j'avais cinquante mille dollars, je ferais beaucoup de choses ; tout d'abord, je visiterais Paris.

Paul. Mais vous ne parlez pas français, et si vous ne savez pas la langue, votre voyage ne sera pas du tout agréable.

Louis. C'est exact, mais si je vais en France, j'étudierai le français.

Paul. Oui, je sais, tout le monde dit cela. Mon frère a dit la même chose et un beau jour, son directeur l'a envoyé à Paris pour affaires. Il a dû partir tout de suite et il ne savait

pas un mot de français. Quand il est revenu il a dit : " Ah !
Si j'avais parlé français, mon voyage aurait été beaucoup plus
intéressant ! "

Louis. A-t-il réussi dans sa mission?

Paul. Oui et non ; mais il aurait mieux réussi s'il avait su
la langue du pays. Mais, revenons à nos moutons. Et alors,
après votre voyage à Paris?

Louis. Je visiterais l'Italie et les grandes villes d'Europe ;
j'achèterais beaucoup de souvenirs dans tous les pays où je
passerais. Je bâtirais ensuite une maison, j'aurais un grand
jardin, j'aurais des poules et des chiens ; j'achèterais une
automobile et je ferais de grandes promenades. Je passerais
l'hiver à la ville et l'été à la campagne.

Paul. Si vous faites tout cela, vos cinquante mille dollars
seront vite dépensés !

Louis. Et vous, comment agiriez-vous si vous receviez
cette somme d'argent?

Paul. Si j'avais cet argent, je le placerais en bonnes
valeurs qui me donneraient six ou sept pour cent d'intérêt,
et je vivrais de mes rentes.

Louis. Cela ferait $3000. Pourriez-vous vivre sans
travailler si vous aviez un revenu de $3000?

Paul. Oui, je pourrais vivre, si j'étais modeste dans mes
désirs.

Louis. Nous reparlerons de cela si nous avons jamais les
cinquante mille dollars, car pour le moment nous faisons
simplement des châteaux en Espagne.

Exercices

A. *Remplacez les infinitifs en italique par le temps convenable du verbe :*

1. Si je vais à la campagne, *aller*-vous avec moi?   2. Si
elle *avoir* le temps, elle finirait ses leçons.   3. Que *faire*-
vous s'il fait beau?   4. Que *faire*-vous s'il faisait beau?
5. Si elle reçoit ce livre, elle le *prêter* à son frère.   6. S'il

avait été ici à l'heure, il *voir* sa cousine.   7. Si nous travaillons bien nous *être* récompensés.   8. Si nous avions bien
étudié, nous *être* récompensés.   9. Nous serions heureux,
si nous *avoir* plus d'amis.   10. S'ils m'avaient écouté, ils
réussir.   11. Que *faire*-vous si vous étiez à [in] ma place?
12. Savez-vous ce que vous *faire*, si vous aviez été à ma place?
13. Je *faire* ce que vous avez fait.   14. Vous *aller* à la campagne s'il n'avait pas plu.   15. Si vous n'êtes pas à l'église
dimanche prochain où vous *trouver*-je?

B. *Traduisez en français :*

1. He will receive ; he would receive.   2. If he will sell ;
if he would sell ; if he sold ; if he sells ; if he were to sell.
3. If he has sold ; if he had sold.   4. We shall go ; we
should go.   5. If we go ; if we were to go.   6. She has
gone ; she had gone ; she will have gone ; she would have
gone.   7. If you see ; if you will see ; if you saw ; if you
had seen.   8. I shall do it, if you speak of it.   9. I should
do it, if you spoke of it.   10. I should have done it, if you
had spoken of it.   11. I will do it, if you will speak of it.
12. Would you do it, if I spoke of it?   13. Will you do it,
if I speak of it?   14. Would you not have done it, if I had
spoken of it?

Exercice-revue

1. Guess what I found?   2. I found a purse ; do you
know what is in that purse?   3. What is useful is not
always beautiful.   4. What is good is often expensive.
5. Look at that, isn't it pretty?   6. Look at this, it is still
prettier.   7. It is those ladies who are so rich.   8. Yes,
it is they.   9. They have their children with them.
10. Here are all the beautiful presents I have received.
11. They like you, that is why you always receive beautiful
presents for your birthday.   12. How old are you now?
When were you born?   13. I am 19, I was born on the
17th of August.   14. It is 2.20, I must leave now, I am late.

15. Take a taxi and you will arrive on time.   16. I am not sure of it.   17. Here are bonbons, take some.   18. No, thank you, I don't need any.   19. I do not like candy. 20. I did not know that you did not like them.   21. Goodby then, I will see you a week from to-day.

*   *   *   *   *   *   *

49ᵉ Leçon: Les pronoms relatifs LEQUEL, DONT, OÙ

Tout est bien, qui finit bien. — *All's well that ends well.*

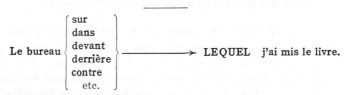

Le bureau { sur / dans / devant / derrière / contre / etc. } ⟶ LEQUEL j'ai mis le livre.

Observe the use of the relative pronoun in the following sentences:

(1) **Voici la table sur** *laquelle* **j'écris.** *Here is the table on which I write.*

(2) **Le crayon avec** *lequel* **j'ai écrit,** *the pencil with which I wrote.*

(3) **Voilà le garçon avec** *lequel* **je joue.** *There is the boy with whom I play.*

The relative pronoun which we translate by **qui** as subject and by **que** as object of a *verb* (Lesson 22) is expressed by **lequel** (**laquelle, lesquels, lesquelles**) for both persons and things when it is used as the object of a *preposition* (**avec, sur, par, dans, sans,** etc.).

de + lequel = **duquel, de laquelle, desquels, desquelles,** *of which.*
à + lequel = **auquel, à laquelle, auxquels, auxquelles,** *to which.*

Dont. — The relative pronoun **dont** is a substitute for **duquel, de laquelle, desquels,** and **desquelles** for persons and things and is generally used by the French, as it is short and invariable.

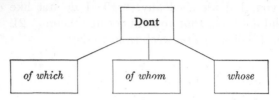

(1) **Apportez-moi le livre *dont* je parle.** *Bring me the book of which I speak.*

(2) **Voici les hommes *dont* vous parliez.** *Here are the men of whom you were speaking.*

(3) **La femme *dont* j'ai vu le fils,** *the woman whose son I saw.*

Attention! Note the order of the words in Example 3. When expressed in French, *the woman whose son I saw* should be changed to *the woman of whom I saw the son.* In other words, the object, in a relative clause introduced by **dont,** *must be placed after the verb*, and not before as in English.

Study the following example :

La femme du fils de laquelle (de qui) nous parlions, *the woman of whose son we were speaking.*

If the object possessed is dependent upon a preposition, then **duquel, de laquelle,** etc., or **de qui** (*persons only*), must be used instead of **dont,** which never follows a preposition.

Instead of **dans lequel, dans laquelle,** etc., **auquel, à laquelle,** etc., meaning *in which, to which*, the French use indifferently **où,** *where*, which, in this case, is considered a relative pronoun.

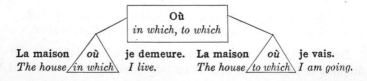

Lire, *to read;* participe passé, **lu,** *read*

Présent	Imparfait	Futur
je lis, *I read.*	je lisais, *I was reading.*	je lirai, *I shall read*
tu lis.	tu lisais.	tu liras.
il lit.	il lisait.	il lira.
nous lisons.	nous lisions.	nous lirons.
vous lisez.	vous lisiez.	vous lirez.
ils lisent.	ils lisaient.	ils liront.

Impératif

Singulier	Pluriel	
lis, *read.*	lisons, *let us read.*	lisez, *read.*

Vocabulaire

rêver, *to dream.*
entendre parler, *to hear.*
former, *to form.*
le cercle, *the circle.*
parfait, *perfect.*
l'île (f.), *the island.*
fameux, *famous.*
la pointe, *the point.*
monter, *to ascend.*
aisément, *easily.*
le toit, *the roof.*

le point de repère, *landmark.*
l'endroit (m.), *the place, the spot.*
le nord, *the north.*
le sud, *the south.*
l'est (ess-t), *the east.*
l'ouest (oo-west), *the west.*
le pas, *the step.*
le chef-d'œuvre (sheh), *the masterpiece.*
notamment, *namely.*
partout, *everywhere.*
le chemin, *the way.*

Lecture

Une promenade dans Paris

Robert.   Voilà enfin ce beau Paris dont j'ai tant lu, dont j'ai tant rêvé, dont j'ai tant entendu parler, et où je suis content d'être maintenant.

Charles.   C'est en effet une ville dont on parle beaucoup et sur laquelle on a beaucoup écrit.

Robert.   C'est aussi une ville où l'on doit se perdre (*get lost*) aisément.

Charles.   Non ; Paris forme presque un cercle parfait dont l'Île de la Cité est le centre et sur laquelle est bâtie la fameuse église de Notre-Dame. La Tour Eiffel dont vous voyez la pointe d'ici, et où nous monterons demain, est votre point de repère ouest.

Robert. Où sommes-nous maintenant?

Charles. Nous sommes près de la Rue de Rivoli, par laquelle on arrive à la Place de la Bastille qui est le point de repère est (*esst*). Au nord, vous avez Montmartre, dont l'Eglise du Sacré-Cœur est fameuse, et au sud, l'Observatoire et le Jardin du Luxembourg, dont vous admirerez la beauté demain.

Robert. Où est la Place de la Concorde au milieu de laquelle il y a l'Obélisque?

Charles. A deux pas d'ici, près du Louvre, où sont les plus beaux chefs-d'œuvre du monde, notamment la Joconde et la Venus de Milo dont vous avez vu des reproductions partout. C'est l'ancien palais des rois de France, dont vous voyez le toit et devant la façade duquel sont les beaux jardins des Tuileries.

Robert. Et moi qui n'ai qu'une semaine pour voir toutes ces belles choses dont vous parlez !

Exercices

A. *Remplacez les tirets par un pronom relatif convenable :*

1. Connaissez-vous cet homme —— arrive? 2. Le livre —— vous lisez est-il intéressant? 3. Donnez-moi la plume avec —— vous avez écrit votre lettre. 4. Voulez-vous me montrer le cadeau —— vous avez reçu et —— vous m'avez parlé hier? 5. La maison dans —— vous demeurez, est très grande. 6. Qui est la dame à —— vous avez donné des fleurs? 7. La dame —— vous avez trouvé le sac n'est plus ici. 8. Voici le papier —— j'ai besoin. 9. Voilà la fenêtre par —— on est entré dans notre appartement. 10. Nous voici dans le parc au milieu —— il y a un petit lac. 11. Où est la maison —— vous êtes né? 12. Avez-vous vu le jardin à l'entrée —— il y a cette belle statue ?

LA PORTE ST. DENIS À PARIS.

B. *Traduisez en français :*

1. The table upon which you will see your letters and news-papers is in the little blue room.   2. Show me the books of which you spoke to my sister.   3. When I was in New York, I used often to see the man of whom you are speaking.
4. The ladies whom you saw yesterday are here to-day.
5. Tell me, please, the name of the city in which you lived two years ago?   6. Of what church are you speaking?
7. I am speaking of the one the roof of which we see from this window.   8. Here is the little boy with whom I used to play when he lived near our house.   9. Is he the one of whom you were speaking a few minutes ago?   10. Here is the man whose daughter and niece arrived yesterday.
11. The lady to whose son I gave my French book is my mother's friend.   12. The man with whom you saw me this morning was my tailor.   13. Is he the tailor of whom you spoke to me yesterday?   14. Yes, he is the one.

Exercice-revue

1. I see you.   2. I see them.   3. Do you see me?
Do you see them?   4. Have you seen us?   Have you seen them?   5. Will you see him?   Will you not see her?
6. Do you not want to see her?   7. Have you seen them?
Had you seen them?   8. Shall I see you?   Shall we see them also?   9. If I could, I should finish this book to-day.
10. What will you do, if it rains?   11. If the weather is fine, we shall take a walk.   12. What would you have done if it had rained?   13. What would you do if it rained?
14. What time will it be when you have finished your lessons?   15. I will have finished them at 9.45, in about three quarters of an hour.   16. I do not see what is so difficult in these lessons.   17. You do not know what I mean.   18. I understand what annoys you.   19. No, I think you do not understand what I say.   20. He knows what is good, but he always does what he should (must) not do.

50ᵉ Leçon : Les pronoms interrogatifs QUI (*who, whom, whose*), QUE et QUOI

Un malheur ne vient jamais seul. — *Misfortunes never come singly.*

Study the following graphs :

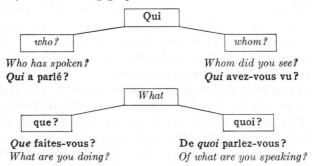

| Qui |
| who? | whom? |

Who has spoken?
Qui a parlé?

Whom did you see?
Qui avez-vous vu?

| What |
| que? | quoi? |

Que faites-vous?
What are you doing?

De *quoi* parlez-vous?
Of what are you speaking?

Interrogative pronouns. — (1) The English interrogative *who, whom* is the French **qui,** the same form for both subject and object.

Qui va là?   *Who goes there?*
Qui avez-vous vu?   *Whom did you see?*
De qui parlez-vous?   *Of whom are you speaking?*

Whose is expressed by **à qui,** *to whom,* and the verb **être.**

Whose house is this?   **A qui est cette maison?**

(2) The interrogative *what* is **que** or more commonly **qu'est-ce que** with verbs, **quoi** with prepositions.

What are you doing? **Que faites-vous?** or Qu'est-ce que vous faites?
Of what are you speaking? **De quoi parlez-vous?**

Il n'y a pas de *quoi* (remercier). { Lit., *There is not of what (to thank).*
Don't mention it, you are welcome.

is an expression used in reply to thanks.   We also say :

Ce n'est pas la peine or **De rien, monsieur (madame, mademoiselle).**

Vocabulaire

quoi de nouveau, *what is the news?*
l'ombrelle (f.), *the parasol.*
neuf, neuve, *new* (never used).
la loge, *the box* (in a theater).
reconnaître, *to recognize.*
poser une question, *to ask a question.*

projeter, *to plan.*
prendre, *to take, to fetch, to call for.*
vous serez des nôtres, *you will be among us.*
passer prendre, *to call and fetch.*
nécessaire, *necessary.*
suivant, *following.*

de tout mon cœur, *with all my heart.*

Lecture

CONVERSATION

Jeanne. Qui est là? Entrez!... Louise! Quelle bonne surprise! Comment allez-vous? Quoi de nouveau?

Louise. Je passais dans votre rue, et alors j'ai pensé: " Tiens, je vais aller dire un petit bonjour à Jeanne!" Et me voici!

Jeanne. C'est charmant, je vous aime de tout mon cœur!

A QUI EST CETTE JOLIE OMBRELLE?

Louise. Oh! A qui est cette jolie ombrelle?

Jeanne. C'est celle de ma sœur.

Louise. Et à qui sont ces beaux souliers neufs?

Jeanne. Ce sont les miens. A propos, qui était dans votre loge hier au théâtre?

Louise. Que me demandez-vous là? C'était mon frère.

Jeanne. Est-ce possible ! Je ne l'ai pas reconnu.

Louise. Qui pensiez-vous que c'était ?

Jeanne. Je ne sais pas, c'est pourquoi je vous ai posé cette question.

Louise. Qu'avez-vous fait avant-hier chez les Durant ? Qui était là ? Avec qui avez-vous dansé ? De quoi a-t-on parlé ?

Jeanne. J'ai oublié de quoi on a parlé. Oh, oui ! On a projeté une excursion pour samedi prochain ; vous serez des nôtres, naturellement.

Louise. Chez qui a-t-on pris rendez-vous ?

Jeanne. Ce ne sera pas nécessaire, on passera nous prendre chez nous.

Louise. Qui passera ?

Jeanne. Nous aurons deux automobiles.

Louise. A qui sont ces autos ? De qui parlez-vous ?

Jeanne. De Paul et de Charles.

Louise. Et s'il pleut ? Qu'est-ce qu'on fera ?

Jeanne. S'il pleut, la partie sera remise à la semaine suivante.

Louise. Maintenant, je rentre chez moi, il est déjà tard.

Jeanne. Au revoir, chère amie, et merci de votre bonne visite.

Louise. Il n'y a pas de quoi. Au plaisir.

Exercices

A. *Remplacez les tirets par le pronom interrogatif :*

1. —— êtes-vous ?   2. —— faites-vous ?   3. A —— parliez-vous ?   4. De —— parlez-vous ?   5. Sur —— écrivez-vous ?   6. Avec —— allez-vous à l'opéra ?   7. A —— est cette jolie robe ?   8. Sans —— ne peut-on pas vivre ?   9. Pour —— travaillez-vous ?   10. —— avez-vous grondé ?   11. —— ont-ils mangé ?   12. A —— sont ces gentils enfants ?

B. *Traduisez en français :*

1. Whom do you want to see?   2. To whom do you want to speak?   3. What do you want to say?   4. What do you mean?   5. Who is that lady?   6. You want something, what [is it]?   7. Whose suit is this?   8. Whose suits are those?   9. Here is a beautiful bracelet, whose is it?   10. From whom did you buy it?   11. Who bought it for [to] you?   12. At whose house shall we spend the evening next Sunday?   13. Who is the richest man in town?   14. Whom are you looking at?   15. What are you looking at?   16. What do you need?   17. What are you afraid of?   18. Whom are you looking for?   19. What are you looking for?   20. Don't mention it.

Exercice-revue

1. Here is the book which I need.   2. This one?   3. The one on the cover[1] of which I wrote my name.   4. What is the name of the little girl to whom you spoke and with whom you often play?   5. I will give you that money if you need it.   6. I would give you that money if you needed it. 7. I should have given you that money, if you had needed it.   8. I never receive what I want.   9. When a man has not what he likes, he must like what he has.   10. I don't understand what you mean.   11. What a nice little boy! How old is he?   12. Is he only seven?   13. I must go home now ; what time is it?   14. Listen to this. 15. What do you think of that?   16. The weather is not good to-day, we will stay home.   17. What kind of weather will it be to-morrow?   18. I do not know, but I think it will rain.   19. If it rains, we will not go to my aunt's. 20. If the weather had been fine, we would have gone to the seashore.

---

[1] cover, *la couverture.*

51ᵉ Leçon: Pronoms interrogatifs (*suite*). LEQUEL

Il n'est pire eau que l'eau qui dort. — *Still waters run deep.*

Study the following graph :

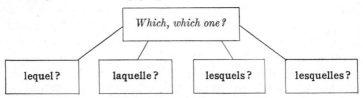

de + lequel = duquel, de laquelle, desquels, desquelles, *of which?*
à + lequel = auquel, à laquelle, auxquels, auxquelles, *to which?*

Attention! Do not confuse the interrogative pronoun **lequel**, *which*, with the interrogative adjective **quel**, *what* (Lesson 42).   **Quel** is always *immediately followed by a noun*; **lequel** is *never* IMMEDIATELY *followed by a noun.*

Quel livre voulez-vous?   WHAT BOOK *do you want?*

Lequel de ces livres voulez-vous?   *Which* of those *books do you want?*

Note. — Notice that as in the case of possessive pronouns (**le mien,** etc.) the article is a part of the interrogative pronoun and contracts with **de** and **à,** when these prepositions precede.

Écrire, *to write;* participe passé, **écrit,** *written*

PRÉSENT	IMPARFAIT	FUTUR
j'écris, *I write.*	j'écrivais, *I was writing.*	j'écrirai, *I shall write.*
tu écris.	tu écrivais.	tu écriras.
il écrit.	il écrivait.	il écrira.
nous écrivons.	nous écrivions.	nous écrirons.
vous écrivez.	vous écriviez.	vous écrirez.
ils écrivent.	ils écrivaient.	ils écriront.

IMPÉRATIF

SINGULIER	PLURIEL	
écris, *write.*	écrivons, *let us write.*	écrivez, *write.*

Vocabulaire

la modiste, *the milliner.*
décider, *to decide.*
le plancher, *the floor.*
d'abord, *first.*

le bal, *the ball.*
le gouverneur, *the governor.*
prêt, *ready.*
ouvrir, *to open.*

Lecture

Conversation

La bonne. Laquelle de vos robes mettrez-vous, mademoiselle?

Suzanne. Ma robe bleue, Marie.

La bonne. La voici.

Suzanne. Mettez-la sur la chaise. La modiste a-t-elle apporté mes deux chapeaux?

La bonne. Oui, mademoiselle; lequel voulez-vous?

Suzanne. Lequel? Le noir, je pense, il ira bien avec ma robe.

La bonne. Avez-vous décidé quels souliers vous porterez?

Suzanne. Lesquels sont les plus légers, les bruns ou les noirs?

La bonne. Si j'étais à votre place, je mettrais mes gris.

Suzanne. Oui, c'est une bonne idée. Où sont mes gants?

La bonne. Lesquels?

Suzanne. Les gris, naturellement, si je mets mes souliers gris.

La bonne. Dans laquelle de ces boîtes les avez-vous mis; dans la boîte rouge?

Suzanne. Oh! Je pense que j'ai perdu mon bracelet!

La bonne. Duquel parlez-vous? De votre bracelet d'or?

Suzanne. Ah! Non; le voici sur le plancher. Quelle émotion j'ai eue!

La bonne. Auxquelles de vos amies devez-vous téléphoner?

Suzanne. Je dois téléphoner à Jeanne et à Marie.

La bonne. Je vais demander la communication. A laquelle voulez-vous téléphoner d'abord?

Suzanne. Je vais téléphoner à Marie.

La bonne. Auquel des bals où vous êtes allée dernière-ment, avez-vous vu les plus jolies robes?

Suzanne. Au bal du gouverneur.

La bonne. Voilà mesdemoiselles Laurent qui viennent vous chercher, et vous n'êtes pas encore prête!

Suzanne. Allez ouvrir et dites-leur que je serai prête dans cinq minutes.

Exercices

A. *Remplacez les tirets par un pronom ou par un adjectif interrogatif:*

1. —— de ces jeunes filles est votre cousine? 2. —— parlez-vous? 3. —— robe avez-vous choisie? 4. Voici trois chapeaux, —— prenez-vous? 5. —— de ces dames avez-vous reçu une invitation? 6. —— dames? 7. —— de ces messieurs devez-vous de l'argent? 8. Tous les gar-çons sont ici, —— des filles sont absentes? 9. Voici plu-sieurs plumes, —— est à vous? 10. —— sont à Jean?

B. *Mettez au pluriel:*

1. Lequel de ces garçons est votre ami? 2. Auquel avez-vous donné votre balle? 3. De laquelle de ces petites filles êtes-vous l'amie? 4. Laquelle est la plus jeune? 5. A laquelle donnez-vous des bonbons?

C. *Traduisez en français:*

1. Which pupils are standing? 2. Which are seated? 3. Of which book are you speaking? 4. Of which of those books are you speaking? 5. Which are the best? 6. Which one is the best? 7. Which of these pictures do you like the best? 8. Which of the animals are the most useful to man? 9. Which of the pupils have finished their exercises? 10. Which of these newspapers have you read?

11. Which one do you want? 12. Which newspaper do you want? 13. In which of these drawers did you put the jewels? 14. Which ones? 15. Which of your lessons is the easiest? 16. Which is the most difficult? 17. Which lesson is the shortest?

Exercice-revue

1. What do you want? I do not know what you want. 2. Whose house is this? 3. Which house? 4. The one in front of which we are now. 5. Here is the park in which we take a walk every morning. 6. Where is the overcoat of which you spoke yesterday? 7. What? Which overcoat? 8. The one you had last week. 9. What book were you reading when I came in? 10. Do you read every day? 11. No, but if I could, I would read [for] one hour every evening. 12. Will you come to my house to-morrow at 2.30, if it is not too cold? 13. I would have gone yesterday if it had not rained. 14. Who will also come? 15. What shall we do? 16. We will make a little music, and Paul will read aloud, you know that he reads very well. 17. By the way, when is he leaving? 18. He will leave a fortnight from to-morrow. 19. He is a good boy, I like him. 20. Everybody likes him.

Une anecdote

MONSIEUR BONJOUR

Le professeur. Mes petits amis, vous avez bien travaillé ; vous méritez une récompense. Je vais vous raconter une petite anecdote.

Monsieur Bonjour, candidat à l'Académie Française, décide un jour de faire visite à quelques (*a few*) académiciens pour préparer sa candidature et savoir approximativement sur combien de voix (*votes*) il pouvait compter.

Il arrive donc à la porte d'un des Quarante et sonne.

Un élève.   Pardon, professeur, " un des Quarante," je ne comprends pas.

Le professeur.   Oui, c'est vrai ; voici : il y a quarante académiciens à l'Académie Française, et souvent ils sont désignés sous la dénomination " Les Quarante."

L'élève.   Merci, monsieur, je comprends maintenant.

Le professeur.   Donc (*so*) monsieur Bonjour sonne.   Une bonne ouvre la porte.

— Votre nom, monsieur ? demande-t-elle.

— Bonjour.

Flattée de cette politesse, la jeune fille répond :

— Bonjour, monsieur ; voulez-vous me dire votre nom ?

BONJOUR MONSIEUR ; QUI DOIS-JE ANNONCER ?

— Je vous dis Bonjour.

— Et moi aussi ; bonjour, monsieur.   Qui dois-je annoncer ?

— Mais Bonjour ; mon nom est Bonjour.

La bonne comprend alors qu'au lieu de (*instead of*) dire " Bonjour monsieur " elle devait dire (*she should say*) " Monsieur Bonjour."

*   *   *   *   *   *   *

52ᵉ Leçon : Idiotismes avec AVOIR

Mon petit doigt me l'a dit. — *A little bird told me.*

The following idioms have **avoir** in French where the verb *to be* is used in English.

avoir chaud, *to be warm.*	avoir soif, *to be thirsty.*
avoir froid, *to be cold.*	avoir sommeil, *to be sleepy.*
avoir faim, *to be hungry.*	avoir honte, *to be ashamed.*
avoir peur, *to be afraid.*	avoir besoin (de), *to need.*
avoir raison, *to be right.*	avoir l'intention (de), *to intend.*
avoir tort, *to be wrong.*	avoir mal à, *to have a pain in, to ache.*

In these expressions **bien** is generally used for *very* or *quite :* **vous avez bien raison, il a bien peur.**

With **mal, froid,** and **chaud,** the person spoken of is made the subject of **avoir.**

Il a mal au bras.	*His arm is sore,* or *aches.*
J'ai bien froid aux mains.	*My hands are very cold.*

Recall the idiomatic use of **avoir** in asking or stating a person's age (Lesson 46).

Quel âge a-t-il ? *How old is he?*
Il a trente ans, et son frère en a vingt-cinq. *He is thirty, and his brother is twenty-five.*

In speaking of parts of the body, the definite article is ordinarily used for *my, his, her,* etc., if the possessor is the subject of the sentence.

Il a le bras cassé.	*His arm is broken.*
Elle a les yeux bleus.	*She has blue eyes.*
Montrez-moi la main droite.	*Show me your right hand.*

Note the following idioms :

Qu'avez-vous ?	*What is the matter with you?*
Je n'ai rien.	*Nothing is the matter with me.*
Il a quelque chose.	*Something ails him.*
Qu'y a-t-il ?	*What is the matter?*
Il n'y a rien.	*There is nothing the matter.*
N'importe.	*No matter, never mind.*

Croire, *to believe;* participe passé, **cru,** *believed*

PRÉSENT	IMPARFAIT	FUTUR
je crois, *I believe.*	je croyais, *I was believing.*	je croirai, *I shall believe*
tu crois.	tu croyais.	tu croiras.
il croit.	il croyait.	il croira.
nous croyons.	nous croyions.	nous croirons.
vous croyez.	vous croyiez.	vous croirez.
ils croient.	ils croyaient.	ils croiront.

IMPÉRATIF

SINGULIER	PLURIEL	
crois, *believe.*	croyons, *let us believe.*	croyez, *believe.*

Vocabulaire

le corps, *the body.*
la tête, *the head.*
la figure, } *the face.*
le visage, }
la bouche, *the mouth.*
la lèvre, *the lip.*
la langue, *the tongue.*
la dent, *the tooth.*
la gorge, *the throat.*
le cou, *the neck.*
l'épaule (f.), *the shoulder.*
la poitrine, *the chest.*
le cœur, *the heart*
partout, *everywhere.*
en un mot, *in short.*
car, *for.*

le dos, *the back.*
le bras, *the arm.*
le coude, *the elbow.*
le poignet, *the wrist.*
la main, *the hand.*
l'oreille (f.), *the ear.*
l'œil (m.), *the eye.*
le menton, *the chin.*
le doigt, *the finger.*
le pouce, *the thumb.*
la jambe, *the leg.*
le genou, *the knee.*
le pied, *the foot.*
remettre, *postpone.*
guéri, *cured.*
une dizaine de, *about ten*

Lecture

CHEZ LE MÉDECIN

Le médecin. Voyons, qu'avez-vous?
Le malade. Docteur, j'ai mal partout.
Le médecin. Comment partout!
Le malade. Oui; j'ai mal à la tête, j'ai mal aux bras, aux jambes, au dos, aux épaules, à la poitrine, en un mot dans

tout le corps. Ce n'est pas tout. Un moment j'ai chaud,
deux minutes après, j'ai froid, je suis sûr que j'ai quelque
chose.

Le médecin. Avez-vous bon appétit?

Le malade. Non, je n'ai pas faim, mais j'ai souvent soif
et j'ai toujours sommeil.

Le médecin. Avez-vous aussi mal à la gorge?

Le malade. Non, mais j'ai quelquefois mal au cœur.

Le médecin. Et les articulations, le coude, le poignet, les
genoux?

Le malade. J'ai surtout mal aux pieds et au cou.

Le médecin. Montrez-moi la langue; donnez-moi la
main; oui, c'est cela. . . .

Le malade. Qu'y a-t-il?

Le médecin. Il n'y a rien, vous avez l'influenza, c'est tout.
Ouvrez la bouche; n'avez-vous pas souvent mal aux dents?

Le malade. Si, docteur, vous avez raison.

Le médecin. Vous n'allez pas assez souvent chez le dentiste et vous avez tort.

Le malade. J'ai souvent l'intention d'aller le voir, mais je
remets toujours ma visite; j'en ai honte maintenant.

Le médecin. Allez le voir quand vous serez guéri. Je
vais vous donner une ordonnance; vous resterez chez vous
pendant une dizaine de jours. La semaine prochaine, je
passerai vous voir; tout me porte (*leads me*) à croire que vous
irez déjà beaucoup mieux.

Le malade. C'est entendu, docteur, à la semaine prochaine.

Exercices

A. *Transposez:* (1) *à l'imparfait,* (2) *au passé indéfini,*
(3) *au plus-que-parfait,* (4) *au futur et* (5) *au conditionnel:*

1. Je n'ai pas trop chaud.   2. N'avez-vous pas froid?
3. Elle a mal à l'œil.   4. Nous n'avons jamais mal aux
yeux.   5. Il en a l'intention.   6. A-t-elle tort?   7. N'avez-

vous pas faim?   8. N'en ont-ils pas honte?   9. Je n'ai
plus soif.   10. Nous avons sommeil.

B. *Traduisez en français:*

1. Are you not too cold so near the window?   2. I was
cold half an hour ago, but now I am too warm.   3. You
are sleepy, are you not?   4. No, but my eyes hurt me.
5. She has a headache.   6. You are hungry perhaps?
7. No, but I am very thirsty.   8. Am I right or wrong?
9. You are always right.   10. Has John a toothache?
11. No, he has a sore throat, he intends to go to the doctor.
12. He is right.   13. What is the matter with her?   Can't
she walk (*marcher*)?   14. No, she fell, and she has a sore
foot.   15. Is it too cold here?   Are your feet cold?
16. Yes, and my ears are cold too.   17. Give me your
hand.   18. What is the matter with you?   19. Nothing
is the matter with me.   20. Nothing is the matter with
her.   21. Nothing is the matter with us.   22. Tell me,
what is the matter with them?   23. What is the matter?
24. Nothing is the matter.   25. No matter.

C. *Traduisez et répondez:*

1. Name ten parts of the head.   2. What have you in
your mouth?   3. Where is your heart?   4. Name two
parts of the hand.   5. What color is your hair?   6. Have
you blue eyes?   7. Show me both hands.

Exercice-revue

1. Which of the metals are the most expensive?   2. Tell
me which.   3. To which of these tailors do you owe 50
dollars?   4. I shall receive my new suit a week from to-day.
5. I will tell you something, listen to this.   6. I do not see
what you find funny in that story.   7. You did not understand what I told you.   8. Will you write to your brother
if I give you my pen?   9. My mother writes him every
week, every Wednesday.   10. How old is he now?   11. He

La Galerie des Glaces du Palais de Versailles.
Le Palais de Versailles; le tapis vert et la fontaine de Neptune.

will be 17 next month.   12. When he is 20, he will come back home.   13. Who are those children who are looking at us?   14. They are our neighbor's.   15. What beautiful children!   16. You have never seen them before?   17. Look out! The chair on which you are seated is broken (*cassée*).   18. What day of the month is it to-day?   19. It is Thursday the 11th.   20. I must go, I have made an appointment with my lawyer, I had forgotten it.

*   *   *   *   *   *   *

53ᵉ Leçon: Les pronoms interrogatifs: QUI EST–CE QUI, QU'EST–CE QUI, etc.

Tel qui rit vendredi, dimanche pleurera. — *Who laughs Friday, will cry Sunday.*

Study the following graph:

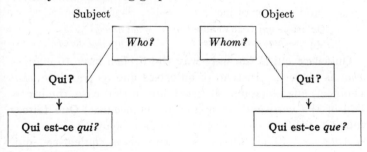

The interrogative pronoun **qui** translates equally the English *who* and *whom*.

  Qui parle si haut? *Who is speaking so loud?*
  Qui voulez-vous voir? *Whom do you want to see?*

Very often, however, especially in conversation, the French use an idiom with **est-ce.** In this case, *who* is translated by **qui est-ce qui,** and *whom* by **qui est-ce que,** the nominative and objective cases being indicated by the *last* relative pronoun ; **qui** for subject and **que** for object (see Lesson 22).

Qui est-ce *qui* parle si haut ?	*Who speaks so loud?*
Qui est-ce *que* vous voulez voir ?	*Whom do you want to see?*

Attention! The pronoun **qui** (subject and object) and the idiomatic expressions **qui est-ce qui** and **qui est-ce que** refer to *persons only.*

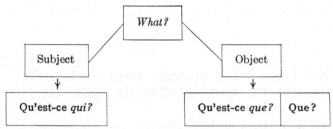

The interrogative pronoun *what* is translated in French by **qu'est-ce qui** when subject and by **qu'est-ce que** when object. Here too, the case is indicated by the last pronoun : **qui** for subject and **que** for object :

Qu'est-ce *qui* vous ennuie ?	*What annoys you?*
Qu'est-ce *que* vous faites ?	*What are you doing?*

Qu'est-ce qui is the only way the French have to express *what* as subject. Instead of **qu'est-ce que** to translate *what* as object, **que** alone may be used, but in that case, the inversion of the verb and pronoun subject occurs. **Que faites-vous?** *What are you doing?* (See note below.)

Attention! The idiomatic expressions **qu'est-ce qui, qu'est-ce que,** and **que** are used for *things only.*

Note. — When **qu'est-ce que** or **qui est-ce que** is used to make a question, the verb and pronoun are not inverted.

Qu'est-ce que vous faites ?	*What are you doing?*
Qui est-ce que vous voulez voir ?	*Whom do you wish to see?*

When the corresponding **que** or **qui** is used, inversion occurs.

Que faites-vous ?
Qui voulez-vous voir ?

Observe also the following expressions :

Qu'est-ce que c'est ?	*What is it?*
Qu'est-ce que c'est que ceci ?	*What is this?*
Qu'est-ce que c'est que cela ?	*What is that?*
Qu'est-ce que c'est qu'une périphrase ?	*What is a paraphrase?*

Ouvrir, *to open;* participe passé, **ouvert,** *open*

PRÉSENT	IMPARFAIT	FUTUR
j'ouvre, *I open.*	j'ouvrais, *I was opening.*	j'ouvrirai, *I shall open.*
tu ouvres.	tu ouvrais.	tu ouvriras.
il ouvre.	il ouvrait.	il ouvrira.
nous ouvrons.	nous ouvrions.	nous ouvrirons.
vous ouvrez.	vous ouvriez.	vous ouvrirez.
ils ouvrent.	ils ouvraient.	ils ouvriront.

IMPÉRATIF

SINGULIER	PLURIEL	
ouvre, *open.*	ouvrons, *let us open.*	ouvrez, *open.*

Vocabulaire

faire entrer, *to show in.*	courir après, *to run after.*
justement, *precisely.*	par terre, *on the ground or floor.*
monter, *to mount.*	laisser tomber, *to drop.*
le buffet, *the cupboard.*	penser à, *to think of.*
le manteau, *the lady's coat.*	penser de, *to think of* (opinion).
envoyer, *to send.*	pleurer, *to cry, to weep.*
arriver, *to happen*	seul(e), *alone.*

Difference between *penser de* **and** *penser à.* — Both expressions are translated in English by *to think of.*

When *to think of* means *to have an opinion,* it is expressed in French by **penser de,** in other words, it is translated literally (Example 3).

When *to think of* means *to have in mind, to think about, to consider,* it is expressed by **penser à.** The French in that case say : *to think to* (Examples 1 and 2).

(1) *A* quoi pensez-vous ?	*What are you thinking about?*
(2) Je pense *à* mon ami Jean.	*I think of my friend John.*
(3) Que pensez-vous *de* lui ?	*What do you think of him?*

Lecture

CONVERSATION

Louise.   Qui est-ce qui sonne?

Jeanne.   Je ne sais pas, je vais voir.

Louise.   Qu'est-ce que c'est?

Jeanne.   C'est le petit garçon de la voisine.

Louise.   Je pensais justement à lui; qu'est-ce qu'il veut?

Jeanne.   Je ne sais pas, je lui ai demandé : " Qui est-ce que vous désirez voir? " et il ne répond pas ; il pleure.

ELLE ÉTAIT MONTÉE SUR UNE CHAISE . . . . .

Louise.   Faites-le entrer.

Henri.   Bonjour, madame.

Louise.   Eh bien! Henri, qu'est-ce qu'il y a? Qu'est-ce que vous avez? Pourquoi pleurez-vous? Qu'est-ce qui est arrivé?

Henri.   Ma petite sœur est tombée.

Louise.   Comment est-elle tombée? Qu'est-ce qu'elle faisait?

Henri.   Elle était montée sur une chaise pour prendre quelque chose dans le buffet ; elle a perdu l'équilibre et est tombée par terre.

Louise.   Qui est-ce qui était dans la maison?

Henri.   J'étais seul, maman est sortie et papa n'est pas encore rentré.

Louise.   Qu'est-ce que vous avez fait?

Henri. J'ai eu peur et je suis vite venu ici. Qu'est-ce que nous allons faire?

Louise. Qu'est ce que vous pensez de cela! Je vais aller chez vous. Marie, donnez-moi mon manteau. Qui est-ce qui passe de l'autre côté de la rue? N'est-ce pas le Docteur Lebon?

Marie. Si, c'est lui.

Louise. C'est la Providence qui l'envoie. Henri, courez vite après lui et dites-lui de venir; moi, je vais chez vous. Allez vite, ne perdez pas de temps.

Exercices

A. *Remplacez les tirets par un des quatre pronoms de la leçon:* **qui est-ce qui,** *etc.:*

1. —— vous faites à l'école? 2. —— est devant la classe? 3. —— est sur la table du maître? 4. —— parle aux élèves? 5. Jean, —— vous avez laissé tomber? 6. —— c'est qu'une grammaire? 7. —— est sorti? 8. A —— vous donnez vos exercices? 9. —— vous fait pleurer? 10. —— vous allez faire dans ce magasin?

B. *Traduisez en français:*

1. What is that? 2. What is a dictionary (*un dictionnaire*)? 3. What do you think of this? 4. Do you often think of me? 5. Whom do you know? 6. Who gave you that beautiful bracelet? 7. What did you drop? 8. What are you going to do? 9. What amuses you? 10. What is it? 11. What is this? 12. Who is there? 13. What do you study at school? 14. What interested you the most in the museum? 15. Whom do you like the better, John or Paul? 16. What can we do? 17. What are you writing? 18. Who writes you so often? 19. Whom do you believe? 20. What do you believe? 21. Whom do you see? 22. What do you see? 23. What

do they know?   24. Who knows that?   25. What do
you know?

Exercice-revue

1. At what time do you eat?   2. I eat promptly at
7 o'clock.   3. I bought two watches; which one do you
want, this one or that one?   4. I will take the one you like
the least.   5. They are both pretty.   6. That is true,
you are right.   7. Who took all that was in this box?
8. It is I.   9. Is it you?   10. If you are ashamed of it,
why don't you say so (it)?   11. If you did not like that,
why did you not say so?   12. If you had told me what you
liked the best, I should have known it.   13. When your
friend comes, tell him that we have written him a letter.
14. Tell him also what annoys you.   15. You have a headache, you are hungry perhaps.   16. If you eat so little
now, you will be hungry in half an hour.   17. I am afraid
so (of it).   18. Open the window if you are too warm.
19. Yes, I shall open it, it is very warm to-day.   20. It
is much warmer than yesterday.

*   *   *   *   *   *   *

54ᵉ Leçon : Formation et place des adverbes

Tout ce qui reluit n'est pas or. — *All that glitters is not gold.*

Study the following formations :

poli (m.), *polite;* poli**ment**, *politely.*
certain (m.), *certain;* certaine (f.), certaine**ment**, *certainly.*
parfait (m.), *perfect;* parfaite (f.), parfaite**ment**, *perfectly.*

Many adverbs in French are formed by adding **-ment** to
the masculine form of the adjective when the latter ends with
a vowel, or to the feminine form when the masculine does
not end with a vowel.

Place des adverbes. — We learned in Lesson 21 that adverbs are generally placed after the verb in simple and compound tenses.

The following adverbs are always placed between the auxiliary verb and the past participle:

bien, *well.*	**guère,**[1] *scarcely.*
mal, *badly.*	**moins,** *less.*
bientôt, *soon.*	**plus,**[1] *more, no longer.*
déjà, *already.*	**toujours,** *always.*
jamais,[1] *never.*	**tant,** *so much, so many.*
enfin, *finally.*	**surtout,** *especially.*
pas,[1] *not.*	**vraiment,** *truly.*
beaucoup, *much, many.*	**encore,** *yet, still, again.*
trop, *too much, too many.*	**souvent,** *often.*
certainement, *certainly.*	**point,**[1] *not at all.*
probablement, *probably.*	**trop,** *too much, too many.*
nullement,[1] *not at all.*	**rien,**[1] *nothing.*
peut-être, *may be.*	**mieux,** *better.*

Hier, aujourd'hui, demain, ici, là, and most adverbial phrases,[2] are placed after the past participle.

Ils sont partis hier.	*They left yesterday.*
Elle a fini tout à l'heure.	*She has just now finished.*

Tout, personne. — Observe the following constructions:

J'ai *tout* perdu.	*I lost everything.*
Je n'ai rencontré *personne.*	*I met nobody.*

As direct object, **tout,** *all, everything,* precedes the past participle, but **personne,** *nobody,* follows it.

Study the following sentences:

*N'*avez-vous vu *personne? Personne.* Have you seen no one? No one.

---

[1] These adverbs of negation are always used with **ne** when a verb is present. **Ne** precedes the verb and the adverb follows it (Lessons 5 and 41).

[2] For example: **tout de suite,** *immediately;* **sur le champ,** *instantly;* **tout à l'heure,** *just now;* **avec plaisir,** *with pleasure.* **A peine,** *hardly,* precedes the past participle. **Tout à fait,** *wholly, quite,* generally precedes.

N'avez-vous rien trouvé? *Rien. Have you found nothing? Nothing.*
Personne n'est absent. *Nobody is absent.*

Rien and **personne** (like **jamais,** *never,* Lesson 41) require **ne** before the verb ; used alone or without a verb, they retain their negative meaning.

Note. — Notice that when **personne** is the subject of the verb, **ne** follows personne, but comes before the verb as usual.

Sortir, *to go out;* participe passé, **sorti,** *gone out*

PRÉSENT	IMPARFAIT	FUTUR
je sors, *I go out.*	je sortais, *I was going out.*	je sortirai, *I shall go out.*
tu sors.	tu sortais.	tu sortiras.
il sort.	il sortait.	il sortira.
nous sortons.	nous sortions.	nous sortirons.
vous sortez.	vous sortiez.	vous sortirez.
ils sortent.	ils sortaient.	ils sortiront.

IMPÉRATIF

SINGULIER	PLURIEL	
sors, *go out.*	sortons, *let us go out.*	sortez, *go out.*

Vocabulaire

ne . . . **pas,** *not.*
ne . . . **point,** *not* (emphatic), *not at all.*
ne . . . **jamais,** *never.*
ne . . . **plus,** *no more, no longer.*
ne . . . **guère,** *scarcely, but little.*
ne . . . **rien,** *nothing, not anything.*
ne . . . **personne,** *nobody, not any-one, no one.*
hier soir, *last evening.*
ce soir, *this evening, to-night.*

cette nuit, *last night, this night.*
être bien mis(e), *to be well dressed.*
être mal mis(e), *to be badly dressed.*
la nouvelle, *the news.*
dernièrement, *lately.*
tout à l'heure, *in a little while, a while ago.*
échouer, *to fail* (in an attempt).
content de, *pleased with.*
sérieusement, *seriously.*
régulièrement, *regularly.*
tout à fait, *quite, entirely.*

Lecture

MADAME CARNOT ATTEND DES VISITES

Mme Carnot. Personne n'est encore arrivé?
Paul. Non, maman, personne.

Mme Carnot. Paul, je vous ai déjà dit vingt fois de mettre votre costume noir quand j'attends des visites. Vous ne m'écoutez jamais ; vous m'avez encore désobéi ; vous êtes toujours mal mis.

Paul. Voilà madame Leblanc et Charles.

Mme Carnot. Bonjour, chère amie ; bonjour, Charles. Quelles bonnes nouvelles ? Quelle robe adorable vous avez ! Comme vous êtes bien mise !

Mme Leblanc. Vous êtes trop aimable ! Et comment va madame votre mère ? Avez-vous reçu dernièrement de ses nouvelles ?

Mme Carnot. Ne saviez-vous pas qu'elle était revenue hier soir ? Elle viendra tout à l'heure, vous la verrez. Eh bien ! Charles, et vos examens ? Avez-vous bien réussi ?

Mme Leblanc. Non, pas du tout ! Il ne travaille guère. Il croit toujours qu'il a tout appris, il ne veut écouter personne, et quand les examens arrivent, il ne sait rien.

Mme Carnot. A-t-il vraiment échoué ?

Mme Leblanc. Mais certainement, il n'a point réussi.

Mme Carnot. Et moi qui pensais qu'il avait très bien travaillé et que vous étiez tout à fait contente de lui.

Mme Leblanc. Non, mais il sait qu'il a mal agi. Il devra beaucoup travailler pendant les vacances, et nous espérons qu'il réussira mieux en septembre. S'il ne réussit pas, il n'ira pas au collège. Son père a déjà décidé cela.

Mme Carnot. Monsieur Leblanc a-t-il vraiment pris cette décision ?

Mme Leblanc. Oui, et Charles a bien compris que son père a parlé sérieusement.

Charles. Je sais parfaitement que j'ai eu tort et que père a raison. Je lui ai promis de travailler régulièrement ; j'ai déjà commencé aujourd'hui et je suis sûr que je passerai certainement mes examens en septembre prochain.

Exercices

A. *Formez les adverbes des adjectifs suivants :*

1. Riche, pauvre, grand. 2. Aimable, aisé, court.
3. Facile, clair, parfait. 4. Difficile, étroit, égal. 5. Exact, froid, grave. 6. Haut, heureux, lent. 7. Joli, identique, ouvert. 8. Large, direct, raisonnable. 9. Simple, triste, nécessaire.

B. *Traduisez en français :*

1. You have written your letter badly. 2. His is written very well. 3. There was nobody here yesterday. 4. When I met your brother in Paris, he had already seen everything. 5. You have not seen anything yet (*yet anything seen*). 6. Those ladies are always well dressed. 7. He has no money and he has scarcely any friends. 8. Nobody has seen anything. 9. Has she lost everything? 10. Yes, she has lost almost everything. 11. Have you seen nobody to-day? 12. Nobody. 13. What did you buy for me yesterday? 14. Nothing. 15. I have not succeeded at all. 16. Will you ever succeed? 17. Nobody has understood what you have said. 18. What can we do? We have scarcely any money. 19. When I saw them, they had not yet seen everything. 20. They have finally seen everything. 21. They will have seen everything to-morrow. 22. Haven't you met anyone? 23. There is not; there was no longer anything; there will be nobody. 24. We have not lost anything. 25. You have not lost everything. 26. Nothing happened yesterday.

Exercice-revue

1. What is the matter with her? 2. Nothing is the matter with her. 3. No, something ails her; has she a headache again? 4. What is a lawyer? 5. What are you doing this afternoon? 6. Do you believe that? 7. I

Une section du palais de Fontainebleau, près de Paris.

shall believe it when I see it. 8. You are right. 9. We shall never believe what we do not see. 10. If I should tell you what I heard, would you believe me? 11. What interests you so much in that book? 12. I cannot tell you exactly what interests me, but the book is very well written. 13. I do not believe that; I read that book before you. 14. It is not the book of which you spoke last week. 15. Which one is it? 16. It is the one my sister gave me yesterday. 17. I shall read it when you have finished it. 18. Take this one until next week. 19. Will you be cold if I open the window? 20. No, open it, the weather is fine to-day; it is not raining any more. 21. Would you have been cold if I had opened the window? 22. Not at all, I like fresh air (*air, m.*).

* * * * ⁙ * *

55ᵉ Leçon : Adverbes interrogatifs

Ne remettez pas au lendemain ce que vous pouvez faire le jour même. — *Do not put off until to-morrow what you can do to-day.*

Study the following questions :

Pourquoi votre frère est-il si malheureux ? *Why is your brother so unhappy?*

Quand votre mère est-elle partie ? *When did your mother leave?*

A quelle heure la vôtre est-elle arrivée chez elle ? *At what time did yours get home?*

The order of words in a sentence beginning with an interrogative adverb (**pourquoi, où, quand, comment,** etc.) is the regular order used in asking questions in French (Lesson 6).

Notice the following example :

Lequel de ses chiens votre frère a-t-il perdu ? *Which of his dogs has your brother lost?*

An interrogative, **lequel, laquelle,** etc., in the objective case, requires the same order.

Study the following questions :

(1) **Où est l'église dont vous parliez?** *Where is the church of which you were speaking?*

(2) **Où demeurent vos amis?** *Where do your friends live?*

(3) **Où vos amis sont-ils allés?** or, **Vos amis, où sont-ils allés?** *Where did your friends go?*

After **où,** when the verb is in a simple tense (Examples 1 and 2), the subject is not usually repeated in the form of a pronoun as in regular questions with a noun subject. But when the verb is in a compound tense (Example 3), the subject is repeated in the form of a pronoun.

Sujets doubles. — When a verb has two or more subjects of *different* grammatical persons, they are usually summed up by **nous** or **vous,** with which the verb agrees.

When **nous** or **vous** is omitted, the verb agrees with whichever pronoun (**nous** or **vous**) is understood.

Ma mère et moi, nous sommes allés chez vous. *My mother and I went to your house.*

Mon frère et vous, vous êtes partis à cinq heures précises. *My brother and you started at exactly five o'clock.*

Lui et moi, nous le verrons demain. *He and I shall see him to-morrow.*

Lui et moi, partirons demain. *He and I will leave to-morrow.*

Monsieur, madame, mademoiselle. — As a mark of respect, the words **monsieur, madame, mademoiselle,** or their plurals, are placed before the adjective **votre** or **vos** followed by **père, mère, frère, sœur, oncle, cousin, ami,** etc., or their plurals.

J'ai rencontré monsieur votre père et madame votre mère. *I met your father and mother.*

Courir, *to run;* participe passé, **couru,** *run*

Présent	Imparfait	Futur
je cours, *I run.*	je courais, *I was running.*	je courrai, *I shall run.*
tu cours.	tu courais.	tu courras.

Présent	Imparfait	Futur
il court.	il courait.	il courra.
nous courons.	nous courions.	nous courrons.
vous courez.	vous couriez.	vous courrez.
ils courent.	ils couraient.	ils courront.

Impératif

SINGULIER	PLURIEL	
cours, *run*.	courons, *let us run*.	courez, *run*.

Vocabulaire

indisposé, *indisposed, unwell.*
supposer, *to suppose.*
prendre froid, } *to catch cold.*
attraper froid, }
le courant d'air, *the draught.*
délicat, *delicate, sensitive.*
fort, *strong.*

sentir, *to feel.*
la santé, *the health.*
grave, *serious, grave.*
le quartier, *the quarter, the ward.*
partout, *everywhere.*
quelque part, *somewhere.*
le bagage, *the baggage.*

tout d'abord, *at first.*
on ne peut mieux, *as well as can be.*
garder la chambre, *to stay indoors.*
dans le courant de la semaine, *during the week.*

Lecture

CONVERSATION

A. Mademoiselle votre sœur est-elle indisposée aujourd'hui?

B. Oui, ma sœur et moi sommes un peu malades.

A. Comment, vous aussi !

COMMENT ! VOUS AUSSI ?

B.   Oui, je suppose que nous avons pris froid.

A.   Où mademoiselle votre sœur et vous avez-vous attrapé froid?   Êtes-vous allées quelque part?

B.   Elle et moi, nous sommes allées à un concert hier dans le quartier Latin, et nous étions dans un courant d'air; ni elle, ni moi, nous n'avons rien remarqué tout de suite.

A.   Comment mademoiselle votre sœur, qui est si délicate, n'a-t-elle pas senti ce courant d'air?

B.   Il faisait très chaud, c'est pourquoi nous n'avons rien remarqué tout d'abord.

A.   Alors, ma mère et moi, nous n'aurions trouvé personne, si nous étions venus chez vous hier à quatre heures de l'après midi?

B.   Non, vous n'auriez trouvé personne.   Et comment madame votre mère va-t-elle?

A.   Merci, elle va on ne peut mieux.   Quand je lui dirai que vous et mademoiselle votre sœur n'êtes pas en bonne santé, elle sera certainement triste d'apprendre cela.

B.   Oh!   Ce ne sera rien de grave.   Vous voyez, je suis debout; ma sœur garde la chambre, car elle n'est pas forte, sa santé est délicate, comme vous le savez.

A.   Quand avez-vous reçu des nouvelles de monsieur votre père?   Quand arrivera-t-il?

B.   Nous avons reçu une lettre hier; il arrivera demain.

A.   Si vous le permettez, mon frère et moi, nous viendrons lui présenter nos respects dans le courant de la semaine prochaine.

B.   Mais certainement, je suis sûre qu'il sera charmé de vous voir tous les deux.

A.   Au revoir, mademoiselle, bien des choses à mademoiselle votre sœur.

B.   Au plaisir, monsieur, faites nos bons compliments à madame votre mère.

Exercices

A. *Traduisez en français :*

1. Henry and I have returned from Paris.   2. When did you and he arrive?   3. Where is your baggage?   4. We left it somewhere.   5. Haven't you looked for it?   6. Yes, we have looked for it everywhere.   7. Mary and I saw it at the station.   8. Why didn't you and she bring it? 9. Because we were not strong enough.   10. What shall we do?   11. I have spoken to John about it ; he will bring it this afternoon.   12. If you had not been there, we should have lost it.   13. When shall you and I go home?   14. Your mother and sister will be here on Tuesday, the 16th, but your father will stay in Paris until the 20th.   15. You forget that you and your brother will have no reward this month, because you have not worked well enough.   16. Which of her friends is your mother visiting?   17. She is visiting a lady who lives in the Latin Quarter.   18. We shall stay home to-day, but to-morrow, Paul and I shall go to the country.

Exercice-revue

1. Give the different meanings of the pronoun **en.** 2. What kind of pronoun is it?   3. Name four of its uses when it means *of it, of them.*   4. Where is it placed? 5. Conjugate rapidly : *I have some,* etc. ; *I haven't any,* etc.   6. What verb is used idiomatically when referring to the weather?   Give five examples.   7. What change occurs in the form of **du, de la, des** when the verb is negative? 8. What do **du, de la, des** become when **ni . . . ni** is used in a sentence?   9. What are the different translations of **jamais** in English?   Give examples.   10. Where is the **que** of **ne . . . que** placed when the verb is in a compound tense? 11. Name the demonstrative pronouns.   12. By what must they always be followed?   Give an example for each case.   13. How is *Mary's* and *my brother's* translated in

French? 14. Name the different uses of **ce**. 15. When are **ceci** and **cela** used? 16. How do they translate *it is* when referring to the time? 17. How is the same *it is* translated when it refers to the days of the week, months, or seasons? 18. What is the difference between the way the age of a person is expressed in French and in English? 19. How is the pluperfect formed? 20. When is it used?

* * * * * * *

56ᵉ Leçon: Pronoms personnels. Revue

Contentement passe richesse. — *Contentment is better than riches.*

We have learned in Lessons 30–32 and 36 that there are two classes of personal pronouns, *disjunctive* and *conjunctive.*

Disjunctive pronouns. —

moi, *I, me.*	**nous,** *we, us.*
toi, *thou, thee.*	**vous,** *you.*
lui, *he, him.*	**eux,** *they, them* (m.).
elle, *she, her.*	**elles,** *they, them* (f.).
moi-même, *myself.*	**nous-mêmes,** *ourselves.*
toi-même, *thyself.*	**vous-mêmes,** *yourselves.*
lui-même, *himself.*	**eux-mêmes,** *themselves* (m.).
elle-même, *herself.*	**elles-mêmes,** *themselves* (f.).

Also, **vous-même,** *yourself.*

A disjunctive pronoun is used:

(*a*) With a preposition: **chez lui,** *at his house.* (Lesson 36.)
(*b*) Alone: **Qui va là? Moi.** *Who goes there? I.* (Lesson 36.)
(*c*) Predicate nominative:

C'est lui.	*It is he.*
Ce sont eux.	*It is they.* (Lesson 44.)

(*d*) For emphasis: (See Lesson 36.)

Moi, je le ferai.	*I shall do it.*
Nous le ferons nous-mêmes.	*We shall do it ourselves.*

(*e*) When separated from the verb by a word (other than **ne** or a conjunctive pronoun) :

Lui seul l'a fait.	*He alone has done it.*
Je n'aime que lui.	*I love no one but him.*
Nous sommes plus riches qu'eux.	*We are richer than they.*

(*f*) To express the different persons of a compound subject or object :

Lui et moi, nous le ferons.	*He and I will do it.*
On nous a invités, vous et moi.	*They have invited you and me.*
Je les ai vus, lui et elle.	*I saw him and her.*

Conjunctive pronouns. — A conjunctive pronoun is used as subject, direct object, or indirect object of a verb expressed. (If the verb is understood, a disjunctive pronoun must be used, as in (*b*), above.)

SUBJECT (NOMINATIVE)	DIRECT OBJECT (ACCUSATIVE)	INDIRECT OBJECT (DATIVE)
je, *I*.	**me,** *me*.	**me,** *to me*.
tu, *thou*.	**te,** *thee*.	**te,** *to thee*.
il, *he, it*.	**le,** *him, it*.	**lui,** *to him*.
elle, *she, it*.	**la,** *her, it*.	**lui,** *to her*.
nous, *we*.	**nous,** *us*.	**nous,** *to us*.
vous, *you*.	**vous,** *you*.	**vous,** *to you*.
ils, *they* (m.).	**les,** *them* (m.).	**leur,** *to them* (m.).
elles, *they* (f.).	**les,** *them* (f.).	**leur,** *to them* (f.).

A personal pronoun used as the direct or indirect object of a verb always precedes the verb, except in the imperative affirmative.

Il me prête un dollar.	*He lends me a dollar.*
Prêtez-moi [1] **encore un dollar.**	*Lend me another dollar.*
Ne lui prêtez rien.	*Don't lend him anything.*
Répondez-vous à votre ami?	*Do you answer your friend?*
Je lui réponds toujours.	*I always answer him.*

[1] The disjunctives **moi** and **toi** are used for **me** and **te** in the imperative affirmative.

Sentir, *to smell; to feel;* participe passé, **senti,** *smelled.*

PRÉSENT	IMPARFAIT	FUTUR
je sens, *I smell.*	je sentais, *I was smelling.*	je sentirai, *I shall smell.*
tu sens.	tu sentais.	tu sentiras.
il sent.	il sentait.	il sentira.
nous sentons.	nous sentions.	nous sentirons.
vous sentez.	vous sentiez.	vous sentirez.
ils sentent.	ils sentaient.	ils sentiront.

IMPÉRATIF

SINGULIER	PLURIEL	
sens, *smell.*	sentons, *let us smell.*	sentez, *smell.*

Lecture

1. Je connais cette dame.   2. La connaissez-vous aussi?
3. Non, je ne la connais pas.   4. Ne lui avez-vous jamais
parlé?   5. Si je la connaissais, je lui parlerais.   6. Lui
parleriez-vous si vous la connaissiez?   7. Je ne vous crois
pas.   8. Pourquoi ne me croyez-vous pas?   9. Nous
vous verrons demain.   10. Qui le dit?   11. Je le dis.
12. Dites-le ou ne le dites pas, cela ne fait rien.   13. Savent-ils que nous les attendrons?   14. Il m'a dit qu'il
m'écrirait.   15. Vous écrira-t-il avant la semaine prochaine?   16. S'il vous écrit, lui répondrez-vous tout de
suite?   17. Je le ferai certainement.   18. Faites-le sans
faute.   19. Cette fenêtre est fermée, ouvrez-la.   20. Ouvrez-la vous-même, mais je pense qu'il y aura un courant d'air.
21. Donnez-moi ce livre, ne le donnez pas à votre sœur.
22. Qui l'a lu, elle ou lui?   23. Lui je pense, mais pas elle.
24. Est-ce lui qui l'a fait?   Non, c'est moi.   25. Lui et
moi, nous irons chez elle demain soir.   26. Vous voici!
Je suis content de vous voir, je dois vous dire quelque chose.

Exercices

A. *Remplacez les mots en italique par des pronoms régimes:*
1. Je comprends *la leçon.*   2. Je parle *au professeur.*
3. Parlez *à Jean.*   4. Je ne vois pas *Jean.*   5. Écrivez *à*

Paul.   6.   N'écrivez pas *à Jeanne.*   7.   Ne voyez-vous pas *ce monsieur?*   8.   Veut-elle *ce bijou?*   9.   Obéissez-vous toujours *à vos parents?*   10.   Obéissez *à vos parents.*
11.   Lisez cette lettre *à votre amie.*   12.   Regardez *ce tableau.*

B.   *Traduisez en français :*

1.   Here I am ; speak to me, don't speak to her.   2.   He does not see me.   3.   Does he not see you?   4.   Speak to them, if they come.   5.   He is waiting for us and we are waiting for him.   6.   Let us not wait for them any longer, they will not come.   7.   Answer me, please.   8.   She will answer you if you speak to her.   9.   Why don't you answer her?   10.   It is for themselves that these children are working.   11.   Who will go, you, she, or I?   12.   She was speaking to you, why did you not listen to her?   13.   She used to sing much better than they (*f.*).   14.   Let us do it.
15.   Never do it.   16.   Don't do it any more.   17.   Why do you scold me?   18.   You never scold him.   19.   If he were not good, I should certainly scold him.   20.   Show your bracelet to her.   21.   I will show it if she wants to see it.   22.   We have not punished them.   23.   I lent him my pen-knife, but he did not bring it back.   24.   He has left it at home.   25.   He has not forgotten to bring it, he has lost it.
26.   There he is, let us punish him for that.

Exercice-revue

1.   What are the different translations of *what* meaning *that which?*   2.   How is the conditional formed?   3.   What other tense has almost the same formation?   4.   In what other tense do we find the same endings as in the conditional?
5.   What prevents confusion between these two tenses?
6.   Give the sequence of tenses in conditional sentences.
7.   What are the only three tenses which can be found after **si** in conditional sentences?   8.   When is **lequel** used instead of **qui** and **que?**   9.   What occurs when **lequel** is pre-

ceded by **de** or **à?**   10. What are the meanings of **dont?**
11. When is **où** a relative pronoun?   12. What are the
translations of **qui?** in English?   13. What are the translations of *what?* in French?   14. How is *whose?* translated
in French?   15. What is the difference between **quel?** and
lequel? Give examples.   16. Name ten idioms with **avoir.**
17. When are *my, his, her,* etc., replaced by the definite
article?   18. Give the different translations of *who? whom?
what?*   19. What is the difference between **penser à** and
penser de?   20. How are adverbs formed and where are
they placed?   21. Name the adverbs of negation.

*   *   *   *   *   *   *

57ᵉ Leçon : Pronoms régimes — directs et indirects

A chaque oiseau son nid est beau. — *To each bird of the air its nest is fair.*

We have learned that conjunctive personal pronouns, when
used as direct or indirect object of a verb, are placed before
the verb. What is to be done when two pronouns, one
direct object, the other indirect object, are the objects of the
same verb? What will be the order of precedence?

Study the following sentences :

   (a) **Je vous le donne.**   *I give it to you.*
   (b) **Il me le donne.**   *He gives it to me.*
   (c) **Je le lui donne.**   *I give it to him.*
   (d) **Je ne le lui donne pas.**   *I do not give it to him.*
   (e) **Je ne vous l'ai pas donné.**   *I did not give it to you.*
   (f) **Ne me le donnez-vous pas?**   *Do you not give it to me?*
   (g) **Ne me l'avez-vous pas donné?**   *Did you not give it to me?*

When two personal pronouns are objects of the same verb,
and are of different persons (Examples *a, b, e, f, g*), the first

L'ÉGLISE DE ST. MACLOU À ROUEN.

and second persons come before the third, *i.e.*, **me, te, nous, vous** come before **le, la, les.**

When both pronouns are of the third person (Examples *c* and *d*), the direct object pronoun precedes the indirect, *i.e.*, **le, la, les** always come before **lui** and **leur.**

CHART

of the different combinations of the object pronouns : **me, te, nous, vous, le, la, les, lui, leur,** before the verb

me ⟨ le / la ③ / ① les	te ⟨ le / la ③ / ② les	nous ⟨ le / la ③ / ① les	vous ⟨ le / la ③ / ② les
le ⟨ lui indirect / direct ⟨ leur	la ⟨ lui indirect / direct ⟨ leur	les ⟨ lui indirect / direct ⟨ leur	

Boire, *to drink ;* participe passé, **bu,** *drunk*

PRÉSENT	IMPARFAIT	FUTUR
je bois, *I drink.*	je buvais, *I was drinking.*	je boirai, *I shall drink.*
tu bois.	tu buvais.	tu boiras.
il boit.	il buvait.	il boira.
nous buvons.	nous buvions.	nous boirons.
vous buvez.	vous buviez.	vous boirez.
ils boivent.	ils buvaient.	ils boiront.

IMPÉRATIF

SINGULIER	PLURIEL	
bois, *drink.*	buvons, *let us drink.*	buvez, *drink.*

Vocabulaire

le souvenir, *the remembrance.*
tourner, *to turn.*

le départ, *the departure.*
le coin, *the corner.*

Lecture

CONVERSATION

Jean. Voici mon meilleur crayon, me le rendrez-vous si ie vous le prête?

Louis.　Je vous le promets.

Jean.　Ma sœur vous a-t-elle montré ses nouveaux joujoux?

Louis.　Oui, elle me les a montrés.

Jean.　Vous a-t-elle dit qui les lui a donnés?

Louis.　Non, elle ne me l'a pas dit.　Qui les lui a apportés?

Jean.　C'est mon oncle Charles qui nous les a envoyés.

Louis.　Pourquoi vous les a-t-il envoyés?　Pourquoi ne vous les a-t-il pas apportés lui-même?

Jean.　Parce qu'il est malade; il nous a écrit une lettre charmante; je vais vous la lire.

Louis.　Je la lirai moi-même.

Jean.　Non, j'aime mieux vous la lire, car il écrit très mal.

Louis.　Vous me la lirez plus tard; voici Paul et Robert qui viennent jouer, vous pourrez leur montrer vos nouveaux jouets.

Jean.　Oui, je vais les leur montrer.

Louis.　Savent-ils que c'est votre fête aujourd'hui?

Jean.　Mais certainement, je le leur ai dit hier, c'est pourquoi ils sont venus aujourd'hui.　J'attends aussi Henri et Alfred.　Les voilà qui tournent le coin de la rue.

Louis.　Combien serons-nous?

Jean.　Ma sœur a invité cinq de ses amies, nous serons douze.　Nous avons des souvenirs pour tout le monde. Voici ceux des petites filles, nous les leur donnerons quand elles partiront.　Ma sœur a les souvenirs pour les garçons; les petites filles nous les donneront aussi au moment du départ.

Exercices

A.　*Conjuguez:*

1.　Je les lui montre, tu les lui, etc.　2.　Je ne la lui lirai pas, tu . . ., etc.　3.　Le leur ai-je porté, etc.　4.　Je les lui montrerai, mais je ne les lui donnerai pas, tu . . ., etc.

B. *Remplacez les noms par les pronoms convenables :*

1. Je ne vous vendrai pas ma balle.   2. Nous avons vendu la maison au voisin.   3. Elle a donné la fleur à Jeanne.   4. Il nous racontera cette histoire.   5. M'avez-vous apporté le livre?   6. J'ai montré mes jouets à mes amis.   7. Vous n'avez pas donné vos jouets à votre sœur. 8. Avez-vous montré vos exercices aux élèves?   9. Ils ne vous prêteront pas leurs livres.   10. Nous ne vous avons pas donné la permission.

C. *Traduisez en français :*

1. He gives it to me.   2. He does not give it to you. 3. Does he give it to you?   4. Doesn't he give it to you? 5. He has not given it to me.   6. Do you give them to them?   7. I ask you for it.   8. Do you ask me for it? 9. Hasn't he asked you for it?   10. I asked you for your handkerchief, but you haven't given it to me.   11. I know it ; I haven't given it to you because I haven't it any longer. 12. I don't understand that ; your sister gave it to you ten minutes ago.   13. I gave it back to her.   14. He will show them to you.   15. Will you lend them to them? 16. Here is a letter, will you read it to me?   17. I shall read it to you with pleasure.   18. He told it to us.   19. We didn't tell it to him.   20. I shall tell it to her if she asks me to.

Exercice-revue

1. Why didn't your brother come to school yesterday? 2. What was the matter with him?   3. Where did your mother go?   4. Which of those pens is the best?   5. The one that is in the ink.   6. What you say is true ; it is the best.   7. If you receive any flowers, will you give me some?   8. I shall not receive any to-day, but if I should receive some, I would give you a dozen.   9. What happened?   You are so happy to-day !   10. You are right, we have received good news from my father.   11. I met your

brother; he was running. Where was he going? 12. He always runs. 13. When he is older, he will not run any more. 14. Has no one come to see you to-day? 15. No, no one. 16. I cannot understand that. 17. Did you read the book of which I spoke to you? 18. Whose book is this? 19. Which one? 20. This one. 21. It is my father's. 22. Can I have it? 23. Yes, it is the book of which they speak so much. 24. I did not know that, but what I know is that that book is very interesting. 25. That is what I shall see when I read it.

* * * * * * *

58e Leçon : Pronoms personnels régimes avec l'impératif

Rira bien, qui rira le dernier. — *He laughs best who laughs last.*

We learned in Lesson 32 that with the imperative affirmative, the personal object pronoun, direct or indirect, comes after the verb.

When two personal pronouns, one direct, the other indirect, are the objects of the same imperative, what will be the order of precedence?

Study the following sentences :

Montrez-*le-lui*.	*Show it to him (to her).*
Donnez-*la-nous*.	*Give it to us.*
Prêtez-*les-leur*.	*Lend them to them.*

The order of the pronouns standing after an *imperative affirmative* is the same as in English, *i.e.*, the direct object precedes the indirect. In French they are joined together and to the verb by hyphens.

Remember that with an *imperative negative*, the pronouns

are placed before the verb, following the general rule (Lessons 30 and 31) :

Ne *les lui* montrez pas.   *Don't show them to him (to her).*
Ne *nous la* donnez pas.   *Don't give it to us.*

Rire, *to laugh;* participe passé, **ri,** *laughed*

Présent	Imparfait	Futur
je ris, *I laugh.*	je riais, *I was laughing.*	je rirai, *I shall laugh.*
tu ris.	tu riais.	tu riras.
il rit.	il riait.	il rira.
nous rions.	nous riions.	nous rirons.
vous riez.	vous riiez.	vous rirez.
ils rient.	ils riaient.	ils riront.

Impératif

SINGULIER	PLURIEL	
ris, *laugh.*	rions, *let us laugh.*	riez, *laugh.*

Vocabulaire

examiner, *to examine.*
la douane, *the custom house.*
la malle, *the trunk.*
la malle-armoire, *the wardrobe trunk.*
le carton à chapeaux, *the hat-box.*
la clé (or clef), *the key.*
déclarer, *to declare.*
le cigare, *the cigar.*
le tabac, *the tobacco.*

la carte à jouer, *the playing card.*
la consommation, *the use.*
personnel, *personal, private.*
éviter, *to avoid, to prevent.*
la difficulté, *the difficulty.*
sur parole, *on one's word.*
le flacon, *the bottle, the vial.*
le parfum, *the perfume.*
garder, *to keep.*

avoir quelque chose à déclarer, *to have anything dutiable.*
demander quelque chose à quelqu'un, *to ask something of somebody, to ask somebody for something.* (Literally : *to ask something to somebody.*)

Lecture

A LA DOUANE

Le voyageur.   Pardon, monsieur, voulez-vous examiner mes bagages?

Le douanier.   Où sont-ils?   Montrez-les-moi.

Le voyageur.   Les voici, ces deux malles-armoires, cette valise et ce carton à chapeaux.   Quelle malle dois-je ouvrir?

Le douanier. Ouvrez-les toutes les deux.

Le voyageur. Je ne puis pas ouvrir celle-ci.

Le douanier. Avez-vous la clé? Donnez-la-moi. Voilà! Avez-vous quelque chose à déclarer : des cigares, du tabac, des cartes à jouer?

Le voyageur. J'ai des cigares pour ma consommation personnelle.

Le douanier. C'est bien, c'est bien, ne me les montrez pas. Si vous avez quelque chose à déclarer, dites-le-nous, cela vous évite des difficultés. Avez-vous de l'eau de Cologne dans cette valise?

AVEZ-VOUS LA CLÉ? DONNEZ-LA-MOI.

Le voyageur. Ne me le demandez pas, je n'en sais rien, c'est celle de ma femme. Ah! la voici; demandez-le-lui.

Le douanier. Madame, avez-vous de l'eau de Cologne dans cette valise? Non, n'ouvrez pas, dites-le-moi, je vous crois sur parole.

La voyageuse. J'ai un ou deux flacons de parfums français.

Le douanier. C'est bien, vous pouvez passer.

Le voyageur. Vous avez gardé la clé de ma malle, rendez-la-moi, s'il vous plaît.

Le douanier. C'est vrai, excusez-moi je vous prie ; la voici.

Exercices

A. *Mettez à la forme affirmative :*

1. Ne la leur donnez pas. 2. Ne nous les montrez pas. 3. Ne la lui passez pas. 4. Ne le lui dites pas. 5. Ne

me les prêtez pas.   6. Ne nous la demandez pas.   7. Ne les lui apportez pas.

B. *Remplacez les noms par des pronoms :*

1. Donnez les exercices aux élèves.   2. Montrez-moi les exercices.   3. Prêtez votre malle à votre frère.   4. Racontez-nous cette histoire.   5. Racontez cette anecdote à votre cousine.   6. Dites-nous la nouvelle.   7. Portez ces fleurs à ces dames.   8. Vendez-nous votre cheval.   9. Lisons notre leçon au professeur.   10. Rendez le parapluie à votre tante.

C. *Traduisez en français :*

1. Give it to me.   2. Give them to her.   3. Give them to them.   4. Give it to us.   5. Give it to him.   6. Show it to her.   7. Show it to us ; to him ; to them.   8. Bring it to us ; to them ; to her ; to me.   9. Tell it to me ; to them ; to us ; to him.   10. Return the pen ; return it to us ; to them ; to me.   11. Lend your books ; lend them to them ; to me ; to her ; to us ; to him.   12. Do not show them to him ; to me ; to her ; to them ; to us.   13. Don't give them to me, give them to her.   14. They do not want your house, don't sell it to them, sell it to us.   15. We know that story, do not tell it to us, tell it to him.   16. Ask for your trunk, ask him for it.   17. Don't ask us for it, ask them for it.   18. Ask them for them.

Exercice-revue

1. Your brother Paul answered his teacher very well yesterday.   2. Yes, he spoke politely.   3. Does he know that his cousin arrived this morning?   4. No, he knows nothing.   5. Nobody knows anything.   6. Have you finished? Have you said everything?   7. Where is the suitcase of which you are speaking?   8. Where did your sister go last evening?   9. Are you hungry? Will you have a piece of bread and some cheese?   10. No, I am cold ;

will you give me a cup of hot tea? 11. Is it cold here? If you are cold, I shall close that window. 12. What do you want? Do you need paper and ink? 13. No, I will tell you what I want. 14. Which of these children is your nephew? 15. The one who plays with the little girl whose hair you admire so much. 16. Is it he? How old is he? 17. He will be ten next month, he was born in July. 18. If I should need money, would you give me some? 19. If you had needed some, I would have given you some. 20. What is money?

Il y en a

Il y a.	Il y en a.	*There are some.*
Y a-t-il?	Y en a-t-il?	*Are there any?*
Il n'y a pas.	Il n'y en a pas.	*There are none.*
N'y a-t-il pas?	N'y en a-t-il pas?	*Aren't there any?*
Il y avait.	Il y en avait.	*There were some.*
Il y a eu.	Il y en a eu.	*There has been some.*
Il y avait eu.	Il y en avait eu.	*There had been some.*
Il y aura.	Il y en aura.	*There will be some.*
Il y aura eu.	Il y en aura eu.	*There will have been some.*
Il y aurait.	Il y en aurait.	*There would be some.*
Il y aurait eu.	Il y en aurait eu.	*There would have been some.*

Une anecdote

Les deux figues

Buffon, le grand naturaliste français du XVIIIe siècle, et le directeur du Jardin des Plantes [1] étaient deux grands amis.

Un jour le directeur rencontre Buffon et lui dit : " Demain, je vais vous envoyer les deux figues du figuier (*fig tree*) très rare qui vous intéresse tant."

Le lendemain (*next day*) il met les deux figues dans une petite boîte et dit à un jeune domestique simple et naïf :

— Portez ces deux figues à monsieur Buffon, et faites attention, elles sont très rares.

---

[1] Botanical garden in Paris.

— Bien, monsieur, dit le domestique.

Mais en route, il ne peut résister à la tentation, et mange la plus grosse des deux figues.

Buffon ouvre la boîte et est très surpris de ne trouver qu'une figue, car il savait que le directeur lui en avait promis deux.

— Où est l'autre figue, demande-t-il?

Le domestique donne des explications confuses et avoue (*confess*) sa faute.

— Polisson (*rascal*), crie Buffon, sais-tu que tu as mangé une figue très rare! Comment as-tu fait cela!

A ces mots, le domestique saisit l'autre figue et l'avale (*swallows*).

— J'ai fait comme ça! dit-il.

* * * * * * *

59e Leçon: **Pronoms personnels** (*suite*)

Abondance de bien ne nuit pas. — *You can't have too much of a good thing.*

Nom complément. — Study the following sentences:

Etes-vous la fille de ce monsieur?	*Are you this gentlemen's daughter?*
Oui, madame, je *la* suis.	*Yes, madam, I am.*
Etes-vous les fils de M. Cadieux?	*Are you the sons of Mr. Cadieux?*
Non, madame, nous ne *les* sommes pas.	*No, madam, we are not.*

If the complement understood in English is a noun (or an adjective used as a noun, as: **le** or **la malade**, *the patient*, **le** or **la coupable**, *the culprit*, etc.), use **le, la, les** in the French translation, according to the gender and number of the noun represented.

The invariable le (adjectif complément). — Observe the following constructions (see also page 363, III, 1):

Etes-vous contentes, mesdames?	*Are you pleased, ladies?*
Nous *le* sommes.	*We are.*
Etes-vous gouvernante?	*Are you a governess?*
Je *le* suis.	*I am.*

If the complement understood in English is an adjective (or a noun used as an adjective), **le** alone is used in French.

Attention! In the examples above, notice that in French every verb must have a complement or an attribute to form a complete sentence. *I am* or *I have,* **Je suis** or **j'ai,** as an answer to the questions **Êtes-vous content?** or **avez-vous le livre?** would be wrong. The French say *I am it* (or *so*) and *I have it:* **je le suis** and **je l'ai.**

Conduire, *to conduct, to lead;* participe passé, **conduit.**

Présent	Imparfait	Futur
je conduis, *I conduct.*	je conduisais, *I was*	je conduirai, *I shall*
tu conduis.	tu conduisais. *conducting.*	tu conduiras. *con-*
il conduit.	il conduisait.	il conduira. *duct.*
nous conduisons.	nous conduisions.	nous conduirons.
vous conduisez.	vous conduisiez.	vos conduirez.
ils conduisent.	ils conduisaient.	ils conduiront.

Impératif

singulier	pluriel	
conduis, *conduct.*	conduisons, *let us conduct.*	conduisez, *conduct.*

Vocabulaire

le beau-frère, *the brother-in-law.*	reconnaître, *to recognize.*
la belle-sœur, *the sister-in-law.*	la directrice, *the principal.*
satisfait, *pleased, satisfied.*	fort, *strong* (adv. *very*).

rappelez-moi au bon souvenir de, *remember me to.*
Je n'y manquerai pas. *I shall not fail from doing so.*

Lecture

Conversation

C. Pardon, madame, n'êtes-vous pas la belle-sœur de mon amie, Mme Delrue?

D. Si, madame, je la suis.

C. J'ai eu l'honneur de vous être présentée chez les Polignac, l'hiver dernier.

D. Parfaitement, je vous reconnais maintenant; mademoiselle Corday n'est-ce pas?

Ewing Galloway

Château de Josselyn en Bretagne.

C.   C'est exact, madame.

D.   Êtes-vous encore maîtresse d'anglais à l'École de Commerce de Paris?

C.   Oui, madame, je le suis.

D.   Êtes-vous toujours satisfaite de votre position?

C.   Oui, je le suis ; je suis directrice de l'école maintenant.

D.   Je suis très heureuse d'apprendre cette bonne nouvelle.

C.   L'êtes-vous réellement?   Cela me fait grand plaisir.

D.   Vos élèves sont-elles aussi contentes de votre nomination?

C.   Je crois qu'elles le sont, et j'espère qu'elles le seront toujours.

D.   J'en suis sûre.   Et vous êtes dans notre ville pour longtemps?

C.   Non, madame, je pars ce soir pour New-York, je suis venue passer quelques jours chez ma sœur et mon beau-frère. Voici leurs deux petites filles : Lucie, huit ans et Suzette, dix.

D.   Bonjour, mes petites.   Êtes-vous les nièces de Mlle Corday?

Suzette.   Oui, madame, nous les sommes.

D.   Comme vous êtes grandes et fortes pour votre âge ! Vous n'êtes jamais malades, n'est-ce pas?

Lucie.   Non, madame, nous ne le sommes jamais.

C.   Et je puis ajouter, madame, qu'elles ne l'ont jamais été.

D.   A la bonne heure !   Je suis sûre qu'elles ne le seront jamais.   Au revoir, mademoiselle Corday ; rappelez-moi au bon souvenir de Mme Polignac quand vous la verrez.

C.   Je n'y manquerai pas.   Au revoir, madame.

Exercices

A. *Répondez aux questions suivantes en employant le pronom convenable :*

1. Êtes-vous couturière?   2. Êtes-vous la couturière?
3. Êtes-vous la sœur de Mme X?   4. Êtes-vous Parisienne?
5. Êtes-vous les messieurs que j'attendais?   6. Mesde-

moiselles vos nièces sont-elles malades? 7. Sont-elles les
filles de votre voisin? 8. Êtes-vous contents de votre
automobile? 9. Vos cousines sont-elles Américaines?
10. Etes-vous les Américains qui sont arrivés hier?

B. *Traduisez en français:*

1. Are you the boy whom the professor punished this
morning? 2. No, madam, I am not. 3. I am glad of it.
4. I am too. 5. If I were to lend you my gold watch,
would you be pleased? 6. I would. 7. Would you?
8. Would your mother be too? 9. I think she would.
10. Are you sure of it? 11. I am. 12. You are rich.
but I am not. 13. Are you happy, Mary? 14. I am, but
my sister is not. 15. Are you John's sister? 16. I am
not. 17. She is always glad and we never are. 18. I
don't know why you aren't. 19. Good morning! Are you
the dressmaker who promised to (*de*) come to-day? 20. Yes,
madam, I am. 21. Are you the men from the department
store? 22. We are. 23. Are you ready to (*à*) work?
24. We are.

Exercice-revue

1. I did not give it to her, she took it. 2. Has he any
money in his coat pocket? 3. I did not hear what you said.
4. Do you believe what he told you? 5. Here is the lady
whose daughter fell in front of our house a month ago.
6. How did the poor girl fall? 7. I don't know, I was not
there and I didn't see her. 8. Her mother says that she
always has a headache now. 9. What is the color of her
eyes? 10. She has blue eyes, I think. 11. Which of his
books has he given you? 12. He didn't give me any book.
13. I thought he had given you the French book of which you
spoke to Paul yesterday. 14. Of what book did I speak?
15. If you open that window, it will be cold in this room.
16. If you were to open that door, there would be a draught.

17. Why did you give her the box in which you had put all of your pencils?

J'ai fait un grand voyage

Je suis allée en France il y a six mois.
Je suis partie de New-York le 11 juillet,
Je suis arrivée à Paris le 17 du même mois,
Je suis descendue à l'Hôtel du Cheval Blanc,
Je suis sortie tous les jours quand il faisait beau,
Je suis entrée dans tous les musées,
Je suis devenue l'amie d'une dame française,
Je suis retournée à Paris après être restée 15 jours à Nice,
Je suis revenue en Amérique au mois de janvier.
Je suis née sous une bonne étoile, car je suis très heureuse.

* * * * * * *

60ᵉ Leçon : Féminin des adjectifs. Irrégularités

Il vaut son pesant d'or. — *He is worth his weight in gold.*

We have seen (Lesson 5) that the feminine of an adjective is formed by adding -e mute to the masculine, while adjectives ending in -e mute remain unchanged.

Exceptions

Adjectives ending in the masculine singular in -el, -eil, -ien, -on, -os, -as, and a number of adjectives ending in -t, double the consonant before adding the mute -e.

Masculine		Feminine	Masculine		Feminine
cruel,	*cruel,*	cruelle.	gros,	*big, stout,*	grosse.
pareil,	*similar,*	pareille.	gras,	*fat,*	grasse.
ancien,	*ancient,*	ancienne.	muet,	*mute, dumb,*	muette.
bon,	*good,*	bonne.	sot,	*foolish,*	sotte.

Adjectives ending in the masculine singular with **-f, -x,** and **-c,** change f to **v,** x to **s,** and **c** to **qu** before adding the mute **-e.**

actif,	*active,*	active.
heureux,	*happy,*	heureuse.
public,	*public,*	publique.

Adjectives ending in **-er** and a number of adjectives ending in **-et** change **e** to **è** before adding the mute **-e.**

léger,	*light,*	légère.
premier,	*first,*	première.
complet,	*complete,*	complète.

The following adjectives have two forms for the masculine singular :

beau, bel,	*beautiful,*	belle.
fou, fol,	*crazy,*	folle.
mou, mol,	*soft,*	molle.
nouveau, nouvel,	*new,*	nouvelle.
vieux, vieil,	*old,*	vieille.

The second form is used only before a noun beginning with a vowel or with silent **h.**

un bel homme,	un nouvel opéra,	un vieil ami.

The following adjectives and a number of others form their feminine irregularly without any fixed rule.

blanc,	*white,*	blanche.
favori,	*favorite,*	favorite.
doux,	*sweet, gentle,*	douce.
flatteur,	*flattering,*	flatteuse.
frais,	*fresh, cool,*	fraîche.

Suivre. *io follow;* participe passé, **suivi,** *followed*

PRÉSENT	IMPARFAIT	FUTUR
je suis, *I follow.*	je suivais, *I was following.*	je suivrai, *I shall follow*
tu suis.	tu suivais.	tu suivras.
il suit.	il suivait.	il suivra.

Présent	Imparfait	Futur
ɒous suivons.	nous suivions.	nous suivrons.
vous suivez.	vous suiviez.	vous suivrez.
ils suivent.	ils suivaient.	ils suivront.

Impératif

Singulier	Pluriel	
suis, *follow*.	suivons, *let us follow*.	suivez, *follow*.

Vocabulaire

inoffensif, *harmless*.
la race, *the breed*.
le mastodonte, *the mastodon*.
sacré, *sacred*.
avancé, *advanced*.
paraît-il, *it appears, they say*.
rugueux, *rough, rugose*.
la démarche, *the walk, the gait*.
vif, *lively, quick, alert*.
jaloux, -se, *jealous*.

la force, *the strength*.
exceptionnel, *exceptional*.
cadet, *younger, junior of two*.
l'étonnement (m.), *the amazement*.
la queue, *the tail*.
puis, *then*.
après tout, *after all*.
franc, *frank*.
je ne saurais, *I couldn't*.
délicieux, -se, *delicious*.

Lecture

Conversation

— Est-ce que l'éléphant est une bête cruelle?

— Non, pas du tout; l'éléphant est une bonne grosse bête inoffensive.

— L'éléphant est le dernier spécimen de l'ancienne race des mastodontes, n'est-ce pas?

— Oui, c'est exact; ce sont les descendants du mammouth; on les trouve surtout en Afrique et en Asie.

— La race africaine et la race asiatique sont-elles pareilles?

— Je ne saurais vous le dire, mais je pense que non. Il y a, je sais, une race blanche. Les éléphants de couleur blanche sont très rares et sont considérés comme des animaux sacrés.

— Ils vivent jusqu'à un âge très avancé, n'est-ce pas?

— Oui, à Londres, j'ai vu un vieil éléphant qui avait, paraît-il, 150 ans. Ils ont la peau très épaisse et très rugueuse. Leur démarche semble lourde, mais est très légère; leur intelligence est vive ; ils ont une force exceptionnelle dans leur trompe.

— L'autre jour nous avons ri. Nous étions au Jardin Zoologique, avec maman et ma sœur cadette. La chère petite

n'a que 5 ans et c'était la première fois qu'elle voyait un éléphant. Elle est d'abord restée muette d'étonnement, puis, savez-vous ce qu'elle a demandé à ma mère ?

— Non, quoi ?

— " Pourquoi lui a-t-on mis aussi une queue dans la bouche ? "

— Voilà certainement un bel exemple de l'imagination des enfants ! Mais sa question n'était pas si sotte après tout !

Exercices

A. *Faites accorder les adjectifs.* (*Make the adjectives agree.*)

1. Elle a mis sa robe *neuf*. 2. Elle est très *heureux*. 3. Quand avez-vous reçu ces *beau* roses *blanc*. 4. Cette *petit* fille est très *gentil*. 5. Elle est toujours très *attentif* en classe. 6. Voici ma couleur *favori*. 7. Cette table est très *ancien*. 8. Ma tante est très *vieux*. 9. Nous habitons dans une *nouveau* maison. 10. Cette soupe est trop *gras*.

B. *Traduisez en français :*

1. Give me those white flowers. 2. Charles is my old friend. 3. This girl is happy, but that one is unhappy. 4. These big strawberries are delicious. 5. I have put on my new shoes (*bottines*) and my feet hurt me. 6. Our

neighbor's wife is very unhappy; her daughter is crazy.
7. She is jealous when she sees that my sister has a new
dress.   8. Will you have a glass of fresh water?   9. This
beautiful muslin is as white as snow.   10. Have you seen
my new full dress (*habit*)?   11. What a foolish question !
12. There is a fine animal.   13. Is this avenue public now?
14. Yes, and it is my favorite promenade.   15. Jane, I
think you will be cold with that light dress.   16. Mary is
not frank, she never says what she thinks.   17. She is
always very flattering.   18. This meat is too fat, don't eat
it.   19. That little girl is very stout for her age.

Exercice-revue

1. Give me the pen if you please.   2. With pleasure,
here it is.   3. I give it to you.   4. You give it to me and
I accept it.   5. I do not like cats, I have already told you
(it to you).   6. Did you tell it to me?   7. I think he is
afraid of me.   8. If he were afraid of you, he would not
come so near you.   9. You are right, you are never wrong.
10. Here is the house of which I speak.   11. Which one?
The one whose façade (*la façade*) is painted (*peinte*) in
blue?   12. Why didn't your brother go out this morning?
13. Which brother, my younger brother?   14. What is a
barometer (*un baromètre*)?   15. Whose barometer is this?
16. What interests you in a barometer?   17. I have ex-
amined (*examiner*) everything and I understand nothing.

*   *   *   *   *   *   *

61e Leçon : Verbes réfléchis ou pronominaux

Ils s'accordent comme chien et chat. — *They agree like cats and dogs.*

A reflexive verb represents the subject as acting upon itself :
(1) most of the time directly : Je me coupe.   *I cut myself*
(2) sometimes indirectly : Je me parle.   *I speak to myself.*

Some verbs in French are always reflexive, although their equivalents in English are not reflexive (*a*). But any transitive verb can be conjugated reflexively (*b*) :

    (*a*) Je *me* couche.　　*I lie down, I go to bed.*
    (*b*) Je lave. *I wash.* ⟶ Je *me* lave. *I wash myself.*

Reflexive verbs are conjugated with a reflexive pronoun object : direct (Example 1) or indirect (Example 2), always of the *same person* as the subject. Because of this reflexive pronoun, they are sometimes called *pronominal* verbs.

Reflexive verbs follow the conjugation to which they belong, and the reflexive pronouns are placed according to the rules governing pronoun objects.

The reflexive pronouns are :

me, *myself, to myself.*　　　　**nous,** *ourselves, to ourselves.*
te, *thyself, to thyself.*　　　　**vous,** *yourselves, to yourselves.*
se, *himself, herself, itself;*　　**se,** *themselves, to themselves.*
  to himself, to herself, to itself.

Conjugaison des verbes réfléchis. —

PREMIÈRE CONJUGAISON

Se laver, *to wash oneself*

PRÉSENT

AFFIRMATIF	NÉGATIF
I wash myself, etc. . . .	*I do not wash myself, etc. . . .*
je *me* lave.	je ne *me* lave pas.
tu *te* laves.	tu ne *te* laves pas.
il (elle) *se* lave.	il (elle) ne *se* lave pas.
nous *nous* lavons.	nous ne *nous* lavons pas.
vous *vous* lavez.	vous ne *vous* lavez pas.
ils (elles) *se* lavent.	ils (elles) ne *se* lavent pas.

IMPARF.　je *me* lavais, *I used to wash myself.*
FUTUR　je *me* laverai, *I shall wash myself.*
CONDIT.　je *me* laverais, *I should wash myself.*
IMPÉRAT. lave-*toi*, lavons-*nous*, lavez-*vous*, *wash yourself, let us wash ourselves, wash yourself (yourselves).*

DEUXIÈME CONJUGAISON	TROISIÈME CONJUGAISON
Se punir, *to punish oneself*	**Se rendre,** *to surrender, to betake oneself*

PRÉSENT	je me punis.	je me rends.
IMPARF.	je me punissais.	je me rendais.
FUTUR	je me punirai.	je me rendrai.
CONDIT.	je me punirais.	je me rendrais.
IMPÉRAT.	punis-toi, punissons-nous, punissez-vous.	rends-toi, rendons-nous, rendez-vous.

Emploi de l'article défini avec les verbes réfléchis. —

Je *me* lave *les* mains.	*I wash my hands.*
Il *se* brosse *les* dents.	*He brushes his teeth.*

In French, the definite article is used instead of the possessive adjective before parts of the body, whenever there is no possible ambiguity (Lesson 52). It is, of course, used with the reflexive verbs, for no ambiguity is possible with such verbs. In these cases, the reflexive pronoun, from direct object that it was, becomes indirect, the literal translation of the two examples above being : *I to myself wash the hands; He to himself brushes the teeth.*

Vocabulaire

s'appeler, *to call oneself.*
se porter bien, *to be well.*
se lever, *to get up.*
se laver, *to wash oneself.*
se coucher, *to go to bed, to lie down.*
se frictionner, *to rub oneself.*
s'essuyer, *to dry oneself.*
se brosser, *to brush oneself.*
s'habiller, *to dress oneself.*
se peigner, *to comb oneself.*

se mettre, *to put oneself, to set oneself to.*
se promener, *to take a walk.*
se salir, *to soil oneself, to get dirty.*
se tromper, *to be mistaken.*
se cacher, *to hide oneself.*
s'apercevoir,[1] *to perceive, to notice.*
se perdre, *to get lost.*
se reposer, *to rest, to take a rest.*
se défendre, *to defend oneself.*

---

[1] **Apercevoir,** *to perceive* or *discover an external object;* **s'apercevoir,** *to perceive a fact.* **J'aperçois mon frère,** *I perceive my brother.* **Je m'aperçois que mon frère est arrivé.** *I perceive that my brother has arrived.*

se **rendre**, *to surrender, to betake oneself.*

se **dépêcher,** *to hurry, to hasten.*

se **préparer,** *to get ready.*

s'**amuser,** *to enjoy oneself.*

se **taire,** *to hold one's tongue.*

dormir comme une marmotte, *to sleep like a top.*

instructif, *instructive.*

le **lit,** *the bed.*

le **devoir,** *the homework.*

la **salle de bain,** *the bathroom.*

la **baignoire,** *the bath tub.*

le **choc,** *the shock.*

la **douche,** *the shower.*

le **crin,** *horse hair.*

la **serviette-éponge,** *turkish towel.*

faire sa toilette, *to make one's toilet.*

Lecture

Voici un bon petit garçon ; il s'appelle Paul Delval. Il travaille bien, il est très ponctuel (*exact*) dans tout ce qu'il fait. Il se porte bien, il n'est jamais malade. Il se lève le matin à 7 heures et se rend immédiatement dans la salle de bain. Il enlève son pyjama, saute dans la baignoire et ouvre la douche froide. Brrr . . . il a d'abord un choc, mais c'est vite passé, il se frictionne avec un gant de crin, ferme la douche et s'essuye avec une grosse serviette-éponge.

Maintenant qu'il s'est lavé, il se brosse les dents, se peigne et retourne dans sa chambre où il s'habille. Quand il a fini sa toilette, il se rend dans la salle à manger où un bon déjeuner l'attend. Il ne se dépêche pas, ce n'est pas nécessaire, car il n'est pas resté dans son lit jusqu'à la dernière minute comme font beaucoup d'autres garçons. Sa mère ne doit jamais lui dire : " Paul, dépêche-toi, tu es encore en retard ! "

Il se prépare maintenant pour aller à l'école où il restera jusqu'à trois heures. Quand il reviendra, il s'amusera avec ses petits voisins pendant une heure ou une heure et demie ; puis il se mettra au travail jusqu'au dîner. Si tous ses devoirs ne sont pas finis, il les continuera le soir ; s'ils sont finis, il lira un livre intéressant et instructif, ou, s'il fait beau il ira se promener avec son père ou sa mère. Tous les jours à 9 heures, il se couche et dort comme une marmotte jusqu'au matin.

Ewing Galloway

MUSICIENS BRETONS.

Exercices

A. *Conjuguez :*

1. Je me porte bien, tu te, etc.   2. Je m'amuse.   3. Je m'habille.   4. Je me salis.   5. Je me perds.   6. Je me défends.   7. Je m'aperçois.

B. *Mettez aux formes négative et interrogative :*

1. Nous nous dépêchons.   2. Elle se fâche.   3. Vous vous habillez.   4. Je me repose.   5. Il se lave la figure. 6. Ils se brossent.   7. Nous nous amusons.   8. Elles se mettront au travail.   9. Vous vous portiez bien.   10. Elle se salissait.   11. Je me promènerai.   12. Il se trompait. 13. Nous nous cacherons.   14. Il se perdrait toujours. 15. Vous vous lèveriez trop tard.

C. *Traduisez en français :*

1. How is your mother to-day?   2. She is well, thank you.   3. At what time do you go to bed?   4. I go to bed at ten o'clock and I get up at six (o'clock).   5. Would you get up so early (*tôt*), if you went to bed at midnight? 6. What is that gentleman's name?   7. His name is Dubois.   8. I beg your pardon, what is your name?   9. My name is John and my sister's is Mary.   10. Don't hide, I see you.   11. You are mistaken, I am not hiding. 12. When you are mistaken, blame yourself and not me. 13. We are going for a walk, hurry up!   14. If you go to the theater, you will enjoy yourself.   15. Will you not get lost if you go alone (*seul*)?   16. I never get lost. 17. Last year, when she was in Paris, she used to get lost all the time.

D. *Exercice oral ou écrit :*

1. He enjoys himself.   2. He is not enjoying himself. 3. Is he not enjoying himself?   4. We shall enjoy ourselves.   5. Let us enjoy ourselves.   6. Enjoy yourself. 7. They used to enjoy themselves.   8. She would enjoy

herself. 9. They surrender. 10. They will not surrender. 11. Let us surrender. 12. Let us not surrender. 13. Do you surrender? 14. I am hurrying. 15. Please hurry (up). 16. Don't hurry. 17. Everybody is hurrying.

Exercice-revue

1. We would do it if we could. 2. I would not say it to her. 3. Would you be willing to tell it to us? 4. She would not be able to do it. 5. They would know that. 6. Would you know it too? 7. He would see you if you stayed here. 8. What would we take? 9. You would not recognize him. 10. Would you come with me? 11. She would put her hat on. 12. They would not leave before me. 13. I thought he would read that book. 14. I believe she would write him. 15. He would not believe you. 16. If he could, he would open the door and (would) go out. 17. Would he run? 18. I would laugh then. 19. Would you feel the draft if I opened that window? 20. If I were thirsty, I would drink one or two glasses of water.

* * * * * * *

62ᵉ Leçon : Verbes pronominaux réciproques

Plus fait douceur que violence. — *Persuasion is better than force.*

Compare the following sentences :

(1) **Nous nous querellons.** *We quarrel.*

(2) **Nous nous blâmons.** *We blame ourselves* or *each other.*

(3) **Nous nous blâmons *l'un l'autre*.** *We blame each other* (two persons).

(4) **Nous nous blâmons *les uns les autres*.** *We blame one another* (more than two).

Some pronominal verbs may be used in the plural either reflexively or reciprocally.

When the verb is used in a reciprocal sense, and no ambiguity is to be feared, the form is that of the reflexive verb (Examples 1 and 2).   Ambiguity is prevented by the use of **l'un l'autre** [1] (**l'une l'autre** for the feminine) if the subject refers to two persons, and by **les uns les autres** (**les unes les autres** for the feminine) if more than two persons are included in the subject.

In Example 1, there is no possible ambiguity; two persons are needed to make a quarrel, and they do not quarrel with themselves, but with each other, therefore the use of **l'un l'autre** is unnecessary.

In Example 2, I may blame myself and you may blame yourself, *i.e.*, *we blame ourselves*, **nous nous blâmons**.   We may also throw the blame on each other.   If in the latter case there is no possible ambiguity, we leave the construction **nous nous blâmons** as it is, but,

Example 3, if the speaker fears that there may be ambiguity or misunderstanding, the use of **l'un l'autre** is required: **nous nous blâmons l'un l'autre**.

Example 4.   The construction and meaning are the same as in Example 3, but more than two persons are involved.

Vocabulaire

assurer, *to assure.*	**se séparer,** *to part.*
attaquer, *to attack.*	**se quereller,** *to quarrel.*
blesser, *to wound.*	**embrasser,** *to embrace, to kiss.*
tuer, *to kill.*	**se sentir,** *to feel.*

Lecture

1. Je pense que vous vous flattez toujours l'un l'autre. 2. Au contraire, votre frère et votre sœur se querellent souvent.   3. C'est vrai, ils se grondent quelquefois; ils ne s'aiment pas trop.   4. Si quelqu'un vous attaque quand vous serez absent, je vous défendrai; et, si quelqu'un m'at-

---

[1] Do not confuse with **l'un et l'autre,** *both:* **Ils sont partis l'un et l'autre.** *They have both left.*   Notice also **l'un ou l'autre,** *either,* and **ni l'un ni l'autre,** *neither.*

taque quand je serai absent, vous me défendrez.   5. Nous nous défendrons ainsi l'un l'autre.   6. Si vous vous séparez dans le bois et si vous perdez votre chemin, nous vous chercherons l'un et l'autre.   7. On me dit que les sœurs ne se querellent jamais.   8. Quelle histoire ! vous vous trompez, je vous assure.   9. Celles-ci se querellent souvent, mais elles finissent par s'embrasser.   10. Vos parents se portent-ils bien ?   11. Toujours bien, merci.   12. Ne vous blessez pas l'une l'autre.   13. Ces messieurs se blâment les uns les autres.

Exercices

A. *Traduisez en français :*

1. We never blame ourselves, I assure you.   2. You know, I suppose, that we always blame each other.   3. Will they not wound each other?   4. Will they kill each other? 5. If this man killed his friend, he would kill himself, too, I think.   6. Why do you not like each other?   7. Who told you that we did (do) not like each other?   8. Nobody ; but you are always scolding each other.   9. We are not quarreling.   10. These two brothers quarrel sometimes, it is true, but in spite of that (*cela*), they are very fond of each other. 11. We always defend one another.   12. Yes, but when you are together you always quarrel.   13. If we lose our way in this wood, we will not separate.   14. If any one attacks us, we will defend ourselves.   15. I will defend myself and you will also defend yourself.   16. We will defend each other.   17. Were you and your brother looking for each other this morning?   18. You forget that I am no longer the young man you saw five years ago.   19. You are mistaken ; I do not forget it.

B. *Exercice oral :*

1. They (*f.*) admire themselves.   2. They (*f.*) admire each other (*two persons*).   3. They admire one another (*more than two persons*).   4. Are you amusing yourselves?

5. Are you amusing each other?   6. Part.   7. Let us not part.   8. Do you blame us?   9. Do you blame yourselves?   10. Do you blame each other?   11. Do not blame us.   12. Do not blame each other.   13. They are fond of her.   14. They are fond of each other.

Exercice-revue

1. You are right and you must be glad to know it.   2. To which of your brothers did you say that?   3. He did not believe me, and he was wrong.   4. He did not always believe me.   5. When I am sleepy, I will go to bed.   6. I would go to bed early if I were tired.   7. What is the matter with you? Are you cold?   8. Not exactly, but I don't feel well.   9. If something ails you, tell it to me.   10. I would certainly tell you.   11. I don't think so ; when something is the matter with you, you never tell me (it to me).   12. What is this, who came here while (*pendant que*) I was out?   13. How is your sister-in-law?   14. She is not well to-day, she has a headache.   15. She is too active and too nervous (*nerveux*).   16. Why doesn't she take a rest?   17. She needs it, she always hurries.   18. What was the matter with your little brother this morning?   19. Go into the bathroom and wash yourself ; you will dress later.   20. Why do you hide? If you think that I do not see you, you are mistaken.

*   *   *   *   *   *   *

63ᵉ Leçon : Verbes pronominaux. — Temps composés

De la coupe aux lèvres, il y a loin. — *There's many a slip 'twixt the cup and the lip.*

The compound or perfect tenses of a verb are formed by combining its past participle with the various tenses of an auxiliary verb. All transitive and most intransitive verbs

form their compound tenses with the auxiliary verb **avoir.**
For intransitive verbs conjugated with **être,** refer to the list
given in Lesson 28.[1]

Donner, *to give*   **Retourner,** *to go back* [2]

COMPOUND TENSES

PASSÉ INDÉFINI

j'ai donné,   je suis retourné.
 I have given.   *I have gone back.*

PLUS-QUE-PARFAIT

j'avais donné,   j'étais retourné,
 I had given.   *I had gone back.*

FUTUR ANTÉRIEUR

j'aurai donné,   je serai retourné,
 I shall have given.   *I shall have gone back.*

CONDITIONNEL PASSÉ

j'aurais donné,   je serais retourné,
 I should have given.   *I should have gone back.*

Reflexive and reciprocal verbs are always conjugated with
être.

Se défendre, *to defend oneself*

PASSÉ INDÉFINI   PLUS-QUE-PARFAIT
je me suis défendu, *I have defended* je m'étais défendu,
tu t'es défendu.   *myself.*   *I had defended myself.*
il s'est défendu.
elle s'est défendue.   FUTUR ANTÉRIEUR
nous nous sommes défendus. je me serai défendu.
vous vous êtes défendus.[3]   *I shall have defended myself.*
ils se sont défendus.
elles se sont défendues.   CONDITIONNEL PASSÉ
                  je me serais défendu.
                  I should have defended myself.

---

[1] Certain verbs are conjugated with **avoir** or **être,** according to the
sense. With **avoir,** attention is called to the action itself, its duration,
etc.; with **être,** the result of the action is indicated: **Vous avez grandi
en peu de temps.** *You have grown up in a short time;* **Vous êtes grandi
maintenant.** *You are grown up now.*

[2] Three French verbs may be translated *return* in English: **rendre,**
to give back, **revenir,** *to come back,* **retourner,** *to go back.*

[3] No **s** in this form if **vous** is singular.

As **être** takes the place of **avoir** with reflexive and reciprocal verbs, the past participle agrees with the *direct* object when the direct object precedes (Lesson 34).

Ils se sont aimés. *They loved each other.*
Ils se sont écrit une lettre. *They have written a letter to each other.*
Les lettres qu'ils se sont écrites. *The letters they have written each other.*
Ma sœur s'est coupée. *My sister has cut herself.*
Ma sœur s'est coupé [1] le doigt. *My sister has cut her finger* (literally, *the finger to herself*).

Observe that in the first, third, and fourth of these examples, the past participle agrees with the preceding direct object. In the second and fifth, however, the direct object does not precede the verb, the reflexive pronoun being in the dative case (*indirect object*).

Vocabulaire

s'enrhumer,[2] *to take cold.*
encore un(e), *another* (additional).
se fâcher, *to get angry.*
adresser, *to address.*

grandir, *to grow tall, to grow up.*
nulle part, *nowhere.*
si tôt, *so soon.*
fort (adv.), *very, hard.*

Lecture

1. A quelle heure vous êtes-vous couché hier soir?   2. Je me suis couché à dix heures et demie.   3. Mon frère s'est levé à sept heures moins un quart.   4. Votre sœur s'est-elle promenée aujourd'hui?   5. Non, elle s'est un peu enrhumée hier soir; c'est pourquoi elle ne se porte pas mieux aujourd'hui.   6. Elles se sont adressées à nous.   7. Elles se sont adressé des lettres.   8. Nous avons vu les lettres qu'elles se sont adressées.   9. Est-ce que vos cousins se sont fâchés lorsque vous leur avez raconté l'affaire?   10. Henri m'a dit

---

[1] Compare: **Ma sœur s'est cassé le bras, Ma sœur a le bras cassé,** and **Ma sœur m'a cassé le bras.**

[2] **s'enrhumer,** *to catch cold;* **être enrhumé,** or **avoir un rhume,** *to have a cold.*

simplement que je me trompais, mais Louise s'est fâchée tout de suite. 11. Est-ce que vous ne vous seriez pas fâché, si j'avais fait cela? 12. Nous nous sommes promenés si long-temps ce matin que ma sœur était fort lasse. 13. Mais ne vous êtes-vous reposés nulle part? 14. Si nous étions restés chez nous hier soir, nous ne nous serions pas enrhumés.

Exercises

A. *Traduisez en français :*

1. I got up at eight this morning. 2. At what time did you get up? 3. We got up at half-past nine. 4. What [a] lazy [man] ! 5. I was not well. 6. What was the matter with you? 7. I caught cold two or three days ago, and I had a toothache this morning. 8. Go to bed at once ! you are sleepy. 9. Don't get angry. 10. Get up, your friends have already arrived. 11. When she has rested a little longer, perhaps another half-hour, you will tell her that we are ready. 12. Where are the letters you sent each other? 13. We have given them back to each other. 14. Would you have gone to bed so soon, if it hadn't been so cold? 15. They went out with their father at quarter of eight ; they walked until quarter past nine, when (and then) they returned. 16. They enjoyed themselves greatly (much), and I think he did also (he also, I think). 17. Go back home now ; and when you are here to-morrow, we will finish together what we began yesterday.

B. *Exercice oral :*

1. I am amusing them. 2. I am enjoying myself. 3. I have amused them. 4. I have enjoyed myself. 5. I used to enjoy myself. 6. I had enjoyed myself. 7. I shall enjoy myself. 8. I should have amused her. 9. I should have enjoyed myself.

Repeat these sentences, making them negative, interrogative, or negative interrogative, and changing the person and gender

*of the subject pronouns to third person singular feminine, first
person plural masculine, etc.*

Exercice-revue

1. At what time does she get up? 2. She gets up at
6 o'clock when she goes to bed early. 3. Yesterday I
went to Mrs. Roxas; why did you not come with me?
4. Whose pen is this? Is it yours or his? 5. Why did he
not answer you politely? 6. He has never answered her
politely. 7. Where is your brother going? 8. Where did
ho go? 9. Get up, I need that chair for your old uncle.
10. John, hurry up, you will be late for school. 11. Is it
so late? I did not know I was late. 12. I was so thirsty
that I drank three cups of tea. 13. Don't tell it to me, I
know it. 14. If you do not need these books, give them to
her. 15. Would you have given them to me if you had
needed them? 16. Give them to us, don't give them to
him. 17. I will give them to him (the one) who can answer
this question. 18. What question? 19. Why do you
quarrel all the time? 20. They quarrel because they do
not love each other. 21. What is a quarrel? 22. I don't
know what a quarrel is. 23. Sometimes we blame each
other and accuse (*s'accuser*) each other, but I cannot say that
we quarrel.

* * * * * * *

64ᵉ Leçon: Les pronoms Y et EN

Qui vivra, verra. — *He who lives will see.*

Y and **en**, although used frequently as adverbs, are pronouns. **Y** = **à** and a noun or pronoun. **En** = **de** and a
noun or pronoun.

For the use of **en**, *of it, of them, some, any*, with words of quantity, numerals, etc., recall Lessons 38 and 39.

Avez-vous des crayons?	*Have you pencils?*
Oui, j'en ai.	*Yes, I have.*
Il n'en a pas.	*He hasn't any.*
Elle en a un.	*She has one.*
Apportez-en.	*Bring some.*

En, *from there, from it, from them,* refers to a place already mentioned, which some one has left. It is used mostly with the verb **venir** or its compound **revenir,** *to come back.*

Êtes-vous allés à l'église? Oui, j'en viens. *Did you go to church? Yes, I come from it (there).*

Avez-vous été aux courses? Oui, j'en reviens. *Have you been at the races? Yes, I am coming back from them (there).*

Y, *to it, to them, there,* is rarely used in reference to persons.

Pensez-vous à vos leçons?	*Are you thinking of your lessons?*
J'y pense.	*I am thinking of them.*
Pensez-y.	*Think of them.*
Pensez-vous à vos amis?	*Are you thinking of your friends?*
Je pense *à eux.*	*I am thinking of them.*

There (expressed or understood in English) is expressed by **y** in referring to a place already mentioned, and by **là** in pointing out a place or thing.

Regardez cette maison. *Look at that house.*

J'y ai demeuré trois mois. *I lived there three months.*

C'est là que vous trouverez ce que vous cherchez. *That is where you will find what you are looking for.*

Y and **en** follow the other pronouns. **Y** precedes **en.**

Je vous les y porterai.	*I shall carry them to you there.*
Je vous y en porterai.	*I shall carry you some there.*
Il y en a beaucoup.	*There are many of them.*

A past participle does not agree with a preceding **en.**[1]

Je n'en ai pas vu. *I haven't seen any.*

---

[1] If **en** is used with an adverb of quantity which precedes the verb, the past participle agrees: **Combien en a-t-on vus?**

LE MONT ST. MICHEL (XIIᵉ SIÈCLE).

In the imperative affirmative, **y** and **en** are joined to the verb, to other pronouns, and to each other.

Prêtez-nous-en.   *Lend us some.*
Donnez-m'en.[1]   *Give me some.*

Vivre, *to live;* participe passé, **vécu,** *lived*

PRÉSENT	IMPARFAIT	FUTUR
je vis, *I live.*	je vivais, *I was living.*	je vivrai, *I shall live.*
tu vis.	tu vivais.	tu vivras.
il vit.	il vivait.	il vivra.
nous vivons.	nous vivions.	nous vivrons.
vous vivez.	vous viviez.	vous vivrez.
ils vivent.	ils vivaient.	ils vivront.

IMPÉRATIF

SINGULIER	PLURIEL	
vis, *live.*	vivons, *let us live.*	vivez, *live.*

Vocabulaire

avoir envie de, *to have a mind to.*
gothique, *gothic.*
sans doute, *no doubt.*
     tout au plus, *at the most.*
     vitrail, pl. vitraux, *stained-glass window.*

voyager, *to travel.*
chaque, *each.*
libre, *free, at liberty.*

Lecture

CONVERSATION

— N'êtes-vous jamais entré dans cette belle église?

— Non ; j'en ai beaucoup entendu parler, mais je n'y suis jamais entré.

— Entrons-y si vous voulez.

— Vous avez peut-être faim, allons d'abord au restaurant.

— Non, j'en sors, mais si vous voulez manger quelque chose, allons-y.

---

[1] Notice that **me** and **te** do not become **moi** and **toi** before **en,** when used with the imperative affirmative.

— Je n'en ai pas envie, je vous assure.

— Entrons alors. Regardez là ; quel magnifique vitrail !
On dit que les vitraux de cette église datent du XIII⁰ siècle.

— Oui, il est de toute beauté et je remarque qu'il y en a
beaucoup.

— Tiens ! Voilà le monsieur américain et sa dame que
j'ai déjà rencontrés ici deux fois.

— Ce sont, comme vous, des admirateurs du style gothique,
sans doute.

— Je le crois. Je suis venu deux fois dans cette église, et
chaque fois je les y ai rencontrés.

— Les Américains voyagent beaucoup maintenant, n'est-ce
pas ?

— Oui ; le mois dernier j'étais à Anvers ; j'ai visité la
cathédrale où sont les plus beaux tableaux de Rubens ; elle
était pleine d'Américains ; j'y en ai compté plus de cinquante.

— Mais j'y pense, il est déjà trois heures, et j'ai rendez-
vous à l'hôtel avec un de mes amis ; je l'avais complètement
oublié ; je dois vous quitter.

— Oh ! c'est dommage.   Prenez un taxi, vous y serez dans
dix minutes, un quart d'heure tout au plus.

— Venez me prendre à l'hôtel demain vers 10 heures, si
vous êtes libre.

— J'y serai certainement, car je n'ai rien à faire demain.

Exercices

A. *Remplacez les mots en italiques par* **y** :

1. Allez-vous *au théâtre ?*   2. Je vais *au cinéma*.   3. Allons *au cinéma* ensemble.   4. Nous avons trouvé nos amis
dans le jardin.   5. Nous entrerons *dans le musée*.   6. Nous
n'allons pas *au concert* ce soir.   7. Vous attendrez vos amis
au coin de la rue.   8. Il a mis ses cravates *dans le tiroir*.
9. J'ai répondu *à cette lettre*.   10. Je pense toujours *à ce
beau tableau*.   11. Pensez *à ce que je vous ai dit*.   12. Ré-

pondez *à ma question.* 13. Ne faites pas attention *à cette remarque.* 14. N'entrons pas *dans l'église maintenant.* 15. Mettez vos crayons *sur cette table.*

B. *Remplacez les mots en italiques par* **en** :

1. J'ai plus *d'argent* que lui. 2. A-t-il beaucoup *de livres?* 3. Il a dix *livres.* 4. N'a-t-il que dix *livres?* 5. Il arrive *de la bibliothèque.* 6. Nous avons assez *de viande.* 7. Elles veulent *des bonbons.* 8. Revient-il *du théâtre?* 9. Montrez-moi *des roses.* 10. Voici *des roses.* 11. Voulez-vous *des violettes?* 12. Sortez *de cette chambre!* 13. Si vous ne sortez pas *de cette chambre,* je vous punirai. 14. Ils reviennent *de la campagne* demain soir. 15. Je ne viens pas *du jardin.*

C. *Traduisez en français :*

1. Do you go to school every day? 2. Yes, I go (there). 3. At what time do you go there? 4. We go there at 9 o'clock. 5. Go there now, you are late. 6. Let us go there. 7. Let us not go there. 8. Last week, we did not go there. 9. Last year, we used to go there every day. 10. If you arrive at the church before me, wait for me there. 11. Did you go to that restaurant? 12. Yes, I am coming from there. 13. Do you see any roses in this garden? 14. Yes, I see two. 15. Do you see only two? 16. I am sure there are more than two. 17. When I was in the country last summer I asked my sister for some books and she sent me a dozen there. 18. Has your mother been to church to-day? 19. She has not been there, but I have. 20. Are you speaking of it? 21. Think of it, but don't speak of it. 22. Are you thinking of it? 23. I think of it all the time. 24. I am glad of it.

Exercice-revue

1. I enjoyed myself very much yesterday at the professor's evening party. 2. And you, Charles, did you not

enjoy yourself? 3. His mother is old, but she is still very active. 4. What a big watch you have! 5. It is [a] big [one] but it is [a] very good [one]. 6. Take me to the hotel. 7. Get up, we must go now. 8. Leave me alone, I do not feel well. 9. What is the matter with you? 10. If I see the doctor, shall I speak to him? 11. Read that book and when you have finished it, you will tell me what you think of it. 12. Don't run, you will fall. 13. Why do you laugh? 14. I do not laugh, I am crying because I cut my finger. 15. How did you cut your finger? 16. I was playing with John, and we cut each other. 17. Were you quarreling? 18. Don't blame each other now. 19. I perceive that you flatter yourself. 20. You are mistaken, I never flatter myself.

*　　*　　*　　*　　*　　*　　*

65ᵉ Leçon: Pronoms personnels. — Revue générale

A l'œuvre on connaît l'artisan. — *A workman is known by his work.*

We have learned that the conjunctive object pronouns are: **me, te, se, nous, vous, le, la, les, lui, leur, y,** and **en.**

The order of precedence is the following:

$$
\left.\begin{array}{l}\text{me}\\\text{te}\\\text{se}\\\text{nous}\\\text{vous}\end{array}\right\} \text{precede} \left.\begin{array}{l}\text{le}\\\text{la}\\\text{les}\end{array}\right\} \text{precede} \left.\begin{array}{l}\text{lui}\\\text{leur}\end{array}\right\} \text{precede } \text{y, precede } \text{en, } + \text{VERB.}
$$

In the imperative affirmative, which requires the pronouns after the verb, **le, la, les** precede the other pronouns, and **me** and **te** become **moi** and **toi**, except before **y** or **en.**

Montrez-*les-moi*.	*Show them to me.*
Mets-*t'y*.	*Stand over there.*
Donnez-*m'en*.	*Give me some.*

Exercice spécial

" Pen " or " pens " being understood by the first pronoun in each phrase below, translate rapidly :

It to her, it to them, it to me, it to him, it to us, some to me, some to us, them to them, them to him, some to them, them to you, some to her.

" Book " or " books " being understood by the first pronoun in each phrase below, translate rapidly :

It to us, it to him, it to them, it to you, it to her, it to himself, it to me, some to us, some to me, them to me, some to her, them to us, some to them, them to them, some to you, some to him.

Résoudre, *to resolve ;* participe passé, **résolu, résous,** *resolved*

Présent	Imparfait	Futur
je résous, *I resolve.*	je résolvais, *I was*	je résoudrai, *I shall*
tu résous.	tu résolvais. *resolving.*	tu résoudras. *resolve.*
il résout.	il résolvait.	il résoudra.
nous résolvons.	nous résolvions.	nous résoudrons.
vous résolvez.	vous résolviez.	vous résoudrez.
ils résolvent.	ils résolvaient.	ils résoudront.

Impératif

Singulier	Pluriel	
résous, *resolve.*	résolvons, *let us resolve.*	résolvez, *resolve.*

Vocabulaire

compris, *understood.*	la tranche, *the slice.*
le roman, *the novel.*	fâché, *angry.*
emprunter, *to borrow.*	le boulanger, *the baker.*
un seul, *a single one.*	le gâteau, *the cake.*
le prix, *the prize.*	planter, *to plant.*
non plus, *either.*	même, adv., *even.*
bien, *very.*	causeur, *talkative.*

Lecture

1. N'avez-vous pas compris ce que je vous ai dit?
2. Vous avez de si bon lait que je vous en demanderai encore

un peu.   3. La bonne en désire aussi ; ne lui en donnerez-vous pas? Volontiers.   4. Votre frère a tant de jolis romans allemands que je lui en emprunterai quelques-uns. 5. Il ne vous les prêtera pas, je vous assure, car il ne m'en a jamais prêté un seul.   6. Elle n'a pas mérité le prix, parce que, si elle l'avait mérité, on le lui aurait donné.   7. Lui, il ne l'a pas mérité non plus.   8. Ce pauvre garçon a bien faim ; coupez-lui une grosse tranche de pain, et donnez-lui aussi du beurre et un verre de lait.   9. J'aime les histoires intéressantes que vous m'avez racontées.   10. Ne lui en racontez pas.   11. Racontez-m'en souvent.   12. Lui répondez-vous, lorsqu'elle vous parle?   13. Voici sa lettre ; répondez-y.   14. N'y pensez plus.

Exercices

A. *Répondez aux questions suivantes en employant des pronoms à la place des noms:*

1. Avez-vous donné votre pain à votre sœur?   2. Avez-vous donné du pain à votre sœur?   3. A-t-il rendu les plumes à son cousin?   4. Avez-vous planté des tulipes dans votre jardin?   5. Avez-vous planté les tulipes dans votre jardin?   6. Avez-vous raconté la nouvelle à votre amie? 7. Donnez-moi un peu de viande, s'il vous plaît.   8. Y a-t-il beaucoup de livres dans votre bibliothèque?   9. Prêtez-vous de l'argent à votre frère?   10. Cherchez-vous vos plumes?   11. Cherchez-vous des plumes?   12. Avez-vous donné des bonbons aux enfants?   13. Avez-vous raconté deux histoires à vos parents?

B. *Traduisez en français:*

1. She asked me for some lemonade and I told her that I would bring her some.   2. Did you bring her some?   3. No, I didn't bring her any, because I hadn't any.   4. I told her so (it).   5. What did she say to you?   6. Don't ask me (it to me), she was very angry.   7. If you had water, why

did you not give some to her?   8. She did not ask me for
any.   9. Speak to her about it.   10. Did I not ask you
what time it was?   11. Our maid went to the baker and
bought bread and cake for us there.   12. Ours bought us
some there too.   13. There are many trees in your garden;
who planted them there?   14. My brother planted many
there.   15. Show them to me.   16. Why don't you show
them to us?   17. I shall give her the flowers if you send
them to me before noon.   18. I shall give them to you
before eleven o'clock.   19. If you do not send them to her
to-day, return them to me.   20. I certainly will.

C. *Exercice supplémentaire:*

1. We lend them to you.   2. Are you lending them to
her?   3. Lend them to her.   4. Lend them some.   5. Lend
me some.   6. Have you lent it to us?   7. Had she lent
me any?   8. Shall you lend them to them?   9. Are you
speaking of it?   10. Are you thinking of it?   11. Let us
think of it.   12. Let us speak of it.   13. Speak of it.
14. Think of it.

Repeat, making each sentence negative.

Exercice-revue

1. We are older than they.   2. She is younger than I.
3. Will you come to our house?   4. We shall be at your
house to-morrow at 5.45, if it does not rain.   5. Come to
my house.   6. I shall be there.   7. I shall wait for you
there.   8. She and I will take a walk.   9. They and I
will wait for you there.   10. Did you take a rest last Sunday?   11. Yes, I got up at 10 o'clock, and stayed home the
whole day.   12. Didn't you take a walk in the park?
13. No, I did not go out, I didn't even dress myself.
14. These two boys played in the street, they lost all their
money, and then they quarreled and blamed each other.
15. Where do you come from (From where do you come)?   Go

in the bathroom and wash your face and hands. 16. Hurry
up, we are waiting for you. 17. Are you ill, Mary? I am.
18. Are you the patient, madam? I am. 19. Are you
pleased with your new maid? I am. 20. She is sweet,
frank, and active; she is neither talkative nor flattering.

* * * * * * *

66e Leçon: Article; prépositions: DE, A, EN, et DANS

Mauvaise herbe croît toujours. — *Ill weeds grow apace.*

Study the following sentences:

(1) **L'Asie est plus grande que l'Europe.**	*Asia is larger than Europe.*
(2) **La France est un beau pays.**	*France is a beautiful country.*
(3) **La Bretagne est intéressante.**	*Brittany is interesting.*
(4) **Le Mont Blanc est très haut.**	*Mount Blanc is very high.*

The definite article is used before names of continents (1),
countries (2), provinces (3), and mountains (4).

However, before names of countries used adjectively, the
article is generally omitted:

> **le roi d'Italie,** *the king of Italy.*
> **du vin de France,** *French wine.*
> **le fromage de Hollande,** *Dutch cheese.*

Study the following sentences:

Je vais *en* France.	*I go to France.*
Je demeure *en* France.	*I live in France.*
J'irai *au* Portugal.	*I shall go to Portugal.*
Mon oncle est *dans* l'Afrique du Nord.	*My uncle is in North Africa.*
Ma tante demeure *à* Paris.	*My aunt lives in Paris.*

The English prepositions *in* and *to* used before the name of
a country or city are both rendered in French by the same
word.

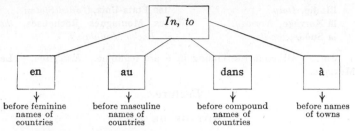

en France,   *au* Portugal,   *dans* l'Afrique du Sud,   *à* Paris
in or *to France.* *in* or *to Portugal.* *in* or *to South Africa.* *in* or *to Paris*

Study the following sentences :

Je viens *de* France.	*I come from France.*
Je viens *de* Paris.	*I come from Paris.*
Je viens *du* Portugal.	*I come from Portugal.*
Je viens *des* États-Unis.	*I come from the United States.*

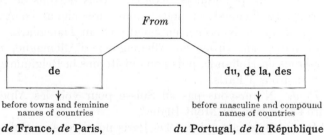

de France, *de* Paris,   *du* Portugal, *de la* République
de Russie, *de* Bruxelles.   Argentine, *des* États-Unis.

Vocabulaire

l'Europe, *Europe.*	le Danemark, *Denmark.*
l'Amérique, *America.*	le Portugal, *Portugal.*
la France, *France.*	le Japon, *Japan.*
l'Allemagne, *Germany.*	le Chili, *Chili.*
l'Angleterre, *England.*	le Pérou, *Peru.*
la Belgique, *Belgium.*	le Mexique, *Mexico.*
la Hollande, *Holland.*	le Mont Blanc, *Mount Blanc.*
la Suisse, *Switzerland.*	le Rhin, *the Rhine.*
la Russie, *Russia.*	les Alpes, *the Alps.*

l'Italie, *Italy*.
la Norvège, *Norway*.
la Suède, *Sweden*.

les États-Unis, *United States*.
les **Montagnes Rocheuses**, *the Rocky Mountains*.

Note. — All countries ending in **e** are feminine.   *Exception.* — **Le Mexique.**

Lecture

Le voyage de Jean

Paul.   Eh bien! Quelles nouvelles? Vous semblez si heureux aujourd'hui.

Jean.   Mon cher, je suis fou de (*with*) joie! Mon frère et moi nous partons dans huit jours; nous allons faire le tour du monde!

Paul.   Non! Pas possible! Oh! le veinard (*lucky fellow*)!

Jean.   Oui, je l'admets (*admit*). Nous partons de New-York, naturellement, et nous allons directement en Angleterre, de là en Norvège, en Suède, et au Danemark. Du Danemark, nous irons en Allemagne; d'Allemagne, nous passerons en Hollande, puis nous visiterons la Belgique et de là nous irons à Paris.

Paul.   N'irez-vous pas en Suisse pour voir les Alpes et faire l'ascension du Mont Blanc?

Jean.   Si, si, attendez. De Paris nous irons en Suisse et nous entrerons en Italie par le tunnel du Simplon. Nous nous embarquerons à Venise et nous visiterons la Grèce, la Turquie et l'Égypte.

Paul.   Alors vous ne verrez pas l'Espagne, ni le Portugal, ni la Russie?

Jean.   Non, on ne peut pas tout voir. A Alexandrie, nous prendrons un bateau qui va au Japon par le Canal de Suez, la Mer Rouge, l'Inde et la Chine.

Paul.   N'irez-vous pas aux Iles Philippines?

Jean.   Je ne sais pas encore, mais je pense que non; du Japon, nous reviendrons en Amérique, mais nous ne savons pas encore quelle route nous prendrons. Nous irons peut-être à Vancouver, au Canada, ou à San Francisco. Si nous allons par la Californie, nous nous arrêterons aux Iles Hawai, à Honolulu.

Paul. Voilà certainement un beau voyage ! Combien de temps serez-vous en route?

Jean. Nous ne savons pas exactement, mais nous comptons que le voyage nous prendra environ trois mois.

Exercices

A. *Remplacez les tirets par* **en, au, à** *ou* **dans,** *selon le cas:*

—— Espagne.   —— Belgique.   —— Venise.

—— Berlin.   —— Danemark.   —— Bruxelles.

—— Japon.   —— Mexique.   —— États-Unis.

—— Asie.   —— Suisse.   —— l'Amérique du Sud

B. *Remplacez les tirets par les mots convenables:*

Je viens d'arriver (*I just arrived*) —— France, —— Paris, —— Canada, —— République de Panama, —— Belgique, —— Boston, —— États-Unis, —— Amérique du Nord, —— Italie, —— Russie, — — New-York, —— Japon, —— Mexique, —— Brésil, —— Indes Orientales, —— Espagne, —— Madrid.

C. *Traduisez en français:*

Charles. Where do you intend to travel this year?

Arthur. I think I shall go to Europe.

Charles. Yes, you were in Japan last year. What countries will you visit in Europe?

Arthur. Two years ago I went to England, Holland, Belgium, France, Spain, and Portugal; this year I think I shall visit Norway, Sweden, Denmark, Germany, Switzerland, and Italy.

Charles. Will you stay long in the capitals of the countries you will visit?

Arthur. I will stay a few (*quelques*) days in London, Oslo, Stockholm, and Copenhagen.

Charles. From Denmark, will you go directly to Berlin?

Arthur. Yes, but I shall not stay there long; I want to spend more time in Switzerland and in Italy.

Charles. How long do you intend to stay in Italy?

Arthur. Probably two weeks, for I want to stay three or four days in Venice, Milan, Naples, and Rome.

Charles. Will you return to the United States from Italy?

Arthur. Yes, I think so.

Charles. What an interesting trip! I should like to accompany you.

Exercice-revue

1. I follow my father because I am his son. 2. Follow him. 3. Take me home, please. 4. Here is some mineral water, but don't drink it if you don't like it. 5. Laugh, my friends, life (*vie*, f.) is short. 6. Run fast if you are late. 7. How do you feel (*se sentir*)? 8. They do not feel as well to-day as yesterday. 9. Don't open that door, it is too cold here. 10. What are you writing? 11. Don't write to him, write to me. 12. Believe me, I don't like that. 13. Will you ever believe me? 14. I have received an interesting letter; I will read it to you. 15. All right, read it to me. 16. Are you already leaving? 17. Yes, we came only for half an hour. 18. I do not know that gentleman, but I know what he does. 19. What will you do next Sunday? 20. I shall walk in the park. 21. If you do that, you will see me, for I shall be there too.

* * * * * * *

Ewing Galloway

STRASBOURG. — VIEILLES MAISONS ET BLANCHISSERIES SUR LE CANAL.

67ᵉ Leçon : DEPUIS. — COMBIEN DE TEMPS. — PENDANT

———

Il faut battre le fer pendant qu'il est chaud. — *Strike while the iron is hot.*

———

Study the following questions :

1. **Depuis quand êtes-vous ici?** *How long have you been here?*
   Depuis quand travaillez-vous? *How long have you been working?*
2. **Combien de temps êtes-vous resté là?** *How long did you stay there?*
   Combien de temps avez-vous travaillé? *How long did you work?*
   Combien de temps travaillerez-vous? *How long will you work?*

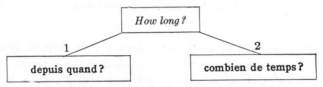

How long?	
1	2
depuis quand?	**combien de temps?**

When an action begun in the past is still going on.

When an action is entirely finished. When an action is in the future.

Depuis quand êtes-vous marié? *How long have you been married?*

Combien de temps avez-vous lu? *Combien de temps* parlerez-vous?

Attention! The English imperfect is not translated by the French imperfect with **combien de temps** when the action is entirely past.

How long were you *in Paris?* **Combien de temps** *avez-vous été* à **Paris?**

Study the following sentences :

1. **Je suis ici depuis trois mois.** *I have been here for three months.*
   Je travaille depuis une heure. *I have been working for one hour.*
2. **Je suis resté là (pendant) trois mois.** *I stayed there for three months.*
   J'ai travaillé (pendant) une heure. *I worked for one hour.*
3. **J'ai du travail pour une semaine.** *I have work for a week.*

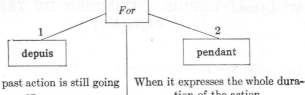

For

1 **depuis**

When the past action is still going on.

Je suis ici depuis trois mois.
I have been here for three months.

2 **pendant**

When it expresses the whole duration of the action.

J'ai parlé (pendant [1]) une heure.
Je parlerai (pendant [1]) une heure.

3 **pour**

When it indicates motive or end.

Nous avons du pain pour deux jours.
We have bread for two days.

Attention! Note that with **depuis** and **depuis quand,** French uses the present where English uses the perfect. The French feel that as long as an action is still going on, it is a present action. In the sentence : **La terre tourne autour du soleil depuis des millions d'années.** *The earth has been turning around the sun for millions of years,* the earth is still turning now, the action is not finished, and is felt by the French as a present action.

Vocabulaire

exactement, *exactly.*
la revue, *the parade.*
superbe, *superb.*
se mêler, *to mix, to meddle with.*
la foule, *the crowd.*
populaire, *popular.*
parmi, *among.*
la chaleur, *the heat.*
les chaleurs, *the hot days.*

la vie, *the life.*
exprimer, *to express.*
merveilleux, *marvelous.*
l'adresse (f.), *the address.*
habiter, *to live.*
s'embarquer, *to embark.*
dépenser, *to spend.*
la Côte d'Azur, *the Riviera.*
une quinzaine, *about fifteen.*

---

[1] **Pendant** in this case is often omitted.

Lecture

CONVERSATION

— Depuis quand êtes-vous à Paris, madame?

— Je suis ici depuis six semaines, je suis arrivée exactement le 30 juin.

— Alors vous étiez ici pendant les fêtes du 14 juillet.

— Oui, et je me suis très bien amusée. La revue a été très intéressante ; le temps était superbe ce jour-là ; le soir, je me suis mêlée à la foule et j'ai dansé dans la rue. J'adore les fêtes populaires.

— Combien de temps resterez-vous encore parmi nous?

— (Pendant) une quinzaine de jours, je pense.

— Comment! Pas plus longtemps que ça? Je pensais que vous vouliez aller à Nice et visiter la Côte d'Azur?

— Mais j'y suis allée il y a un mois, avant les grandes chaleurs.

— Vous avez eu raison. Comment avez-vous trouvé la Riviera? Combien de temps y avez-vous passé?

— J'y suis restée (pendant) quinze jours, et j'aurais voulu y rester toute ma vie ; je ne trouve pas de mots pour exprimer mon admiration ; c'est merveilleux !

— Si j'avais su que vous y alliez, je vous aurais donné l'adresse d'une de mes tantes qui habite Cannes.

— Oh! Quel dommage! Depuis combien de temps madame votre tante demeure-t-elle à Cannes?

— Elle y demeure depuis un an, elle y a acheté une villa l'année dernière. Avez-vous aussi visité plusieurs autres villes?

— Oui, je suis restée trois jours à Marseille, deux à Lyon et deux à Dijon. D'ici je partirai pour Londres.

— Combien de temps resterez-vous à Londres?

— Deux ou trois jours au plus. De là j'irai à Southampton où je m'embarquerai pour New-York. Je ne puis pas rester plus longtemps ; j'ai déjà dépensé beaucoup d'argent ; j'en ai encore assez pour deux ou trois semaines, c'est-à-dire juste assez pour finir mon voyage.

Exercices

A. *Remplacez les tirets par l'expression ou le mot convenable :*

1. —— demeurez-vous dans cette maison? 2. J'y demeure —— dix ans. 3. —— y demeurerez-vous encore? 4. Peut-être —— deux ou trois ans. 5. —— Jean est-il dans sa chambre? 6. —— ce matin. 7. —— y restera-t-il encore? 8. Je pense qu'il travaillera encore —— une heure. 9. Moi, j'ai fini mes devoirs, j'ai étudié —— trois heures. 10. J'ai encore du travail —— quelques jours, et alors je serai prêt pour les examens.

B. *Traduisez en français :*

1. Isn't it your uncle who lives in that old house? 2. Yes, it is he ; he has been living in it for over twenty years. 3. How long have your father and mother been traveling in Europe? 4. They have been there for several months. 5. They have visited all the most interesting cities of France, Germany, and Holland. 6. How long were they in Rotterdam? 7. They were there two or three weeks. 8. Haven't they been in Switzerland yet? 9. How long have they been there? 10. For seven or eight weeks, I think. 11. Are they fond of the Alps? 12. Where will they spend the winter? 13. They will be in Rome four months ; then they will go to Naples. 14. How long have you been here? 15. How long shall you stay here? 16. How long did they stay? 17. Have you lived there long? 18. How long? 19. I have been looking for my pen for ten minutes ; have you seen it?

Exercice-revue

1. What is the order of words in a sentence beginning with an interrogative adverb? Give two examples. 2. Is

that rule the same when **où** is used? 3. What happens
when a verb has two subjects of different grammatical
persons? 4. Name the disjunctive personal pronouns.
5. When are they used? 6. How are they made emphatic?
7. Name the direct object conjunctive pronouns. 8. Name
the indirect object conjunctive pronouns. 9. Give the
present indicative of **sentir.** 10. Give the order of precedence of conjunctive object pronouns when they are of different grammatical persons. 11. What is the order when they
are of the 3rd person? 12. What is the order with the
imperative affirmative? 13. Give the imperfect of **boire.**
14. Conjugate **il y en a** in all the tenses already studied.
15. Give the present of **rire.** 16. Give the different ways
to translate *so* or *it :* (a) with a noun complement, (b) with an
adjective complement. 17. Give the present of **suivre.**
18. Give the definition of a reflexive verb. 19. Name the
reflexive pronouns. 20. Are the reflexive pronouns always
the direct object?

* * * * * * *

68ᵉ Leçon : Le passé défini

On connaît ses amis au besoin. — *A friend in need is a friend indeed.*

CONJUGAISON DU PASSÉ DÉFINI (PRETERITE)

Avoir	Être
j'eus, *I had.*	je fus, *I was.*
tu eus.	tu fus.
il eut.	il fut.
nous eûmes.	nous fûmes.
vous eûtes.	vous fûtes.
ils eurent.	ils furent.

Donner	Finir	Rendre
je donnai, *I gave.*	je finis, *I finished.*	je rendis, *I gave back.*
tu donnas.	tu finis.	tu rendis.
ii donna.	il finit.	il rendit.
nous donnâmes.	nous finîmes.	nous rendîmes.
vous donnâtes.	vous finîtes.	vous rendîtes.
ils donnèrent.	ils finirent.	ils rendirent.

Using the above paradigms as models, learn to conjugate the past definite of any regular verb; also, of the irregular verbs already given: **aller, j'allai, tu allas,** *etc.;* **faire, je fis,** *etc.;* **dire, je dis,** *etc.;* **savoir, je sus,** *etc.;* **voir, je vis,** *etc.;* **recevoir, je reçus,** *etc.* (The past definite of the irregular verbs is given in full in the grammar summary at the end of this book.) *Observe that the only change of vowel occurs in the third person plural of the first conjugation.*

Use of past tenses. — (1) We have seen (Lesson 14) that the conversational past tense, denoting what happened, is the *past indefinite* (perfect).

(2) We have also seen (Lesson 25) that the *imperfect* is used to express a customary or continued past action, or a description of the state of things when something took place or while it was taking place; also with **si** in conditional clauses (Lesson 48).

(3) The *past definite* is used only in a formal narrative or historical style to denote an action or state which was definitely completed in past time.

(4) The *past anterior* (compound of the past definite) expresses an action immediately prior to that expressed by the past definite. It is used only after **quand, aussitôt que, à peine,** etc. It is formed with the past definite of **avoir** (sometimes **être,** Lesson 28) and the past participle of the verb.

(5) The *pluperfect* (compound of the imperfect, Lesson 46) expresses an action entirely finished when another past action took place. It is used like the past perfect in English.

The names, *descriptive past,* given to the imperfect, and the *narrative past,* given to the past definite, in the Grandgent grammars, are highly suggestive of the proper use of these tenses.

Study carefully the following examples:

(1) **J'ai vu votre cousine il y a quelques jours.** *I saw your cousin a few days ago.*

(1) **Êtes-vous allés la voir?** *Did you go to see her?*

(2) **Où était-elle? Elle était chez elle.** *Where was she? She was at home.*

(2) **Quand j'étais à Paris, j'allais souvent à l'opéra.** *When I was in Paris, I often went (used to go) to the opera.*

(2) **Les anciens Égyptiens embaumaient les morts, les Grecs et les Romains les brûlaient.** *The ancient Egyptians embalmed the dead, the Greeks and Romans burned them.*

(3) **On embauma le corps d'Alexandre et on le transporta en Égypte.** *They embalmed the body of Alexander and carried it to Egypt.*

(3) **Le prince Édouard dans cette bataille ne perdit pas soixante hommes.** *Prince Edward in that battle did not lose sixty men.*

(4–3) **Après qu'il eut parlé, il s'assit.** *After he had spoken, he sat down.*

(4–3) **A peine fut-il arrivé que midi sonna.** *He had scarcely arrived when it struck twelve.*

(5) **J'avais fini quand vous êtes entrés.** *I had finished when you entered.*

Vocabulaire

gronder, *to rumble.*
le lointain, *the distance.*
s'assombrir, *to become dark.*
de plus en plus, *more and more.*
le peuple, *the people.*
s'agiter, *to be restless.*
imbu, *imbued.*
répandre, *to spread out.*
obliger, *to oblige.*
de bon cœur, *heartily, willingly.*
tarder, *to be long in.*
fuir, *to flee.*
ramener, *to take back, to bring back.*
forcer, *to force, to oblige.*
prêter serment, *to take the oath.*
affolé, *frantic.*

faire appel, *to call on.*
la goutte, *the drop.*
déborder, *to overflow.*
retenir, *to retain, to keep.*
le parlement, *the congress.*
décapiter, *to behead.*
le juge, *the judge.*
la fermeté, *the firmness.*
l'âme, *the soul.*
remporter, *to win* (a prize).
gagner, *to win.*
le soldat, *the soldier.*
l'ennemi, *the enemy.*
la bataille, *the battle.*
l'épée, *the sword.*
s'écrier, *to exclaim, to cry out.*

Lecture

Quand le professeur eut fini la leçon de grammaire, il prit un livre qui était sur sa table et nous lut le passage suivant :

" Mais le tonnerre de la révolution grondait dans le lointain, et l'horizon politique de la France s'assombrissait de plus en plus.   Le peuple commençait à s'agiter, les soldats de La Fayette étaient revenus d'Amérique imbus des idées et des grands préceptes contenus dans la Déclaration de l'Indépendance, qu'ils répandaient dans la populace.   Louis XVI fut obligé de convoquer à Versailles les États Généraux. Il fit la chose de bon cœur, car il aimait vraiment son peuple, mais il ne tarda cependant pas à perdre sa popularité par ses hésitations dues toujours à l'influence des nobles et de la reine qui faisaient cause commune.   Devenant de plus en plus impopulaire, il décida de fuir à l'étranger, mais il fut reconnu et ramené à Paris, où on l'obligea à prêter serment à la constitution.   De plus en plus affolé, Louis XVI fit appel aux souverains étrangers pour venir à son secours.   Ce fut la goutte d'eau qui fait déborder le vase.   Le roi qu'on avait gardé captif à Versailles, fut transporté à Paris, aux Tuileries où il fut retenu prisonnier.   Il fut accusé de trahison, jugé par le Convention, c'est-à-dire le parlement d'alors, et reconnu coupable de conspiration contre la liberté de la nation. Il fut condamné à mort et décapité le 21 janvier 1793.

Louis XVI montra devant ses juges et devant la mort une fermeté d'âme remarquable qui, malheureusement, lui avait manqué dans son gouvernement.

Voilà ce que rappelle Versailles à ceux qui connaissent l'histoire de France."

Exercices

A. *Traduisez en français :*

1. The tree fell and killed the man who was cutting it.
2. Their daughter won the prize and afterwards received a

beautiful book.   3. After the death of the queen, they beheaded her son.   4. The old man often told us stories, and one day he told us the story of his life.   5. My father says that he used to forget everything when he was at school. 6. Who won the battle, the English or the French?   7. Napoleon lost the battle of Waterloo.   8. Was he not a great general in spite of that?   9. At last the general saw the enemy.   10. He noticed that the soldiers were not far from the city which he was defending.   11. What did he do? 12. He seized his sword and cried, " Let us receive them well ! "   13. What happened then?   14. His men obeyed him immediately and defended the city.   15. The king praised the general and gave him a magnificent sword.

Exercice-revue

1. I cut my hand yesterday.   2. How did you cut your finger?   3. He did not cut his finger; he tells you that he cut his hand.   4. Excuse me, I was mistaken.   5. Be careful; don't cut yourself.   6. When children play with penknifes, they cut themselves.   7. Yes, and very often they cut one another.   8. When did your brother leave for France?   9. I am sure he was glad.   10. He was. 11. Were you too?   12. No, I wasn't, I would have liked (wanted) to go with him.   13. When will he be in Paris? 14. He will be there the 11th of June.   15. How long will he stay there?   16. He will stay there for a month, maybe five weeks.   17. How long have you been waiting for me? 18. I have been waiting for ten minutes ; I was in front of that store.   19. That's funny ; I just came out of it, and I did not see you.   20. Let us walk now.

*   *   *   *   *   *   *

69ᵉ Leçon : Remarques sur les verbes en –ER

Je jette ma langue aux chiens. — *I give it up.*

All the verbs of the first conjugation but two (**aller,** *to go,* and **envoyer,** *to send*) are regular, and are conjugated like **donner.** A few present some peculiarities caused by changes made for the sake of pronunciation. These verbs are :

1. Those having **e** mute before their last syllable, such as **mener, lever, appeler, jeter.**
2. Those having an **é** before their last syllable, as **célébrer, préférer, espérer.**
3. Those ending in **-yer.** ⎱
4. Those ending in **-cer** or **-ger.** ⎰ See Lesson 70.

E **mute before a final syllable.** — Verbs of the first conjugation having an **e** mute in the syllable next before the ending of the infinitive, change that **e** mute to **è,** when, in the course of the conjugation, the syllable following contains **e** mute.

Lever, *to lift*

PRÉSENT. **je lève, tu lèves, il lève, nous levons, vous levez, ils lèvent.**

IMPARFAIT INDICATIF. **je levais, tu levais,** etc.

PASSÉ INDÉFINI. **j'ai levé.**

PASSÉ DÉFINI. **je levai,** etc.

FUTUR. **je lèverai,** etc.

CONDITIONNEL. **je lèverais,** etc.

IMPÉRATIF. **lève, levons, levez.**

Exceptions in *-eler* **and** *-eter.* — Most verbs ending in -eler, as **appeler,** and -eter, as **jeter,** double the l or the t, instead of changing **e** mute to **è,** the effect on the pronunciation being the same.

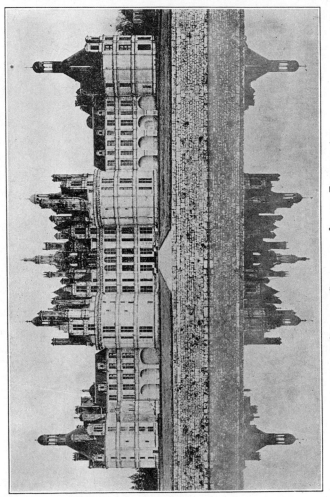

Le Château de Chambord, bâti par François 1er.

Appeler, *to call;* jeter, *to throw*

PRÉSENT

j'appelle, je jette.
tu appelles, tu jettes.
il appelle, il jette.
nous appelons, nous jetons.
vous appelez, vous jetez.
ils appellent, ils jettent.

IMPARFAIT

j'appelais, je jetais.
etc.

PASSÉ DÉFINI

j'appelai, je jetai.

FUTUR

j'appellerai, je jetterai.

CONDITIONNEL

j'appellerais, je jetterais.

IMPÉRATIF

appelle, jette.
appelons, jetons.
appelez, jetez.

Acheter, *to buy,* geler, *to freeze,* and a few other verbs follow the rule for lever, instead of doubling l or t :

j'achète, tu achètes, il achète, nous achetons, etc.; j'achèterai, etc.
je gèle, tu gèles, il gèle, nous gelons, etc., je gèlerai, etc.

É before a final syllable. — All verbs of the first conjugation having é in the syllable next before the ending of the infinitive change that é into è, when the following syllable contains e mute, except in the future and in the conditional.

Célébrer, *to celebrate*

PRÉSENT. je célèbre, tu célèbres, il célèbre, nous célébrons, vous célébrez, ils célèbrent.

IMPARFAIT. je célébrais, etc.

PASSÉ INDÉFINI. j'ai célébré, etc.

PASSÉ DÉFINI. je célébrai, etc.

FUTUR. je célébrerai, tu célébreras, etc.

CONDITIONNEL. je célébrerais, etc.

IMPÉRATIF. célèbre, célébrons, célébrez.

Note carefully that there is no change of accent in the future or conditional of these verbs.

Vocabulaire

mener,[1] *io guide, to lead, to take.*
amener, *to bring* (to escort hither).
ramener, *to bring back.*
emmener, *to take away.*
promener, *to take out for a walk, a
    drive,* etc.
le libraire, *the bookseller.*
se fâcher, *to get angry.*
jeter, *to throw.*
geler, *to freeze.*
exagérer, *to exaggerate.*
patiner, *to skate.*

espérer, *to hope.*
régner, *to reign.*
préférer, *to prefer.*
répéter, *to repeat.*
posséder, *to possess.*
la poupée, *the doll.*
le cas, *the case.*
le chiffre, *the figure, the number.*
la glace, *the ice.*
ailleurs, *elsewhere.*
d'ailleurs, *besides.*
amer, *bitter.*

Lecture

1. Ma petite sœur préfère ces poupées-ci à celles-là, mais
je trouve celles-là bien plus belles que celles-ci.   2. Est-ce
que vous n'exagérez pas un peu?   3. J'exagère peut-être
quelquefois, mais je n'exagère pas dans ce cas-ci.   4. Je
pense que ma fête tombe le 13 du mois prochain.   5. Le
13 ! c'est un bien vilain chiffre !   Je préférerais le 12 ou le 14.
6. D'ailleurs le 13 est un dimanche, nous célébrerons cette
fête le 12.   7. Espérons que le temps fera beau ; l'année
dernière il a fait très mauvais.   8. Vous devez être bien
content ce soir : il gèle très fort, vous pourrez patiner demain.
9. Nous n'avons pas patiné l'hiver dernier ; il n'a presque
jamais gelé.   10. J'achète mes livres, mes plumes et mes
journaux chez le libraire au coin de notre rue.   11. Comment t'appelles-tu, mon enfant?   12. Marie ! c'est un bien
joli nom ; Marie, mène-moi près de ta maman.   13. La
bonne promènera les enfants ce soir ; ils ne sont pas prêts
maintenant.   14. N'est-ce pas vous qui possédez tant de
grandes maisons?

---

[1] Distinguish carefully difference in meaning of **mener** and its compounds and **porter** and its corresponding compounds : **porter,** *to carry,
to bear;* **apporter,** *to bring;* **rapporter,** *to bring back;* **emporter,** *to carry
away.*

Exercices

A. *Traduisez en français :*

1. Would they not prefer these books to those?   2. Let us hope that they will always be happy.   3. Do you not exaggerate his fortune?   4. I never exaggerate anything; he possesses many houses.   5. When will you celebrate my birthday?   6. [On] what day does it fall?   7. On the 13th of the month. I think it is also on a Friday.   8. Unfortunate [man], we shall never celebrate your birthday; choose another day, if you please, but do not choose the 23d, because we shall be too busy that day.   9. If you bring your friends, we will take them with us.   10. When will the maids take the children out to walk?   11. I shall buy those pictures for my mother.   12. Where are you taking my brother?   13. I am taking him to school.   14. Throw away that pear, it is very bitter.   15. I hope that we shall skate to-morrow.   16. Is it freezing a little this evening?   17. I think it is freezing hard; it has been freezing for [the last] twenty-four hours.   18. The ice will be strong enough to-morrow.

Exercice-revue

1. How did your sister enjoy herself in England?   2. She enjoyed herself very much; she always enjoys herself. 3. She is very happy, is she not?   4. Yes, she is, she does not get angry easily.   5. Do you get angry very often? 6. He always does his work himself, so he is sure it is well done.   7. You did not hurry, and you were right.   8. Are there many pupils in your French class?   9. Yes, there are many, there are more than fifty.   10. Do you often think of your French lessons?   11. Of course, I think of them every day.   12. What do you think of the French language?   13. I think that French is a beautiful language, very smooth and very useful.   14. I think so too. 15. Have you ever been in France?   16. Yes, I went there

last year. 17. I also visited Belgium, Holland, and Germany. 18. How long did you stay in Holland? 19. I remained there but a few days. 20. Which do you like better, Belgium or Holland? 21. I like Belgium better, but France is the country I like the best.

* * * * * * *

70ᵉ Leçon : Remarques sur les verbes en –ER (suite)

A cheval donné on ue regarde pas la bride. — *Never look a gift horse in the mouth.*

Verbs ending in -yer. — 1. In verbs ending in **-oyer** or **-uyer,** the **y** becomes **i** before **e** mute.

2. Verbs ending in **-ayer** may keep the **y** throughout or change to **i** before **e** mute : **payer,** *to pay,* **je paye** or **je paie, je payerai** or **je paierai.**

3. In verbs in **-eyer** the **y** remains unchanged.

Employer, *to employ, to use*

Présent	Passé défini
j'emploie.	j'employai.
tu emploies.	tu employas.
il emploie.	il employa.
nous employons.	nous employâmes.
vous employez.	vous employâtes.
ils emploient.	ils employèrent.

Imparfait	Futur
j'employais, etc.	j'emploierai, etc.
nous employions, etc.	

Conditionnel présent
j'emploierais, etc.

Passé indéfini	Impératif
j'ai employé,	emploie.
etc.	employons.
	employez.

Verbs ending in -cer or -ger. — In a verb ending in -cer
or -ger, c or g, being soft in the infinitive, must be kept soft
throughout the verb.   When, therefore, in any tense, c or g
would be followed by a or o, a cedilla is placed under the c
and a silent e [1] is placed after the g, to keep them soft.

placer, *to place;* plaçant, *placing;* nous plaçons, *we place.*
manger, *to eat;* mangeant, *eating;* nous mangeons, *we eat.*

Commencer, *to begin*   **Protéger,** *to protect*

PRÉSENT

je commence.	je protège.
tu commences.	tu protèges.
il commence.	il protège.
nous commençons.	nous protégeons.
vous commencez.	vous protégez.
ils commencent.	ils protègent.

IMPARFAIT

je commençais, etc.	je protégeais, etc.
nous commencions, etc.	nous protégions, etc.

PASSÉ DÉFINI

je commençai, etc.	je protégeai, etc.
ils commencèrent.	ils protégèrent.

FUTUR

je commencerai.	je protégerai.

CONDITIONNEL PRÉSENT

je commencerais.	je protégerais.

Vocabulaire

appuyer, *to support, to lean.*	corriger, *to correct.*
aboyer, *to bark.*	déranger, *to disturb.*
effrayer, *to frighten.*	se déranger, *to disturb oneself, to*
nettoyer, *to clean.*	*be disturbed.*
essayer, *to try (on).*	le devoir, *duty, exercise* (lesson).
annoncer, *to announce.*	autrefois (adv.), *formerly.*

[1] Observe that the e inserted after g to keep it soft is merely an ortho-
graphical sign, and has no effect except on the quality of the g.   See
Introduction.

prononcer, *to pronounce.*
menacer, *to threaten.*
envoyer, *to send.* Future and conditional, irregular: **j'enverrai,**
j'enverrais.

sale, *dirty.*
assez, *rather, somewhat.*

Lecture

1. Essayez ce crayon-ci, c'est mon meilleur.   2. Vraiment, il est très bon ; j'essaierai aussi votre plume.   3. Je paie très cher les plumes et les crayons que j'achète chez le libraire du coin.   4. Nettoyez un peu cette table, elle est toujours sale.   5. Monsieur, je nettoie cette table tous les matins.   6. Ce vilain petit chien que vous amenez toujours avec vous, aboie presque tout le temps.   7. On dit que les chiens qui aboient ne mordent jamais.   8. Appuyez, s'il vous plaît, ma chaise contre cette table. Merci.   9. Je mangeais, je pense, lorsque vous êtes entré.   10. Nous ne prononçons pas les langues anciennes mieux que vous. 11. Si nous dérangeons votre frère, maintenant qu'il est occupé, il ne sera pas content.   12. Protégeons les malheureux.   13. Ne menaçons personne.

Exercices

Traduisez en français :

1. You will frighten your mother if you break that glass. 2. They would pay us this evening what they owe us, if they had money enough.   3. She is very lazy ; she does not employ her time well.   4. Why does he not send that book to his cousin?   5. Why will you not send my letters to your sister as soon as you receive them?   6. Those dogs bark all night.   7. Do not try his pen ; it is a poor one.   8. My brother was eating his breakfast, when my aunt came in this morning.   9. He used to correct all my letters and all my exercises. 10. Let us always oblige our friends.   11. Formerly they pronounced very well.   12. Why do we always disturb your uncle?   13. They announced the sad news to their friends as soon as your letter arrived.   14. Don't dis-

turb yourself.   15. I will buy this watch next week ; I have
not money enough to-day.

Exercice-revue

1. He always gets up at 6 o'clock in (of) the morning.
2. What is he doing?   Why does he throw his books on the
table?   3. What is that little girl's name?   4. Do they
take a walk every day?   5. My brother does, but I don't.
6. How long will he walk?   7. How long has he been
walking?   8. Let us see, what time is it now?   He has been
walking for two hours.   9. Does he always walk as long as
that?   10. Yes, sometimes, when the weather is fine, he
walks for three hours.   11. I hope he will come back soon,
I must speak to him.   12. What do they possess?   Nothing !   13. That's true, they possess nothing, but they are
happy.   14. I am sure they are.   15. Let us go to the
Durands.   16. No, I have come from there, there is nobody
home.   17. We went to the store this afternoon and we
bought some silk ties and lace handkerchiefs there.   18. Did
you see my mother there?   19. Did she go there too this
afternoon?   20. Yes, she did.

*   *   *   *   *   *   *

71e Leçon : Subjonctif : doute, émotion, désir

Aucun chemin de fleurs ne conduit à la gloire. — *There is no pathway
of flowers leading to glory.*

Study the present subjunctive of the regular verbs :

Donner	Finir	Rendre
That I (may) give, etc. . . .	*That I (may) finish,* etc. . . .	*That I (may) give back,* etc. . . .
Que je donne.	**Que je finisse.**	**Que je rende.**
Que tu donnes.	**Que tu finisses.**	**Que tu rendes.**

Donner	Finir	Rendre
Qu'il donne.	Qu'il finisse.	Qu'il rende.
Que nous donnions.	Que nous finissions.	Que nous rendions.
Que vous donniez.	Que vous finissiez.	Que vous rendiez.
Qu'ils donnent.	Qu'ils finissent.	Qu'ils rendent.

Recevoir

That I (may) receive, etc.

Que je reçoive.	Que nous recevions.
Que tu reçoives.	Que vous receviez.
Qu'il reçoive.	Qu'ils reçoivent.

Formation. — The present subjunctive is formed by replacing the ending **-ent**[1] of the third person plural of the present indicative by the endings :

-e, -es, -e, -ions, -iez, -ent.

Notice that the endings of the three persons singular and of the 3d person plural are the same as those of the present indicative of the verbs of the first conjugation ; the 1st and 2d plural have the endings of the imperfect.

Notice also that the verbs ending in **-ier,** like **étudier, oublier,** have two *i*'s in the first and second person plural of the present subjunctive : **Que nous étudi*ions*, que vous oubli*iez*.**

Notes. — 1. All French verbs (with the exception of **avoir** and **être**) have the same endings in the subjunctive.

2. The subjunctive mood has no future tense; the present subjunctive is used instead.

Emploi du subjonctif. —

Study the following sentences :

(1) **Je doute que vous *réussissiez*.** *I doubt that you will succeed.*

(2) **Je suis content que vous *finissiez* ce travail.** *I am pleased that you are finishing this work.*

---

[1] This rule applies to all regular verbs and also to nearly all irregular verbs. The most important exceptions are **avoir** and **être** (Lesson 72) ; **aller, faire, pouvoir, savoir** and **vouloir** (Lesson 73).

(3) **Je crains qu'il (ne)** [1] ***vende* sa maison.**   *I fear that he will sell his house.*

Special Note. — The **ne** spoken of below is dropped more and more by modern writers and is bound to disappear very shortly from subordinate clauses, as it is often pleonastic and always confusing. For that reason we have discarded it entirely in this modern grammar.

---

(4) **Je désire que vous lui *parliez*.**   *I wish you to speak to him.*

(5) **Je veux que vous l'*attendiez*.**   *I want you to wait for him.*

(6) **Je suis surpris que vous le *grondiez*.**   *I am surprised that you scold him.*

(7) **Il a peur de *tomber*.** **He *fears* he *will fall*.**

Verbs expressing *doubt* (1), *emotion, joy* (2), *fear* (3), *surprise* (6), *sorrow, complaint,* etc., *wish* or *desire* (4 and 5) are followed by the subjunctive, when the person speaking is not the subject of the verb in the subordinate clause.

When the subject is the same in both clauses, the infinitive is used instead of the subjunctive (Example 7).

Vocabulaire

précipité, *hasty.*	**exiger,** *to exact, to insist.*
au moins, *at least.*	**s'impatienter,** *to grow impatient.*
le préparatif, *the preparation.*	**arrêter,** *to stop.*
en avant, *ahead.*	**s'occuper de,** *to get busy with,*
enregistrer, *to check.*	*to take care of.*

Lecture

Le départ précipité

— Dépêchez-vous si vous voulez que nous arrivions à la gare au moins une demi-heure avant le départ du train.

---

[1] Formerly, after verbs meaning *fear* (**craindre, avoir peur, trembler,** etc.) and the two verbs **prendre garde,** *to take care,* and **empêcher,** *to prevent, to keep from,* **ne** was required before the verb of the subordinate clause although affirmative. According to the new rules, **ne** may be left out (see page 359).

— Pourquoi ne m'avez-vous pas dit qu'il était si tard? J'ai peur que nous manquions le train.　Quelle heure est-il exactement?

— Il est neuf heures et quart ; je doute que vous finissiez vos préparatifs avant 9 h. 30, et vous n'avez pas encore déjeuné.

— Je ne veux pas que vous m'attendiez ; partez seul.

<small>Je ne veux pas que vous m'attendiez, partez seul.</small>

— Non, je désire que vous m'accompagniez.

— Comme vous êtes drôle !　Je suis surpris que vous désiriez que je vous accompagne.　Ne pouvez-vous pas partir en avant, prendre les billets et faire enregistrer la grande malle?

— Si, mais j'ai peur que vous arriviez en retard et que vous manquiez le train.

— Que voulez-vous que je vous réponde?　Si vous exigez que je parte avec vous, dites à la bonne qu'elle se rende au coin de la rue et qu'elle arrête le premier taxi qui passera.

— Elle n'est pas encore revenue du marché.

— Cela ne fait rien.　Me voilà prêt.　Voulez-vous que nous descendions la malle?

— Elle est en bas, j'ai ordonné qu'on la porte dans le hall il y a un quart d'heure.

— Eh bien !　Partons.

— Mais je veux que vous déjeuniez.

— Non, je crains que vous vous impatientiez.　Si j'ai le

temps, je prendrai une tasse de café au buffet de la gare
pendant que vous vous occuperez des bagages et des billets.

Exercices

A. *Mettez les verbes en italique au subjonctif :*

1. Il veut que j'*arriver* à la gare avant lui.   2. Je veux
que vous l'*attendre*.   3. Désirez-vous que nous *acheter* cette
grande malle-armoire?   4. Elle est bien contente que vous
penser toujours à elle.   5. Elle est fâchée que ses enfants
lui *désobéir*.   6. N'est-ce pas Voltaire qui a dit : " Obéis si
tu veux qu'on t'*obéir* un jour "?   7. Je crains que vous
manquer l'omnibus.   8. Nous sommes surpris qu'ils *vendre*
tous leurs bijoux.   9. Êtes-vous heureux que nous *parler*
si bien français?   10. Ils veulent que vous *réussir*.

B. *" Ils sont contents " étant sous-entendu* (understood),
faites les changements nécessaires dans les phrases suivantes :

1. Je vends ma maison.   2. Il attend son frère.   3. Il
réussit ses examens.   4. Nous arrivons à l'heure.   5. Vous
finissez votre leçon.   6. J'obéis au professeur.   7. Elle
punit le petit garçon.   8. Nous commençons la leçon.
9. Je réponds à sa lettre.   10. Vous étudiez votre français.

C. *Traduisez en français :*

1. I am glad you never arrive late at school.   2. My
mother wants me to get up at 6.30.   3. I want you to
speak to me.   4. Does he wish me to speak to him?   5. Do
you want him to speak to you about it?   6. I am surprised
you speak to him after all he has said and done.   7. I want
you to stay home, you have not studied your lessons yet.
8. I doubt you will arrive before her.   9. I am pleased
that I sing so well.   10. He wants us to obey him.   11. I
am afraid they will never obey him.   12. He fears that
he may arrive before us.   13. Will you permit my sister
and me to play a little in the garden?   14. No, I do not

want you to play to-day, I have a headache.   15. The
telephone rings; do you want me to answer?   16. I am
surprised that he does not punish that child.   17. I doubt
that he will succeed.   18. Do you want me to carry your
suitcase? It is too heavy for you.   19. They wish us to
dine with them on Monday.   20. I doubt if (that) we will
accept their invitation.

Exercice-revue

1. We always correct what we have written.   2. Paul
is not here, he is trying on his new suit at the tailor's.
3. What pencil is she using now?   4. Let us begin the
lesson, it is already late.   5. When I was young, I always
used to disturb my old uncle.   6. Will you send her that
letter?   7. Hold your tongue, we are eating now.   8. I
know all he possesses.   9. I hope you will buy that large
white house.   10. Help one another is a maxim (une
maxime) we too often forget.   11. Give it to me, if you do
not want to give it to her.   12. Why should I give it to you
when I need it myself?   13. How long will you need it?
14. I will need it for at least two weeks.   15. How long
will you stay in the country this summer?   16. Will you
be glad to go there?   17. I will be glad to go there.
18. Come there too.   19. Would he be glad to come there
with me?   20. He would be glad to accompany you there.

*   *   *   *   *   *   *

72ᵉ Leçon: Subjonctif: verbes impersonnels

Honi soit qui mal y pense. — *Evil to him who evil thinks.*

Observe the use of the subjunctive in the following sentences:

Il faut que vous étudiiez la leçon.   *You must study the lesson.*
Il se peut qu'elle soit ici demain.   *She may be here to-morrow.*
Il semble qu'il ait réussi.   *It seems that he has succeeded.*

Ewing Galloway

LYON, SUR LE RHÔNE, LA GRANDE VILLE INDUSTRIELLE DU SUD DE LA FRANCE.

The subordinate clause depending on impersonal verbs implying *necessity, uncertainty, possibility,* etc., requires the subjunctive.

Study the following graph :

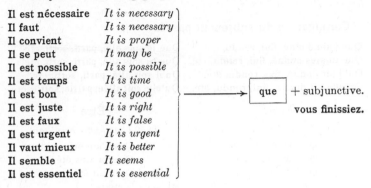

Il est nécessaire	*It is necessary*	
Il faut	*It is necessary*	
Il convient	*It is proper*	
Il se peut	*It may be*	
Il est possible	*It is possible*	
Il est temps	*It is time*	
Il est bon	*It is good*	$\longrightarrow$ que + subjunctive.
Il est juste	*It is right*	vous finissiez.
Il est faux	*It is false*	
Il est urgent	*It is urgent*	
Il vaut mieux	*It is better*	
Il semble	*It seems*	
Il est essentiel	*It is essential*	

Note. **Il faut** translates also the English *must.*

$$I \; must = \text{il faut que je}$$
$$We \; must = \text{il faut que nous} \quad \Big\} + \text{verb (subjunctive).}$$
$$John \; must = \text{il faut que Jean}$$

Subjonctif présent des verbes auxiliaires. —

Avoir	Être
Que j'aie, *That I (may) have.*	Que je sois, *That I (may) be.*
Que tu aies.	Que tu sois.
Qu'il ait.	Qu'il soit.
Qu'elle ait.	Qu'elle soit.
Que nous ayons.	Que nous soyons.
Que vous ayez.	Que vous soyez.
Qu'ils aient.	Qu'ils soient.
Qu'elles aient.	Qu'elles soient.

Impératif

aie, *have.* ayons, *let us have.*   sois, *be.* soyons, *let us be.*
   ayez, *have.*   soyez, *be.*

The imperative of the two auxiliary verbs is taken from the present subjunctive.

Subjonctif passé. —

Je suis content qu'elle ait reçu ce cadeau. *I am pleased that she has received that present.*

Je suis surpris que vous *soyez parti* si tôt. *I am surprised that you left so early.*

Conjugaison du subjonctif passé. —

Que j'aie donné, fini, rendu, etc.	Que je sois allé, parti, sorti, etc.
Que tu aies donné, fini, rendu, etc.	Que tu sois allé, parti, sorti, etc.
Qu'il ait donné, fini, rendu, etc.	Qu'il soit allé, parti, sorti, etc.
Qu'elle ait donné, fini, rendu, etc.	Qu'elle soit allée, partie, sortie, etc.

Avoir

That I may have had, etc.

Que j'aie eu.
Que tu aies eu.
Qu'il ait eu.
etc.

Être

That I may have been, etc.

Que j'aie été.
Que tu aies été.
Qu'il ait été.
etc.

The past or perfect subjunctive is formed with the present subjunctive of the auxiliary verb **avoir** (sometimes **être**, Lesson 28) and a past participle.

Emploi du subjonctif passé. — The past or perfect subjunctive is used when the subordinate clause expresses a past action.

Note. — In such a case, the principal clause need not necessarily be in the past. We may be glad, surprised, etc., *now*, that something happened yesterday, a month or ten years ago. In the first example under **subjonctif passé**, I am pleased *now* that she has received that present, maybe two weeks or two months ago.

Vocabulaire

s'étonner, *to be surprised.*
rester au lit, *to stay in bed.*
se prononcer, *to pronounce oneself.*
la pneumonie, *the pneumonia.*
le refroidissement, *the cold.*
guérir, *to cure.*
le cours, *the course.*

d'un autre côté, *on the other hand.*
prudent, *careful, prudent.*
faire venir, *to send for.*
du moins, *at any rate.*
l'absent (m.), *the absentee.*
la douleur, *the pain.*
sur pieds, *sitting up, astir.*

Lecture

LÉON EST MALADE

Léon.   Qui est là?

Paul.   C'est moi, Paul.

Léon.   Entrez, mon ami ; ne vous étonnez pas, il faut que je reste au lit.

Paul.   Je regrette infiniment que vous soyez malade. Qu'avez-vous?

Léon.   Le médecin ne s'est pas encore prononcé. Il se peut que j'aie la grippe ; il est aussi possible que ce soit une pneumonie.

Paul.   J'espère que ce ne sera rien de tout cela ; ce n'est probablement qu'un simple refroidissement.

JE REGRETTE INFINIMENT QUE VOUS SOYEZ MALADE.

Léon.   Il est possible que ce ne soit que cela, du moins espérons-le. Il est important que je sois vite guéri. Nous sommes à la fin des cours, et il faut que je finisse de préparer mes examens.

Paul.   Oui ; il est certainement malheureux que vous deviez rester chez vous maintenant, mais d'un autre côté, il vaut mieux que vous soyez prudent.

Léon.   Je suis content que ma mère ait fait venir le docteur tout de suite. Savez-vous qu'il se peut que j'aie pris froid avant-hier à la partie de football.

Paul.   Il est très possible que ce soit la cause de votre indisposition ; vous rappelez-vous comme il a fait froid vers la fin de l'après-midi? Je doute que vous soyez le seul malade ; il y avait plusieurs absents dans notre classe ce matin. Qu'avez-vous, vous devenez tout pâle?

Léon. Oui, voilà mes douleurs dans la tête qui reviennent.

Paul. Je vais vous laisser. D'ailleurs, il est temps que je vous quitte ; il faut que je rentre à la maison ; il est nécessaire que je prépare mon examen de " math " (prononcez *matt*), vous savez comme je suis faible dans cette branche (*subject*) et il faut que je travaille plus que les autres. Au revoir, voulez-vous que je passe vous dire un petit bonjour demain?

Léon. Mais certainement, je suis très heureux que vous soyez venu aujourd'hui.

Paul. Entendu alors, je viendrai à la même heure, et si vous allez mieux, nous préparerons ensemble les nouvelles leçons. A demain, je souhaite de tout mon cœur que vous soyez sur pieds.

Exercices

A. *Remplacez les tirets par le présent du subjonctif d'*avoir *ou d'*être :

1. Il faut que je —— à l'école à 9 heures.   2. Il se peut que Louis —— déjà là quand j'arriverai.   3. Je désire qu'ii —— le premier prix.   4. Il est temps que nous —— une semaine de vacances.   5. Il est possible que Paul et Charles —— malades, car ils étaient absents aujourd'hui.   6. Il vaut mieux que vous ne —— pas en retard à l'école.   7. Il est important que nous —— tous nos livres avec nous. 8. Il est désirable qu'il y —— beaucoup d'élèves dans cette école.   9. Faut-il qu'elle —— partie quand vous arriverez? 10. Il est heureux qu'ils —— venus.

B. *Traduisez en français :*

1. It is possible that you are right, but I think that you are wrong.   2. Is it right that he should be punished?

3. Yes, because I want him to be polite to (*envers*) everybody.
4. John, it is necessary that you be punctual at school.
5. Yes, I know, it is essential for us to be on time.   6. It
may be that your brother and sister have already arrived.
7. I must have some paper, pens, and ink at once.   8. My
father has been traveling for some time, and it is possible
that he is now in Paris.   9. It is time that I should have
news of him (of his news).   10. She must have her new
dress to-night.   11. It is certain that she will not have it
before to-morrow.   12. It is possible that she has already
received it.   13. No, it is impossible that they have brought
it so early.   14. Must you be at the lawyer's to-day?
15. I must be there to-day or to-morrow.   16. Is it possible that he is so rich?   17. I doubt that he has bought
that large white house of which you were speaking.   18. I
am glad you are finishing your work.   19. We regret that
he has not finished it yet.   20. It is essential that he succeed.   21. I fear you will not succeed.   22. I fear he has
not succeeded.   23. Is she glad we enjoyed ourselves
yesterday?   24. I am afraid you may think I do not want
him to succeed.

Exercice-revue

1. The two men killed each other.   2. Why did they kill
each other?   3. Why don't you go to bed if you are tired?
4. Why didn't you go to bed if you were tired?   5. Did
he not hurry?   6. Why should he have hurried, he was not
late.   7. How long have you been going to school?   8. We
have been going to school for five years.   9. When does
your father intend to visit France, Belgium, and Switzerland?   10. He will go to Europe next summer.   11. Will
you go with him to Paris?   12. I do not know anything
about it.   13. Would you like (*vouloir*) to go there?   14. I
went there two years ago, I know Paris.   15. Did you live
there?   16. Yes, I lived there for several months.

17. What (how) do they call that beautiful square near the Louvre? 18. Why were you laughing five minutes ago? 19. We travel in South America every year. 20. If you pass your examination, I shall take you with me.

* * * * * * *

73ᵉ Leçon : Subjonctif : superlatifs ; relatifs

Il faut saisir l'occasion aux cheveux. — *You must seize time by the forelock.*

1. Subjonctif après un superlatif. —

Observe the construction of the following sentences :

(1) C'est *le plus beau* livre que j'aie.   *It is the finest book I have.*

(1) C'est *le plus beau* livre que j'aie jamais lu.   *It is the finest book I ever read.*

(2) C'est *le premier* (*dernier, seul*) homme qui l'*ait* fait.   *He is the first (last, only) man who did it.*

(3) C'est le plus beau *des* livres que j'ai lus.   *It is the finest of the books that I have read.*

(4) La meilleure élève, *qui était malade*, n'a pas reçu son diplôme.   *The best pupil, who was ill, did not receive her diploma.*

When there is a superlative in the main clause, the subordinate clause introduced by **que** must be in the subjunctive (Examples 1). The same rule applies after **le premier, le dernier, le seul,** when they have superlative force.

When the superlative is followed by **de** (Example 3), or when the subordinate clause is merely explanatory (Example 4), the subjunctive is *not* used.

2. Subjonctif après un pronom relatif. — Compare the two following sentences :

(1) Je cherche quelqu'un *qui* me *rende* service.   *I am looking for some one to do me a favor.*

(2) J'ai un ami qui me rendra service.   *I have a friend who will do me a favor.*

After a relative pronoun (**qui, que, dont, où,** etc.), the subjunctive is used when doubt, uncertainty, or purpose is implied (Example 1).

When there is no doubt or purpose in the mind of the speaker, of course, the subjunctive is *not* used (Example 2).

SUBJONCTIF PRÉSENT DES VERBES IRRÉGULIERS DÉJÀ MENTIONNÉS

Aller	Faire	Savoir
Que j'aille.	je fasse.	je sache.
Que tu ailles.	tu fasses.	tu saches.
Qu' il aille.	il fasse.	il sache.
Que nous allions.	nous fassions.	nous sachions.
Que vous alliez.	vous fassiez.	vous sachiez.
Qu' ils aillent.	ils fassent.	ils sachent.

Pouvoir	Vouloir
Que je puisse.	je veuille.
Que tu puisses.	tu veuilles.
Qu' il puisse.	il veuille.
Que nous puissions.	nous voulions.
Que vous puissiez.	vous vouliez.
Qu' ils puissent.	ils veuillent.

Note. — These verbs, with **avoir** and **être,** are the only irregular verbs the present subjunctive of which is formed irregularly.

Remarques sur *vouloir* **et** *savoir.* —

Je veux.	*I wish, want, command.*
Je veux bien.	*I am willing, consent.*
Je voudrais or je voudrais bien.	*I should like.*

Notice the difference in meaning between the present indicative and the conditional of the verb **vouloir.**

Il veut le faire.   *He wishes (wills, means) to do it.*
Il voudrait le faire.   *He would like to do it.*
Je veux être à Paris avant le 1er mai.   *I wish (intend) to be in Paris before the first of May.*

Je voudrais y être maintenant. *I should like to be there now,* or *I wish I were there now.*

Observe the use of the present subjunctive of **savoir** to express a softened assertion:

Je ne sache rien de plus charmant. *I know nothing more charming.*
Est-il venu quelqu'un pendant mon absence? Pas que je sache. *Has any one come during my absence? Not that I know of.*
Il se porte bien, autant que je sache. *He is well, so far as I know.*

Vocabulaire

répéter, *to repeat.*   **bien élevé,** *well-bred, well-mannered.*
mal élevé, *ill-bred.*   **aller bien,** *to fit well.*
distraire, *to entertain.*

Lecture

— Mère, puis-je aller jouer avec Émile?

— Non. Faut-il que je vous répète que je n'aime pas que vous jouiez avec lui? C'est, je crois, le seul de vos camarades de classe qui soit mal élevé.

— Il est possible que son éducation ne soit pas aussi bonne que celle des autres garçons, mais Émile est certainement le garçon le plus intelligent que nous ayons jamais eu dans notre classe. C'est le premier élève qui ait jamais reçu le maximum en algèbre, en anglais, en latin et en français.

— C'est possible, mais Émile est-il vraiment le seul qui puisse vous distraire? Choisissez un autre camarade de classe qui soit bien élevé; l'éducation, mon cher fils, est la plus belle chose qu'un homme ou une femme puisse avoir dans la vie; il faut que vous vous rappeliez cela tout le temps.

— C'est entendu, mère; Émile n'est pas le meilleur des amis que j'ai, mais c'est certainement le plus intéressant que je connaisse.

— Nous allons sortir maintenant. Il faut que je vous

achète un costume qui vous aille bien, car le dernier que vous avez acheté avec votre père ne vous allait pas du tout.   Il vaut mieux que, cette fois, ce soit moi qui le choisisse.

— N'est-il pas possible que nous fassions cet achat demain ?

— Demain il se peut que je fasse visite à tante Julie.

— Partons tout de suite alors car il faut que je sois rentré dans une heure car Paul doit venir travailler avec moi.

Exercices

A. Remplacez les tirets par le temps convenable du verbe entre parenthèses :

1. (être) Ma mère est la meilleure femme qui —— au monde.   2. (avoir) C'est le seul livre qui m'—— jamais intéressé.   3. (pouvoir) Ce n'est pas la meilleure chose que vous —— faire.   4. (aller) Voilà la première robe qui lui —— bien.   5. (savoir) Nous cherchons une bonne qui —— le français.   6. (vouloir) Avez-vous trouvé un ami qui —— vous aider ?   7. (connaître) De ces deux dames, c'est la plus jeune que je ——.   8. (faire) Jean n'est-il pas le seul élève qui —— toujours les mêmes fautes ?   9. (savoir) Nous avons une bonne qui —— le français et l'espagnol.   10. (entendre) C'est la musique la plus charmante que j'—— jamais ——.

B. Traduisez en français :

1. She is the prettiest girl I have ever seen.   2. She certainly is the prettiest of all the girls I know.   3. This is the most beautiful horse you ever had.   4. At any rate (*en tout cas*) it is the most beautiful of the horses that were on the race track (*champ de courses*, m.) yesterday.   5. Give me back my beautiful French dictionary, please, it is the best one that one can buy.   6. We are looking for a house where we shall be happy.   7. We have found a house where we shall be happy.   8. Is it the youngest of his

daughters who is dead? 9. Isn't she the poorest woman
you know? 10. She is the happiest of the women I know
here. 11. Is there a man who is content with (*de*) what
he possesses? 12. I doubt there is one. 13. He is the
only friend who has remained faithful to me. 14. Paris is
the most beautiful city I have ever visited. 15. This is the
first lesson we find difficult. 16. Is that the only thing you
can say? 17. It is the only story I know.

Exercice-revue

1. Did you get up before him or after him yesterday?
2. I do not remember exactly, but I think he got up before
me. 3. I know nothing about it. 4. Give them to them
if you do not want to give her some. 5. Have you ever
been in Portugal? 6. I went there several times.
7. How long did you stay the last time you were there?
8. As soon as the professor had finished the lesson, he left
(*quitter*) the classroom. 9. My little brother tries to (*de*)
speak French, but he can't. 10. To which of these gentlemen do you want me to introduce you? 11. I wish you
to introduce me to the one who is standing near the window.
12. Mr. Dufour, allow me to introduce to you my good
friend Henri Mombel. 13. I am afraid she may know what
has happened. 14. Why do you want us to know it?
15. It is better that you do not know it. 16. It is good
that we have not known it. 17. They are surprised that
you speak so little. 18. I doubt that you will finish this
work before to-morrow evening.

* * * * * * *

CARCASSONNE ET SES FORTIFICATIONS.

74ᵉ Leçon: Subjonctif; négation; interrogation

Il faut que tout le monde vive. — *Live and let live.*

Observe and compare the following sentences :

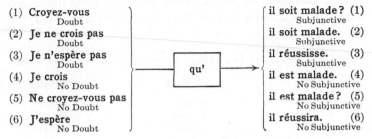

(1) **Croyez-vous**
Doubt

(2) **Je ne crois pas**
Doubt

(3) **Je n'espère pas**
Doubt

(4) **Je crois**
No Doubt

(5) **Ne croyez-vous pas**
No Doubt

(6) **J'espère**
No Doubt

qu'

il soit malade? (1)
Subjunctive

il soit malade. (2)
Subjunctive

il réussisse. (3)
Subjunctive

il est malade. (4)
No Subjunctive

il est malade? (5)
No Subjunctive

il réussira. (6)
No Subjunctive

Remarques sur les examples ci-dessus.

(1) I am asking for information because I am in doubt, hence the subjunctive.   If, however, I believed that he was ill and if I were merely trying to find out if you also believed it, the indicative would be used.   **Croyez-vous que je suis malade?   Il ne croit pas que je suis ici.   Croyez-vous que je ferai cela?**   In these three examples there is no doubt in the mind of the speaker.

(2) I do not believe he is ill (but he may be ill), therefore doubt.

(3) When **espérer** is used negatively or interrogatively, the subjunctive is used because the result hoped for is doubtful in the mind of the speaker.

(4) I do not know that he is ill, but I do not doubt it.

(5) A negative-interrogative question, calling for an affirmative answer.   There is no doubt in the mind of the speaker who is just asking for a confirmation of what he believes; therefore the indicative is used and *not* the subjunctive.   **Ne pensez-vous pas qu'il a tort?   Ne trouvez-vous pas que cette petite fille est gentille?**

(6) Although **espérer** is a verb of emotion, it does not require the subjunctive when used affirmatively, because, when we hope, we do not want to let subsist any doubt about the realization of the thing hoped for.

Emploi. — Verbs used interrogatively or negatively and implying *doubt, uncertainty*, are followed by the subjunctive. This is particularly true with verbs of *thinking* and *believing*.

If, however, there is no doubt in the mind of the speaker, the indicative is used.

The subjunctive is not used after **est-ce que? n'est-ce pas que?** nor generally after such verbs as **savoir,** *to know,* **faire savoir,** *to let know,* **dire,** *to tell,* **apprendre,** *to learn, to hear, to inform,* **informer,** *to inform,* when they are used interrogatively or negatively, if there is no doubt in the mind of the speaker.

SUBJONCTIF PRÉSENT DES VERBES IRRÉGULIERS DÉJÀ MENTIONNÉS

Dire
Que	je dise.
Que	tu dises.
Qu'	il dise.
Que	nous disions.
Que	vous disiez.
Qu'	ils disent.

Voir
je voie.
tu voies.
il voie.
nous voyions.
vous voyiez.
ils voient.

Prendre
je prenne.
tu prennes.
il prenne.
nous prenions.
vous preniez.
ils prennent.

Connaître
Que	je connaisse.
Que	tu connaisses.
Qu'	il connaisse.
Que	nous connaissions.
Que	vous connaissiez.
Qu'	ils connaissent.

Mettre
je mette.
tu mettes.
il mette.
nous mettions.
vous mettiez.
ils mettent.

Vocabulaire

l'atelier (m.), *the studio.*
servir de, *to serve as.*
le modèle, *the model.*
tomber amoureux, *to fall in love.*
partager, *to share.*
l'audace (f.), *the audacity.*
un tel, *such a.*
le pinceau, *the brush* (painting).
mettre les pieds, *to set foot.*
claquer, *to slam* (a door).
l'anxiété (f), *the anxiety.*

le chevalet, *the easel.*
l'ébauche (f.), *the drawing, the sketch.*
le bol, *the bowl.*
le lait, *the milk.*
dessiner, *to design.*
la mouche, *the fly.*
poser, *to pose.*
la laitière, *the milkmaid.*
la colère, *the anger.*
le bout, *the extremitu.*

en larmes, *in tears.*

se marier, *to get married.*

empoigner, *to grab.*

enlever, *to take off, to remove.*

venir de (+ inf.), *to just have.*

la supercherie, *the trickery.*

un mauvais sujet, *a worthless fellow, a bad boy.*

Lecture

VAN DYCK ET LA MOUCHE

La fille de Rubens visitait souvent l'atelier de son père et, très souvent aussi, lui servait de modèle. Van Dyck, le meilleur élève de Rubens, était tombé amoureux de la jeune fille qui partageait ses sentiments.

Un jour qu'il était seul avec le maître, Van Dyck se décide à lui demander la main de sa fille.

— Se peut-il que vous ayez tant d'audace ! s'écrie Rubens furieux. Il faut que vous soyez devenu fou pour me faire

LA FILLE DE RUBENS VISITAIT SOUVENT L'ATELIER DE SON PÈRE.

une telle demande ! Croyez-vous que vous sachiez déjà tenir un pinceau ! Et vous voulez que je vous donne ma fille. Vraiment, vous êtes le plus impertinent petit monsieur qui ait jamais mis les pieds chez moi ! Et il sortit en claquant la porte.

Sa fille qui attendait avec anxiété le résultat de l'entrevue, entre dans l'atelier et trouve Van Dyck en larmes.

— Je ne pense pas que nous puissions jamais nous marier, dit-il à la jeune fille. Je suis le plus malheureux garçon qui soit au monde ; il faut que j'abandonne mes rêves les plus chers.　Il est impossible que je reste plus longtemps ici, il ne faut plus que je vous voie ! J'irai à Paris, je travaillerai.　Mais avant de partir, il faut que je joue un tour au maître.

Sur un chevalet, se trouvait une ébauche à laquelle Rubens travaillait ; c'était une jeune fille tenant un bol de lait. Van Dyck prit sa palette et dessina une mouche sur le bord du bol.

Il avait à peine terminé que Rubens rentre.　Voyant (*seeing*) sa fille, il dit :

— Ah ! Te voilà !　C'est bien, mets-toi là et pose ; il faut que je finisse ma laitière.

Apercevant la mouche, il entre dans une colère terrible :

— Oh, cette sale mouche !　J'avais ordonné qu'on n'ouvre pas les fenêtres, mais quand je demande qu'on fasse quelque chose, il faut qu'on me désobéisse, naturellement !　Et du bout de son pinceau, il essaie d'enlever la mouche.

Van Dyck avait saisi sa boîte à couleurs et courait vers la porte.　Mais Rubens, qui venait de s'apercevoir de la supercherie, et reconnaissant le talent de son élève favori, se lève, se précipite sur lui, l'empoigne par le cou, et le conduisant devant sa fille, lui dit :

— Embrasse ta fiancée, mauvais sujet !

Exercices

A. *Questions sur la lecture :*

1. Croyez-vous que Van Dyck soit impertinent?
2. Pense-t-il que la fille de Rubens puisse devenir un jour sa femme?　3. Qu'est-ce que Rubens lui dit?　4. Van Dyck est-il heureux?　5. Qu'est-ce qu'il dit à la fille du maître?　6. Que faut-il qu'il fasse avant de partir?
7. Quand Rubens rentre, que dit-il à sa fille?　8. Qu'avait-il ordonné?　9. Pensez-vous qu'on lui ait désobéi?
10. Que dit-il à Van Dyck en le conduisant devant sa fille?

B. *Traduisez en français :*

1. She does not think that her father has come.   2. She thinks that her mother has come.   3. Does she think that we have come?   4. It may be that they have come. 5. She must finish her work at once.   6. I do not pretend that he is right, but I think you are wrong.   7. I hope you will answer your sister's letter ; do you forget that she is ill? 8. I do not forget that she is ill, but I shall not answer her letter yet.   9. I do not suppose you will give her all that money.   10. She does not hope that her father will give her any, but I think that he will.   11. Did you tell them that I would thank them myself?   12. Don't you find [that] this water [is] very good?   13. Do you believe that they are in London?   14. Do (*est-ce que*) you believe that (*cela*)?   15. Is (*est-ce que*) not that true?

Exercice-revue

1. Name the reciprocal pronouns.   2. When are they used?   3. Can they be used with a verb in the singular? 4. How are the compound tenses of reflexive verbs formed? 5. How does the past participle of reflexive verbs agree? 6. Give the different translations of the adverbial pronouns **y** and **en.**   7. When are they used?   8. Conjugate **vivre** in the present indicative.   9. Give the order of precedence of all the objective personal pronouns.   10. Conjugate **craindre** in the present indicative.   11. How are *in* and *to* translated in French when referring to countries and towns? 12. How is *from* translated in identical cases?   13. Which are the two translations of *how long?* Give examples. 14. What tense is used in French to express an action begun in the past but still going on?   15. How is *for* translated? 16. Give the uses of the past tenses of the indicative mood. 17. After which words is the past anterior used?   18. Mention the peculiarity of the verbs of the first conjugation having **e** mute before the last syllable.   19. What are the

peculiarities of those ending in -yer? 20. And of those ending in -cer and -ger?

* * * * * * *

75ᵉ Leçon : Subjonctif ; conjonctions

En toute chose il faut considérer la fin. — *Look before you leap.*

Observe the use of the subjunctive in the following sentences :

J'attendrai *que* vous le fassiez.	*I shall wait until you do it.*
*Quoiqu'*il soit jeune, il a déjà les cheveux gris.	*Although he is young, he already has gray hair.*
Ne partez pas *sans que* je le sache.	*Do not leave without my knowing it.*

The subjunctive is used after the following conjunctions of *purpose, condition, fear, time,* etc., and also after the two pronouns **qui . . . que,** *whoever,* and **quoi . . . que,** *whatever.*

que, *until* (after **attendre**).

afin que,
pour que, } *in order that.*

à moins que,[1] *unless.*

au cas que, *in case (that).*

bien que,
quoique, } *although.*

de peur que,[1]
de crainte que,[1] } *lest.*

jusqu'à ce que, *until.*

avant que,[1] *before.*

pourvu que, *provided.*

de sorte que, *in such a way that.*

supposé que, *suppose.*

sans que, *without.*

non que, *not (that).*

qui que, *whoever* (pron.).

quoi que, *whatever* (pron.).

que (used for any of the above conjunctions and for **si,** *if*).

soit que . . . ou que, *either . . . or.*

si (with adj. or adv.) . . . que, *however.*

However, it must not be taken as a general rule that all conjunctions must be followed by the subjunctive; those which are used to state a positive fact govern, of course, the indicative. Examples : **dès que, pendant que, puisque, lorsque,** etc.

---

[1] After these conjunctions, **ne** may be omitted (see Special Note, page 279, Lesson 71, and new rules, page 359).

Compare the two following examples :

(1) **Il agira de telle sorte que tout le monde *sera* content.** *He will act in such a way that everybody will be pleased.*

(2) **Agissez de telle sorte que tout le monde *soit* content.** *Act in such a way that everybody (will) be pleased.*

In the second example, there is a doubt, therefore the subjunctive ; in the first example, there is *no* doubt, therefore *no* subjunctive.

Subjonctif présent des verbes irréguliers déjà mentionnés

Partir	Venir	Lire
Que je parte.	je vienne.	je lise.
Que tu partes.	tu viennes.	tu lises.
Qu' il parte.	il vienne.	il lise.
Que nous partions.	nous venions.	nous lisions.
Que vous partiez.	vous veniez.	vous lisiez.
Qu' ils partent.	ils viennent.	ils lisent.

Écrire	Croire
Que j'écrive.	je croie.
Que tu écrives.	tu croies.
Qu' il écrive.	il croie.
Que nous écrivions.	nous croyions.
Que vous écriviez.	vous croyiez.
Qu' ils écrivent.	ils croient.

Vocabulaire

de nouveau, *again.*
changer, *to change.*
la mi-mai, *the middle of May.*
revoir, *to review.*
à fond, *thoroughly.*
puisque, *since.*

appliqué, *diligent.*
le congé, *the holiday.*
illustrer, *to illustrate.*
remporter, *to win (a prize).*
oser, *to dare.*
aider, *to help.*

Lecture

— Voilà de nouveau la pluie ! Je ne pense pas que nous puissions partir à la campagne ce mois-ci, à moins que le temps change.

— C'est vrai ; bien que nous soyons à la mi-mai, le temps est exécrable, et il fait très froid pour la saison.

— Allons-nous commencer nos leçons tout de suite ou attendrons-nous que Paul arrive?

— C'est très bien d'attendre qu'il arrive pourvu qu'il vienne ; mais supposé qu'il ne vienne pas, nous aurons perdu beaucoup de temps et il se peut que nous ne finissions pas nos leçons avant le dîner.

— Vous avez raison ; il est très rare que Paul soit à l'heure, et vous verrez qu'avant qu'il arrive, au cas qu'il vienne, il se peut que nous ayons déjà fini une bonne partie de notre travail.

— Commençons par notre leçon de français. Le professeur a dit que nous devions revoir le subjonctif afin que nous le sachions à fond pour notre examen au commencement du mois prochain.

— Il est un fait certain que nous ne pouvons pas espérer passer notre examen sans que nous sachions le subjonctif sur le bout des doigts.

— Quoique le professeur l'ait expliqué très clairement, le subjonctif est un mode que je ne comprends pas ; je regrette qu'il existe. Pour que je le comprenne, il faudra, je crois, que j'aille étudier dans une école de Paris.

— Je ne pense pas que Paul vienne maintenant, sa mère ne l'aura pas laissé sortir de peur qu'il s'enrhume.

— Allons ! travaillons, si difficile que soit le subjonctif, il faut que nous l'apprenions et que nous le sachions.

Exercices

A. *Mettez les verbes en italique aux temps convenables :*

1. Quoique je *faire*, je ne réussis pas.   2. Bien qu'il *savoir* toujours ses leçons, il n'est pas le premier de sa classe. 3. Ils le feront pourvu que vous le leur *demander*.   4. Bien que vous *connaître* ce monsieur, vous ne lui parlez jamais. 5. Qui que vous *être* et quoi que vous lui *dire*, il ne vous

écoutera pas. 6. Nous attendrons jusqu'à ce que vous *revenir*, pourvu que vous ne nous *faire* pas attendre trop longtemps. 7. Au cas que je ne *pouvoir* pas partir, je vous téléphonerai, de façon que vous le *savoir*. 8. Je vous verrai encore avant que vous *partir*. 9. Ils ne porteront pas ses bagages à moins qu'il le *vouloir*. 10. Pour que vous *comprendre* le subjonctif, il faut que vous l'*étudier*.

B. *Traduisez en français :*

1. I like him, although he does not always obey me. 2. You must work until I am ready. 3. I do not think he will reply to your letter before we arrive from the country. 4. In case you need money, he will send you all of his. 5. Since he has a great deal more than I, I will accept his offer. 6. He will not give me the money he has promised me, unless I obey him. 7. I shall not punish you to-day, although you deserve it. 8. You must be diligent so that your mother will be pleased with you. 9. Although you have promised me a holiday, you have not given it to me. 10. I shall give you a beautiful book illustrated by Gustave Doré, provided you win the first prize in (*de*) French. 11. I shall not win that prize unless you help me a little. 12. She does not dare to come here, for fear you will scold her. 13. She stayed at home until we came back. 14. He flatters us so that we may forgive him [for] what he has done. 15. If you get here before twelve and if (*que*) I am not ready, wait for me until I have finished my work. 16. Before he goes to France, he must know French. 17. However rich one may be, one never has money enough.

Exercice-revue

1. Louis XVI was beheaded on the 21st of January, 1793. 2. He was a good king. 3. He showed much courage before death. 4. How long was he king of France? 5. I do not remember exactly. 6. I do not think he had

been very happy. 7. Although he loved his people, he did not know how to govern them (it). 8. Do you think he paid for the mistakes of Louis XIV and Louis XV? 9. It may be that he paid for them, but I doubt that he could have stopped the revolution. 10. I must go now; it may be that they are waiting for me at home. 11. I regret that you will not stay a little longer. 12. So am I, I am very sorry (*désolé*) I must leave so soon. 13. I do not think I shall be able to see you before next week. 14. What a pity that you are living so far from us! 15. You are the best friend I have. 16. You are the best of the friends I have. 17. She is the best friend I ever had. 18. She is the most beautiful girl I know. 19. She is the most beautiful of the girls I know. 20. I am looking for an apartment (which is) big enough for my whole family.

* * * * * * *

76e Leçon : Subjonctif : concordance des temps ; imparfait

Faute de grives on mange des merles. — *Half a loaf is better than no bread.*[1]

After the present or future in the principal clause or, in conversation, after the conditional, the present of the subjunctive is used; after any other tense, the imperfect subjunctive. However, this tense is seldom used.

Je veux		Je voulais
Je voudrai	qu'il le fasse.	Je voulus
Je voudrais		Je voudrais [2] qu'il le fît.
		J'ai voulu
		J'avais voulu
		J'aurais voulu

---

[1] Literally, *For want of a thrush, one may eat a blackbird.*
[2] In a formal, dignified style.

PANORAMA D'AVIGNON MONTRANT LE PALAIS DES PAPES.

When the subjunctive is in a compound tense, the tense of the auxiliary **avoir** or **être** depends on the tense of the verb in the principal clause.

Espérez-vous qu'il l'*ait* fait ?	*Do you hope he has done it ?*
Espériez-vous qu'il l'*eût* fait ?	*Did you hope he had done it ?*

The imperfect subjunctive, though common in French classics, is now usually avoided in French. If an infinitive construction cannot be substituted, the present subjunctive is used.

Compare :

Il empêchait que nous n'arrivassions à temps.	*He prevented us from*
Il nous empêchait d'arriver à temps.	*arriving in time.*
Je voudrais que vous m'accompagnassiez.	*I should like you to go*
Je voudrais que vous m'accompagniez.	*with me.*

Formation de l'imparfait du subjonctif. — The imperfect subjunctive of any French verb may be formed by adding to the second person singular of the past definite the endings :

-se, -ses, ^t,[1] -sions, -siez, -sent.

PASSÉ DÉFINI		SUBJONCTIF IMPARFAIT
1ST PERSON	2D PERSON	
je donnai.	tu donnas.	que je donnasse.
j'allai.	tu allas.	que j'allasse.[2]
je reçus.	tu reçus.	que je reçusse.
j'eus.	tu eus.	que j'eusse.
je fus.	tu fus.	que je fusse.

Donner	**Finir**	**Rendre**
That I gave (should, might give), etc.	*That I finished (should, might finish),* etc.	*That I gave back (should, might give back),* etc.
Que je donnasse.	Que je finisse.	Que je rendisse.
Que tu donnasses.	Que tu finisses.	Que tu rendisses.
Qu'il donnât.	Qu'il finît.	Qu'il rendît.
Que nous donnassions.	Que nous finissions.	Que nous rendissions.
Que vous donnassiez.	Que vous finissiez.	Que vous rendissiez.
Qu'ils donnassent.	Qu'ils finissent.	Qu'ils rendissent.

[1] The s has disappeared before t and has been replaced by a circumflex (^) on the preceding vowel.

[2] For the imperfect subjunctive of irregular verbs, see appendix.

Avoir	Être
That I had (should, might have), etc.	*That I was (should, might be), etc.*
Que j'eusse.	Que je fusse.
Que tu eusses.	Que tu fusses.
Qu'il eût.	Qu'il fût.
Que nous eussions.	Que nous fussions.
Que vous eussiez.	Que vous fussiez.
Qu'ils eussent.	Qu'ils fussent.

Lecture

1. Je veux que vous soyez plus attentif. 2. Je voudrais que vous soyez (fussiez) plus attentif. 3. Il est indispensable qu'il ait ses livres ce soir. 4. Il était indispensable qu'il eût ses livres ce soir. 5. Mon père craint que vous soyez fatigué. 6. Mon père craignait que vous fussiez fatigué. 7. Il est temps qu'il finisse sa lettre et qu'il la mette à la poste. 8. Il était temps qu'il finît sa lettre et qu'il la mît à la poste. 9. Je préfère qu'elle choisisse elle-même ce qu'elle désire. 10. Je préférerais qu'elle choisît elle-même ce qu'elle désire. 11. J'ai préféré qu'elle choisît elle-même ce qu'elle désirait. 12. J'empêcherai qu'il ferme la porte. 13. J'ai empêché qu'il fermât la porte. 14. C'est le plus beau morceau de musique que j'aie jamais entendu. 15. C'était le plus beau morceau de musique que j'eusse jamais entendu. 16. Ne lui parlez pas, de peur qu'elle fonde (*to burst*) en larmes. 17. Je ne lui ai pas parlé de peur qu'elle fondît en larmes.

Exercices

Traduisez en français :

1. It is time for her to choose (that she should choose). 2. It was time for her to choose. 3. You are the only man whom (*à qui*) she obeys. 4. You were the only man whom she obeyed. 5. It is certain that I am right. 6. It was certain that I was right. 7. I should like to have him receive these letters in time (*à temps*). 8. I wished him to

receive those letters in time. 9. I shall not accept their invitation unless I have the permission of my father and mother. 10. Do you believe they are guilty? 11. Did you believe they were guilty? 12. He approves of my being (he finds good that I am) idle (*paresseux*). 13. He approved of my being idle. 14. Do you think that he is right? 15. Did you think that he was right? 16. I think that he is wrong. 17. I fear that he is wrong. 18. I do not think he is wrong. 19. I did not think that he was wrong. 20. I feared he was wrong.

Épître amoureuse d'un puriste

"Ah ! Fallait-il [1] que je vous visse,
Fallait-il que vous me plussiez, [2]
Qu'ingénûment je vous le disse,
Qu'avec orgueil [3] vous vous tussiez. [4]
Fallait-il que je vous aimasse,
Que vous me désespérassiez, [5]
Et qu'en vain je m'opiniâtrasse, [6]
Et que je vous idolâtrasse, [7]
Pour que vous m'assassinassiez ?"

* * * * * * *

77e Leçon : Subjonctif : clauses indépendantes ; plus-que-parfait ; revue générale

Mieux vaut sagesse que richesse. — *Wisdom is better than riches.*

Study the following sentences :

Vive la **France!**	*Long live France!*
Dieu me *soit* **en aide!**	*God help me!*
Ainsi *soit*-il.	*So let it be.*
Honni *soit* **qui mal y pense.**	*Evil to him who evil thinks.*

[1] was necessary. [2] to please. [3] pride. [4] to keep silent. [5] to drive to despair. [6] to be obstinate. [7] to idolize.

The subjunctive is sometimes used in independent clauses. However, strictly speaking, these independent clauses are subordinate clauses with the principal clauses suppressed or understood : (**je désire que**) **la France vive.** *I wish France may live;* (**je désire que**) **Dieu me soit en aide.** *I wish God to help me;* etc.

Observe also the subjunctive in the following sentences :

Que tout le monde *fasse* **son devoir.** *Let every one do his duty.*
Qu'il *vienne* **s'il veut me voir.** *Let him come if he wants to see me.*

The 3rd person of the subjunctive (singular and plural) is also used independently to supply the 3rd person of the imperative (singular and plural).

Plus-que-parfait du subjonctif

avoir,	**que j'eusse eu,** etc.	*that I might have had,* etc.
être,	**que j'eusse été,** etc.	*that I might have been,* etc.
donner,	**que j'eusse donné,** etc.	*that I might have given,* etc.
finir,	**que j'eusse fini,** etc.	*that I might have finished,* etc.
rendre,	**que j'eusse rendu,** etc.	*that I might have given back,* etc.
aller,	**que je fusse allé,** etc.	*that I might have gone,* etc.
venir,	**que je fusse venu,** etc.	*that I might have come,* etc.
rester,	**que je fusse resté,** etc.	*that I might have stayed,* etc.

The pluperfect subjunctive is formed with the imperfect subjunctive of the auxiliary verb **avoir** (sometimes **être,** Lesson 28) and a past participle.

Emploi du plus-que-parfait du subjonctif. — Like the perfect subjunctive, the pluperfect is used, when the subordinate clause expresses a past action and follows a principal clause also in the past. (See Lesson 76, 2d paragraph.)

The pluperfect subjunctive, like the imperfect, is avoided, whenever possible, especially in conversation, where it sounds affected.

	Ouvrir	Sortir	Courir
Que	j'ouvre.	je sorte.	je coure.
Que	tu ouvres.	tu sortes.	tu coures.
Qu'	il ouvre.	il sorte.	il coure.
Que	nous ouvrions.	nous sortions.	nous courions.
Que	vous ouvriez.	vous sortiez.	vous couriez.
Qu'	ils ouvrent.	ils sortent.	ils courent.

	Sentir	Boire
Que	je sente.	je boive.
Que	tu sentes.	tu boives.
Qu'	il sente.	il boive.
Que	nous sentions.	nous buvions.
Que	vous sentiez.	vous buviez.
Qu'	ils sentent.	ils boivent.

Revue générale

The subjunctive is used:

1. With verbs expressing doubt, wish, will, or an emotion such as joy, sorrow, fear, surprise, expectation, etc.

2. After impersonal verbs implying necessity, uncertainty, possibility, etc.

3. After a superlative, and after **le premier, le dernier, le seul,** when they have superlative force.

4. After a relative pronoun when doubt, uncertainty, or purpose is implied.

5. After negative and interrogative verbs, especially those of thinking and believing and implying doubt or uncertainty.

6. After certain conjunctions or conjunctive locutions of purpose, fear, time, condition, etc.

7. In independent clauses expressing a wish, and to supply the 3rd person of the imperative.

*The subjunctive is **not** used:*

1. After **espérer** used affirmatively.

2. After impersonal verbs when the thought is stated as a fact or probability.

3. After a superlative followed by **de**.

4. After a relative pronoun when no doubt or purpose is implied.

5. After a negative or interrogative verb when there is no doubt in the mind of the speaker.

6. After certain conjunctions or conjunctive locutions implying no doubt or purpose.

Vocabulaire

le siècle, *the century.*
l'ouest, *the west.*
l'époque (f.), *the time, the epoch.*
la diligence, *the stagecoach.*
à cheval, *horseback.*
à pied, *on foot.*
l'auberge (f.), *the inn.*
l'aubergiste (m.), *the innkeeper.*
le loup, *the wolf.*
le repas, *the repast, the meal.*
plaire, *to please.*
l'occasion (f.), *the opportunity.*
prouver, *to prove.*
avancer, *to advance.*
régler, *to settle.*
ajouter, *to add.*

le plat, *the dish, the course.*
goûter, *to taste.*
admettre, *to admit.*
aucun, *any, none.*
excepter, *to except.*
même, *even.*
la coutume, *the custom.*
l'aventure (f.), *the adventure.*
en même temps, *in the same time.*
condamner, *to condemn.*
l'amende (f.), *the fine.*
l'emprisonnement, *the confinement.*
exaspérer, *to exasperate.*
échapper, *to escape.*
la chrétienté, *Christendom.*
se tourner, *to turn.*

Lecture

Excepté le lord-maire

Le grand acteur anglais du XVIIIe siècle, Samuel Foote, voyageait un jour dans l'ouest de l'Angleterre. A cette époque, les chemins de fer n'existaient pas, et il fallait qu'on fasse (fît) les voyages en diligence, à cheval et même souvent à pied.

Notre acteur s'arrête donc dans une auberge pour dîner.

— Monsieur l'aubergiste, dit-il, j'ai une faim de loup ; y a-t-il quelqu'un ici qui puisse me préparer un bon repas?

— Je ne doute pas une minute que mon dîner vous plaise,

répondit l'aubergiste ; mon établissement est, autant que je sache, le meilleur qui soit dans cette partie de l'Angleterre, et je suis bien aise que vous me donniez l'occasion de prouver ce que j'avance.

Lorsque Foote voulut régler l'addition, l'aubergiste lui dit :

— Je ne crois pas qu'il soit nécessaire que je vous demande si vous avez bien dîné ; je suis heureux que vous ayez fait honneur à tous mes plats.

— C'est exact, votre cuisine est la plus succulente que j'aie jamais goûtée ; j'ai dîné comme personne en Angleterre.

— Excepté le lord-maire, ajoute l'aubergiste avec vivacité.

JE NE CONNAIS PAS UN HOMME QUI SOIT . . . .

— Je n'admets pas que vous fassiez une seule exception répond Foote.

— Il faut que vous exceptiez le lord-maire.

— Pas même le lord-maire.

— Si, monsieur.

— Non, monsieur !

— Monsieur, vous êtes le premier qui refusiez de vous conformer à nos coutumes locales, et comme je suis magistrat en même temps qu'aubergiste, je vais vous mener devant le lord-maire, à moins que vous consentiez à excepter ce digne personnage.

— Voilà certainement la plus sotte aventure qui me soit jamais arrivée, s'écrie Foote. Allons voir le lord-maire, monsieur l'aubergiste ; bien que je n'aie pas de temps à perdre, je serai enchanté de le voir, pourvu qu'il ne me fasse pas attendre trop longtemps.

Et ils partirent.

— Monsieur Foote, lui dit le vénérable magistrat, il faut que vous sachiez que c'est une habitude ici, depuis des temps immémoriaux, qu'on fasse toujours une exception pour le lord-maire, et qui que vous soyez et quoi que vous fassiez dans la vie, il convient que vous vous y conformiez. Afin que vous ne l'oubliiez pas une autre fois, je vous condamne à un shilling d'amende ou à cinq heures d'emprisonnement ; que vous choisissiez l'un ou l'autre, cela m'est parfaitment égal.

Foote, exaspéré, vit qu'il était impossible qu'il échappe (échappât) au verdict du lord-maire, et qu'il valait mieux qu'il paye (payât).

Il sortit de la salle en disant :

— Je ne connais pas, dans toute la chrétienté, un homme qui soit plus fou que cet aubergiste — excepté le lord-maire, ajouta-t-il en se tournant respectueusement du côté de Sa Seigneurie.

Exercices

A. *Relevez, dans l'historiette ci-dessus, les verbes au subjonctif et expliquez dans chaque cas, pourquoi le subjonctif a été employé.*

B. *Traduisez en français :*

1. Our friends wish us to stay with them this week.
2. The children must stay home, their mother does not want them to go out.   3. Have patience, but you must not have too much.   4. I must finish this letter first.   5. If you wish to go to his house, you may go there, but if you wish us to go (there) I must tell you frankly that we won't.
6. Our teacher told us that we should write our exercises in our note-books.   7. Why does he want you to write them?   8. I should like you to buy me some books.

9. I am very sorry he did not come. 10. It is already late, I doubt he will come. 11. We are very glad you came. 12. It is very late, it is time for us to leave. 13. It is not necessary for you to leave so soon, you must stay a little longer. 14. Don't you want to have dinner (to dine) with us? 15. It is too bad that I cannot accept your kind invitation, but I must be home before the children come back from school. 16. I am afraid they may already be home now. 17. It is good that they should do that. 18. It seems that he has not received my letter. 19. I do not doubt that you will receive an answer to-day or to-morrow. 20. I am surprised that I have not received one yet.

21. I did not tell him anything, for fear he should repeat what I said. 22. He is a good man, I hope he will succeed. 23. Are you sure you saw him yesterday? 24. I saw him, but I do not think he recognized me. 25. I am looking for a French book where I can find good exercises. 26. Don't you think that Chardenal is the book you need? 27. Is there any one (*quelqu'un*) who is willing to help me? Not that I know of. 28. You are the first (one) who has ever told me that I am a rich man. 29. Whoever you are, you must obey the law. 30. I explained that to him for fear he would not understand what you mean. 31. Although you explained it to him, he did not understand me. 32. He is the most stupid man I ever met. 33. Long live America! 34. Let them go if they do not want to stay here. 35. This dress is the most stylish you ever had. 36. Don't you think it fits me well? 37. I bought it without my mother knowing it. 38. Suppose she sees it, what will she say? 39. I hope she will not scold you. 40. We shall get up early to-morrow, so that we can go to the station and say good-by to our friends before they leave.

*　　*　　*　　*　　*　　*　　*

78ᵉ Leçon : Infinitif

Promettre et tenir sont deux. — *It is easier to promise than to perform.*

The infinitive expresses an action in a vague and indeterminate way : **parler,** *to speak,* **vendre,** *to sell.*

Infinitif avec prépositions. — Observe the infinitive in the following sentences :

(1) **Il est parti sans** *voir* **son frère.** *He left without seeing his brother.*
Nous mangerons avant de *partir.* *We shall eat before leaving.*
(2) **Nous partirons après** *avoir mangé.* *We shall leave after eating.*

When a verb comes after a preposition, it should be in the infinitive form (Examples 1). The preposition **après** always requires the *past infinitive* (Example 2), which is formed with the infinitive of **avoir** (sometimes **être,** Lesson 28) and a past participle.

Note. — Notice that very often the *present participle* is used in English after a preposition to translate the *French infinitive.*

Infinitif sans préposition. — A great number of French verbs are followed by either **à** or **de** which, of course, call for an infinitive when another verb follows. This will be dealt with in the next lesson. However, certain verbs are followed by the infinitive *without* any preposition. The most common [1] of these verbs are :

aimer mieux, *to like better.*	**pouvoir,** *to be able.*
aller, *to go.*	**préférer,** *to prefer.*
compter, *to intend.*	**prétendre,** *to pretend.*
croire, *to believe.*	**regarder,** *to look at.*
désirer, *to desire, to wish.*	**savoir,** *to know.*
écouter, *to listen.*	**sembler,** *to seem.*
entendre, *to hear.*	**venir,** *to come.*
espérer, *to hope.*	**voir,** *to see.*
faire, *to make.*	**vouloir,** *to wish.*
laisser, *to let.*	**il faut,** *it is necessary.*
oser, *to dare.*	**il vaut mieux,** *it is better.*

---

[1] For complete list see page 434.

Vue extérieure du fameux amphithéâtre d'Arles. (Ruine romaine.)
L'Aqueduc romain de Batthant, aux environs de Lyon.

Infinitif comme sujet ou complément. — Study the following sentences :

(1) *Promettre* est facile, *tenir* est difficile.	*To promise (promising) is easy, to keep (keeping) a promise is difficult.*
(2) Je crois *avoir* raison.	*I think I am right.*
(3) Il va *chanter*.	*He is going to sing.*
(4) Nous préférons ne pas *sortir*.	*We prefer not to go out.*

An infinitive can be used as a *subject* (Example 1). In that case it corresponds to the English verbal noun and present participle.

It can also be used as an *object* (Example 2).

When two verbs have the same subject and are used in the same clause, the second one is put in the infinitive (Examples 3 and 4). Of course exception should be made for the two auxiliary verbs **avoir** and **être,** which are always followed by a past participle to form the compound tenses.

Attention! **Ne . . . pas,** before an infinitive come together. This is the only case when they are not separated. With the infinitive of **avoir** and **être** they may be separated ; **n'être pas** or **ne pas être.** (The same applies to the other negatives, **ne . . . jamais, ne . . . rien,** etc.)

Emploi de l'infinitif. — Notice the use of the infinitive in the following cases :

(1) Que faire?	*What is to be done?*
(2) Agir ainsi!	*Act thus!*
(3) Voir page **60.**	*See page 60.*

An infinitive is sometimes used as a question (1), an exclamation (2), or an imperative (3).

Observe the infinitive in the following sentences :

(1) Il est allé *parler* au professeur.	*He went and spoke to the professor.*
(2) Elle est venue nous *aider*.	*She came and helped us.*
(3) Il vaut mieux *rire* que de *pleurer*.	*It is better to laugh than to cry.*
(4) Il viendra pour vous *parler* de cette affaire.	*He will come to speak to you of that matter.*

Aller and **venir** followed by an infinitive (Examples 1 and 2) often have the meaning of *go and* and *come and*.

Than before an infinitive (Example 3) is expressed by **que de**.

When the English *to* means *in order to, for the purpose of,* it is generally expressed by **pour** (Example 4).

Vocabulaire

s'**accouder**, *to lean on one's elbow.*
l'**infini** (m.), *the infinite.*
sombre, *dark.*
distinguer, *to distinguish.*
le **buisson**, *the bush.*
l'**allée** (f.), *the lane.*
l'**étoile** (f.), *the star.*
pétiller, *to sparkle.*
la **voûte**, *the canopy.*

céleste, *celestial.*
augmenter, *to increase.*
abandonner, *to give up, to abandon.*
le **désir**, *the desire.*
la **lune**, *the moon.*
argenté, *silvery.*
éclairer, *to light, to illuminate.*
avoir l'air, *to look as if, to seem to.*
se rendre compte, *to realize.*

pâlir, *to grow pale.*

Lecture

A MA FENÊTRE

J'adore m'accouder à ma fenêtre qui se trouve en face d'un grand parc. Le soir surtout, quand la nature semble dormir, je puis y rester des heures et laisser courir ma pensée dans l'infini de la nuit. Tout est sombre, silencieux, et le grand calme me fait supposer que je suis seul sur la terre. Je ne puis distinguer ni arbres, ni buissons, ni allées. Des étoiles pétillent dans la voûte céleste ; je crois pouvoir les compter, je commence toujours, je ne finis jamais, car leur nombre semble augmenter si rapidement que je dois abandonner mon projet. Mais voilà la lune, là-bas à l'horizon ; on ne peut voir que son grand front argenté ; elle semble ne pas vouloir se montrer ; on dirait qu'elle veut se cacher encore un peu. Mais non, la voilà qui monte ; elle vient regarder de ses yeux vagues cette terre qu'elle doit éclairer, car elle sait que ni hommes ni bêtes ne peuvent rester dans l'obscurité. Cepen-

J'ADORE M'ACCOUDER À MA FENÊTRE.

dant, elle a l'air d'hésiter encore un moment, mais elle se rend compte, sans doute, que tout le monde l'a vue et qu'il vaut mieux se montrer que de rester à demi-cachée, et la voilà qui apparaît dans toute sa splendeur de reine de la Nuit, faisant pâlir d'envie les étoiles jalouses.

Exercices

Traduisez en français :

1. We went and saw (We went to see) our aunt this morning ; she is much better.   2. I hope to see you on Thursday.
3. She did not dare to look at them.   4. She does not wish to come to-day, unless you think that she will find her father here.   5. Seeing is believing.   6. I like better to go to-day than to stay until the eleventh.   7. She will not be willing to accompany us.   8. They may come and see us this morning.   9. They came to see us last evening, but we were out.   10. We shall do our very best to receive him with honor.   11. She did it to please you.   12. I do not know how to thank her.   13. Thank her?   14. Do you think they can return soon?   15. You do not seem to believe what I say.   16. Let them come ! I would rather (I prefer to) see them to-day than wait until a week from Friday.
17. May I come too?   18. You may come, and you may bring all your friends with you.   19. It seems to me that you are mistaken ; I do not believe that I am acquainted with this lady.

79ᵉ Leçon : Infinitif après les prépositions A et DE

Il faut des raisons pour parler, mais il n'en faut point pour se taire. — *We must have reasons for speech, but we need none for silence.*

Infinitif avec *à*. — Study the following graph :

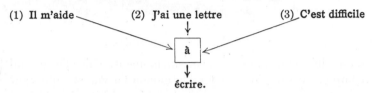

A great number of French verbs require **à** before the infinitive (Example 1).

The verb **avoir** followed by a *noun* requires **à** before the next verb if that verb can be changed into an infinitive passive (Example 2).   *I have a letter to be written.*

An *adjective* preceded by **c'est, c'était, cela est,** etc., requires **à** before the following infinitive (Examples 3).   *That is easy to be written* (passive idea).

Infinitif avec *de*. — Study also the following graph :

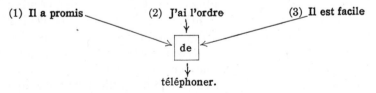

Another great number of French verbs require the preposition **de** before an infinitive (Example 1).

The verb **avoir,** followed by a *noun*, requires **de** before the next verb if that verb can *not* be changed into an infinitive passive (Example 2).

When an *adjective* is preceded by **il est, il était,** etc., it requires **de** before the infinitive (Example 3).

Remark. — No specific rule can be given regarding the preposition which follows a verb. Certain verbs take **à**, others take **de**; some take either; some do not take any (Lesson 78).

The same applies to adjectives : some take **à**, some take **de** before an infinitive. Practice alone will accustom the student to use the proper preposition. The only invariable rules on the adjectives are those applying to both Examples 3. (**C'est . . . à ; il est . . . de.**)

The most common verbs requiring the prepositions **à** or **de** are given in the following columns (for complete list see pages 434–435).

VERBS FOLLOWED BY **à** :	VERBS FOLLOWED BY **de** :
aider à, *to help to.*	**cesser de,** *to cease from.*
aimer à, *to like to.*	**commander de,** *to command from.*
s'appliquer à, *to apply oneself to.*	**conseiller de,** *to advise to.*
apprendre à, *to learn, to teach to.*	**craindre de,** *to fear to.*
s'attendre à, *to expect to.*	**défendre de,** *to forbid to.*
consentir à, *to consent to.*	**dire de,** *to tell to.*
décider à, *to persuade to.*	**décider de,** *to decide to.*
se décider à, *to decide to.*	**essayer de,** *to try to.*
engager à, *to induce to.*	**être désolé de,** *to be sorry to.*
enseigner à, *to teach to.*	**négliger de,** *to neglect to.*
s'habituer à, *to get accustomed to.*	**ordonner de,** *to order to.*
inviter à, *to ask, invite to.*	**permettre de,** *to allow to.*
se mettre à, *to begin to.*	**promettre de,** *to promise to.*
renoncer à, *to renounce, to give up.*	**recommander de,** *to recommend to.*
réussir à, *to succeed in.*	**refuser de,** *to refuse to.*
tarder à, *to be late in, to delay in.*	**remercier de,** *to thank for.*
venir à, *to chance to.*	**venir de,** *to have just.*

Lecture

UNE LETTRE DE PARIS

Paris le 31 juillet 19—

Mon cher Louis,

Je me décide enfin à vous envoyer quelques mots avant de quitter Paris. J'aurais aimé à rester plus longtemps ici, mais il m'a été impossible de décider mes parents à consentir à rester ici un peu plus longtemps ; ils ont refusé de m'accorder ce que je demandais ; nous partons ce soir.

Nous allons d'abord voir ma sœur qui, comme vous le savez, est à Lausanne.   Les cours de l'école où elle est en pension viennent de finir, et ma mère désire beaucoup ne pas la faire attendre.   De Suisse, nous irons visiter l'Italie où nous avons l'intention de passer plusieurs semaines.   Je suis impatient de voir la Suisse et l'Italie, mais je vous assure que je suis désolé de quitter ce beau Paris.   Il y a tant de choses à voir ici !   Je dois aussi renoncer à un voyage en

JE ME DÉCIDE ENFIN À VOUS ENVOYER QUELQUES MOTS.

automobile dans la région des châteaux, que nous avons été forcés de remettre à cause du mauvais temps.   Les projets sont faciles à faire, mais difficiles à exécuter.

J'avais promis de vous faire une description de Paris que vous désirez tant connaître, mais il est impossible de faire cela par lettre, il serait absurde d'essayer.   Ce que j'essayerai de faire, ce sera de vous donner plus régulièrement de mes nouvelles.   Jusqu'à maintenant, j'ai eu très peu de temps à consacrer à ma correspondance, mon cher ami, et je vous prie de m'excuser d'avoir négligé de vous écrire ; je ne cesse cependant de penser à vous.

J'espère que vous vous portez bien.   Inutile de vous dire de faire attention à votre santé ; je vous invite à être prudent ; ne négligez pas de bien vous couvrir le soir, les nuits sont froides dans les montagnes.   Faites-moi aussi le plaisir de présenter mes respects à madame votre mère, et recevez une bonne poignée de main de

Votre ami,

Charles.

Exercices

A. *Remplacez les tirets par la préposition convenable :*

1. C'est difficile —— faire.   2. Il est difficile —— faire ce travail.   3. Je suis prêt —— vous aider —— le faire. 4. Je viens —— voir Henri.   5. A-t-il été content —— vous voir?   6. Il a demandé à son père la permission —— venir avec moi.   7. Avez-vous réussi —— lui faire comprendre l'importance —— savoir le français?   8. J'ai oublié —— prendre mon parapluie.   9. Que ferez-vous s'il vient —— pleuvoir?   10. Je ne pense pas qu'il pleuve encore, il vient —— pleuvoir pendant deux heures. 11. Pourquoi Jeanne a-t-elle refusé —— répondre à la maîtresse?   12. Je ne sais pas, au lieu —— répondre, elle s'est mise —— pleurer.   13. Vous êtes-vous décidé —— partir la semaine prochaine?   14. Oui, nous avons décidé —— partir d'aujourd'hui en huit.   15. Maintenant que j'ai consenti —— accompagner mon cousin à Paris, je ne cesse plus —— y penser.

B. *Traduisez en français :*

1. They have letters to write.   2. I had the pleasure of meeting your uncle last night.   3. He refused to come with me.   4. He succeeded in winning the second prize. 5. That is not easy to do.   6. No, it is easier to say it than to do it.   7. It is absurd to speak so.   8. Allow me to take your watch.   9. Promise to give it back to me. 10. What a beautiful apple ! Is it good to eat?   11. You must get accustomed to studying five hours every day. 12. I mean that I cannot allow you to do nothing.   13. Do you need to see them?   14. Is it time to leave now? 15. Will you be so good as to shut the door?   16. I beg your pardon, but we have just done it.   17. I am glad to hear that.   18. She is always late in answering me. 19. When she entered, everybody began to sing and dance.

20. I just finished what I had to say.   21. If you begin to work now, I promise to take you to the theater to-night. 22. Don't you think he is right to forget that quarrel? 23. Yes, he avoided speaking to them.   24. Haven't you a house to sell?   25. No, sir, but they have one to let (*louer*).

*   *   *   *   *   *   *

80ᵉ Leçon: L'infinitif au lieu du subjonctif

A quelque chose malheur est bon. — *It's an ill wind that blows nobody any good.*[1]

When the subjunctive mode can be avoided by using the infinitive in the secondary clause, it should be done, since the frequent use of the subjunctive makes the style heavy.

Emploi de l'infinitif au lieu du subjonctif. — Study the following sentences :

(1) **Est-ce que vous craignez de lui parler?** *Do you fear to speak to him?*

(2) **Venez me voir avant de lui parler.** *Come to see me before speaking to him.*

When two verbs have the same person for subject (Example 1), the second is generally in the infinitive (Lesson 78).

If two clauses have the same person for subject, the conjunction which joins them may often be changed to a preposition, and the following verb put in the infinitive (Example 2).

[1] Literally, *For something misfortune is good.*

List of conjunctions which may be changed to prepositions :

CONJUNCTION		PREPOSITION
afin que,	*in order that,*	afin de.
pour que,	*in order that,*	pour.
avant que,	*before,*	avant de.
sans que,	*without,*	sans.
à moins que,	*unless,*	à moins de.
de crainte que,	*for fear that, lest,*	de crainte de.
de peur que,	*for fear that, lest,*	de peur de.
jusqu'à ce que,	*till, until,*	jusque.

Traduction de *must*. — Analyze the following sentences :

		CONJUGATION OF falloir
Il faut que Jean le fasse.	*John must do it.*	il faut.
Il faut qu'il le fasse.	⎱ *He must do it.*	il fallait.
Il *lui* faut le faire.	⎰	il a fallu.
Il *me* faut le faire.	*I must do it.*	il avait fallu.
Il *nous* faut le faire.	*We must do it.*	il eut fallu.
Il *vous* faut le faire.	*You must do it.*	il faudra.
Il *leur* faut le faire.	*They must do it.*	il faudrait.
Il faut qu'on le fasse.	⎱ *One must do it* or	il aura fallu.
Il faut le faire.	⎰ *it must be done.*	il aurait fallu.
Un homme comme il faut, *a gentleman.*		qu'il faille.
		qu'il ait fallu.

If the subject of *must* is a noun, **falloir** is followed by the subjunctive ; if the subject is a personal pronoun, or if the statement is general, **falloir** may be followed by the infinitive by changing the subject pronoun of the second clause to an indirect object pronoun which is placed before **falloir**.

Lecture

1. Mon père a ordonné que les enfants descendissent au salon.   2. Mon père a ordonné aux enfants de descendre tout de suite au salon.   3. Elle commande que je lui achète un journal français.   4. Elle m'a commandé de lui acheter un journal français.   5. Je ne sortirai pas avant qu'il

nous ait donné sa parole.   6. Je ne sortirai pas avant
d'avoir obtenu votre promesse.   7. Il craint qu'elle meure.
8. Il craint de mourir.   9. Elle dit vous avoir écrit.
10. Elle dit que vous m'avez écrit.   11. Elle me dit de
vous écrire.   12. Il prétend avoir raison.   13. Il prétend
que je n'ai pas raison.   14. Il croit avoir bien fait.   15. Il
croit que vous avez bien fait.   16. Combien de temps faut-il
pour apprendre à parler français?   17. Cela dépend de
bien des choses.   (Bien des, see page 364, 2.)

Exercices

A. *Reconstruisez les phrases suivantes en employant l'infinitif
au lieu du subjonctif :*

1. Elle a demandé que vous achetiez un dictionnaire.
2. Faut-il que je lui en achète un?   3. Ils m'ont dit de
leur écrire avant que je parte.   4. Faut-il qu'il soit stupide
pour qu'il ait fait cela !   5. Il est parti depuis une heure
de peur qu'il vous rencontre ici.   6. Nous avions ordonné
que vous fussiez (soyez) ici à cinq heures, pourquoi êtes-vous
en retard?   7. Le médecin a défendu que je mange de la
viande.   8. Il faut que nous partions tout de suite.   9. De
peur que je manque mon train je me suis levé à six heures, ce
matin.   10. Vous n'arriverez pas à l'heure, à moins que
vous preniez une voiture.

B. *Traduisez en français :*

1. I fear I am wrong.   2. I feared I was wrong.   3. I
am sorry I am late.   4. I was sorry I was late.   5. The
doctor has ordered me to run a little every day.   6. I
thought I had seen you somewhere.   7. He pretends he
has spoken to you.   8. He will not try it for fear he should
make a mistake.   9. I shall speak to him before I write
to you.   10. I wish I were in the country that I might
(*pour pouvoir*) rest.   11. Is it possible to do that?
12. That is impossible to do.   13. Must one always do

Ewing Galloway

LES ARÈNES DE NÎMES, QUI DATENT DE L'OCCUPATION ROMAINE.

one's best?   14. Must you stay here long?   15. He now believes she is dead.   16. We (*on*) must not believe all we hear.   17. The poor old woman of whom I was speaking to you the other day died yesterday.

Exercice-revue

1. If you want to go and see him, you may go, but I doubt that you will find him home.   2. Don't you think he should be home now?   3. I don't think he has come back from the country.   4. He must be here, unless he has missed his train.   5. I am glad you put on your straw hat to-day, it is very warm.   6. Are you not glad you put on your white dress, Mary?   7. Be here to-morrow at nine.   8. In case I am not here at nine promptly, have a little patience and wait for me.   9. How long do you want me to wait for you?   10. It will not be necessary for you to wait a long time.   11. I do not think you will have to wait more than ten minutes, a quarter of an hour at the most.   12. Let them do what they want, because I doubt they will ever obey you.   13. John, don't you know that your mother does not want you to run all the time?   14. She is afraid you may fall ill.   15. He is the tallest man we ever saw.   16. He is the tallest of all the men I know.

*   *   *   *   *   *   *

81e Leçon: Participe présent; participe passé

En forgeant on devient forgeron. — *Practice makes perfect.*

Participe présent. — The present participle is used to denote action simultaneous with that of the main verb. It is formed by replacing the endings **-er, -ir,** and **-re** of the infinitive by **-ant.**

donnant, *giving.*   **finissant,** *finishing.*   **rendant,** *giving back.*
ayant, *having.*   **étant,** *being.*

To prevent confusion between the first and second conjugations, -iss- is inserted between the stem and the ending in the verbs of the second conjugation.

The present participle is *never* used in the conjugation of a French verb as it is used in English :

I am giving.	**Je donne.**	*I have been giving.*	**J'ai donné.**
I was giving.	**Je donnais.**	*I had been giving.*	**J'avais donné.**

Participe présent avec en. — **En,** *in, while, by,* is the *only preposition* that may be used with a present participle. With other prepositions, where the participle is used in English, the infinitive is required in French (Lesson 78).

Ce n'est pas en *pleurant*, mais en *travaillant* que vous réussirez. *It is not by crying, but by working that you will succeed.*

Je l'ai vu en *revenant*.	*I saw him while coming back.*
Il lisait tout en *marchant*.	*Still walking, he was reading.*

Participe présent composé. — The present participle has a compound tense which is formed with the present participle of the auxiliary verbe **avoir** (sometimes **être,** Lesson 28) and a past participle.

Ayant pris son chapeau, il sortit. *Having taken his hat, he went out.*

Autres emplois. — Analyze the following sentences :

(1) **Ces hommes, prévoyant le danger, se sont mis sur leurs gardes.** *These men, foreseeing the danger, put themselves on their guard.*

(2) **Ces hommes prévoyants ont aperçu le danger.** *These farsighted men have perceived the danger.*

A present participle may be used as a *verb* or as an *adjective*. As a verb it is invariable and usually refers to the subject (1). As an adjective, it follows the noun and agrees with it in gender and in number as a regular adjective (2).

Compare the following sentences :

Je l'entends chanter.	*I hear him singing.*	**Je l'entends qui chante.**
Je le vois jouer.	*I see him playing.*	**Je le vois qui joue.**
Je l'ai vu jouer.	*I saw him playing.*	**Je l'ai vu qui jouait.**

After the following verbs the present participle is generally used in English, and the infinitive in French. Instead of the infinitive, a tense of the indicative with **qui** may be used with all except **paraître** and **sembler** :

apercevoir, *to perceive.*	**sentir**, *to feel.*
écouter, *to listen.*	**voir**, *to see.*
entendre, *to hear.*	**paraître**, *to appear.*
regarder, *to look at.*	**sembler**, *to seem.*

Participe passé. — As already learned, the past participle is used with the different tenses of the auxiliary verbs **avoir** or **être** to form all compound tenses.

Study the following sentences :

(1) **Qui a écrit les lettres que vous avez reçues?**
(2) **Votre sœur s'est-elle blessée?   Oui, elle s'est cassé la jambe.**
(3) **Voici les choses désirées.**
(4) **Les chansons que j'ai entendu chanter sont très belles.**

A past participle used with **avoir** agrees with a preceding *direct object* (Example 1) ; with **être,** it agrees with the *subject*, except in the case of pronominal verbs (which are conjugated with **être** instead of **avoir**) when it agrees with the reflexive pronoun if that is the direct object (Example 2) (Lessons 28, 34, 63).

A past participle used as an adjective agrees with the noun or pronoun to which it relates (Example 3).

According to the new syntax, a past participle conjugated with **avoir** and followed by an infinitive, may remain invariable (Example 4) when the object precedes, while, according to the old rule, the past participle had to agree with the preceding object.

Noms collectifs. — Study the following sentences :

La foule des spectateurs que j'ai vue était immense. *The crowd of spectators that I saw was immense.*

Une foule d'enfants le suivaient partout. *A crowd of children followed him everywhere.*

A collective noun representing the *whole* number of the persons or things mentioned requires its verb, adjective, and pronoun in the singular; otherwise the verb, adjective, or pronoun is in the plural. In general, collective nouns preceded by **le** or **la** take the singular; preceded by **un** or **une,** the plural.

Vocabulaire

la plupart des, *most.*
causer, *to talk, to chat.*
couvrir, *to cover.*
faire mal à, *to hurt.*

se donner la main, *to shake hands.*
l'acteur, l'actrice, *actor, actress.*
la pièce, *the play.*
la foule, *the crowd.*

Note. — Notice that **la plupart** takes **des** and not **de** before a noun.

Lecture

1. J'ai vu courir la foule.   2. J'ai vu la foule qui courait. 3. J'entends rire ma sœur.   4. Écoutez-la rire; il me semble que ce rire est peu naturel.   5. Il travaille en chantant et en causant avec tout le monde.   6. Ces messieurs sont vraiment amusants, n'est-ce pas?   7. Le champ de bataille était couvert de soldats mourants.   8. Ces photographies sont bien ressemblantes.   9. Voilà un chien qui aboie.   10. Tout en refusant, elle semble accepter. 11. De quoi riez-vous?   12. Ne riez pas de moi, je vous prie.   13. La plupart des soldats se sont bien défendus. 14. Pendant une année entière elles se sont défendu tout amusement.   15. Ces deux hommes se sont querellés, mais après ils se sont donné la main.   16. J'ai entendu dire que madame votre mère est revenue ce matin.   17. Qui a fait mal à cette petite fille?   18. Elle s'est fait mal elle-même. 19. Est-ce que vous vous rappelez cette pièce que nous avons vu jouer un soir à la Comédie Française?   20. Oui, et je me rappelle aussi la plupart des acteurs que nous avons vu jouer.

Exercice

Traduisez en français :

1. I hear your brother speaking.   2. I heard him speaking to his friend.   3. Did you see him running with those children?   4. We have watched him eating.   5. We looked at it while [we were] eating.   6. This lady is truly amusing.   7. Whom is she amusing?   8. By amusing us, she enjoys herself.   9. What a charming lady!   10. She is also a very obliging person.   11. They came without bringing us what we asked for.   12. There they are; they are reading the papers.   13. [One's] appetite comes while eating.   14. This woman appears to suffer (the infinitive or the adjective).   15. I have heard that your sisters have arrived.   16. A large number (*nombre*, m.) of their friends came to see them last evening.   17. My cousins, Mary and Jane, have often written to each other.   18. The books he dropped are mine.   19. Who are those men I saw walking in your garden?   20. A crowd of children were running and playing in the yard behind the school. 21. The crowd of men and women who were watching the children play was still larger.   22. A poor old lady has fallen in the street in front of our house. Did you see her fall? 23. I am afraid she hurt herself.   24. Most pens are poor.

*   *   *   *   *   *   *

82ᵉ Leçon : Le verbe DEVOIR

A qui veut, rien n'est impossible. — *Where there's a will there's a way.*[1]

Devoir, *ought, must, to owe, to have to*

PARTICIPE PRÉSENT, **devant.**   PARTICIPE PASSÉ, **dû, due.**

IND. PRÉS., **je dois, tu dois, il doit; nous devons, vous devez, ils doivent.**

---

[1] Literally, *To him who will, nothing is impossible.*

PASSÉ IND., **j'ai dû.**

IMPARF.	je devais.	PL.-QUE-P.	j'avais dû.
PASSÉ DÉF.	je dus.	PASSÉ ANT.	j'eus dû.
FUTUR	je devrai.	FUT. ANT.	j'aurai dû.
CONDIT.	je devrais.	COND. PASSÉ	j'aurais dû.
SUBJ. PRÉS.	que je doive.	SUBJ. PARF.	que j'aie dû.
SUBJ. IMP.	que je dusse.	SUBJ. PLPF.	que j'eusse dû.

IMPÉRATIF, **dois, devons, devez.**

The verb **devoir** is expressed in English in many more different ways than any other verb. In many cases the translation depends upon the tense in which the verb is used in French ; sometimes also, it depends upon the object of the verb.

Study the following sentences :

(1) **Je** *dois* **dix francs à Paul.**   *I owe Paul ten francs.*
    Je lui *dois* **dix francs.**   *I owe him ten francs.*

Followed by a *noun*, **devoir** expresses the idea of *debt*, and corresponds to the English *to owe.*

(2)   (*a*) **Je** *dois* **lui dire cela.**   *I must tell him that.*
    (*b*) **Je** *devrais* **lui dire cela.**   *I ought to tell him that.*
    (*c*) **J'***aurais dû* **lui dire cela.**   *I ought to have told him that.*

Generally speaking, **devoir,** followed by an infinitive expresses *duty, obligation.*

(*a*) **Devoir** in the *present* + an infinitive expresses a strong obligation, with the understanding that the action expressed in the infinitive will be performed by the speaker : *I must tell him that* (and I will). It corresponds to the English *must.*

(*b*) **Devoir** in the *present conditional* + an infinitive, expresses an obligation, but with the understanding that the action expressed by the infinitive will not, or may not be performed by the speaker : *I ought to tell him that* (but I won't or I don't know if I will). It corresponds to the English *ought to.*

(c) **Devoir** in the *past conditional* + an infinitive expresses a past obligation that it is too late for the speaker to perform. As *ought* has no past in English, the English present infinitive which followed *ought* in Example *b* is changed to a past infinitive. It corresponds to the English *ought to have.*

Notice the translation of **devoir** in the following sentences :

(3) (a) **Nous *devrions* partir plus tôt.** *We should leave earlier.*
   (b) **Nous *aurions dû* partir plus tôt.** *We should have left earlier.*

Similarly, when *should* may be changed to *ought to*, and *should have* to *ought to have*, translate : *I should* by **je devrais,** and *I should have* by **j'aurais dû.**

(4) (a) **Je *dois* être à l'école à 8 heures.** *I must be at school at 8 o'clock.*
   Nous *devons* partir dans une heure. *We have to go in an hour.*
   (b) **Elle *devait* prendre le train de minuit.** *She was to take the midnight train.*

(a) **Devoir** in the present indicative, followed by an infinitive, often conveys the English idea of *to be to*, or *to have to*, expressing future obligation.

(b) **Devoir** in the imperfect indicative + an infinitive conveys the idea of something which was to have happened.

(5) **Il *doit* être en route maintenant.** *He must be on his way now.*
   Vous *devez* être fatigué, reposez-vous. *You must be tired, rest.*
   Il *a dû* être surpris de vous voir. *He must have been surprised to see you.*

When **devoir** implies *supposition* or *inference* on the part of the speaker, it is translated by *must* (**je dois, tu dois,** etc.) or *must have* (**j'ai dû, tu as dû,** etc.), with the verb following in the infinitive.

(6) ***Dussé-je* faire toute la route à pied, j'irai le voir.** *Even though I have to (even if I must) walk the whole way, I shall go to see him.*

At the beginning of a sentence, **devoir** in the imperfect subjunctive translates the English *even though, even if.*

Vocabulaire

la **banque,** *the bank.*
le **banquier,** *the banker.*
malhonnête, *dishonest.*
la **faute,** *the fault.*
   se **faire du mauvais sang,** *to worry.*
plaie d'argent n'est pas mortelle, *money losses may be repaired.*

le **bateau,** *the ship, the boat.*
à quoi bon? *what is the use?*
le **plan,** *the plan, the project.*
se **passer,** *to happen.*

Lecture

LA PERTE D'ARGENT

— Vous devez être très malheureux d'avoir perdu tout votre argent?

— Oui, surtout que je dois beaucoup à mon ami Maurice; je lui dois plus de dix mille francs.

— Vous devriez lui dire que votre banquier était un homme malhonnête; Maurice doit savoir que ce n'est pas votre faute.

— Oui, j'aurais dû lui dire tout de suite ce qui est arrivé, maintenant je ne peux plus; je viens d'apprendre qu'il est parti hier soir pour l'Amérique, il doit être en route maintenant.

— Ne devait-il pas partir la semaine prochaine seulement?

VOUS NE DEVEZ PAS VOUS FAIRE DU MAUVAIS SANG.

— Si, mais il a dû changer ses plans à cause de son oncle qui a dû partir une semaine plus tôt.

— Ne devriez-vous pas lui télégraphier?

— Non, à quoi bon; il saura toujours la mauvaise nouvelle

assez tôt ; je ne dois pas lui dire cela en quelques mots ; je
lui écrirai une longue lettre en lui expliquant comment les
choses se sont passées.

— Vous ne devez pas vous faire du mauvais sang, Maurice
comprendra.

— J'en suis certain, et je vous assure qu'il ne perdra rien,
car, dussé-je travailler toute ma vie, je le rembourserai
jusqu'au dernier sou.

— Oui, oui, vous êtes jeune encore, et " plaie d'argent n'est
pas mortelle," dit le proverbe. Comment ! Deux heures
moins le quart ! Mon ami, je dois vous quitter, je dois être
chez mon avocat à 2 heures. Je devrais déjà être en route
maintenant ; j'aurais dû partir il y a vingt minutes.

— Au revoir, mon cher. Merci de votre bonne visite.

Exercice

Traduisez en français :

1. You owe me fifty dollars. 2. You ought to pay me
now. 3. I have to go to the bank to-morrow. 4. You
should have gone this morning. 5. You ought to have
told me before that you were to have that money to-day.
6. Was he not to go to New York last Saturday? 7. Certainly, he must be there now. 8. You must be thirsty after
running so long ; here is a glass of lemonade. 9. I do not
like lemonade ; even though I were to be thirsty all my life,
I would not drink lemonade. 10. There is your aunt,
she must have been very beautiful when she was young.
11. You should have seen her twenty years ago, she was
really beautiful. 12. Must you go now? 13. Yes, I
ought to be gone already. 14. You should stay here and
have dinner (*dîner*) with me. 15. I am sorry, but I am
to have dinner with the Duvals. 16. You ought to telephone them that you are ill, and we would spend the evening
together. 17. No, I cannot ; it is Mrs. Duval's birthday.
I have to be with them to-night.

Exercice-revue

1. Did you hear me singing yesterday?   2. Yes, I heard you while passing (*passer devant*) your house.   3. Is it not better to sing than to cry?   4. Will you help me to do this, please?   5. Is it so difficult to do it?   6. Yes, it is not easy to do.   7. If you chance to see Charles, please speak to him.   8. I think that Mrs. Barnier and her sister are two charming women.   9. Did you see them last Sunday while going to church?   10. I saw them entering the church.   11. Miss Magloire is hurt; what is the matter with her?   12. She fell and broke her finger.   13. I am very sorry she hurt herself.   14. I do not think it is very serious.   15. Don't you think she is the most charming girl to whom one can speak?   16. Be kind to her.   17. I would like to be introduced to him.   18. You wish you were in Paris, do you not?   19. Yes, I wish I could live there. 20. Do you want us to go there next summer?

*   *   *   *   *   *   *

83ᵉ Leçon: Formation des temps; voix passive

Chacun pour soi, et Dieu pour tous. — *Every one for himself, and God for us all.*

The five tenses from which we may form the other parts of regular verbs and of most of the irregular verbs are called **primitive tenses,** or principal parts.   They are as follows : Infinitive, Present Participle, Past Participle, Present Indicative, Past Definite.

By the use of + and — signs, the formation of tenses may be clearly shown by the following

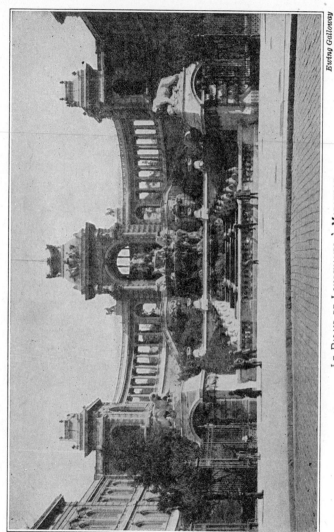

Ewing Galloway

LE PALAIS DE LONGCHAMPS À MARSEILLE.

Table of forms

INFINITIVE, $\left\{\begin{array}{l} \text{+ ai = FUTURE.} \\ \text{+ ais = CONDITIONAL PRESENT.} \end{array}\right.$

PRES. PARTICIPLE, $\left\{\begin{array}{l} \text{− ant + ons = 1st person plural PRESENT INDICATIVE.} \\ \text{− ant + ais = IMPERFECT INDICATIVE.} \\ \text{− ant + e = PRESENT SUBJUNCTIVE.} \end{array}\right.$

PAST PARTICIPLE: after **avoir** or **être** = Compound Tenses.

PRES. INDICATIVE, $\left\{\begin{array}{l} \text{1st person sing. = 2d person sing. IMPERATIVE.} \\ \text{3d person plural − nt = PRES. SUBJUNCTIVE.} \end{array}\right.$

PAST DEF.: 2d person sing. + se = IMPERFECT SUBJUNCTIVE.

Example : **Suivre,** *to follow*

Suivre, $\left\{\begin{array}{l} \text{je suivrai, FUTURE.} \\ \text{je suivrais, CONDITIONAL PRES.} \end{array}\right.$

Suivant, $\left\{\begin{array}{l} \text{nous suivons, 1st person plural, PRESENT INDICATIVE.} \\ \text{je suivais, IMPERFECT INDICATIVE.} \\ \text{que je suive, PRESENT SUBJUNCTIVE.} \end{array}\right.$

Suivi, $\left\{\begin{array}{l} \text{j'ai suivi, PAST INDEFINITE.} \\ \text{j'avais suivi, PLUPERFECT INDICATIVE.} \\ \text{j'eus suivi, PAST ANTERIOR.} \\ \text{j'aurai suivi, FUTURE PERFECT.} \\ \text{j'aurais suivi, CONDITIONAL PERFECT.} \\ \text{que j'aie suivi, PERFECT (PAST) SUBJUNCTIVE.} \\ \text{que j'eusse suivi, PLUPERFECT SUBJUNCTIVE.} \\ \text{avoir suivi, PERFECT INFINITIVE.} \\ \text{ayant suivi, PERFECT PARTICIPLE.} \end{array}\right.$

je suis, $\left\{\begin{array}{l} \text{suis, IMPERATIVE.} \\ \text{que je suive, PRESENT SUBJUNCTIVE.} \end{array}\right.$

je suivis: que je suivisse, IMPERFECT SUBJUNCTIVE.

Practice drill

Form the tenses of the following irregular verbs from their principal parts :

(1) **Dormir,** *to sleep,* **dormant, dormi, je dors, je dormis.**

Also : **partir,** *to go away,* **sortir,** *to go out,* **servir,** *to serve,* **se repentir** (**de**), *to repent,* **sentir,** *to feel,* **mentir,** *to (tell a) lie,* **s'endormir,** *to go to sleep,* etc., and their compounds.

Observe that the final consonant of the stem is dropped in the singular of the Present Indicative of these verbs : **pars, sers, sens,** etc.

(2) **Offrir,** *to offer,* **offrant, offert, j'offre, j'offris.**

Also : **souffrir,** *to suffer,* **ouvrir,** *to open,* **couvrir,** *to cover,* and their compounds.

(3) **Prendre,** *to take,* **prenant, pris, je prends, je pris.**

Also the compounds of **prendre: apprendre,** *to learn, to teach,* **comprendre,** *to understand,* **entreprendre,** *to undertake,* etc.

(4) **Plaindre,** *to pity,* **plaignant, plaint, je plains, je plaignis.**

Also : **se plaindre,** *to complain,* and all verbs in **-aindre, -eindre, -oindre,** such as **craindre,** *to fear,* **peindre,** *to paint,* **éteindre,** *to extinguish,* **teindre,** *to tint,* **atteindre,** *to reach,* **joindre,** *to join,* etc.

(5) **Naître,** *to be born,* **naissant, né, je nais, je naquis.**

Like **connaître** and **paraître,** this verb has î in the stem everywhere before **t.**

(6) **Plaire,** *to please,* **plaisant, plu, je plais, je plus.**

Third singular, present indicative, **il plaît.**
Also : **se taire,** *to be silent* (no î in third singular, present indicative).

(7) **Vivre,** *to live,* **vivant, vécu, je vis, je vécus.**

(8) **Battre,** *to strike,* **battant, battu, je bats, je battis.**

Also : **se battre,** *to fight,* **combattre,** *to combat,* etc.

(9) **Conduire,** *to conduct,* **conduisant, conduit, je conduis, je conduisis.**

Also all verbs in **-uire** (**instruire, traduire, produire, introduire,** etc.), except **luire,** *to shine* (past participle, **lui,** and no past definite), and **nuire,** *to injure* (past participle, **nui**).

Voix passive. — As in English, any tense of the Passive Voice of a transitive verb is the same as the corresponding tense of the auxiliary verb followed by the past participle of the verb in question.

Elle est aimée de tout le monde.   *She is loved by everybody.*
Nous avons été reçus avec honneur.   *We were received with honor.*

The passive is used far less frequently than in English, its place being taken by **on** with the active or by a reflexive construction.

On m'a dit que ce n'est pas vrai.   *I have been told that it's not true.*
On leur a donné des livres.   *Some books have been given to them.*
La porte s'ouvre, mais personne n'entre.   *The door is opened, but no one comes in.*
Cela ne se dit pas.   *No one says that.*

Vocabulaire

se repentir, *to repent.*
offenser, *to offend.*
le porte-monnaie, *the purse.*
se servir de, *to use.*
par cœur, *by heart.*

suivre, *to follow.*
se plaindre, *to complain.*
peindre, *to paint.*
se plaire, *to enjoy oneself.*
faire l'enfant, *to be childish.*

Lecture

1. Ne vous repentez-vous pas d'avoir offensé un de vos meilleurs amis?   2. Voici mon porte-monnaie; servez-vous-en, je vous prie.   3. N'ouvrez pas cette fenêtre; j'ai peur d'un courant d'air.   4. En hiver je souffre toujours du froid.   5. Madame N. est née à Dinan, en Bretagne, le 12 février, 1881, d'une famille honnête et ancienne.   6. Napoléon naquit en 1769 et mourut en 1821.   7. Il faut qu'on prenne les choses comme elles viennent et les hommes comme ils sont.   8. Apprenez ces vers par cœur.   9. La plupart des hommes estiment ce qu'ils ne comprennent pas.   10. Allez devant; je suis à vous, et je vous suis.   11. Desquels de ses amis se plaint-elle?   12. Voici l'atelier où un grand artiste peignait.   13. Cela ne plaît pas à tout le monde.   14. Il paraît que vous vous plaisiez à Paris, lorsque vous y demeuriez.   15. Comment traduit-on cette phrase?   16. Faites taire votre chien.   17. Avez-vous jamais entendu ceci? — je suis ce que je suis; je ne suis pas ce que je suis; si j'étais ce que je suis, je ne serais pas ce que je suis.

Exercice

Traduisez en français :

1. Take an umbrella, if you go out ; it will rain in less than (before) an hour.   2. Follow us ; do not follow them. 3. Take me to Mr. B's house ; I am to see him on (*pour*) business.   4. Those boys quarrel very often, but I have forbidden them to fight.   5. Tell him to hold his tongue. 6. Is it polite to say, " Hold your tongue "?   7. My brother has been given a gold watch.   8. My grandfather always falls asleep while reading the newspaper.   9. Let us not fall asleep while we are reading ; we are too young to do that.   10. Your cousin is not [a] reasonable [man] ; nothing pleases him.   11. I know that he always complains of everything.   12. Let us offer these flowers to (our) mother ; they are the most beautiful ones we have ever offered her. 13. If you wish us to open our books, please tell us at what page we are to open them.   14. Don't be childish ; put on your hat and go take a walk with them.

*   *   *   *   *   *   *

84e Leçon : Résumé des pronoms relatifs et interrogatifs ; adjectifs et pronoms indéfinis

Nous avons tous assez de force pour supporter les maux d'autrui. — *We all have strength enough to bear the misfortunes of others.*

Pronoms relatifs. —

NOMINATIVE, **qui,** *who, which, that.*

GENITIVE,
- de qui, *of whom.*
- **dont,** *of whom, of which, whose.*
- **duquel, de laquelle,** } *of whom, of which,*
- **desquels, desquelles,** } *whose.*

DATIVE, **à qui,** *to whom.*
- **auquel, à laquelle,** } *to whom, to which.*
- **auxquels, auxquelles,** }

ACCUSATIVE, **que,** *whom, which, that.*

Pronoms interrogatifs. —

PERSONS	THINGS

NOMINATIVE

qui? qui est-ce qui? *who?*	qu'est-ce qui? *what?*

GENITIVE

de qui? *of whom?*   de quoi? *of what?*

duquel? de laquelle? ⎱ *of which*   duquel? de laquelle? ⎱ *of which*
desquels? desquelles? ⎰ *(one(s))?*   desquels? desquelles? ⎰ *(one(s))?*

DATIVE

à qui? *to whom?*   à quoi? *to what?*

auquel? à laquelle? ⎱ *to which*   auquel? à laquelle? ⎱ *to which*
auxquels? auxquelles? ⎰ *(one(s))?*   auxquels? auxquelles? ⎰ *(one(s))?*

ACCUSATIVE

qui? qui est-ce que? *whom?*   que? qu'est-ce que? *what?*

                                         quoi? *what?* used alone as an exclamation or as the object of a verb understood.

Adjectifs et pronoms indéfinis. — (1) The following are adjectives only :

chaque, *each, every.*
quelque, *some;* pl., *few.*
quelconque (after the noun), *whatever.*
maint, *many a.*

certain, *certain.*
différent(e)s,
divers, diverses, ⎱ *various.*
même, *self, same, even.*

    Also : quel . . . que (with subjunctive of être), ⎱ *whatever.*
           quelque . . . que (with subjunctive), ⎰

Chaque homme; il y a quelque temps; des livres quelconques; maintes fois; une certaine histoire; différentes (diverses) affaires; la même justice (*the same justice*); la justice même (*justice herself*); aujourd'hui même; quelles que soient ses idées; quelques amis qu'il ait.

(2) The following are pronouns only :

chacun(e), *each, each one.*
quelqu'un(e), *some one, any one.*
quelques-uns (unes), *some, few.*
quelque chose, *something.*

rien, *nothing.*
personne, *nobody.*
on, *one, people,* etc. (Lesson 39.)
autrui, *others* (with preposition only).

Chacun de ces hommes; on le dit; les bêtises que l'on dit; les fautes d'autrui.

Quelqu'un, quelque chose, personne, and rien take de before an adjective. **Donnez-moi quelque chose de joli,** *give me something pretty.* **N'avez-vous rien de plus joli?** *have you nothing prettier?*

(3) The following are adjectives or pronouns :

aucun(e),   ⎫
nul(le),   ⎬ (ne with verb)
pas un(e), ⎭ *no, nobody.*
plusieurs, *several.*

tel(le), *such.*
autre, *other.*
tout, toute,   ⎫
tous,[1] toutes, ⎬ *every, whole, all.*

Aucune (nulle, pas une) femme ne le croit; sans aucune faute; aucun d'eux ne l'accepte; j'en ai plusieurs; de tels hommes; des lits tels quels (*such as they are*)**; monsieur un tel** (*Mr. So and So*)**; tel père, tel fils; tous les hommes sont mortels; c'est tout; nous sommes tous [1] ici; tous les deux (tous deux); l'un et l'autre; autres temps, autres mœurs** (*customs*)**; il y en a d'autres; vous autres soldats** (*you soldiers*).

Tout, quite, wholly. — **Tout** used as an adverb varies for the sake of euphony before a feminine adjective beginning with a consonant or an **h** aspirate.

    Elle est toute surprise.   *She is quite surprised.*
    Elles sont toutes honteuses.   *They are greatly ashamed.*
But : **Elle est tout aimable.**   *She is very agreeable.*
    Tout poli qu'il est.   *However polite he is.*

Observe indicative.

Soi (rarely used), oneself, himself. — **Soi,** the disjunctive form of **se,** generally refers to **on, chacun, personne,** etc., and is used only with a preposition.

    Chacun pour soi.   *Every man for himself.*
    On est heureux lorsqu'on est content de soi.   *One is happy when one is satisfied with oneself.*

Vocabulaire

la manière, *manner, way.*
le remords, *remorse.*

la confiance, *the confidence.*
le soin, *the care.*

---

[1] S pronounced when **tous** is a pronoun.

Lecture

1. Avez-vous encore le moindre doute? Aucun.
2. Chaque élève de cette classe l'admire.   3. Chacun a sa manière de voir.   4. On ne doit pas se moquer d'autrui.
5. D'autres prendraient cela d'une autre façon.   6. Il n'y a personne qui en soit fâché.   7. Il n'y a pas une personne qui en soit fâchée.   8. Nous sommes tous à vous.
9. Nous sommes tout à vous.   10. Ecoutez! qu'on me laisse tout seul!   11. Le crime traîne après soi des remords.
12. La valeur, toute héroïque qu'elle est, ne suffit pas pour faire des héros.   13. Toute ville a ses coutumes.   14. Toutes les villes de la France ont quelque chose d'intéressant.
15. Toute confiance est dangereuse, si elle n'est pas entière.
16. Lisez avec beaucoup de soin les quelques pages qui suivent.   17. Qui que ce soit qui vous l'ait dit, il s'est trompé.

Exercice

1. He has been waiting here a long time for some one.
2. We Americans are never content with what we possess.
3. Give me any (a) book whatever.   4. A certain man was speaking to me about various things, and he asked me what I have just asked you.   5. No man is perfect.   6. I was looking for something to eat.   7. Something good, I suppose.   8. Such is the kindness of this gentleman, that we no longer need anything.   9. Whoever (see Lesson 75) you may be and whatever you may do, your duty is to obey the law (*loi*, f.).   10. Whatever your intentions (*f.*) may be, you must not forget the rights of others.   11. Both are guilty.   12. Every man is mortal.   13. Did you ever see such a man?   14. I know nobody more agreeable than his wife.   15. We have heard that said many a time, but we do not believe it.   16. His brothers are quite happy, but his sisters are quite sad.   17. Whom have you met to-day?
18. What are you going to do now?   19. Did I ask you of

whom or of what you are thinking? 20. The woman whose son died yesterday is very poor, is she not? 21. Isn't the one whose sons are living poorer still? 22. What do you write with? 23. Do you wish me to give you what I have in my pocket? 24. Who is the boy I saw you speaking to this morning? 25. Is he the one you were telling me about yesterday? 26. What is this book? 27. Whose is it? 28. What color is it? 29. Which of these books is yours? 30. What is that? 31. What is a cat? 32. Whose friend is that man?

* * * * * * *

85ᵉ Leçon : Curiosités et particularités

La fin couronne l'œuvre. — *The end crowns the work.*

Adjectifs. —

1. **Demi** and **nu** are invariable before the noun, but agree when placed after it ; **nu-pieds,** *barefoot,* **les pieds nus; une demi-pomme, une pomme et demie.**

2. A number of adjectives are used literally and figuratively. They are usually literal when they follow a noun, figurative when they precede. Some of those are :

un abîme profond, *a deep abyss.*	**un profond silence,** *a deep silence.*
un cheval noir, *a black horse.*	**un noir soupçon,** *a dark suspicion.*
une maison chère, *an expensive house.*	**une chère amie,** *a dear friend.*
une histoire vraie, *a true story.*	**une vraie histoire,** *a regular yarn.*

For other adjectives with meanings varying according to position, see pages 377–378.

3. With **plus . . . plus,** *the more . . . the more,* the adjective stands after the verb.

Beaucoup de gens pensent que, plus on est *riche,* **plus on est** *heureux.* *Many people think that, the richer a man is, the happier he is.*

4. Some adjectives may be used as adverbs ; they are then invariable :

parler bas (haut), *to speak low (loud).*

chanter juste (faux), *to sing in (out of) tune.*

sentir bon (mauvais), *to smell good (bad).*

viser haut, *to aim high.*

tenir bon, *to stand firm.*

aller droit, *to go straight.*

arrêter court, *to stop short.*

voir clair, *to see clearly.*

Il l'a fait exprès. *He did it purposely.*

5. Compound adjectives of color are invariable :

des robes *bleu-clair*, *light blue dresses.*

Noms composés. —

(a)	le chou-fleur,	*the cauliflower,*	les choux-fleurs.
(b)	le grand-père,	*the grandfather,*	les grands-pères.
(c)	le chef-d'œuvre,	*the masterpiece,*	les chefs-d'œuvre.
(d)	le contre-courant,	*the counter-current,*	les contre-courants.
(e)	la grand'mère,	*the grandmother,*	les grand'mères.

When a compound noun is formed of two nouns (*a*), or of a noun and an adjective (*b*), the plural is formed by putting the two words in the plural.

If it is composed of two nouns connected by a preposition (*c*), the first noun only is made plural.

If it is formed of a noun and an invariable word (*d*), the noun alone is made plural.

Note that in feminine compound nouns formed with **grande** (*e*), for euphony the **e** of **grande** is dropped and replaced by the (**'**), to prevent sounding the **d**.

Nouns used as adjectives of color are invariable :

des robes *citron*, *lemon yellow dresses.*

des bas *orange*, *orange color stockings.*

Prépositions. — Notice the difference between :

une tasse *à* café, *a coffee cup.*

une tasse *de* café, *a cup of coffee.*

The preposition **à** is placed between two nouns to denote purpose, fitness, or style.

une machine à coudre, *a sewing-machine.*
un couteau à papier, *a paper-knife.*
un moulin à vent, *a windmill.*
du papier à lettres, *letter-paper.*
une tasse à thé, *a tea-cup.*
un bateau à vapeur, *a steamboat.*

En and *dans.* —

1. J'ai un livre *en* main.   *I have a book in my hand.*
   J'ai un sou *dans* la main.   *I have a sou in my hand.*

Dans carries the idea of *into, inside of,* while **en** doesn't.

2. Il partira *dans* une semaine.   *He will start in a week.*
   Il finira ce travail *en* une semaine.   *He will finish that work in a week (it will take him a week to finish that work).*

Dans is used in this case to express the time at the end of which an act will take place.   **En** expresses the time taken to perform the action.

Vers and *envers.* —

Il est allé *vers* la ville *vers* deux heures.   *He went toward the city about two o'clock.*
Il est cruel *envers* les pauvres.   *He is harsh to the poor.*

Vers expresses direction or time; **envers,** feeling or behavior.

Vocabulaire

la pensée, *the thought.*
sérieux, -se, *serious.*
la bottine, *high shoe.*
l'oiseau-mouche, m., *humming bird.*
la mouche, *fly.*
la cuiller, *spoon.*
haut, *loud, high.*
sourd, *deaf.*
viser, *to aim.*
droit, *straight.*

Lecture

1. Pourquoi vous promenez-vous tête nue dans la rue?
2. J'aime à me promener nu-tête et vous?   3. Moi pas.
4. Cet homme a toujours de profondes pensées.   5. Plus il est vieux, plus il devient sérieux, et plus on le connaît, plus

La Cascade de St. Benoît, en Savoie.

LA MARSEILLAISE.

on l'aime.   6. Nous serons chez vous dans une demi-heure,
trois quarts d'heure au plus tard.   7. Je préfère que vous
me disiez à quelle heure vous serez ici.   8. Nous arriverons
vers deux heures et demie au plus tard.   9. Pourquoi avez-
vous mis vos bottines brun-clair ; il va pleuvoir.   10. Tiens !
Vous avez des oiseaux-mouches ?   11. Oui, mes beaux-
frères viennent de revenir des Indes Orientales ; ils les ont
rapportés avec eux.   12. Ces petits oiseaux sont de véri-
tables chefs-d'œuvre de la création !   13. Marie, apportez-
moi un verre d'eau et une cuiller à thé.   14. Qu'avez-vous
en main ? J'ai mes gants.   15. Devinez ce que j'ai dans
la main ? J'ai une mouche.   16. Soyons bons envers les
animaux.   17. Ne parlez pas si haut, je ne suis pas sourd.
18. Quand j'étais jeune, mon père ne cessait de me répéter
ceci : " Visez haut, allez droit et tenez bon."   19. Dans un
mois nous serons à Paris.

Exercices

A. *Mettez les mots suivants au pluriel :*

1. Le grand-oncle.   2. Nu-tête.   3. Tête nue.   4. Un
chef-lieu (*country town*).   5. Un gant jaune-clair.   6. Ma
grand'mère.   7. Le vice-roi.   8. Une demi-orange.

B. *Remplacez les tirets par les prépositions convenables :*

1. Je vois ce que vous avez —— poche.   2. Mon mouchoir et mes clés sont —— ma poche.   3. Soyez prêt ——
une heure.   4. Non, je ne puis finir mes leçons —— une
heure, elles sont trop longues.   5. Par aéroplane, on peut
aller de New-York à Paris —— trente heures.   6. Regardez, voilà Paul qui vient —— nous.   7. Il n'a pas été gentil
—— moi hier, il a été impoli.   8. Je suis obligé de vous
offrir du café dans une tasse —— thé.

C. *Traduisez en français :*

1. We intend to come back to the city about nine in the
evening.   2. Now it is possible to go from here to Chicago

in eighteen hours.　3. Come into the house, we shall be
better to read the letter there.　4. Read aloud, I like to
hear you reading.　5. What beautiful letter-paper !　6. Is
your grandmother in town to-day?　7. Don't go barefoot
in that room, the dressmaker has worked there all day.
8. She left half an hour ago.　9. She sings all the time, but
unfortunately, she never sings in tune.　10. She finished
to-day my dark blue dress.　11. Do not tease (*taquiner*)
that dog, you must be good to animals.　12. Turn (*se
tourner*) toward me, I want to see how the dress fits you.
13. Your two grandfathers will come to-night.　14. Give
me a cup of tea and a tea-spoon.　15. All of the tea-cups
are broken.　16. The richer a man is, the more cares (*souci*)
he has.　17. That's true, I never thought of it.　18. We
will go to the seashore in a month.　19. I am glad of it, for
you need a rest.　20. So do we, and I am glad our French
course is finished.

*　*　*　*　*　*　*

MORCEAUX CHOISIS

1. Le Normand et le boulanger

Un Normand entre un jour chez un boulanger et demande un pain de deux livres. Le boulanger en met un sur le comptoir. Le Normand en demande le prix. " Cinquante centimes," répond le boulanger. — " Il n'a pas le poids," dit l'acheteur en le pesant dans sa main. — " N'importe," réplique l'autre, " il 5 sera plus facile à porter." Le Normand dépose alors quarante centimes sur le comptoir. " Ce n'est pas assez," dit le boulanger. — " N'importe," réplique le Normand, " ce sera plus facile à compter."

2. L'opération inutile

Un officier anglais ayant reçu une balle dans la jambe, fut 10 transporté chez lui, où deux médecins furent appelés. Pendant trois jours ils ne firent que sonder et fouiller la plaie. L'officier, qui souffrait beaucoup, leur demanda ce qu'ils cherchaient : " Nous cherchons la balle qui vous a blessé. — C'est trop fort ! s'écria le patient, pourquoi ne le disiez-vous pas plus tôt? je 15 l'ai dans ma poche."

3. A quoi sert la vaccine ?

Un homme très crédule disait qu'il n'avait pas de confiance dans la vaccine. " A quoi sert-elle, ajoute-t-il ; je connais un enfant beau comme le jour, que sa famille avait fait vacciner . . . eh bien ! il est mort deux jours après . . . — Comment ! deux 20 jours après? . . . — Oui . . . il est tombé du haut d'un arbre, et s'est tué raide . . . Faites donc vacciner vos enfants après cela ! "

4. Comment on devient maréchal de France

Le maréchal Lefebvre avait un camarade de régiment qui vint le voir un jour et qui admirait, non sans un sentiment 25

d'envie, son bel hôtel, ses belles voitures, sa nombreuse livrée,
ses magnifiques appartements, tout le train enfin d'un grand
dignitaire de l'empire : " Parbleu, lui dit-il, il faut avouer que
tu es bien heureux, et que le ciel t'a bien traité ! — Veux-tu, lui
5 répondit le maréchal, avoir tout cela? — Oui, certainement. —
La chose est très simple : tu vas descendre dans la cour de
mon hôtel ; je mettrai à chaque fenêtre deux soldats qui tireront
sur toi. Si tu échappes aux balles, je te donnerai tout ce que
tu m'envies. C'est comme cela que je l'ai obtenu."

5. Scène d'omnibus

10　La scène se passe dans un omnibus, à Paris. Deux vieilles
dames sont assises l'une à côté de l'autre. L'une veut que la
portière soit fermée, l'autre la veut ouverte. On appelle le
conducteur pour décider la question. " Monsieur, dit la première, si cette fenêtre reste ouverte, je suis sûre d'attraper un
15 rhume qui m'emportera. — Monsieur, si on la ferme, je suis
certaine de mourir d'un coup d'apoplexie." Le conducteur ne
savait que (what) faire, lorsqu'un vieux monsieur, qui jusque
là s'était tenu tranquille dans un coin de la voiture, le tira
d'embarras. " Ouvrez donc la portière, mon cher ami, cela fera
20 mourir l'une ; puis vous la fermerez, cela nous débarrassera de
l'autre, et nous aurons la paix."

6. Un marché

Un vieil harpagon fait venir un médecin pour voir sa femme
très malade. Le médecin, qui connaissait son homme, de-
mande à s'arranger d'abord pour ses honoraires.
25　" Soit ! " dit l'harpagon ; " je vous donnerai 200 francs, que
vous tuiez ma femme ou que vous la guérissiez."
Le médecin accepte ; mais, malgré ses soins, la femme meurt.
Quelque temps après, il vient réclamer son argent.
" Quel argent? " dit l'harpagon : " avez-vous guéri ma
30 femme? "
" Non, je ne l'ai pas guérie."
" Alors, vous l'avez tuée? "
" Tuée? Oh ! quelle horreur ! Vous savez bien que non."

" Eh bien, puisque vous ne l'avez ni guérie ni tuée, que demandez-vous ? "

7. La plus grande ganache [1] de l'empire

Un jour Napoléon, fort mécontent à la lecture d'une dépêche de Vienne, dit à Marie-Louise, " Votre père est une *ganache*." Marie-Louise, qui ignorait beaucoup de termes français, 5 s'adressa au premier chambellan : " L'empereur dit que mon père est une *ganache*, que veut dire cela ? " A cette demande inattendue, le courtisan balbutia que cela voulait dire un homme sage, de poids, de bon conseil. A quelques jours de là, et la mémoire encore toute fraîche de sa nouvelle acquisition, Marie- 10 Louise présidait le conseil de famille. Voyant la discussion plus animée qu'elle ne voulait, elle interpella, pour y mettre fin, M. R. . . . ., qui, à ses côtés (*at her side*), bayait aux corneilles.[2] " C'est à vous à nous mettre d'accord dans cette occasion impor- tante, lui dit-elle ; vous serez notre oracle, car je vous tiens pour 15 la plus grande *ganache* de l'empire."

8. Joseph II et le sergent

L'empereur Joseph II n'aimait ni la représentation ni l'ap- pareil. Un jour, revêtu d'une simple redingote boutonnée, accompagné d'un seul domestique à cheval et sans livrée, il était allé, dans une calèche à deux places qu'il conduisait lui- 20 même, faire une promenade du matin dans les environs de Vienne. Comme il reprenait le chemin de la ville, il fut sur- pris par la pluie.

Il en était encore éloigné, lorsqu'un piéton, qui regagnait aussi la capitale, fait signe au conducteur d'arrêter, ce que 25 Joseph II fait aussitôt. " Monsieur, lui dit le militaire (car c'était un sergent), y aurait-il de l'indiscrétion à vous deman- der une place à côté de vous ? Cela ne vous gênerait pas pro- digieusement, puisque vous êtes seul dans votre calèche, et ménagerait mon uniforme que je mets aujourd'hui pour la 30 première fois. — Ménageons votre uniforme, mon brave, lui dit.

---

[1] Blockhead.
[2] *Was gaping at the crows*, that is, was staring into the air.

Joseph, et mettez-vous là. D'où venez-vous? — Ah! dit le
sergent, je viens de chez un garde-chasse de mes amis, où
j'ai fait un fier déjeuner. — Qu'avez-vous donc mangé de si
bon? — Devinez. — Que (*how*) sais-je, moi; une soupe à la
5 bière? — Ah! bien, oui une soupe; mieux que ça. — De la
choucroute? — Mieux que ça. — Une longe de veau? — Mieux
que ça, vous dit-on. — Oh! ma foi, je ne puis plus deviner,
dit Joseph. — Un faisan, mon digne homme, un faisan tiré sur
les plaisirs de Sa Majesté, dit le camarade en lui frappant
10 sur le genou. — Tiré sur les plaisirs de Sa Majesté, il n'en
devait être que meilleur. — Je vous en réponds."

Comme on approchait de la ville, et que la pluie tombait
toujours, Joseph demanda à son compagnon dans quel quartier
il logeait, et où il voulait qu'on le descendît. "Monsieur, c'est
15 trop de bonté, je craindrais d'abuser de . . . — Non, non, dit
Joseph, votre rue?" Le sergent, indiquant sa demeure,
demanda à connaître celui dont il recevait tant d'honnêtetés.
"A votre tour, dit Joseph, devinez. — Monsieur est militaire,
sans doute? — Comme dit monsieur. — Lieutenant? — Ah!
20 bien, oui, lieutenant; mieux que ça. — Capitaine? — Mieux
que ça. — Colonel, peut-être? — Mieux que ça, vous dit-on. —
Comment! s'écrie le sergent, en se rencognant aussitôt dans la
calèche, seriez-vous feld-maréchal? — Mieux que ça. — Ah!
mon Dieu, c'est l'empereur! — Lui-même, dit Joseph, se dé-
25 boutonnant pour montrer ses décorations." Il n'y avait pas
moyen de tomber à genoux dans la voiture; le sergent se con-
fond en excuses et supplie l'empereur d'arrêter pour qu'il
puisse descendre. "Non pas, lui dit Joseph; après avoir
mangé mon faisan vous seriez trop heureux de vous débarras-
30 ser de moi aussi promptement; j'entends bien que vous ne me
quittiez qu'à votre porte." Et il l'y descendit.

9. Le maréchal Ney (1769–1815)

Les habitants des frontières étant d'un patriotisme plus
ardent et d'une âme plus militaire que ceux de l'intérieur, il
est tout naturel que l'Alsace et la Lorraine aient donné à la
35 Révolution et à Napoléon tant de vaillants soldats et de grands
généraux: Custine, Westermann, Kellermann, Kléber, Drouot,

Richepanse, Lasalle, Rapp, Lefebvre, glorieux prédécesseurs
des héros alsaciens et lorrains au service de la France en 1870
et en 1914.   Un autre, le plus fameux, est le maréchal Ney
dont la statue se trouve à l'entrée de l'Esplanade de Metz, la
plus belle promenade de la ville.   5

Michel Ney, né à Sarrelouis en 1769, était le fils d'un tonnelier.   A l'âge de 19 ans, il devint soldat et se fit aussitôt remarquer par ses rares aptitudes militaires.   Mais il n'avait
aucune chance de devenir officier à cause de sa basse origine.
Heureusement la Révolution vint changer l'ordre social et lui 10
donner l'occasion de montrer ses grandes qualités de soldat.
Il prit part à la campagne de 1792 et se distingua dans de
nombreux combats.   Par sa valeur et son énergie sur les
champs de bataille, il gagna le surnom d'*Infatigable* et le grade
de chef d'escadron.   Devenu un peu plus tard général de bri- 15
gade, il se montra aussi généreux après la victoire que terrible
pendant le combat.

En 1799, il se fit remarquer par un exploit de rare audace.
Ayant reçu l'ordre de prendre Mannheim, il entra secrètement
dans la ville avec cent cinquante hommes déterminés et s'en 20
empara.   Pour le récompenser, on le nomma général de division.
Quand Bonaparte établit le Consulat (1799), Ney continua à
servir dans les armées du Rhin et du Danube.   Comme toujours, il se montra héroïque soldat et contribua beaucoup aux
succès des campagnes de 1800–1801.   25

Quand Bonaparte devint empereur sous le nom de Napoléon
en mai 1804, il nomma Ney maréchal de France.   Dans la
campagne de 1805 contre l'Autriche, alliée de l'Angleterre et
de la Russie, le maréchal Ney, à la tête du sixième corps,
marcha de victoire en victoire.   Pendant la campagne suivante, 30
il donna tant de nouvelles preuves de son courage et de son
audace qu'il reçut le surnom de *Brave des braves*.   Ses soldats
qui l'adoraient avaient en lui la plus grande confiance.   Ils
l'appelaient à cause de ses cheveux roux *le Lion rouge*.

En 1808, Napoléon organisa une nouvelle noblesse militaire 35
et Ney reçut le titre de duc d'Elchingen, en souvenir de sa
belle conduite à la bataille de ce nom où il avait remporté une
brillante victoire sur les Autrichiens.

Toujours à la tête du fameux sixième corps, il fut envoyé en Espagne, puis en Portugal, où, pendant la retraite de l'armée française, il fut chargé de résister aux attaques de l'armée anglo-portugaise. En cette circonstance, il fit preuve d'une 5 connaissance profonde de l'art des retraites et excita par sa conduite l'admiration de l'ennemi.

Pendant la campagne de Russie, il continua à se distinguer et se conduisit avec tant d'éclat à la bataille de la Moskowa (1812) que Napoléon le nomma prince de la Moskowa. Mais 10 ce fut surtout pendant la désastreuse retraite de Russie que Ney rendit les plus grands services en sauvant la vie à de nombreux soldats.

Au milieu des scènes de douleur et de mort qui se répétaient à chaque pas, il gardait une force d'âme, une présence d'esprit, 15 une énergie inaltérables, et, à pied, le fusil à la main, il se battait comme le dernier de ses soldats. "Toujours combattant, reculant et ne fuyant pas, marchant toujours après les autres, et, pour la centième fois, pendant quarante jours et quarante nuits, exposant sa vie et sa liberté pour sauver quelques Fran-20 çais de plus, il sortit enfin le dernier de cette fatale Russie."

Cette désastreuse campagne allait hâter la chute de l'empire. Bientôt l'ennemi passa la frontière et entra en France. Ney montra autant d'activité que d'intrépidité, mais tous ses efforts furent vains. Napoléon fut forcé d'abdiquer et de se retirer 25 à l'île d'Elbe.

Quelques mois plus tard, après le retour de Napoléon, Ney combattait héroïquement à la terrible bataille de Waterloo. Il eut cinq chevaux blessés sous lui. "En sueur, la flamme aux yeux, l'écume aux lèvres, l'uniforme déboutonné, 30 une de ses épaulettes à demi coupée par un coup de sabre, . . . sanglant, fangeux, magnifique, une épée cassée à la main, il disait : 'Venez voir comment meurt un maréchal de France sur un champ de bataille ! '" Mais il ne mourut pas. Il était destiné à tomber sous des balles françaises. Après l'abdication 35 de Napoléon et le retour de Louis XVIII, Ney fut jugé par la Chambre des pairs pour haute trahison, et condamné à mort.

L'incident suivant eut lieu pendant le procès. Comme le maréchal était né à Sarrelouis qui venait d'être enlevé à la

La statue de Napoléon à Ajaccio, en Corse.
Ajaccio en Corse. Vue prise du port.

France par la traité de Vienne (1815), un de ses avocats argua que son client n'était plus sous la juridiction du roi de France. Ney bondit en entendant cet argument et s'écria :

"Je remercie mon avocat de ses bons sentiments, mais je préfère ne pas être défendu que d'être défendu de la sorte."   5

Puis il ajouta solennellement :

"Je suis Français et je mourrai Français."

Le 7 décembre 1815, il fut fusillé à Paris, avenue de l'Observatoire, sur le lieu même où se trouve la statue par Rude, qui lui fut élevée en 1848.   L'officier, chargé de l'exécution, 10 lui demanda la permission de lui bander les yeux.

"Ne savez-vous pas," lui répondit-il, "que depuis vingt-cinq ans j'ai l'habitude de regarder les balles en face ? "

Alors Ney s'avança de quelques pas, leva son chapeau de la main gauche, comme il avait l'habitude de le faire sur le champ 15 de bataille pour exciter ses soldats, et plaça la main droite sur sa poitrine en disant : "Soldats, visez droit au cœur !"   On n'entendit qu'un seul coup : le *Brave des braves* tomba immédiatement, frappé de dix balles.

Telles furent la vie et la mort de celui à la droite de la statue 20 duquel se tenait le maréchal Pétain le 8 décembre 1918 quand les libérateurs de l'Alsace-Lorraine défilèrent devant lui sur l'Esplanade de Metz.

APPENDIX A

TRANSLATION HELPS

How to translate *he*, *she*, and *they*

1. When subject : **il, elle, ils, elles.**
2. When separated from the verb by a preposition : **lui, elle, eux, elles.**
3. For emphasis : **lui, elle, eux, elles.**
4. Before *who* or *whom* when these pronouns begin a clause indispensable to the understanding of the sentence : **celui, celle, ceux, celles.**
5. Before *who* or *whom* when these pronouns begin a clause not indispensable to the understanding of the sentence : **lui, elle, eux, elles.**

How to translate *it*

1. When it is subject : **il** or **elle** according to the gender.
2. When it answers the question *what? :* **le, la, l', les.**
3. When preceded by *of, from, with :* **en.**
4. When preceded by *in, to :* **y.**
5. When subject of an impersonal verb : **il.**
6. When subject of **être** : **ce, c'.**
7. When followed by *self :* **lui-même, elle-même, même.**

How to translate *his*

1. When possessive adjective (followed by a noun) : **son, sa, ses.**
2. When possessive pronoun : **le sien, la sienne, les siens, les siennes.**

How to translate *this* and *that*

1. When adjectives, *i.e.*, when followed by a noun : **ce, cet, cette, ces.**

2. When adjectives, and both in the same sentence : **-ci** and **-là** added to the noun, following **ce, cet, cette, ces.**
3. When pronouns : **celui, celle, ceux, celles.**
4. When used in opposition to each other, or in comparisons :

$$\text{celui} \begin{cases} \text{-ci} \\ \text{-là} \end{cases} \quad \text{celle} \begin{cases} \text{-ci} \\ \text{-là} \end{cases} \quad \text{ceux} \begin{cases} \text{-ci} \\ \text{-là} \end{cases} \quad \text{celles} \begin{cases} \text{-ci} \\ \text{-là} \end{cases}$$

5. When pointing at, but not mentioning the object : **ceci, cela, ça.**

How to translate *that* (relative pronoun)

1. When it can be changed into *which:* **qui** or **que.**

How to translate *who*

1. When relative pronoun : **qui.**
2. When interrogative pronoun : **qui** or **qui est-ce qui.**

How to translate *whom*

1. After a preposition : **qui.**
2. In all other cases : **que.**
3. When interrogative pronoun : **qui** or **qui est-ce que.**

How to translate *whose*

1. When relative pronoun : **dont.**
2. When interrogative pronoun : **à qui ?, de qui ?,** sometimes **quel ?**

How to translate *which*

1. When interrogative adjective or before **être : quel, quelle,** etc. . . .
2. When relative pronoun subject : **qui.**
3. When relative pronoun object : **que.**
4. When relative pronoun, object of a preposition : **lequel,** etc.
5. When relative pronoun referring to a whole clause, or meaning *that which* and subject : **ce qui.**
6. When relative pronoun, referring to a whole clause, or meaning *that which* but object : **ce que.**
7. After a preposition and relating to a whole clause : **quoi.**
8. When interrogative pronoun, meaning *which one*, and followed by **de : lequel, laquelle, lesquels, lesquelles.**

How to translate *of which*

1. When relative pronoun : **dont.**
2. When interrogative pronoun : **duquel, de laquelle, desquels,** etc.

How to translate *to which*

Either relative or interrogative pronoun : **auquel, à laquelle, auxquels, auxquelles.**

How to translate *what*

1. When interrogative adjective (followed by a noun) : **quel, quelle, quels, quelles.**
2. When relative pronoun and meaning *that which* and subject : **ce qui.**
3. When relative pronoun and meaning *that which* object : **ce que.**
4. When interrogative pronoun and subject : **qu'est-ce qui.**
5. When interrogative pronoun and object : **qu'est-ce que.**
6. When before an adjective preceded by *more* or *less :* **quoi de.**
7. When after a preposition : **quoi.**
8. When used alone, either interrogative or exclamatory : **quoi.**

How to translate **lui**

1. When it answers the question to whom : *to him, to her.*
2. After a preposition : *him.*
3. After **c'est :** *he.*
4. For emphasis : *he.*
5. After a verb, when *to* is understood, as with *to give : him, her.*

How to translate **le**

1. As an object of a verb : *him* or *it.*
2. Before the verb **être :** *he.*
3. With certain verbs (*to think, to believe, to say,* etc.) : *so.*

How to translate **leur**

1. When it answers the question to whom : *to them.*
2. When it precedes a noun, it is a possessive adjective and it means : *their.*
3. When a possessive pronoun preceded by **le** or **la :** *theirs.*

How to translate **le leur**

1. When possessive pronoun : *theirs.*
2. When **le** and **leur** are separated pronouns : *it to them, him to them.*

How to translate **en**

1. When strictly personal pronoun : *of it, of them* (sometimes *of him, of them,* referring to people).
2. When pártitive pronoun : *some, any, some of it, some of them.*
3. When adverbial pronoun : *from it, from them, from there.*

How to recognize **que**

1. When it can be replaced by **lequel** : relative pronoun.
2. When it *cannot* be replaced by **lequel** : conjunction.

APPENDIX B

FRENCH SYNTAX AND ORTHOGRAPHY

Adopted by the Minister of Public Instruction, February, 1901

Le Ministre de l'Instruction publique et des Beaux-Arts,
Vu l'article 5 de la loi du 27 février, 1880 ;
Vu l'arrêté du 31 juillet, 1900 ;
Le Conseil supérieur de l'Instruction publique entendu, Arrête :

ARTICLE 1er. — Dans les examens ou concours dépendant du Ministère de l'Instruction publique, qui comportent des épreuves spéciales d'orthographe, il ne sera pas compté de fautes aux candidats pour avoir usé des tolérances indiquées dans la liste annexée au présent arrêté.

La même disposition est applicable au jugement des diverses compositions rédigées en langue française, dans les examens ou concours dépendant du Ministère de l'Instruction publique qui ne comportent pas une épreuve spéciale d'orthographe.

Pluriel des noms propres. — La plus grande obscurité régnant dans les règles et les exceptions enseignées dans les grammaires, on tolérera dans tous les cas que les noms propres, précédés de l'article pluriel, prennent la marque du pluriel. Ex. : *les Corneilles* comme *les Gracques*, — *des Virgiles* (exemplaires) comme *des Virgiles* (éditions).

Il en sera de même pour les noms propres de personnes désignant les œuvres de ces personnes. Ex. : *des Meissoniers.*

Pluriel des noms empruntés à d'autres langues. — Lorsque ces mots sont tout à fait entrés dans la langue française, on tolérera que le pluriel soit formé suivant la règle générale. Ex. : *des exéats* comme *des déficits.*

Noms composés. — Les mêmes noms composés se rencontrent aujourd'hui tantôt avec le trait d'union, tantôt sans trait d'union. Il est inutile de fatiguer les enfants à apprendre des contradictions que rien ne justifie. L'absence de trait d'union dans l'expression *pomme de terre* n'empêche pas cette expression de former un véritable mot composé aussi bien que *chef-d'œuvre*, par exemple. Ces mots pourront toujours s'écrire sans trait d'union.

Article partitif. — On tolérera *du, de la, des*, au lieu de *de*, partitif, devant un substantif précédé d'un adjectif. Ex. : *de* ou *du bon pain, de bonne viande* ou *de la bonne viande, de* ou *des bons fruits.*

Adjectif construit avec plusieurs substantifs. — Lorsqu'un adjectif qualificatif suit plusieurs substantifs de genres différents, on tolérera toujours que l'adjectif soit construit au masculin pluriel, quel que soit le genre du substantif le plus voisin. Ex. : *appartements et chambres meublés.* On tolérera aussi l'accord avec le substantif le plus rapproché. Ex. : *un courage et une foi nouvelle.*

Nu, demi, feu. — On tolérera l'accord de ces adjectifs avec le substantif qu'ils précèdent. Ex. : *nu* ou *nus pieds, une demi* ou *demie heure* (sans trait d'union entre les mots), *feu* ou *feue la reine.*

Adjectifs numéraux. — *Vingt, cent.* La prononciation justifie dans certains cas la règle actuelle, qui donne un pluriel à ces deux mots quand ils sont multipliés par un autre nombre. On tolérera le pluriel de *vingt* et de *cent*, même lorsque ces mots sont suivis d'un autre adjectif numéral. Ex. : *quatre-vingt* ou *quatre-vingts dix hommes; quatre cent* ou *quatre cents trente hommes.*

Le trait d'union ne sera pas exigé entre le mot désignant les unités et le mot désignant les dizaines. Ex. : *dix sept.*

Dans la désignation du millésime, on tolérera *mille* au lieu de *mil*, comme dans l'expression d'un nombre. Ex. : *l'an mil huit cent quatre vingt dix* ou *l'an mille huit cents quatre vingts dix.*

Tout. — On tolérera l'accord du mot *tout* aussi bien devant les adjectifs féminins commençant par une voyelle ou par une *h* muette que devant les adjectifs féminins commençant par une consonne ou par une *h* aspirée. Ex. : *des personnes tout heureuses* ou *toutes heureuses; l'assemblée tout entière* ou *toute entière.*

Trait d'union. — On tolérera l'absence de trait d'union entre le verbe et le pronom sujet placé après le verbe. Ex. : *est il ?*

Accord du verbe quand le sujet est un mot collectif. — Toutes les fois que le collectif est accompagné d'un complément au pluriel, on tolérera l'accord du verbe avec le complément. Ex. : *un peu de connaissances suffit* ou *suffisent.*

C'est, ce sont. — Comme il règne une grande diversité d'usage relativement à l'emploi régulier de *c'est* et de *ce sont,* et que les meilleurs auteurs ont employé *c'est* pour annoncer un substantif au pluriel ou un pronom de la troisième personne au pluriel, on tolérera dans tous les cas l'emploi de *c'est* au lieu de *ce sont.* Ex. : *c'est* ou *ce sont des montagnes et des précipices.*

Participe passé. — Il n'y a rien à changer à la règle d'après laquelle le participe passé construit comme épithète doit s'accorder avec le mot qualifié, et construit comme attribut avec le verbe *être* ou un verbe intransitif doit s'accorder avec le sujet. Ex. : *des fruits gâtés; ils sont tombés; elles sont tombées.*

Pour le participe passé construit avec l'auxiliaire *avoir,* lorsque le participe passé est suivi soit d'un infinitif, soit d'un participe présent ou passé, on tolérera qu'il reste invariable, quels que soient le genre et le nombre des compléments qui précèdent. Ex. : *les fruits que je me suis laissé* ou *laissés prendre; — les sauvages que l'on a trouvé* ou *trouvés errant dans les bois.* Dans le cas où le participe passé est précédé d'une expression collective, on pourra à volonté le faire accorder avec le collectif ou avec son complément. Ex. : *la foule d'hommes que j'ai vue* ou *vus.*

Ne dans les propositions subordonnées. — L'emploi de cette négation dans un très grand nombre de propositions subordonnées donne lieu à des règles compliquées, difficiles, abusives, souvent en contradiction avec l'usage des écrivains les plus classiques.

Sans faire de règles différentes suivant que les propositions dont elles dépendent sont affirmatives ou négatives ou interrogatives, on tolérera la suppression de la négation *ne* dans les propositions subordonnées dépendant de verbes ou de locutions signifiant :

Empêcher, défendre, éviter que, etc. Ex. : *défendre qu'on vienne* ou *qu'on ne vienne;*

Craindre, désespérer, avoir peur, de peur que, etc. Ex. : *de peur qu'il aille* ou *qu'il n'aille;*

Douter, contester, nier que, etc.   Ex. : *je ne doute pas que la chose soit vraie* ou *ne soit vraie.*

On tolérera de même la suppression de cette négation après les comparatifs et les mots indiquant une comparaison : *autre, autrement que*, etc.   Ex. : *l'année a été meilleure qu'on l'espérait* ou *qu'on ne l'espérait; les résultats sont autres qu'on le croyait* ou *qu'on ne le croyait.*

De même, après les locutions *à moins que, avant que.*   Ex. : *à moins qu'on accorde le pardon* ou *qu'on n'accorde le pardon.*

APPENDIX C

GRAMMAR SUMMARY

The present Grammar Summary is a complete résumé of all grammatical rules contained in this book. It will help the student to make a rapid review of all the elements of grammar included in a complete French Course in the shortest possible time; this will be particularly helpful before examination periods.

To the rules of grammar mentioned above have been added certain syntactical facts and peculiarities, purposely omitted in the lessons as non-essential, but which students may need for reference in their advanced work — translation and composition.

THE ARTICLES

	SINGULAR				PLURAL
	Before a consonant or **h** aspirate		Before a vowel or **h** mute		Before all nouns
Definite	*Masc.*	*Fem.*	*Both genders*		*Both genders*
the	le	la	l'		les
of, from } *the*	du	de la	de l'		des
to, at the	au	à la	à l'		aux
Indefinite			*Masc.*	*Fem.*	
a, an	un	une	un	une	——
of or from } *a, an*	d'un	d'une	d'un	d'une	——
to, at a, an	à un	à une	à un	à une	——

The article is repeated in French before every noun, but may be omitted in order to give rapidity to the speech.

I. Use of the definite article

(1) Before general nouns:

    J'aime les arbres et les fleurs.   *I like trees and flowers.*

(2) Before names of continents, countries, provinces, mountains, rivers, etc.

l'Europe, *Europe;* **la France,** *France;* **la Normandie,** *Normandy,* etc.

(3) After verbs of coming and returning from, before names of countries *not* ending in **e** (except **Mexique**), and before compound names of countries:

Il arrive du Canada.	*He arrives from Canada.*
Nous venons des États-Unis.	*We come from the United States.*

(4) Instead of a possessive adjective:

J'ai mal à la tête.	*I have a headache.*
Donnez-moi la main.	*Give me your hand.*

(5) With titles or professions, or before a proper noun preceded by an adjective:

le docteur Mombel, *Doctor Mombel;* **le professeur Grosjean,** *Professor Grosjean.*

le petit Louis, *little Louis;* **le grand Jackson,** *big Jackson.*

(6) For *a* or *an* (in prices) before nouns of weight, measure, quantity, numbers, etc.

cinq francs la livre (le mètre, la douzaine, les trois, etc.).
five francs a pound (a meter, a dozen, a set of three, etc.).

(7) Before days of the week and also the names of seasons (unless preceded by **en** in the latter case) to express regular occurrence:

Je reste chez moi le dimanche.	*I stay at home (on) Sundays.*
L'été nous allons à la campagne.	*In summer we go to the country.*

(8) Before names of languages, unless preceded by **en.** (After the verb **parler,** the use of the article is optional, but generally omitted.)

J'étudie le français et l'espagnol.	*I study French and Spanish.*
Parlez-vous (le) français?	*Do you speak French?*

II. Omission of the definite article

(1) In a number of expressions made up of a verb + a noun, such as:

avoir besoin, *to need.*	**prendre congé,** *to take leave.*
avoir faim, *to be hungry,* etc.	**rendre visite,** *to pay a visit,* etc.

(2) In titles of sovereigns:

> **François Premier,** *Francis the First.*
> **Louis Seize,** *Louis the Sixteenth.*

(3) Before feminine names of countries when **en** or **de** is used:

> **Je vais en France.**   *I go to France.*
> **Je viens de Russie.**   *I come from Russia.*

(4) Before names of countries used adjectively:

> **l'histoire de France,** *French history;* **la reine de Hollande,** *the queen of Holland.*

(5) In condensed sentences, such as advertisements, addresses, etc.:

> **Maison à vendre,** *House for sale;* **Rue Lafayette,** *Lafayette Street.*

III. Omission of the indefinite article

(1) Before nouns used adjectively (profession, trade, nationality):

> **Je suis Américain.**   *I am an American.*
> **Il est médecin.**   *He is a doctor.*

(2) Before **cent** and **mille:**

> **Il m'a donné cent (mille) francs.**   *He gave me one hundred (thousand) francs.*

(3) In exclamations after **quel** or **quelle** and their plurals:

> **Quel beau tableau !**   *What a beautiful picture!*
> **Quelles jolies robes !**   *What pretty dresses!*

IV. Use of the partitive article

The partitive articles **du, de la, de l', des** translate *some* or *any* (expressed or understood), followed by a noun, to express that the noun is used in a partitive sense:

> **Avez-vous du pain et de l'eau ?**   *Have you (any) bread and water?*
> **J'ai de la viande et des légumes.**   *I have (some) meat and vegetables.*

V. Modification of the partitive articles

De alone is used instead of **du, de la, de l',** or **des:**

(1) After a negation or a negative verb:

> **Pas d'argent, pas de plaisirs.**   *No money, no pleasures.*
> **Je n'ai pas de pain.**   *I have no bread.*

(2) After adverbs of quantity (except **bien,** *many,* sometimes used instead of **beaucoup**) :

> **trop de sucre,** *too much sugar;* **beaucoup de pain,** *much bread;* **moins de fromage,** *less cheese.*
> But : **bien** *des* **enfants,** *many children* (for **beaucoup d'enfants**).

(3) After nouns of quantity or measurement (except **la plupart,** *most*) :

> **une tasse de café,** *a cup of coffee;* **un mètre de soie,** *a meter of silk.*
> But : **la plupart** *des* **hommes,** *most men.*

(4) Before a noun preceded by an adjective : [1]

> **J'ai de bon lait.**   *I have good milk.*
> **Elle a de jolies robes.**   *She has pretty dresses.*

VI. Omission of the partitive article

(1) After **ni . . . ni,** *neither . . . nor;* **sans,** *without;* **avec,** *with;* and a few other prepositions :

> **Je n'ai ni argent ni amis.**   *I have neither money nor friends.*
> **Je suis sans argent.**   *I am without money.*
> **Il marche avec peine.**   *He walks with difficulty.*

(2) In long enumerations :

> **Il y avait dans la rue: hommes, femmes, enfants, vieilles gens,** etc.
> *There were in the street: men, women, children, old people,* etc.

(3) After a verb requiring **de** (see Lesson 39) before a noun complement, and in phrases formed with **de** + a noun :

> **Il manque d'argent.**   *He lacks money.*
> **Elle a une robe de soie.**   *She has a silk dress.*

(4) When a noun is repeated after a preposition :

> **Il m'a raconté histoire après histoire.**   *He told me story after story.*

THE NOUN

I. The gender of inanimate objects

A short and satisfactory rule for the gender of French nouns is as follows :

---

[1] See also modifications of syntax, page 358.

Nouns having the following terminations are feminine :

ale, ole, ule ; ure, ère, eur ;
rre, lle, ie, ié ; ée, ue, ion ;
be, ce, de ; fe, ne, pe ;
se, te, té ; ve, he, aison.

As **cathédrale, école, nature, faveur, terre, conversation, clémence, cité, beauté, moitié, marche, maison, liaison.**

All other nouns are masculine.

As **port, cheval, café, crime, village.**

There are, of course, exceptions to this rule, but it holds good in 95 cases out of 100.

Observe that the rule does not apply to nouns evidently denoting males, as **prince, homme,** etc. ; or to nouns evidently denoting females, as **princesse, dame,** etc.

II. Formation of the feminine in nouns representing animate beings

Nouns representing animate beings usually have a particular form for each sex, and their feminine, like the feminine of adjectives, is more or less regularly formed :

un **Français,**	*a Frenchman,*	une **Française.**
un **Prussien,**	*a Prussian,*	une **Prussienne.**
un **jardinier,**	*a gardener,*	une **jardinière.**
un **baron,**	*a baron,*	une **baronne.**
un **jumeau,**	*a twin,*	une **jumelle.**
un **époux,**	*a husband,*	une **épouse.**
un **compagnon,**	*a companion,*	une **compagne.**

(1) Those ending with an *e mute* are the same for both genders :

un **Russe,**	*a Russian,*	une **Russe.**
un **esclave,**	*a slave,*	une **esclave.**
un **artiste,**	*an artist,*	une **artiste.**

PRINCIPAL EXCEPTIONS

	un **âne,**	*an ass,*	une **ânesse.**
	un **comte,**	*a count,*	une **comtesse.**
	un **hôte,**	*a host,*	une **hôtesse.**
	un **maître,**	*a master,*	une **maîtresse.**
	un **nègre,**	*a negro,*	une **négresse.**
	un **prêtre,**	*a priest,*	une **prêtresse.**
	un **Suisse,**	*a Swiss,*	une **Suissesse.**
	un **tigre,**	*a tiger,*	une **tigresse.**
	un **traître,**	*a traitor,*	une **traîtresse.**
also	un **abbé,**	*an abbot,*	**une abbesse.**

(2) Substantives ending in **-eur** and derived from a present participle change **-eur** into **-euse** :

le danseur (from **dansant**),	*the dancer,*	**la danseuse.**
le plaideur (from **plaidant**),	*the suitor,*	**la plaideuse.**
le buveur (from **buvant**),	*the drinker,*	**la buveuse.**

(3) Substantives ending in **-teur,** and which are not derived from a present participle, change **-teur** into **-trice** :

l'accusateur,	*the accuser,*	**l'accusatrice.**
l'acteur,	*the actor,*	**l'actrice.**
l'instituteur,	*the teacher,*	**l'institutrice.**

Add to these : **le débiteur,** *debtor;* **l'inspecteur,** *the inspector;* **l'exécuteur,** *the executor;* **l'inventeur,** *the inventor;* **le persécuteur,** *the persecutor.*

(4) Some in **-eur** change it into **-eresse** for the feminine, such as : **l'enchanteur,** *the enchanter,* **l'enchanteresse** ; **le pécheur,** *the sinner,* **la pécheresse** ; **le vengeur,** *the avenger,* **la vengeresse** ; **le défendeur,** *the defendant,* **la défenderesse** ; **le chasseur,** *the hunter,* **la chasseresse.** — **Chanteur** has two feminines, **chanteuse** and **cantatrice** : the latter is used only of professional singers. **Empereur** makes **impératrice** ; **gouverneur, gouvernante** ; **serviteur, servante** ; **compagnon, compagne** ; **héros, héroïne** ; **dieu, déesse** ; **duc, duchesse.** **Témoin** is used for both genders, and also **auteur, poète, philosophe, peintre, juge, guide,** etc., and even **possesseur, successeur,** and **professeur. Ange,** *angel,* is always masculine.

(5) Some nouns originally feminine keep that gender, even when applied to man : **la dupe,** *the dupe;* **la sentinelle,** *the sentry;* **la recrue,** *the recruit;* **la victime,** *the victim;* **la personne,** *the person;* **la ganache,** *the blockhead;* **la connaissance,** *the acquaintance,* etc.

(6) Some names of animals form their feminine irregularly :

le bélier,	*the ram,*	**la brebis.**
le bouc,	*the he-goat,*	**la chèvre.**
le cheval,	*the horse,*	**la jument.**
le mouton,	*the sheep,*	**la brebis.**
le sanglier,	*the wild boar,*	**la laie.**
le singe,	*the monkey,*	**la guenon.**
le canard,	*the duck,*	**la cane.**

le chat,	the cat,	la chatte.
le mulet,	the mule,	la mule.
le perroquet,	the parrot,	la perruche.
le loup,	the wolf,	la louve.
le dindon,	the turkey,	la dinde.
le bœuf,	the ox,	la vache.
le coq,	the cock,	la poule.

(7) Most of the names of animals have only one form for both genders such are :

ALL MASCULINE

le castor, *the beaver.*	le cigne, *the swan.*
le chameau, *the camel.*	le hibou, *the owl.*
l'écureuil, *the squirrel.*	le vautour, *the vulture.*
l'éléphant, *the elephant.*	le merle, *the blackbird.*
le léopard, *the leopard.*	le saumon, *the salmon.*

ALL FEMININE

la baleine, *the whale.*	l'alouette, *the lark.*
la girafe, *the giraffe.*	l'hirondelle, *the swallow.*
la panthère, *the panther.*	la perdrix, *the partridge.*
l'hyène, *the hyena.*	la pie, *the magpie.*
la souris, *the mouse.*	la tortue, *the tortoise.*

To all these nouns, when we wish to determine the sex, we add **mâle** or **femelle** : la panthère **mâle**, la panthère **femelle** ; l'éléphant **mâle**, l'éléphant **femelle**.

(8) Some nouns are of double gender ; for example :

un(e) artiste, *an artist.*	un(e) esclave, *a slave.*
un(e) enfant, *a child.*	un(e) camarade, *a comrade.*
un(e) malade, *a patient.*	un(e) propriétaire, *an owner.*

(9) A number of nouns change their meaning according to the gender ; the following are a few of them :

MASCULINE		FEMININE
book,	livre,	*pound.*
page (attendant),	page,	*page (of a book).*
veil,	voile,	*sail.*
turn, trick,	tour,	*tower.*
post, position,	poste,	*post-office.*
pendulum,	pendule,	*clock.*
critic,	critique,	*criticism.*
politician,	politique,	*politics.*

MASCULINE		FEMININE
handle,	**manche,**[1]	*sleeve.*
mode, mood,	**mode,**	*fashion.*
cabin-boy,	**mousse,**	*moss.*
guide,	**guide,**	*rein.*
stove,	**poêle,**	*frying-pan.*

III. Formation of the plural

Nouns and adjectives form their plural by adding **s** to the singular : Lesson 31.

EXCEPTIONS. — (1) Nouns and adjectives ending in **s, x, z,** in the singular, are the same in the plural : Lesson 31.

(2) Nouns and adjectives ending in **-au** or **-eu** take **x** in the plural : Lesson 31.

But the noun **landau,** *a landau* (sort of carriage), and the adjective **bleu,** *blue,* take **s** in the plural.

(3) Nouns and adjectives in **-al** change **al** into **aux ;** Lesson 31.

But **s** is added in the plural to the nouns **bal, carnaval, chacal, régal,** and to the adjectives **fatal, final, glacial, initial, matinal, naval, pénal,** and a few others seldom used.

(4) The following nouns ending in **-ail** change **ail** into **aux :**

le bail,	*the lease,*	**les baux.**
le corail,	*the coral,*	**les coraux.**
l'émail,	*the enamel,*	**les émaux.**
le soupirail,	*the air-hole,*	**les soupiraux.**
le travail,	*the work, the labor,*	**les travaux.**
le vitrail,	*the glass window,*	**les vitraux.**

Bétail, *cattle,* has no plural ; **bestiaux** is the plural word for *cattle.*

(5) Seven nouns ending in **-ou** take **x :**

le bijou,	*the jewel,*	**les bijoux.**
le caillou,	*the pebble,*	**les cailloux.**
le chou,	*the cabbage,*	**les choux.**
le genou,	*the knee,*	**les genoux.**
le hibou,	*the owl,*	**les hiboux.**
le joujou,	*the toy,*	**les joujoux**
le pou,	*the louse,*	**les poux.**

(6) **Aïeul, ciel,** and **œil,** generally make **aïeux,** *ancestors;* **cieux,** *heavens;* **yeux,** *eyes.* But **aïeul** makes **aïeuls,** when it means

---

[1] **La Manche,** *the English Channel.*

the paternal and maternal grandfathers ; **ciel** makes **ciels** when it means the testers of beds, the roofs of quarries, or " skies " in painting ; and in the cases when **œil** does not mean properly *eye*, it makes **œils**, as, **des œils-de-bœuf**, *oval windows.*

(7) Foreign words, which have not yet been naturalized in France by custom, remain invariable, such as : **des alibi, des errata, des infolio, des in-quarto, des post-scriptum, des fac-simile, des Te Deum,** etc.

But the following take the mark of the plural : **des bravos, des duos, des trios, des numéros, des opéras, des zéros, des impromptus, des échos, des déficits,** etc.

IV. Plural of compound nouns

GENERAL RULES. — To form the plural of a compound noun :

(*a*) If the noun is composed of two nouns or an adjective and a noun, connected by a hyphen, both parts are made plural.

le chou-fleur,	*the cauliflower,*	les choux-fleurs.
l'oiseau-mouche,	*the humming-bird,*	les oiseaux-mouches.
le petit-fils,	*the grandson,*	les petits-fils.
le beau-frère,	*the brother-in-law,*	les beaux-frères.
le grand-père,	*the grandfather,*	les grands-pères.
But la grand'mère,	*the grandmother,*	les grand'mères.
une demi-heure,	*a half hour,*	des demi-heures.

(*b*) If the noun is composed of two nouns connected by a preposition and hyphens, the first noun only is made plural.

le chef-d'œuvre,	*the masterpiece,*	les chefs-d'œuvre.
l'arc-en-ciel,	*the rainbow,*	les arcs[1]-en-ciel.

(*c*) If the noun is composed of a noun and a verb, adverb, or preposition, the noun only takes the sign of the plural.

le tire-bouchon,	*the corkscrew,*	les tire-bouchons.
l'arrière-grand-père,	*the great-grandfather,*	les arrière-grands-pères.

Some compound nouns have a plural form when their meaning is singular : **le cure-dents,** *the tooth-pick;* **le casse-noisettes,** *the nut-cracker;* **le porte-clefs,** *the turnkey;* **un essuie-mains** (or **main**), *a towel.*

---

[1] s not heard.

(*d*) If the noun is composed of two verbs or of any two invariable words, it remains unchanged in the plural.

le ouï-dire,	*hearsay,*	les ouï-dire.
le dit-on,	*saying, rumor,*	les dit-on.
le passe-partout,	*pass-key,*	les passe-partout.

THE ADJECTIVE

I. Formation of the feminine of adjectives

GENERAL RULE. — To form the feminine of adjectives, add *e mute* to the masculine (Lesson 5).

EXCEPTIONS. — (1) Adjectives ending with *e mute* in the masculine are the same in the feminine (Lesson 5).

(2) Adjectives ending in **-el, -en, -on, -et,** double the last consonant, and take an *e mute* after it (Lesson 56).

(3) Several adjectives also double their last consonant in the feminine (Lesson 60).

(4) Adjectives ending in **-f** change **f** into **ve** (Lesson 60).

(5) Adjectives ending in **-x** change **x** into **se** (Lesson 60).

(6) Adjectives ending in **-eur,** and derived from a present participle, change **eur** into **euse**: **flatteur** (from **flattant**), **flatteuse**; **grondeur** (from **grondant**), **grondeuse**.

(7) Adjectives ending in **-teur,** and not derived from a present participle, change **teur** into **trice**:

Profanateur, profanatrice; corrupteur, corruptrice.
Adjectives ending in **-érieur,** not belonging to either of the above exceptions, follow the general rule: **inférieur, inférieure; ultérieur, ultérieure.** Add to these **meilleur, majeur,** and **mineur.**

(8) Many adjectives form their feminines irregularly (see Lesson 60).

The plural of adjectives is formed in the same way as that of nouns (see Lesson 35).

II. Agreement of adjectives

(1) An adjective agrees in gender and number with the noun it modifies:

| **Les petits enfants sont amusants.** | *Little children are amusing.* |
| **Elle est grande.** | *She is tall.* |

(2) An adjective qualifying two or more nouns is made plural and agrees in gender with both, if of the same gender; if of different genders, the adjective is masculine.

L'eau et la limonade sont froides. *The water and the lemonade are cold.*
Les plumes et les crayons sont bons. *The pens and pencils are good.*

(3) When two adjectives denoting different singular objects refer to one noun, the noun is made plural and the adjectives are in the singular :

> **les races latine et slave,** *Latin and Slavonic races.*
> **les cinquième et sixième étages,** *the fifth and sixth stories.*

(4) Compound adjectives of color and nouns serving as adjectives of color are invariable :

> **des yeux marron,** *chestnut color eyes.*
> **des gants brun-clair,** *light brown gloves.*

(5) **Demi** and **nu** are invariable when placed before the noun, but agree when they follow the noun :

> **nu-tête,** *bareheaded;* **pieds nus,** *barefooted.*

III. Position of adjectives

(1) Predicate adjectives are placed, in general, as in English :

Je suis pauvre. *I am poor.*
Heureux et content, il partit. *Happy and satisfied he left.*

Notice that with **assez,** and in exclamations, the position of the adjectives is reversed, compared to the English :

Il est assez grand pour marcher seul. *He is big enough to walk alone.*
Que vous êtes gentil ! *How kind you are!*

(2) Adjectives of physical quality (size, color, dimension), nationality, religion, past and present participles used as adjectives, are placed after the noun :

un chapeau rouge, *a red hat;* **une table carrée,** *a square table;* **un écrivain anglais,** *an English writer;* **une histoire amusante,** *an amusing story;* **un travail fini,** *a finished work.*

(3) The following adjectives usually precede the noun :

beau	grand	joli	meilleur	vilain	cher
bon	gros	long	moindre	sot	méchant
court	jeune	mauvais	petit	vieux	gentil

IV. Comparison of adjectives

(1) The comparison of adjectives is formed by placing **plus,** *more,* for superiority ; **moins,** *less,* for inferiority ; and **aussi,** *as,* for equality, before the adjective and **que,** *than* or *as,* after it.

> **Je suis plus (moins, aussi) grand que mon frère.**
> *I am taller (less tall, as tall) than (as) my brother.*

(2) The superlative is formed by placing the definite article or a possessive adjective before the comparatives of superiority or inferiority, and dropping the **que.**

> **la plus belle bague du magasin,** *the prettiest ring in the store.*
> **mon plus grand crayon,** *my largest pencil.*
> **le plus grand des deux,** *the taller of the two.*

Notes. — (*a*) After a superlative *in* = **de** (Ex. 1).

(*b*) In French there is no difference between *the taller* and *the tallest, the richer* and *the richest,* etc. (Ex. 3).

(3) Adjectives compared irregularly :

> **bon, meilleur, le meilleur,** *good, better, best.*
> **mauvais, pire, le pire,** *bad, worse, worst.*
> **petit, moindre, le moindre,** *small, smaller, smallest.*

Note. — **Pire** is not so common as **plus mauvais** and it serves also as the comparative of **méchant,** *bad, evil, wicked.* Generally, **moindre** is used to denote *less* (in importance) and **plus petit,** *less* (in size).

V. Possessive adjectives

	SINGULAR		PLURAL
	Masculine	*Feminine*	*Both genders*
My	**mon** [1]	**ma**	**mes**
Thy	**ton**	**ta**	**tes**
His, her, its	**son**	**sa**	**ses**
Our	**notre**		**nos**
Your	**votre**		**vos**
Their	**leur**		**leurs**

Note. — **Mon, ton,** and **son** are used instead of **ma, ta, sa,** before feminine nouns beginning with a vowel or **h** mute.

The possessive adjectives are repeated before each noun they modify.

VI. Agreement of possessive adjectives

Possessive adjectives agree in gender and number with the noun representing the object possessed and *not* with the possessor.

Il
Elle } a *son* chapeau.   *He (she) has his (her) hat.*

VII. Omission of the possessive adjective

The possessive adjective is omitted and replaced by the definite article when used with a part of the body, if no ambiguity is possible :

Je me suis cassé le bras.   *I broke my arm.*
Ouvrez la bouche.   *Open your mouth.*

VIII. Demonstrative adjectives

	MASCULINE		FEMININE
SINGULAR *This* or *that*	Before a consonant ce	Before a vowel or **h** mute cet	Before any letter cette
PLURAL *These* or *those*	ces		

-ci and **-là** are respectively added to the noun when two or more persons or things are in sight and sharp distinction is to be made between *this* and *that* or *these* and *those*.

IX. Numeral adjectives

Cardinal numbers

0	zéro (*zay-ro*).	10	dix (*diss*).
1	un, une.	11	onze.
2	deux (x *silent*).	12	douze (*dooze*).
3	trois (s *silent*).	13	treize (*trèze*).
4	quatre (u *silent*).	14	quatorze (*catorze*)
5	cinq (q *sounded*).	15	quinze (*cainze*).
6	six (*siss*).	16	seize (*sèze*).
7	sept (*sètt*).	17	dix-sept (*diss-sètt*).
8	huit (*üitt, short*).	18	dix-huit (*diz-witt*).
9	neuf (f *sounded*).	19	dix-neuf (*diz-neuff*).

20	vingt (*vin*).	60	soixante (*soissante*).
21	vingt et un (*vinté-un*).	61	soixante et un, *etc.*
22	vingt-deux (*vint'*).	70	soixante-dix.
23	vingt-trois (*vint'*).	71	soixante et onze (*té onz*), *etc.*
24	vingt-quatre (*vint'*).	80	quatre-vingts (gts *silent*).
25	vingt-cinq (*vint'*).	81	quatre-vingt-un, *etc.*
26	vingt-six (*vint'*).	90	quatre-vingt-dix.
27	vingt-sept (*vint'*).	91	quatre-vingt-onze, *etc.*
28	vingt-huit (*vint'*).	100	cent (t *silent*).
29	vingt-neuf (*vint'*).	101	cent un, *etc.* (t *silent*).
30	trente.	200	deux cents (ts *silent*).
31	trente et un.	250	deux cent cinquante.
32	trente-deux.	1,000	mille.
40	quarante (*carante*).	1,001	mille un.
41	quarante et un, *etc.*	1,100	mille cent *or* onze cents.[1]
50	cinquante (*cincante*).	1,000,000	un million.
51	cinquante et un, *etc.*	1,000,000,000	un milliard, *etc.*

(1) **Et** is used in 21, 31, 41, 51, 61, 71 (sometimes omitted with 71). It is not used in 81, 91, and 101.

(2) **Le** and **la** are not elided before **huit** and **onze,** or their ordinals, and the **s** of **les** is *not* carried over with these numbers.

> **le huit mai.**　　　　**le onze juin.**
> **le huitième mois.**　　**la onzième semaine.**

(3) **Quatre-vingts** takes **s** when the number stands alone ; if it is followed by another number, the **s** is dropped : **quatre-vingt trois.**

Cent follows the same rule ; it takes **s** in its multiples when those are used alone : **deux cents, cinq cents,** but the **s** is dropped when another numeral follows : **cinq cent un.**

Note that the **t** of **cent** is silent before another numeral ; 101 is pronounced **cen un.**

(4) **Mille** is always invariable : **cinq *mille* soldats.** In dates, **mille** may be spelled *mil:* **en *mil* sept cent dix,** in *1710.*

---

[1] Instead of *mille cent, mille deux cents*, etc., the French say *onze, douze cents*, until *dix neuf cents;* but they do not say *dix cents* for **mille,** nor *vingt* or *trente cents*, etc., for **deux** or **trois mille**, etc., nor *vingt et un, vingt deux* or *trente et un, trente deux cents*, etc., for **deux mille cent, deux mille deux cents, trois mille cent, trois mille deux cents,** etc.

Ordinal numbers

1st	premier, première.	18th	dix-huitième.
2d	deuxième, *or* second (*gon*).	19th	dix-neuvième.
3d	troisième.	20th	vingtième.
4th	quatrième.	21st	vingt et unième.
5th	cinquième.	22d	vingt-deuxième.
6th	sixième.	30th	trentième.
7th	septième.	40th	quarantième.
8th	huitième.	50th	cinquantième.
9th	neuvième.	60th	soixantième.
10th	dixième.	70th	soixante-dixième.
11th	onzième.	80th	quatre-vingtième.
12th	douzième.	90th	quatre-vingt-dixième.
13th	treizième.	100th	centième.
14th	quatorzième.	101st	cent unième.
15th	quinzième.	200th	deux centième.
16th	seizième.	1,000th	millième.
17th	dix-septième.	1,000,000th	millionième.

Fractions. — Except for ½, **un demi**; ⅓, **un tiers,** and ¼, **un quart,** fractions are expressed in French as in English, using a cardinal for the numerator and an ordinal for the denominator.

Dates. — Cardinal numbers and not ordinal are used in dates as well as in titles of sovereigns, except for **premier,** *first.*
On in dates and *the* in titles are omitted in French.

Quel jour du mois sommes-nous?	*What day of the month is it?*
C'est aujourd'hui le 11 mai.	*To-day is the 11th of May.*
Il est né le 19 octobre.	*He was born on October the 19th.*
Henri Quatre.	*Henry the Fourth.*

Time of the day. —

Quelle heure est-il?	*What time is it?*
Il est dix heures à ma montre.	*It is 10 o'clock by my watch.*
Votre montre avance.	*Your watch is fast.*
Sa montre retarde.	*His watch is slow.*
Ma montre va juste.	*My watch is right.*

Note. — *It is* = **il est** when referring to the time of the day. **Heure(s)** is never omitted. **Minutes** is often omitted.

Age. —

Quel âge avez-vous?	*How old are you?*
J'ai vingt ans.	*I am twenty (years old).*
Je suis âgé de trente ans.	*I am thirty years old.*

Dimensions are expressed as follows :

De quelle hauteur est cette église ? ⎱
Quelle est la hauteur de cette église ? ⎰ *What is the height of this church?*

Une église haute de cent pieds, *A church one hundred feet in height.*
Une maison d'une largeur de trente pieds, *A house thirty feet wide.*
Un jardin de cent pieds de longueur,[1] *A garden a hundred feet long.*

L'escalier est large de dix pieds, ⎱
L'escalier a dix pieds de largeur,[1] ⎬ *The staircase is ten feet broad.*
L'escalier a une largeur de dix pieds, ⎰

Cette table a six pieds de longueur sur quatre de largeur.
This table is six feet by four.

Cet arbre-ci est plus haut que celui-là de vingt pieds.
This tree is twenty feet taller than that.

Numeral adverbs. —

première*ment*,   troisième*ment*,
deuxième*ment*,   etc.

Also : **primo, secondo, tertio,** etc., from the Latin, and abbreviated in 1°, 2°, 3°, etc.

Multiplicative. — Nouns or adjectives. —

double, *double.*   décuple, *tenfold.*
triple, *triple.*   centuple, *hundredfold.*
quadruple, *quadruple.*

are the most used.

Collectives. —

une huitaine, *about eight.*   une quarantaine, *about forty.*
une dizaine, *about ten.*   une cinquantaine, *about fifty.*
une douzaine, *a dozen.*   une soixantaine, *about sixty.*
une quinzaine, *about fifteen.*   une centaine, *about a hundred.*
une vingtaine, *about twenty.*   un millier, *about a thousand.*
une trentaine, *about thirty.*   une paire, *a pair.*

un couple, *a couple* (male and female).
une couple, *a couple* (two of a kind).

X. Adjectives with a preposition

(1) Adjective **+ à** : When the adjective denotes *fitness, tendency, disposition* or their opposites :

Il n'est bon *à* rien.   *He is good for nothing.*
Il est enclin *à* la paresse.   *He is inclined to laziness.*
Il est utile *à* ses amis.   *He is useful to his friends.*

---

[1] **Long, large,** and **haut** may be used for **longueur, largeur,** and **hauteur,** in this construction ; **épais** and **profond** are not so used instead of **épaisseur** and **profondeur.**

(2) Adjective + **de :** When the adjective denotes *origin, abundance,* or *separation, lack* or *want.*

Je suis originaire *de* **France.** *I am of French origin.*
Il est heureux *de* **vous voir.** *He is happy to see you.*
Nous sommes privés *de* **votre amitié.** *We are deprived of your friendship.*

(3) Adjective + **en :** When the adjective denotes skill or abundance.

Il est riche *en* **terres.** *He is rich in land.*
Je suis fort *en* **français.** *I am strong (learned) in French.*

(4) Adjective + **envers :** When the adjective expresses feeling towards.

Il est bon *envers* **les animaux.** *He is kind to animals.*
Nous sommes polis *envers* **lui.** *We are polite towards him.*

XI. Adjectives which change their signification according as they are placed before or after the noun

Bon. Un homme bon, *a good man;* un bon homme, *a simple man;* un bon mot, *a pun;* une bonne parole, *a good word.*

Brave. Un homme brave, *a brave man;* un brave homme, *a worthy man.*

Certain. Une chose certaine, *a positive thing;* une certaine chose, *a particular thing.*

Cher. Mon cher ami, *my dear friend;* une maison chère, *a costly house.*

Commun. Une voix commune, *a common voice;* d'une commune voix, *unanimously.*

Dernier. Le mois dernier, *last month;* le dernier mois, *the last month* (of the year, of my stay in London, etc.).

Différent; divers. Les différentes (diverses) choses, *various things;* les choses différentes (diverses), *different things.*

Faux. Une fausse clef, *a skeleton key;* une clef fausse, *a wrong key;* une fausse porte, *a secret door;* une porte fausse, *a false door.*

Furieux. Un furieux menteur, *a terrible liar;* un homme furieux, *an enraged man.*

Galant. Un galant homme, *a well-bred man;* un homme galant, *a man polite to ladies.*

Gentil. Un gentilhomme, *a nobleman;* un homme gentil, *a delightful, polite man.*

Grand. Un grand homme, *a great man;* un homme grand, *a tall man.* But if, after *grand homme*, some other external qualities are added, it means *tall: C'est un grand homme blond, bien fait.* In like manner if, after *un homme grand*, some moral qualification is added, *grand* does not refer to the size : *Un homme grand dans ses desseins.* Le grand air, *noble manners;* l'air grand, *a noble look.*

Haut. Le haut ton, *an arrogant manner;* le ton haut, *a loud voice.*

Honnête. Un honnête homme, *an honest man;* un homme honnête, *a polite man.*

Mauvais. Le mauvais air, *vulgar appearance;* l'air mauvais, *ill-natured look.*

Méchant. Une méchante épigramme, *a poor epigram;* une épigramme méchante, *a wicked epigram.*

Même. La même femme, *the same woman;* les rues mêmes, *even the streets*, or *the very streets.*

Mortel. Un mortel ennemi, *a deadly enemy;* l'homme mortel, *mortal man.*

Neuf. Un habit neuf, *a new-made coat;* un habit nouveau, *a coat of new fashion.*

Nouveau. Le nouveau vin, *wine different from that which was drunk before, newly broached wine;* du vin nouveau, *wine newly made.*

Pauvre. When placed before the noun, it has the various significations which the word *poor* has in English : *assister un pauvre vieillard, une pauvre veuve, un pauvre homme*, means to assist one in poverty ; *le pauvre enfant, les pauvres innocents, le pauvre animal*, are terms of endearment ; *un pauvre orateur, de pauvre vin*, are terms of contempt. When placed after the noun it always signifies poverty : un homme pauvre, *a needy man.*

Petit. Un petit homme, *a little man;* un homme petit, *a mean man.* Observe that *petit* has its natural meaning when placed before the noun, its figurative, when placed after. It is the reverse with *grand*.

Plaisant. Un plaisant conte, *an unlikely, absurd tale;* un conte plaisant, *an amusing story.* Un plaisant homme, *a ridiculous man;* un homme plaisant, *a humorous man.*

Propre. Mon propre habit, *my own coat;* un habit propre, *a clean coat.*

Seul. Un seul homme, *a single man;* un homme seul, *a man alone.*

Triste. Un triste homme, *a poor kind of a man;* un homme triste, *a sorrowful man.*

Vilain. Un vilain homme, *a disagreeable man;* un homme fort vilain, *an ugly man.*

THE ADVERB

I. Formation of adverbs

(1) Many adverbs are formed from adjectives.

When the adjective ends in a vowel, **ment** is added directly to the adjective :

poli, poli*ment*. **facile, facile*ment*.**

(2) When the adjective does not end in a vowel, **ment** is added to the *feminine* of the adjective :

sûr,	sûre,	sûre*ment*,	*surely.*
parfait,	parfaite,	parfaite*ment*,	*perfectly.*
actif,	active,	acti*vement*,	*actively.*

(3) Some adjectives ending in **e** change **e** to **é** on adding **ment**.

énorme,	énor*mé*ment,	*enormously.*
immense,	immen*sé*ment,	*immensely.*

(4) Some adjectives change the added **e** of the feminine to **é**.

précis,	précise,	préci*sé*ment,	*precisely.*
profond,	profonde,	profon*dé*ment,	*profoundly.*
commun,	commune,	commu*né*ment,	*commonly.*

(5) Adjectives in **ant, ent,** change **nt** of the masculine to **m** and add **ment**.

constant,	consta*mm*ent	*constantly.*
élegant,	élé*ga*mment,	*elegantly.*
prudent,	prude*mm*ent,	*prudently.*

EXCEPTIONS. — **lent** and **présent,** which are regular.

(6) Other exceptions :

gentil,	**gentiment,**	*gently.*
bref,	**brièvement,**	*briefly.*
impuni,	**impunément,**	*with impunity.*

II. Comparison of adverbs

(1) Adverbs are regularly compared like adjectives :

Il parle plus (moins) lentement que moi. *He speaks more (less) slowly than I.*
Il parle aussi facilement que moi. *He speaks as easy as I.*

(2) The following are irregularly compared :

bien, *well.*   **mieux,** *better.*   **beaucoup,** *much.*   **plus,** *more.*
mal, *badly, ill.*   { **pis,** *worse.* / **plus mal,** *worse.* }   **peu,** *little.*   **moins,** *less.*

(3) The superlative is formed by placing **le** (invariable) before the comparative of superiority or inferiority :

De toutes ces jeunes filles, c'est elle qui parle *le* moins vite, mais *le* plus poliment. *Of all these young girls, it is she who speaks the least rapidly but the most politely.*

(4) After adverbs of quantity, **de** is always used :

beaucoup *de* livres.   **trop *de* travail.**

(5) Notice that *more than* and *less than* are translated by **plus de** and **moins de** before a number.

plus *de* dix livres.   **moins *de* onze élèves.**

III. Position of adverbs

(1) Adverbs regularly stand immediately after the verb :

Il parle *prudemment*. *He speaks prudently.*
Il a parlé *prudemment*. *He has spoken prudently.*

(2) Short adverbs like : **bien, mal, beaucoup, trop, peu, encore,** etc., are placed between the auxiliary and the past participle.

Vous avez bien (mal, trop, beaucoup, peu, encore, etc.) chanté.
You sang well (badly, too much, much, little, again, etc.).

(3) Adverbs of time and place, like **aujourd'hui, demain, hier, tôt, tard, ici, là, ailleurs, partout,** etc., never come between the auxiliary and the past participle. Sometimes they even may be placed at the very beginning of the sentence for emphasis :

J'ai compris maintenant.	*I have understood now.*
Maintenant je comprends.	*Now I understand.*

IV. Distinctions in the use of certain adverbs

Oui — Si. — **Oui** is a plain *yes* in affirmations. **Si** contradicts a statement and is generally used for answering affirmatively a negative question :

> **Irez-vous ? Oui, j'irai.**
> **N'irez-vous pas ?** *Si,* **j'irai.**

Autant — Tant. — **Autant** means *as much, as many.* **Tant** means *so much, so many :*

J'ai *autant* **de livres que vous.**	*I have as many books as you.*
J'ai *tant* **marché que je suis fatigué.**	*I walked so much that I am tired.*

Plus — Davantage. — Both mean *more,* but **davantage** is not used in comparisons. It is used absolutely, and usually stands at the end of the sentence :

> **Je suis** *plus* **pauvre que vous, mais Paul l'est davantage.**
> *I am poorer than you, but Paul is more so.*

(4) *Ne . . . que — Seulement.* — Both mean *only.* **Seulement** is used in preference to **ne . . . que :** (*a*) when there is no verb, (*b*) when *only* refers to the subject, (*c*) when *only* refers to the verb :

Seulement **deux,**	*Only two.*
Seulement **ma sœur le fera.**	*Only my sister will do it.*
Ne parlez pas, écoutez *seulement.*	*Don't speak, only listen.*

THE PRONOUN

I. Definition

A pronoun is a word used instead of a noun to avoid its repetition ; while an adjective accompanies a noun to qualify it or determine it.

In the sentence **Ma plume est bonne, la tienne est bonne aussi, ma** is an adjective determining the noun **plume,** that is to say, expressing whose pen it is ; **la tienne,** on the contrary, is a pronoun standing for **ta plume** and is used to avoid the repetition of that noun.

II. Possessive pronouns

	SINGULAR		PLURAL	
	Masculine	*Feminine*	*Masculine*	*Feminine*
Mine	le mien	la mienne	les miens	les miennes
Thine	le tien	la tienne	les tiens	les tiennes
His, hers, its	le sien	la sienne	les siens	les siennes
Ours	le or la nôtre		les nôtres	
Yours	le or la vôtre		les vôtres	
Theirs	le or la leur		les leurs	

Observe that the article is a part of the possessive pronoun and contracts with **de** and **à** when preceded by those prepositions : **du mien,** *of mine,* **au mien,** *to mine,* etc.

Possessive pronouns agree in gender and number with the noun represented (the object possessed) and *not* with the possessor of the object :

J'ai mon livre et Louise a *le sien*.   *I have my book and Louise has hers.*
Louise a sa plume et Jean a *la sienne*.   *Louise has her pen and John has his.*

III. Demonstrative pronouns

This (one), that (one), the one $\left\{\begin{array}{l}\textbf{celui}\\\textbf{celle}\end{array}\right\}$ + **de,** or **qui,** or **que,** or **dont,** or **-ci,** or **-là.**

These, those (ones), the ones $\left\{\begin{array}{l}\textbf{ceux}\\\textbf{celles}\end{array}\right\}$ + **de,** or **qui,** or **que,** or **dont,** or **-ci,** or **-là.**

ce, *this, that, these, those, he, she it, they.*

$\left.\begin{array}{l}\textbf{ceci,} \text{ } this\\\textbf{cela,} \text{ } that\end{array}\right\}$ object pointed out, but not mentioned.

Uses of *ce*. — (1) **Ce** + **être,** when real subject of **être,** is translated by *it, this,* or *that.*

C'est vrai.   *It (this, that) is true.*

(2) **Ce + être,** when the predicate is a noun, a pronoun, or a superlative is translated by *he, she, it, they, this, that, these, those.*

C'est le professeur.	*He (it, she) is the professor.*
C'est nous.	*It is we.*
Ce sont nos plus jolies robes.	*They (or these) are our prettiest dresses.*

(3) **Ce +** a relative (**qui, que, dont**) means *that which, what, which.*

Je vois *ce qui* vous amuse.	*I see what amuses you.*
Je comprends *ce que* vous dites.	*I understand what you say.*
Je sais *ce dont* vous parlez.	*I know what you are speaking of.*
Je devine *ce à quoi* vous pensez.	*I guess what you are thinking of.*

Ceci — cela. — **Ceci,** *this,* and **cela,** *that,* are neuter pronouns, because having no antecedent, they are neither masculine nor feminine. They are used to express something indicated or pointed out, but not mentioned:

Prenez *ceci* et donnez-moi *cela.*   *Take this and give me that.*

Note. — Had the object been mentioned, **celui-ci** (**celle-ci**) and **celui-là** (**celle-là**) should have been used.

Ceci may also refer to what is about to be said, and **cela** to what has just been said:

Ecoutez *ceci.*   *Listen to this.*
Ne parlez plus, *cela* (*ca*) m'ennuie.   *Don't speak any more, that annoys me.*

Ça is the colloquial form of **cela.**

IV. Personal pronouns

CONJUNCTIVES			DISJUNCTIVES
Subject	*Direct Object*	*Indirect Object*	*Subject and Object*
je	me	me	moi
tu	te	te	toi
il	le, se	lui, se	lui, soi
elle	la, se	lui, se	elle, soi
nous	nous	nous	nous
vous	vous	vous	vous
ils	se, les	se, leur	soi, eux
elles	se, les	se, leur	soi, elles

Note. — The disjunctive pronoun **soi** is generally used when it takes the place of an indefinite pronoun :

On doit travailler pour *soi.*   *One must work for oneself.*
Chacun pour *soi.*   *Every one for himself.*

Agreement. — Personal pronouns agree in gender, number, and person with their antecedents :

Voici vos lettres, nous *les* **avons lues.**   *Here are your letters, we have read them.*

Cases. — *Nominative :* The nominative form stands as *subject* of the verb : *il* donne.

Accusative : The accusative form stands as *object* of the verb : **il** *le* **donne.**

Dative: The dative form stands as *indirect object* of the verb and is governed by the preposition **à,** expressed or *understood :*

Je *lui* **parle.**   *I speak to him.*

In dative cases in English, the preposition **à,** *to* (or *for, from*) is generally expressed, while in French it is generally understood.

When the preposition **à** is expressed in French, the disjunctive pronoun is used instead of the conjunctive :

Il l'a dit à *moi* **et à** *eux.*

Note. — When the conjunctive object pronoun *is not* **le, la,** or **les,** the preposition **à** and a disjunctive pronoun should be used :

Il vous a envoyé *à moi.*   *He sent you to me.*
Je me suis présenté *à eux.*   *I introduced myself to them.*
But : **Je les lui ai envoyés.**   *I sent them to him.*

Impersonal: **Il** is the sole impersonal pronoun, used as subject of impersonal verbs. (See Lessons 40, 45 and 72.)

Il **pleut.**   *It is raining.*

Predicative: (1) **Le, la** and **les** are used as predicate when referring to a noun or to an adjective used as a noun.

Etes-vous sa sœur ?   **Je** *la* **suis.**   *Are you his sister? I am.*
Etes-vous les malades ?   **Nous** *les* **sommes.**   *Are you the sick ones? We are.*

(2) **Le** *invariable* is used as predicate when referring to an adjective or to a noun used as an adjective :

Etes-vous contente Jeanne ?   **Je** *le* **suis.**   *I am.*
Sont-elles Américaines ?   **Elles** *le* **sont.**   *They are.*

Note. — In the latter case (2) **le** is pleonastic, as compared with English.

V. Position of personal object pronouns

(1) These pronouns (direct or indirect) are placed *immediately before* the verb of which they are the object, except in the imperative affirmative.

Je *le* verrai et je *lui* parlerai.	*I shall see him and speak to him.*
Voyez-*le* et parlez-*lui*.	*See him and speak to him.*
Je l'ai vu et je *lui* ai parlé.	*I saw him and spoke to him.*

Notice in tne last example that, in compound tenses, the auxiliary is considered as a real verb.

(2) The personal pronoun objects always precede **voici** and **voilà**.

Nous **voici.**	*Here we are.*	*La* **voilà.**	*There she is.*

(3) When a verb has more than one pronoun object, the first person precedes the second and third, and the second precedes the third. If both pronouns are third person, the direct (**le, la, les**) always precedes the indirect (**lui, leur**).

ORDER OF PRECEDENCE

je me
tu te
il
elle } se
on
nous nous
vous vous
ils
elles } se

le
before la } before lui leur } before y en } and y before en + verb.
les

(4) With a verb in the imperative affirmative, the object pronouns come after the verb, and the order is the same as in English :

Donnez-*le-moi*.	*Give it to me.*
Montrez-*lui-en*.	*Show him some.*
Conduisez-*nous-y*.	*Take us there.*

Notice that **me** and **te** become **moi** and **toi** when following the verb.

TABLE SHOWING THE POSSIBLE COMBINATIONS OF TWO OBJECT
PRONOUNS BEFORE AND AFTER THE VERB

BEFORE THE VERB	AFTER THE VERB	BEFORE THE VERB	AFTER THE VERB	BEFORE THE VERB		AFTER THE VERB
me le	-le-moi	te le	-le-toi	se le	le lui	-le-lui
me la	-la-moi	te la	-la-toi	se la	la lui	-la-lui
me les	-les-moi	te les	-les-toi	se les	les lui	-les-lui
nous le	-le-nous	vous le	-le-vous	se le	le leur	-le-leur
nous la	-la-nous	vous la	-la-vous	se la	la leur	-la-leur
nous les	-les-nous	vous les	-les-vous	se les	les leur	-les-leur
m'en	-m'en	t'en	-t'en	s'en	lui en	-lui-en
m'en	-m'en	t'en	-t'en	s'en	l'en	-l'en
nous en	-nous-en	vous en	-vous-en	s'en	leur en	-leur-en
nous en	-nous-en	vous en	-vous-en	s'en	les en	-les-en
m'y		t'y		s'y		
m'y		t'y		s'y	l'y	-l'y
nous y	-nous-y	vous y	-vous-y	s'y	leur y	-leur-y
nous y	-nous-y	vous y	-vous-y	s'y	les y	-les -y
		y en	y-en			

VI. Disjunctive pronouns

The disjunctive pronouns are used:

(1) *Absolutely, i.e.,* when the verb is *not* expressed:

Qui parle? Moi (lui, elle, eux).   *Who speaks? I (he, she, they).*

(2) *After a preposition:*

Il ira avec eux (moi, lui, elle).   *He will go with them (me, him, her).*

(3) *As logical subject of* **ce + être:**

C'est moi (toi, lui, elle).   *It is I (you, he, she).*

(4) *In comparisons:*

Il est plus fort que moi.   *He is stronger than I.*

(5) *For emphasis:*

Lui le fera, et moi, je me reposerai.   *He will do it and I will rest.*

(6) *In composite subjects:*

Elle et moi, nous comprenons.   *She and I (we) understand.*

VII. Relative pronouns

qui, *who, which, that* (*whom*, after a preposition).
que, *whom, which, that.*
dont, *whose, of whom, of which,* etc.
où, *in which, into which, at which, to which,* etc.
lequel, lesquels, }
laquelle, lesquelles, } *who, whom, which, that.*
quoi, *what, which.*

Agreement. — A relative pronoun is of the gender, number, and *person* of its antecedent :

C'est vous *qui parlerez* d'abord.   *It is you who will speak first.*
C'est nous *qui chantons.*   *It is we who sing.*
Les maisons que j'ai vu*es.*   *The houses which I have seen.*

Uses of the relative pronouns. — (1) **Qui,** *who, which, that,* is *always subject* and is used for persons or things :

le monsieur *qui* parle, *the gentleman who speaks.*
le livre *qui* est sur la table, *the book which (that) is on the table.*

(2) **Qui,** *whom,* after a preposition refers to persons only :

la dame à *qui* je parle, *the lady to whom I speak.*

(3) **Que,** *whom, which, that,* is used as direct object, and refers to persons or things :

les enfants *que* vous voyez, *the children whom you see.*
les livres *que* j'ai achetés, *the books which (that) I bought.*

(4) **Dont,** *whose, of whom, of which* = **de** + a relative :

l'homme *dont* j'ai vu le fils, *the man whose son I saw.*

Remember that, in a relative clause introduced by **dont,** the object must be placed *after the verb,* and not before as in English.

Note. — The relative pronoun, often omitted in English, is never omitted in French.

(5) **Où,** *where,* is used as a relative pronoun when it means **dans, à, vers** + *a relative:*

la maison *où* vous êtes, *the house where (in which) you are.*
la maison *où* vous allez, *the house where (to which, toward which) you go.*

(6) **Lequel, laquelle,** and their plurals, *who, whom, which, that,* are used where **qui** and **que,** etc., may not be used. They

refer to persons as well as things.   They are used mainly after a
preposition.

> la chaise sur *laquelle* vous êtes assis, *the chair on which you are seated.*

Remember that **lequel, lesquels** contract with **de** and **à** to
duquel, desquels, auquel, auxquels.   Dont is generally used
instead of **duquel, desquels, de laquelle** and **desquelles.**

> *Note.* — When depending on a noun depending itself on a preposition,
> *whose* is expressed by **duquel,** etc., which follows the noun.

> le monsieur à la fille *duquel* je parle, *the gentleman to whose daughter I speak.*

(7) **Quoi,** *what, which,* is used instead of **que** after a preposition.

> Je sais de *quoi* il parle.   *I know what he is speaking of.*

(8) **Ce qui** (subj.), **ce que** (obj.) translate the English *what*
when the latter has the sense of *that which,* and **ce dont** translates *that of which.*

> Je vois *ce qui* vous intéresse.   *I see what interests you.*
> Je comprends *ce que* vous dites.   *I understand what you say.*
> Je sais *ce dont* vous parlez.   *I know what you are speaking of.*

VIII. Interrogatives

ADJECTIVES		PRONOUNS	
quel? quelle? quels? quelles? } *which? what?* + noun	Variable	lequel? laquelle? lesquels? lesquelles? }	*which? Which* or *what one(s)?* not followed by noun
	Invariable	Qui? Qui est-ce qui? } *who?* Qui? Qui est-ce que? } *whom?* Qu'est-ce qui? *what?* (subj.) Que? Qu'est-ce que? } *what?* (obj.)	

Uses of interrogative pronouns. — (1) **Qui,** *who? whom?* used
for persons only, stands in both direct and indirect questions and
may be subject or object.

> (a) *Qui* chante?   *Qui* est là?   *Who sings?   Who is there?*
> (b) *Qui* avez-vous vu?   *Whom have you seen?*
> (c) De *qui* parlez-vous?   *Of whom are you speaking?*

(2) **Que,** *what?* is always object and refers to things only :

> *Que* dites-vous?   *What do you say?*

(3) **Quoi,** *what?* is the disjunctive form of **que.** It is used :
(*a*) Absolutely (without a verb), (*b*) after a preposition.

Vous voulez quelque chose, *quoi?*	*You want something, what?*
Quoi? **Vous partez déjà?**	*What? You are leaving already?*
De *quoi* **parlez-vous?**	*Of what are you speaking?*
En *quoi* **puis-je vous être utile?**	*In what can I help you?*

(4) **Qui est-ce qui** (*who*), **qui est-ce que** (*whom*) are old gal-licisms, still extensively used in conversation (for persons only).

Qui (est-ce qui) **chante?**	*Who sings?*
Qui (est-ce que) **vous avez vu?**	*Whom have you seen?*

Notice that, when **est-ce que** is part of an interrogative locution, there is no inversion of the verb and the pronoun subject. (Compare with Example (*b*) (1) above.)

(5) **Qu'est-ce qui** (subj.), **qu'est-ce que** (obj.) are in the same class with the locutions of the preceding paragraph (4), but they refer to things only.

Qu'est-ce qui **vous amuse?**	*What amuses you?*
Qu'est-ce que **vous voulez?**	*What do you want?*
Qu'est-ce que **c'est?**	*What is it?*

(6) **Qu'est-ce que c'est que,** *what is?* is an old gallicism much used in asking questions, when the person or object is mentioned or pointed out.

Qu'est-ce que c'est que **ceci?**	*What is this?*
Qu'est-ce que c'est que **cela?**	*What is that?*
Qu'est-ce que c'est qu'un **aéroplane?**	*What is an airplane?*

(7) **Lequel,** etc., *which (one),* etc., refer either to persons or things and are used as subject, object, or after a preposition :

Lequel **de ces livres voulez-vous?**	*Which of these books do you want?*
Duquel **avez-vous besoin?**	*Which (one) do you need?*
A laquelle **de ces dames . . . ?**	*To which of those ladies . . . ?*

Attention! Do not confuse **lequel** with **quel** (adjective). The latter is always followed immediately by a noun :

Quel livre voulez-vous?	*Which book do you want?*

(8) **A qui** + **être,** *whose?* denotes possession :

A qui **est cette maison?**	*Whose house is that?*

IX. Indefinites

Some indefinites are used as *adjectives*, others as *pronouns*, and some have both uses.

(1) Adjectives (only). —

chaque, *each, every.*
divers, *many.*
maint(e), *many.*

quelque(s), *some, (pl.) a few.*
quelconque(s), *after a noun, whatever.*

chaque élève, *each pupil.*
quelques livres, *a few books.*
un livre quelconque, *any book whatever.*

(2) Pronouns (only). —

on, *one, they, people.*
personne . . . ne, *nobody.*
rien . . . ne, *nothing.*
chacun(e), *each one.*
quelqu'un(e), *some one, any one.*

quelques-uns(unes), *some, a few.*
quelque chose, *something.*
quiconque, *whoever.*
qui que + subj., *whoever.*
quoi que + subj., *whatever.*

On dit que c'est vrai.	*They (people) say that it is true.*
Ici *on* parle français.	*Here French is spoken.*
*Personne n'*est venu.	*Nobody has come.*
Chacun pour soi.	*Each one for himself.*
*Rien n'*est impossible.	*Nothing is impossible.*
Quelqu'un est à la porte.	*Some one is at the door.*
Dites *quelque chose.*	*Say something.*
Quiconque parlera sera puni.	*Whoever speaks will be punished.*
Qui que vous soyez.	*Whoever you may be.*
Quoi que vous disiez.	*Whatever you may say.*

(3) Adjectives or pronouns. —

aucun(e) . . . ne, *no, nobody, none.*
autre, *other.*
même, *same.*
nul . . . ne, *no, nobody.*

plusieurs, *several.*
tel, telle, *such a.*
l'un et l'autre, *both.*
pas un . . . ne, *not a, not one.*

tout(e), tous,[1] toutes, *all, every.*

Aucun ami n'est venu.	*No friend came.*
Aucun n'est venu.	*None came.*
*Nul n'*est venu.	*Nobody came.*
Pas un homme n'est venu.	*Not one man came.*
*Pas un n'*a échappé.	*Not one has escaped.*

---

[1] When **tous** is pronoun, the **s** is sounded.

THE NEGATION

(1) The negation, without verb, is **non**.

Avez-vous fait cela ? *Non.*	*Did you do that? No.*
Oui ou *non,* **l'avez-vous fait ?**	*Did you do it, yes or no?*

(2) The negation, with a verb, consists of two parts : **ne** placed before the verb, and the second part after it. In compound tenses, the auxiliary is considered as the real verb, and therefore, the second part of the negation is placed after the auxiliary verb, *i.e.,* before the past participle.

The principal negations are :

ne . . . **pas,** *not.*		ne . . . **personne,** *nobody.*	
ne . . . **point,** *not.*		ne . . . **aucunement,**	} *not at all.*
ne . . . **guère,** *hardly.*		ne . . . **nullement,**	
ne . . . **jamais,** *never.*		ne . . . **aucun,**	
ne . . . **plus,** *no more.*		ne . . . **nul,**	} *no, none.*
ne . . . **que,** *only.*		ne . . . **pas un,**	
ne . . . **rien,** *nothing.*		ne . . . **ni** (. . . **ni**), *neither . . . nor.*	

Je *ne* **le lui ai** *pas* **donné.**	*I did not give it to him.*
Ne **lui en donnez** *plus.*	*Don't give him any more.*

When there is one or more personal object pronouns in a negative sentence, **ne,** the first part of the negation, is pushed to the left, together with the subject, in order to make room for the pronouns which should be placed immediately before the verb or the auxiliary.

(3) With an *infinitive, both parts* of the negation come together and are placed before the infinitive. **Que** and **personne,** however, follow the verb :

Il parle de *ne pas* **venir.**	*He speaks of not coming.*
Il parle de *ne* **venir** *que* **demain.**	*He speaks of coming only to-morrow.*

(4) *Ne* **alone as negative.** — With certain verbs, especially **pouvoir, savoir, oser, cesser** (the latter followed by an infinitive), the second part of the negation is generally omitted :

Pourquoi ? Je *ne* **sais.**	*Why? I don't know.*
Il *ne* **cesse de chanter.**	*He does not stop singing.*

(5) *Ne* **omitted.** — When the verb is not expressed, the second part of the negation is used alone :

Qui est là ? *Personne.*	*Who is there? No one.*
Que dites-vous ? *Rien.*	*What do you say? Nothing.*
Fumez-vous ? *Jamais.*	*Do you smoke? Never.*

THE PREPOSITION

(1) The most common prepositions are :

à, *to, at, in, on,* etc.
après, *after, next to.*
avant, *before* (time).
avec, *with.*
chez, *with, at—'s.*
contre, *against.*
dans, *in*(*to*).
de, *of, from, with,* etc.
depuis, *since, from.*
derrière, *behind.*
dès, *from, since.*
devant, *before* (place).

durant, *during.*
en, *in, to.*
entre, *between, among.*
envers, *towards.*
hormis, *except.*
jusque, *till, until.*
malgré, *in spite of.*
moyennant, *by means of.*
nonobstant, *notwithstanding.*
outre, *besides.*
par, *by, through.*

parmi, *among.*
pendant, *during.*
pour, *for.*
sans, *without.*
sauf, *save, except.*
selon, *according to.*
sous, *under.*
suivant, *according to.*
sur, *on, upon.*
vers, *towards.*
voici, *here is* (*are*).
voilà, *there is* (*are*).

(2) **Prepositional locutions.** — Besides the single prepositions mentioned in the preceding paragraph, there are prepositional locutions, made of several words and generally ending with **de** or **à.** Such are :

à cause de, *on account of.*
à côté de, *by the side of.*
à force de, *by dint of.*
à l'égard de, *with regard to.*
à l'exception de, *except.*
à l'insu de, *unknown to.*
à travers, *across, through.*
au delà de, *beyond.*
au-dessous de, *under.*
au-dessus de, *above.*
au devant de, *in front of.*
au lieu de, *instead of.*
au milieu de, *in the midst of.*
au moyen de, *by means of.*
auprès de, *near by.*

autour de, *around.*
au travers de, *across, through.*
d'après, *according to.*
en deçà de, *on this side* (*of*).
en dépit de, *in spite of.*
en face de, *in front of.*
faute de, *for want of.*
jusqu'à, *as far as, until.*
par delà, *beyond.*
par-dessous, *under.*
par-dessus, *over.*
près de, *near.*
quant à, *as for.*
vis-à-vis de, *opposite.*

(3) **Position.** — Prepositions precede the word they govern, as in English :

Je pense *à* ma mère.   *I think of my mother.*
Je parle *de* lui.   *I speak of him.*

(4) **Repetition.** — The prepositions are repeated before each word they govern :

la mère *de* **Paul** et *de* **Jeanne,** *the mother of Paul and Jane.*

(5) **Prepositions followed by a verb.** — A verb following a preposition is always in the infinitive. **En** is the only exception, being followed by the present participle. **Après** is followed by the past infinitive.

Il aime *à* rire et *à* chanter.	*He likes to laugh and to sing.*
Il est parti *en chantant.*	*He left singing.*
Après avoir parlé, il partit.	*After speaking, he left.*

Idiomatic uses

Prepositions greatly vary as to their uses, meanings, and translations in both English and French. This can only be acquired by practice. A few examples follow :

(1) **A,** *to, at, in, on,* etc. —

à Paris,	*in(to) Paris.*
à la maison,	*at home.*
à la campagne,	*in(to) the country.*
à pieds,	*on foot.*
à haute voix,	*with a loud voice.*
à quoi pensez-vous ?	*what are you thinking about?*
à la main,	*by hand.*
à partir de demain,	*from to-morrow.*
à cette condition,	*under that condition.*
mot *à* mot,	*word for word.*
un *à* un,	*one by one.*
du matin *au* soir,	*from morning till evening.*
la dame *à* la robe bleue,	*the lady with the blue dress.*

(2) **De,** *of, from.* —

de Paris,	*from Paris.*
de jour,	*by day.*
de cinq à six heures,	*between five and six o'clock.*
de tout mon cœur,	*with all my heart.*
de cette façon,	*in this way.*
de jour en jour,	*day after day.*
*d'*un autre côté,	*on the other hand.*
Je vous remercie *de* cela,	*I thank you for that.*
tenir *de*,	*to take after.*
le train *de* Chicago,	*the train to Chicago.*
connaître *de* vue,	*to know by sight.*

(3) **En,** *in, to, at.* —

en amont, *en* aval,	*upstream, downstream.*
en France,	*in(to) France.*

en route,	*on the way.*
en liberté,	*at liberty.*
en même temps,	*at the same time.*
en pure perte,	*to no purpose.*
en aucune façon,	*by no means.*
aller (se promener) *en* voiture,	*to drive, to ride,*
en automobile, *en* bateau,	*to go boat riding.*

(4) **Dans,** *in, into.* —

dans ce but,	*to that end.*
copier *dans* un livre,	*to copy out of a book.*

(5) **Par,** *by, through.* —

par ici, *par* là,	*this way, that way.*
par une belle journée,	*on a beautiful day.*
par exemple,	*for instance, for example, the idea!*
par jour, semaine, **an,**	*per day, week, year.*
par terre,	*on the ground, on the floor, by land.*
par bateau,	*by boat.*
par la pluie,	*in the rain.*
par pitié,	*for pity's sake.*
par le temps qui court,	*as time goes.*
par la fenêtre,	*out of the window.*

(6) **Chez,** *at, to, in the house of, among, with.* —

chez Duval,	*at (to, in) the house of Duval.*
chez les Grecs,	*among the Greeks.*
il dîne *chez* nous,	*he dines with us.*

(7) **Pour,** *for.* —

pour affaires, *on business.*

(8) **Sur,** *on, upon.* —

un *sur* cent, *one out of a hundred.*

(9) **Depuis,** *since.* —

Je parle *depuis* deux heures. *I have been speaking for two hours.*

(10) **Pendant,** *during.* —

J'ai parlé *pendant* deux heures. *I have spoken for two hours.*

CONJUNCTIONS

The principal conjunctions are. —

et, *and.*	**ou,** *or.*
ni, *nor.*	**or,** *now.*
mais, *but.*	**car,** *for.*
que, *that, than, as.*	**donc,** *now, thus.*
si, *if.*	**comme,** *as.*
quoique, *though, although.*	**lorsque,** *when.*
puisque, *since.*	**quand,** *when.*
afin que, *so that.*	**dès que,** *as soon as.*
pour que, *in order that.*	**tandis que,** *whilst.*
pendant que, *while.*	**parce que,** *because.*
de peur que, *for fear that.*	**après que,** *after.*
encore, *yet, still.*	**avant que,** *before.*
cependant, *however.*	**jusqu'à ce que,** *until.*
toutefois, *yet, nevertheless.*	**ainsi,** *therefore.*

THE VERB

Auxiliary verbs

There are only two auxiliary verbs in French, **avoir** (*to have*) and **être** (*to be*).

I. Avoir

INFINITIVE PRESENT	INFINITIVE PAST
avoir, *to have.*	**avoir eu,** *to have had.*

PARTICIPLE PRESENT	PARTICIPLE PAST
ayant, *having.*	**eu,** *had.*

INDICATIVE PRESENT	PAST INDEFINITE
I have, am having.	*I have had, I had.*
j'ai.	**j'ai eu.**
tu as.	**tu as eu.**
il or **elle a.**	**il** or **elle a eu.**
nous avons.	**nous avons eu.**
vous avez.	**vous avez eu.**
ils or **elles ont.**	**ils** or **elles ont eu.**

<table>
<tr><td colspan="2">

IMPERFECT

I had, was having, used to have.

j'avais.
tu avais.
il or elle avait.
nous avions.
vous aviez.
ils or elles avaient.

</td><td colspan="2">

PLUPERFECT

I had had.

j'avais eu.
tu avais eu.
il or elle avait eu.
nous avions eu.
vous aviez eu.
ils or elles avaient eu.

</td></tr>
</table>

PAST DEFINITE

I had.

j'eus.
tu eus.
il or elle eut.
nous eûmes.
vous eûtes.
ils or elles eurent.

PAST ANTERIOR

I had had.

j'eus eu.
tu eus eu.
il or elle eut eu.
nous eûmes eu.
vous eûtes eu.
ils or elles eurent eu.

FUTURE

I shall have.

j'aurai.
tu auras.
il or elle aura.
nous aurons.
vous aurez.
ils or elles auront.

FUTURE ANTERIOR

I shall have had.

j'aurai eu.
tu auras eu.
il or elle aura eu.
nous aurons eu.
vous aurez eu.
ils or elles auront eu.

CONDITIONAL PRESENT

I should have.

j'aurais.
tu aurais.
il or elle aurait.
nous aurions.
vous auriez.
ils or elles auraient.

CONDITIONAL PAST

I should have had.

j'aurais eu.
tu aurais eu.
il or elle aurait eu.
nous aurions eu.
vous auriez eu.
ils or elles auraient eu.

SUBJUNCTIVE PRESENT
(that) I (may) have, etc.[1]

que j'aie.
que tu aies.
qu'il or qu'elle ait.
que nous ayons.
que vous ayez.
qu'ils (elles) aient.

SUBJUNCTIVE PAST
(that) I (may) have had, etc.

que j'aie eu.
que tu aies eu.
qu'il or qu'elle ait eu.
que nous ayons eu.
que vous ayez eu.
qu'ils (elles) aient eu.

SUBJUNCTIVE IMPERFECT
(that) I might have, (that) I had, etc.

que j'eusse.
que tu eusses.
qu'il or qu'elle eût.
que nous eussions.
que vous eussiez.
qu'ils (elles) eussent.

SUBJUNCTIVE PLUPERFECT
(that) I (might) have had, etc.

que j'eusse eu.
que tu eusses eu.
qu'il or qu'elle eût eu.
que nous eussions eu.
que vous eussiez eu.
qu'ils (elles) eussent eu.

IMPERATIVE

SINGULAR

aie, *have (thou).*
(qu'il ait, *let him have.*)[1]

PLURAL

ayons, *let us have.*
ayez, *have.*
(qu'ils aient, *let them have.*)[2]

II. Avoir used interrogatively

INDICATIVE PRESENT
have I?

ai-je?
as-tu?
a-t-il?   a-t-elle?
avons-nous?
avez-vous?
ont-ils?   ont-elles?

PAST INDEFINITE
have I had?   had I?

ai-je eu?
as-tu eu?
a-t-il eu?   a-t-elle eu?
avons-nous eu?
avez-vous eu?
ont-ils eu?   ont-elles eu?

---

[1] The subjunctive has no English equivalent. Its translation depends upon the preceding construction.

[2] Third person, present subjunctive, used as imperative.

IMPERFECT	PLUPERFECT
had I?	*had I had?*

avais-je?
avais-tu?
avait-il?   avait-elle?
avions-nous?
aviez-vous?
avaient-ils?   avaient-elles?

avais-je eu?
avais-tu eu?
avait-il eu?   avait-elle eu?
avions-nous eu?
aviez-vous eu?
avaient-ils (elles) eu?

PAST DEFINITE	PAST ANTERIOR
had I?	*had I had?*

eus-je?
eus-tu?
eut-il?   eut-elle?
eûmes-nous?
eûtes-vous?
eurent-ils?   eurent-elles?

eus-je eu?
eus-tu eu?
eut-il eu?   eut-elle eu?
eûmes-nous eu?
eûtes-vous eu?
eurent-ils (elles) eu?

FUTURE	FUTURE ANTERIOR
shall I have?	*shall I have had?*

aurai-je?
auras-tu?
aura-t-il?   aura-t-elle?
aurons-nous?
aurez-vous?
auront-ils?   auront-elles?

aurai-je eu?
auras-tu eu?
aura-t-il eu?   aura-t-elle eu?
aurons-nous eu?
aurez-vous eu?
auront-ils (elles) eu?

CONDITIONAL PRESENT	CONDITIONAL PAST
should I have?	*should I have had?*

aurais-je?
aurais-tu?
aurait-il?   aurait-elle?
aurions-nous?
auriez-vous?
auraient-ils (elles)?

aurais-je eu?
aurais-tu eu?
aurait-il eu?   aurait-elle eu?
aurions-nous eu?
auriez-vous eu?
auraient-ils (elles) eu?

OBSERVATION FOR ALL VERBS USED NEGATIVELY. — Instead of **pas,** put **point** for a stronger negation, **jamais** for *never,* and **plus** for *no more* or *no longer.* (See Lesson 54.)

III. Avoir used negatively

INDICATIVE PRESENT	PAST INDEFINITE
I have not.	*I have not had, I did not have.*

je n'ai pas.	je n'ai pas eu.
tu n'as pas.	tu n'as pas eu.
il or elle n'a pas.	il or elle n'a pas eu.
nous n'avons pas.	nous n'avons pas eu.
vous n'avez pas.	vous n'avez pas eu.
ils or elles n'ont pas.	ils or elles n'ont pas eu.

IMPERFECT	PLUPERFECT
I had not.	*I had not had.*

je n'avais pas.	je n'avais pas eu.
tu n'avais pas.	tu n'avais pas eu.
il or elle n'avait pas.	il or elle n'avait pas eu.
nous n'avions pas.	nous n'avions pas eu.
vous n'aviez pas.	vous n'aviez pas eu.
ils or elles n'avaient pas.	ils or elles n'avaient pas eu.

PAST DEFINITE	PAST ANTERIOR
I had not.	*I had not had.*

je n'eus pas	je n'eus pas eu,
tu n'eus pas.	tu n'eus pas eu.
il or elle n'eut pas.	il or elle n'eut pas eu.
nous n'eûmes pas.	nous n'eûmes pas eu.
vous n'eûtes pas.	vous n'eûtes pas eu.
ils or elles n'eurent pas.	ils or elles n'eurent pas eu.

FUTURE	FUTURE ANTERIOR
I shall not have.	*I shall not have had.*

je n'aurai pas.	je n'aurai pas eu.
tu n'auras pas.	tu n'auras pas eu.
il or elle n'aura pas.	il or elle n'aura pas eu.
nous n'aurons pas.	nous n'aurons pas eu.
vous n'aurez pas.	vous n'aurez pas eu.
ils or elles n'auront pas.	ils or elles n'auront pas eu.

CONDITIONAL PRESENT	CONDITIONAL PAST
I should not have.	*I should not have had.*

je n'aurais pas.	je n'aurais pas eu.
tu n'aurais pas.	tu n'aurais pas eu.
il or elle n'aurait pas.	il or elle n'aurait pas eu.
nous n'aurions pas.	nous n'aurions pas eu.
vous n'auriez pas.	vous n'auriez pas eu.
ils or elles n'auraient pas.	ils or elles n'auraient pas eu.

SUBJUNCTIVE PRESENT

(that) I may not have.

que je n'aie pas.
que tu n'aies pas.
qu'il or qu'elle n'ait pas.
que nous n'ayons pas.
que vous n'ayez pas.
qu'ils (elles) n'aient pas.

SUBJUNCTIVE PAST

(that) I may not have had.

que je n'aie pas eu.
que tu n'aies pas eu.
qu'il or qu'elle n'ait pas eu.
que nous n'ayons pas eu.
que vous n'ayez pas eu.
qu'ils (elles) n'aient pas eu.

SUBJUNCTIVE IMPERFECT

(that) I might not have.

que je n'eusse pas.
que tu n'eusses pas.
qu'il or qu'elle n'eût pas.
que nous n'eussions pas.
que vous n'eussiez pas.
qu'ils (elles) n'eussent pas.

SUBJUNCTIVE PLUPERFECT

(that) I might not have had.

que je n'eusse pas eu.
que tu n'eusses pas eu.
qu'il or qu'elle n'eût pas eu.
que nous n'eussions pas eu.
que vous n'eussiez pas eu.
qu'ils (elles) n'eussent pas eu.

IMPERATIVE

SINGULAR

n'aie pas, *do not have.*
(qu'il n'ait pas, *let him not have.*)

PLURAL

n'ayons pas, *let us not have.*
n'ayez pas, *do not have.*
(qu'ils n'aient pas, *let them not have.*)

IV. Avoir used negatively and interrogatively

INDICATIVE PRESENT

have I not?

n'ai-je pas?
n'as-tu pas?
n'a-t-il (elle) pas?
n'avons-nous pas?
n'avez-vous pas?
n'ont-ils (elles) pas?

PAST INDEFINITE

have I not had?

n'ai-je pas eu?
n'as-tu pas eu?
n'a-t-il (elie) pas eu?
n'avons-nous pas eu?
n'avez-vous pas eu?
n'ont-ils (elles) pas eu?

IMPERFECT

n'avais-je pas? *had I not?*
etc.

PLUPERFECT

n'avais-je pas eu? *had I not had?*
etc.

PAST DEFINITE

n'eus-je pas? *had I not?*
etc.

PAST ANTERIOR

n'eus-je pas eu? *had I not had?*
etc.

FUTURE

shall I not have?

n'aurai-je pas?
etc.

FUTURE ANTERIOR

shall I not have had?

n'aurai-je pas eu?
etc.

CONDITIONAL PRESENT
should I not have?

n'aurais-je pas?
etc.

CONDITIONAL PAST
should I not have had?

n'aurais-je pas eu?
etc.

V. Être

INFINITIVE PRESENT
être, *to be.*

INFINITIVE PAST
avoir été, *to have been.*

PARTICIPLE PRESENT
étant, *being.*

PARTICIPLE PAST
été, *been.*

INDICATIVE PRESENT
I am.

je suis.
tu es.
il or elle est.
nous sommes.
vous êtes.
ils or elles sont.

PAST INDEFINITE
I have been, I was.

j'ai été.
tu as été.
il or elle a été.
nous avons été.
vous avez été.
ils or elles ont été.

IMPERFECT
I was, used to be, etc

j'étais.
tu étais.
il or elle était.
nous étions.
vous étiez.
ils or elles étaient.

PLUPERFECT
I had been.

j'avais été.
tu avais été.
il or elle avait été.
nous avions été.
vous aviez été.
ils or elles avaient été.

PAST DEFINITE
I was.

je fus.
tu fus.
il or elle fut.
nous fûmes.
vous fûtes.
ils or elles furent.

PAST ANTERIOR
I had been.

J'eus été.
tu eus été.
il or elle eut été.
nous eûmes été.
vous eûtes été.
ils or elles eurent été.

FUTURE
I shall be, etc.

je serai.
tu seras.
il or elle sera.
nous serons.
vous serez.
ils or elles seront.

FUTURE ANTERIOR
I shall have been.

j'aurai été.
tu auras été.
il or elle aura été.
nous aurons été.
vous aurez été.
ils or elles auront été.

CONDITIONAL PRESENT	CONDITIONAL PAST
I should be.	*I should have been.*

je serais.	j'aurais été.
tu serais.	tu aurais été.
il or elle serait.	il or elle aurait été.
nous serions.	nous aurions été.
vous seriez.	vous auriez été.
ils or elles seraient.	ils or elles auraient été.

SUBJUNCTIVE PRESENT	SUBJUNCTIVE PAST
(that) I (may) be.	*(that) I (may) have been.*

que je sois.	que j'aie été.
que tu sois.	que tu aies été.
qu'il or qu'elle soit.	qu'il or qu'elle ait été.
que nous soyons.	que nous ayons été.
que vous soyez.	que vous ayez été.
qu'ils (elles) soient.	qu'ils (elles) aient été.

SUBJUNCTIVE IMPERFECT	SUBJUNCTIVE PLUPERFECT
(that) I (might) be.	*(that) I (might) have been.*

que je fusse.	que j'eusse été.
que tu fusses.	que tu eusses été.
qu'il or qu'elle fût.	qu'il or qu'elle eût été.
que nous fussions.	que nous eussions été.
que vous fussiez.	que vous eussiez été.
qu'ils or qu'elles fussent.	qu'ils or qu'elles eussent été.

IMPERATIVE

SINGULAR	PLURAL
	soyons, *let us be.*
sois, *be.*	soyez, *be.*
(qu'il soit, *let him be.*)	(qu'ils soient, *let them be.*)

VI. Etre used interrogatively

INDICATIVE	PAST INDEFINITE
am I?	*have I been? was I?*

suis-je ?	ai-je été ?
es-tu ?	as-tu été ?
est-il ? est-elle ?	a-t-il été ? a-t-elle été ?
sommes-nous ?	avons-nous été ?
êtes-vous ?	avez-vous été ?
sont-ils ? sont-elles ?	ont-ils été ? ont-elles été ?

<table>
<tr><th>IMPERFECT
was I?</th><th>PLUPERFECT
had I been?</th></tr>
</table>

IMPERFECT *was I?*	PLUPERFECT *had I been?*
étais-je ?	avais-je été ?
étais-tu ?	avais-tu été ?
était-il ? était-elle ?	avait-il été ? avait-elle été ?
étions-nous ?	avions-nous été ?
étiez-vous ?	aviez-vous été ?
étaient-ils ? étaient-elles ?	avaient-ils (elles) été ?

PAST DEFINITE *was I?*	PAST ANTERIOR *had I been?*
fus-je ?	eus-je été ?
fus-tu ?	eus-tu été ?
fut-il ? fut-elle ?	eut-il été ? eut-elle été ?
fûmes-nous ?	eûmes-nous été ?
fûtes-vous ?	eûtes-vous été ?
furent-ils ? furent-elles ?	eurent-ils (elles) été ?

FUTURE *shall I be?*	FUTURE ANTERIOR *shall I have been?*
serai-je ?	aurai-je été ?
seras-tu ?	auras-tu été ?
sera-t-il ? sera-t-elle ?	aura-t-il été ? aura-t-elle été ?
serons-nous ?	aurons-nous été ?
serez-vous ?	aurez-vous été ?
seront-ils ? seront-elles ?	auront-ils (elles) été ?

CONDITIONAL PRESENT *should I be?*	CONDITIONAL PAST *should I have been?*
serais-je ?	aurais-je été ?
serais-tu ?	aurais-tu été ?
serait-il ? serait-elle ?	aurait-il été ? aurait-elle été ?
serions-nous ?	aurions-nous été ?
seriez-vous ?	auriez-vous été ?
seraient-ils ? seraient-elles ?	auraient-ils (elles) été ?

VII. Etre used negatively

INDICATIVE PRESENT *I am not.*	PAST INDEFINITE *I have not been, I was not.*
je ne suis pas.	je n'ai pas été.
tu n'es pas.	tu n'as pas été.
il or elle n'est pas.	il or elle n'a pas été.
nous ne sommes pas.	nous n'avons pas été.
vous n'êtes pas.	vous n'avez pas été.
ils or elles ne sont pas.	ils or elles n'ont pas été.

IMPERFECT
I was not.

je n'étais pas.
tu n'étais pas.
il or elle n'était pas.
nous n'étions pas.
vous n'étiez pas.
ils or elles n'étaient pas.

PAST DEFINITE
I was not.

je ne fus pas.
tu ne fus pas.
il or elle ne fut pas.
nous ne fûmes pas.
vous ne fûtes pas.
ils or elles ne furent pas.

FUTURE
I shall not be.

je ne serai pas.
tu ne seras pas.
il or elle ne sera pas.
nous ne serons pas.
vous ne serez pas.
ils or elles ne seront pas.

CONDITIONAL PRESENT
I should not be.

je ne serais pas.
tu ne serais pas.
il or elle ne serait pas.
nous ne serions pas.
vous ne seriez pas.
ils or elles ne seraient pas.

SUBJUNCTIVE PRESENT
(that) I may not be.

que je ne sois pas.
que tu ne sois pas.
qu'il (elle) ne soit pas.
que nous ne soyons pas.
que vous ne soyez pas.
ou'ils (elles) ne soient pas.

PLUPERFECT
I had not been.

je n'avais pas été.
tu n'avais pas été.
il or elle n'avait pas été.
nous n'avions pas été.
vous n'aviez pas été.
ils or elles n'avaient pas été.

PAST ANTERIOR
I had not been.

je n'eus pas été.
tu n'eus pas été.
il or elle n'eut pas été.
nous n'eûmes pas été.
vous n'eûtes pas été.
ils or elles n'eurent pas été.

FUTURE ANTERIOR
I shall not have been.

je n'aurais pas été.
tu n'auras pas été.
il or elle n'aura pas été.
nous n'aurons pas été.
vous n'aurez pas été.
ils or elles n'auront pas été.

CONDITIONAL PAST
I should not have been.

je n'aurais pas été.
tu n'aurais pas été.
il or elle n'aurait pas été.
nous n'aurions pas été.
vous n'auriez pas été.
ils or elles n'auraient pas été.

SUBJUNCTIVE PAST
(that) I might not have been.

que je n'aie pas été.
que tu n'aies pas été.
qu'il (elle) n'ait pas été.
que nous n'ayons pas été.
que vous n'ayez pas été.
qu'ils (elles) n'aient pas été.

SUBJUNCTIVE IMPERFECT	SUBJUNCTIVE PLUPERFECT
(that) I might not be.	*(that) I might not have been.*
que je ne fusse pas.	que je n'eusse pas été.
que tu ne fusses pas.	que tu n'eusses pas été.
qu'il or qu'elle ne fût pas.	qu'il or qu'elle n'eût pas été.
que nous ne fussions pas.	que nous n'eussions pas été.
que vous ne fussiez pas.	que vous n'eussiez pas été.
qu'ils (elles) ne fussent pas.	qu'ils (elles) n'eussent pas été.

IMPERATIVE

SINGULAR	PLURAL
	ne soyons pas, *let us not be.*
ne sois pas, *do not be.*	ne soyez pas, *be not, do not be.*
(qu'il ne soit pas, *let him not be.*)	(qu'ils ne soient pas, *let them not be.*)

VIII. Etre used negatively and interrogatively

INDICATIVE PRESENT	PAST INDEFINITE
am I not?	*have I not been? was I not?*
ne suis-je pas?	n'ai-je pas été?
n'es-tu pas?	n'as-tu pas été?
n'est-il pas? n'est-elle pas?	n'a-t-il pas été? n'a-t-elle pas été?
ne sommes-nous pas?	n'avons-nous pas été?
n'êtes-vous pas?	n'avez-vous pas été?
ne sont-ils (elles) pas?	n'ont-ils (elles) pas été?

IMPERFECT	PLUPERFECT
was I not?	*had I not been?*
n'étais-je pas?	n'avais-je pas été?
etc.	etc.

PAST ANTERIOR	PAST DEFINITE
was I not?	*had I not been?*
ne fus-je pas?	n'eus-je pas été?
etc.	etc.

FUTURE	FUTURE ANTERIOR
shall I not be?	*shall I not have been?*
ne serai-je pas?	n'aurai-je pas été?
etc.	etc.

CONDITIONAL PRESENT	CONDITIONAL PAST
should I not be?	*should I not have been?*
ne serais-je pas?	n'aurais-je pas été?
etc.	etc.

IX. Terminations of the three regular conjugations

Conjugation	Infinitive	Present Participle	Past Participle	Present Indicative	Imperfect	Preterite
1.	er	ant	é	e es e ons ez ent	ais ais ait ions iez aient	ai as a âmes âtes èrent
2.	ir	(iss)ant	i	is is it issons issez issent	ais ais ait ions iez aient	is is it îmes îtes irent
3.	re	ant	u	s s t ons ez ent	ais ais ait ions iez aient	is is it îmes îtes irent

Observations on these terminations

(1) All verbs in the French language terminate in the same way in four of their tenses :

The present participle in -ant.

The imperfect and the conditional in -ais, -ais, -ait, -ions, -iez, -aient.

The future in -ai, -as, -a, -ons, -ez, -ont.

(2) The endings of the future and of the conditional are always preceded by r.

Terminations of the three regular conjugations

Future	Conditional	Imperative	Subjunctive Present	Subjunctive Imperfect
ai	ais		e	asse
as	ais	e	es	asses
a	ait	e	e	ât
ons	ions	ons	ions	assions
ez	iez	ez	iez	assiez
ont	aient	ent	ent	assent
ai	ais		isse	isse
as	ais	is	isses	isses
a	ait	isse	isse	ît
ons	ions	issons	issions	issions
ez	iez	issez	issiez	issiez
ont	aient	issent	issent	issent
ai	ais		e	isse
as	ais	s	es	isses
a	ait	e	e	ît
ons	ions	ons	ions	issions
ez	iez	ez	iez	issiez
ont	aient	ent	ent	issent

(3) The termination of the past participle is most important, as all compound tenses are formed by that participle preceded by **avoir** or **être**.

(4) Three forms of the imperative are like the corresponding persons of the present indicative. It must, however, be remarked that the **s** of the second person singular of the present indicative in verbs of the 1st conjugation does not appear in the imperative. The third person, singular and plural, is taken from the present subjunctive.

X. The three conjugations

First Verbs in **-er**	Second Verbs in **-ir**	Third Verbs in **-re**

PRESENT INFINITIVE

| porter, *to carry.* | finir, *to finish.* | rendre, *to give back.* |

PAST INFINITIVE

| avoir porté. | avoir fini. | avoir rendu. |

PRESENT PARTICIPLE

| portant. | finissant. | rendant. |

PAST PARTICIPLE

| porté. | fini. | rendu. |

PRESENT INDICATIVE

je porte.	je finis.	je rends.
tu portes.	tu finis.	tu rends.
il porte.	il finit.	il rend.
nous portons.	nous finissons.	nous rendons.
vous portez.	vous finissez.	vous rendez.
ils portent.	ils finissent.	ils rendent.

PAST INDEFINITE

j'ai porté.	j'ai fini.	j'ai rendu.
tu as porté.	tu as fini.	tu a rendu.
il a porté.	il a fini.	il a rendu.
nous avons porté.	nous avons fini.	nous avons rendu.
vous avez porté.	vous avez fini.	vous avez rendu.
ils ont porté.	ils ont fini.	ils ont rendu.

IMPERFECT INDICATIVE (*Descriptive Past*)

je portais.	je finissais.	je rendais.
tu portais.	tu finissais.	tu rendais.
il portait.	il finissait.	il rendait.
nous portions.	nous finissions.	nous rendions.
vous portiez.	vous finissiez.	vous rendiez.
ils portaient.	ils finissaient.	ils rendaient.

PLUPERFECT

j'avais porté.	j'avais fini.	j'avais rendu.
tu avais porté.	tu avais fini.	tu avais rendu.
il avait porté.	il avait fini.	il avait rendu.
nous avions porté.	nous avions fini.	nous avions rendu.
vous aviez porté.	vous aviez fini.	vous aviez rendu.
ils avaient porte.	ils avaient fini.	ils avaient rendu.

First	Second	Third

PAST DEFINITE (*Preterite or Narrative Past*)

je portai.	je finis.	je rendis.
tu portas.	tu finis.	tu rendis.
il porta.	il finit.	il rendit.
nous portâmes.	nous finîmes.	nous rendîmes.
vous portâtes.	vous finîtes.	vous rendîtes.
ils portèrent.	ils finirent.	ils rendirent.

PAST ANTERIOR

j'eus porté.	j'eus fini.	j'eus rendu.
tu eus porté.	tu eus fin.	tu eus rendu.
il eut porté.	il eut fini.	il eut rendu.
nous eûmes porté.	nous eûmes fini.	nous eûmes rendu.
vous eûtes porté.	vous eûtes fini.	vous eûtes rendu.
ils eurent porté.	ils eurent fini.	ils eurent rendu.

FUTURE

je porterai.	je finirai.	je rendrai.
tu porteras.	tu finiras.	tu rendras.
il portera.	il finira.	il rendra.
nous porterons.	nous finirons.	nous rendrons.
vous porterez.	vous finirez.	vous rendrez.
ils porteront.	ils finiront.	ils rendront.

FUTURE ANTERIOR

j'aurai porté.	j'aurai fini.	j'aurai rendu.
tu auras porté.	tu auras fini.	tu auras rendu.
il aura porté.	il aura fini.	il aura rendu.
nous aurons porté.	nous aurons fini.	nous aurons rendu.
vous aurez porté.	vous aurez fini.	vous aurez rendu.
ils auront porté.	ils auront fini.	ils auront rendu.

CONDITIONAL PRESENT

je porterais.	je finirais.	je rendrais.
tu porterais.	tu finirais.	tu rendrais.
il porterait.	il finirait.	il rendrait.
nous porterions.	nous finirions.	nous rendrions.
vous porteriez.	vous finiriez.	vous rendriez.
ils porteraient.	ils finiraient.	ils rendraient.

CONDITIONAL PAST

j'aurais porté.	j'aurais fini.	j'aurais rendu.
tu aurais porté.	tu aurais fini.	tu aurais rendu.
il aurait porté.	il aurait fini.	il aurait rendu.
nous aurions porté.	nous aurions fini.	nous aurions rendu
vous auriez porté.	vous auriez fini.	vous auriez rendu.
ils auraient porté.	ils auraient fini.	ils auraient rendu.

First	Second	Third

SUBJUNCTIVE PRESENT

First	Second	Third
que je porte.	que je finisse.	que je rende.
que tu portes.	que tu finisses.	que tu rendes.
qu'il porte.	qu'il finisse.	qu'il rende.
que nous portions.	que nous finissions.	que nous rendions.
que vous portiez.	que vous finissiez.	que vous rendiez.
qu'ils portent.	qu'ils finissent.	qu'ils rendent.

SUBJUNCTIVE PAST

First	Second	Third
que j'aie porté.	que j'aie fini.	que j'aie rendu.
que tu aies porté.	que tu aies fini.	que tu aies rendu.
qu'il ait porté.	qu'il ait fini.	qu'il ait rendu.
que nous ayons porté.	que nous ayons fini.	que nous ayons rendu.
que vous ayez porté.	que vous ayez fini.	que vous ayez rendu.
qu'ils aient porté.	qu'ils aient fini.	qu'ils aient rendu.

SUBJUNCTIVE IMPERFECT

First	Second	Third
que je portasse.	que je finisse.	que je rendisse.
que tu portasses.	que tu finisses.	que tu rendisses.
qu'il portât.	qu'il finît.	qu'il rendît.
que nous portassions.	que nous finissions.	que nous rendissions.
que vous portassiez.	que vous finissiez.	que vous rendissiez.
qu'ils portassent.	qu'ils finissent.	qu'ils rendissent.

SUBJUNCTIVE PLUPERFECT

First	Second	Third
que j'eusse porté.	que j'eusse fini.	que j'eusse rendu.
que tu eusses porté.	que tu eusses fini.	que tu eusses rendu.
qu'il eût porté.	qu'il eût fini.	qu'il eût rendu.
que nous eussions porté.	que nous eussions fini.	que nous eussions rendu.
que vous eussiez porté.	que vous eussiez fini.	que vous eussiez rendu.
qu'ils eussent porté.	qu'ils eussent fini.	qu'ils eussent rendu.

IMPERATIVE

First	Second	Third
porte.	finis.	rends.
(qu'il porte.)	(qu'il finisse.)	(qu'il rende.)
portons.	finissons.	rendons.
portez.	finissez.	rendez.
(qu'ils portent.)	(qu'ils finissent.)	(qu'ils rendent.)

XI. Peculiarities in verbs of the first conjugation

All the verbs of the 1st conjugation, but two, are regular, and consequently conjugated like **porter**. But a few, besides those which have been seen in Lessons 69, 70, present some peculiarities :

(1) Verbs in -ier, such as **prier, crier, oublier,** have two consecutive **i**'s in the 1st and 2d persons plural of the imperfect indicative and present subjunctive : **priions, priiez, criions, criiez, oubliions, oubliiez;** the first **i** belongs to the root, the second to the termination.

(2) In verbs in -yer, after the **y** of the root, there is an **i** belonging to the termination in the same parts of the verb : **employions, employiez.**

XII. The passive form

Verbs have two Voices, namely :

The Active Voice, when the subject does something, as, —

Mon père me punit.	*My father punishes me.*
Mon père m'a puni.	*My father has punished me.*

The Passive Voice, when the subject has something done to it, as, —

Je suis puni par mon père.	*I am punished by my father.*
J'ai été puni par mon père.	*I was punished by my father.*

Only transitive verbs have a passive voice. The passive is used much less frequently than in English, its place being taken by **on** with the active or by a reflexive construction.

Conjugation of the passive verb être frappé

PRESENT INFINITIVE	PAST INFINITIVE
être frappé, *to be struck.*	**avoir été frappé,** *to have been struck.*

PRESENT PARTICIPLE	PAST PARTICIPLE
étant frappé, *being struck.*	**ayant été frappé,** *having been struck.*

PRESENT INDICATIVE	PAST INDEFINITE
I am struck, etc.	*I have been struck, I was struck, etc.*
je suis frappé (ée).	j'ai été frappé (ée).
tu es frappé (ée).	tu as été frappé (ée).
il (elle) est frappé (ée).	il (elle) a été frappé (ée).
nous sommes frappés (ées).	nous avons été frappés (ées).
vous êtes frappés (ées).	vous avez été frappés (ées).
ils (elles) sont frappés (ées).	ils (elles) ont été frappés (ées).

IMPERFECT	PLUPERFECT
I was struck.	*I had been struck.*
j'étais frappé (ée).	j'avais été frappé (ée).

XIII. Conjugation of a reflexive verb

PRESENT INFINITIVE	PAST INFINITIVE
se laver, *to wash one's self.*	s'être lavé, *to have washed one's self.*

PRESENT PARTICIPLE	PAST PARTICIPLE
se lavant, *washing one's self.*	s'étant lavé, *having washed one's self.*

PRESENT INDICATIVE	PAST INDEFINITE
I wash myself.	*I have washed myself.*
je me lave.	je me suis lavé (ée).
tu te laves.	tu t'es lavé (ée).
il se lave.	il (elle) s'est lavé (ée).
nous nous lavons.	nous nous sommes lavés (ées).
vous vous lavez.	vous vous êtes lavés (ées).
ils se lavent.	ils (elles) se sont lavés (ées).

IMPERFECT	PLUPERFECT
I was washing myself.	*I had washed myself.*
je me lavais.	je m'étais lavé (ée).

IMPERATIVE

	lavons-nous, *let us wash ourselves.*
lave-toi, *wash thyself.*	lavez-vous, *wash yourselves (yourself).*
(qu'il se lave, *let him wash himself.*)	(qu'ils se lavent, *let them wash themselves.*)

Observe that the pronoun object is placed after the imperative. See Lesson 32. If the imperative is negative, the pronoun is placed before, according to the general rule, as :

> ne nous lavons pas, *let us not wash ourselves.*
> ne vous lavez pas, *do not wash yourselves (yourself).*

XIV. Conjugation of a reciprocal verb

PRESENT INDICATIVE

	Speaking of two persons only	Speaking of more than two
nous nous flattons	l'un l'autre,	les uns les autres.
vous vous flattez	l'un l'autre,	les uns les autres.
ils se flattent	l'un l'autre,	les uns les autres.

All through the conjugation, put **l'une l'autre** if speaking of *two feminine* subjects, and **les unes les autres** if speaking of more than two.

PAST INDEFINITE

nous nous sommes flattés	l'un l'autre,	les uns les autres.
vous vous êtes flattés	l'un l'autre,	les uns les autres.
ils se sont flattés	l'un l'autre,	les uns les autres.

IMPERFECT

nous nous flattions	l'un l'autre,	les uns les autres.
vous vous flattiez	l'un l'autre,	les uns les autres.
ils se flattaient	l'un l'autre,	les uns les autres.

And so on to the

IMPERATIVE AFFIRMATIVE

flattons-nous	l'un l'autre,	les uns les autres.
flattez-vous	l'un l'autre,	les uns les autres.
qu'ils se flattent	l'un l'autre,	les uns les autres.

IMPERATIVE NEGATIVE

ne nous flattons pas	l'un l'autre,	les uns les autres.
ne vous flattez pas	l'un l'autre,	les uns les autres.
qu'ils ne se flattent pas	l'un l'autre,	les uns les autres.

If the reciprocal verb requires the preposition **à** before its object, it is conjugated in this way :

PRESENT INDICATIVE
We speak to each other.

nous nous parlons	l'un à l'autre,	les uns aux autres.
vous vous parlez	l'un à l'autre,	les uns aux autres.
ils se parlent	l'un à l'autre,	les uns aux autres.

If the reciprocal verb requires any other preposition before its object, the preposition is likewise placed between **l'un** and **l'autre,** or **les uns** and **les autres,** as :

PAST INDEFINITE
We fought against each other.

nous nous sommes battus	l'un contre l'autre,	les uns contre les autres.
vous vous êtes battus	l'un contre l'autre,	les uns contre les autres.
ils se sont battus	l'un contre l'autre,	les uns contre les autres.

Infinitive and Participles	Indicative			
	PRESENT	IMPERFECT	PAST DEFINITE	FUTURE
Acquérir	acquier s	acquér ais	acqu is	acquer rai
acquérant	acquier s	acquér ais	acqu is	acquer ras
acquis	acquier t	acquér ait	acqu it	acquer ra
To acquire	acquér ons	acquér ions	acqu îmes	acquer rons
	acquér ez	acquér iez	acqu îtes	acquer rez
	acquièr ent	acquér aient	acqu irent	acquer ront
Aller	vai s	all ais	all ai	i rai
allant	va s	all ais	all as	i ras
allé*	va	all ait	all a	i ra
To go	all ons	all ions	all âmes	i rons
	all ez	all iez	all âtes	i rez
	vont	all aient	all èrent	i ront
Assaillir	assaill e	assaill ais	assaill is	assailli rai
assaillant	assaill es	assaill ais	assaill is	assailli ras
assailli	assaill e	assaill ait	assaill it	assailli ra
To assault	assaill ons	assaill ions	assaill îmes	assailli rons
(*assail*)	assaill ez	assaill iez	assaill îtes	assailli rez
	assaill ent	assaill aient	assaill irent	assailli ront
Asseoir	assied s	assey ais	ass is	assié rai
asseyant	assied s	assey ais	ass is	assié ras
assis	assied	assey ait	ass it	assié ra
(reflexive)	assey ons	assey ions	ass îmes	assié rons
To sit	assey ez	assey iez	ass îtes	assié rez
	assey ent	assey aient	ass irent	assié ront
Battre	bat s	batt ais	batt is	batt rai
battant	bat s	batt ais	batt is	batt ras
battu	bat	batt ait	batt it	batt ra
To beat	batt ons	batt ions	batt îmes	batt rons
	batt ez	batt iez	batt îtes	batt rez
	batt ent	batt aient	batt irent	batt ront

*Verbs or past participles marked with a * are conjugated with **être**.

irregular verbs

Conditional	Imperative	Subjunctive		Verbs Conjugated in Same Manner
		PRESENT	IMPERFECT	
acquer rais	——	acquièr e	acquis se	Conquérir
acquer rais	acquier s	acquièr es	acquis ses	Enquérir (s') *
acquer rait	——	acquièr e	acqu ît	Reconquérir
acquer rions	acquér ons	acquér ions	acquis sions	Requérir
acquer riez	acquér ez	acquér iez	acquis siez	
acquer raient	——	acquièr ent	acquis sent	
i rais	——	aill e	allas se	
i rais	va	aill es	allas ses	
i rait	——	aill e	all ât	Aller (s'en) *
i rions	all ons	all ions	allas sions	
i riez	all ez	all iez	allas siez	
i raient	——	aill ent	allas sent	
assailli rais	——	assaill e	assaillis se	Faillir
assailli rais	assaill e	assaill es	assaillis ses	Tressaillir
assailli rait	——	assaill e	assaill ît	
assailli rions	assaill ons	assaill ions	assaillis sions	
assailli riez	assaill ez	assaill iez	assaillis siez	
assailli raient	——	assaill ent	assaillis sent	
assié rais	——	assey e	assis se	Rasseoir (se) *
assié rais	assied s	assey es	assis ses	Surseoir
assié rait	——	assey e	ass ît	In the future and con-ditional, one may also
assié rions	assey ons	assey ions	assis sions	say, *j'asseyerai*, *j'as-*
assié riez	assey ez	assey iez	assis siez	*soirai*, etc., *j'asseyerais*,
assié raient	——	assey ent	assis sent	*j'assoirais*, etc.
batt rais	——	batt e	battis se	Abattre
batt rais	bat s	batt es	battis ses	Battre (se) *
batt rait	——	batt e	batt ît	Combattre
batt rions	batt ons	batt ions	battis sions	Débattre
batt riez	batt ez	batt iez	battis siez	Débattre (se) *
batt raient	——	batt ent	battis sent	Ebattre (s') *
				Rabattre
				Rebattre

List of

Infinitive and Participles	Indicative			
	PRESENT	IMPERFECT	PAST DEFINITE	FUTURE
Boire	boi s	buv ais	b us	boi rai
buvant	boi s	buv ais	b us	boi ras
bu	boi t	buv ait	b ut	boi ra
To drink	buv ons	buv ions	b ûmes	boi rons
	buv ez	buv iez	b ûtes	boi rez
	boiv ent	buv aient	b urent	boi ront
Bouillir	bou s	bouill ais	bouill is	bouilli rai
bouillant	bou s	bouill ais	bouill is	bouilli ras
bouilli	bou t	bouill ait	bouill it	bouilli ra
To boil	bouill ons	bouill ions	bouill îmes	bouilli rons
	bouill ez	bouill iez	bouill îtes	bouilli rez
	bouill ent	bouill aient	bouill irent	bouilli ront
Conclure	conclu s	conclu ais	concl us	conclu rai
concluant	conclu s	conclu ais	concl us	conclu ras
conclu	conclu t	conclu ait	concl ut	conclu ra
To conclude	conclu ons	conclu ions	concl ûmes	conclu rons
	conclu ez	conclu iez	concl ûtes	conclu rez
	conclu ent	conclu aient	concl urent	conclu ront
Conduire	condui s	conduis ais	conduis is	condui rai
conduisant	condui s	conduis ais	conduis is	condui ras
conduit	condui t	conduis ait	conduis it	condui ra
To conduct	conduis ons	conduis ions	conduis îmes	condui rons
	conduis ez	conduis iez	conduis îtes	condui rez
	conduis ent	conduis aient	conduis irent	condui ront
Connaître	connai s	connaiss ais	conn us	connaît rai
connaissant	connai s	connaiss ais	conn us	connaît ras
connu	connaî t	connaiss ait	conn ut	connaît ra
To know (be	connaiss ons	connaiss ions	conn ûmes	connaît rons
acquainted	connaiss ez	connaiss iez	conn ûtes	connaît rez
with)	connaiss ent	connaiss aient	conn urent	connaît ront

irregular verbs

Conditional	Imperative	Subjunctive		Verbs Conjugated in Same Manner
		PRESENT	IMPERFECT	
boi rais	——	boiv e	bus se	
boi rais	boi s	boiv es	bus ses	
boi rait	——	boiv e	b ût	Reboire
boi rions	buv ons	buv ions	bus sions	
ɔoi riez	buv ez	buv iez	bus siez	
boi raient	——	boiv ent	bus sent	
bouilli rais	——	bouill e	bouillis se	Rebouillir
bouilli rais	bou s	bouill es	bouillis ses	*Bouillir* is used with
bouilli rait	——	bouill e	bouill ît	*faire: je fais bouillir le*
bouilli rions	bouill ons	bouill ions	bouillis sions	*lait.*
bouilli riez	bouill ez	bouill iez	bouillis siez	
bouilli raient	——	bouill ent	bouillis sent	
conclu rais	——	conclu e	conclus se	
conclu rais	conclu s	conclu es	conclus ses	
conclu rait	——	conclu e	concl ût	Exclure
conclu rions	conclu ons	conclu ions	conclus sions	Inclure
conclu riez	conclu ez	conclu iez	conclus siez	
conclu raient	——	conclu ent	conclus sent	
condui rais	——	conduis e	conduisis se	Déduire Produire
condui rais	condui s	conduis es	conduisis ses	Econduire Réduire
condui rait	——	conduis e	conduis ît	Introduire Traduire
condui rions	conduis ons	conduis ions	conduisis sions	Construire Détruire
condui riez	conduis ez	conduis iez	conduisis siez	Cuire Instruire
condui raient	——	conduis ent	conduisis sent	and their compounds.
connaît rais	——	connaiss e	connus se	Apparaître
connaît rais	connai s	connaiss es	connus ses	Comparaître
connaît rait	——	connaiss e	conn ût	Disparaître
connaît rions	connaiss ons	connaiss ions	connus sions	Méconnaître
connaît riez	connaiss ez	connaiss iez	connus siez	Paraître
connaît raient	——	connaiss ent	connus sent	Reconnaître Reparaître

Infinitive and Participles	Indicative			
	PRESENT	IMPERFECT	PAST DEFINITE	FUTURE
Coudre	coud s	cous ais	cous is	coud rai
cousant	coud s	cous ais	cous is	coud ras
cousu	coud	cous ait	cous it	coud ra
To sew	cous ons	cous ions	cous îmes	coud rons
	cous ez	cous iez	cous îtes	coud rez
	cous ent	cous aient	cous irent	coud ront
Courir	cour s	cour ais	cour us	cour rai
courant	cour s	cour ais	cour us	cour ras
couru	cour t	cour ait	cour ut	cour ra
To run	cour ons	cour ions	cour ûmes	cour rons
	cour ez	cour iez	cour ûtes	cour rez
	cour ent	cour aient	cour urent	cour ront
Craindre [1]	crain s	craign ais	craign is	craind rai
craignant	crain s	craign ais	craign is	craind ras
craint	crain t	craign ait	craign it	craind ra
To fear	craign ons	craign ions	craign îmes	craind rons
	craign ez	craign iez	craign îtes	craind rez
	craign ent	craign aient	craign irent	craind ront
Croire	croi s	croy ais	cr us	croi rai
croyant	croi s	croy ais	cr us	croi ras
cru	croi t	croy ait	cr ut	croi ra
To believe	croy ons	croy ions	cr ûmes	croi rons
	croy ez	croy iez	cr ûtes	croi rez
	croi ent	croy aient	cr urent	croi ront
Croître [2]	croî s	croiss ais	cr ûs	croît rai
croissant	croî s	croiss ais	cr ûs	croît ras
crû	croî t	croiss ait	cr ût	croît ra
To grow	croiss ons	croiss ions	cr ûmes	croît rons
	croiss ez	croiss iez	cr ûtes	croît rez
	croiss ent	croiss aient	cr ûrent	croît ron

[1] The verbs ending in **aindre** or **eindre** preserve the **d** only in the future and conditional present.

[2] When **croître** is spelled as **croire**, a circumflex accent is placed over the **i** or the **u** to distinguish it from **crois**. **Je crois** without accent means I *believe*, and **Je croîs** with accent *I grow*.

irregular verbs

Conditional	Imperative	Subjunctive		Verbs Conjugated in Same Manner
		PRESENT	IMPERFECT	
coud rais	——	cous e	cousis se	
coud rais	coud s	cous es	cousis ses	
coud rait	——	cous e	cousis ît	Découdre
coud rions	cous ons	cous ions	cousis sions	Recoudre
coud riez	cous ez	cous iez	cousis siez	
coud raient	——	cous ent	cousis sent	
cour rais	——	cour e	courus se	Accourir
cour rais	cour s	cour es	courus ses	Concourir
cour rait	——	cour e	cour ût	Discourir
cour rions	cour ons	cour ions	courus sions	Encourir
cour riez	cour ez	cour iez	courus siez	Parcourir
cour raient	——	cour ent	courus sent	Recourir Secourir
craind rais	——	craign e	craignis se	Adjoindre
craind rais	crain s	craign es	craignis ses	Contraindre
craind rait	——	craign e	craignis ît	Enjoindre
craind rions	craign ons	craign ions	craignis sions	Joindre
craind riez	craign ez	craign iez	craignis siez	Plaindre
craind raient	——	craign ent	craignis sent	Se plaindre Rejoindre
croi rais	——	croi e	crus se	
croi rais	croi s	croi es	crus ses	
croi rait	——	croi e	cr ût	
croi rions	croy ons	croy ions	crus sions	
croi riez	croy ez	croy iez	crus siez	
croi raient	——	croi ent	crus sent	
croît rais	——	croiss e	crûs se	
croît rais	croî s	croiss es	crûs ses	
croît rait	——	croiss e	cr ût	Accroître
croît rions	croiss ons	croiss ions	crûs sions	Décroître
croît riez	croiss ez	croiss iez	crûs siez	Recroître
croît raient	——	croiss ent	crûs sent	

Infinitive and Participles	Indicative			
	PRESENT	IMPERFECT	PAST DEFINITE	FUTURE
Cueillir	cueill e	cueill ais	cueill is	cueille rai
cueillant	cueill es	cueill ais	cueill is	cueille ras
cueilli	cueill e	cueill ait	cueill it	cueille ra
To gather	cueill ons	cueill ions	cueill îmes	cueille rons
	cueill ez	cueill iez	cueill îtes	cueille rez
	cueill ent	cueill aient	cueill irent	cueille ront
Devoir	doi s	dev ais	d us	dev rai
devant	doi s	dev ais	d us	dev ras
dû due	doi t	dev ait	d ut	dev ra
To owe	dev ons	dev ions	d ûmes	dev rons
(*must, ought,*	dev ez	dev iez	d ûtes	dev rez
etc.)	doiv ent	dev aient	d urent	dev ront
Dire	di s	dis ais	d is	di rai
disant	di s	dis ais	d is	di ras
dit	di t	dis ait	d it	di ra
To say (*tell*)	dis ons	dis ions	d îmes	di rons
	di tes	dis iez	d îtes	di rez
	dis ent	dis aient	d irent	di ront
Dormir	dor s	dorm ais	dorm is	dormi rai
dormant	dor s	dorm ais	dorm is	dormi ras
dormi	dor t	dorm ait	dorm it	dormi ra
To sleep	dorm ons	dorm ions	dorm îmes	dormi rons
	dorm ez	dorm iez	dorm îtes	dormi rez
	dorm ent	dorm aient	dorm irent	dormi ront
Écrire	écri s	écriv ais	écriv is	écri rai
écrivant	écri s	écriv ais	écriv is	écri ras
écrit	écri t	écriv ait	écriv it	écri ra
To write	écriv ons	écriv ions	écriv îmes	écri rons
	écriv ez	écriv iez	écriv îtes	écri rez
	écriv ent	écriv aient	écriv irent	écri ront

irregular verbs

Conditional	Imperative	Subjunctive		Verbs Conjugated in Same Manner
		PRESENT	IMPERFECT	
cueille rais	——	cueill e	cueillis se	
cueille rais	cueill e	cueill es	cueillis ses	
cueille rait	——	cueill e	cueill ît	Accueillir
cueille rions	cueill ons	cueill ions	cueillis sions	Recueillir
cueille riez	cueill ez	cueill iez	cueillis siez	Se recueillir *
cueille raient	——	cueill ent	cueillis sent	
dev rais	——	doiv e	dus se	
dev rais	doi s	doiv es	dus ses	Redevoir
dev rait	——	doiv e	d ût	*See* Recevoir.
dev rions	dev ons	dev ions	dus sions	
dev riez	dev ez	dev iez	dus siez	
dev raient	——	doiv ent	dus sent	
				Redire
				The following are conjugated like *dire* except in second person plural present indicative and imperative (*contredisez*, etc.): —
di rais	——	dis e	dis se	
di rais	di s	dis es	dis ses	
di rait	——	dis e	dî t	
di rions	dis ons	dis ions	dis sions	Contredire Interdire
di riez	di tes	dis iez	dis siez	Se dédire Médire
di raient	——	dis ent	dis sent	Prédire
				Maudire makes *maudissant, nous maudissons, je maudissais.*
dormi rais	——	dorm e	dormis se	
dormi rais	dor s	dorm es	dormis ses	
dormi rait	——	dorm e	dorm ît	
dormi rions	dorm ons	dorm ions	dormis sions	Endormir
dormi riez	dorm ez	dorm iez	dormis siez	S'endormir
dormi raient	——	dorm ent	dormis sent	Se rendormir
écri rais	——	écriv e	écrivis se	
écri rais	écri s	écriv es	écrivis ses	Circonscrire
écri rait	——	écriv e	écriv ît	Décrire
écri rions	écriv ons	écriv ions	écrivis sions	Inscrire
écri riez	écriv ez	écriv iez	écrivis siez	Prescrire
écri raient	——	écriv ent	écrivis sent	Proscrire
				Souscrire
				Transcrire

List of

Infinitive and Participles	Indicative			
	PRESENT	IMPERFECT	PAST DEFINITE	FUTURE
Envoyer	envoi e	envoy ais	envoy ai	enver rai
envoyant	envoi es	envoy ais	envoy as	enver ras
envoyé	envoi e	envoy ait	envoy a	enver ra
To send	envoy ons	envoy ions	envoy âmes	enver rons
	envoy ez	envoy iez	envoy âtes	enver rez
	envoi ent	envoy aient	envoy èrent	enver ront
Faire	fai s	fais ais	f is	fe rai
faisant	fai s	fais ais	f is	fe ras
fait	fai t	fais ait	f it	fe ra
To do	fais ons	fais ions	f îmes	fe rons
(make)	fai tes	fais iez	f îtes	fe rez
	f ont	fais aient	f irent	fe ront
Fuir	fui s	fuy ais	fu is	fui rai
fuyant	fui s	fuy ais	fu is	fui ras
fui	fui t	fuy ait	fu it	fui ra
To flee	fuy ons	fuy ions	fu îmes	fui rons
	fuy ez	fuy iez	fu îtes	fui rez
	fui ent	fuy aient	fu irent	fui ront
Lire	li s	lis ais	l us	li rai
lisant	li s	lis ais	l us	li ras
lu	li t	lis ait	l ut	li ra
To read	lis ons	lis ions	l ûmes	li rons
	lis ez	lis iez	l ûtes	li rez
	lis ent	lis aient	l urent	li ront
Mettre	met s	mett ais	m is	mett rai
mettant	met s	mett ais	m is	mett ras
[mis	met	mett ait	m it	mett ra
To put	mett ons	mett ions	m îmes	mett rons
	mett ez	mett iez	m îtes	mett rez
	mett ent	mett aient	m irent	mett ront

irregular verbs

Conditional	Imperative	Subjunctive		Verbs Conjugated in Same Manner
		PRESENT	IMPERFECT	
enver rais	——	envoi e	envoyas se	
enver rais	envoi e	envoi es	envoyas ses	
enver rait	——	envoi e	envoy ât	Renvoyer
enver rions	envoy ons	envoy ions	envoyas sions	
enver riez	envoy ez	envoy iez	envoyas siez	
enver raient	——	envoi ent	envoyas sent	
fe rais	——	fass e	fis se	
fe rais	fai s	fass es	fis ses	Contrefaire Parfaire
fe rait	——	fass e	f ît	Défaire Refaire
fe rions	fais ons	fass ions	fis sions	Défaire (se*) Satisfaire
fe riez	fai tes	fass iez	fis siez	Surfaire
fe raient	——	fass ent	fis sent	
fui rais	——	fui e	fuis se	
fui rais	fui s	fui es	fuis ses	
fui rait	——	fui e	fu ît	
fui rions	fuy ons	fuy ions	fuis sions	S'enfuir *
fui riez	fuy ez	fuy iez	fuis siez	
fui raient	——-	fui ent	fuis sent	
li rais	——	lis e	lus se	
li rais	li s	lis es	lus ses	
li rait	——	lis e	l ût	Élire
li rions	lis ons	lis ions	lus sions	Réélire
li riez	lis ez	lis iez	lus siez	Relire
li raient	——	lis ent	lus sent	
mett rais	——	mett e	mis se	Admettre Premettre
mett rais	met s	mett es	mis ses	Commettre Remettre
mett rait	——	mett e	m ît	Démettre Soumettre
mett rions	mett ons	mett ions	mis sions	Omettre Transmettre
mett riez	mett ez	mett iez	mis siez	Compromettre
mett raient	——	mett ent	mis sent	Entremettre (s') *

List of

Infinitive and Participles	Indicative			
	PRESENT	IMPERFECT	PAST DEFINITE	FUTURE
Moudre	moud s	moul ais	moul us	moud rai
moulant	moud s	moul ais	moul us	moud ras
moulu	moud	moul ait	moul ut	moud ra
To grind	moul ons	moul ions	moul ûmes	moud rons
	moul ez	moul iez	moul ûtes	moud rez
	moul ent	moul aient	moul urent	moud ront
Mourir	meur s	mour ais	mour us	mour rai
mourant	meur s	mour ais	mour us	mour ras
mort *	meur t	mour ait	mour ut	mour ra
To die	mour ons	mour ions	mour ûmes	mour rons
	mour ez	mour iez	mour ûtes	mour rez
	meur ent	mour aient	mour urent	mour ront
Mouvoir	meu s	mouv ais	m us	mouv rai
mouvant	meu s	mouv ais	m us	mouv ras
mû mue	meu t	mouv ait	m ut	mouv ra
To move	mouv ons	mouv ions	m ûmes	mouv rons
	mouv ez	mouv iez	m ûtes	mouv rez
	meuv ent	mouv aient	m urent	mouv ront
Naître	nai s	naiss ais	naqu is	naît rai
naissant	nai s	naiss ais	naqu is	naît ras
né *	naît t	naiss ait	naqu it	naît ra
To be born	naiss ons	naiss ions	naqu îmes	naît rons
	naiss ez	naiss iez	naqu îtes	naît rez
	naiss ent	naiss aient	naqu irent	naît ront
Nuire	nui s	nuis ais	nuis is	nui rai
nuisant	nui s	nuis ais	nuis is	nui ras
nui	nui t	nuis ait	nuis it	nui ra
To hurt	nuis ons	nuis ions	nuis îmes	nui rons
	nuis ez	nuis iez	nuis îtes	nui rez
	nuis ent	nuis aient	nuis irent	nui ront
Ouvrir	ouvr e	ouvr ais	ouvr is	ouvri rai
ouvrant	ouvr es	ouvr ais	ouvr is	ouvri ras
ouvert	ouvr e	ouvr ait	ouvr it	ouvri ra
To open	ouvr ons	ouvr ions	ouvr îmes	ouvri rons
	ouvr ez	ouvr iez	ouvr îtes	ouvri rez
	cuvr ent	ouvr aient	ouvr irent	ouvri ront

irregular verbs

| Conditional | Imperative | Subjunctive | | Verbs conjugated in Same Manner |
		PRESENT	IMPERFECT	
moud rais	——	moul e	moulus se	
moud rais	moud s	moul es	moulus ses	
moud rait	——	moul e	moul ût	Émoudre
moud rions	moul ons	moul ions	moulus sions	Rémoudre
moud riez	moul ez	moul iez	moulus siez	Remoudre
moud raient	——	moul ent	moulus sent	
mour rais	——	meur e	mourus se	
mour rais	meur s	meur es	mourus ses	
mour rait	——	meur e	mour ût	
mour rions	mour ons	mour ions	mourus sions	
mour riez	mour ez	mour iez	mourus siez	
mour raient	——	meur ent	mourus sent	
mouv rais	——	meuv e	mus se	Émouvoir
mouv rais	meu s	meuv es	mus ses	The past participles
mouv rait	——	meuv e	m ût	*ému* and *promu* do not
mouv rions	mouv ons	mouv ions	mus sions	take the circumflex
mouv riez	mouv ez	mouv iez	mus siez	accent.
mouv raient	——	meuv ent	mus sent	
naît rais	——	naiss e	naquis se	
naît rais	nai s	naiss es	naquis ses	
naît rait	——	naiss e	naqu ît	
naît rions	naiss ons	naiss ions	naquis sions	Renaître
naît riez	naiss ez	naiss iez	naquis siez	
naît raient	——	naiss ent	naquis sent	
nui rais	——	nuis e	nuisis se	
nui rais	nui s	nuis es	nuisis ses	
nui rait	——	nuis e	nuis ît	
nui rions	nuis ons	nuis ions	nuisis sions	Luire
nui riez	nuis ez	nuis iez	nuisis siez	Reluire
nui raient	——	nuis ent	nuisis sent	
ouvri rais	——	ouvr e	ouvris se	Couvrir
ouvri rais	ouvr e	ouvr es	ouvris ses	Découvrir
ouvri rait	——	ouvr e	ouvr ît	Entr'ouvrir
ouvri rions	ouvr ons	ouvr ions	ouvris sions	Offrir
ouvri riez	ouvr ez	ouvr iez	ouvris siez	Recouvrir
ouvri raient	——	ouvr ent	ouvris sent	Rouvrir
				Souffrir

List of

Infinitive and Participles	Indicative			
	PRESENT	IMPERFECT	PAST DEFINITE	FUTURE
Partir	par s	part ais	part is	parti rai
partant	par s	part ais	part is	parti ras
parti *	par t	part ait	part it	parti ra
To set out	part ons	part ions	part îmes	parti rons
	part ez	part iez	part îtes	parti rez
	part ent	part aient	part irent	parti ront
Peindre [1]	pein s	peign ais	peign is	peind rai
peignant	pein s	peign ais	peign is	peind ras
peint	pein t	peign ait	peign it	peind ra
To paint	peign ons	peign ions	peign îmes	peind rons
	peign ez	peign iez	peign îtes	peind rez
	peign ent	peign aient	peign irent	peind ront
Plaire	plai s	plais ais	pl us	plai rai
plaisant	plai s	plais ais	pl us	plai ras
plu	plaî t	plais ait	pl ut	plai ra
To please	plais ons	plais ions	pl ûmes	plai rons
	plais ez	plais iez	pl ûtes	plai rez
	plais ent	plais aient	pl urent	plai ront
Pourvoir	pourvoi s	pourvoy ais	pourv us	pourvoi rai
pourvoyant	pourvoi s	pourvoy ais	pourv us	pourvoi ras
pourvu	pourvoi t	pourvoy ait	pourv ut	pourvoi ra
To provide	pourvoy ons	pourvoy ions	pourv ûmes	pourvoi rons
	pourvoy ez	pourvoy iez	pourv ûtes	pourvoi rez
	pourvoi ent	pourvoy aient	pourv urent	pourvoi ront
Pouvoir	peu x *or* puis	pouv ais	p us	pour rai
pouvant	peu x	pouv ais	p us	pour ras
pu	peu t	pouv ait	p ut	pour ra
To be able	pouv ons	pouv ions	p ûmes	pour rons
	pouv ez	pouv iez	p ûtes	pour rez
	peuv ent	pouv aient	p urent	pour ront
Prendre	prend s	pren ais	pr is	prend rai
prenant	prend s	pren ais	pr is	prend ras
pris	prend	pren ait	pr it	prend ra
To take	pren ons	pren ions	pr îmes	prend rons
	pren ez	pren iez	pr îtes	prend rez
	prenn ent	pren aient	pr irent	prend ront

[1] The verbs in **eindre** preserve the d only in the Future and Conditional tenses.

irregular verbs

Conditional	Imperative	Subjunctive		Verbs conjugated in Same Manner
		PRESENT	IMPERFECT	
parti rais	——	part e	partis se	
parti rais	par s	part es	partis ses	Départir
parti rait	——	part e	part ît	Se départir *
parti rions	part ons	part ions	partis sions	Repartir
parti riez	part ez	part iez	partis siez	
parti raient	——	part ent	partis sent	Astreindre
peind rais	——	peign e	peignis se	Atteindre
peind rais	pein s	peign es	peignis ses	Ceindre
peind rait	——	peign e	peign ît	Dépeindre
peind rions	peign ons	peign ions	peignis sions	Éteindre
peind riez	peign ez	peign iez	peignis siez	Étreindre
peind raient	——	peign ent	peignis sent	Feindre
				Repeindre
				Restreindre
plai rais	——	plais e	plus se	Teindre
plai rais	plai s	plais es	plus ses	
plai rait	——	plais e	pl ût	
plai rions	plais ons	plais ions	plus sions	Complaire
plai riez	plais ez	plais iez	plus siez	Déplaire
plai raient	——	plais ent	plus sent	Taire
				Se taire
pourvoi rais	——	pourvoi e	pourvus se	
pourvoi rais	pourvoi s	pourvoi es	pourvus ses	
pourvoi rait	——	pourvoi e	pourv ût	
pourvoi rions	pourvoy ons	pourvoy ions	pourvus sions	Dépourvoir
pourvoi riez	pourvoy ez	pourvoy iez	pourvus siez	
pourvoi raient	——	pourvoi ent	pourvus sent	
pour rais		puiss e	pus se	The first person singu-
pour rais		puiss es	pus ses	lar present indicative is
pour rait		puiss e	p ût	*je peux* or *je puis;* but
pour rions		puiss ions	pus sions	the interrogative form
pour riez		puiss iez	pus siez	is always *puis-je ?*
pour raient		puiss ent	pus sent	
prend rais	- ——	prenn e	pris se	Apprendre
prend rais	prend s	prenn es	pris ses	Comprendre
prend rait	——	prenn e	pr ît	Désapprendre
prend rions	pren ons	pren ions	pris sions	Entreprendre
prend riez	pren ez	pren iez	pris siez	Se méprendre *
prend raient	——	prenn ent	pris sent	Reprendre
				Surprendre

List of

Infinitive and Participles	Indicative			
	PRESENT	IMPERFECT	PAST DEFINITE	FUTURE
Recevoir	reçoi s	recev ais	reç us	recev rai
recevant	reçoi s	recev ais	reç us	recev ras
reçu	reçoi t	recev ait	reç ut	recev ra
To receive	recev ons	recev ions	reç ûmes	recev rons
	recev ez	recev iez	reç ûtes	recev rez
	reçoiv ent	recev aient	reç urent	recev ront
Résoudre	résou s	résolv ais	résol us	résoud rai
résolvant	résou s	résolv ais	résol us	résoud ras
résolu [1]	résou t	résolv ait	résol ut	résoud ra
To resolve	résolv ons	résolv ions	résol ûmes	résoud rons
	résolv ez	résolv iez	résol ûtes	résoud rez
	résolv ent	résolv aient	résol urent	résoud ront
Rire	ri s	ri ais	r is	ri rai
riant	ri s	ri ais	r is	ri ras
ri	ri t	ri ait	r it	ri ra
To laugh	ri ons	ri ions	r îmes	ri rons
	ri ez	ri iez	r îtes	ri rez
	ri ent	ri aient	r irent	ri ront
Savoir	sai s	sav ais	s us	sau rai
sachant	sai s	sav ais	s us	sau ras
su	sai t	sav ait	s ut	sau ra
To know	sav ons	sav ions	s ûmes	sau rons
	sav ez	sav iez	s ûtes	sau rez
	sav ent	sav aient	s urent	sau ront
Sentir	sen s	sent ais	sent is	senti rai
sentant	sen s	sent ais	sent is	senti ras
senti	sen t	sent ait	sent it	senti ra
To feel	sent ons	sent ions	sent îmes	senti rons
	sent ez	sent iez	sent îtes	senti rez
	sent ent	sent aient	sent irent	senti ront
Servir	ser s	serv ais	serv is	servi rai
servant	ser s	serv ais	serv is	servi ras
servi	ser t	serv ait	serv it	servi ra
To serve	serv ons	serv ions	serv îmes	servi rons
	serv ez	serv iez	serv îtes	servi rez
	serv ent	serv aient	serv irent	servi ront

[1] This verb has a second past participle **résous** (invariable) used in chemistry

irregular verbs

Conditional	Imperative	Subjunctive		Verbs Conjugated in Same Manner
		PRESENT	IMPERFECT	
recev rais	——	reçoiv e	reçus se	Apercevoir
recev rais	reçoi s	reçoiv es	reçus ses	Concevoir
recev rait	——	reçoiv e	reç ût	Décevoir
recev rions	recev ons	recev ions	reçus sions	Percevoir
recev riez	recev ez	recev iez	reçus siez	*See* Devoir
recev raient	——	reçoiv ent	reçus sent	
résoud rais	——	résolv e	résolus se	
résoud rais	résou s	résolv es	résolus ses	
résoud rait	——	résolv e	résol ût	
résoud rions	résolv ons	résolv ions	résolus sions	
résoud riez	résolv ez	résolv iez	resolus siez	
résoud raient	——	résolv ent	résolus sent	
ri rais	——	ri e	ris se	
ri rais	ri s	ri es	ris ses	
ri rait	——	ri e	r ît	
ri rions	ri ons	ri ions	ris sions	Sourire
ri riez	ri ez	ri iez	ris siez	
ri raient	——	ri ent	ris sent	
sau rais	——	sach e	sus se	
sau rais	sach e	sach es	sus ses	
sau rait	——	sach e	s ût	
sau rions	sach ons	sach ions	sus sions	
sau riez	sach ez	sach iez	sus siez	
sau raient	——	sach ent	sus sent	
senti rais	——	sent e	sentis se	Consentir
senti rais	sen s	sent es	sentis ses	Pressentir
senti rait	——	sent e	sent ît	Se repentir*
senti rions	sent ons	sent ions	sentis sions	Ressentir
senti riez	sent ez	sent iez	sentis siez	Mentir
senti raient	——	sent ent	sentis sent	Démentir
servi rais	——	serv e	servis se	
servi rais	ser s	serv es	servis ses	
servi rait	——	serv e	serv ît	Desservir
servi rions	serv ons	serv ions	servis sions	Resservir
servi riez	serv ez	serv iez	servis siez	
servi raient	——	serv ent	servis sent	

Infinitive and Participles	Indicative			
	PRESENT	IMPERFECT	PAST DEFINITE	FUTURE
Sortir	sor s	sort ais	sort is	sorti rai
sortant	sor s	sort ais	sort is	sorti ras
sorti *	sor t	sort ait	sort it	sorti ra
To go out	sort ons	sort ions	sort îmes	sorti rons
	sort ez	sort iez	sort îtes	sorti rez
	sort ent	sort aient	sort irent	sorti ront
Suffire	suffi s	suffis ais	suff is	suffi rai
suffisant	suffi s	suffis ais	suff is	suffi ras
suffi	suffi t	suffis ait	suff it	suffi ra
To suffice	suffis ons	suffis ions	suff îmes	suffi rons
	suffis ez	suffis iez	suff îtes	suffi rez
	suffis ent	suffis aient	suff irent	suffi ront
Suivre	sui s	suiv ais	suiv is	suiv rai
suivant	sui s	suiv ais	suiv is	suiv ras
suivi	sui t	suiv ait	suiv it	suiv ra
To follow	suiv ons	suiv ions	suiv îmes	suiv rons
	suiv ez	suiv iez	suiv îtes	suiv rez
	suiv ent	suiv aient	suiv irent	suiv ront
Tenir	tien s	ten ais	t ins	tiend rai
tenant	tien s	ten ais	t ins	tiend ras
tenu	tien t	ten ait	t int	tiend ra
To hold	ten ons	ten ions	t înmes	tiend rons
(keep)	ten ez	ten iez	t întes	tiend rez
	tienn ent	ten aient	t inrent	tiend ront
Vaincre	vainc s	vainqu ais	vainqu is	vainc rai
vainquant	vainc s	vainqu ais	vainqu is	vainc ras
vaincu	vainc	vainqu ait	vainqu it	vainc ra
To conquer	vainqu ons	vainqu ions	vainqu îmes	vainc rons
(vanquish)	vainqu ez	vainqu iez	vainqu îtes	vainc rez
	vainqu ent	vainqu aient	vainqu irent	vainc ront

irregular verbs

Conditional	Imperative	Subjunctive		Verbs Conjugated in Same Manner
		PRESENT	IMPERFECT	
sorti rais	——	sort e	sortis se	
sorti rais	sor s	sort es	sortis ses	
sorti rait	——	sort e	sort ît	Ressortir
sorti rions	sort ons	sort ions	sortis sions	
sorti riez	sort ez	sort iez	sortis siez	
sorti raient	——	sort ent	sortis sent	
suffi rais	——	suffis e	suffis se	*Confire*, to preserve;
suffi rais	suffi s	suffis es	suffis ses	past participle *confit*.
suffi rait	——	suffis e	suff ît	
suffi rions	suffis ons	suffis ions	suffis sions	
suffi riez	suffis ez	suffis iez	suffis siez	
suffi raient	——	suffis ent	suffis sent	
suiv rais	——	suiv e	suivis se	
suiv rais	sui s	suiv es	suivis ses	
suiv rait	——	suiv e	suiv ît	Poursuivre
suiv rions	suiv ons	suiv ions	suivis sions	
suiv riez	suiv ez	suiv iez	suivis siez	
suiv raient	——	suiv ent	suivis sent	
tiend rais	——	tienn e	tins se	S'abstenir *
tiend rais	tien s	tienn es	tins ses	Appartenir
tiend rait	——	tienn e	t înt	Contenir Détenir
tiend rions	ten ons	ten ions	tins sions	Entretenir
tiend riez	ten ez	ten iez	tins siez	Maintenir Obtenir
tiend raient	——	tienn ent	tins sent	Retenir Soutenir
vainc rais	——	vainqu e	vainquis se	
vainc rais	vainc s	vainqu es	vainquis ses	Convaincre
vainc rait	——	vainqu e	vainqu ît	
vainc rions	vainqu ons	vainqu ions	vainquis sions	
vainc riez	vainqu ez	vainqu iez	vainquis siez	
vainc raient	——	vainqu ent	vainquis sent	

Infinitive and Participles	Indicative			
	PRESENT	IMPERFECT	PAST DEFINITE	FUTURE
Valoir	vau x	val ais	val us	vaud rai
valant	vau x	val ais	val us	vaud ras
valu	vau t	val ait	val ut	vaud ra
To be worth	val ons	val ions	val ûmes	vaud rons
	val ez	val iez	val ûtes	vaud rez
	val ent	val aient	val urent	vaud ront
Venir	vien s	ven ais	v ins	viend rai
venant	vien s	ven ais	v ins	viend ras
venu *	vien t	ven ait	v int	viend ra
To come	ven ons	ven ions	v înmes	viend rons
	ven ez	ven iez	v întes	viend rez
	vienn ent	ven aient	v inrent	viend ront
Vivre	vi s	viv ais	véc us	viv rai
vivant	vi s	viv ais	véc us	viv ras
vécu	vi t	viv ait	véc ut	viv ra
To live	viv ons	viv ions	véc ûmes	viv rons
	viv ez	viv iez	véc ûtes	viv rez
	viv ent	viv aient	véc urent	viv ront
Voir	voi s	voy ais	v is	ver rai
voyant	voi s	voy ais	v is	ver ras
vu	voi t	voy ait	v it	ver ra
To see	voy ons	voy ions	v îmes	ver rons
	voy ez	voy iez	v îtes	ver rez
	voi ent	voy aient	v irent	ver ront
Vouloir	veu x	voul ais	voul us	voud rai
voulant	veu x	voul ais	voul us	voud ras
voulu	veu t	voul ait	voul ut	voud ra
To wish (will,	voul ons	voul ions	voul ûmes	voud rons
be willing,	voul ez	voul iez	voul ûtes	voud rez
want)	veul ent	voul aient	voul urent	voud ront

irregular verbs

Conditional	Imperative	Subjunctive		Verbs Conjugated in Same Manner
		PRESENT	IMPERFECT	
vaud rais	——	vaill e	valus se	Équivaloir
vaud rais	vau x	vaill es	valus ses	Prévaloir
vaud rait	——	vaill e	val ût	Revaloir
vaud rions	val ons	val ions	valus sions	The present subjunctive of *prévaloir* is
vaud riez	val ez	val iez	valus siez	*prévale, prévales, prévale,*
vaud raient	——	vaill ent	valus sent	*prévalent.*
viend rais	——	vienn e	vins se	Advenir Parvenir
viend rais	vien s	vienn es	vins ses	Convenir(à)[1] Prévenir [1]
viend rait	——	vienn e	v înt	Convenir Provenir
viend rions	ven ons	ven ions	vins sions	(de) Revenir
viend riez	ven ez	ven iez	vins siez	Devenir Se souvenir
viend raient	——	vienn ent	vins sent	Disconvenir (de)
				Intervenir Subvenir [1]
				Survenir
				[1] Conjugated with *avoir.*
viv rais	——	viv e	vécus se	
viv rais	vi s	viv es	vécus ses	
viv rait	——	viv e	véc ût	Revivre
viv rions	viv ons	viv ions	vécus sions	Survivre
viv riez	viv ez	viv iez	vécus siez	
viv raient	——	viv ent	vécus sent	
ver rais	——	voi e	vis se	Revoir Pourvoir
ver rais	voi s	voi es	vis ses	Entrevoir Prévoir
ver rait	——	voi e	v ît	Differ only in the future and conditional
ver rions	voy ons	voy ions	vis sions	which become regular;
ver riez	voy ez	voy iez	vis siez	but *pourvoir* takes *u* in-
ver raient	——	voi ent	vis sent	stead of *i* in the past definite and imperfect subjunctive.
voud rais	——	veuill e	voulus se	
voud rais	veuill e	veuill es	voulus ses	
voud rait	——	veuill e	voul ût	
voud rions	veuill ons	voul ions	voulus sions	
voud riez	veuill ez	voul iez	voulus siez	
voud raient	——	veuill ent	voulus sent	

List of verbs governing the infinitive *without* a preposition

accourir, *to hasten.*
affirmer, *to affirm.*
aimer mieux, *to prefer.*
aller, *to go, to be about to.*
apercevoir, *to perceive.*
assurer, *to assert.*
avoir beau, *to be in vain.*
avouer, *to confess.*
compter, *to expect.*
concevoir, *to conceive, to represent to one's self.*
confesser, *to confess.*
courir, *to run.*
croire, *to believe.*
daigner, *to deign.*
déclarer, *to declare.*
déposer, *to depose* (as a witness).
désirer, *to desire.*

devoir, *to be to, to have to, must.*
écouter, *to listen.*
entendre, *to hear.*
envoyer, *to send.*
espérer, *to hope.*
faillir, *to come near (doing).*
faire, *to cause, to get, to have.*
falloir, *to be necessary.*
s'imaginer, *to fancy.*
laisser, *to allow, to let.*
mener, *to take.*
nier, *to deny.*
observer, *to observe.*
oser, *to dare.*
ouïr, *to hear.*
paraître, *to appear.*
penser, *to be near to.*

pouvoir, *to be able.*
préférer, *to prefer.*
prétendre, *to pretend.*
rapporter, *to relate.*
reconnaître, *to acknowledge.*
regarder, *to look at.*
retourner, *to go back.*
revenir, *to come back.*
savoir, *to know how (to be able).*
sembler, *to seem.*
sentir, *to feel.*
souhaiter, *to wish.*
soutenir, *to maintain.*
témoigner, *to testify.*
valoir mieux, *to be better.*
venir, *to come.*
voir, *to see.*
vouloir, *to be willing.*

List of verbs requiring *de* before an infinitive

s'abstenir, *to abstain.*
accorder, *to permit.*
achever, *to finish.*
affecter, *to affect.*
ambitionner, *to be ambitious to.*
s'apercevoir, *to perceive.*
appréhender, *to apprehend, to fear.*
avertir, *to warn.*
s'aviser, *to bethink one's self, to think (of).*
blâmer, *to blame for.*
brûler, *to be impatient.*
cesser, *to cease.*
charger, *to charge.*
se charger, *to undertake.*
choisir, *to choose.*
commander, *to command.*
conjurer, *to entreat.*
conseiller, *to advise.*
consoler, *to console for.*

se contenter, *to be satisfied.*
craindre, *to fear.*
crier, *to cry out.*
dédaigner, *to disdain.*
défendre, *to forbid.*
se dépêcher, *to hasten.*
détester, *to detest.*
dire, *to tell, to bid.*
discontinuer, *to discontinue.*
écrire, *to write.*
s'efforcer, *to exert one's self, to try.*
éluder, *to elude.*
empêcher, *to prevent.*
s'ennuyer, *to be bored with.*
s'enorgueillir, *to be proud.*
entreprendre, *to undertake.*
essayer, *to try.*

s'étonner, *to wonder at.*
éviter, *to shun, to avoid.*
s'excuser, *to excuse one's self from.*
faire bien, *to do well.*
feindre, *to pretend.*
féliciter, *to congratulate.*
finir, *to finish.*
se flatter, *to flatter one's self, to hope.*
frémir, *to shudder.*
gager, *to wager.*
se garder, *to take care not to.*
gémir, *to groan.*
gêner, *to trouble.*
gronder, *to scold for.*
se hâter, *to make haste.*
s'imaginer, *to take into one's head.*
s'indigner, *to be indignant.*

inspirer, *to inspire.*
interdire, *to forbid.*
jouir, *to enjoy.*
jurer, *to swear.*
louer, *to praise for.*
mander, *to bid.*
manquer, *to fail to.*
méditer, *to contemplate.*
se mêler, *to interfere, to meddle.*
menacer, *to threaten.*
mériter, *to deserve.*
mourir, *to die; to long.*
négliger, *to neglect.*
obliger, *to oblige, to do a service.*
obtenir, *to obtain.*
s'occuper, *to be intent on.*
offrir, *to offer.*
omettre, *to omit.*
oublier, *to forget.*

ordonner, *to prescribe.*
pardonner, *to forgive.*
parier, *to bet.*
parler, *to speak.*
se passer, *to do without.*
permettre, *to permit.*
persuader, *to persuade.*
se piquer, *to pride one's self on.*
plaindre, *to pity.*
se plaindre, *to complain.*
se presser, *to hasten.*
prier, *to request, to beg.*
projeter, *to intend.*
promettre, *to promise.*
proposer, *to propose.*
se proposer, *to purpose.*
protester, *to protest.*
recommander, *to recommend.*
redouter, *to fear.*
refuser, *to refuse.*

regretter, *to regret.*
se réjouir, *to rejoice.*
remercier, *to thank.*
se repentir, *to repent.*
reprocher, *to reproach.*
se réserver, *to reserve to one's self a right.*
résoudre, *to resolve.*
rire, *to laugh.*
risquer, *to risk.*
rougir, *to blush.*
sommer, *to summon.*
se soucier, *to mind, to care.*
soupçonner, *to suspect.*
se souvenir, *to remember.*
suggérer, *to suggest.*
tâcher, *to try.*
tenter, *to attempt.*
trembler, *to fear.*
se vanter, *to boast.*
venir, *to have just.*

List of verbs requiring *à* before an infinitive

s'abaisser, *to stoop to.*
aboutir, *to end in.*
s'accorder, *to agree in.*
s'accoutumer, *to accustom one's self.*
s'acharner, *to be eager, to be determined.*
admettre, *to admit.*
s'aguerrir, *to inure.*
aider, *to help.*
aimer, *to like.*
s'amuser, *to amuse one's self.*
appeler, *to call.*
s'appliquer, *to apply.*
apprendre, *to learn, to teach.*
s'apprêter, *to prepare one's self.*
aspirer, *to aspire.*
assigner, *to summon.*
assujettir, *to compel.*

s'assujettir, *to submit.*
s'attacher, *to be determined.*
s'attendre, *to expect.*
autoriser, *to authorize.*
s'avilir, *to stoop.*
avoir, *to have.*
balancer, *to hesitate.*
se borner, *to confine one's self.*
chercher, *to seek, to try.*
commencer, *to begin.*
se complaire, *to delight in.*
concourir, *to concur.*
condamner, *to condemn.*
condescendre, *to condescend.*
consentir, *to consent.*
consister, *to consist in.*
conspirer, *to conspire.*
se consumer, *to ruin one's health.*

contribuer, *to contribute.*
convier, *to invite.*
coûter, *to cost.*
décider, *to persuade.*
se décider, *to decide.*
descendre, *to stoop.*
destiner, *to destine, to design.*
déterminer, *to induce.*
se déterminer, *to determine, to resolve.*
dévouer, *to devote.*
disposer, *to prepare, to fit.*
se disposer, *to prepare.*
dresser, *to train.*
employer, *to employ, to occupy.*
encourager, *to encourage.*
engager, *to induce.*
s'engager, *to bind one's self.*

s'enhardir, *to make bold, to venture.*
enseigner, *to teach.*
s'entendre, *to know how.*
s'étudier, *to apply one's self.*
exceller, *to excel.*
exciter, *to urge.*
s'exercer, *to exercise one's self.*
exhorter, *to exhort.*
s'exposer, *to expose one's self.*
se fatiguer, *to fatigue one's self.*
gagner, *to gain by.*
habituer, *to accustom.*
se hasarder, *to venture.*
hésiter, *to hesitate.*
instruire, *to instruct.*
inviter, *to invite, to ask.*
se mettre, *to set about, to begin.*

s'obstiner, *to persist in.*
occuper, *to occupy, to employ.*
s'occuper, *to be engaged.*
s'offrir, *to offer, to stand forth.*
s'opiniâtrer, *to be obstinate.*
parvenir, *to succeed in.*
passer, *to spend in.*
pencher, *to lean.*
penser, *to think of.*
persévérer, *to persevere.*
persister, *to persist.*
se plaire, *to delight.*
plier, *to bend.*
porter, *to induce.*
prendre plaisir, *to take pleasure in.*
préparer, *to prepare.*
se préparer, *to prepare one's self.*
prétendre, *to aspire.*

provoquer, *to provoke.*
réduire, *to reduce.*
se refuser, *to refuse one's self, not to admit.*
renoncer, *to renounce.*
se résigner, *to resign, to submit one's self.*
se résoudre, *to resolve.*
réussir, *to succeed.*
servir, *to serve.*
songer, *to think of.*
suffire, *to be sufficient.*
tarder, *to delay, to be long.*
travailler, *to work, to study, to endeavor.*
se tuer, *to kill one's self, to take much trouble.*
venir, *to chance, to happen.*
viser, *to aim, to aspire.*
vouer, *to devote.*
se vouer, *to devote, to apply one's self.*

LIST OF MOST COMMON VERBAL IDIOMS USED IN CONVERSATION

Aller, *to go*

Aller à pied,	*to walk.*
Aller à cheval,	*to ride horseback.*
Aller en voiture (en automobile),	*to ride.*
Aller à la rencontre de,	*to go to meet.*
Aller faire des emplettes,	*to go shopping.*
Aller bien,	*to fit, to suit, to be well.*
Aller de mal en pis,	*to grow worse and worse.*
Ne pas y aller par quatre chemins,	*to go straight to the point.*
Cela va sans dire.	*That goes without saying.*
Comme vous y allez!	*You go at it tooth and nail!*
Allons donc!	*No! Nonsense!*

Avoir, *to have*

Avoir l'air,	*to look.*
Avoir l'air de,	*to look as if.*
Avoir mal à,	*to have a pain in.*
Avoir chaud, froid, faim, etc.	*to be warm, cold, hungry,* etc.

Avoir envie de,	to have a mind to.
Avoir beau,	in vain.
Qu'est-ce qu'il y a ?	What is the matter ?
Il y a que,	the matter is . . .
Il peut y avoir,	there can (may) be.
Il doit y avoir,	there must be.
Il devrait y avoir,	there should be.

Connaître, to know

Connaître de vue,	to know by sight.
Connaître de nom,	to know by name.
Se connaître en,	to be a judge of.
S'y connaître,	to be a judge of it.

Courir, to run

Courir le risque,	to run the chance.
Courir à toutes jambes,	to run as fast as one's legs will carry one.
Courir après son argent,	to try to get one's money back.
Courir un danger,	to be exposed to a danger.
Le bruit court.	The report is spread that . . .
Par le temps qui court,	as times go.

Dire, to say

Dire du bien de,	to speak well of.
Dire du mal de,	to speak ill of.
Dire sa façon de penser,	to speak one's mind freely.
A vrai dire,	to tell the truth.
On dit.	They say, it is said.

Dormir, to sleep

Dormir à la belle étoile,	to sleep in the open air.
Dormir sur les deux oreilles,	to have nothing to fear.
Dormir comme un loir,	to sleep like a dormouse.

Être, to be

Être en train de,	to be in the act of.
Être en avance,	to be early.
Être en retard,	to be late.
Être à l'heure,	to be on time.
Être de retour,	to be back.
Être à même de,	to be able.
Être au courant de,	to be posted on.
Être de l'avis de,	to agree with.
Être enrhumé,	to have a cold.
N'y être pour rien,	to have nothing to do with it.
N'être pas dans son assiette,	to be out of sorts.
N'être pas si bête,	to know better.

Faire, *to make, to do*

Il fait beau, mauvais,	*The weather is fine, bad.*
Il fait chaud, froid,	*It is warm, cold.*
Faire grand cas de,	*to think a great deal of.*
Faire peu de cas de,	*to think a little of.*
Faire attendre,	*to keep waiting.*
Faire faire,	*to have made, to cause to be made.*
Faire la sourde oreille,	*to turn a deaf ear.*
Faire d'une pierre deux coups,	*to kill two birds with one stone.*
Cela ne fait rien.	*That does not matter.*
Cela ne me fait rien.	*I do not care.*
Faire mal à,	*to hurt.*
Faire une promenade,	*to take a walk.*

Se faire, *to become*

Se faire à,	*to get used to.*
S'y faire,	*to get used to it.*
Se faire du mauvais sang, Se faire des cheveux gris,	*to be much annoyed, to worry, to fret.*
Se faire moquer de soi,	*to make a fool of one's self.*
Il se fait tard.	*It is getting late.*
Comment se fait-il?	*How is it that?*
Il peut se faire que.	*It may be that.*
Il pourrait se faire que.	*It might be that.*

Falloir, *to be necessary*

Il s'en faut de beaucoup que je . . .	*I am far from . . .*
Il s'en faut de beaucoup qu'il . . .	*He is far from . . .*
Il s'en faut de beaucoup que vous. . .	*You are far from . . .*
Tant s'en faut,	*far from it.*
Peu s'en faut,	*nearly, not far from it.*
Il le faut.	*It or that must be done.*
Il fallait voir, il aurait fallu voir.	*You should have seen.*
Il faudrait voir.	*You should see.*

Fuir, *to fly, to run away*

Fuir le danger,	*to avoid danger.*
Fuir le monde,	*to shun the world.*
Fuir le travail,	*to shrink from work.*

Mettre, *to put*

Mettre dehors,	*to put out.*
Mettre en doute,	*to question.*
Mettre à bout,	*to put out of patience.*
Mettre au courant de,	*to acquaint with.*
Mettre à même de,	*to enable.*
Mettre en colère,	*to anger.*
Mettre à la porte,	*to send away, to turn out.*

Se mettre, *to begin, to set about*

Se mettre à,	*to set about, to begin.*
S'y mettre,	*to set about it.*
Se mettre en route,	*to set off, to start.*
Se mettre en colère,	*to get angry.*
Se mettre bien,	*to dress well.*
Se mettre en quatre pour,	*to sacrifice oneself for.*

Passer, *to pass*

Passer chez,	*to call on.*
En passer par,	*to submit to.*
Se passer de,	*to do without.*
S'en passer,	*to do without it.*
Se passer,	*to take place, to occur.*

Plaire, *to please*

Je fais ce qu'il me plaît.	*I do what I please.*
Nous faisons ce qu'il nous plaît.	*We do what we please.*
S'il vous plaît.	*If you please.*
Plaît-il?	*What do you say?*
A Dieu ne plaise que . . .	*God forbid that . . .*

Pouvoir, *to be able, can, may*

N'en pouvoir plus,	*to be exhausted.*
N'y pouvoir rien,	*to be unable to help.*
Je n'y puis rien.	*I cannot help it.*
Il se peut que.	*It may be that.*
Il se pourrait que.	*It might be that.*
Cela se peut.	*That is possible, that can be done.*
Sauf qui peut!	*Let him save himself who can.*

Prendre, *to take*

Prendre la clef des champs,	*to take to one's heels.*
Prendre quelqu'un au dépourvu,	*to take a person unawares.*
Prendre quelqu'un sur le fait,	*to catch a person in the very act.*
Prendre un parti,	*to take a resolution.*
Prendre parti pour,	*to take sides with.*
Prendre en grippe,	*to take a strong dislike to.*
Prendre son courage à deux mains,	*to screw up one's courage.*
S'en prendre à,	*to blame.*
S'y prendre,	*to go about it.*

Revenir, *to come back*

Ne pas revenir de,	*to be very much surprised at.*
N'en pas revenir,	*not to go over it.*
Cela revient au même,	*that amounts to the same.*

Rire, *to laugh*

Rire aux éclats,	*to roar with laughter.*
Rire aux larmes,	*to laugh till tears come.*
Rire de bon cœur,	*to laugh heartily.*
Rire sous cape,	*to laugh in one's sleeve.*
Rire jaune,	*to give a forced laugh.*
Rire du bout des lèvres,	*to give a faint laugh.*
Rire au nez de quelqu'un,	*to laugh in some one's face.*
Un pince-sans-rire,	*a dry joker.*
Il est à mourir de rire.	*He is killing.*
Rira bien qui rira le dernier.	*He laughs best who laughs last.*

Savoir, *to know*

Savoir à fond,	*to know thoroughly.*
Savoir gré de,	*to be thankful for.*
Savoir vivre,	*to know how to behave.*
Savoir mauvais gré de,	*to be ill-pleased with.*
En savoir long,	*to know a thing or two.*
Ne savoir à quel saint se vouer,	*not to know which way to turn.*
Que je sache,	*so far as I know.*

Servir, *to serve, to help to, to wait on*

Servir,	*to be of service, of use to.*
Servir de,	*to serve as, to do instead of.*
Servir de père à,	*to be a father to.*
A quoi sert de,	*what is the use of.*
Ne servir à rien,	*to be of no use.*
Se servir,	*to use, to help one's self.*

Sortir, *to go out, to come out*

Sortir quelqu'un d'embarras,	*to get a person out of trouble.*
En sortir,	*to get along, to get out of it.*

Tenir, *to hold, to keep*

Tenir à,	*to care, to like, to be anxious.*
Y tenir,	*to care about it.*
Tenir de,	*to take after.*
Tenir le bon bout,	*to have the better hand.*
Je n'y tiens plus !	*I cannot wait any longer!*
Il ne tient qu'à vous de,	*It only depends on you to . . .*
Qu'à cela ne tienne,	*Never mind that.*
Tiens! Tiens! Tiens!	*Well! Well! Well!*
Tenez,	*Here! see now, take it.*

Se tenir, *to stand, to keep oneself*

Se tenir debout,	*to stand up.*
Se tenir droit,	*to stand straight.*
S'en tenir à,	*to abide by.*
S'en tenir là,	*to go no further.*
Savoir à quoi s'en tenir,	*to know what to think of.*

Valoir, *to be worth*

Valoir la peine,	*to be worth while.*
Valoir son pesant d'or,	*to be worth one's weight of gold.*
Ne pas valoir grand'chose,	*not to be good for much.*
Le jeu n'en vaut pas la chandelle.	*The game is not worth the candle.*
Se faire valoir,	*to praise oneself, to boast.*
Il vaut mieux or Mieux vaut.	*It is better.*
Il vaut autant or Autant vaut.	*It is just as well.*

Venir, *to come*

Venir à (+ infin.),	*to happen to.*
Venir de (+ infin.),	*to have just.*
En venir aux mains,	*to come to blows.*
Venir à bout de,	*to succeed in.*
En venir à bout,	*to succeed in doing it.*
D'où vient que . . .	*How is it that . . .*
Où voulez-vous en venir ?	*What are you aiming at?*
Venir au fait,	*to come to the point.*

Vivre, *to live*

Vivre au jour le jour,	*to live from hand to mouth.*
Vivre de ses rentes,	*to live on one's income.*
Vivre en grand seigneur,	*to live like a lord.*
Il faut que tout le monde vive.	*Live and let live.*

Voir, *to see*

Voir quelqu'un d'un bon œil,	*to be favorable to a person.*
Voir beaucoup de pays,	*to travel much.*
Voir tout en beau,	*to see the bright side of everything.*
Voir venir quelqu'un,	*to see what a person is driving at.*
N'avoir rien à voir à,	*to have nothing to do with.*
Faire voir,	*to show.*
En avoir vu bien d'autres,	*not to be so easily frightened.*

Vouloir, *to want, to wish*

Vouloir bien,	*to be willing, good enough, to like.*
Vouloir du bien à,	*to bear good will to.*
Vouloir du mal à,	*to bear ill will to.*
En vouloir à,	*to have a grudge against, to be angry with.*
Vouloir dire,	*to mean.*
Veuillez (+ an infinitive).	*Please (+ a verb).*
Vouloir en venir à,	*to be aiming at.*

CLASSIFIED VOCABULARY

LA FAMILLE. *The family*

le père, *the father.*	la mère, *the mother.*
le fils, *the son.*	la fille, *the daughter.*
le frère, *the brother.*	la sœur, *the sister.*
le grand-père, *the grandfather.*	la grand'mère, *the grandmother.*
le petit-fils, *the grandson.*	la petite-fille, *the granddaughter.*
l' oncle (m.), *the uncle.*	la tante, *the aunt.*
le neveu, *the nephew.*	la nièce, *the niece.*
le cousin, *the cousin.*	la cousine, *the cousin.*
le cousin germain, *the first cousin* (m.).	la cousine germaine, *the first cousin* (f.).
le beau-père, *the father-in-law.*	la belle-mère, *the mother-in-law.*
le beau-frère, *the brother-in-law.*	la belle-sœur, *the sister-in-law.*
le beau-fils, *the stepson.*	la belle-fille, *the stepdaughter.*
le gendre, *the son-in-law.*	la bru, *the daughter-in-law.*
l' aîné (m.), *the eldest son.*	l' aînée (f.), *the eldest daughter.*
le cadet, *the youngest son.*	la cadette, *the youngest daughter.*
les parents, *the parents.*	le parent, *the relative.*

LA MAISON. *The house*

la façade, *the front, the façade.*	le salon, *the parlor.*
le mur, *the wall.*	la salle à manger, *the dining room.*
la porte d'entrée, *the front door.*	le fumoir, *the smoking room.*
la fenêtre, *the window.*	la chambre à coucher, *the bedroom.*
le toit, *the roof.*	le boudoir, *the boudoir.*
la girouette, *the weathercock.*	la salle de bain, *the bathroom.*
la gouttière, *the gutter.*	la mansarde, *the garret.*
la cheminée, *the chimney.*	le rez-de-chaussée, *the groundfloor.*
le vestibule, *the vestibule, foyer.*	l' étage (m.), *the floor, the story.*
l' escalier (m.), *the stairs.*	le grenier, *the attic.*
l' ascenseur (m.), *the elevator, lift.*	la cave, *the cellar.*
le monte-charge, *the dumb-waiter.*	le balcon, *the balcony.*

LES MEUBLES. *The furniture*

la table, *the table.*
la chaise, *the chair.*
le fauteuil, *the armchair.*
le sofa, *the sofa.*
le canapé, *the divan.*
la console, *the console.*
la cheminée, *the mantel-piece.*
le miroir, *the mirror.*
la pendule, *the clock.*
le candélabre, *the candlestick.*
le lustre, *the chandelier.*
le poste de T.S.F.,[1] *the radio set.*
le cadre, *the frame* (picture).
le buffet, *the cupboard.*
l' armoire (f.), *the china-closet, the wardrobe.*
la servante, *the dinner-wagon.*
le tapis, *the rug.*
le bureau, *the desk.*
le rideau, *the curtain.*

le lit, *the bed.*
le matelas, *the mattress.*
l' oreiller (m.), *the pillow.*
le drap, *the sheet.*
la taie d'oreiller, *the pillow-case.*
la couverture, *the blanket.*
l' édredon (m.), *the comforter.*
la commode, *the chiffonier.*
la table de toilette, *the dresser.*
la table de nuit, *the night table.*
la garde-robe, *the wardrobe.*
le placard, *the closet.*
la descente de lit, *the carpet.*
le porte-manteau, *the coat-hanger.*
le porte-parapluies, *the umbrella-stand.*
le rayon, *the shelf.*
le ventilateur, *the fan.*
le poêle, *the stove.*
le fourneau, *the kitchen-stove.*

NOURRITURE. *Food*

Hors-d'œuvre. *Relishes, side-dishes*

des anchois, *anchovies.*
du caviar, *caviar.*
des sardines, *sardines.*
du hareng, *herring.*

des crevettes, *shrimps.*
du saucisson, *sausage.*
du jambon, *ham.*
des olives, *olives.*

Potages. *Soups*

un potage julienne, ⎤ *vegetable*
un potage jardinière, ⎦ *soup.*
le bouillon, *broth.*
un potage bisque, *bisque soup.*
une soupe à l'oignon, *onion soup.*

une soupe à l'oseille (f.), *sorrel soup.*
une soupe au vermicelle, *vermicelli soup.*
une soupe aux poireaux, *leek soup.*

Poissons. *Fish*

du saumon, *salmon.*
du turbot, *turbot.*
de la sole, *sole.*
du maquereau, *mackerel.*
de la raie, *skate, ray.*

de la morue, *codfish.*
de l'esturgeon, *sturgeon.*
de l'églefin (m.), *haddock.*
du brochet, *pike.*
de la limande, *flounder.*

Crustacés et coquillages. *Crustacea and shell-fish*

du homard, ⎤
de la langouste, ⎦ *lobster.*
des écrevisses, *crawfish.*

des huîtres, *oysters.*
des moules, *mussels.*
des crevettes, *shrimps.*

---

[1] T.S.F. means télégraphie sans fil (wireless telegraphy).

Viandes. *Meat*

du rosbif, *roastbeef.*

un bifteck, *beefsteak.*

du ragoût, *stew.*

du rôti de veau, *roast veal.*

du gigot, *leg of lamb.*

un entrecôte, *porter-house steak.*

une côtelette de veau, *veal chop.*

une côtelette de mouton, *mutton chop.*

une côtelette d'agneau, *lamb chop.*

une côtelette de porc, *pork chop.*

des rognons, *kidneys.*

des ris de veau, *sweet-bread.*

Volaille et gibier. *Poultry and game*

du poulet, *chicken.*

du poulet de grain, *spring chicken.*

du poulet au blanc, *chicken fricassee.*

du canard, *duck.*

du dindon, *turkey.*

du caneton, *young duck.*

de l'oie (f.), *goose.*

du pigeon, *pigeon.*

des pigeonneaux, *squabs.*

du lièvre, *hare.*

du faisan, *pheasant.*

des perdrix, *partridges.*

des cailles, *quails.*

de la bécasse, *woodcock.*

Légumes. *Vegetables*

des asperges, *asparagus.*

des aubergines, *egg-plants.*

des betteraves, *beets.*

des carottes, *carrots.*

du céléri, *celery.*

des choux, *cabbage.*

du chou-fleur, *cauliflower.*

des choux de Bruxelles, *Brussel sprouts.*

des épinards, *spinach.*

des flageolets, *green beans.*

des haricots, *beans.*

des haricots verts, *string beans.*

des navets, *turnips.*

de l'oseille (f.), *sorrel.*

des petits pois, *green peas.*

des poireaux, *leeks.*

des pommes de terre, *potatoes.*

des tomates, *tomatoes.*

FRUITS ET ARBRES FRUITIERS. *Fruit and fruit trees*
(Most fruits are feminine; most fruit trees, masculine)

la poire, *the pear.*

la pomme, *the apple.*

la prune, *the plum.*

la pêche, *the peach.*

l' abricot (m.), *the apricot.*

la cerise, *the cherry.*

la fraise, *the strawberry.*

la framboise, *the raspberry*

la mûre, *the mulberry.*

la groseille, *currant.*

la noix, *the walnut.*

la noisette, *the hazel-nut.*

l' amande (f.), *the almond.*

le raisin, *the grape.*

le poirier, *the pear tree.*

le pommier, *the apple tree.*

le prunier, *the plum tree.*

le pêcher, *the peach tree.*

l' abricotier (m.), *the apricot tree.*

le cerisier, *the cherry tree.*

le fraisier, *the strawberry vine.*

le framboisier, *the raspberry bush.*

le mûrier, *the mulberry tree.*

le groseillier, *currant bush.*

le noyer, *the walnut tree.*

le noisetier, *the hazel tree.*

l' amandier (m.), *the almond tree.*

la vigne, *the grapevine.*

le marron, *the chestnut.*
la figue, *the fig.*
la datte, *the date.*
l' olive (f.), *the olive.*
le citron, *the lemon.*
l' orange (f.), *the orange.*
la mandarine, *the tangerine.*
le pamplemousse, *the grape-fruit.*

la grenade, *the pomegranate.*
le melon, *the melon.*
l' ananas (m.), *the pineapple.*

le marronnier, *the chestnut tree.*
le figuier, *the fig tree.*
le dattier, *the date tree.*
l' olivier (m.), *the olive tree.*
le citronnier, *the lemon tree.*
l' oranger (m.), *the orange tree.*
le mandarinier, *the tangerine tree.*
le pamplemousse, *the grape-fruit tree.*

le grenadier, *pomegranate tree.*
le melon, *the melon.*
l' ananas (m.), *the pineapple.*

SALADES. *Salads*

la laitue, *lettuce.*
la romaine, *romaine.*
l' endive (f.), *endive.*

la chicorée, *chicory.*
l' escarole (f.), *escarole.*
le cresson, *watercress.*

FROMAGES. *Cheese*

le camembert, *camembert.*
le brie, *brie.*
le gruyère, *Swiss-cheese.*
le roquefort, *roquefort.*

le Hollande, *Holland-cheese.*
l' Edam (m.), *Edam-cheese.*
le Chester, *Chester-cheese.*
le petit suisse, *cream cheese.*

DESSERTS. *Sweets*

des pâtisseries, *pastries.*
du gâteau, *cake.*
des sorbets, *sherbets.*
de la tarte, *tart.*
des tartelettes, *tartlets.*
du chausson, *fruit-pie.*
du baba, *baba.*
du chocolat, *chocolate.*
des pralines, *chocolate-candy.*

des biscuits, *biscuits.*
de la compote, *stewed fruits.*
des bonbons, *candy.*
de la glace, *ice-cream.*
de la confiture, *jam.*
de la gelée, *jelly.*
des petits fours, *petits fours.*
du cacao, *cocoa.*
des dragées, *Jordan almonds.*

VAISSELLE ET ARGENTERIE. *China and silverware*

le plat, *the dish.*
l' assiette (f.), *the plate.*
l' assiette à soupe, *the soup-plate.*
l' assiette à dessert, *the dessert plate.*
le couteau de table, *the knife.*
le couteau à dessert, *the dessert-knife.*
le couteau à poisson, *the fish-knife.*
la corbeille à pain, *the bread-basket.*

la cafetière, *the coffee-pot.*
la pelle à tarte, *the pie-knife.*
la pince à sucre, *the sugar-tong.*
la soupière, *the soup-tureen.*
le ravier, *radish-dish.*
la saucière, *the sauce-boat.*
le légumier, *the vegetable-dish.*
le coquetier, *the egg-cup.*
la salière, *the salt-cellar.*

la cuiller de table, *the table-spoon.*
la cuiller à dessert, *the dessert-spoon.*
la cuiller à thé, *the tea-spoon.*
la cuiller à café, *the coffee-spoon.*
la cuiller à sel, *the salt-spoon.*
la fourchette de table, *the table-fork.*
la fourchette à dessert, *the dessert-fork.*
la fourchette à poisson, *the fish-fork.*
la fourchette à huître, *the oyster-fork.*
le service à découper, *the carving set.*
le service à salade, *the salad set.*
la louche, *the soup-ladle.*

la poivrière, *the pepper-box.*
l' huilier (m.), *the oil-pitcher.*
le beurrier, *the butter-dish.*
le sucrier, *the sugar-bowl.*
le compotier, *the fruit-dish.*
le saladier, *the salad-bowl.*
la bonbonnière, *the sweet-box.*
le verre, *the glass.*
la coupe, *the drinking cup.*
la tasse, *the cup.*
la soucoupe, *the saucer.*
le bol, *the bowl.*
la carafe, *the decanter.*
la théière, *the tea-pot.*

Les vêtements. *Clothing*

Hommes

l' habit (m.), *the full dress.*
le smoking, *the tuxedo.*
la jaquette, *the cutaway.*
la redingote, *the frock-coat.*
le complet, *the business suit.*
le veston, *the coat.*
le gilet, *the vest.*
le pantalon, *the pants.*
la culotte, *the short pants.*
la chemise, *the shirt.*
le col (dur, mou), *the collar (hard, soft).*
la cravate, *the tie.*
le sous-vêtement, *the underwear.*
les bretelles, *the suspenders.*
le caleçon, *the hose.*
la chaussette, *the sock.*
le pyjama, *the pajama.*
le pardessus, *the overcoat.*
la pelisse, *the fur-coat.*
la canne, *the walking stick.*

Femmes

la robe, *the dress.*
le corsage, *the corsage.*
la jupe, *the skirt.*
le manteau, *the coat.*
la fourrure, *the fur-coat.*
le tour de cou, *the neck-piece.*
le tailleur, *the tailor-suit.*
le jupon, *the petticoat.*
la chemise de nuit, *the night gown.*
la brassière, *the brassière.*
la combinaison, *the slip, the step in.*
le pantalon, *the knickers.*
le bas, *the stocking.*
le tablier, *the apron.*
le fourreau, *the slip.*
la dentelle, *the lace.*
le filet, *the hair-net.*
le nœud, *the bow.*
le sac à main, *the hand-bag.*
l' ombrelle (f.), *the parasol.*

Mixtes

le soulier, *the low-shoe.*
la bottine, *the high-shoe.*
la pantoufle, *the slipper.*
le chapeau, *the hat.*
le gant, *the glove.*

le bouton, *the button.*
le parapluie, *the umbrella.*
le mouchoir, *the handkerchief.*
la jarretière, *the garter.*
le porte-monnaie, *the purse.*

PAYS ET HABITANTS. *Countries, inhabitants, and their languages*

la France,	les Français,	le français.
les États-Unis (m.),	les Américains,	l' anglais.
l' Allemagne (f.),	les Allemands,	l' allemand.
l' Angleterre (f.),	les Anglais,	l' anglais.
la Belgique,	les Belges,	le français et le flamand.
la Bulgarie,	les Bulgares,	le bulgare.
le Danemark,	les Danois,	le danois.
l' Espagne (f.),	les Espagnols,	l' espagnol.
la Grèce,	les Grecs,	le grec moderne.
la Hollande,	les Hollandais,	le hollandais.
la Hongrie,	les Hongrois,	le hongrois.
l' Italie (f.),	les Italiens,	l' italien.
la Norvège,	les Norvégiens,	le norvégien.
la Pologne,	les Polonais,	le polonais.
le Portugal,	les Portugais,	le portugais.
la Roumanie,	les Roumains,	le moldo-valaque.
la Russie,	les Russes,	le russe.
la Suède,	les Suédois,	le suédois.
la Suisse,	les Suisses,	le français, l'allemand, l'italien.
la Turquie,	les Turcs,	le turc.
la Yugoslavie,	les Yugoslaves,	le serbe.

PROFESSIONS ET MÉTIERS. *Professions and trades*

le médecin, *the physician.*
l' avocat (m.), *the lawyer.*
le notaire, *the notary.*
le professeur, *the professor.*
l' institutrice (f.), *the (lady) teacher.*
l' ingénieur (m.), *the engineer.*
l' architecte (m.), *the architect.*
le vétérinaire, *the veterinary.*
le pharmacien, *the pharmacist.*
le droguiste, *the druggist.*
le dentiste, *the dentist.*
le musicien, *the musician.*
l' artiste (m. or f.), *the artist.*
le sculpteur, *the sculptor.*
l' écrivain (m. or f.), *the writer.*
le banquier, *the banker.*
le directeur, *the director.*
le gérant, *the manager.*
le secrétaire, *the secretary.*
le comptable, *the bookkeeper.*
le fabricant, *the manufacturer.*

l' infirmier (ère), *the nurse.*
l' ouvrier (m.), *the workman.*
le charpentier, *the carpenter.*
le menuisier, *the joiner.*
le serrurier, *the locksmith.*
le forgeron, *the blacksmith.*
le mécanicien, *the mechanic.*
le maçon, *the bricklayer.*
le peintre, *the painter.*
le plombier, *the plumber.*
l' électricien (m.), *the electrician.*
le gazier, *the gas-man.*
le poêlier, *the stove-maker.*
le photographe, *the photographer.*
le boulanger, *the baker.*
le boucher, *the butcher.*
le charcutier, *the pork-butcher.*
l' épicier (m.), *the grocer.*
le pâtissier, *the pastry-cook.*
le cuisinier, *the chef, the cook.*
le mercier, *the haberdasher.*

le (la) sténographe, *the stenograph.*
le (la) dactylographe, *the typist.*
le (la) sténo-dactylo, *the steno-typist.*
le correspondancier, *the correspondant.*
le représentant, *the representative.*
le voyageur, *the traveling-salesman.*
le patron, *the boss.*
le commis, *the clerk.*
l' employé (m.), *the employee.*
le garçon de course, *the errand-boy.*
l' hôtelier (m.), *the hotel-keeper.*
l' aubergiste (m.), *the inn-keeper.*
le restaurateur, *the restaurant-keeper.*
la coiffeur, *the hairdresser.*
le barbier, *the barber.*
le garçon de cabine, *the steward.*

le tailleur, *the tailor.*
le chapelier, *the hat-maker.*
le cordonnier, *the shoemaker.*
le savetier, *the cobbler.*
le tapissier, *the upholsterer.*
l' imprimeur (m.), *the printer.*
le papetier, *the stationer.*
le boutiquier, *the shop-keeper.*
le portier, *the doorman.*
le concierge, *the janitor.*
le chauffeur, *the taxi-driver.*
le facteur, *the post-man, the porter.*
le domestique, *the servant.*
la servante, *the maid.*
la femme de chambre, *the chamber-maid.*
le valet, *the valet.*
la blanchisseuse, *the laundress.*
la nourrice, *the nurse* (children).

ARMÉE ET MARINE. *Army and Navy*

l' officier (m.), *the officer.*
le maréchal, *the marshal.*
le général, *the general.*
le colonel, *the colonel.*
le major, *the major.*
le capitaine, *the captain.*
le lieutenant, *the lieutenant.*
l' adjudant, *the adjutant.*

le sous-officier, *the non-commissioned officer.*
le sergent, *the sergeant.*
le caporal, *the corporal.*
l' amiral (m.), *the admiral.*
l' enseigne (m.), *the ensign.*
le matelot, *the sailor.*
le mousse, *the ship-boy.*
le quartier-maître, *the quartermaster.*

ARTS ET SCIENCES. *Arts and Sciences*

la musique, *music.*
la poésie, *poetry.*
la peinture, *painting.*
la sculpture, *sculpture.*
l' architecture (f.), *architecture.*
le chant, *singing.*

la physique, *physic.*
la chimie, *chemistry.*
la minéralogie, *mineralogy.*
l' histoire (f.), *history.*
la géographie, *geography.*
la pédagogie, *pedagogy.*

LA NATURE. *Nature*

le ciel, *the sky.*
la terre, *the earth.*
le firmament, *the firmament.*
le soleil, *the sun.*
la lune, *the moon.*
l' étoile (f.), *the star.*
l' astre (m.), *the heavenly body.*
le nuage, *the cloud.*

la montagne, *the mountain.*
la vallée, *the valley.*
le fleuve, *the river.*
la rivière, *the river.*
la mer, *the sea.*
l' océan (m.), *the ocean.*
la vague, *the wave.*
la marée, *the tide.*

la comète, *the comet.*
le volcan, *the volcano.*
le tremblement de terre, *the earth-quake.*
le minerai, *the ore.*
le vent, *the wind.*
la tempête, *the tempest.*
le typhon, *the typhoon.*
la mine, *the mine.*
le gouffre, *the abyss.*
le précipice, *the precipice.*
la pluie, *the rain.*
la neige, *the snow.*
la grêle, *the hail.*
l' orage (m.), *the storm.*
le tonnerre, *the thunder.*

LA VILLE. *The city*

la rue, *the street.*
l' avenue (f.), *the avenue.*
le boulevard, *the boulevard.*
le parc, *the park.*
l' hôtel (m.) de ville,
la mairie, } *the city hall.*
l' hôtel (m.) des postes, *the post-office.*
la gare, *the railroad station.*
le télégraphe, *the telegraph office.*
le réverbère, *the lamp-post.*
le tram, *the tramway.*
l' omnibus (m.), *the omnibus.*
le métro, *the subway.*
le conseil municipal, *the town council.*
le maire, *the mayor.*
l' échevin (m.), *the alderman.*
le juge, *the judge.*
l' égout (m.), *the sewer.*
la centrale électrique, *the power station.*
le monument, *the monument.*
le musée, *the museum.*
l' église (f.), *the church.*
la villa, *the mansion.*
le palais, *the palace.*
l' hôtel (m.), *the hotel.*
le restaurant, *the restaurant.*
le théâtre, *the theater.*
le cinéma, *the movie-house.*
l' agent (m.) de police, *the policeman.*
l' officier (m.) de police, *the police officer.*
le commissaire de police, *the sheriff.*
le préfet de police, *the police commissioner.*

LES PARTIES DU CORPS. *Parts of the body*

le corps, *the body.*
la tête, *the head.*
les cheveux, *the hair.*
le front, *the forehead.*
l' œil (m.), *the eye;* les yeux, *the eyes.*
les sourcils, *the eye-brows.*
les cils, *the eye-lashes.*
la tempe, *the temple.*
l' oreille (f.), *the ear.*
la joue, *the cheek.*
le nez, *the nose.*
la narine, *the nostril.*
la lèvre, *the lip.*
la dent, *the tooth.*
la langue, *the tongue.*
le palais, *the palate.*
le menton, *the chin.*
la poitrine, *the chest.*
le cœur, *the heart.*
le bras, *the arm.*
le coude, *the elbow.*
le poignet, *the wrist.*
la main, *the hand.*
le doigt, *the finger.*
le pouce, *the thumb.*
l' index (m.), *the index.*
le dos, *the back.*
le ventre, *the abdomen.*
l' estomac (m.), *the stomach.*
la hanche, *the hip.*
la cuisse, *the thigh.*
la jambe, *the leg.*
le mollet, *the calf.*
le pied, *the foot.*

le cou, *the neck.*
la gorge, *the throat.*
l' épaule (f.), *the shoulder.*

la cheville, *the ankle.*
l' orteil (m.), *the toe.*
le talon, *the heel.*

MALADIES. *Diseases*

la fièvre, *the fever.*
le refroidissement, *the cold.*
la grippe, *the grippe.*
l' influenza (f.), *the influenza.*
la pneumonie, *the pneumonia.*
la pleurésie, *the pleurisy.*
le croup, *the croup, diphtheria.*
la scarlatine, *the scarlet fever.*
la rougeole, *the measles.*
la coqueluche, *the whooping cough.*
la migraine, *the headache.*

le rhumatisme, *the rheumatism.*
la goutte, *the gout.*
le lumbago, *the lumbago.*
l' urticaire (f.), *the rash, the hives.*
l' ophthalmie (f.), *the ophthalmy.*
la paralysie, *the paralysis.*
l' indigestion (f.), *the indigestion.*
l' apoplexie (f.), *the apoplexy.*
le délire, *the delirium.*
la phtisie, *the consumption.*
la bronchite, *the bronchitis.*

LES ANIMAUX. *Animals*

Domestiques

le cheval, *the horse.*
la vache, *the cow.*
le bœuf, *the ox.*
le taureau, *the bull.*
le veau, *the calf.*
le mouton, *the sheep.*
la brebis, *the ewe.*
l' agneau (m.), *the lamb.*
le chien, *the dog.*
le chat, *the cat.*
le cochon, *the pig.*
la chèvre, *the goat.*
le lapin, *the rabbit.*
la poule, *the hen.*
le coq, *the rooster.*
le poulet, *the chicken.*
le poussin, *the chick.*
le canard, *the duck.*
le dindon, *the turkey.*
l' oie (f.), *the goose.*
le faisan, *the pheasant.*

Sauvages

le tigre, *the tiger.*
le léopard, *the leopard.*
l' ours (m.), *the bear.*
le chacal, *the jackal.*
l' éléphant (m.), *the elephant.*
le singe, *the monkey.*
le gorille, *the gorilla.*
la panthère, *the panther.*
le loup, *the wolf.*
le sanglier, *the wild boar.*
le renard, *the fox.*
la girafe, *the giraffe.*
le rhinocéros, *the rhinoceros.*
le lièvre, *the hare.*
le zèbre, *the zebra.*
le buffle, *the buffalo.*
l' antilope (f.), *the antelope.*
l' hippopotame (m.), *the hippopotamus.*
le crocodile, *the crocodile.*
la tortue, *the turtle.*

LES MÉTAUX. *Metals*

l' or (m.), *the gold.*
l' argent (m.), *the silver.*
le platine, *the platinum.*
le cuivre, *the copper.*
le plomb, *the lead.*
l' étain (m.), *the tin.*

le fer, *the iron.*
le nickel, *the nickel.*
le laiton, *the brass.*
le bronze, *the bronze.*
l' acier (m.), *the steel.*
l' aluminium (m.), *the aluminium.*

VOCABULARY

A

a, has. **il y a,** there is, there are; ago.

à, to, at, in.

abandonner, to abandon.

abeille, *f.* bee.

abhorré de, abhorred by.

abondant, -e, abundant.

d'abord, at first.

abord, *m.* approach. **d'—,** first. **de prime —,** at first sight.

aboyer, to bark.

abreuver, to water, to drench.

abricot, *m.* apricot.

absent, -e, absent. (*as a noun*) absent, absentee.

absolu, absolute.

absolument, entirely, absolutely.

s'abstenir (de), to abstain (from).

abstinence, *f.* abstinence.

abuser, to abuse, to deceive.

accepté, -e, accepted.

accepter, to accept.

accès, *m.* fit, attack.

accident, *m.* accident.

accompagner, to accompany.

accord, *m.* agreement.

s'accorder, to lean on one's elbow.

accoutumer, to accustom.

accueil, *m.* reception, welcome.

accueillir, to receive, to welcome.

accuser, to accuse.

acheté, -e, bought.

acheter (à), to buy from.

acheteur, *m.* purchaser.

achever, to finish.

acier, *m.* steel.

acquérir, to acquire.

s'acquitter, to perform.

acte, *m.* act.

actif, active, active.

action, *f.* engagement, action.

adjectif, *m.* adjective.

admettre, to admit.

admirer, to admire.

adresse, *f.* address.

adresser, to send to. **s'adresser (à),** to address.

adverbe, *m.* adverb.

adversité, *f.* adversity.

aéroplane, *m.* airplane.

affaire, *f.* affair, matter.

affaires, *f. pl.* business.

affliger, to afflict, to distress.

affolé, frantic.

affreux, -se, frightful.

afin de, in order to (*with infin.*).

afin que, so that (*with subjun.*).

Afrique, *f.* Africa.

âge, *m.* age. **moyen âge,** Middle Ages.

âgé, -e, old, aged.

agi, behaved.

agir, to act, to behave.

agiter, to wave. **s'—,** to get restless.

agneau, *m.* lamb.

agréable, pleasant, agreeable.

aide, *f.* help.

aider, to help.

aïeul, *m.* grandfather. **aïeuls,** *m.* grandfathers. **aïeux,** *m.* ancestors.

aigu, aiguë, sharp, acute.

aiguille, *f.* needle.
ailleurs, elsewhere.   d'ailleurs, besides.
aimable, amiable, kind.
aimer, to like, to love.   **aimer
  mieux,** to prefer.
aîné, -e, elder, oldest.
ainsi, thus, so.
aise, bien aise, glad.
aisément, easily.
ajouter, to add.
ajuster, to adjust, to fit.
allé, -e, gone.
allée, *f.* alley.
allécher, to allure, to attract.
Allemagne, *f.* Germany.
allemand, -e, German.
aller, to go.   — bien, to be well.
allons! come! allons donc! non-
  sense!
allumer, to light, to kindle.
allumette, *f.* match.
almanach, *m.* almanac.
alors, then, at that time.
les Alpes, *f.* the Alps.
ambition, *f.* ambition.
âme, *f.* soul, spirit.
amende, *f.* fine, penalty.
amener, to bring (*a person*).
amer, bitter.
américain, -e, American.
Amérique, *f.* America.
ami, *m.*, amie, *f.* friend.
amitié, *f.* friendship.
amphithéâtre,   *m.*   amphitheatre,
  arena.
amusant, -e, amusing.
amusement, *m.* fun.
amuser, to amuse.   s'amuser, to
  enjoy one's self.
an, *m.* year.
ananas, *m.* pineapple.
ancien, ancienne, old, ancient.
ange, *m.* angel.
anglais, -e, English.
Angleterre, *f.* England.

animal, *m.* animal.
animé, -e, animated.
année, *f.* year.   l'année dernière, *f.*
  last year.
anniversaire, *m.* anniversary, birthday.
annoncer, to announce.
annuaire téléphonique,   *m.*   tele
  phone book.
anxiété, *f.* anxiety.
août, *m.* August.
apercevoir, to perceive; s'—, to
  notice (*a fact*).
apoplexie, *f.* apoplexy.
appareil, *m.* form, display.
appartement, *m.* apartment, rooms.
appartenir, to belong.
appel, *m.* appeal.   faire —, to call
  on (*for help*).
appeler, to call, to summon.   s'appeler, to call one's self, to be
  called.
appétit, *m.* appetite.
appliqué, -e, diligent.
s'appliquer, to apply one's self.
apporté, -e, brought.
apporter, to bring.
apportez-moi, bring me.
apprendre, to learn, to inform.
appris, -e, learned.
approbation, *f.* approbation.
s'approcher de, to go up to, to come
  near.
approuver, to approve.
appui, *m.* support.
appuyer, to support, to rest on.
après, after, afterwards (*time only*).
  après-demain, the day after to-
  morrow.   après-midi, *f.* afternoon.   — tout, after all, anyhow.
aqueduc, *m.* aqueduct.
arbre, *m.* tree.
architecte, *m.* architect.
ardemment, eagerly.
ardoise, *f.* slate.
arènes, *pl.* arena, **amphitheatre.**

argent, *m.* money, silver.
argenté, -e, silvery.
argument, *m.* argument.
Aristote, *m.* Aristotle.
arracher, to tear out, to pull up.
arranger, to arrange.
s'arranger, to settle.
arrêter, to stop.
arrivé, -e, arrived.
arrivée, *f.* arrival.
arriver, to arrive, to happen.
arroser, to water.
article, *m.* article. — **défini,** definite article. — **indéfini,** indefinite article.
artillerie, *f.* artillery.
Asie, *f.* Asia.
assemblée, *f.* assembly, meeting.
asseoir, to seat. **s'asseoir,** to sit down.
assez, enough; rather, somewhat.
assiette, *f.* plate.
assigner, to assign.
assis, -e, seated, sitting.
assister à, to be present at.
assortiment, choice, line.
s'assombrir, to become dark.
assurer, to affirm, to maintain, to assure.
atelier, *m.* workshop, studio.
attaquer, to attack.
attendre, to wait (for); expect. **se faire —,** to be long in coming. **faire —,** to keep waiting.
attentif, attentive, attentive.
attention, *f.* attention, notice.
attentivement, attentively.
attirer, to attract; to drag.
attraper, to catch. — **froid,** to catch cold.
au, to the, at the. **au moins,** at the least. **au lieu de,** instead of.
auberge, *f.* inn.
aubergiste, *m.* innkeeper.
aucun, -e, any, none, no.
audace, *f.* audacity.

au-devant, before.
augmenter, to increase.
aujourd'hui, to-day.
auparavant (*adv.*), before.
auquel, à laquelle, auxquels, auxquelles, to which, to whom.
aussi, also, as; *at beginning of a clause,* therefore, and so.
aussitôt, immediately, at once.
aussitôt que, as soon as.
autant, as much, as many.
auteur, *m.* author.
automne, *m.* autumn.
autour (de), around.
autre, other.
autrefois, formerly.
autrement, otherwise.
Autriche, *f.* Austria.
autrichien, *m.* **-enne,** *f.* an Austrian.
aux, to the, at the.
il y avait, there was, there were.
avaler, to swallow.
plus avancé, better off.
avancement, *m.* promotion.
avance, *f.* advance. **en —, d'—,** ahead of time.
avancer, to advance, to be fast.
avant (*prep. of time*), before. **avant-hier,** the day before yesterday. **en -,** forward, **d'—,** ahead.
avec, with.
aventure, *f.* adventure.
avenue, *f.* avenue.
avertir, to warn, to notify.
aveugle, blind.
avocat, *m.* lawyer.
avoir, to have.
avouer, to confess, to admit.
avril, *m.* April.
ayant, having.
azur, azure.

B

bagage, *m.* luggage.
bague, *f.* ring.

3

baignoire, *f.* bath tub.
baisser, to stoop, to lower.
bal, *m.* ball, dance, party.
balai, *m.* broom.
balayer, to sweep.
balbutier, to stammer.
balle, *f.* ball, bullet.
balustrade, *f.* railing.
banane, *f.* banana.
banc, *m.* bench.
banque, *f.* bank.
banquier, *m.* banker.
bas, basse, low. au bas, at the foot.
bataille, *f.* battle.
bataillon, *m.* battalion.
bateau, *m.* boat. bateau à vapeur, steamer.
bâtir, to build.
bâton, *m.* stick.
batterie, *f.* battery.
battre, to beat; to flap. se battre, to fight.
battu, -e, beaten.
beau, bel, belle, beautiful, fine, handsome.
beaucoup, much, many, a great deal, plenty.
beau-frère, *m.* brother-in-law.
bec, *m.* beak.
Belgique, *f.* Belgium.
belle-sœur, *f.* sister-in-law.
benin, -igne, benign, kindly.
besogne, *f.* task, job.
besoin (avoir), to be in need, to need.
bête, *f.* beast, animal.
bête (*adj.*), stupid.
beurre, *m.* butter.
bévue, *f.* blunder.
bibliothèque, *f.* library.
bien, well, very, a great many, most; much, quite; indeed. eh bien! well! bien aise, glad. c'est —, that's all right.
bientôt, soon. à —, see you soon.

bière, *f.* beer.
bijou, *m.* jewel.
billet, *m.* note.
bise, *f.* north wind.
blâmer, to blame.
blanc, blanche, white.
blanchisserie, wash-house, bleachery, laundry.
blé, *m.* wheat.
blessé, -e, wounded.
blesser, to wound.
blessure, *f.* wound.
bleu, -e, blue.
bœuf, *m.* ox.
boire, to drink.
bois, *m.* wood, grove.
boisson, *f.* drink.
boîte, *f.* box.
boiter, to limp, to walk lame.
bol, *m.* bowl.
bombe, *f.* bomb.
bon, bonne, good, kind. à quoi —? what is the use?
bonheur, *m.* happiness, pleasure.
bonhomme, *m.* fellow, "little man."
bonne, *f.* maid, servant, nursemaid.
bonté, *f.* goodness.
bord, *m.* edge, bank, shore. au bord de la mer, at the coast.
borgne, blind.
bottine, *f.* boot.
bouche, *f.* mouth.
boucle d'oreille, *f.* earring.
boulanger, *m.* baker.
bouquet, *m.* bouquet.
bourgeois, *m.* middle-class man.
bourse, *f.* purse. la Bourse, stock exchange.
bout, *m.* end, extremity.
bouteille, *f.* bottle.
bouton, *m.* button.
bracelet, *m.* bracelet.
bras, *m.* arm.
brave, brave; honest.
braver, to brave, to defy.
brebis, *f.* sheep, ewe.

4

bref, brève, short, brief.
Brésil, *m.* Brazil.
breton, Briton, of Brittany.
Bretagne, *f.* Brittany.
bride, *f.* bridle.
brillant, bright, sparkling, glittering.
broche, *f.* brooch.
brosse, *f.* brush.
brosser, to brush.
brouillard, *m.* fog.
bruit, *m.* noise, report, rumor.
brûler, to burn.
brun, -e, brown.
brusquement, rudely, bruskly.
bruyant, -e, noisy, boisterous.
bu, -e, drunk.
buffet, buffet, cupboard.
buisson, *m.* bush.
bureau, *m.* desk, office.

C

ça (*a familiar contraction for* **cela**), that. **ça et là,** here and there.
cabaret, *m.* tavern.
cache-nez, *m.* muffler.
caché, -e, hidden.
cacher, to hide, to conceal.
cadeau, *m.* present.
cadet, -te, younger, junior.
café, *m.* coffee.
cage, *f.* cage.
cahier, *m.* copy-book, note-book.
caisse, *f.* box.
caisse d'épargne, savings-bank.
calèche, *f.* carriage.
calendrier, *m.* calendar.
calme, calm.
camarade, *m.* comrade.
campagne, *f.* country; campaign. **à la campagne,** in the country.
canadien, -enne, Canadian.
canal, *m.* canal.
canif, *m.* penknife.
canne, *f.* cane.
canot, *m.* rowboat.

canotage, *m.* boat riding.
capitaine, *m.* captain.
capitale, *f.* capital.
captiver, to captivate; to take up.
car (*conj.*), for.
carafe, *f.* carafe, decanter.
cargaison, *f.* cargo.
carré, -e, square.
carte, *f.* card, bill of fare, map.
— **à jouer,** playing card.
carton, *m.* cardboard, box. — **à chapeaux,** hat box.
cas, *m.* case, circumstance. **en tout cas,** at any rate.
cascade, *f.* cascade, waterfall.
casque, *m.* helmet.
casquette, *f.* cap.
casser, to break. — **la croûte,** to eat.
cathédrale, *f.* cathedral.
cause, *f.* cause. **à** — **de,** on account of, because of.
causer, to talk, to chat.
causeur, talkative.
ce, cet, cette, this, that. **ce qui, ce que,** what (*rel.*). **ce sont,** they are, those are.
ceci, this (thing).
céder, to yield, to give way *or* place. — **le pas,** to give precedence.
cela, that (thing).
célèbre (*adj.*), celebrated, famous.
célébrer, to celebrate.
céleste, celestial, heavenly.
celle, *f.* that, this. **celle-ci,** this, this one. **celle-là,** that, that one.
celles, *f.* those, these. **celles-ci,** these. **celles-là,** those.
celui, *m.* that, this. **celui qui,** he who. **celui-ci,** the latter, this, this one. **celui-là,** that, that one.
cent, hundred.
centime, *m.* centime, *about one-fifth of a cent.*
cependant, however, meanwhile.

cercle, *m.* circle, club.
cerise, *f.* cherry.
certain, -e, certain.
certainement, certainly.
ces (*adj.*), these, those.
cesser, to cease.
c'est, he is, she is, it is.
cet, cette. *See* ce.
ceux, *m.* those, these. ceux-ci,
these, the latter. ceux-là, those,
the former.
chacun, -e, each, every one.
chagrin, *m.* grief, trouble.
chagrin, -e, sad, vexed, sorry.
chaîne, *f.* chain.
chaise, *f.* chair.
chaleur, *f.* warmth, heat. les —s,
the hot season.
chambellan, *m.* chamberlain.
chambre, *f.* room.
chameau, *m.* camel.
champ, *m.* field. — de course,
race-course.
chance, *f.* luck, chance.
changement, *m.* change.
changer, to change.
chanson, *f.* song.
chanter, to sing.
chapeau, *m.* hat.
chapelle, *f.* chapel.
chaque, each, every.
charger, to load, to charge.
Charles, *m.* Charles.
charmant, -e, charming.
charmé, -e, delighted.
charpentier, *m.* carpenter.
chasse, *f.* hunt.
chasser, to drive, to hunt.
chasseur, *m.* huntsman.
chat, *m.* chatte, *f.* cat.
château, *m.* castle.
châtié, clean-cut, severe, chaste.
chaud, -e, hot, warm. avoir chaud,
to be warm.
chauffer, to warm.
chaussette, *f.* sock.

chaussure, *f.* footwear.
chef, *m.* chief. — d'œuvre, masterpiece.
chemin, *m.* way, road.
chemise, *f.* shirt, chemise.
cher, chère, dear.
cherché, -e, looked for, sought.
chercher, to look for, to seek, to
try to find.
chétif, -ive, paltry, puny.
cheval, *m.* horse. à —, on horseback.
cheveux, *m. pl.* the hair.
chez, at, in, *or* to the house of.
chic (*invar.*), smart.
chien, *m.* dog.
chiffre, *m.* number.
Chili, *m.* Chili.
Chine, *f.* China.
choc, *m.* shock.
choisi, -e, chosen.
choisir, to choose.
choix, *m.* choice.
chose, *f.* thing. autre —, *f.* something else.
choucroute, *f.* sauerkraut.
chrétienté, *f.* Christendom.
ci, here.
ciel, *m.* heaven, sky.
cigale, *f.* grasshopper.
cigare, *m.* cigar.
cinq, five.
cinquante, fifty.
cinquième, fifth.
circonstance, *f.* circumstance.
cirque, *m.* circus.
ciseaux, *m. pl.* scissors.
citadin, *m.* townsman.
citoyen, *m.* citizen.
civil, -e, polite.
clair, *m.* light. clair de lune, moon-
light.
clair, -e (*adj.*), clear, obvious, light.
clameur, *f.* noise.
classe, *f.* class. salle de —, classroom.

claquer, to slam.
clé, f. key.
clef, f. key.
clergé, m. clergy.
clou, m. nail.
cœur, m. heart, courage. de tout mon —, with all my heart. de bon —, heartily, willingly.
coiffeur, m. barber.
coin, m. corner.
col, m. collar.
colère, f. anger, passion.
collier, m. necklace.
colonel, m. colonel.
combattre, to fight.
combien, how much, how many. combien de temps, how long.
comédien, m. actor.
comique, comical.
commandant, m. commander.
commandé, -e, ordered.
commander, to order, to bid.
comme, as, like, how. — à l'ordinaire, as usual. — il faut, well mannered.
commencer, to begin, to commence.
comment, how, what.
commettre, to commit.
commission, f. errand.
compagne, f. comrade.
compagnon, m. companion.
complet, -plète, complete.
complet, m. three-piece suit.
complètement, completely.
complexe, complex, varied, unusual.
composé, -e, composed.
comprendre, to understand, past part. compris.
compte, m. account. se rendre —, to realize.
compter, to count; to intend.
comptoir, m. counter.
concevoir, to conceive, to plan.
concourir, to take part.
condamner, to condemn.

condition, f. position.
conducteur, m. driver, guide, conductor.
conduire, to take to; to drive. se —, to behave.
conduite, f. conduct.
confiance, f. confidence.
confier, to trust, to intrust.
confiture, f. jam.
se confondre, to be lost in, to become confused.
confus, -e, confused.
congé, m. vacation leave.
congédier, to dismiss.
connaissance, f. acquaintance, knowledge.
connaître, to know, to judge.
conquérir, to conquer.
conseil, m. advice; council.
conseiller, to advise, to recommend.
consentir, to consent.
considérer, to consider, to think, to hold to be.
consommation, f. refreshment, drink; use.
constamment, constantly.
consulter, to consult.
conte, m. story, tale, anecdote.
content, -e, satisfied, pleased.
conter, to relate.
continuellement, continually.
continuer, to continue.
contraindre, to compel.
contraire, contrary, reverse. au —, on the contrary.
contre, against, contrary to.
convaincre, to convince.
convaincu, -e, convinced.
convenable, becoming, proper.
convenablement, properly.
convenir, to agree. il convient, it is proper.
convenu, -e, appointed, agreed upon.
conversation, f. conversation.

corail, *m.* coral.
corbeau, *m.* crow.
corbeille, *f.* basket.
cordialité, *f.* cordiality.
Corniche, *f. a famous road along and above the coast of the Riviera in Southern France.*
corps, *m.* body.
correspondance, *f.* correspondence.
corriger, to correct, to improve.
corrompre, to taint.
Corse, Corsica.
costume, *m.* suit.
côte, *f.* coast. la Côte d'Azur, the Riviera.
côté, *m.* side. à —, near, on one side. de l'autre —, on the other side. d'un autre —, on the other hand.
coton, *m.* cotton.
cou, *m.* neck.
se coucher, to go to bed, to lie down.
coude, *m.* elbow.
couleur, *f.* color.
coup, *m.* shot, blow, stroke. — de canon, cannon-shot. — de pied, kick. — de téléphone, telephone call. tout à —, suddenly.
coupable, guilty.
coupé, -e, cut.
couper, to cut, to cut off.
cour, *f.* court, courtyard, yard.
courage, *m.* courage.
courageux, -se, courageous.
courant, *m.* current. courant d'air, draught.
courir, to run.
couronner, to crown.
cours, *m.* course.
course, *f.* errand; race.
court, -e, short.
courtisan, *m.* courtier.
cousin, *m.* -e, *f.* cousin.
couteau, *m.* knife.
coûter, to cost.

coutume, *f.* habit, custom. avoir —, to be accustomed.
couturière, *f.* dressmaker.
couvert, -e (de), covered (with).
couvrir, to cover.
craie, *f.* chalk.
craindre, to fear.
crainte, *f.* fear.
cravate, *f.* necktie, cravat.
crayon, *m.* pencil.
créateur, -trice, creative, inventive
crédule, credulous.
créer, to create.
crème, *f.* cream.
crever, to burst.
cri, *m.* cry.
crier, to cry, to cry out, to shout. s'écrier, to exclaim.
crime, *m.* crime.
crin, *m.* horsehair.
croire, to believe.
cruel, -le, cruel.
cruellement, cruelly.
cueillir, to gather, to harvest.
cuiller, *f.* spoon.
cuir, *m.* leather.
cuirasse, *f.* cuirass.
cuisine, *f.* kitchen.
cuisinière, *f.* cook.
cuivre, *m.* copper.
curieux, -se, curious.

D

dame, *f.* lady.
Danemark, *m.* Denmark.
dans, in.
danse, *f.* dance.
date, *f.* date.
dater, to date (from).
davantage, more.
de, of, from, in, with, by; some, any; than.
dé, *m.* thimble.
débarrasser, to rid.
se débattre, to struggle.
décapiter, to behead.

8

débiter, to recite.

déborder, to overflow.

debout, standing up.

déboutonner, to unbutton.

décembre, *m.* December.

décevoir, to deceive.

décider, to decide; to persuade.

déclarer, to declare.

décoration, *f.* decoration.

décourager, to discourage.

découvert, -e, discovered.

découvrir, to uncover. se —, to take off one's hat.

dédire, to contradict.

défaut, *m.* fault, defect.

défendre, to forbid. se —, to defend one's self *or* each other; to deny one's self.

défendu, -e, forbidden.

définitivement, positively.

dégoût, *m.* dislike.

déjà, already.

déjeuner, *m.* breakfast.

déjeuner, *v.* to breakfast.

de l', de la, of the; some, any.

délicat, -e, delicate.

délicieux, -se, delicious, delightful.

demain, *m.* to-morrow.

demande, *f.* inquiry.

demander, to ask (for). se —, to ask one's self, to wonder.

démarche, *f.* step.

déménager, to move.

demeure, *f.* dwelling.

demeuré, -e, lived.

demeurer, to remain, to live, to dwell.

demi, -e, à demi, half. **demi-douzaine,** *f.* half-dozen. **demi-livre,** *f.* half-pound.

demoiselle, *f.* young lady, unmarried lady.

démontrer, to prove.

dénoter, to show, to denote, to evidence.

dent, *f.* tooth.

dentelle, *f.* lace.

dentiste, *m.* dentist.

départ, *m.* departure.

dépêche, *f.* dispatch.

dépêcher, to hasten.

dépendre de, to depend upon.

dépens, *m. pl.* expense.

dépenser, to spend.

déplaire, to displease.

déposer, to lay down.

dépourvu, -e, unprepared.

depuis, since, for, from. **depuis quand,** how long.

déranger, to disturb. se —, to get disturbed.

dernier, dernière, last; utmost, worst.

dernièrement, lately.

derrière, behind (*of place*).

des, of the, from the; some, any.

désagréable, disagreeable.

descendre, to come down, to let out, to get out.

déserter, to desert.

déserteur, *m.* deserter.

désir, *m.* wish, desire.

désirer, to wish.

désobéir, to disobey.

désolé, -e, grieved.

désormais, in future, henceforth.

dès que, as soon as.

dessert, *m.* dessert.

dessin, *m.* design, drawing.

dessiner, to draw.

dessous, underneath, below.

dessus, upon, above.

détail, *m.* detail.

détaler, to pack up; to take to one's heels.

déterminer, to determine.

détester, to detest.

détruire, to destroy.

deuil, *m.* mourning.

deux, two.

deuxième, second.

devant, in front of, before.

devenir, to become.
devenu, -e, become.
deviner, to guess.
devoir, *m.* duty, home work.
devoir, *v.* to owe, must.
diable, *m.* devil.
diamant, *m.* diamond.
dictée, *f.* dictation.
dictionnaire, *m.* dictionary.
Dieu, God, the Lord; the heavens.
différent, -e, different.
difficile, difficult.
difficulté, *f.* difficulty.
digne, worthy.
dignitaire, *m.* dignitary.
diligence, *f.* stage-coach.
dimanche, *m.* Sunday.
dimensions, *f.* dimensions.
dîner, *m.* dinner.
dîner, *v.* to dine.
dire, to say.
directrice, *f.* directress, principal.
dirigeable, *m.* dirigible, balloon, airship.
diriger, to direct.
discret, discrète, discreet.
discussion, *f.* discussion.
disgrâce, *f.* displeasure.
disparaître, to disappear.
disparu, -e, disappeared.
disposé, -e, inclined.
distinguer, to distinguish, to tell from.
dit, -e, said.
divin, -e, divine.
dix, ten.
dix-huit, eighteen.
dixième, tenth.
dix-neuf, nineteen.
dix-sept, seventeen.
dizaine, *f.* about ten.
docteur, *m.* doctor.
doigt, *m.* finger.
domestique, *m. or f.* servant.
dommage, *m.* harm, injury. c'est dommage, that is too bad.

don, *m.* gift.
donc, then, so, therefore.
donné, -e, given.
donner, to give, to ascribe. donner dans, to come into; to strike.
donnez, give.
dont, of which, of whom, whose.
dormi, slept.
dormir, to sleep.
dos, *m.* back.
douane, *f.* custom-house.
douche, *f.* shower bath.
doué, -e, gifted.
douleur, *f.* grief, pain.
douloureux, -se, painful.
doute, *m.* doubt. sans —, doubtless, of course.
douter, to doubt.
doux, douce, sweet, gentle.
douzaine, *f.* dozen.
douze, twelve.
douzième, twelfth.
dramatique, dramatic.
drap, *m.* cloth.
droit, *m.* right.
droit, -e (*adj.*), right, straight.
droite, *f.* right hand. à droite, on or to the right.
droiture, *f.* uprightness.
drôle, *m.* rogue, scamp.
drôle (*adj.*), odd, queer, funny.
du, of the, from the; some, any.
dû, due, due, must, been obliged.
duel, *m.* duel.
duquel, de laquelle, desquels, desquelles, of which.
dur, -e, hard.
durer, to last.

E

eau, *f.* water.
ébauche, *f.* sketch, drawing.
échapper, to escape.
écharpe, *f.* scarf.
échouer, to fail.
éclair, *m.* lightning.
éclairer, to light, to illuminate.

éclat, *m.* brightness, luster.
éclater, to burst.
école, *f.* school.
écossais, -e, Scotch, Scotchman.
Écosse, *f.* Scotland.
écouter, to listen (to).
écran, *m.* screen.
s'écrier, to exclaim.
écrire, to write.
écrit, -e, written.
écriture, *f.* handwriting.
écrivain, *m.* writer.
écu, *m.* crown (*silver coin*).
écurie, *f.* stable.
édifice, *m.* building.
Edimbourg, *m.* Edinburgh.
édition, *f.* edition.
effet, effect, fact, deed. en —, truly, indeed.
effrayer, to frighten. s'effrayer, to be frightened.
effrontément, impudently.
égal, -e, equal. cela m'est égal, it is all the same to me.
égarer, to mislay. s'égarer, to lose one's way.
église, *f.* church.
égorger, to cut the throat of.
égratignure, *f.* scratch.
eh bien! well!
élaboré, -e, contrived.
éléphant, *m.* elephant.
élevé, -e, high. bien —, well mannered. mal —, ill mannered.
élève, *m. or f.* pupil.
elle, *f.* she, her, it. elle-même, *f.* herself. elles, *f.* they, them. elles-mêmes, themselves.
éloigné, -e, distant.
éloigner, to move away.
élysée, Elysian; Les Champs Élysées, the Elysian Fields, *a broad boulevard in Paris, extending from the Tuileries Gardens to the Arch of Triumph.*
s'embarquer, to sail, to embark.

embarras, *m.* perplexity.
embrasser, to embrace.
emmener, to lead away.
s'émouvoir, to be moved.
s'emparer de, to take possession of.
empêcher, to hinder, to prevent.
empereur, *m.* emperor.
empire, *m.* empire.
emplette, *f.* purchase.
employer, to employ.
empoigner, to seize, to grab.
emporter, to carry off.
s'empresser, to hasten.
emprisonnement, imprisonment, custody.
emprunter (à), to borrow (from).
ému, -e, moved, agitated.
en (*pron.*), some, any; of it, of him, of her, of them, for it; hence, thence.
en (*prep.*), in, while, at.
enchanté, -e, delighted.
enclume, *f.* anvil.
encore, still, as yet, again; too. — un, another.
encourir, to incur.
encre, *f.* ink.
encrier, *m.* inkwell.
endroit, *m.* place, spot.
enfant, *m. or f.* child.
enfermer, to shut up.
enfin, at last.
enfler, to swell.
enlever, to carry off, to take off. s'enlever, to rise.
ennemi, *m.* enemy.
ennuyer, to annoy, to bother.
s'enquérir, to inquire.
enregistrer, to check (*luggage*).
s'enrhumer, to catch cold. être enrhumé, -e, to have a cold.
enseigner, to teach.
ensemble, together.
ensuite, afterwards, next.
s'ensuivre, to follow, to result.
entendre, to hear; to mean. —

dire, to hear, to learn. — **parler de,** to hear from. **bien entendu,** of course.

enthousiasmé, carried away.

entourer, to surround.

entre, between.

entré, -e, entered, come in.

entreprise, *f.* undertaking.

entrer (dans), to go in, to enter.

entretenir, to converse, to entertain.

envers, towards.

envie, *f.* desire, fancy; envy. **avoir — de,** to have a mind to.

envier, to envy, to begrudge.

envieux, -se, envious.

environ, about. **les environs,** *m.* neighborhood.

envoyer, to send.

épais, épaisse, thick.

épaisseur, *f.* thickness.

épaule, *f.* shoulder.

épée, *f.* sword.

épingle, *f.* pin.

époque, *f.* period, time.

éprouver, to feel, to experience.

épuisé, -e, exhausted.

équilibre, *m.* balance.

Ernest, *m.* Ernest.

erreur, *f.* mistake.

es, art (*pres. ind.,* 2d *per. sing.* of **être**).

escalier, *m.* staircase.

espace, *m.* space.

Espagne, *f.* Spain.

espagnol, -e, Spanish.

espèce, *f.* kind, sort.

espérer, to hope, to expect.

esprit, *m.* spirit, wit.

essai, *m.* test, trial.

essayer, to try, to try on, to test.

essentiel, -le, essential, material.

s'essuyer, to dry one's self.

est, is; belongs. **n'est-ce pas?** is it not? is it? **il en fut surpris, n'est-ce pas?** he was surprised at it, wasn't he? **le train n'est pas arrivé, n'est-ce pas?** the train isn't in, is it? **je n'ai rien dit, n'est-ce pas?** I didn't say anything, did I?

est, *m.* east.

estimer, to esteem, to value highly.

et, and.

établir, to establish, to secure.

étage, *m.* story (*of a house*), floor.

étant, being.

état, *m.* condition.

les États-Unis, *m.* the United States.

été, *m.* summer.

été (*part.*), been.

éteindre, to put out.

étendard, *m.* standard.

étendre, to stretch.

étinceler, to flash.

étoile, *f.* star.

étonnement, *m.* astonishment.

étonner, to astonish. **s'—,** to be surprised.

étourdi, -e, heedless.

étrange, strange.

étranger, *m.* stranger. **à l'—,** abroad.

être, *m.* being.

être (*v.*), to be. **être à,** to belong to; to be busy about. [**en être.**] **où en êtes-vous?** how far have you got? **j'en suis pour mes peines,** I had my trouble for nothing. **il n'en est rien,** it's nothing of the sort. [**c'est que.**] **venez-vous? c'est que nous ne pouvons pas,** are you coming? The fact is we can't. *See* **est.**

étroit, -e, narrow, tight.

étude, *f.* study.

étudier, to study.

eu, had.

Europe, *f.* Europe.

eux, they, them.

eux-mêmes, themselves.

12

événement, *m.* event.
éventail, *m.* fan.
éventualité, *f.* contingency.
évident, -e, evident.
éviter, to avoid, to prevent.
exactement, exactly.
exactitude, *f.* punctuality.
exagérer, to exaggerate.
examiner, to examine.
exaspérer, to exasperate.
excepté, except.
exceptionnel, -le, exceptional.
excuse, *f.* excuse.
excuser, to excuse.
exécuter, to execute.
exemple, *m.* example. par —, for instance; you don't say so.
exercice, *m.* exercise, drill.
exiger, to demand, to require, to insist upon.
expédition, *f.* expedition.
expérience, *f.* experience.
expliquer, to explain.
s'exposer, to expose one's self.
exprès, purposely.
expression, expression.
exprimer, to express.
extérieur, outside, exterior, from without.
extravagance, *f.* extravagance.
extrême, extreme.

F

face, *f.* face, surface. en face de, opposite.
fâché, -e, vexed, angry.
fâcher, to vex. se —, to get angry.
facile, easy.
facilement, easily.
façon, *f.* fashion, way.
faim, *f.* hunger. avoir —, to be hungry.
faire, to do, to make. — beau (temps), to be fine (weather). — le malade, to pretend to be ill. — dire, to send word.

avoir beau —, to be no use trying. — faire, to get *or* have done. — bâtir, to build. — savoir, to let know. — des affaires, to do business. — de son mieux, to do one's best. ne — rien, to make no difference. — entrer, to show in. — appel à, to apply to, to call on. se — du mauvais sang, to be annoyed, to fret, to worry.
faisan, *m.* pheasant.
fait, *m.* fact, act.
fait, *v.* does, makes.
fait (*part.*), done, made, shaped. tout —, ready made.
falloir, to be necessary, must, want.
fameux, -se, famous.
famille, *f.* family.
farine, *f.* flour.
fatigant, -e, tiresome.
fatigué, -e, tired, fatigued.
il faut, it is necessary, must.
faute, *f.* fault, offense, mistake.
fauteuil, *m.* arm-chair.
faux, fausse, false, artificial, adulterated.
favori, favorite, favorite.
feignit, *from* feindre.
feindre, to feign, to pretend to.
feld-maréchal, *m.* field-marshal.
féliciter, to congratulate.
femme, *f.* woman, wife.
fenêtre, *f.* window.
fer, *m.* iron. fers, fetters. — à cheval, horse-shoe. — blanc, *m.* tin.
fermé, -e, shut.
fermer, to shut, to close.
fermeté, *f.* firmness.
fermier, *m.* farmer.
féroce, fierce, ferocious.
festin, *m.* feast.
fête, *f.* birthday.
feu, *m.* fire.
feuille, *f.* leaf (*of book or tree*).

février, *m.* February.
fi! fie!
fidèle, faithful.
fier, fière, proud.
figure, *f.* face.
se figurer, to fancy.
fil, *m.* thread.
fille, *f.* daughter, girl.
fils, *m.* son.
fin, *f.* end. à la —, after all.
fini, -e, ended, finished.
finir, to finish.
fixer, to fix.
flacon, vial, bottle.
flambeau, *m.* torch.
flatter, to flatter. se —, to hope;
    to flatter one's self.
flatteur, *m.* flatterer.
flegmatiquement, calmly.
fleur, *f.* flower.
fleuriste, *m.* florist.
fleuve, *m.* river.
flocon, *m.* flake.
foire, *f.* fair.
fois, *f.* time. bien des —, many
    a time.
foncé, -e, dark (*in color*).
fonction, *f.* function.
fondre, to melt. — en larmes, to
    burst into tears.
font, *v.* make.
fontaine, *f.* fountain, fount.
force, *f.* strength, power.
forcer, to force, to oblige.
forêt, *f.* forest.
forgeron, *m.* blacksmith.
former, to form.
fort, -e (*adj.*), strong, hard, learned;
    (*adv.*), much, very. trop —, too
    much, too bad.
fortification, *f.* fortification.
fortune, *f.* fortune.
fou, fol, folle, mad, foolish, crazy.
foudre, *f.* lightning.
fouiller, to ransack.
foule, *f.* crowd.

fourchette, *f.* fork.
fourmi, *f.* ant.
fournir, to furnish.
fourrure, *f.* fur.
frais, fraîche, fresh, cool.
fraise, *f.* strawberry.
fraisier, *m.* strawberry plant.
framboise, *f.* raspberry.
franc, *m.* franc, 20 sous.
franc, franche, straightforward,
    frank.
français, -e, French.
France, *f.* France.
frapper, to strike.
fréquenter, to frequent.
frère, *m.* brother.
se frictionner, to rub one's self.
fripon, *m.* rogue.
froid, -e, cold. avoir —, to be cold.
froideur, *f.* coldness.
fromage, *m.* cheese.
frugal, -e, frugal.
fruit, *m.* fruit.
fruitier, -ère (*adj.*), fruit.
fuir, to flee.
fumée, *f.* smoke.
fumer, to smoke.
fureur, *f.* fury. en —, wild.
furieux, -se, furious.
fusil, *m.* gun.

G

gagner, to reach, to gain.
gai, -e, cheerful, merry.
gaiement, cheerfully.
galerie, *f.* gallery, hall.
ganache, *f.* blockhead.
gant, *m.* glove.
garçon, *m.* boy; waiter; bachelor.
garde, *m.* keeper, guard. — chasse,
    m. gamekeeper.
garde, *f.* notice. prendre —, to
    look out, to take care.
garder, to keep, to take care of.
gare, *f.* railway station.
gâteau, *m.* cake.

gâter, to spoil.
gauche (*adj.*), left.
gauche, *f.* left-hand. **à —,** to *or* on the left.
geler, to freeze.
gêner, to inconvenience.
général, *m.* general.
généreux, -se, generous.
genou, *m.* knee.
genre, *m.* kind, sort.
gens, *m. or f.* people.
gentil, -le, pretty, nice, amiable.
géographie, *f.* geography.
géographique, geographical.
giberne, *f.* cartridge-pouch.
gibier, *m.* game.
gilet, *m.* waistcoat, vest.
glace, *f.* ice; mirror.
gloire, *f.* glory.
gomme, *f.* eraser.
gorge, *f.* throat.
gothique, gothic.
goût, *m.* taste.
goûter, to taste; to lunch.
goutte, *f.* drop.
gouvernante, *f.* governess.
gouverneur, *m.* governor.
grâce, *f.* charm, favor. **— à,** thanks to. **de —,** pray, I pray you.
gracieux, -se, graceful.
grammaire, *f.* grammar.
grand, -e, large, tall, great.
grandir, to grow up.
grand-père, *m.* grandfather.
grange, *f.* barn.
gras, grasse, fat.
gratter, to scratch.
grave, grave, severe.
gravement, gravely.
gravure, *f.* engraving.
grec, grecque, Greek.
grêle, *f.* hail.
grelotter, to shiver.
grenade, *f.* pomegranate.
grenadier, *m.* grenadier.

grenouille, *f.* frog.
gris, -e, gray.
gronder, to growl, to scold, to rumble.
groom, *m.* lackey.
gros, grosse, stout, big, large, rough.
grosseur, *f.* size.
guère (**ne** *before verb*), scarcely, hardly.
guérir, to cure.
guerre, *f.* war.
Guillaume, *m.* William.

H

(*Aspirate* h *is indicated by* '.)
habile, clever.
habilement, skillfully.
habiller, to dress. **s'—,** to dress (one's self).
habit, *m.* coat, clothes.
habitant, *m.* inhabitant.
habitation, *f.* habitation.
habiter, to dwell in, to live in.
habitude, *f.* habit.
habitué, *m.* frequenter.
habituer, to accustom.
'haïr, to hate.
haleine, *f.* breath.
'haricots, *m.* beans.
harpagon, *m.* miser.
'hasard, *m.* chance. **par —,** per-chance; I suppose.
'hâter, to hasten.
'haut, *m.* height, top.
'haut, -e (*adj.*), high, tall; (*adv.*), loud.
'hauteur, *f.* height.
La 'Haye, The Hague.
Henri, *m.* Henry.
hériter, to inherit.
heure, *f.* hour, o'clock. **tout à l'heure,** just now.
heureusement, happily.
heureux, -se, happy, fortunate.

'**hibou,** *m.* owl.
hier, yesterday. — **soir,** last night.
histoire, *f.* history, story.
hiver, *m.* winter.
'**hollandais, -e,** Dutch.
hommage, *m.* homage.
homme, *m.* man.
honnête, honest, civil, respectable.
honnêteté, *f.* kindness, courtesy.
honoraires, *m. pl.* fee.
'**honte,** *f.* shame.
'**honteux, -se,** ashamed, shameful.
horloge, *f.* clock.
horreur, *f.* shocking thing.
horrible, horrible.
horriblement, dreadfully.
hors-d'œuvres, *m. pl.* relishes, side-dish.
hôte, *m.* host; occupant.
hôtel, *m.* hotel, mansion, hall.
hôtel de ville, city hall.
'**huit,** eight.
'**huitième,** eighth.
humeur, *f.* temper.
humide, damp, moist.

I

ici, here.
idée, *f.* idea.
identique, identical, like.
ignorer, to be ignorant of.
il, he, it.
il y a, there is, there are.
île, *f.* island.
illustre, famous.
illustrer, to illustrate.
ils, they.
s'imaginer, to fancy.
imbu, -e, imbued, impressed with.
imiter, to imitate.
immense, immense.
s'impatienter, to become restless, *or* impatient.
impeccable, irreproachable, impeccable.

impératrice, *f.* empress.
imperméable, waterproof, raincoat.
impertinence, *f.* impertinence.
impertinent, *m.* impertinent fellow.
impitoyable, pitiless.
importance, *f.* importance, weight, consequence.
important, -e, important.
il importe, it is important. **n'importe,** no matter, never mind.
impossible, impossible.
impur, -e, impure.
inattendu, -e, unexpected.
incertain, -e, uncertain.
incliner, to bend. **s'incliner,** to bow.
inconnu, unknown.
incroyable, incredible.
indiquer, to indicate.
indiscrétion, *f.* indiscretion.
indispensable, indispensable.
indisposé, -e, indisposed.
industriel, industrial, manufacturing.
infâme, infamous, disgraceful.
inférieur, -e, lower.
infiniment, infinitely.
influence, *f.* influence.
infortune, *f.* misfortune.
ingrat, -e, ungrateful.
injustement, unjustly.
inoffensif, -ve, harmless.
inquiet, -ète, uneasy, troubled.
inquiéter, to annoy. **s'inquiéter,** to trouble one's self, to be uneasy.
inscription, *f.* notice.
inscrire, to write down.
insecte, *m.* insect.
instant, *m.* moment.
instructif, -ve, instructive.
instruire, to teach. **s'instruire,** to learn.
instruit, -e, wise.
insulter, to insult.
intelligence, *f.* intelligence.

16

intention, *f.* meaning.
interdire, to forbid.
intéressant, -e, interesting.
intéresser, to interest.
intérêt, *m.* interest.
interpeller, to speak to.
interprète, *m.* interpreter.
interrompre, to interrupt.
inutile, useless.
invalide, *m.* veteran.
inventif, -tive, inventive, imaginative.
invitation, *f.* invitation.
invité, *m.* guest.
inviter, to invite.
Irlande, *f.* Ireland.
irrésolu, -e, irresolute.
Italie, *f.* Italy.
italien, -ne, Italian.

J

j' *stands for* **je.**
Jacques, *m.* James.
jalousie, *f.* jealousy; Venetian blind.
jaloux, -se, jealous.
jamais, ever. **ne . . . jamais,** never.
jambe, *f.* leg. **à toutes —,** at full speed.
janvier, *m.* January.
Japon, *m.* Japan.
jaquette, *f.* jacket, cut-away coat.
jardin, *m.* garden. **— des Plantes,** public garden in Paris.
jardinier, *m.* gardener.
jaune, yellow.
je, I.
Jean, *m.* John.
Jeanne, *f.* Jane.
jeter, to cast, to throw.
jeu, *m.* game, play.
jeudi, *m.* Thursday.
jeune, young.
jeûner, to fast.
jeunesse, *f.* youth.

joie, *f.* joy.
joindre, to join, to meet.
joli, -e, pretty.
jonquille, *f.* jonquil.
joue, *f.* cheek.
joué, -e, played.
jouer, to play.
jouet, *m.* toy, plaything.
jouir de, to enjoy.
joujou, *m.* toy.
jour, *m.* day.
journal, -aux, *m.* newspaper.
journée, *f.* day.
jovial, -e, jovial.
joyeux, -se, cheerful.
juge, *m.* judge.
juillet, *m.* July.
juin, *m.* June.
jumeau, *m.* **jumelle,** *f.* twin.
jurer, to swear.
jusqu'à, as far as, till.
juste, just. **tout —,** exactly.
justement, just, exactly, justly.

K

kilogramme, *m.* kilogram.
kilomètre, *m.* kilometer.

L

l' *stands for* **le** *or* **la.**
la, the; her, it.
là, there.
laborieux, -se, industrious.
lâche, cowardly.
laconisme, *m.* conciseness.
laid, -e, ugly.
laine, *f.* wool.
laisser, to let, to allow, to leave, let alone. **— tranquille,** to let alone. **— tomber,** to drop.
lait, *m.* milk.
laitière, *f.* milkmaid.
lampe, *f.* lamp.
lancer, to throw.
langue, *f.* tongue, language.

languir, to languish.

lapin, *m.* rabbit.

laquelle, which.

large, broad, loose.

largeur, *f.* breadth.

larme, *f.* tear.

las, lasse, tired.

latin, -e, Latin.

laver, to wash.

le, the; him, it.

leçon, *f.* lesson.

lecture, *f.* reading.

léger, légère (*adj.*), light (*in weight*).

légume, *m.* vegetable.

lendemain, *m.* next day.

lent, -e, slow.

lentement, slowly.

léopard, *m.* leopard.

lequel, laquelle, lesquels, lesquelles, which.

les, the; them.

lest, *m.* ballast.

lettre, *f.* letter.

leur (*pron.*), to them; (*adj.*), their. le —, la —, les leurs, theirs, their.

lever, to raise. se —, to rise, to get up.

lèvre, *f.* lip.

libraire, *m.* bookseller.

librairie, *f.*, library.

libre, free, disengaged, at liberty.

lieu, *m.* place. au — de, instead of.

lieue, *f.* league.

lieutenant, *m.* lieutenant.

ligne, *f.* line.

linge, *m.* linen.

lion, *m.* lion. lionne, *f.* lioness.

lionceau, *m.* cub.

lire, to read; *past part.* lu.

lisière, *f.* verge, border.

lit, *m.* bed.

litre, *m.* liter = $1\frac{3}{4}$ *pints*.

littérateur, *m.* man of letters, scholar.

livre, *m.* book.

livre, *f.* pound.

livrée, *f.* livery; retinue of servants.

loge, *f.* box (*theater*).

loger, to lodge.

loi, *f.* law.

l'on *stands for* on, one, people.

loin, far. — de, far from. de —, from afar. — de là, far from it.

lointain, *m.* distance.

loisir, *m.* leisure.

Londres, *m.* London.

long, longue, long. le — de, through, along.

longe, *f.* loin.

longtemps, a long time, long.

longueur, *f.* length.

lorsque, when, while.

louer, to praise.

louer, to hire, to rent.

Louis, *m.* Louis.

louis, — d'or, *m.* louis, twenty-franc piece.

Louise, *f.* Louise.

loup, *m.* wolf.

lourd, -e, heavy.

loyal, -e, loyal, true.

lu, -e, read.

lucratif, -ve, lucrative.

lueur, *f.* gleam, flash, light.

lui, he, to him, to her, to it. lui-même, himself. de lui-même, of his own accord.

luire, to shine, to glitter.

lumière, *f.* light.

luncher, to lunch.

lundi, *m.* Monday.

lune, *f.* moon.

lunettes, *f.* spectacles.

lutte, *f.* struggle.

lutter, to struggle, to fight.

M

m' *stands for* me.

M. *stands for* monsieur, Sir, Mr.

ma, my.
madame, *f.* Madam, Mrs.
mademoiselle, *f.* Miss.
magasin, *m.* shop, store. — de nouveautés, department store.
magnanime, magnanimous.
magnifique, magnificent.
mai, *m.* May.
main, *f.* hand. donner la —, to shake hands. en —, in hand.
maint, -e, many, many a.
maintenant, now, by this time. — que, now that.
maintenir, to maintain.
mairie, *f.* city-hall.
mais, but; why!
maison, *f.* house. à la —, at home.
maître, *m.* teacher, master.
maîtresse, *f.* mistress, school-teacher.
majesté, *f.* majesty.
mal, *m.* harm, evil.
mal (*adv.*), ill, badly. de — en pis, from bad to worse. se porter —, to be sick.
malade (*adj.*), ill, sick; (*n.*), patient.
maladie, *f.* illness.
malentendu, *m.* misunderstanding.
malgré, in spite of.
malheur, *m.* misfortune.
malheureusement, unfortunately.
malheureux, -se, unhappy, unfortunate.
malhonnête, dishonest.
malin, maligne, cunning, clever, sly.
malle, *f.* trunk. — armoire, wardrobe trunk.
maman, *f.* mamma.
manchon, *m.* muff.
mangé, -e, eaten.
manger, to eat.
manière, *f.* way, manner. — de voir, point of view.
manquer, to miss, to fail. — de, to lack, to be in need of.

manteau, *m.* cloak.
marbre, *m.* marble.
marchand, *m.* dealer, merchant.
marchander, to bargain for.
marche, *f.* step.
marché, *m.* market.
marcher, to walk, to march; to go to work.
mardi, *m.* Tuesday.
maréchal, *m.* marshal.
mari, *m.* husband.
le Maroc, Morocco.
mars, *m.* March.
mastodonte, *m.* mastodon.
matin, *m.* morning.
mauvais, bad. — sujet, bad boy, bad fellow.
me, me, to me, myself, to myself.
méchant, -e, naughty, wicked.
mécontent, -e, displeased.
mécontenter, to displease.
médecin, *m.* doctor.
meilleur, -e, better (*adj.*).
mêler, to mix. se — de, to meddle with.
même, same, even. de —, likewise.
mémoire, *f.* memory, remembrance.
menace, *f.* threat.
menacer, to threaten.
ménager, to save, to spare.
ménagerie, *f.* menagerie.
mener, to take to, to lead.
mensonge, *m.* deceit, lie.
mentionner, to mention.
mentir, to lie, speak falsely.
menton, *m.* chin.
mer, *f.* sea.
merci, thank you.
mercier, *m.* haberdasher.
mercredi, *m.* Wednesday.
mère, *f.* mother.
mériter, to merit.
merveilleux, -se, marvelous.
mes, my.
mesdames, *f.* ladies, Mesdames.

mesdemoiselles, *f.* Misses, the Misses.

message, *m.* message.

Messieurs, *m.* sirs, gentlemen.

mesure, *f.* measure. **sur —s,** on measure.

métal, *m.* metal.

métier, *m.* trade, profession.

mètre, *m.* meter.

mettre, to put, to put on. **se — à,** to go to, to set about. **— les pieds,** to set foot.

le Mexique, Mexico.

mi, half, middle. **mi-mai,** the middle of May.

midi, *m.* noon; south.

miel, *m.* honey.

le mien, la mienne, les miens, les miennes, mine.

mieux, better (*adv.*). **faire de son —,** to do one's best.

mil, one thousand (*used in dates only*).

milieu, *m.* middle. **au — de,** in the middle of, among.

militaire, *m.* soldier.

mille, *m.* thousand; mile.

milliard, *m.* a billion.

million, *m.* million.

ministre, *m.* minister.

minuit, *m.* midnight.

minute, *f.* minute.

miroir, *m.* mirror.

mis, mise, put, dressed.

misérable, miserable; wretch.

misère, *f.* misery.

Mlle. *stands for* **mademoiselle,** Miss.

Mlles. *stands for* **mesdemoiselles,** Misses, the Misses.

MM. *stands for* **messieurs,** gentlemen, Messrs.

Mme. *stands for* **madame,** Madam, Mrs.

Mmes. *stands for* **mesdames,** ladies.

modèle, *m.* model.

moderne, modern.

modiste, *f. or m.* milliner.

mœurs, *f.* manners, customs.

moi, I, me, to me, as for me. **à moi!** help! **moi-même,** myself.

moindre, less. **le —,** least.

moins, less, fewer. **à — que,** unless. **au —,** at the least, at any rate. **du —,** at least.

mois, *m.* month. **le — dernier,** last month.

moitié, à moitié, *f.* half.

moment, *m.* moment. **moments perdus,** spare moments.

mon, ma, mes, my.

monde, *m.* world. **beaucoup de —,** many people. **personne au —,** nobody in the world. **tout le —,** everybody.

Monsieur, *m.* Sir, Mr., gentleman.

mont, *m.* hill, mount.

les montagnes Rocheuses, Rocky Mountains.

montagne, *f.* mountain.

monter, to go up, to carry up; to ride, to climb.

montre, *f.* watch.

montrer, to show, to point to.

se moquer de, to sneer at, laugh at.

morceau, *m.* piece.

mordre, to bite.

morsure, *f.* bite.

mort, *f.* death.

mort, -e (*part.*), dead.

mot, *m.* word.

mou, (mol), molle, soft.

mouche, *f.* fly.

mouchoir, *m.* handkerchief.

moulin, *m.* mill.

mourant, -e, dying.

mourir, to die.

mousseline, *f.* muslin.

moutarde, *f.* mustard.

mouton, *m.* sheep.

mouvement, *m.* movement.

mouvoir, to move, to stir.

moyen, *m.* means, way. — **âge,** *m.* Middle Ages.

muet, -ette, mute, silent.

mugir, to bellow, to roar.

muguet, *m.* lily-of-the-valley.

mur, *m.* wall.

mûr, -e, ripe.

mûrir, to ripen.

musée, *m.* museum.

musicien, *m.* musician.

musique, *f.* music.

N

naître, to be born. **faire —,** to produce, to give rise to.

nature, *f.* nature.

naturel, -le, natural.

naturellement, naturally, of course.

naufrage, *m.* shipwreck. **faire —,** to be wrecked.

n'est-ce pas. *See* **être.**

ne . . . pas, not.

ne . . . personne, nobody, no one.

ne . . . plus, no longer.

ne . . . que, only, nothing but.

né, née, born.

nécessaire, necessary.

négociant, *m.* merchant.

neige, *f.* snow.

neiger, to snow.

nenni, no, no.

net, nette, clean.

nettoyer, to clean.

neuf, nine.

neuf, neuve, new-made.

neuvième, ninth.

neveu, *m.* nephew.

nez, *m.* nose.

ni . . . ni, neither . . . nor.

nièce, *f.* niece.

Noël, *m.* Christmas.

noir, -e, black.

noix, *f.* nut.

nom, *m.* name.

nombre, *m.* number.

nombreux, -se, numerous.

nommer, to name.

non, no. **ni moi — plus,** nor I either.

nord, *m.* North.

Normand, *m.* Norman.

nord-ouest, northwest.

nos, our.

notamment, namely.

notre (*adj.*), our.

le nôtre, la —, les nôtres (*pron.*), ours.

nourriture, *f.* food.

se nourrir de, to live on.

nous, we, us, to us; ourselves, to ourselves. **nous-mêmes,** ourselves.

nouveau, nouvel, nouvelle, new. **de —,** again. **quoi de —?** what news?

nouvelle, *f.* report; story, novel, romance; (*plur.*), news.

novembre, *m.* November.

nu, nue, bare.

nuire, to injure.

nuit, *f.* night. **cette —,** last night (*from* 12 *till this morning*).

nul, nulle (*adj.*), no.

nullement, not at all.

nulle part, nowhere.

numéro, *m.* number.

O

obéir, to obey.

objet, *m.* object.

obligé, -e, obliged.

obliger, to oblige.

obscur, -e, obscure, dark.

observer, to observe, to keep.

obtenir, to obtain.

occasion, *f.* opportunity; bargain.

occupation, *f.* occupation.

occupé, -e, busy, engaged.

occuper, to occupy. **s'—,** to get busy with.

octobre, *m.* October.
odeur, *f.* smell.
œil, *m.* (*pl.* yeux), eye.
œuf, *m.* egg.
œuvre, *f.* work, production, deed.
offenser, to offend.
offert, -e, offered.
office, *m.* office, duty. bons offices, kind offices.
officier, *m.* officer.
offre, *f.* offer.
offrir, to offer.
oiseau, *m.* bird.
ombrelle, *f.* parasol.
omettre, to omit.
omnibus, *m.* omnibus.
on, one, people, we, you, they.
oncle, *m.* uncle.
ont, have (*third person pl.*).
onze, eleven.
onzième, eleventh.
opéra, *m.* opera.
opération, *f.* operation.
opticien, *m.* optician.
s'opposer (à), to object to.
opprimer, to oppress.
or, *m.* gold.
oracle, *m.* oracle.
orage, *m.* storm.
orageux, -se, stormy.
orange, *f.* orange.
ordinaire, common. à l'—, as usual.
ordonnance, *f.* prescription.
ordonner, to order.
ordre, *m.* order.
oreille, *f.* ear. boucle d'—, *f.* earring.
orphelin, *m.* orphan.
ortolan, *m.* ortolan (*a delicate bird*).
oser, to dare.
ôter, to take off *or* away.
ou, or.
où, where. par —, which way?
oublier, to forget.
ouest, *m.* west.

oui, yes. je crois que —, I think so.
ours, *m.* bear.
oût, *for* août, *m.* August.
outre, beyond, besides.
ouvert, -e (*adj.*), open; (*part.*), opened.
ouverture, *f.* opening.
ouvrage, *m.* work; book.
ouvrier, *m.* workman.
ouvrir, to open.

P

page, *f.* page.
paille, *f.* straw.
pain, *m.* bread, loaf.
paire, *f.* pair.
paix, *f.* peace.
palais, *m.* palace; palate.
pâle, pale.
pâlir, to grow pale.
panier, *m.* basket.
panorama, *m.* panorama.
pantalon, *m.* pants.
pantoufle, *f.* slipper.
pape, *m.* pope.
papier, *m.* paper. — à lettres, note paper.
Pâques, *f. m.* Easter.
paquet, *m.* parcel, bundle.
par, by, through; *before words expressing time*, a *or* an. — ici, this way, in this direction.
paraître, to appear. vient de —, just published. paraît-il, they say.
parapluie, *m.* umbrella.
parbleu! upon my word!
parc, *m.* park.
parce que, because.
parcourir, to go over, to run through.
par-dessous, under.
par-dessus, over.
pardessus, *m.* overcoat.
pardon, *m.* pardon; excuse me!
pardonner, to forgive.

pareil, -le, like, alike, such.
parent, *m.* parent, relative.
paresseux, -se, lazy, idle.
parfait, -e, perfect.
parfaitement, perfectly, quite.
parfum, *m.* perfume.
par ici, this way.
parier, to wager.
parisien, -enne, Parisian.
parlé, -e, spoken.
parlement, *m.* parliament, congress.
parler, to speak.
parmi, among.
parole, *f.* word. **sur —,** on one's word.
part, *f.* part, share. **de ma (ta, sa) —,** from me (thee, him, her). **quelque —,** somewhere. **nulle —,** nowhere.
partager, to share, to divide.
parti, -e, gone away, departed, set out, left.
particularité, *f.* peculiarity.
en particulier, privately.
partie, *f.* part ; party, excursion.
partir, to set out, to leave.
partout, everywhere.
parvenir, to reach, succeed.
pas (*adv.*), not, not any. **— du tout,** not at all. *See* **ne.**
pas, *m.* step.
passage, *m.* passage.
passer, to spend; to hand; to escape, to go, to pass. **se —,** to take place, occur. **se — de,** to do without. **— chez,** to call on. **— prendre,** to call and fetch.
pasteur, *m.* pastor.
patiner, to skate.
pauvre, poor.
payer, to pay (for).
pays, *m.* country.
paysan, *m.* peasant.
peau, *f.* skin, leather. **gant de —,** kid glove.

pêche, *f.* peach.
pécore, *f.* silly goose.
peigne, *m.* comb.
peigner, *m.* to comb.
peine, *f.* trouble, labor, grief. **à —,** scarcely, just. **donnez-vous la —, prenez la —,** please.
peintre, *m.* painter.
pendant, during, for. **— que,** during, while.
pénible, painful.
pensée, *f.* thought.
penser, to think. **— à,** to think of. **— de,** to think of (*opinion*).
pension, *f.* boarding-school. **— bourgeoise,** boarding house.
percher, to perch.
perdre, to lose. **se —,** to get lost.
perdu, -e, lost.
père, *m.* father.
perfectionner, to perfect.
permettre, to permit.
permission, *f.* permission.
Perses, *m.* Persians.
personnage, *m.* personage.
personnalité, *f.* personality.
personne, *f.* person, people, any one. **jeune —,** *f.* young lady. **ne . . . personne,** *m.* nobody, no one. **— au monde,** nobody in the world.
personnel, -le, personal.
persuader, to persuade.
peser, to weigh.
pétiller, to sparkle.
petit, -e, little, small, short.
peu, *m.* few, a little. **avant —,** before long. **sous —,** in a little while.
peu, little, few, not very. **— à —,** by degrees, gradually. **à — près,** about, nearly.
peuple, *m.* people, nation.
peur, *f.* fear. **avoir —,** to be afraid. **de — de,** for fear of.
peut-être, perhaps.

23

philosophie, *f.* philosophy.
phosphorique, phosphorescent.
photographie, *f.* photograph.
phrase, *f.* sentence.
pièce, *f.* piece; (*theat.*), play.
pied, *m.* foot. **à —,** on foot. **sur —,** standing, sitting up.
pierre, *f.* stone.
pierreux, -se, stony.
piéton, *m.* pedestrian.
pinceau, *m.* painting brush.
se piquer de, to pride one's self.
pire, worse.
pis (*adv.*), worse.
pitié, *f.* pity.
pivoine, *f.* peony.
place, *f.* place, situation; square; seat.
placer, to place.
plaie, *f.* wound.
plaindre, to pity. **se —,** to complain.
plaire, to please. **se —,** to enjoy.
s'il vous plaît, if you please.
plaît-il, what did you say?
plaisir, *m.* pleasure.
plancher, *m.* floor.
plante, *f.* plant.
planter, to plant.
plat, *m.* dish, course.
plein, -e, full, open.
pleuré, -e, wept, cried.
pleurer, to weep.
pleuvoir, to rain.
pluie, *f.* rain.
plume, *f.* feather, pen.
plumier, *m.* pencil-box.
la plupart, most.
plus, more. **ne . . . plus,** not again, no more, no longer. **de — en —,** more and more. **— tôt,** sooner.
plusieurs, several.
plutôt, rather.
pluvieux, -se, rainy.
pneumonie, *f.* pneumonia.

poche, *f.* pocket.
poète, *m.* poet.
poids, *m.* weight.
poignet, *m.* wrist.
point, *m.* point. **— de repère,** landmark.
ne . . . point, not, not at all.
pointe, *f.* point.
poire, *f.* pear.
poisson, *m.* fish.
poitrine, *f.* chest, breast.
poivre, *m.* pepper.
poli, -e (*adj.*), polite.
poliment, politely.
politesse, *f.* politeness.
pomme, *f.* apple. **— de terre,** *f.* potato.
pont, *m.* bridge.
populaire, popular.
port, *m.* port, harbor.
portant : bien portant, well.
porte, *f.* door, gate.
porté, -e, carried.
porte-monnaie, *m.* purse.
porte-plume, *m.* pen-holder.
porter, to carry, to bear, to wear, to put. **— à,** to take to. **se —,** to be.
portière, *f.* door.
portrait, *m.* portrait.
poser, to place, to put down, to pose.
posséder, to possess.
possible, possible.
poste, *m.* post, station.
poste, *f.* post-office.
pot, *m.* pot, jug. **— de terre,** earthen pot.
potage, *m.* soup, broth.
pouce, *m.* thumb, inch.
poule, *f.* hen.
poulet, *m.* chicken.
poupée, *f.* doll.
pour, for, to, in order to.
pourquoi, why.
poursuivre, to pursue.

pourtant, yet, however.
pourvoir, to provide.
pourvu que, provided.
pousser, to push; to utter.
poussière, *f.* dust.
pouvoir, to be able.
pré, *m.* meadow.
précieux, -se, precious.
précipiter, to precipitate.
précipité, hasty.
précis, exact, careful, precise.
précisément, exactly.
préférable, preferable.
préférer, to prefer.
premier, -ère, first, former.
prendre, to take, to catch. —
 garde, to beware, to take care.
 — rendez-vous, to make an
 appointment. — froid, to catch
 cold.
prenez, take.
préparatifs, *m. pl.* preparation.
préparer, to prepare. se —, to
 get ready.
près de, near, beside, closely, on
 the point of.
présence, *f.* presence.
présent, *m.* present. à —, now.
présenter, to show, to present.
président, *m.* president.
présider, to preside over.
presque, almost.
pressé, -e, pressed, hurried, in a
 hurry.
prêt, prête, ready.
prêté, lent.
prétendre, to pretend.
prêter, to lend. — serment, to
 take an oath.
prétexte, *m.* pretense.
prêteur, *m.* prêteuse, *f.* lender.
prêtre, *m.* priest.
preuve, *f.* proof.
prévenir, to warn.
prévenu, -e, warned.
prévoir, to foresee.

prier, to pray, to beg.
prière, *f.* prayer, entreaty.
prince, *m.* prince.
princesse, *f.* princess.
principal, principaux, principal.
printemps, *m.* spring.
pris, -e, taken.
prison, *f.* prison.
prisonnier, *m.* prisoner.
prix, *m.* prize; price, value.
probablement, probably.
procès, *m.* trial.
prochain, -e, next. le mois —,
 next month.
prodigieusement, greatly.
professeur, *m.* teacher, professor.
profit, *m.* benefit.
profond, -e (*adj.*), deep.
profondeur, *f.* depth.
proie, *f.* prey.
projeter, to plan, to make plans.
promenade, *f.* walk; ride.
promener, to take out to walk.
 se —, to take a walk.
promesse, *f.* promise.
promettre, to promise.
promis, -e, promised.
promptement, quickly.
prononcer, to pronounce, to utter.
 se —, to declare one's self, to
 speak out.
propos, *m.* talk. à —, by the way.
proposition, *f.* proposal.
propre à, fit for.
propriétaire, *m.* landlord.
propriété, *f.* property.
protection, *f.* patronage.
protéger, to protect.
prouver, to prove.
proverbe, *m.* proverb.
provoquer, to provoke.
prudence, *f.* prudence.
prudent, -e, careful, prudent.
prune, *f.* plum.
la Prusse, Prussia.
prussien, -ne, Prussian.

pu, been able.
public, publique, public.
puis, then.
puisque, since, as.
puissant, -e, mighty.
punir, to punish.
punition, *f.* punishment.
pupitre, *m.* desk.

Q

qu' *stands for* **que.**
qualité, *f.* quality.
quand, when. **depuis —,** how long.
quant à, as for.
quarante, forty.
quart, quarter, fourth. **— d'heure,** quarter of an hour.
quartier, *m.* quarter, ward. **Quartier Latin,** the Latin Quarter, *a part of Paris in which many colleges and schools are situated.*
quatorze, fourteen.
quatre, four.
quatre-vingts, eighty.
quatre-vingt-dix, ninety.
quatrième, fourth.
que *(pron.),* whom, which, that; *(interr.),* what.
que *(conj.),* than, as, since; how; let.
quel, quels, quelle, quelles, what, which; what a . . .!
quelconque *(after the noun),* whatever.
quelque *(adj.),* some, any. **— chose,** something. **— part,** somewhere. **— temps,** sometime.
quelque *(adv.),* however, whatever.
quelqu'un, somebody. **quelques-uns,** a few.
quelquefois, sometimes.
se quereller, to quarrel.
qu'est-ce que . . .? what?
question, *f.* question.
queue, *f.* tail. **faire —,** to stand in line.

qui, who, which, that; *(interr. or after prep.),* who, whom.
quinzaine, *f.* fortnight; fifteen.
quinze, fifteen.
quitter, to leave; to change.
quoi, which, what. **de quoi,** wherewith.
quoique, although.

R

race, *f.* race, breed.
raconter, to relate, to tell.
rafraîchir, to refresh.
rageur, -se, passionate.
raide, stiff.
raison, *f.* reason. **avoir —,** to be right.
raisonnable, reasonable, sensible.
ramasser, to pick up.
ramener, to bring back.
rang, *m.* rank.
ranger, to range, to arrange.
rapidement, quickly.
rappeler, to remind, to recall.
se rapporter, to correspond to.
rapprocher, to bring near.
rare, rare.
rat, *m.* rat.
ravir, to charm. **à —,** admirably.
rayon, *m.* counter; ray; shelf.
réaliste, realistic, realist.
recevoir, to receive.
recherché, -e, sought after, select.
réciproquement, reciprocally.
réclamer, to claim.
recommander, to recommend, to order.
recommencer, to begin again.
récompense, *f.* reward.
récompenser, to reward.
reconnaissant, -e, grateful.
reconnaître, to recognize.
se recoucher, to go to bed again.
reçu, -e, received.
recueil, *m.* selection, collection, extract.

recueillir, to harvest.
reculer, to go back.
redemander, to ask back or again.
réduire, to reduce.
réfléchir, to reflect.
réforme, f. reform.
refroidissement, m. cold, cooling.
refuser, to refuse.
regagner, to get back to.
régal, m. treat, feast.
regard, m. look; (plur.), glances, eyes.
regarder, to look at; to concern.
régiment, m. regiment.
règle, f. rule.
régler, to settle.
régner, to reign.
regretter, to regret.
régulier, -ère, regular.
régulièrement, regularly.
reine, f. queen.
réjouir, to rejoice.
relever, to lift up, to push up.
reliefs, m. pl. scraps.
relire, to read again.
reluire, to shine, to glitter.
remarquable, remarkable.
remarquer, to notice.
remercier, to thank.
remettre, to put on again; to send.
remords, m. remorse.
remplir, to fill, to fulfill.
remporter, to carry back; to win.
remuer, to move.
renard, m. fox.
se rencogner, to get into a corner.
rencontrer, to meet.
rendez-vous, m. meeting place, appointment. donner —, prendre —, to fix an appointment.
rendre, to render, to make, to return, to restore, to yield. — visite, to pay a visit. se —, to surrender one's self; to go. se — compte, to realize.

rendu, -e, given back; returned.
renoncer, to renounce.
rente, f. income, property.
rentrer, to enter, to return; to come home again.
répandre, to spread.
reparler, to speak again.
repartir, to set off again; to answer.
repas, m. meal.
se repentir, to repent.
repère, m. mark, datum. point de —, land-mark.
répéter, to repeat.
réplique, f. reply. sans —, without replying, at once.
répliquer, to reply, to retort.
répondre, to answer.
réponse, f. answer.
repos, m. rest.
se reposer, to rest one's self.
reprendre, to regain, to get back; to resume; to reply.
représentation, f. representation, show.
représenter, to assure.
réprimer, to repress, to curb.
reprocher, to reproach.
république, f. republic.
respect, m. respect. manquer de —, to be disrespectful.
respectueusement, respectfully.
ressemblant, -e, a good likeness.
ressembler, to resemble.
ressortir, to go out again.
reste, m. remainder. du —, however, after all.
resté, -e, remained, stayed.
rester, to remain, to stay. — au lit, to stay in bed.
résulter, to follow.
rétabli, -e, recovered.
se rétablir, to be restored to health.
retenir, to engage, to keep.
retentir, to resound.
retirer, to withdraw, to draw back.

retour, *m.* return. **de —,** returned, back again.
retourner, to return, to go back.
retrouver, to find, to find again.
réussir, to succeed, to be successful.
rêve, *m.* dream.
réveiller, to awaken.
revenant, *m.* ghost.
revenir, to come back.
revenu, -e, come back, returned.
revenu, *m.* income.
rêver, to dream.
revoir, to see again.
revue, *f.* review, revision, parade.
le Rhin, the Rhine.
rhume, *m.* cold.
ri, laughed.
riant, -e, laughing.
riche, rich.
richement, richly.
rien, nothing.
rire, *m.* laughter.
rire (*v.*), to laugh.
rive, *f.* bank, shore.
rivière, *f.* river.
robe, *f.* dress, robe.
robuste, robust, hardy, vigorous, strong.
roi, *m.* king.
rôle, *m.* character, part.
romain, Roman.
roman, *m.* novel, romance.
romancier, novelist.
rompre, to break.
rond, -e, round.
rosbif, *m.* roast beef.
rose, *f.* rose.
rôt, *for* **rôti,** *m.* roast.
rouge, red.
rougir, to blush.
rouler, to roll.
route, *f.* road, way.
roux, rousse, red.
royal, -e, royal.
royaume, *m.* kingdom.

ruban, *m.* ribbon.
rue, *f.* street.
rugueux, -se, coarse, rough.
ruine, *f.* ruin.
ruisseau, *m.* stream.
ruse, *f.* cunning, trick.
russe, Russian.
la Russie, Russia.

S

s' *stands for* **se;** *before* **il** *or* **ils** *for* **si.**
sa, his, her, its.
sable, *m.* sand.
sac, *m.* bag. **sac de nuit,** *m.* traveling-bag.
sacré, -e, sacred.
sacrifier, to sacrifice.
sage, wise, good.
saint, -e, holy.
saisir, to seize.
saison, *f.* season.
salade, *f.* salad.
sale, dirty.
salir, to soil. **se —,** to get dirty.
salle, *f.* hall, room. **— à manger,** dining-room. **— de classe,** *f.* classroom. **— de bain,** bathroom.
salon, *m.* drawing-room, parlor.
samedi, *m.* Saturday.
sang, *m.* blood.
sanglant, -e, bloody.
sans, without, but for.
santé, *f.* health.
satisfait, -e, pleased, satisfied.
sauce, *f.* gravy.
sauf, except. **sain et —,** safe and sound.
sauvage, wild.
sauver, to save. **se —,** to escape.
savamment, cunningly.
savant, -e, learned.
savoir, to know.
savon, *m.* soap.

la **Saxe,** Saxony.

scandaleux, -se, scandalous.

scélérat, *m.* scoundrel.

scène, *f.* scene, incident.

science, *f.* science.

scientifique, scientific.

sculpture, *f.* sculpture.

se, himself, to himself; herself, to herself; one's self, to one's self; themselves, to themselves.

sec, sèche, dry.

sécher, to dry up.

second, -e (*adj.*), second.

seconde, *f.* second (*of time*).

secouer, to shake.

secourir, to assist.

secret, *m.* secret.

secret, secrète (*adj.*), secret, hidden.

secrètement, secretly.

section, *f.* section, part, division, wing.

seigneur, *m.* lord.

la **Seine,** the Seine.

seize, sixteen.

séjour, *m.* stay, sojourn.

sel, *m.* salt.

selon, according to.

semaine, *f.* week.

semblant, *m.* appearance.

semestre, *m.* semester.

sembler, to appear, to seem. **ce me semble,** it seems to·me.

sens, *m.* sense, meaning.

sentier, *m.* path.

sentiment, *m.* feeling.

sentir, to feel; to smell.

séparer, to separate. **se —,** to part.

sept, seven.

septembre, *m.* September.

septième, seventh.

sergent, *m.* sergeant.

sérieux, -se, serious.

sérieusement, seriously.

serment, *m.* oath.

serpent, *m.* serpent.

serrure, *f.* lock.

service, *m.* service.

serviette, *f.* napkin, towel. — **éponge,** Turkish towel.

servir, to serve, to be of use. **se — de,** to use.

ses, his, her, its.

seul, -e, alone.

seulement, only.

sévère, severe.

sévèrement, severely.

si, if, so; yes. **si fait,** yes, indeed. **que si,** to be sure.

siècle, *m.* century.

siège, *m.* seat; siege.

le **sien, les siens, la sienne, les siennes,** his, hers, its.

siffler, to whistle.

sifflet, *m.* a whistle.

signe, *m.* sign, signal.

signer, to sign.

sillons, *m. plur.* plains, fields.

simple, simple, foolish.

simplement, simply, merely.

sincère (*adj.*), sincere.

singe, *m.* monkey.

sire, *m.* sire.

sitôt, so soon.

six, six.

sixième, sixth.

smoking, *m.* dinner jacket, tuxedo.

sobre, sober, restrained.

sœur, *f.* sister.

soi, one's self, himself, herself.

soie, *f.* silk.

soif, *f.* thirst. **avoir —,** to be thirsty.

soigner, to nurse.

soin, *m.* care.

soir, *m.* evening. **ce —,** this evening, to-night. **hier —,** last evening.

soirée, *f.* evening; evening party.

soit, *interj.* agreed, all right.

soixante, sixty.

soixante-dix, seventy.
soldat, *m.* soldier.
soleil, *m.* sun.
solide, solid, strong.
somme, *f.* sum.
sommeil, *m.* sleep. **avoir —,** to be sleepy.
son, *m.* sound.
son, sa, ses, his, her, its.
sonder, to probe.
songer, to think.
sonner, to ring the bell.
sonnette, *f.* bell.
sont, are, belong. **sont à,** belong to.
sort, *m.* fate.
sortant, -e, going out, retiring.
sorti, -e, gone out.
sortir, to go out, to issue.
sot, sotte, foolish, stupid.
sou, *m.* cent; sou (*five centimes*).
soudain, suddenly.
souffler, to blow.
souffrir, to suffer; to allow.
souhaiter, to wish; to hope.
soulier, *m.* shoe.
soupçon, *m.* suspicion.
soupe, *f.* soup.
souper (*v.*), to sup.
souper, *m.* supper.
souple, pliant, many-sided.
sourd, -e (*adj.*), deaf.
sourire, *m.* smile.
sourire (*v.*), to smile.
souris, *f.* mouse.
sous, under, below, beneath. **— peu,** in a little while. **— vêtement,** underwear.
sous-marin, *m.* submarine.
sous-officier, non-commissioned officer.
soutenir, to bear, to maintain.
se souvenir, to remember.
souvenir, *m.* token.
souvent, often.
spectacle, *m.* sight, play.

splendeur, *f.* splendor, brightness.
station, *f.* station.
statue, *f.* statue, monument.
studieux, -se, studious.
stupide, stupid.
style, *m.* style, manner of writing.
subitement, suddenly.
subtilité, *f.* subtlety.
succès, *m.* success.
sucre, *m.* sugar.
sud, *m.* south.
suffire, to suffice.
la Suisse, Switzerland.
suite, *f.* train; what follows. **tout de —,** at once, directly.
suivant, -e, following.
suivre, to follow.
sujet, sujette, subject.
superbe, superb, beautiful.
supercherie, *f.* deceit, swindle.
supérieur, -e, superior.
supplier, to implore.
supporter, to support.
supposer, to suppose.
sur, on, upon.
sûr, -e, sure, certain.
surprendre, to surprise.
surpris, -e, surprised.
sursaut, *m.* start. **en —,** with a start.
surtout, above all.

T

ta, thy.
tabac, *m.* tobacco.
table, *f.* table.
tableau, *m.* picture.
tâcher, to try.
taille, *f.* figure, build.
tailleur, *m.* tailor.
taire, to say nothing about, to be silent. **se —,** to hold one's tongue, keep quiet.
talent, *m.* talent.
tandis que, while.

30

tant, so much, so many. — soit peu, however little.

tante, *f*. aunt.

tantôt, by and by; sometimes.

tapis, *m*. carpet.

taquiner, to tease.

tard, -e, late.

tarder à, to be late in, to delay, to be long in.

tasse, *f*. cup.

te, thee, to thee; thyself, to thyself.

tel, telle, such. un —, such a.

télégramme, *m*. telegram.

télégraphier, to telegraph.

téléphone, *m*. telephone.

téléphoner, to telephone.

tellement, so much so.

témoigner, to show, to express.

tempête, *f*. tempest, storm.

temps, *m*. time; weather. à —, in *or* on time. combien de —, how long. de — en —, now and then. en même —, at the same time.

tendre (*v*.), to hold out, to stretch.

tenez! see here! I say! stop a moment.

tenir, to hold, to keep; — de, to take after. — compte, to take into consideration.

tenter, to attempt; to tempt.

terme, *m*. term, expression; end.

terminer, to end.

terrain, *m*. soil, ground.

terre, *f*. land, earth. par —, on the floor.

terrible, awful. enfant —, plague of a child, nuisance.

territoire, *m*. territory.

tes, thy.

tête, *f*. head.

thé, *m*. tea.

théâtre, *m*. scene, theater.

thème, *m*. exercise.

Thérèse, *f*. Theresa.

le tien, la tienne, les tiens, les tiennes, thine.

tiens! there! I say! indeed!

tiers, *m*. a third.

tigre, *m*. tiger.

timide, timid, modest.

tiré, -e, drawn; shot.

tirer, to draw; to fire. se tirer, to get out.

tiroir, *m*. drawer.

titre, title; à juste —, rightly, deservedly.

toi, thou, thee, to thee. toi-même, thyself.

toile, *f*. linen.

toilette, *f*. toilet.

toit, *m*. roof.

Tolède, *f*. Toledo.

tombe, *f*. tomb.

tombé, -e, fallen.

tombeau, *m*. tomb, sepulchre, sarcophagus.

tomber, to fall. — amoureux de, to fall in love with.

ton, ta, tes, thy.

ton, *m*. tone.

tonnelier, *m*. cooper.

tonnerre, *m*. thunder.

tort, *m*. wrong. avoir —, to be wrong.

tôt, soon, early.

toujours, always, still.

tour, *m*. turn, trick. faire un —, to take a turn. jouer un —, to play a trick.

tour, *f*. tower.

tourment, *m*. torment.

tourmenter, to tease.

tourner, to turn round.

tousser, to cough.

tout, -e, tous, toutes, all, whole, every, everything.

tout (*adv*.), quite. — à coup, suddenly. — à fait, quite. — à l'heure, a little while ago, just now. — au moins, at the very least. — de suite, at once. — en, while. — juste, exactly

— **d'abord,** at first. — **au plus,** at the most. **pas du** —, not at all.

traduire, to translate.

tragédie, *f.* tragedy.

tragique, tragic.

trahir, to betray.

trahison, *f.* treason, treachery.

train, *m.* train; style. **être en** —, to be in full swing. **être en** — **de,** to be in the act of.

traîneau, *m.* sledge.

traîner, to drag. **se** —, to creep along, to trudge.

traiter, to treat, to serve. — **de,** to treat as *or* like.

tranche, *f.* slice.

tranquille, easy, calm, tranquil, in peace.

transporter, to carry, to take.

travail, travaux, *m.* work.

travaillé, -e, worked.

travailler, to work. **se** —, to try one's best.

à travers, through, across.

traverser, to cross, to go across.

treize, thirteen.

tremblant, -e, trembling.

trembler, to shake, to shiver.

trente, thirty.

très, very; very much (*before a past part.*).

tressaillir, to tremble, to start.

tribune, *f.* gallery.

trimestre, *m.* trimester.

triste, sad, sorry.

trois, three.

troisième, third.

trompe, *f.* trunk (*of an elephant*).

trompé, -e, mistaken, deceived.

tromper, to deceive. **se** —, to be mistaken.

trop, too much, too many, too. **de trop,** in the way.

troupeau, *m.* flock.

trousses, *f.*: **à mes** —, at my heels.

trouvé, -e, found.

trouver, to find; to think; to like. **se** —, to be; to happen. — **bon,** approve, think fit. — **mauvais,** disapprove.

tu, thou.

tuer, to kill. **se tuer,** to kill one's self *or* each other.

tulipe, *f.* tulip.

tumulte, *m.* uproar.

turc, turque, Turkish.

Turquie, *f.* Turkey.

tuteur, *m.* guardian.

U

un, une, a, an, one. **l'un et l'autre,** both. **l'un l'autre,** each other.

uniforme, *m.* uniform.

univers, *m.* universe.

université, *f.* university.

urgent, -e, urgent, pressing.

utile, useful.

utilement, usefully.

V

vaccine, *f.* vaccination.

vache, *f.* cow.

vague, *f.* wave.

en vain, in vain.

vaincre, to overcome, to conquer.

vaincu, -e, vanquished, conquered.

vainqueur, *m.* conqueror.

vaisseau, *m.* boat, ship.

valet, *m.* valet.

valeur, *f.* bravery; value; security.

valoir, to be worth. — **mieux,** to be better.

se vanter, to extol one's self *or* each other.

vaste, vast.

veau, *m.* veal.

veiller, to watch; to lie awake.

velours, *m.* velvet.

venant, *m.* comer. **à tout** —, to all comers.

vendre, to sell. se —, to be sold;
  to fetch (a price).
vendredi, m. Friday.
vendu, -e, sold.
vengeance, f. vengeance.
venir, to come. — de, to have
  just. faire —, to call for.
vent, m. wind.
vente, f. sale.
venu, -e, come.
vérité, f. truth.
vermisseau, m. little worm.
verre, m. glass.
vers (prep.), towards.
vers, m. verse, line.
vert, -e, green.
vertu, f. virtue.
veston, m. coat.
vêtement, m. clothing.
veuve, f. widow.
viande, f. meat.
victoire, f. victory.
victorieux, -se, victorious.
vide, empty.
vider, to empty.
vie, f. life, living; " good time."
  de ma vie, as long as I live.
Vienne, f. Vienna.
vieux, vieil, vieille, old.
vif, vive, lively, quick, keen, alive.
vigne, f. vine.
vilain, -e, ugly, bad, wretched.
village, m. village.
ville, f. town, city. en —, in town
  (down town).
vin, m. wine.
vingt, twenty.
vingtième, twentieth.
violer, to violate.
violet, -te, purple, violet color.
violette, f. violet.
visage, m. face, look.
viser, to aim.
vision, f. vision.
visite, f. visit.
visité, -e, visited.

visiter, to visit.
vite, quickly, quick.
vitrail, m. stained-glass window.
vivement, sharply, eagerly, keenly.
vivre, to live.
voici, here is, here are.
voilà, there is, there are.
voir, to see.
voisin, m., voisine, f. neighbor.
voisin, -e (adj.), next, near.
voiture, f. carriage.
voix, f. voice.
voler, to fly; to steal.
voleur, m. thief.
volontiers, willingly.
votre, vos, your.
le vôtre, la —, les vôtres, yours.
voulez-vous, will you have? do
  you wish?
vouloir, to like, to wish, to will.
  — bien, to consent, to permit.
  en — à, to have a grudge against.
  — dire, to mean.
vous, you, to you; yourself, to
  yourself; yourselves, to yourselves. vous-même, yourself.
voûte, f. arch, canopy.
voyage, m. voyage, journey.
voyager, to travel.
voyageur, m. traveller.
vrai, -e, true. c'est —, it is true.
vraiment, truly, really.
vu, -e, seen.
vue, f. sight; view, picture.

W

wagon, m. railway carriage.
whist, m. whist.

Y

y, there; to it, to them; in it, in
  them.
yeux, m. (plur. of œil), eyes.

Z

zéro, m. zero, nought.

A

a, an, un, une.
to be able, pouvoir.
about, environ, près de. around, autour de.
abroad, à l'étranger.
absent, absent, -e.
absolute, absolu, -e.
absolutely, absolument.
to abstain, s'abstenir (de).
absurd, absurde.
abundant, abondant, -e.
to accept, accepter.
to accompany, accompagner.
according to, selon.
on account of, à cause de.
to accuse, accuser.
to accustom, habituer.
to act, agir.
active, actif, active.
acute, aigu, -ë.
to add, ajouter.
address, adresse, *f.*
to address, adresser, s'adresser à.
admirably, à ravir, admirablement.
to admire, admirer. to — one's self *or* each other, s'admirer.
to admit, admettre.
advance, avance, *f.*
adventure, aventure.
adverb, adverbe, *m.*
to advise, conseiller.
affair, affaire, *f.*
to affirm, affirmer.
to be afraid, avoir peur, craindre.
Africa, l'Afrique, *f.*
after, après.
afternoon, après-midi, *f.*

afterwards, ensuite.
again, encore, de nouveau.
against, contre.
age, âge, *m.*
aged, âgé, -e.
agitated, ému, -e.
ago, il y a.
agreeable, aimable, agréable.
airplane, aeroplane.
ale, bière, *f.*
all, tout, -e, tous, toutes. not at all, pas du tout, point.
to allow, permettre.
almost, presque.
alone, seul, -e.
already, déjà.
also, aussi.
although, quoique, bien que.
always, toujours.
ambition, ambition, *f.*
America, l'Amérique, *f.*
American, américain, -e.
amiable, aimable.
among, parmi.
to amuse, amuser.
amusing, amusant, -e.
an, un, une.
ancestor, aïeul, *plur.* aïeux.
ancient, ancien, -ne.
and, et.
anecdote, anecdote, *f.*
angel, ange, *m.*
anger, colère, *f.*
angry, fâché, rageur, -euse. to get angry, se fâcher.
animal, animal, *m.* ; bête, *f.*
anniversary, anniversaire, *m.*
to announce, annoncer.
to annoy, ennuyer.

answer, réponse, *f.*
to answer, répondre (à).
anxiety, anxiété, *f.*
any, du, de la, de l', des; en.
any one, quelqu'un.
anything, quelque chose.
anywhere, quelque part.
apiece, la pièce.
to appear, sembler, paraître.
appetite, appétit, *m.*
apple, pomme, *f.*
appointment, rendez-vous, *m.* to make an —, donner rendez-vous.
to apply to, s'adresser, faire appel à.
approach, abord, *m.*
to approve, approuver, trouver bon.
apricot, abricot, *m.*
April, avril, *m.*
arch, voûte, *f.*
architect, architecte, *m.*
architecture, architecture, *f.*
arm, bras, *m.*
arm-chair, fauteuil, *m.*
army, armée, *f.*
to arrange, arranger.
arrival, arrivée, *f.*
to arrive, arriver.
arrived, arrivé, -e.
article, article, *m.*
artist, artiste, *m. or f.*
as, comme. as . . . as, aussi . . . que. as for, quant à. as many, as much, autant. as soon as, dès que, aussitôt que. as usual, comme à l'ordinaire.
ashamed, honteux, -se. to be —, avoir honte.
Asia, l'Asie, *f.*
to ask, to ask for, demander. to — back, redemander. to — pardon, demander pardon à.
to assassinate, assassiner.
to assure, assurer.
astonishing, étonnant, -e.
astonishment, étonnement, *m.*

at, à. at last, enfin. at once, tout de suite. at present, à présent.
to be attached to, se tenir à.
to attack, attaquer.
to attend to, se mêler de; soigner.
attention, attention, *f.*; (*good care*), bons soins, *m.*
attentive, attentif, -ve.
audacity, audace, *f.*
August, août, *m.*
aunt, tante, *f.*
Austria, l'Autriche, *f.*
Austrian, autrichien, -ne.
author, écrivain, auteur, *m.*
autumn, automne, *m.*
avenue, avenue, *f.*
to avoid, éviter.

B

bad, mauvais, -e, vilain, -e. bad boy, mauvais sujet, *m.*
badly, mal.
bag, sac, *m.* traveling —, sac de nuit.
baggage, bagage, *m.*
baker, boulanger, *m.*
balance, équilibre, *m.*
ball, balle, *f.* (*plaything*); bal, *m.* (*dancing party*).
banana, banane, *f.*
bank, banque, *f.*
banker, banquier, *m.*
barber, coiffeur, *m.*
bargain, marché, *m.*
to bargain for, marchander.
to bark, aboyer.
barn, grange, *f.*
basket, panier, *m.*; corbeille, *f.*
bath, bain, *m.* — room, salle de bain, *f.* — tub, baignoire, *f.*
battle, bataille, *f.*
to be, être. (*health*), se porter, aller. — well, se porter bien. — ill, se porter mal. — afraid, avoir peur. — ashamed, avoir honte. — cold, avoir froid. —

hungry, avoir faim. — **off,** s'en aller. — **right,** avoir raison. — **sleepy,** avoir sommeil. — **thirsty,** avoir soif. — **in want,** avoir besoin. — **warm,** avoir chaud. — **wrong,** avoir tort.

bear, ours, *m.*

to bear, porter.

beast, bête, *f.*

to beat, battre

beautiful, beau, belle, superbe.

because, parce que. **because of,** à cause de.

to become, devenir. **to — dark,** s'assombrir.

become (*part.*), devenu, -e.

bed, lit, *m.* **to go to —,** se coucher.

bee, abeille, *f.*

been, été.

beer, bière, *f.*

before (*prep. of time*), avant; (*prep. of place*), devant, en présence de; (*adv. of time*), auparavant; (*conj.*), avant que; (*followed by an infin.*), avant de, avant que de.

to begin, commencer, se mettre à.

beginning, commencement, *m.*

to behave, agir.

to behead, décapiter.

behind (*prep. of place*), derrière.

to believe, croire.

Belgium, la Belgique.

to belong, appartenir, être à.

bench, banc, *m.*

benign, bénin, -igne.

besides, d'ailleurs.

best (*adj.*), le meilleur; (*adv.*), le mieux.

better (*adj.*), meilleur; (*adv.*), mieux.

better off, plus avancé.

to be better (*health*), se porter mieux, aller mieux. **to be worth more,** valoir mieux.

to betray, trahir. **to — one's self,** se trahir.

between, entre.

to bid, commander, dire.

big, gros, -se.

bill, billet, *m.*

billion, billion, *m.*; milliard, *m.*

bird, oiseau, *m.*

birthday, fête, *f.*, fête de naissance.

to bite, mordre.

bitter, amer, -ère.

black, noir, -e.

blackboard, tableau noir, *m.*

to blame, blâmer. **— one's self o**; **each other,** se blâmer.

to bless, bénir.

blind (*adj.*), aveugle.

blue, bleu, -e.

to blush, rougir.

boarding-school, pension, *f.*

boat, bateau, *m.*

body, corps, *m.*

boldness, audace, *f.*

bonnet, chapeau, *m.*

book, livre, *m.*

bookseller, libraire, *m.*

boot, bottine, *f.*

born, né, -e.

to borrow, emprunter (à).

bottle, bouteille, *f.*; flacon, *m.*

bought, acheté, -e.

bouquet, bouquet, *m.*

bowl, bol, *m.*

box, boîte, *f.* loge (*theater*).

boy, garçon, *m.*

bracelet, bracelet, *m.*

Brazil, le Brésil.

bread, pain, *m.*

breadth, largeur, *f.*

to break, casser.

to breakfast, déjeuner.

breast, poitrine, *f.*; sein, *m.*

bridge, pont, *m.*

brief, bref, brève.

bright, brillant.

to bring, amener, apporter. bring me, apportez-moi. to bring back, ramener.

broad, large.

brooch, broche, *f.*

broom, balai, *m.*

broth, potage, *m.*

brother, frère, *m.*

brother-in-law, beau-frère, *m.*

brown, brun, -e.

to brush, brosser.

buffet, buffet, *m.*

to build, bâtir.

building, édifice, *m.*; bâtiment, *m.*

bush, buisson, *m.*

business, affaires, *f. plur.* — suit, complet.

busy, occupé, -e. to get —, s'occuper.

but, mais. but for, sans.

butter, beurre, *m.*

button, bouton, *m.*

to buy, acheter.

by, par. by far, de beaucoup. by that road, par cette route.

C

cabbage, chou, *m.*

cage, cage, *f.*

cake, gâteau, *m.*

calendar, calendrier, *m.*

to call, appeler. to — one's self, s'appeler. to -- on, passer chez.

call: telephone —, coup (*m.*) de téléphone.

calm, tranquille.

camel, chameau, *m.*

can (*to be able*), pouvoir; (*to know how*), savoir.

Canada, le Canada.

Canadian, canadien, -enne.

canne, canne, *f.*

cannon shot, coup de canon, *m.*

canopy, voûte, *f.*

cap, casquette, *f.*

to captivate, captiver.

carafe, carafe, *f.*

card, carte, *m.* visit, calling —, carte de visite *f.* playing —, carte à jouer, *f.*

cardboard, carton, *m.*

care, soin, *m.* good —, bons soins.

to care about, se soucier de.

careful, prudent.

carpenter, charpentier, *m.*

carpet, tapis, *m.*

carriage, voiture, *f.*

to carry, porter. to carry off, emporter, remporter.

case, cas, *m.*

castle, château, *m.*

cat, chat, *m.*; chatte, *f.*

to catch cold, s'enrhumer.

to cease to, cesser de.

to celebrate, célébrer.

celebrated, *adj.* célèbre.

celestral, céleste.

cent, sou, *m.*

century, siècle.

certain, certain, -e.

certainly, certainement.

chain, chaîne, *f.*

chair, chaise, *f.*

chalk, craie, *f.*

to change, changer.

to charge, accuser de.

Charles, Charles, *m.*

to charm, ravir.

charming, charmant, -e.

chat, causer.

cheap, à bon marché.

check, enregistrer (bagages).

cheek, joue, *f.*

cheer: three cheers! vive!

cheerful, gai, -e.

cheerfully, gaiement.

cheese, fromage, *m.*

cherry, cerise, *f.*

chest, poitrine, *f.*

chicken, poulet, *m.*

chief, chef, *m.*

child, enfant, *m. or f.*

chin, menton, *m.*
China, la Chine.
choice, choix, *m.* assortiment, *m.*
to choose, choisir.
chosen, choisi, -e.
christiandom, chrétienté, *f.*
Christmas, Noël, *m.*
church, église, *f.*
cigar, cigare, *m.*
circle, cercle, *m.*
circus, cirque, *m.*
city, ville, *f.*
city hall, hôtel de ville, *m.*, mairie, *f.*
to claim, réclamer.
class, classe, *f.*
classroom, salle de classe, *f.*
clean, *adj.* net, nette.
to clean, nettoyer.
clever, habile; malin, maligne.
clock, horloge, *f.*
to close, fermer.
closed, fermé, -e.
cloth, drap, *m.*
clothes for the wash, linge, *m.*
clothing, vêtement, *m.*
club, cercle, *m.*
coarse, rugueux, -se.
coast, bord (*m.*) de la mer.
coat, habit, *m.* veston, *m.*
coffee, café, *m.*
cold, froid, refroidissement, *m.*
  to be —, avoir froid. to have a —, être enrhumé. to take —, s'enrhumer.
collar, col, *m.*
to collect, ramasser.
collection, collection, *f.*
color, couleur, *f.*
to comb, peigner.
to come, venir; (*part.*), venu, -e.
  — back, revenir; (*part.*), revenu, -e. — in, entrer. — down, descendre; (*part.*), descendu, -e.
come! voyons! allons!
to command, commander.

to commence, commencer, se mettre à.
to commit, commettre.
committee, comité, *m.*
common, ordinaire.
company, compagnie, *f.*
to compel, contraindre.
to complain, se plaindre.
complete, complet, complète.
to complete, achever, terminer.
completely, complètement.
comrade, camarade, *m. or f.*; ami, *m.*
to conceal, cacher.
to conceive, concevoir.
to concern, regarder.
to condemn, condamner.
condition, condition, *f.*
conduct, conduite, *f.*
congratulate, féliciter.
to confess, avouer.
conscience, conscience, *f.*
to consent, consentir (à), vouloir bien.
to consider, trouver.
Constantinople, Constantinople, *m.*
constantly, constamment.
construction, construction, *f.*
contented, content, -e.
continent, continent, *m.*
continually, continuellement.
to contradict, contredire.
contrary, contraire, *m.* on the —, au contraire.
conversation, conversation, *f.*
cook, cuisinière, *f.*
cool, frais, fraîche.
copper, cuivre, *m.*
copy-book, cahier, *m.*
cordiality, cordialité, *f.*
corner, coin, *m.*
to correct, corriger.
to cost, coûter.
cotton, coton, *m.*
to cough, tousser.
to count, compter.

country, pays, *m.*; (*in distinction from the town*), campagne, *f.* **in the country,** à la campagne.
courage, courage, *m.*, cœur, *m.*
courageous, courageux, -se.
course, cours, *m.*
court, cour, *f.*
courtier, courtisan, *m.*
cousin, cousin, *m.*, cousine, *f.*
cow, vache, *f.*
cream, crème, *f.*
to crown, couronner.
cruel, cruel, -le.
to cry, crier; (*to weep*), pleurer.
cub, lionceau, *m.*
cunning, malin, maligne.
cup, tasse, *f.*
to cure, guérir.
to curse, maudire.
custody, emprisonnement, *m.*
to cut, couper; **cut down,** abattre.

D

to dance, danser.
to dare, oser.
dark, foncé.
daughter, fille, *f.*
day, jour, *m.*, journée, *f.* **every —,** tous les jours. **all —,** toute la journée. **— before yesterday,** avant-hier, *m.*
to dazzle, éblouir.
dead, mort, -e.
deaf, sourd, -e.
a great deal, beaucoup, bien.
dear, cher, chère.
death, mort, *f.*
decanter, carafe, *f.*
to deceive, tromper, décevoir.
December, décembre, *m.*
to decide, se décider.
decidedly, décidément.
to declare, déclarer.
deep, profond, -e.
defect, défaut, *m.*

to defend, défendre.
definite, défini, -e.
to delay, tarder.
delicious, délicieux, -se.
Denmark, le Danemark.
dentist, dentiste, *m.*
to depart, partir.
departed, parti, -e.
to depend upon, dépendre de.
depth, profondeur, *f.*
to descend, descendre.
to deserve, mériter (de).
to desire, désirer.
desk, pupitre, *m.*, bureau, *m.*
detail, détail, *m.*
to detest, détester.
diamond, diamant, *m.*
dictionary, dictionnaire, *m.*
did. *See* do.
to die, mourir.
differently, autrement.
difficult, difficile.
difficulty, difficulté, *f.*
diligent, appliqué, -e.
dimensions, dimensions, *f.*
to dine, dîner.
dining-room, salle à manger, *f.*
dinner, dîner, *m.* **— jacket,** smoking, *m.*
dirty, sale. **to get —,** se salir.
disapprove, trouver mauvais.
to discover, découvrir.
discussion, discussion, *f.*
dish, plat, *m.*
dishonest, malhonnête.
to disobey, désobéir (à).
displeasure, déplaisir, *m.*, disgrâce, *f.*
disposition, caractère, *m.*
distance, distance, *f.*, lointain, *m.*
to disturb, déranger.
to do, faire; (*of one's health*) se porter. **— one's hair,** se coiffer. **to do without,** se passer de. (*As an auxiliary.*) **He knows better than I do,** Il le sait mieux que

moi. (*In urging, rendered by* donc *or* prier.) **Do speak to me!** Parlez-moi donc! (*In replying.*) [Did he say so?] **He did.** Mais oui. [He came yesterday.] **Did he?** Vraiment?
doctor, médecin, *m.*
dog, chien, *m.*
doll, poupée, *f.*
domestic, domestique, *m. or f.*
done, fait, -e.
door, porte, *f.*
to doubt, douter.
dozen, douzaine, *f.*
draught, courant d'air, *m.*
to draw, dessiner.
drawer, tiroir, *m.*
drawing, dessin, *m.*, ébauche, *f.*
drawing-room, salon, *m.*
dream, rêve, *m.*
to dream, rêver.
dress, robe, *f.*
to dress, habiller.
dressed, mis, mise; habillé, -e.
dressmaker, couturière, *f.*
drink, boisson, *f.*
to drink, boire.
to drive, aller en voiture.
drop, goutte, *f.*
to drop, laisser tomber.
drunk, bu, -e.
dry, sec, sèche.
to dry one's self, s'essuyer, se sécher.
in a duel, en duel.
dumb, muet, muette.
during, pendant.
dust, poussière, *f.*
Dutch, hollandais, -e.
duty, devoir, *m.*
to dwell, demeurer.
dying, mourant, -e.

E

each, chaque, *adj.*, chacun, *pron.*
each other, l'un l'autre.
to earn, gagner.

ear-rings, boucles d'oreilles, *f.*
earth, terre, *f.*
easily, facilement, aisément.
Easter, Pâques, *f. pl.*
easy, facile; (*calm*), tranquille.
to eat, manger.
eaten, mangé, -e.
edge, bord, *m.*
Edinburgh, Edimbourg, *m.*
effect, effet, *m.* **in —** (*in reality*), en effet.
effort, effort, *m.*
egg, œuf, *m.*
eight, huit.
eighteen, dix-huit.
eighth, huitième.
eighty, quatre-vingts.
either, l'un ou l'autre; (*after negation*), non plus.
elbow, coude, *m.*
elephant, éléphant, *m.*
eleven, onze.
eleventh, onzième.
elsewhere, ailleurs.
emperor, empereur, *m.*
to employ, employer.
empress, impératrice, *f.*
empty, vide.
encourage in, encourager à.
end (*conclusion*), fin, *f.*; (*extremity*), bout, *m.*
to end, finir, achever.
enemy, ennemi, *m.*
engaged, occupé, -e.
England, l'Angleterre, *f.*
English, anglais, -e.
engraving, gravure, *f.*
to enjoy one's self, s'amuser.
enough, assez.
to enter, entrer (dans).
enterprise, entreprise, *f.*
to entreat, prier, supplier.
equal, égal, -e.
equality, égalité, *f.*
eraser, gomme, *f.*
Ernest, Ernest, *m.*

error, faute, *f.*, erreur, *f.*
especially, surtout.
essential, essentiel, -elle.
to establish, établir.
even, même.
evening, soir, *m.*
event, événement, *m.*
ever, jamais.
every, tout, -e, tous, toutes; chaque.
everybody, tout le monde.
every one, chacun; tout le monde.
everything, tout, *m.*
everywhere, partout.
evident, évident, -e.
exactly, précisément.
to exaggerate, exagérer.
example, exemple, *m.*
to exasperate, exaspérer.
excellent, excellent, -e.
exceptional, exceptionnel.
to exclaim, s'écrier.
excuse, excuse, *f.*
to excuse, excuser.
exercise, exercice, *m.*, thème, *m.*
to expect (*before noun*), attendre; (*before infin.*), s'attendre à.
expense, dépens, *m. plur.*
experience, expérience, *f.*
to experience, éprouver.
to explain, expliquer.
to express, exprimer.
to extol, vanter, louer.
extremity, extrémité, *f.*, bout, *m.*
eye, œil, *m.*; *plur.* yeux.

F

face, visage, *m.*, figure, *f.*; (*a wry face*), grimace, *f.*
to fail in respect, manquer de respect.
faithful, fidèle.
to fall, tomber. — in with, rencontrer. — out, se brouiller. to — in love, tomber amoureux de.

fallen, tombé, -e.
false, faux, fausse.
family, famille, *f.*
famous, fameux, -se.
fan, éventail, *m.*
to fancy, s'imaginer.
far, loin. by far, de beaucoup.
fast, vite.
fat, gras, grasse.
father, père, *m.*
fault (*defect*), défaut, *m.*; (*error*), faute, *f.*
favor, faveur, *f.*
favorite, favori, favorite.
fear, peur, *f.* for fear of, de crainte de, de peur de.
to fear, craindre, avoir peur.
February, février, *m.*
fellow, garçon, *m.*
firmness, fermeté, *f.*
ferocious, féroce.
few, peu. a few, quelques (*adj.*), quelques-uns (*pron.*).
fewer, moins.
field, champ, *m.*
fifteen, quinze.
fifth, cinquième.
fifty, cinquante.
to fight, se battre.
to fill, remplir.
to find, trouver; (*a thing lost*), retrouver.
fine, beau, belle.
fine, amende, *f.*
finger, doigt, *m.*
to finish, finir, achever.
fire, feu, *m.*
first, premier, première.
fish, poisson, *m.*
to fit, aller.
fit of anger, accès (*m.*) de colère.
five, cinq.
to flatter, flatter.
flatterer, flatteur, *m.*, -euse, *f.*
flattering, flatteur, -euse.
to flee, fuir.

flock, troupeau, *m.*
floor, plancher, *m.*
florist, fleuriste, *m.*
flour, farine, *f.*
flower, fleur, *f.*
fly, mouche, *f.*
fog, brouillard, *m.*
to follow, suivre.
food, nourriture, *f.*
foolish, fou, folle; ,sot, sotte.
foot, pied, *m.*
footwear, chaussure, *f.*
for, pour; (*during*), pendant; (*marking the beginning*), depuis; (*conj.*), car.
to forbid, défendre.
to force, forcer.
forenoon, matin, *m.*
to forget, oublier.
to forgive, pardonner.
fork, fourchette, *f.*
to form, former.
formerly, autrefois.
fortnight, quinze jours, *m.*; quinzaine, *f.*
fortunate, heureux, -se.
fortune, fortune, *f.*
forty, quarante.
found, trouvé, -e.
four, quatre.
fourteen, quatorze.
fourth, quatrième. **a fourth,** un quart.
tranc, franc, *m.*
frank, franc, franche.
frantic, affolé, -e.
free, libre.
freely, librement.
to freeze, geler.
French, français, -e.
Frenchman, Français, *m.*
fresh, frais, fraîche.
Friday, vendredi, *m.*
friend, ami, *m.*, amie, *f.*
friendship, amitié, *f.*
to frighten, effrayer.

frightful, affreux, -euse.
from, de. — **me,** de ma part.
— **him,** de sa part.
fruit, fruit, *m.*
fruit (*adj.*), fruitier, -ère.
to fulfill, remplir.
full, plein, -e.
fur, fourrure, *f.*
to furnish, fournir.

G

game, jeu, *m.*
garden, jardin, *m.*
gardener, jardinier, *m.*, -ère, *f.*
general, général, *m.*
generous, généreux, -se.
genius, génie, *m.*
gentle, doux, douce; gentil, gentille.
gentleman, monsieur, *m.*
geography, géographie, *f.*
George, Georges, *m.*
German. allemand, -e.
Germany, l'Allemagne, *f.*
to get, avoir, recevoir. — **here,** arriver. — **rid,** se défaire. — **up,** se lever.
ghost, revenant, *m.*
gift, cadeau, *m.*
girl, fille, *f.*
to give, donner. — **back,** rendre.
— **me,** donnez-moi.
given, donné, -e. — **back,** rendu.
glad, bien aise.
Glasgow, Glasgow, *m.*
glass, verre, *m.* **stained- — window,** vitrail, *m.*
glory, gloire, *f.*
glove, gant, *m.*
to go, aller. — **away,** s'en aller, partir. — **out,** sortir. — **to bed,** se coucher. — **without,** se passer de.
gold, or, *m.*
gone, allé, -e, parti, -e.
gone out, sorti, -e.

good, bon, bonne; (in conduct), sage. **to be so good as,** avoir la bonté de.

gothic, gothique.

governess, gouvernante, f.

government, gouvernement, m.

governor, gouverneur, m.

to grab, empoigner, saisir.

grammar, grammaire, f.

grand, magnifique.

grandfather, grand-père, aïeul, m.

grateful, reconnaissant, -e.

gravy, sauce, f.

gray, gris.

great, grand, -e.

greatcoat, paletot, m.

greatness, grandeur, f.

Greek, grec, grecque.

green, vert, -e.

on what ground, à quel titre.

to grow up, grandir. **to — pale,** pâlir.

to guarantee, garantir.

guardian, tuteur, m.

to guess, deviner.

guest, invité, m.

to guide, mener.

guilty, coupable.

H

haberdasher, mercier, m.

habit, habitude, f.

had (part.), eu.

The Hague, La Haye.

hair, cheveu, m.

half, demi, -e, moitié, f., mi.

half-hour, demi-heure, f.

hand, main, f. **in —,** en main(s).

handkerchief, mouchoir, m.

handsome, beau, belle.

to happen, arriver, se passer.

happy, heureux, -se.

hard, dur, -e; fort, -e; difficile.

hardly, à peine.

harmless, inoffensif, -ve.

harmonious, harmonieux, -se.

hasty, précipité.

hat, chapeau, m.

to have, avoir. **will you —,** voulez-vous?

he, il, lui. **he who,** celui qui.

head, tête, f.

health, santé, f.

to hear, entendre. **to hear it said,** entendre dire. **to — from,** entendre parler de.

heart, cœur, m. **with all my heart,** de tout mon cœur.

heaven, ciel, m.

heavy, lourd, -e.

heedless, étourdi, -e.

heedlessness, étourderie, f.

height, hauteur, f.

to help, aider.

hen, poule, f.

Henry, Henri, m.

her (pron.), elle, la. **to her,** lui. (adj.), son, sa, ses.

here, ici.

here is or **here are,** voici.

herself, se, elle-même.

hesitation, hésitation, f.

to hide, cacher. **to — one's self,** se cacher.

high, haut, -e.

him, le, lui. **to him,** lui.

himself, se, lui-même.

his (adj.), son, sa, ses; (pron.), le sien, la sienne, les siens, les siennes.

historian, historien, m.

history, histoire, f.

hold! tenez!

holiday, congé, m.; jour de congé, m.

Holland, la Hollande.

at home, à la maison; chez . . .

honey, miel, m.

honor, honneur, m.

to hope (before a future), espérer; (before a pres. or past), aimer à croire, aimer à penser.

horse, cheval, chevaux, *m.*
on horseback, à cheval.
horse-shoe, fer à cheval, *m.*
horse-hair, crin, *m.*
hot, chaud, -e.
hotel, hôtel, *m.*
hour, heure, *f.*
house, maison, *f.* at the — of, chez.
  custom —, douane, *f.*
how, comment, comme, que. —
  long? combien de temps? depuis
  quand? — **many?** — **much?**
  combien?
however, pourtant, cependant.
humanity, humanité, *f.*
hundred, cent.
hundredth, centième.
hunger, faim, *f.* **to be hungry,**
  avoir faim.
hurry: to be in a, être pressé.
husband, mari, *m.*

I

I, je; moi.
ice, glace, *f.*
idea, idée, *f.*
identical, identique.
idle, paresseux, -se.
if, si.
ill (*adj.*), malade; (*adv.*), mal. **to**
  be —, être malade, se porter
  mal.
illness, maladie, *f.*
to illustrate, illustrer.
illustrated, illustré, -e.
illustrious, illustre.
imaginary, imaginaire.
imbued, imbu.
immediately, tout de suite.
impertinent, impertinent, -e.
important, important, -e.
to be important, importer.
impossible, impossible.
impudence, impudence, *f.*
in, à, dans; en.
inch, pouce, *m.*

income, revenu, *m.*, rente, *f.*
increase, augmenter.
incredible, incroyable.
indeed, bien.
indefinite, indéfini, -e.
indifference, indifférence, *f.*
indispensable, indispensable.
indisposed, indisposé, -e.
indisputable, incontestable.
to induce, engager (à).
industrious, laborieux, -se.
infinite, infini, -e.
inhabitants, les habitants, *m.*
ink, encre, *f.*
inkwell, encrier, *m.*
inn, auberge, *f.*
innkeeper, aubergiste, *m.*
innocence, innocence, *f.*
insect, insecte, *m.*
to insist, exiger.
insolence, insolence, *f.*
instant, instant, *m.*
instead of, au lieu de.
instructive, instructif, -ve.
to insult, insulter.
to intend, compter.
interest, intérêt, *m.*
interesting, intéressant, -e.
to interfere, se mêler de.
to intimidate, intimider.
into, dans.
to invite, inviter.
iron, fer, *m.*
it, il, le, la, lui. **of it,** en. **to it,** y.
  it is the tenth, c'est le dix. **it is**
  I, c'est moi. **it is they,** ce sont
  eux. **it is said,** on dit. **that's**
  it, c'est ça.
Italian, italien, -ne.
Italy, l'Italie, *f.*
its, son, sa, ses.

J

jacket, jaquette, *f.*
jam, confiture, *f.*
James, Jacques, *m.*

Jane, Jeanne, *f.*
January, janvier, *m.*
Japan, Japon, *m.*
jealous, jaloux, -se.
jest, plaisanterie, *f.*
jewel, bijou, *m.*
John, Jean, *m.*
jonquil, jonquille, *f.*
journey, voyage, *m.*
judge, juge, *m.*
July, juillet, *m.*
June, juin, *m.*
just (*adj.*), juste; (*adv.*), justement. to have —, venir de. —
now, tout à l'heure.
justice, justice, *f.*

K

to keep, garder.
key, clef, *f.*
to kill, tuer.
kilogram, kilogramme, *m.*
kind, sorte, *f.*, genre, *m.*
kind, bon, bonne.
to kindle, allumer.
kindness, bonté, *f.*
king, roi, *m.*
to kiss each other, s'embrasser.
kitchen, cuisine, *f.*
knife, couteau, *m.*
to knock, frapper.
to know, connaître, savoir.

L

to labor, travailler.
labor, travail, *m.*
laborious, laborieux, -se.
lace, dentelle, *f.*
ladder, échelle, *f.*
lady, dame, *f.* young lady, jeune
fille, jeune personne, demoiselle, *f.*
lamb, agneau, *m.*
lamp, lampe, *f.*
land, terre, *f.*
landlord, propriétaire, *m.*
land-mark, point de repère, *m.*

language, langue, *f.*, langage, *m.*
large, grand, -e; gros, -se.
last, dernier, dernière. — month,
le mois dernier. — evening, hier
soir. — night, cette nuit. at
last, enfin.
late, tard, -e. to be — in, tarder à.
lately, dernièrement.
Latin, latin, -e.
to laugh, rire.
laughed (*part.*), ri.
law, loi, *f.*
lawyer, avocat, *m.*
laziness, paresse, *f.*
lazy, paresseux, -se.
to lead, mener. — to, amener. —
back, ramener. — away, emmener.
leaf, feuille, *f.*
to lean on one's elbow, s'accouder.
to learn, apprendre.
learned, instruit, -e. appris, -e.
at least, du moins. at the —, au
moins.
leather, cuir, *m.*
to leave (*go away*), partir; (*leave
behind*), laisser; quitter.
left (*adj.*), gauche.
leg, jambe, *f.*
to lend, prêter.
length, longueur, *f.*
lent, prêté, -e.
leopard, léopard, *m.*
less (*adj.*), moindre; (*adv.*), moins.
lesson, leçon, *f.*
lest, de peur que, de crainte que;
(*after verbs expressing fear*), que.
to let, laisser; (*a house*), louer.
letter, lettre, *f.*
liberty, liberté, *f.* at —, libre.
library, bibliothèque, *f.*
life, vie, *f.*
light (*adj.*), léger, légère; clair.
light (*noun*), lumière, *f.*
to light, allumer.
lightning, éclair, *f.*

like (*adj.*), pareil, -le; (*adv.*), comme.
to like, aimer.
to be like, ressembler (à).
likely, probable, vraisemblable.
lily-of-the-valley, muguet, *m.*
linen, linge, *m.*
lion, lion, *m.*, lionne, *f.*
lip, lèvre, *f.*
to listen, écouter.
little (*adj.*), petit, -e; (*adv.*), peu.
to live, demeurer; vivre. live in, habiter.
lively, vif, vive.
living, vie, *f.*
to lock, fermer à clef.
London, Londres, *m.*
long, long, longue. a — time, longtemps.
no longer, ne . . . plus.
to look, avoir l'air. — at, regarder. — for, chercher.
to lose, perdre.
loose, large.
lost, perdu, -e.
Louis, Louis, *m.*
to love, aimer.
low, bas, basse.
luck, chance, *f.*
to lunch, luncher.

M

mad, fou, folle.
made, fait, -e. ready —, tout fait, -e.
magnanimity, magnanimité, *f.*
magnificent, magnifique.
maid-servant, bonne, *f.*
to maintain, maintenir.
to make, faire. — haste, se dépêcher.
malignant, malin, maligne.
mamma, maman, *f.*
man, homme, *m.*
manners, manières, *f. plur.*

many, beaucoup. as — as, autant que. too —, trop.
many a, maint, -e.
marble, marbre, *m.*
March, mars, *m.*
to march, marcher.
market, marché, *m.*
to marry, épouser.
marvelous, merveilleux, -se.
Mary, Marie, *f.*
master, maître, *m.*
mastodon, mastodonte, *m.*
match, allumette, *f.*
May, mai, *m.*
it may be, il se peut, il est possible.
me, me, moi.
meadow, pré, *m.*, prairie, *f.*
to mean, vouloir dire.
meaning, intention, *f.*
meat, viande, *f.*
to meddle with, se mêler de.
to meet, rencontrer. to go to —, aller au devant de.
to mend, raccommoder.
merchant, négociant, *m.*
merry, gai, -e.
metal, métal, *m.*
meter, mètre, *m.*
Mexico, le Mexique.
Middle Ages, moyen âge, *m.*
midnight, minuit, *m.*
mile, mille, *m.*
milk, lait, *m.*
milkmaid, laitière, *f.*
milkman, laitier, *m.*
milliner, modiste, *f.*
million, million, *m.*
mind: to have a — to, avoir envie de.
mine, le mien, la mienne, les miens, les miennes.
minister, ministre, *m.*
minute, minute, *f.*
mirror, miroir, *m.*
misery, misère, *f.*
misfortune, malheur, *m.*

to mislay, égarer.
Miss, Mademoiselle *or* Mlle., *f.*
mistake, faute, *f.*
to be mistaken, se tromper.
mistress, maîtresse, *f.*
to mock, se moquer de.
modern, moderne.
moment, moment, *m.*
Monday, lundi, *m.*
money, argent, *m.*
monkey, singe, *m.*
Mont Blanc, le Mont Blanc.
month, mois, *m.* in the — of, au mois de.
moon, lune, *f.*
more, plus, davantage. no more, ne . . . plus.
morning, matin, *m.*
mortal, mortel, mortelle.
most, la plupart, *f.*
mother, mère, *f.*
mountain, montagne, *f.*
mouse, souris, *f.*
mouth, bouche, *f.*
movement, mouvement, *m.*
Mr., monsieur *or* M., *m.*
Mrs., madame *or* Mme., *f.*
much, beaucoup; fort. so —, autant. too —, trop.
muff, manchon, *m.*
museum, musée, *m.*
music, musique, *f.*
musician, musicien, *m.*
muslin, mousseline, *f.*
must, il faut que; devoir.
mute, muet, -ette.
mutton, mouton, *m.*
my, mon, ma, mes.
myself, moi-même.
mystery, mystère, *m.*

N

nail, clou, *m.*
name, nom, *m.*
to name, nommer.
namely, notamment.

napkin, serviette, *f.*
Napoleon, Napoléon, *m.*
naturally, naturellement.
naughty, méchant, -e.
near, près de.
nearly, presque.
necessary, nécessaire.
to be necessary, falloir.
neck, cou, *m.* — tie, cravate, *f.*
to need, avoir besoin de; falloir de.
needle, aiguille, *f.*
to neglect, négliger.
neighbor, voisin, *m.*; voisine, *f.*
neither . . . nor, ni . . . ni.
nephew, neveu, *m.*
never, ne . . . jamais.
new (*another*), nouveau, nouvelle.
new-made, neuf, neuve.
news, nouvelles, *f. plur.* what — ? quoi de nouveau?
newspaper, journal, *m.*
next, prochain, -e.
nice, gentil, gentille.
niece, nièce, *f.*
night, nuit, *f.* at —, le soir. last —, cette nuit.
nine, neuf.
nineteen, dix-neuf.
ninety, quatre-vingt-dix.
ninth, neuvième.
no, non, ne . . . pas, ne . . . point. — longer, — more, ne . . . plus. — one, personne . . . ne. — money, pas d'argent.
no (*adj.*), nul, nulle.
nobody, personne . . . ne.
noise, bruit, *m.*
noon, midi, *m.*
nor, ni. — I either, ni moi non plus.
north, nord, *m.*
nose, nez, *m.*
not, ne . . . pas. — at all, pas du tout, point. — yet, pas encore.
note, billet, *m.*
note-book, cahier, *m.*

nothing, ne . . . rien.
to notice, remarquer.
novel, roman, *m.*
November, novembre, *m.*
now, à présent, maintenant.
nowhere, nulle part.
number, chiffre, *m.* ; nombre, *m.*
numerous, nombreux, -se.
nut, noix, *f.*

O

oath, serment, *m.*
to obey, obéir (à).
to oblige, obliger.
obstinate, obstiné, -e.
to obtain, obtenir.
October, octobre, *m.*
of, de ; du ; de la ; des.
offense, faute, *f.*
offer, offre, *f.*
offered, offert, -e.
office, bureau, *m.*
officer, officier, *m.*
often, souvent.
old, vieux, vieil, vieille.
to omit, omettre.
omnibus, omnibus, *m.*
on, sur. on *before a day or date is
    not translated.*
once, une fois.   at —, tout de suite.
one (*adj.*), un, une ; (*pron.*), on,
    l'on. no one, personne . . . ne.
    the one, celui, celle.
one's self, se, soi.
only (*adj.*), seul, -e ; (*adv.*), seule-
    ment, ne . . . que.
to open, ouvrir.
opened, ouvert, -e.
opera, opéra, *m.*
opportunity, occasion, *f.*
to oppose, opposer.
or, ou.
orange, orange, *f.*
order, ordre, *m.*
to order, ordonner, commander.
ordered, commandé, -e.

in order that, afin que, pour que.
other (*different*), autre ; (*addi-
    tional*), encore un (une).
otherwise, autrement.
our, notre, nos.
ours, le nôtre, la nôtre, les nôtres.
ourselves, nous, nous-mêmes.
out, hors.   to go —, sortir.   to set
    —, partir.
to overflow, déborder.
to owe (*ought*), devoir.
owl, hibou, *m.*
own : my own, le mien.
overcoat, pardessus, *m.*
ox, bœuf, *m.*

P

to pack, emballer.
package, paquet, *m.*
pain, douleur, *f.*
painful, douloureux, -se.
paint, couleur, *f.*
to paint, peindre.
painter, peintre, *m.*
painting, tableau, *m.* ; peinture, *f.*
painting brush, pinceau, *m.*
pair, paire, *f.*
palace, palais, *m.*
pamphlet, brochure, *f.*
pants, pantalon, *m.*
paper, papier, *m.* ; journal, *m.*
parade, revue, *f.*
parasol, ombrelle, *f.*
parcel, paquet, *m.*
pardon, pardon, *m.*   to ask —, de-
    mander pardon à.
to pardon, pardonner.
parents, parents, *m.*
Parisian, parisien, -enne.
park, parc, *m.*
parlor, salon, *m.*
part, partie, *f.*
to part, séparer.   — from each
    other, se séparer.
to pass, passer.   to come to —, se
    passer.

passage, passage, *m.*
patience, patience, *f.*
to pay for, payer.
peace, paix, *f.*
peach, pêche, *f.*
pear, poire, *f.*
peasant, paysan, *m.*
pen, plume, *f.*
pencil, crayon, *m.* — box, plumier, *m.*
pen-holder, porte-plume, *m.*
pen-knife, canif, *m.*
peony, pivoine, *f.*
people, gens; on, l'on. so many —, tant de monde.
pepper, poivre, *m.*
to perceive, apercevoir.
perfect, parfait.
to perfect, perfectionner.
perfectly, parfaitement.
perfume, parfum, *m.*
perhaps, peut-être.
perishable, périssable.
permission, permission, *f.*
to permit, permettre.
person, personne, *f.*
personnage, personnage, *m.*
personal, personnel.
to persuade to, décider à.
philosophy, philosophie, *f.*
photograph, photographie, *f.*
physician, médecin, *m.*
to pick up, ramasser.
picture, tableau, *m.*
piece, morceau, *m.*; pièce, *f.*
pin, épingle, *f.*
to pinch, serrer; blesser.
pineapple, ananas, *m.*
to pity, plaindre.
place, place, *f.*; lieu, *m.*, endroit, *m.*
to place, placer.
to plan, projeter.
plate, assiette, *f.*
play, jeu, *m.*
to play, jouer.
plaything, joujou, *m.*

pleasant, agréable, aimable.
please, veuillez (*with infin.*).
to please, plaire, faire plaisir à. if you —, s'il vous plaît.
pleased with, content (-e) de.
pleasure, plaisir, *m.*
pliant, souple.
plum, prune, *f.*
pneumonia, pneumonie, *f.*
pocket, poche, *f.*
pocket-book, porte-monnaie, *m.*
point, pointe, *f.*
policeman, sergent (*m.*) de ville.
polite, poli, -e.
politely, poliment.
poor, pauvre; (*bad*), mauvais, -e.
pope, pape, *m.*
popular, populaire.
portrait, portrait, *m.*
positively, définitivement.
to possess, posséder.
possible, possible.
post, poste, *m.*
posterity, postérité, *f.*
post-office, poste, *f.*
potato, pomme de terre, *f.*
pound, livre, *f.*
to praise, louer.
precious, précieux, -euse.
to precipitate, précipiter.
to predict, prédire.
to prefer, préférer, aimer mieux.
preferable, préférable.
preparation, préparatifs, *m. pl.*
to prepare, préparer.
prescription, ordonnance, *f.*
present, cadeau, *m.*; présent, *m.*
preserve, confiture, *f.*
president, président, *m.*
pressed, pressé.
to pretend, prétendre.
pretty (*adj.*), joli, -e.
to prevent, éviter.
price, prix, *m.*
priest, prêtre, *m.*
prince, prince, *m.*

princess, princesse, *f.*
principal, principal, -e.
principle, principe, *m.*
prize, prix, *m.* **to gain a —,**
    gagner *or* remporter un prix.
probably, probablement.
probity, probité, *f.*
professor, professeur, *m.*
to promise, promettre.
promised, promis, -e.
to pronounce, prononcer.
proof, preuve, *f.*
proper, convenable.
to be proper, convenir.
property, propriété, *f.*
in proportion as, à mesure que.
proposal, proposition, *f.*
to propose, proposer.
to protect, protéger.
protection, protection, *f.*
proud, fier, fière.
to prove, prouver.
proverb, proverbe, *m.*
provided that, pourvu que.
to provide for, pourvoir à.
province, province, *f.*
Prussia, la Prusse.
Prussian, prussien, -ne.
public, public, publique.
punctuality, exactitude, *f.*
to punish, punir.
punishment, punition, *f.*
pupil, élève, *m.* or *f.*
purple, violet.
purse, porte-monnaie, *m.*
to pursue, poursuivre.
put, mis, -e, placé, -e.
to put, placer, mettre; **— up** (*at a*
    hotel), descendre.

Q

quality, qualité, *f.*
to quarrel, se quereller.
quarter (*the 4th part*), quart, *m.*
quarter (*district*) quartier, *m.*
queen, reine, *f.*

question, question, *f.*
quite, tout à fait, tout.

R

rabbit, lapin, *m.*
railroad, chemin de fer, *m.*
railway-carriage, wagon, *m.*
railway station, gare, *f.*
rain, pluie, *f.*
to rain, pleuvoir.
raincoat, imperméable, *m.*
rainy, pluvieux, -se.
rare, rare.
raspberry, framboise, *f.*
rat, rat, *m.*
to read, lire.
read, lu, -e.
ready, prêt, prête.
to realize, réaliser.
really, vraiment.
reason, raison, *f.*
reasonable, raisonnable.
to receive, recevoir.
received, reçu, -e.
reciprocally, réciproquement.
to reckon, compter.
to recommend, conseiller.
red, rouge; (*of hair*), roux, rousse.
to reflect, réfléchir.
refreshment, rafraîchissement, *m.*,
    consommation, *f.*
to refuse, refuser.
to regret, regretter.
regular, régulier, régulière.
regularly, régulièrement.
to reign, régner.
to relate, raconter.
relative, parent, *m.*
relish, hors-d'œuvre, *m.*
to remain, rester.
remained, resté, -e.
remarkable, remarquable.
remedy, remède, *m.*
to remember, se souvenir (de).
remembrance, souvenir, *m.*
to remind, rappeler.

to remit, remettre.
to renounce, renoncer (à).
to repeat, répéter.
reply, réponse, *f.*
to reply, répondre.
report, bruit, *m.*
representation, représentation, *f.*
to reproach for, reprocher à
to resign, se démettre.
resistance, résistance, *f.*
respect, respect, *m.* **to fail in —,** manquer de respect à.
rest (*remainder*), reste, *m.* ; **repos,** *m.*
to rest, se reposer.
restless: to become —, s'impatienter.
to resume, reprendre.
to return (*to give back*), rendre ; (*to come back*), revenir ; (*to go back*), retourner.
returned (*come back*), revenu, -e ; (*given back*), rendu, -e.
review, revue, *f.*
revolution, révolution, *f.*
reward, récompense, *f.*
to reward, récompenser.
Rhine, le Rhin.
ribbon, ruban, *m.*
rich, riche.
to ride, monter. **— horseback,** monter à cheval. **to go riding,** aller à cheval.
right, droit, -e, juste. **to be —,** avoir raison.
ring, bague, *f.*
to ring, sonner.
ripe, mûr, -e.
to ripen, mûrir.
to rise, se lever.
river, rivière, *f.* ; fleuve, *m.*
road, route, *f.* ; chemin, *m.*
roastbeef, rosbif, *m.*
roasted, rôti, -e.
Rome, Rome, *f.*
roof, toit, *m.*

room, chambre, *f.* ; salle, *f.*
rose, rose, *f.*
round, rond, -e.
to rub, frictionner.
rule, ruler, règle, *f.*

S

sacred, sacré, -e.
to sacrifice, sacrifier.
sad, triste ; chagrin, -e.
safely, sans accident.
said, dit.
sail, s'embarquer.
salad, salade, *f.*
salt, sel, *m.*
same, même.
sand, sable, *m.*
satisfied, content, -e.
Saturday, samedi, *m.*
savage, sauvage, *m.*
Savoy, la Savoie.
scandal, scandale, *m.*
scarcely, à peine, ne . . . guère.
scarf, écharpe, *f.*
scenery, paysage, *m.*
school, école, *f.* **at —,** à l'école. **boarding-—,** pension, *f.* **— teacher,** maître, *m.* ; maîtresse, *f.*
science, science, *f.*
scissors, ciseaux, *m. pl.*
to scold, gronder.
Scotland, l'Écosse, *f.*
scoundrel, scélérat, *m.*
to scratch, gratter.
sculpture, sculpture, *f.*
sea, mer, *f.*
seashore, at the, au bord de la mer.
season, saison, *f.*
seated, assis, -e.
second, second, -e ; deuxième.
second (*of time*), seconde, *f.*
secret, secret, *m.*
secret (*adj.*), secret, secrète.
securities, valeurs, *f. pl.*
to see, voir.
see! tenez !

to seek, chercher.
to seem, sembler.
seen, vu, -e.
to seize, saisir, empoigner.
selfish, égoïste.
to sell, vendre.
to send, envoyer.
sentence, phrase, f.
September, septembre, m.
seriously, sérieusement.
serpent, serpent, m.
servant, bonne, f.; domestique, m.
    or f.
to serve, servir.
service, service, m.
to set out, partir.
seven, sept.
seventeen, dix-sept.
seventh, septième.
seventy, soixante-dix.
several, plusieurs.
severely, sévèrement.
shall: I — buy it, je l'achèterai.
    he — do it, je veux qu'il le fasse.
    — I buy some? faut-il en ache-
    ter? I — come at once, je vais
    venir tout de suite.
shame, honte, f.
sharp, aigu, -ë.
she, elle. she who, celle qui.
sheep, mouton, m.; brebis, f.
shelf, rayon, m.
ship, vaisseau, m.
to be shipwrecked, faire naufrage.
shirt, chemise, f.
shock, choc, m.
shoe, soulier, m.
shop, magasin, m.
to go shopping, faire des emplettes.
shore, bord, m.
short, court, -e, petit, -e.
shoulder, épaule, f.
to show, montrer. — me, mon-
    trez-moi. to — in, faire entrer.
shower-bath, douche, f.
shut, fermé, -e.

to shut, fermer.
sick, malade.
silent, muet, muette.
silk, soie, f.
silver, argent, m.
silvery, argenté.
simple, simple.
simply, simplement.
since, depuis; puisque.
sincere, sincère.
to sing, chanter.
sir, monsieur, m.
sister, sœur, f.
sister-in-law, belle-sœur, f.
to sit, s'asseoir.
sitting, assis, -e.
situation, place, f.
six, six.
sixteen, seize.
sixth, sixième.
sixty, soixante.
to skate, patiner.
sketch, ébauche, f.
skin, peau, f.
sky, ciel, m.
to slam, claquer.
to slander, calomnier, médire de.
slate, ardoise, f.
slave, esclave, m. or f.
to sleep, dormir. to be sleepy,
    avoir sommeil.
sleepless night, une nuit blanche.
slept, dormi.
slice, tranche, f.
slipper, pantoufle, f.
slow, lent.
slowly, lentement.
small, petit, -e.
smart, chic (invar.).
to smell, sentir.
to smoke, fumer.
snake, serpent, m.
snow, neige, f.
to snow, neiger.
so, si; (after a transitive verb), le;
    (after an intransitive), ainsi. —

many, — much, tant. — soon,
sitôt. — long as, tant que. —
do I, moi aussi.
soap, savon, *m.*
sock, chaussette, *f.*
soft, mou, molle.
to soil, salir.
sold, vendu, -e.
soldier, soldat, *m.*
solid, solide.
some, du, de la, de l', des; en;
quelques, quelques-uns.
somebody, quelqu'un.
something, quelque chose. —
else, autre chose.
sometime, quelque temps.
sometimes, quelquefois.
somewhat, un peu, assez.
somewhere, quelque part.
son, fils, *m.*
song, chanson, *f.*
soon, bientôt. see you —, à bientôt.
sooner, plus tôt.
sorrowful, chagrin, -e.
sorry, fâché, triste, chagrin, -e. to
be —, être fâché de.
soul, âme, *f.*
soup, soupe, *f.*; potage, *m.*
south, midi, *m.*, sud, *m.*
Spain, l'Espagne, *f.*
Spanish, espagnol, -e.
to sparkle, pétiller.
to speak, parler. to — again, reparler.
to spend, passer, dépenser.
in spite of, malgré.
splendid, magnifique, superbe.
spoken, parlé, -e.
spoon, cuiller, *f.*
spring, printemps, *m.*
to sprain, démettre.
square (*adj.*), carré, -e.
stage-coach, diligence, *f.*
staircase, escalier, *m.*
stake : to be at stake, y aller de.

to stand still, ne pas bouger.
standing, debout.
star, étoile, *f.*
to start for, partir pour.
station, gare, *f.*
to stay, rester.
stayed, resté, -e.
in his stead, à sa place.
steamboat, bateau (*m.*) à vapeur.
steel, acier, *m.*
stick, canne, *f.*
still, encore.
store, magasin, *m.* department
—, magasin de nouveautés.
storm, orage, *m.*
stormy, orageux, -se.
story, histoire, *f.* (*of a house*),
étage, *m.*
stout, gros, grosse.
straight, droit, -e.
strange, étrange.
stranger, étranger, *m.*
straw, paille, *f.*
strawberry, fraise, *f.*
stream, ruisseau, *m.*
street, rue, *f.*
strength, force, *f.*
to strike, frapper.
strong, fort, -e.
studious, studieux, -se.
to study, étudier.
subject, sujet, *m.*
subject (*adj.*), sujet, sujette.
to submit, soumettre.
to succeed, réussir.
such, pareil, -le; tel, telle.
to suffer, souffrir.
suffering, souffrant, -e.
sugar, sucre, *m.*
suit, costume, *m.*
sum, somme, *f.*
summer, été, *m.*
sun, soleil, *m.*
Sunday, dimanche, *m.*
support, appui, *m.*
to support, appuyer.

suppose — Vocabulary — thunder

sure, sûr, -e, certain, -e.
to surprise, surprendre.
to surrender, se rendre.
to sweep, balayer.
sweet, doux, douce; parfumé, -e.
Switzerland, la Suisse.
sword, épée, *f.*

T

table, table, *f.*
tailor, tailleur, *m.*
to take, prendre. — to, mener,
conduire. — a walk, se promener. — after, tenir de. —
away, enlever. — off, ôter.
taken, pris, prise.
talent, talent, *m.*
to talk, parler.
talkative, causeur, -euse.
tall, grand, -e.
tea, thé, *m.*
to teach, enseigner (à), apprendre.
teacher, maître, *m.*; maîtresse, *f.*,
professeur, *m.*
to tear, déchirer.
to tear out, arracher.
to tease, taquiner.
to telegraph, télégraphier.
telephone, téléphone, *m.* — book,
annuaire téléphonique, *m.*
to telephone, téléphoner.
to tell, raconter, dire à.
temper, humeur, *f.*
temple, temple, *m.*
ten, dix.
tender, tendre, délicat, -e.
tenth, dixième.
Thames, the, la Tamise.
than, que; (*before a number*), de.
to thank, remercier. thank you,
merci. thanks to, grâce à.
that (*adj.*), ce, cet, cette. (*demon.
pron.*), celui, celle; celui-là,
celle-là; cela. (*rel. pron.*), qui

(*nom.*), que (*acc.*). (*conj.*), que.
that's all, voilà tout.
the, le, la, les.
theater, théâtre, *m.*
thee, te, toi.
theft, vol, *m.*
their, leur, leurs.
theirs, le leur, la leur, les leurs.
them, les; eux, elles. to —, leur.
themselves, se; eux-mêmes, elles-
mêmes.
then (*afterwards*), ensuite, alors,
puis; (*therefore*), donc.
there, là, y. — is, are, il y a, voilà.
— was, were, il y avait.
therefore, donc.
these (*adj.*), ces. (*pron.*), ceux-ci,
celles-ci.
they, ils, on. — who, ceux qui,
celles qui.
thick, épais, -se.
thickness, épaisseur, *f.*
thimble, dé, *m.*
thine, le tien, la tienne, les tiens, les
tiennes.
thing, chose, *f.*
to think, penser; trouver.
third, troisième. a —, un tiers.
thirst, soif. to be thirsty, avoir soif.
thirteen, treize.
thirty, trente.
this (*adj.*), ce, cet, cette; (*pron.*),
celui-ci, celle-ci; ceci.
those (*adj.*), ces. (*pron.*), ceux,
celles; ceux-là, celles-là.
thou, tu, toi.
though, quoique, cependant.
thousand, mille (mil, *in dates*).
thousandth, millième.
thread, fil, *m.*
to threaten, menacer.
three, trois.
throat, gorge, *f.*
to throw, jeter.
thumb, pouce, *m.*
thunder, tonnerre, *m.*

54

Thursday, jeudi, *m.*
thus, ainsi; *at the beginning of a sentence*, aussi.
thy, ton, ta, tes.
thyself, te, toi-même.
tiger, tigre, *m.*
till, jusqu'à; *(conj.)*, jusqu'à ce que *(with subj.).*
time, temps, *m.*; fois, *f.* a long —, longtemps. by this —, maintenant. from — to —, de temps en temps.
in time, à temps.
tin, fer-blanc, *m.*
tipsy, gris, grise.
tired, las, lasse; fatigué, -e; *(bored)*, ennuyé, -e.
to, à, jusqu'à.
tobacco, tabac, *m.*
to-day, aujourd'hui.
together, ensemble.
told, dit, dite, raconté, -e.
toilet, la toilette, *f.*
to-morrow, demain.
tongue, langue, *f.*
to-night, ce soir.
too *(also)*, aussi; *(before adj. or adv.)*, trop. — many, — much, trop.
tooth, dent, *f.*
tuxedo, smoking, *m.*
toward, vers.
town, ville, *f.*
toy, joujou, *m.*
trade, métier, *m.*
train, train, *m.*
to transmit, transmettre.
to travel, voyager.
treason, trahison, *f.*
to treat, traiter.
tree, arbre, *m.*
to tremble, trembler.
trembling, tremblant, -e.
trial, procès, *m.*
trifle, misère, *f.*; rien, *m.*
to trouble, déranger.
troubled *(adj.)*, inquiet, -ète.

troublesome, fatigant, -e; ennuyeux, -se.
true, vrai, -e.
trunk, trompe, *f.*
trunk, malle, *f.*
to trust, se fier à.
truth, vérité, *f.*
to try, essayer, tâcher de.
Tuesday, mardi, *m.*
tulip, tulipe, *f.*
Turkish, turc, turque.
turn, tour, *m.*
tutor, précepteur, *m.*
twelve, douze.
twenty, vingt.
twice, deux fois.
twin, jumeau, *m.*, jumelle, *f.*
two, deux.

U

ugly, vilain, -e.
umbrella, parapluie, *m.*
uncertain, incertain.
uncle, oncle, *m.*
under, sous.
uneasy, inquiet, inquiète.
unfortunate, malheureux, -se.
unfortunately, malheureusement.
ungrateful, ingrat, -e.
unhappy, malheureux, -se; mécontent, -e.
United States, les États-Unis, *m.*
unjustly, injustement.
unless, à moins que.
until, jusqu'à ce que.
unwell, malade.
upon, sur.
us, to us, nous.
use, usage, *m.*
useful, utile.
useless, inutile.
as usual, comme à l'ordinaire.

V

vacation, congé, *m.*
various, divers, -es, différents, -es.

vegetable, légume, *m.*

very, très, bien. — much, beaucoup. — well! très bien!

vest, gilet, *m.*

to vex, fâcher.

vial, flacon, *m.*

victory, victoire, *f.*

Vienna, Vienne, *f.*

village, village, *m.*

to violate, trahir.

violet, violette, *f.*

virtue, vertu, *f.*

visit, visite, *f.* to pay a —, rendre visite.

to visit, visiter, aller chez.

voice, voix, *f.*

voyage, voyage, *m.*

W

waistcoat, gilet, *m.*

to wait for, attendre.

walk, promenade, *f.* to take a —, se promener. to go out for a —, aller faire une promenade.

to walk, aller à pied. — lame, boiter.

want, besoin, *m.* to be in —, avoir besoin; falloir. to —, vouloir.

war, guerre, *f.*

warm, chaud, -e. to be —, avoir chaud.

to wash, laver.

to waste, perdre.

watch, montre, *f.*

to watch, regarder.

water, eau, *f.*

to water, arroser.

waterproof, imperméable.

to wave, agiter.

way, chemin, *m.*

we, nous; on.

to wear, porter.

weather, temps, *m.* in this cold —, par le froid qu'il fait.

Wednesday, mercredi, *m.*

week, semaine, *f.*

to weep, pleurer.

to welcome, accueillir.

well, bien. to be —, se porter bien.

what, quel, quelle; quels, quelles; ce qui, ce que.

whatever, quelconque (*after the noun*).

when, quand, lorsque; (*interr.*), quand.

where, où.

west, ouest, *m.*

which, *rel. pron.* (*nom.*) qui, (*acc.*) que; (*inter. pron. after prep. or followed by* of), lequel, laquelle; lesquels, lesquelles. from —, of —, duquel, de laquelle; desquels, desquelles; dont. to —, auquel, à laquelle; auxquels, auxquelles. (*interr. adj.*), quel.

while, en (*with pres. part.*), pendant que, tandis que.

whist, whist, *m.*

to whistle, siffler.

whistle, sifflet, *m.*

white, blanc, blanche.

who, qui.

whoever, qui que.

whole, tout, -e; tous, toutes.

whom, que; (*after prep.*), qui.

whose, dont; à qui.

why? pourquoi?

why! mais!

wicked, méchant, -e.

wide, large.

width, largeur, *f.*

wife, femme, *f.*

wild, féroce, sauvage.

William, Guillaume, *m.*

to be willing, vouloir (bien).

willingly, volontiers, de bon cœur.

will you have? voulez-vous?

to win, gagner; remporter.

wind, vent, *m.*

window, fenêtre, *f.*

wine, vin, *m.*

winter, hiver, *m.*

wise, sage.
to wish, désirer, souhaiter, vouloir.
with, avec.
without, sans.
wolf, loup, *m.*
woman, femme, *f.*
wonderful, merveilleux, -se.
wood, bois, *m.*
wooden, de bois.
wool, laine, *f.*
word, mot, *m.* in a —, en un mot. on one's —, sur parole.
work, ouvrage, *m.*; travail, *m.*
to work, travailler.
workman, ouvrier.
world, monde, *m.*
to worry, se faire du mauvais sang.
worse, plus mauvais, pire.
to be worth, valoir.
worthy, digne.
to wound one's self *or* each other, se blesser.
wrist, poignet, *m.*
to write, écrire.
writer, écrivain.

written, écrit, -e.
to be wrong, avoir tort.
wrought, travaillé, -e.

Y

yard, cour, *f.*
year, an, *m.*; année, *f.* last —, l'année dernière, *f.*
yellow, jaune.
yes, oui; si.
yesterday, hier.
yet (*again, still*), encore; (*however*), pourtant.
you, vous; on.
young, jeune. — lady, jeune fille, demoiselle, *f.*
your, votre, vos.
yours, le vôtre, la vôtre, les vôtres.
yourself, vous, vous-même.
yourselves, vous, vous-mêmes.
youth, jeunesse, *f.*

Z

zero, zéro, *m.*

LEXIQUE

Numbers refer to pages.

Note. — As a complete list of irregular verbs of common use is given, in alphabetical order, at the end of the grammar summary in this book, no separate mention of any irregular verb is made in the present index. They are conjugated *in full* in pages 414–433.

59

l'on, use, 129.
lui, after a preposition, 124, 214, 252, 383–386; after a verb, 215, 219.

matin, distinguished from *matinée*, 86.
même, 337; with emphatic pronouns, 125, 214.
mien, 37.
mille, mil, 56.
million, followed by *de*, 56.
moi, use, 124–125.
mon, before a feminine word, 34 (2).
months, name of, 60.
more, translation, 381.
must, 283, 327–329.

names of places, with or without the article, 257.
nasal vowels, xx.
ne, 9; without *pas*, 391; with *ni . . . ni*, 144; *ne . . . que*, 145.
negation, 144; *see* ne.
neither, 64.
neuf, pronunciation, 49.
ni . . . ni, 144.
not, *see* ne.
notre, 33.
nôtre, 37.
nouns, formation of plural, 17–18; of feminine, 365; plural of compound nouns, 341; collective, 325; gender of, 365; nouns of measure or quantity, 96–97; of material, 111–112; used in a general sense, 76; in a partitive sense, 76.
numbers, cardinal, 55; ordinal, 59; with *et*, 56.

obéir, object, 105 (*footnote*).
on, use of, 129.
only, 145.
onze, no liaison, 59.

ordinals, *see* numbers.
où, relative use, 182.
oui and si, 12.

participle, past, as adjective, 325; agreement after *être*, 93–94; after *avoir*, 115; of reflexive verbs, 244.
participle, present, 324; compared with infinitive, 313.
partitive article, 75–76.
pas, omission, 391; precedes the infinitive, 313.
passive form, 334; translation, 335; conjugation, 334.
past anterior, conjugation, 266; use, 266–267.
past definite, 265; use, 266–267.
past indefinite, 41; distinguished from past definite, 266–267.
past participle, *see* participle.
pendant, distinguished from *depuis* and *pour*, 262.
personal pronouns, *see* pronouns.
personne, position, 206; in partitive sense with *de*, 338.
petit, comparison, 63.
peu s'en faut, 438.
peur (*avoir*), followed by the subjunctive, 279; *de peur que*, 298.
places, names of, with or without the article, 257.
plupart (*la*), followed by *des*, 316.
pluperfect, indicative, 168; subjunctive, 306.
plural, nouns, 17–18; adjectives, 17, 119–120; compound nouns, 341; article, 17–18.
plus, used in comparisons, 63–66.
possessive adjectives, 33; repetition, 33.
possessive case, 20.
possessive pronouns, 37.
pour, distinguished from *depuis* and *pendant*, 262; with infinitive, 314.

pouvoir, used without *pas*, 391.
premier, with names of rulers and in dates, 60 (*footnote*), 168.
prepositions, 341, 392–394.
present indicative; 1st conjugation, 28; 2d conj., 52; 3d conj., 73; use, 28, 261–262.
present participle, *see* participle.
present subjunctive, formation, 278; use, 277–311.
primitive tenses, 332.
pronominal verbs, 235–236; conjugation, 236–237; compound tenses, 243–245; used instead of English passive, 335.
pronoun, conjunctive, 100, 215, 252, 385; demonstrative, 154–157; disjunctive, 124, 214; indefinite, 337; interrogative, 186, 199, 200, 337; order of, 252, 385; personal, 100, 104, 124, 214, 215; possessive, 37; relative, 70, 171, 181, 336.
pronunciation, xiv-xxiii; syllables, xxiii; words for practice, xxiv; linking of words, xxiv-xxv.
punctuation, xxvi.

quand, with the future, 90.
quatre-vingt, with or without *s*, 56.
que, pronoun object, 70.
que, elision of *e*, 70; cannot be omitted, 70; used to avoid the repetition of other conjunctions, 298; with the subjunctive, 298; used for " *how!*," " *how much!*," 371, note 2, last example.
quel, 84, 148.
question, form of, 7; first singular, 30, noun subject, 12.
qui, does not admit elision, 70. *See* pronoun, interrogative and relative.
qui est-ce qui, qu'est-ce qui, 199, 200.

quoi, 186.
quoique, with subjunctive, 298.

reciprocal verbs, conjugation, 240.
reflexive verbs, conjugation, 235, 243.
relative pronoun, 70, 171, 181, 336.
rien, position of, 206; in partitive sense with *de*, 338.

savoir, used negatively without *pas*, 391; subjunctive of softened assertion, 298; distinguished from *connaître*, 149.
se, 236.
seasons, 60.
sept, pronunciation of, 49.
seul, with the subjunctive, 288.
si (*so*), in comparisons, 63; meaning " *yes*," 12.
si, conjunction, 177; elision of *i*, 178.
sien, 37.
six, pronunciation of, 49.
so, translation, 63.
soi, 338.
soir, distinguished from *soirée*, 86.
some, before a noun, 75, 76; exceptional uses, 76, 144; without a noun, 133.
son, before a feminine word beginning with a vowel or *h* mute, 34 (2).
subject, repeated when of different persons, 210; in interrogative sentences, 12, 209.
subjunctive mood, 277; formation and conjugation of the present, 278; after impersonal verbs, 282; after negative or interrogative verbs, 293; after verbs of emotion, 279; after relative pronouns and after superlatives. 288; after certain conjunctions, 298; compared with the indica-

64 Lexique

tive, 294, 299; compared with the infinitive, 320; formation and conjugation of the imperfect, 303; sequence of tenses, 302; subjunctive in independent clauses, 305; with *que*, 298; used for imperative, 306; pluperfect formation, 306.

superlative, formation, 63; with *c'est* or *ce sont*, 158; when placed after its noun requires the article to be repeated, 64.

syllables, division of, xxiii.

syntax, modification of, 357.

t, euphonic, 7; pronunciation in numbers, 55.

tenses, formation, 333; compound, 244; primitive, 330.

than, 63, 66; when translated by *de*, 380; or by *que de*, 314.

that, relative pronoun, 70; demonstrative adjective, 45; demonstrative pronoun, 154–157; conjunction, 298; must always be expressed, 70.

them, 100, 134, 215, 219, 383.

they, 214–215.

this, demonstrative adjective, 45; demonstrative pronoun, 154–157.

tien, 37.

time, of day, 162; duration of, 261; expressions of, 342.

titles of sovereigns, 60 (footnote), 168.

ton, before a feminine word beginning with a vowel or *h* mute, 34 (2).

tout, position, 85, 205; variable as an adverb, 338; used with *en* and present participle, 324.

trouver, meanings, 31.

union of words, xxiv.

venir, idiomatic use of, 441.

verbal adjectives, 324.

verbs, conjugated with *être*, 93; auxiliary, 395; irregular, 414; reciprocal, 240; reflexive, 235; regular, 407; used with the infinitive without a preposition, 312; requiring *de* before an infinitive, 317; requiring *à* before an infinitive, 317.

vers, distinguished from *envers*, 342.

vingt, final *t*, 48, 55.

voilà, distinguished from *il y a*, 50.

votre, 33.

vôtre, 37.

vouloir, with *bien*, 289.

vous, use, 5 (note); use as singular, 5 (note).

vowels, simple, xv; compound, xix; nasal, xx.

we, used indefinitely, 129.

weather, ways of expressing, 140.

week, days of the, 59.

what, adjective, 148; interrogative pronoun, 186, 337; relative pronoun, 171.

which, adjective, 148; interrogative pronoun, 190, 337; relative pronoun, 70, 336.

who, relative pronoun, 70, 181–182, 336; interrogative pronoun, 186, 199, 337.

whom, 70, 181–182, 186, 199, 336, 337.

whose, interrogative, 186; relative, 182.

y, meaning and position, 247–248.

-yer, verbs ending in, 274.